Microsoft® Official Academic Course

Windows Server® 2008 Applications Infrastructure Configuration (70-643)

Craig T. Zacker

WILEY

Credits

EXECUTIVE EDITOR	John Kane
DIRECTOR OF MARKETING AND SALES	Mitchell Beaton
MICROSOFT STRATEGIC RELATIONSHIPS MANAGER	Merrick Van Dongen of Microsoft Learning
DEVELOPMENT AND PRODUCTION	Custom Editorial Productions, Inc.
EDITORIAL ASSISTANT	Jennifer Lartz
PRODUCTION MANAGER	Micheline Frederick
PRODUCTION EDITOR	Kerry Weinstein
CREATIVE DIRECTOR	Harry Nolan
COVER DESIGNER	Michael St. Martine
TECHNOLOGY AND MEDIA	Lauren Sapira/Elena Santa Maria

This book was set in Garamond by Aptara, Inc. and printed and bound by Bind Rite Graphics. The covers were printed by Phoenix Color.

Microsoft, ActiveX, Excel, InfoPath, Microsoft Press, MSDN, OneNote, Outlook, PivotChart, PivotTable, PowerPoint, SharePoint SQL Server, Visio, Windows, Windows Mobile, and Windows Vista are either registered trademarks or trademarks of Microsoft Corporation in the United States and/or other countries. Other product and company names mentioned herein may be the trademarks of their respective owners.

The example companies, organizations, products, domain names, e-mail addresses, logos, people, places, and events depicted herein are fictitious. No association with any real company, organization, product, domain name, e-mail address, logo, person, place, or event is intended or should be inferred.

The book expresses the author's views and opinions. The information contained in this book is provided without any express, statutory, or implied warranties. Neither the authors, John Wiley & Sons, Inc., Microsoft Corporation, nor their resellers or distributors will be held liable for any damages caused or alleged to be caused either directly or indirectly by this book.

ISBN 978-0-470-22513-4

Printed in the United States of America

10 9 8 7 6 5

Foreword from the Publisher

Wiley's publishing vision for the Microsoft Official Academic Course series is to provide students and instructors with the skills and knowledge they need to use Microsoft technology effectively in all aspects of their personal and professional lives. Quality instruction is required to help both educators and students get the most from Microsoft's software tools and to become more productive. Thus our mission is to make our instructional programs trusted educational companions for life.

To accomplish this mission, Wiley and Microsoft have partnered to develop the highest quality educational programs for Information Workers, IT Professionals, and Developers. Materials created by this partnership carry the brand name "Microsoft Official Academic Course," assuring instructors and students alike that the content of these textbooks is fully endorsed by Microsoft, and that they provide the highest quality information and instruction on Microsoft products. The Microsoft Official Academic Course textbooks are "Official" in still one more way—they are the officially sanctioned courseware for Microsoft IT Academy members.

The Microsoft Official Academic Course series focuses on *workforce development*. These programs are aimed at those students seeking to enter the workforce, change jobs, or embark on new careers as information workers, IT professionals, and developers. Microsoft Official Academic Course programs address their needs by emphasizing authentic workplace scenarios with an abundance of projects, exercises, cases, and assessments.

The Microsoft Official Academic Courses are mapped to Microsoft's extensive research and job-task analysis, the same research and analysis used to create the Microsoft Certified Technology Specialist (MCTS) exam. The textbooks focus on real skills for real jobs. As students work through the projects and exercises in the textbooks they enhance their level of knowledge and their ability to apply the latest Microsoft technology to everyday tasks. These students also gain resume-building credentials that can assist them in finding a job, keeping their current job, or in furthering their education.

The concept of life-long learning is today an utmost necessity. Job roles, and even whole job categories, are changing so quickly that none of us can stay competitive and productive without continuously updating our skills and capabilities. The Microsoft Official Academic Course offerings, and their focus on Microsoft certification exam preparation, provide a means for people to acquire and effectively update their skills and knowledge. Wiley supports students in this endeavor through the development and distribution of these courses as Microsoft's official academic publisher.

Today educational publishing requires attention to providing quality print and robust electronic content. By integrating Microsoft Official Academic Course products, *WileyPLUS*, and Microsoft certifications, we are better able to deliver efficient learning solutions for students and teachers alike.

Bonnie Lieberman

General Manager and Senior Vice President

Preface

Welcome to the Microsoft Official Academic Course (MOAC) program for Microsoft Windows Server 2008. MOAC represents the collaboration between Microsoft Learning and John Wiley & Sons, Inc. publishing company. Microsoft and Wiley teamed up to produce a series of textbooks that deliver compelling and innovative teaching solutions to instructors and superior learning experiences for students. Infused and informed by in-depth knowledge from the creators of Windows Server 2008, and crafted by a publisher known worldwide for the pedagogical quality of its products, these textbooks maximize skills transfer in minimum time. Students are challenged to reach their potential by using their new technical skills as highly productive members of the workforce.

Because this knowledgebase comes directly from Microsoft, architect of the Windows Server operating system and creator of the Microsoft Certified Technology Specialist and Microsoft Certified Professional exams (www.microsoft.com/learning/mcp/mcts), you are sure to receive the topical coverage that is most relevant to students' personal and professional success. Microsoft's direct participation not only assures you that MOAC textbook content is accurate and current; it also means that students will receive the best instruction possible to enable their success on certification exams and in the workplace.

■ The Microsoft Official Academic Course Program

The *Microsoft Official Academic Course* series is a complete program for instructors and institutions to prepare and deliver great courses on Microsoft software technologies. With MOAC, we recognize that, because of the rapid pace of change in the technology and curriculum developed by Microsoft, there is an ongoing set of needs beyond classroom instruction tools for an instructor to be ready to teach the course. The MOAC program endeavors to provide solutions for all these needs in a systematic manner in order to ensure a successful and rewarding course experience for both instructor and student—technical and curriculum training for instructor readiness with new software releases; the software itself for student use at home for building hands-on skills, assessment, and validation of skill development; and a great set of tools for delivering instruction in the classroom and lab. All are important to the smooth delivery of an interesting course on Microsoft software, and all are provided with the MOAC program. We think about the model below as a gauge for ensuring that we completely support you in your goal of teaching a great course. As you evaluate your instructional materials options, you may wish to use the model for comparison purposes with available products.

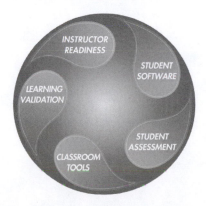

▪ Pedagogical Features

The MOAC textbook for Windows Server 2008 Applications Infrastructure Configuration is designed to cover all the learning objectives for that MCTS exam, which is referred to as its "objective domain." The Microsoft Certified Technology Specialist (MCTS) exam objectives are highlighted throughout the textbook. Many pedagogical features have been developed specifically for *Microsoft Official Academic Course* programs.

Presenting the extensive procedural information and technical concepts woven throughout the textbook raises challenges for the student and instructor alike. The Illustrated Book Tour that follows provides a guide to the rich features contributing to *Microsoft Official Academic Course* program's pedagogical plan. Following is a list of key features in each lesson designed to prepare students for success on the certification exams and in the workplace:

- Each lesson begins with an **Objective Domain Matrix.** More than a standard list of learning objectives, the Domain Matrix correlates each software skill covered in the lesson to the specific MCTS "objective domain."

- Concise and frequent **Step-by-Step** instructions teach students new features and provide an opportunity for hands-on practice. Numbered steps give detailed, step-by-step instructions to help students learn software skills. The steps also show results and screen images to match what students should see on their computer screens.

- **Illustrations:** Screen images provide visual feedback as students work through the exercises. The images reinforce key concepts, provide visual clues about the steps, and allow students to check their progress.

- **Key Terms:** Important technical vocabulary is listed at the beginning of the lesson. When these terms are used later in the lesson, they appear in bold italic type and are defined. The Glossary contains all of the key terms and their definitions.

- Engaging point-of-use **Reader aids,** located throughout the lessons, tell students why this topic is relevant (*The Bottom Line*), provide students with helpful hints (*Take Note*), or show alternate ways to accomplish tasks (*Another Way*). Reader aids also provide additional relevant or background information that adds value to the lesson.

- **Certification Ready?** features throughout the text signal students where a specific certification objective is covered. They provide students with a chance to check their understanding of that particular MCTS objective and, if necessary, review the section of the lesson where it is covered. MOAC offers complete preparation for MCTS certification.

- **Knowledge Assessments** provide three progressively more challenging lesson-ending activities.

www.wiley.com/college/microsoft *or*
call the MOAC Toll-Free Number: 1+(888) 764-7001 (U.S. & Canada only)

■ Lesson Features

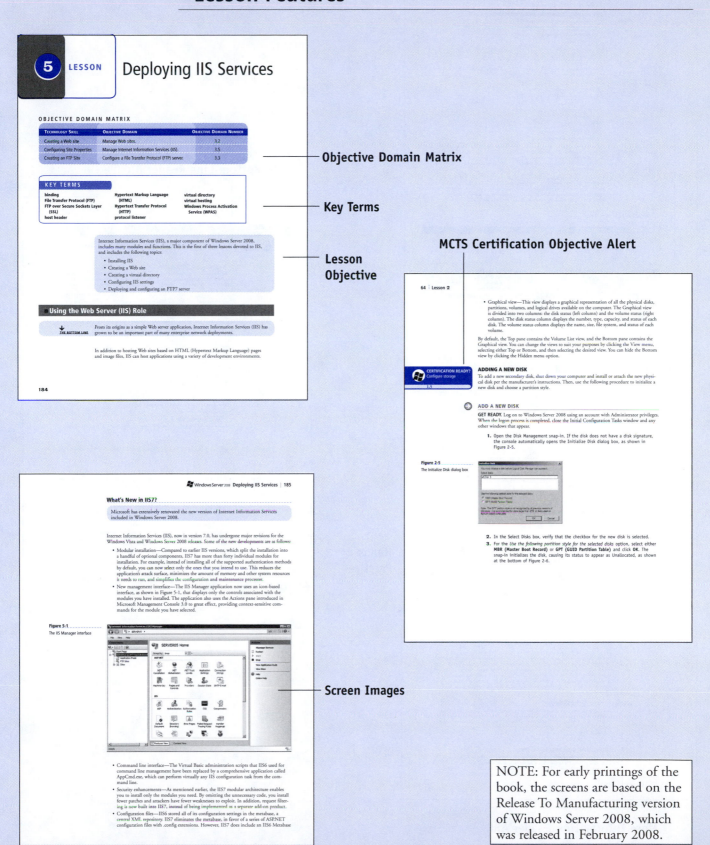

Objective Domain Matrix

Key Terms

Lesson Objective

MCTS Certification Objective Alert

Screen Images

NOTE: For early printings of the book, the screens are based on the Release To Manufacturing version of Windows Server 2008, which was released in February 2008.

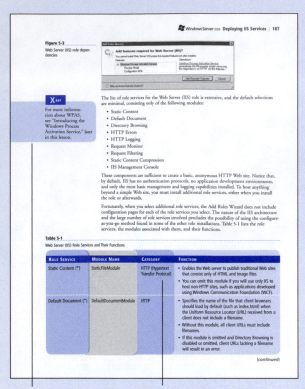

X Ref Reader Aid   **Easy-to-Read Tables**

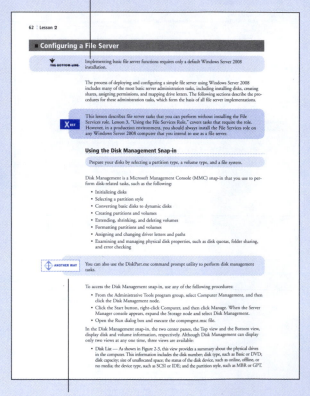

The Bottom Line Reader Aid

Another Way Reader Aid

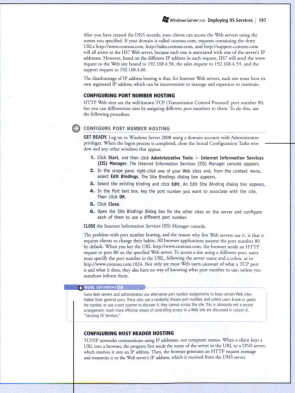

Hands-on Practice

More Information Reader Aid

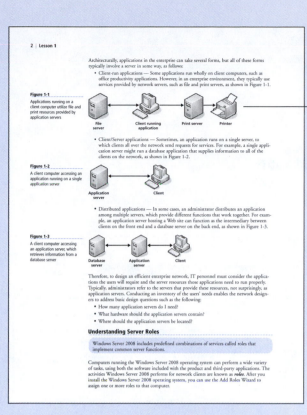

Informative Diagrams

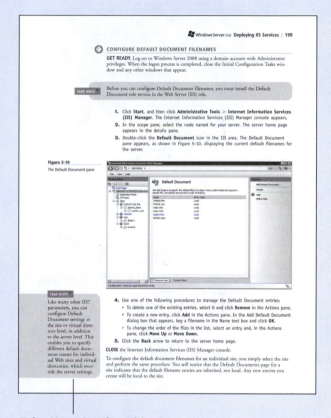

Take Note Reader Aid

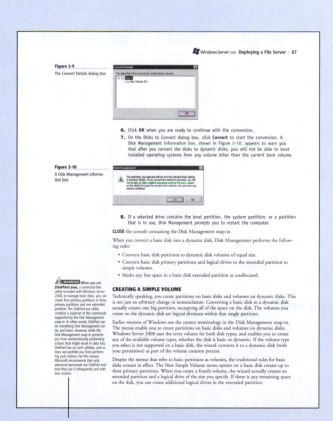

Warning Reader Aid

Summary Skill Matrix

Review Questions

Cases Scenarios

Knowledge Assessment Questions

Conventions and Features Used in This Book

This book uses particular fonts, symbols, and heading conventions to highlight important information or to call your attention to special steps. For more information about the features in each lesson, refer to the Illustrated Book Tour section.

CONVENTION	MEANING
NEW FEATURE ✓	This icon indicates a new or greatly improved Windows feature in this version of the software.
↓ **THE BOTTOM LINE**	This feature provides a brief summary of the material to be covered in the section that follows.
CLOSE	Words in all capital letters and in a different font color than the rest of the text indicate instructions for opening, saving, or closing files or programs. They also point out items you should check or actions you should take.
CERTIFICATION READY?	This feature signals the point in the text where a specific certification objective is covered. It provides you with a chance to check your understanding of that particular MCTS objective and, if necessary, review the section of the lesson where it is covered.
TAKE NOTE	Reader aids appear in shaded boxes found in your text. *Take Note* provides helpful hints related to particular tasks or topics.
◆ **ANOTHER WAY**	*Another Way* provides an alternative procedure for accomplishing a particular task.
X REF	These notes provide pointers to information discussed elsewhere in the textbook or describe interesting features of Windows Server 2008 that are not directly addressed in the current topic or exercise.
Alt + **Tab**	A plus sign (+) between two key names means that you must press both keys at the same time. Keys that you are instructed to press in an exercise will appear in the font shown here.
A *shared printer* can be used by many individuals on a network.	Key terms appear in bold italic.
Key **My Name is.**	Any text you are asked to key appears in color.
Click **OK.**	Any button on the screen you are supposed to click on or select will also appear in color.

The *Microsoft Official Academic Course* programs are accompanied by a rich array of resources that incorporate the extensive textbook visuals to form a pedagogically cohesive package. These resources provide all the materials instructors need to deploy and deliver their courses. Resources available online for download include:

- The **MSDN Academic Alliance** is designed to provide the easiest and most inexpensive developer tools, products, and technologies available to faculty and students in labs, classrooms, and on student PCs. A free 3-year membership is available to qualified MOAC adopters.

  Note: Microsoft Windows Server 2008 can be downloaded from MSDN AA for use by students in this course

- **Windows Server 2008 Evaluation Software.** DVDs containing an evaluation version of Windows Server 2008 is bundled inside the front cover of this text.

- The **Instructor's Guide** contains Solutions to all the textbook exercises as well as chapter summaries and lecture notes. The Instructor's Guide and Syllabi for various term lengths are available from the Book Companion site (http://www.wiley.com/college/microsoft) and from *WileyPLUS*.

- The **Test Bank** contains hundreds of questions in multiple-choice, true-false, short answer, and essay formats and is available to download from the Instructor's Book Companion site (http://www.wiley.com/college/microsoft) and from *WileyPLUS*. A complete answer key is provided.

- **PowerPoint Presentations and Images.** A complete set of PowerPoint presentations is available on the Instructor's Book Companion site (http://www.wiley.com/college/micro-soft) and in *WileyPLUS* to enhance classroom presentations. Tailored to the text's topical coverage and Skills Matrix, these presentations are designed to convey key Windows Server concepts addressed in the text.

  All figures from the text are on the Instructor's Book Companion site (http://www.wiley.com/college/microsoft) and in *WileyPLUS*. You can incorporate them into your PowerPoint presentations, or create your own overhead transparencies and handouts.

  By using these visuals in class discussions, you can help focus students' attention on key elements of Windows Server and help them understand how to use it effectively in the workplace.

- When it comes to improving the classroom experience, there is no better source of ideas and inspiration than your fellow colleagues. The Wiley Faculty Network connects teachers with technology, facilitates the exchange of best practices, and helps to enhance instructional efficiency and effectiveness. Faculty Network activities include technology training and tutorials, virtual seminars, peer-to-peer exchanges of experiences and ideas, personal consulting, and sharing of resources. For details visit www.WhereFacultyConnect.com.

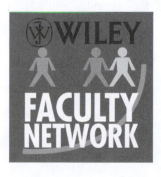

WileyPLUS

Broad developments in education over the past decade have influenced the instructional approach taken in the Microsoft Official Academic Course program. The way that students learn, especially about new technologies, has changed dramatically in the Internet era. Electronic learning materials and Internet-based instruction is now as much a part of classroom instruction as printed textbooks. *WileyPLUS* provides the technology to create an environment where students reach their full potential and experience academic success that will last them a lifetime!

WileyPLUS is a powerful and highly-integrated suite of teaching and learning resources designed to bridge the gap between what happens in the classroom and what happens at home and on the job. *WileyPLUS* provides instructors with the resources to teach their students new technologies and guide them to reach their goals of getting ahead in the job market by having the skills to become certified and advance in the workforce. For students, *WileyPLUS* provides the tools for study and practice that are available to them 24/7, wherever and whenever they want to study. *WileyPLUS* includes a complete online version of the student textbook, PowerPoint presentations, homework and practice assignments and quizzes, image galleries, test bank questions, gradebook, and all the instructor resources in one easy-to-use Web site.

Organized around the everyday activities you and your students perform in the class, *WileyPLUS* helps you:

- **Prepare & Present** outstanding class presentations using relevant PowerPoint slides and other *WileyPLUS* materials—and you can easily upload and add your own.

- **Create Assignments** by choosing from questions organized by lesson, level of difficulty, and source—and add your own questions. Students' homework and quizzes are automatically graded, and the results are recorded in your gradebook.

- **Offer context-sensitive help to students, 24/7.** When you assign homework or quizzes, you decide if and when students get access to hints, solutions, or answers where appropriate—or they can be linked to relevant sections of their complete, online text for additional help whenever—and wherever they need it most.

- **Track Student Progress:** Analyze students' results and assess their level of understanding on an individual and class level using the *WileyPLUS* gradebook, or export data to your own personal gradebook.

- **Administer Your Course:** *WileyPLUS* can easily be integrated with another course management system, gradebook, or other resources you are using in your class, providing you with the flexibility to build your course, your way.

Please view our online demo at **www.wiley.com/college/wileyplus.** Here you will find additional information about the features and benefits of *WileyPLUS*, how to request a "test drive" of *WileyPLUS* for this title, and how to adopt it for class use.

MSDN ACADEMIC ALLIANCE—FREE 3-YEAR MEMBERSHIP AVAILABLE TO QUALIFIED ADOPTERS!

The Microsoft Developer Network Academic Alliance (MSDN AA) is designed to provide the easiest and most inexpensive way for universities to make the latest Microsoft developer tools, products, and technologies available in labs, classrooms, and on student PCs. MSDN AA is an annual membership program for departments teaching Science, Technology, Engineering, and Mathematics (STEM) courses. The membership provides a complete solution to keep academic labs, faculty, and students on the leading edge of technology.

Software available in the MSDN AA program is provided at no charge to adopting departments through the Wiley and Microsoft publishing partnership.

As a bonus to this free offer, faculty will be introduced to Microsoft's Faculty Connection and Academic Resource Center. It takes time and preparation to keep students engaged while giving them a fundamental understanding of theory, and the Microsoft Faculty Connection is designed to help STEM professors with this preparation by providing articles, curriculum, and tools that professors can use to engage and inspire today's technology students.

* Contact your Wiley rep for details.

For more information about the MSDN Academic Alliance program, go to:

http://msdn.microsoft.com/academic/

Note: Microsoft Windows Server 2008 can be downloaded from MSDN AA for use by students in this course.

Important Web Addresses and Phone Numbers

To locate the Wiley Higher Education Rep in your area, go to the following Web address and click on the *"Who's My Rep?"* link at the top of the page.

http://www.wiley.com/college

Or Call the MOAC Toll Free Number: 1 + (888) 764-7001 (U.S. & Canada only).

To learn more about becoming a Microsoft Certified Professional and exam availability, visit www.microsoft.com/learning/mcp.

Book Companion Web Site (www.wiley.com/college/microsoft)

The students' book companion site for the MOAC series includes any resources, exercise files, and Web links that will be used in conjunction with this course.

WileyPLUS

WileyPLUS is a powerful and highly-integrated suite of teaching and learning resources designed to bridge the gap between what happens in the classroom and what happens at home and on the job. For students, *WileyPLUS* provides the tools for study and practice that are available 24/7, wherever and whenever they want to study. *WileyPLUS* includes a complete online version of the student textbook, PowerPoint presentations, homework and practice assignments and quizzes, image galleries, test bank questions, gradebook, and all the instructor resources in one easy-to-use Web site.

WileyPLUS provides immediate feedback on student assignments and a wealth of support materials. This powerful study tool will help your students develop their conceptual understanding of the class material and increase their ability to answer questions.

- A **Study and Practice** area links directly to text content, allowing students to review the text while they study and answer.

- An **Assignment** area keeps all the work you want your students to complete in one location, making it easy for them to stay on task. Students have access to a variety of interactive self-assessment tools, as well as other resources for building their confidence and understanding. In addition, all of the assignments and quizzes contain a link to the relevant section of the multimedia book, providing students with context-sensitive help that allows them to conquer obstacles as they arise.

- A **Personal Gradebook** for each student allows students to view their results from past assignments at any time.

Please view our online demo at www.wiley.com/college/wileyplus. Here you will find additional information about the features and benefits of *WileyPLUS*, how to request a "test drive" of *WileyPLUS* for this title, and how to adopt it for class use.

Wiley Desktop Editions

Wiley MOAC Desktop Editions are innovative, electronic versions of printed textbooks. Students buy the desktop version for 50% off the U.S. price of the printed text, and get the added value of permanence and portability. Wiley Desktop Editions provide students with numerous additional benefits that are not available with other e-text solutions.

Wiley Desktop Editions are NOT subscriptions; students download the Wiley Desktop Edition to their computer desktops. Students own the content they buy to keep for as long as they want. Once a Wiley Desktop Edition is downloaded to the computer desktop, students have instant access to all of the content without being online. Students can also print out the sections they prefer to read in hard copy. Students also have access to fully integrated resources within their Wiley Desktop Edition. From highlighting their e-text to taking and sharing notes, students can easily personalize their Wiley Desktop Edition as they are reading or following along in class.

Windows Server 2008 Evaluation Edition

All MOAC Windows Server 2008 textbooks are packaged with an evaluation edition of Windows Server 2008 on the companion DVDs. Installing the Windows Server Evaluation Edition provides students with the state-of-the-art system software, enabling them to use a full version of Windows Server 2008 for the course exercises. This also promotes the practice of learning by doing, which can be the most effective way to acquire and remember new computing skills.

Evaluating Windows Server 2008 software does not require product activation or entering a product key. The Windows Server 2008 Evaluation Edition provided with this textbook may be installed without activation and evaluated for an initial 60 days. If you need more time to evaluate Windows Server 2008, the 60-day evaluation period may be reset (or re-armed) three times, extending the original 60-day evaluation period by up to 180 days for a total possible evaluation time of 240 days. After this time, you will need to uninstall the software or upgrade to a fully licensed version of Windows Server 2008.

System Requirements

The following are estimated system requirements for Windows Server 2008. If your computer has less than the minimum requirements, you will not be able to install this product correctly. Actual requirements will vary based on your system configuration and the applications and features you install.

PROCESSOR

Processor performance depends not only on the clock frequency of the processor, but also on the number of processor cores and the size of the processor cache. The following are the processor requirements for this product:

- Minimum: 1 GHz (for x86 processors) or 1.4 GHz (for x64 processors)
- Recommended: 2 GHz or faster

TAKE NOTE*
An Intel Itanium 2 processor is required for Windows Server 2008 for Itanium-Based Systems.

RAM

The following are the RAM requirements for this product:

- Minimum: 512 MB
- Recommended: 2 GB or more
- Maximum (32-bit systems): 4 GB (for Windows Server 2008 Standard) or 64 GB (for Windows Server 2008 Enterprise or Windows Server 2008 Datacenter)
- Maximum (64-bit systems): 32 GB (for Windows Server 2008 Standard) or 2 TB (for Windows Server 2008 Enterprise, Windows Server 2008 Datacenter, or Windows Server 2008 for Itanium-Based Systems)

Disk space requirements

TAKE NOTE *

Computers with more than 16 GB of RAM will require more disk space for paging, hibernation, and dump files.

The following are the approximate disk space requirements for the system partition. Itanium-based and x64-based operating systems will vary from these estimates. Additional disk space may be required if you install the system over a network. For more information, see http://www.microsoft.com/windowsserver2008.

- Minimum: 10 GB
- Recommended: 40 GB or more
- DVD-ROM drive
- Super VGA (800 x 600) or higher-resolution monitor
- Keyboard and Microsoft mouse (or other compatible pointing device)

Important Considerations for Active Directory Domain Controllers

The upgrade process from Windows Server 2003 to Windows Server 2008 requires free disk space for the new operating system image, for the Setup process, and for any installed server roles.

For the domain controller role, the volume or volumes hosting the following resources also have specific free disk space requirements:

- Application data (%AppData%)
- Program files (%ProgramFiles%)
- Users' data (%SystemDrive%\Documents and Settings)
- Windows directory (%WinDir%)

The free space on the %WinDir% volume must be equal or greater than the current size of the resources listed above and their subordinate folders when they are located on the %WinDir% volume. By default, dcpromo places the Active Directory database and log files under %Windir%—in this case, their size would be included in the free disk space requirements for the %Windir% folder.

However, if the Active Directory database is hosted outside of any of the folders above, then the hosting volume or volumes must only contain additional free space equal to at least 10% of the current database size or 250 MB, whichever is greater. Finally, the free space on the volume that hosts the log files must be at least 50 MB.

A default installation of the Active Directory directory service in Windows Server 2003 has the Active Directory database and log files under %WinDir%\NTDS. With this configuration, the NTDS .DIT database file and all the log files are temporarily copied over to the quarantine location and then copied back to their original location. This is why additional free space is required for those resources. However, the SYSVOL directory, which is also under %WinDir% (%WinDir%\SYSVOL), is moved and not copied. Therefore, it does not require any additional free space.

After the upgrade, the space that was reserved for the copied resources will be returned to the file system.

Installing and Re-Arming Windows Server 2008

WARNING Although you can reset the 60-day evaluation period, you cannot extend it beyond 60 days at any time. When you reset the current 60-day evaluation period, you lose whatever time is left on the previous 60-day evaluation period. Therefore, to maximize the total evaluation time, wait until close to the end of the current 60-day evaluation period before you reset the evaluation period.

Evaluating Windows Server 2008 software does not require product activation. The Windows Server 2008 Evaluation Edition may be installed without activation, and it may be evaluated for 60 days. Additionally, the 60-day evaluation period may be reset (re-armed) three times. This action extends the original 60-day evaluation period by up to 180 days for a total possible evaluation time of 240 days.

How To Install Windows Server 2008 Without Activating It

1. Run the Windows Server 2008 Setup program.

2. When you are prompted to enter a product key for activation, do not enter a key. Click No when Setup asks you to confirm your selection.

3. You may be prompted to select the edition of Windows Server 2008 that you want to evaluate. Select the edition that you want to install.

4. When you are prompted, read the evaluation terms in the Microsoft Software License Terms, and then accept the terms.

5. When the Windows Server 2008 Setup program is finished, your initial 60-day evaluation period starts. To check the time that is left on your current evaluation period, run the Slmgr.vbs script that is in the System32 folder. Use the **-dli** switch to run this script. The **slmgr.vbs -dli** command displays the number of days that are left in the current 60-day evaluation period.

How To Re-Arm the Evaluation Period

This section describes how to extend, or re-arm, the Windows Server 2008 evaluation period. The evaluation period is also known as the "activation grace" period.

When the initial 60-day evaluation period nears its end, you can run the Slmgr.vbs script to reset the evaluation period. To do this, follow these steps:

1. Click **Start**, and then click **Command Prompt**.

2. Type **slmgr.vbs -dli**, and then press **ENTER** to check the current status of your evaluation period.

3. To reset the evaluation period, type **slmgr.vbs –rearm**, and then press **ENTER**.

4. Restart the computer.

This resets the evaluation period to 60 days.

How To Automate the Extension of the Evaluation Period

You may want to set up a process that automatically resets the evaluation period every 60 days. One way to automate this process is by using the Task Scheduler. You can configure the Task Scheduler to run the Slmgr.vbs script and to restart the server at a particular time. To do this, follow these steps:

1. Click **Start**, point to **Administrative Tools**, and then click **Task Scheduler**.

2. Copy the following sample task to the server, and then save it as an .xml file. For example, you can save the file as **Extend.xml**.

```xml
<?xml version="1.0" encoding="UTF-16"?> <Task version="1.2"
xmlns="http://schemas.microsoft.com/windows/2004/02/mit/task">
<RegistrationInfo> <Date>2007-09-17T14:26:04.433</Date>
<Author>Microsoft Corporation</Author> </RegistrationInfo>
<Triggers> <TimeTrigger id="18c4a453-d7aa-4647-916b-
af0c3ea16a6b"> <Repetition> <Interval>P59D</Interval>
<StopAtDurationEnd>false</StopAtDurationEnd> </Repetition>
<StartBoundary>2007-10-05T02:23:24</StartBoundary>
<EndBoundary>2008-09-17T14:23:24.777</EndBoundary>
<Enabled>true</Enabled> </TimeTrigger> </Triggers>
<Principals> <Principal id="Author">
<UserId>domain\alias</UserId>
```

```
<LogonType>Password</LogonType>
<RunLevel>HighestAvailable</RunLevel> </Principal>
</Principals> <Settings> <IdleSettings>
<Duration>PT10M</Duration> <WaitTimeout>PT1H</WaitTimeout>
<StopOnIdleEnd>true</StopOnIdleEnd>
<RestartOnIdle>false</RestartOnIdle> </IdleSettings>
<MultipleInstancesPolicy>IgnoreNew</MultipleInstancesPolicy>
<DisallowStartIfOnBatteries>true</DisallowStartIfOnBatteries>
<StopIfGoingOnBatteries>true</StopIfGoingOnBatteries>
<AllowHardTerminate>true</AllowHardTerminate>
<StartWhenAvailable>false</StartWhenAvailable>
<RunOnlyIfNetworkAvailable>false</RunOnlyIfNetworkAvailable>
<AllowStartOnDemand>true</AllowStartOnDemand>
<Enabled>true</Enabled> <Hidden>false</Hidden>
<RunOnlyIfIdle>false</RunOnlyIfIdle>
<WakeToRun>true</WakeToRun>
<ExecutionTimeLimit>P3D</ExecutionTimeLimit>
<DeleteExpiredTaskAfter>PT0S</DeleteExpiredTaskAfter>
<Priority>7</Priority> <RestartOnFailure>
<Interval>PT1M</Interval> <Count>3</Count>
</RestartOnFailure> </Settings> <Actions Context="Author">
<Exec> <Command>C:\Windows\System32\slmgr.vbs</Command>
<Arguments>-rearm</Arguments> </Exec> <Exec>
<Command>C:\Windows\System32\shutdown.exe</Command>
<Arguments>/r</Arguments> </Exec> </Actions> </Task>
```

3. In the sample task, change the value of the following "UserID" tag to contain your domain and your alias:

   ```
   <UserId>domain\alias</UserId>
   ```

4. In the Task Scheduler, click **Import Task** on the **Action** menu.
5. Click the sample task .xml file. For example, click **Extend.xml**.
6. Click **Import**.
7. Click the **Triggers** tab.
8. Click the **One Time** trigger, and then click **Edit**.
9. Change the start date of the task to a date just before the end of your current evaluation period.
10. Click **OK**, and then exit the Task Scheduler.

The Task Scheduler will now run the evaluation reset operation on the date that you specified.

Preparing to Take the Microsoft Certified Technology Specialist (MCTS) Exam

The Microsoft Certified Technology Specialist (MCTS) certifications enable professionals to target specific technologies and to distinguish themselves by demonstrating in-depth knowledge and expertise in their specialized technologies. Microsoft Certified Technology Specialists are consistently capable of inplementing, building, troubleshooting, and debugging a particular Microsoft Technology.

For organizations, the new generation of Microsoft certifications provides better skills verification tools that help with assessing not only in-demand skills on Windows Server, but also the ability to quickly complete on-the-job tasks. Individuals will find it easier to identify and work towards the certification credential that meets their personal and professional goals.

To learn more about becoming a Microsoft Certified Professional and exam availability, visit www.microsoft.com/learning/mcp.

Microsoft Certifications for IT Professionals

The new Microsoft Certified Technology Specialist (MCTS) and Microsoft Certified IT Professional (MCITP) credentials provide IT professionals with a simpler and more targeted framework to showcase their technical skills in addition to the skills that are required for specific developer job roles.

The Microsoft Certified Database Administrator (MCDBA), Microsoft Certified Desktop Support Technician (MCDST), Microsoft Certified System Administrator (MCSA), and Microsoft Certified Systems Engineer (MCSE) credentials continue to provide IT professionals who use Microsoft SQL Server 2000, Windows XP, and Windows Server 2003 with industry recognition and validation of their IT skills and experience.

Microsoft Certified Technology Specialist

The new Microsoft Certified Tehnology Specialist (MCTS) credential highlights your skills using a specific Microsoft technology. You can demonstrate your abilities as an IT professional or developer with in-depth knowledge of the Microsoft technology that you use today or are planning to deploy.

The MCTS certifications enable professionals to target specific technologies and to distinguish themselves by demonstrating in-depth knowledge and expertise in their specialized technologies. Microsoft Certified Technology Specialists are consistently capable of implementing, building, troubleshooting, and debugging a particular Microsoft technology.

You can learn more about the MCTS program at www.microsoft.com/learning/mcp/mcts.

Microsoft Certified IT Professional

The new Microsoft Certified IT Professional (MCITP) credential lets you highlight your specific area of expertise. Now, you can easily distinguish yourself as an expert in database administration, database development, business intelligence, or support.

By becoming certified, you demonstrate to employers that you have achieved a predictable level of skill not only in the use of the Windows Server operating system, but with a comprehensive set of Microsoft technologies. Employers often require certification either as a condition of employment or as a condition of advancement within the company or other organization.

You can learn more about the MCITP program at www.microsoft.com/learning/mcp/mcitp.

The certification examinations are sponsored by Microsoft but administered through Microsoft's exam delivery partner Prometric.

Preparing to Take an Exam

Unless you are a very experienced user, you will need to use a test preparation course to prepare to complete the test correctly and within the time allowed. The *Microsoft Official Academic Course* series is designed to prepare you with a strong knowledge of all exam topics, and with some additional review and practice on your own, you should feel confident in your ability to pass the appropriate exam.

After you decide which exam to take, review the list of objectives for the exam. You can easily identify tasks that are included in the objective list by locating the Objective Domain Matrix at the start of each lesson and the Certification Ready sidebars in the margin of the lessons in this book.

To take the MCTS test, visit www.microsoft.com/learning/mcp/mcts to locate your nearest testing center. Then call the testing center directly to schedule your test. The amount of advance notice you should provide will vary for different testing centers, and it typically depends on the number of computers available at the testing center, the number of other testers who have already been scheduled for the day on which you want to take the test, and the number of times per week that the testing center offers MCTS testing. In general, you should call to schedule your test at least two weeks prior to the date on which you want to take the test.

When you arrive at the testing center, you might be asked for proof of identity. A driver's license or passport is an acceptable form of identification. If you do not have either of these items of documentation, call your testing center and ask what alternative forms of identification will be accepted. If you are retaking a test, bring your MCTS identification number, which will have been given to you when you previously took the test. If you have not prepaid or if your organization has not already arranged to make payment for you, you will need to pay the test-taking fee when you arrive.

About the Author

Craig Zacker is a writer, editor, and networker whose computing experience began in the days of teletypes and paper tape. After making the move from minicomputers to PCs, he worked as an administrator of Novell NetWare networks and as a PC support technician while operating a freelance desktop publishing business. After earning a Master's Degree in English and American Literature from New York University, Craig worked extensively on integrating Microsoft Windows operating systems into existing internetworks, supported fleets of Windows workstations, and was employed as a technical writer, content provider, and webmaster for the online services group of a large software company. Since devoting himself to writing and editing full-time, Craig has authored or contributed to dozens of books on networking topics, operating systems, and PC hardware, including *Microsoft Official Academic Course: Windows Vista Configuration Exam 70-620* and *Windows XP Pro: The Missing Manual.* He developed educational texts for college courses, designed online training courses for the Web, and published articles with top industry publications.

Acknowledgments

MOAC Instructor Advisory Board

We would like to thank our Instructor Advisory Board, an elite group of educators who has assisted us every step of the way in building these products. Advisory Board members have acted as our sounding board on key pedagogical and design decisions leading to the development of these compelling and innovative textbooks for future Information Workers. Their dedication to technology education is truly appreciated.

Charles DeSassure, Tarrant County College

Charles DeSassure is Department Chair and Instructor of Computer Science & Information Technology at Tarrant County College Southeast Campus, Arlington, Texas. He has had experience as a MIS Manager, system analyst, field technology analyst, LAN Administrator, microcomputer specialist, and public school teacher in South Carolina. DeSassure has worked in higher education for more than ten years and received the Excellence Award in Teaching from the National Institute for Staff and Organizational Development (NISOD). He currently serves on the Educational Testing Service (ETS) iSkills National Advisory Committee and chaired the Tarrant County College District Student Assessment Committee. He has written proposals and makes presentations at major educational conferences nationwide. DeSassure has served as a textbook reviewer for John Wiley & Sons and Prentice Hall. He teaches courses in information security, networking, distance learning, and computer literacy. DeSassure holds a master's degree in Computer Resources & Information Management from Webster University.

Kim Ehlert, Waukesha County Technical College

Kim Ehlert is the Microsoft Program Coordinator and a Network Specialist instructor at Waukesha County Technical College, teaching the full range of MCSE and networking courses for the past nine years. Prior to joining WCTC, Kim was a professor at the Milwaukee School of Engineering for five years where she oversaw the Novell Academic Education and the Microsoft IT Academy programs. She has a wide variety of industry experience including network design and management for Johnson Controls, local city fire departments, police departments, large church congregations, health departments, and accounting firms. Kim holds many industry certifications including MCDST, MCSE, Security+, Network+, Server+, MCT, and CNE.

Kim has a bachelor's degree in Information Systems and a master's degree in Business Administration from the University of Wisconsin Milwaukee. When she is not busy teaching, she enjoys spending time with her husband Gregg and their two children—Alex, 14, and Courtney, 17.

Penny Gudgeon, Corinthian Colleges, Inc.

Penny Gudgeon is the Program Manager for IT curriculum at Corinthian Colleges, Inc. Previously, she was responsible for computer programming and web curriculum for twenty-seven campuses in Corinthian's Canadian division, CDI College of Business, Technology and Health Care. Penny joined CDI College in 1997 as a computer programming instructor at one of the campuses outside of Toronto. Prior to joining CDI College, Penny taught productivity software at another Canadian college, the Academy of Learning, for four years. Penny has experience in helping students achieve their goals through various learning models from instructor-led to self-directed to online.

Before embarking on a career in education, Penny worked in the fields of advertising, marketing/sales, mechanical and electronic engineering technology, and computer programming. When not working from her home office or indulging her passion for lifelong learning, Penny likes to read mysteries, garden, and relax at home in Hamilton, Ontario, with her Shih-Tzu, Gracie.

Margaret Leary, Northern Virginia Community College

Margaret Leary is Professor of IST at Northern Virginia Community College, teaching Networking and Network Security Courses for the past ten years. She is the co-Principal Investigator on the CyberWATCH initiative, an NSF-funded regional consortium of higher education institutions and businesses working together to increase the number of network security personnel in the workforce. She also serves as a Senior Security Policy Manager and Research Analyst at Nortel Government Solutions and holds a CISSP certification.

Margaret holds a B.S.B.A. and MBA/Technology Management from the University of Phoenix, and is pursuing her Ph.D. in Organization and Management with an IT Specialization at Capella University. Her dissertation is titled "Quantifying the Discoverability of Identity Attributes in Internet-Based Public Records: Impact on Identity Theft and Knowledge-based Authentication." She has several other published articles in various government and industry magazines, notably on identity management and network security.

Wen Liu, ITT Educational Services, Inc.

Wen Liu is Director of Corporate Curriculum Development at ITT Educational Services, Inc. He joined the ITT corporate headquarters in 1998 as a Senior Network Analyst to plan and deploy the corporate WAN infrastructure. A year later he assumed the position of Corporate Curriculum Manager supervising the curriculum development of all IT programs. After he was promoted to the current position three years ago, he continued to manage the curriculum research and development for all the programs offered in the School of Information Technology in addition to supervising the curriculum development in other areas (such as Schools of Drafting and Design and Schools of Electronics Technology). Prior to his employment with ITT Educational Services, Liu was a Telecommunications Analyst at the state government of Indiana working on the state backbone project that provided Internet and telecommunications services to the public users such as K-12 and higher education institutions, government agencies, libraries, and healthcare facilities.

Wen Liu has an M.A. in Student Personnel Administration in Higher Education and an M.S. in Information and Communications Sciences from Ball State University, Indiana. He used to be the director of special projects on the board of directors of the Indiana Telecommunications User Association, and used to serve on Course Technology's IT Advisory Board. He is currently a member of the IEEE and its Computer Society.

Jared Spencer, Westwood College Online

Jared Spencer has been the Lead Faculty for Networking at Westwood College Online since 2006. He began teaching in 2001 and has taught both on-ground and online for a variety of institutions, including Robert Morris University and Point Park University. In addition to his academic background, he has more than fifteen years of industry experience working for companies including the Thomson Corporation and IBM.

Jared has a master's degree in Internet Information Systems and is currently ABD and pursuing his doctorate in Information Systems at Nova Southeastern University. He has authored several papers that have been presented at conferences and appeared in publications such as the Journal of Internet Commerce and the Journal of Information Privacy and Security (JIPC). He holds a number of industry certifications, including AIX (UNIX), A+, Network+, Security+, MCSA on Windows 2000, and MCSA on Windows 2003 Server.

MOAC Windows Server Reviewers

We also thank the many reviewers who pored over the manuscript, providing invaluable feedback in the service of quality instructional materials.

Windows Server® 2008 Applications Infrastructure Configuration Exam 70-643

Chris Aburime, Inver Hills Community College

Ron Handlon, Remington College — Tampa

Steve Strom, Butler Community College

Bonnie Willy, Ivy Tech

Focus Group and Survey Participants

Finally, we thank the hundreds of instructors who participated in our focus groups and surveys to ensure that the Microsoft Official Academic Courses best met the needs of our customers.

Jean Aguilar, Mt. Hood Community College

Konrad Akens, Zane State College

Michael Albers, University of Memphis

Diana Anderson, Big Sandy Community & Technical College

Phyllis Anderson, Delaware County Community College

Judith Andrews, Feather River College

Damon Antos, American River College

Bridget Archer, Oakton Community College

Linda Arnold, Harrisburg Area Community College–Lebanon Campus

Neha Arya, Fullerton College

Mohammad Bajwa, Katharine Gibbs School–New York

Virginia Baker, University of Alaska Fairbanks

Carla Bannick, Pima Community College

Rita Barkley, Northeast Alabama Community College

Elsa Barr, Central Community College–Hastings

Ronald W. Barry, Ventura County Community College District

Elizabeth Bastedo, Central Carolina Technical College

Karen Baston, Waubonsee Community College

Karen Bean, Blinn College

Scott Beckstrand, Community College of Southern Nevada

Paulette Bell, Santa Rosa Junior College

Liz Bennett, Southeast Technical Institute

Nancy Bermea, Olympic College

Lucy Betz, Milwaukee Area Technical College

Meral Binbasioglu, Hofstra University

Catherine Binder, Strayer University & Katharine Gibbs School–Philadelphia

Terrel Blair, El Centro College

Ruth Blalock, Alamance Community College

Beverly Bohner, Reading Area Community College

Henry Bojack, Farmingdale State University

Matthew Bowie, Luna Community College

Julie Boyles, Portland Community College

Karen Brandt, College of the Albemarle

Stephen Brown, College of San Mateo

Jared Bruckner, Southern Adventist University

Pam Brune, Chattanooga State Technical Community College

Sue Buchholz, Georgia Perimeter College

Roberta Buczyna, Edison College

Angela Butler, Mississippi Gulf Coast Community College

Rebecca Byrd, Augusta Technical College

Kristen Callahan, Mercer County Community College

Judy Cameron, Spokane Community College

Dianne Campbell, Athens Technical College

Gena Casas, Florida Community College at Jacksonville

Jesus Castrejon, Latin Technologies

Gail Chambers, Southwest Tennessee Community College

Jacques Chansavang, Indiana University–Purdue University Fort Wayne

Nancy Chapko, Milwaukee Area Technical College

Rebecca Chavez, Yavapai College

Sanjiv Chopra, Thomas Nelson Community College

Greg Clements, Midland Lutheran College

Dayna Coker, Southwestern Oklahoma State University–Sayre Campus

Tamra Collins, Otero Junior College

Janet Conrey, Gavilan Community College

Carol Cornforth, West Virginia Northern Community College

Gary Cotton, American River College

Edie Cox, Chattahoochee Technical College

Rollie Cox, Madison Area Technical College

David Crawford, Northwestern Michigan College
J.K. Crowley, Victor Valley College
Rosalyn Culver, Washtenaw Community College
Sharon Custer, Huntington University
Sandra Daniels, New River Community College
Anila Das, Cedar Valley College
Brad Davis, Santa Rosa Junior College
Susan Davis, Green River Community College
Mark Dawdy, Lincoln Land Community College
Jennifer Day, Sinclair Community College
Carol Deane, Eastern Idaho Technical College
Julie DeBuhr, Lewis-Clark State College
Janis DeHaven, Central Community College
Drew Dekreon, University of Alaska–Anchorage
Joy DePover, Central Lakes College
Salli DiBartolo, Brevard Community College
Melissa Diegnau, Riverland Community College
Al Dillard, Lansdale School of Business
Marjorie Duffy, Cosumnes River College
Sarah Dunn, Southwest Tennessee Community College
Shahla Durany, Tarrant County College–South Campus
Kay Durden, University of Tennessee at Martin
Dineen Ebert, St. Louis Community College–Meramec
Donna Ehrhart, State University of New York–Brockport
Larry Elias, Montgomery County Community College
Glenda Elser, New Mexico State University at Alamogordo
Angela Evangelinos, Monroe County Community College
Angie Evans, Ivy Tech Community College of Indiana
Linda Farrington, Indian Hills Community College
Dana Fladhammer, Phoenix College
Richard Flores, Citrus College
Connie Fox, Community and Technical College at Institute of Technology West Virginia University
Wanda Freeman, Okefenokee Technical College
Brenda Freeman, Augusta Technical College
Susan Fry, Boise State University
Roger Fulk, Wright State University–Lake Campus
Sue Furnas, Collin County Community College District

Sandy Gabel, Vernon College
Laura Galvan, Fayetteville Technical Community College
Candace Garrod, Red Rocks Community College
Sherrie Geitgey, Northwest State Community College
Chris Gerig, Chattahoochee Technical College
Barb Gillespie, Cuyamaca College
Jessica Gilmore, Highline Community College
Pamela Gilmore, Reedley College
Debbie Glinert, Queensborough Community College
Steven Goldman, Polk Community College
Bettie Goodman, C.S. Mott Community College
Mike Grabill, Katharine Gibbs School–Philadelphia
Francis Green, Penn State University
Walter Griffin, Blinn College
Fillmore Guinn, Odessa College
Helen Haasch, Milwaukee Area Technical College
John Habal, Ventura College
Joy Haerens, Chaffey College
Norman Hahn, Thomas Nelson Community College
Kathy Hall, Alamance Community College
Teri Harbacheck, Boise State University
Linda Harper, Richland Community College
Maureen Harper, Indian Hills Community College
Steve Harris, Katharine Gibbs School–New York
Robyn Hart, Fresno City College
Darien Hartman, Boise State University
Gina Hatcher, Tacoma Community College
Winona T. Hatcher, Aiken Technical College
BJ Hathaway, Northeast Wisconsin Tech College
Cynthia Hauki, West Hills College – Coalinga
Mary L. Haynes, Wayne County Community College
Marcie Hawkins, Zane State College
Steve Hebrock, Ohio State University Agricultural Technical Institute
Sue Heistand, Iowa Central Community College
Heith Hennel, Valencia Community College
Donna Hendricks, South Arkansas Community College
Judy Hendrix, Dyersburg State Community College
Gloria Hensel, Matanuska-Susitna College University of Alaska Anchorage
Gwendolyn Hester, Richland College

www.wiley.com/college/microsoft or
call the MOAC Toll-Free Number: 1+(888) 764-7001 (U.S. & Canada only)

Tammarra Holmes, Laramie County Community College
Dee Hobson, Richland College
Keith Hoell, Katharine Gibbs School–New York
Pashia Hogan, Northeast State Technical Community College
Susan Hoggard, Tulsa Community College
Kathleen Holliman, Wallace Community College Selma
Chastity Honchul, Brown Mackie College/ Wright State University
Christie Hovey, Lincoln Land Community College
Peggy Hughes, Allegany College of Maryland
Sandra Hume, Chippewa Valley Technical College
John Hutson, Aims Community College
Celia Ing, Sacramento City College
Joan Ivey, Lanier Technical College
Barbara Jaffari, College of the Redwoods
Penny Jakes, University of Montana College of Technology
Eduardo Jaramillo, Peninsula College
Barbara Jauken, Southeast Community College
Susan Jennings, Stephen F. Austin State University
Leslie Jernberg, Eastern Idaho Technical College
Linda Johns, Georgia Perimeter College
Brent Johnson, Okefenokee Technical College
Mary Johnson, Mt. San Antonio College
Shirley Johnson, Trinidad State Junior College–Valley Campus
Sandra M. Jolley, Tarrant County College
Teresa Jolly, South Georgia Technical College
Dr. Deborah Jones, South Georgia Technical College
Margie Jones, Central Virginia Community College
Randall Jones, Marshall Community and Technical College
Diane Karlsbraaten, Lake Region State College
Teresa Keller, Ivy Tech Community College of Indiana
Charles Kemnitz, Pennsylvania College of Technology
Sandra Kinghorn, Ventura College
Bill Klein, Katharine Gibbs School–Philadelphia
Bea Knaapen, Fresno City College
Kit Kofoed, Western Wyoming Community College
Maria Kolatis, County College of Morris
Barry Kolb, Ocean County College
Karen Kuralt, University of Arkansas at Little Rock

Belva-Carole Lamb, Rogue Community College
Betty Lambert, Des Moines Area Community College
Anita Lande, Cabrillo College
Junnae Landry, Pratt Community College
Karen Lankisch, UC Clermont
David Lanzilla, Central Florida Community College
Nora Laredo, Cerritos Community College
Jennifer Larrabee, Chippewa Valley Technical College
Debra Larson, Idaho State University
Barb Lave, Portland Community College
Audrey Lawrence, Tidewater Community College
Deborah Layton, Eastern Oklahoma State College
Larry LeBlanc, Owen Graduate School– Vanderbilt University
Philip Lee, Nashville State Community College
Michael Lehrfeld, Brevard Community College
Vasant Limaye, Southwest Collegiate Institute for the Deaf – Howard College
Anne C. Lewis, Edgecombe Community College
Stephen Linkin, Houston Community College
Peggy Linston, Athens Technical College
Hugh Lofton, Moultrie Technical College
Donna Lohn, Lakeland Community College
Jackie Lou, Lake Tahoe Community College
Donna Love, Gaston College
Curt Lynch, Ozarks Technical Community College
Sheilah Lynn, Florida Community College– Jacksonville
Pat R. Lyon, Tomball College
Bill Madden, Bergen Community College
Heather Madden, Delaware Technical & Community College
Donna Madsen, Kirkwood Community College
Jane Maringer-Cantu, Gavilan College
Suzanne Marks, Bellevue Community College
Carol Martin, Louisiana State University– Alexandria
Cheryl Martucci, Diablo Valley College
Roberta Marvel, Eastern Wyoming College
Tom Mason, Brookdale Community College
Mindy Mass, Santa Barbara City College
Dixie Massaro, Irvine Valley College
Rebekah May, Ashland Community & Technical College
Emma Mays-Reynolds, Dyersburg State Community College

Timothy Mayes, Metropolitan State College of Denver

Reggie McCarthy, Central Lakes College

Matt McCaskill, Brevard Community College

Kevin McFarlane, Front Range Community College

Donna McGill, Yuba Community College

Terri McKeever, Ozarks Technical Community College

Patricia McMahon, South Suburban College

Sally McMillin, Katharine Gibbs School–Philadelphia

Charles McNerney, Bergen Community College

Lisa Mears, Palm Beach Community College

Imran Mehmood, ITT Technical Institute–King of Prussia Campus

Virginia Melvin, Southwest Tennessee Community College

Jeanne Mercer, Texas State Technical College

Denise Merrell, Jefferson Community & Technical College

Catherine Merrikin, Pearl River Community College

Diane D. Mickey, Northern Virginia Community College

Darrelyn Miller, Grays Harbor College

Sue Mitchell, Calhoun Community College

Jacquie Moldenhauer, Front Range Community College

Linda Motonaga, Los Angeles City College

Sam Mryyan, Allen County Community College

Cindy Murphy, Southeastern Community College

Ryan Murphy, Sinclair Community College

Sharon E. Nastav, Johnson County Community College

Christine Naylor, Kent State University Ashtabula

Haji Nazarian, Seattle Central Community College

Nancy Noe, Linn-Benton Community College

Jennie Noriega, San Joaquin Delta College

Linda Nutter, Peninsula College

Thomas Omerza, Middle Bucks Institute of Technology

Edith Orozco, St. Philip's College

Dona Orr, Boise State University

Joanne Osgood, Chaffey College

Janice Owens, Kishwaukee College

Tatyana Pashnyak, Bainbridge College

John Partacz, College of DuPage

Tim Paul, Montana State University–Great Falls

Joseph Perez, South Texas College

Mike Peterson, Chemeketa Community College

Dr. Karen R. Petitto, West Virginia Wesleyan College

Terry Pierce, Onandaga Community College

Ashlee Pieris, Raritan Valley Community College

Jamie Pinchot, Thiel College

Michelle Poertner, Northwestern Michigan College

Betty Posta, University of Toledo

Deborah Powell, West Central Technical College

Mark Pranger, Rogers State University

Carolyn Rainey, Southeast Missouri State University

Linda Raskovich, Hibbing Community College

Leslie Ratliff, Griffin Technical College

Mar-Sue Ratzke, Rio Hondo Community College

Roxy Reissen, Southeastern Community College

Silvio Reyes, Technical Career Institutes

Patricia Rishavy, Anoka Technical College

Jean Robbins, Southeast Technical Institute

Carol Roberts, Eastern Maine Community College and University of Maine

Teresa Roberts, Wilson Technical Community College

Vicki Robertson, Southwest Tennessee Community College

Betty Rogge, Ohio State Agricultural Technical Institute

Lynne Rusley, Missouri Southern State University

Claude Russo, Brevard Community College

Ginger Sabine, Northwestern Technical College

Steven Sachs, Los Angeles Valley College

Joanne Salas, Olympic College

Lloyd Sandmann, Pima Community College–Desert Vista Campus

Beverly Santillo, Georgia Perimeter College

Theresa Savarese, San Diego City College

Sharolyn Sayers, Milwaukee Area Technical College

Judith Scheeren, Westmoreland County Community College

Adolph Scheiwe, Joliet Junior College

Marilyn Schmid, Asheville-Buncombe Technical Community College

Janet Sebesy, Cuyahoga Community College

Phyllis T. Shafer, Brookdale Community College

Ralph Shafer, Truckee Meadows Community College

Anne Marie Shanley, County College of Morris

Shelia Shelton, Surry Community College

Merilyn Shepherd, Danville Area Community College

Susan Sinele, Aims Community College

Beth Sindt, Hawkeye Community College

Andrew Smith, Marian College

Brenda Smith, Southwest Tennessee Community College

Lynne Smith, State University of New York–Delhi

Rob Smith, Katharine Gibbs School–Philadelphia

Tonya Smith, Arkansas State University–Mountain Home

Del Spencer – Trinity Valley Community College

Jeri Spinner, Idaho State University

Eric Stadnik, Santa Rosa Junior College

Karen Stanton, Los Medanos College

Meg Stoner, Santa Rosa Junior College

Beverly Stowers, Ivy Tech Community College of Indiana

Marcia Stranix, Yuba College

Kim Styles, Tri-County Technical College

Sylvia Summers, Tacoma Community College

Beverly Swann, Delaware Technical & Community College

Ann Taff, Tulsa Community College

Mike Theiss, University of Wisconsin–Marathon Campus

Romy Thiele, Cañada College

Sharron Thompson, Portland Community College

Ingrid Thompson-Sellers, Georgia Perimeter College

Barbara Tietsort, University of Cincinnati–Raymond Walters College

Janine Tiffany, Reading Area Community College

Denise Tillery, University of Nevada Las Vegas

Susan Trebelhorn, Normandale Community College

Noel Trout, Santiago Canyon College

Cheryl Turgeon, Asnuntuck Community College

Steve Turner, Ventura College

Sylvia Unwin, Bellevue Community College

Lilly Vigil, Colorado Mountain College

Sabrina Vincent, College of the Mainland

Mary Vitrano, Palm Beach Community College

Brad Vogt, Northeast Community College

Cozell Wagner, Southeastern Community College

Carolyn Walker, Tri-County Technical College

Sherry Walker, Tulsa Community College

Qi Wang, Tacoma Community College

Betty Wanielista, Valencia Community College

Marge Warber, Lanier Technical College–Forsyth Campus

Marjorie Webster, Bergen Community College

Linda Wenn, Central Community College

Mark Westlund, Olympic College

Carolyn Whited, Roane State Community College

Winona Whited, Richland College

Jerry Wilkerson, Scott Community College

Joel Willenbring, Fullerton College

Barbara Williams, WITC Superior

Charlotte Williams, Jones County Junior College

Bonnie Willy, Ivy Tech Community College of Indiana

Diane Wilson, J. Sargeant Reynolds Community College

James Wolfe, Metropolitan Community College

Marjory Wooten, Lanier Technical College

Mark Yanko, Hocking College

Alexis Yusov, Pace University

Naeem Zaman, San Joaquin Delta College

Kathleen Zimmerman, Des Moines Area Community College

We also thank Lutz Ziob, Jim DiIanni, Merrick Van Dongen, Jim LeValley, Bruce Curling, Joe Wilson, Rob Linsky, Jim Clark, and Scott Serna at Microsoft for their encouragement and support in making the Microsoft Official Academic Course programs the finest instructional materials for mastering the newest Microsoft technologies for both students and instructors.

Brief Contents

Contents

Deploying an Application Server

OBJECTIVE DOMAIN MATRIX

TECHNOLOGY SKILL	OBJECTIVE DOMAIN	OBJECTIVE DOMAIN NUMBER
Installing Windows Deployment Services	Deploy images by using Windows Deployment Services.	1.1
Activating Windows	Configure Microsoft Windows activation.	1.2

KEY TERMS

application
application services
client machine ID (CMID)
directory services
feature
infrastructure services
Key Management Service (KMS)

KMS activation threshold
MAK Independent Activation
MAK Proxy Activation
Multiple Activation Key (MAK)
preboot execution environment (PXE)
role
ServerManagerCmd.exe

thin client
virtual server
Windows Deployment Services (WDS)
Windows PE (Preinstallation Environment) 2.1

■ Introducing Windows Server 2008 Application Services

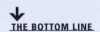
THE BOTTOM LINE Windows Server 2008 includes support services that enable administrators to deploy applications in several different ways.

Two basic types of computers can be on an enterprise network: clients and servers. In computer networking, a server is, by definition, a system that responds to requests for resources originating from clients on the same network. The resources provided by a server can take many forms, including information, document files, Web pages, and security services.

Designing an enterprise network is a complex undertaking that must consider many factors, not all of them technical. Certainly, technical elements such as hardware platforms and operating systems are important, but the designers of a large network also have to consider other elements, including management, political, and economic factors.

One of the primary considerations in the enterprise network design process is what the users of the network need to do with their computers. After all, companies supply their employees with computers so that they can get work done, and to accomplish this goal, the users need computer programs designed to aid them in the performance of specific tasks. These programs are also known as *applications*.

Architecturally, applications in the enterprise can take several forms, but all of these forms typically involve a server in some way, as follows:

- Client-run applications — Some applications run wholly on client computers, such as office productivity applications. However, in an enterprise environment, they typically use services provided by network servers, such as file and print servers, as shown in Figure 1-1.

Figure 1-1

Applications running on a client computer utilize file and print resources provided by application servers

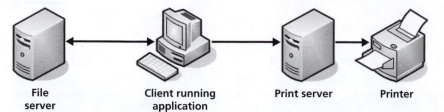

File server   **Client running application**   **Print server**   **Printer**

- Client/Server applications — Sometimes, an application runs on a single server, to which clients all over the network send requests for services. For example, a single application server might run a database application that supplies information to all of the clients on the network, as shown in Figure 1-2.

Figure 1-2

A client computer accessing an application running on a single application server

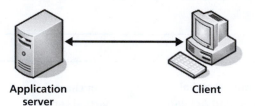

Application server   **Client**

- Distributed applications — In some cases, an administrator distributes an application among multiple servers, which provide different functions that work together. For example, an application server hosting a Web site can function as the intermediary between clients on the front end and a database server on the back end, as shown in Figure 1-3.

Figure 1-3

A client computer accessing an application server, which retrieves information from a database server

Database server   **Application server**   **Client**

Therefore, to design an efficient enterprise network, IT personnel must consider the applications the users will require and the server resources those applications need to run properly. Typically, administrators refer to the servers that provide these resources, not surprisingly, as application servers. Conducting an inventory of the users' needs enables the network designers to address basic design questions such as the following:

- How many application servers do I need?
- What hardware should the application servers contain?
- Where should the application servers be located?

Understanding Server Roles

Windows Server 2008 includes predefined combinations of services called roles that implement common server functions.

Computers running the Windows Server 2008 operating system can perform a wide variety of tasks, using both the software included with the product and third-party applications. The activities Windows Server 2008 performs for network clients are known as *roles*. After you install the Windows Server 2008 operating system, you can use the Add Roles Wizard to assign one or more roles to that computer.

The roles provided by the Add Roles Wizard fall into three basic categories, as follows:

- *Directory services* — Store, organize, and supply information about a network and its resources.
- *Infrastructure services* — Provide support services for network clients.
- *Application services* — Provide communications services, operating environments, or programming interfaces for specific applications.

 TAKE NOTE * The Add Roles Wizard and the Add Features Wizard are accessible from the Initial Configuration Tasks window or the Server Manager application. You can also install and remove roles and features from the command line, using the ServerManagerCmd.exe utility.

Table 1-1 lists the specific roles that Microsoft has supplied with Windows Server 2008. This book is devoted to the roles providing the Windows Server 2008 application services, but the directory and infrastructure services also play a part in providing network clients with access to the applications they need.

Table 1-1

Windows Server 2008 Server Roles

DIRECTORY SERVICES	INFRASTRUCTURE SERVICES	APPLICATION SERVICES
Active Directory Certificate Services — Implements certification authorities (CAs) and other services that facilitate the creation and management of the public key certificates employed by the identity and access control elements of the Windows Server 2008 security infrastructure.	DHCP (Dynamic Host Configuration Protocol) Server — Provides network clients with dynamically-assigned IP addresses and other TCP/IP configuration settings, such as subnet masks, default gateway addresses, DNS (Domain Name system) server addresses, and WINS (Windows Internet Naming System) server addresses.	Application Server — Provides an integrated environment for deploying and running server-based business applications designed within (or expressly for) the organization, such as those requiring the services provided by Internet Information Services (IIS), Microsoft.NET Framework 2.0 and 3.0, COM+, ASP.NET, Message Queuing, or Windows Communication Foundation (WCF).
Active Directory Domain Services — Configures the server to function as an Active Directory domain controller, which stores and manages a distributed database of network resources and application-specific information.	DNS Server — Provides name-to-address and address-to-name resolution services for Active Directory and Internet clients. The Windows Server 2008 DNS server implementation also supports dynamic DNS and DHCP integration.	Fax Server — Enables administrators to manage fax devices and clients to send and receive faxes over the network.
Active Directory Federation Services — Creates a single sign-on environment by implementing trust relationships that enable users on one network to access applications on other networks without providing a secondary set of logon credentials.	Network Policy and Access Services (NPAS) — Implements services such as Routing and Remote Access (RRAS), Network Policy Server (NPS), Health Registration Authority (HRA), and Host Credential Authorization Protocol (HCAP), which provide network connectivity and secure network access to local and remote users.	File Services — Installs tools and services that enhance Windows Server 2008's basic ability to provide network clients with access to files stored on server drives, including Distributed File System (DFS), DFS Replication, Storage Manager for Storage Area Networks (SANs), fast file searching, and file services for UNIX clients.

(continued)

Table 1-1 (*continued*)

DIRECTORY SERVICES	INFRASTRUCTURE SERVICES	APPLICATION SERVICES
Active Directory Lightweight Directory Services — Implements a Lightweight Directory Access Protocol (LDAP) directory service that provides support for directory-enabled applications without incurring the extensive overhead of Active Directory Domain Services.	Windows Deployment Services (WDS) — Enables administrators to remotely install Windows operating systems on computers throughout the enterprise.	Print Services — Provides clients with access to printers attached to the server or to the network, as well as centralized network printer and print server management, and printer deployment using Group Policy.
Active Directory Rights Management Services (AD RMS) — Client/server system that uses certificates and licensing to implement persistent usage policies, which can control access to information, no matter where a user moves it.		Streaming Media Services — Enables the server to transmit digital media content to network clients in real time. (This role is not included with Windows Server 2008, but it is available as a free download from Microsoft's Web site.)
		Terminal Services — Enables clients on the network or on the Internet to remotely access server-based applications or the entire Windows desktop, using server resources.
		UDDI Services — Implements Universal Description, Discovery, and Integration (UDDI), which enables the organization to publish information about its Web services for use by intranet, extranet, and/or Internet clients.
		Web Server (IIS) — Installs Internet Information Services (IIS) 7.0, which enables the organization to publish Web sites and ASP.NET, WCF, or Windows SharePoint-based applications for use by intranet, extranet, and/or Internet clients.

Understanding Server Features

Windows Server 2008 includes a large collection of individual modules called *features,* which you can install in any combination.

In addition to its roles, Windows Server 2008 includes a collection of features, which you can select individually. You can also augment a given role by adding features that increase its capabilities.

The features that are installable using the Add Features Wizard are as follows:

- .NET Framework 3.0 — A software package containing code that provides solutions to a large number of common programming requirements, including user interface, database access, cryptographic security, and network communications routines. Software developers can utilize these routines, with their own code, to build Windows applications more easily.

- BitLocker Drive Encryption — Encrypts entire hard disk volumes, allowing access to the volumes only after validating the integrity of the computer's boot components and confirming that no one has moved the drive to another computer.

- BITS Server Extensions — The Background Intelligent Transfer Service (BITS) enables client computers to transmit and receive files without utilizing resources needed by other processes. These server extensions enable the Windows Server 2008 computer to receive files uploaded by BITS clients.
- Connection Manager Administration Kit (CMAK) — Enables administrators to create customized service profiles for the Connection Manager client dialer application.
- Desktop Experience — Implements a collection of Windows Vista features on the Windows Server 2008 computer, including Windows Media Player and desktop themes.
- Failover Clustering — Enables multiple servers to work together at performing the same tasks, to provide high availability for applications and services.
- Group Policy Management — Installs the Group Policy Management Console, a Microsoft Management Console snap-in that simplifies the process of deploying, managing, and troubleshooting Group Policy Objects (GPOs).
- Internet Printing Client — Enables users to send print jobs to remote Web server-based printers, using an Internet connection.
- Internet Storage Name Server (iSNS) — Provides discovery services for clients accessing storage area networks running the Internet Small Computer System Interface (iSCSI), including registration, deregistration, and queries.
- LPR (Line Printer Remote) Port Monitor — Enables the computer to send print jobs to a UNIX computer with a compatible line printer daemon (LPD) implementation running on it.
- Message Queuing — Provides a variety of messaging services that enable applications to communicate, even when they run on different operating systems, use different types of networks, run at different times, or are temporarily offline.
- Multipath I/O (MPIO) — Provides multiple data paths to a single server storage device.
- Network Load Balancing (NLB) — Distributes incoming client traffic evenly among servers running the same application, enabling administrators to scale the application up or down by adding or removing servers as needed.
- Peer Name Resolution Protocol (PNRP) — A name resolution service that enables computers to register their peer names and associate them with their IPv6 addresses. Other computers on the network can then use the service to resolve a name into an address, enabling them to establish a connection to the named computer.
- Quality Windows Audio Video Experience (qWave) — Provides flow control and traffic prioritization services for applications that stream audio and video content over a network.
- Remote Assistance — Enables one user to provide technical support or training to another user at a remote computer by observing the remote user's desktop or by taking control of it.
- Remote Differential Compression (RDC) — Enables applications to conserve network bandwidth by determining what parts of a file have changed and transmitting only the modifications over the network.
- Remote Server Administration Tools — Enables administrators to access management tools on remote computers running Windows Server 2003 and Windows Server 2008.
- Removable Storage Manager (RSM) — Creates catalogs of removable media and operates drives that use removable media.
- RPC Over HTTP Proxy — Enables objects to receive Remote Procedure Calls (RPC) messages using the Hypertext Transfer Protocol (HTTP), even if someone has moved the object to another server on the network.
- Simple TCP/IP Services — Implements the Character Generator, Daytime, Discard, Echo, and Quote of the Day services, as defined in the TCP/IP standards.
- SMTP Server — The Simple Mail Transfer Protocol (SMTP) provides communication between email servers, and between email clients and servers.

- SNMP Services — Installs support for the Simple Network Management Protocol (SNMP), which enables network management applications to communicate with the agents for managed devices on the network.
- Storage Manager for SANs — Enables administrators to create and manage logical unit numbers (LUNs) for storage subsystems on a storage area network (SAN).
- Subsystem for UNIX-based Applications — Enables Windows Server 2008 to compile and run UNIX-based applications.
- Telnet Client — Enables the computer to connect to a Telnet server and access a command-line administration interface.
- Telnet Server — Enables remote users running Telnet clients to connect to the computers and access a command-line administration interface.
- TFTP (Trivial File Transfer Protocol) Client — Enables the computer to send files to and receive them from a TFTP server on the network, without the need for authentication.
- Windows Internal Database — Implements a relational data store that other Windows Server 2008 roles and features can utilize.
- Windows PowerShell — Implements a command-line shell and scripting language that provides improved administration and automation capabilities.
- Windows Process Activation Service (WAS) — Implements an environment that generalizes the IIS process model by removing the dependency on HTTP, thus enabling WCF applications to use non-HTTP protocols. This feature is required to run the Web Server (IIS) role.
- Windows Server Backup Features — Enables administrators to perform full or partial server backups at scheduled intervals.
- Windows System Resource Manager (WSRM) — Enables administrators to allocate specific amounts of CPU and memory resources to specific applications, services, or processes.
- WINS Server — Provides NetBIOS name registration and resolution services for down level Windows clients.
- Wireless LAN Service — Implements the Wireless LAN (WLAN) AutoConfig service, which detects and configures wireless network adapters, and manages wireless networking profiles and connections.

■ Planning an Enterprise Application Server Deployment

THE BOTTOM LINE
Planning an enterprise server deployment requires an understanding of the Windows Server 2008 roles and how they interact.

A Windows Server 2008 computer can perform one role or many roles, depending on the requirements of the organization. A small business might have only one server that fulfills all of the roles the company requires. A large enterprise network, on the other hand, typically has many servers and distributes the required roles among them. It is also possible to separate roles by deploying multiple virtual machines on a single computer and installing a different role on each one.

Assigning Multiple Roles

Windows Server 2008 computers can perform multiple roles at the same time.

The concept of assigning multiple roles to a single Windows Server 2008 computer makes it possible to utilize each computer's hardware resources more efficiently. For example, a computer that is functioning only as a DHCP server will probably only utilize a small percentage of its

CPU resources, as shown in Figure 1-4. This is because the only thing the DHCP service has to do is assign TCP/IP configuration settings to computers as they start, and then renew those settings, usually several days later. Most of the time, the service is idle.

Figure 1-4

Running a single role on a server can often be a waste of system resources

DHCP

To take full advantage of that DHCP server, a designer can assign other roles to it as well. The number of roles a server can perform depends on the computer's hardware configuration, the hardware requirements of the role, and the size and scope of the enterprise. For example, on a large enterprise network hosting 10,000 clients, a dedicated DHCP server would make sense. However, in a small to medium-sized enterprise, that DHCP server might also be able to function as a DNS server and an Active Directory domain controller without overtaxing its hardware, as shown in Figure 1-5.

Figure 1-5

Many servers can support several roles simultaneously

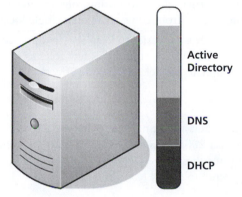

Active Directory

DNS

DHCP

In fact, the computer might have the hardware capacity to function as a Web server also. However, before adding that role, you must consider some other factors. Will the Web server be hosting a low-volume intranet Web site or a high-traffic Internet site? A greater amount of Web client traffic requires more resources.

With that consideration in mind, you might think it is a good idea to purchase the most powerful computer you can find, one with sufficient hardware resources to run all of the server roles the enterprise needs. For some organizations, this is a viable option, but distributing server roles among several computers has several distinct advantages, including the following:

- Fault tolerance — A single server provides a single point of failure. If one computer is performing all of the roles your enterprise needs to function, and that computer malfunctions, then you lose all of the services. Running multiple servers enables the business to better tolerate a single failure.

- Resource allocation — The hardware resources needed by specific server roles can fluctuate wildly, depending on a number of factors. A Web server, for example, might require more server resources during periods of heavy incoming network traffic, which occur at certain times of the day. If the Web server's peak utilization period happens to coincide with the peak utilization of the computer's other roles, the server could become a bottleneck, forcing performance of all the roles to suffer.

- Availability — Distributing roles among several computers enables you to build high availability into your network design. For example, you might configure one computer with the Web server role, and another computer to perform infrastructure roles, such as DHCP and DNS. To add high availability to the design, you would install the Web server role on the infrastructure server and the DHCP and DNS roles on the Web server, disabling the redundant services for the time being. This way, in the event that either server fails, the other one can take over its roles at a few minutes notice.

- Scalability — Having multiple servers on the network enables administrators to reallocate resources as needed. If, for example, a sudden increase in traffic to the company's Internet Web server causes that computer's CPU utilization to consistently spike at 100 percent, you could conceivably redeploy the Web server role on one of the company's other servers, one with a faster processor. Alternatively, you could add a second Web server and configure the two computers to split the traffic load between them.

- Security — Different roles can have different security requirements. For example, you might have a server functioning as an Active Directory domain controller that has sufficient resources to take on another role, but it would be a bad idea to use that computer as an Internet Web server. Computers exposed to the Internet are points of vulnerability, and for that reason, many enterprises put them on perimeter networks, isolated from internal resources, such as infrastructure servers. Generally speaking, the more roles a server has to perform, the more ports it has to leave open for incoming network traffic, and more open ports increase the attack surface of the computer.

- Network traffic — Running a variety of roles on a single server can consolidate a lot of network traffic onto a single subnet. Even if the server is capable of handling many different types of requests from clients all over the enterprise, the network might become a serious performance bottleneck. Distributing roles among servers on different subnets can prevent too much traffic from converging on a single location.

- Update management — It is far easier to keep servers updated with the latest operating system patches if each computer is running as few roles as is practical. In addition, fewer problems occur if an update has deleterious side effects.

TAKE NOTE* Another factor to consider when allocating roles to servers is the dependencies between many of the Windows Server 2008 roles and services. The Add Roles Wizard and the Add Features Wizard both enforce these dependencies by prompting you to install the correct antecedents with your selected roles and features.

Selecting Application Server Roles

Most Windows Server 2008 roles include a variety of options that you can use to customize the installation.

As mentioned earlier in this lesson, the complexity of the design and implementation process for an enterprise network's application servers is largely dependent on the types of applications the users need. The first step of the design process is to inventory those needs. Then, you can consider the various ways of providing for those needs.

The application services Microsoft includes with Windows Server 2008 provide administrators with several ways to deploy even the simplest applications. The method you choose depends on several factors, including economy, security, and ease of administration. The following sections examine the major application service roles listed earlier in this lesson, list the services that compose each one, and discuss how to use them to implement applications on an enterprise network.

USING THE FILE SERVICES ROLE

Virtually all enterprise networks have some (or maybe all) users who spend much of their time working with standard, off-the-shelf productivity applications, such as word processors, spreadsheets, email clients, and so forth. Even though the simplest way to deploy these applications is to install them on the users' individual workstations, employees can use application servers on the network in several ways.

The first consideration is where the users will store their documents. Storing document files on local workstation drives is a simple solution, but one with significant drawbacks. If users have to collaborate on documents, they would have to create shares on their local drives. This could result in dozens or hundreds of additional shares on the network, making navigation difficult. This practice also creates access control problems; the users would have to either set their own permissions or rely on administrators to do so. Finally, storing documents on workstation drives complicates the process of backing them up on a regular basis.

The more common, and more practical, solution is to have users store their documents on network servers, which means deploying one or more file servers on the network. Windows Server 2008 does not need a special role to provide basic file services. Administrators can share folders on any server drive and make them available to users by assigning the appropriate permissions.

However, installing the File Services role on a Windows Server 2008 computer provides additional capabilities that can aid in the management of document storage, such as the following:

- Distributed File System — Consists of two role services: DFS Namespace, which enables administrators to create a virtual directory tree consisting of folders stored on different servers, and DFS Replication, which maintains duplicate copies of the DFS namespace in remote locations.

- File Server Resource Manager (FSRM) — Enables administrators to create and enforce storage quotas, specify file types that are permitted on network volumes, and generate storage reports.

- Services for Network File System — Implements the Network File System (NFS) on the Windows Server 2008 computer. NFS is the standard file-sharing solution for UNIX-based operating systems, so this service enables UNIX clients to access files stored on a Windows server.

- Single Instance Store (SIS) — Conserves disk space on Windows servers by creating a single master copy of duplicate files stored in several locations, and deleting the duplicates.

- Windows Search Service — Creates an index that enables clients to rapidly search for files stored on server drives, without having to access each drive in turn.

- Windows Server 2003 File Services — Provides down level replication and indexing services that enable the server to participate on legacy networks with Windows Server 2003 storage services.

- Share and Storage Management — A new snap-in for Microsoft Management Console (MMC) that provides a centralized administration tool for file server resources.

In addition to the services provided by the File Services role, additional Windows Server 2008 applications and services provide management capabilities for storage area network (SAN) technology, including the following:

- Storage Manager for SANs — Provides configuration and management capabilities for SANs implemented using Fibre Channel or iSCSI networking technologies.

- Storage Explorer — An MMC snap-in that generates a tree view of a SAN and provides access to the configuration interfaces of individual SAN devices.

- iSCSI Initiator — Internet Small Computer System Interface (iSCSI) is an open standard SAN technology that provides a lower cost alternative to Fibre Channel. The iSCSI Initiator enables a Windows Server 2008 computer to access storage devices connected with a standard Gigabit Ethernet switch.

- iSCSI Remote Boot — Enables a Windows Server 2008 computer (or a group of Windows Server 2008 computers) to boot from a remote disk on a SAN.

X REF

For more information on the File Services role and other Windows Server 2008 storage technologies, see Lesson 2, "Deploying a File Server."

- iSNS Server — The Internet Storage Naming Service (iSNS) associates iSCSI initiators with specific SAN storage devices, thus emulating an iSCSI SAN function built into Fibre Channel switches.
- Multipath I/O — Provides an additional level of fault tolerance for storage technologies, such as Redundant Array of Independent Disks (RAID) arrays, that are designed to provide high availability.

USING THE TERMINAL SERVICES ROLE

Installing productivity applications on an individual workstation is a simple task, unless you have to repeat the process on hundreds or thousands of computers. In addition, after you have installed the applications, you must consider the prospect of upgrading and maintaining them as needed. Methods for automating the deployment and maintenance of applications on large groups of computers can require extensive planning and preparation, as well as the additional expense of a management software product.

Windows Server 2008 provides an alternative to individual workstation installations in the form of Terminal Services. Terminal Services is a technology that enables users working at another computer on the company network or on the Internet to establish a connection to a server and open an application or desktop session there.

Deploying applications using Terminal Services offers several advantages to the network administrator, including the following:

- Single application installation — Because the applications run on the Terminal Services server, it is only necessary to install them on that one computer. This ensures that all of the users are running the same application versions, and simplifies maintenance and upgrade tasks for the administrators, because they only have to work on a single installation.
- Low bandwidth consumption — Unlike virtual private network (VPN) or direct dial-up connections, a Terminal Services connection uses relatively little network bandwidth because the applications are running on the server computer. The only data exchanged by the Terminal Services client and the server is data needed to relay the keyboard, mouse, and display information.
- Broad-based client support — A user connecting to the Terminal Services server only has to run a simple client program because the resources needed to run the applications are on the server. This means that the client workstations can be low-end computers, non-Windows computers, or even ***thin client*** devices, which are minimal computers designed only for server communication.
- Conservation of licenses — Instead of purchasing application licenses for individual workstations, which might or might not be in use at any given time, you can maintain a pool of licenses on the Terminal Services server, which the system allocates to users as they log on. For example, an office with 100 workstations would require 100 licenses for an application installed on each computer, even if there were never more than 50 users running the application at any one time. Using Terminal Services, 50 application licenses would be sufficient, because only the users actually connected to the server need a license.

The Terminal Services role included in Windows Server 2008 implements the following role services:

- Terminal Server — Implements the service that enables remote users to connect to the computer and run applications or a full desktop session.
- TS Licensing — Manages the client access licenses that remote computers need to access the Terminal Server.
- TS Session Broker — On enterprise networks with multiple, load-balanced Terminal Servers, enables clients to reconnect to an existing session on a specific Terminal Server.
- TS Gateway — Enables remote users on the Internet to access a Terminal Server on an enterprise network using HTTP.
- TS Web Access — Enables remote users to access Terminal Servers using a Web-based client.

TAKE NOTE*

Microsoft provides the Remote Desktop feature, based on Terminal Services, with the Windows XP Professional and Windows Vista desktop operating systems.

TAKE NOTE*

Using Terminal Services might yield savings on application licenses, but a computer connecting to a terminal server requires a Terminal Server client access license (CAL) as well. The only exceptions to this are the two client licenses included with Windows Server 2008 for Remote Desktop administration purposes.

For more information on the Terminal Services role and other Windows Server 2008 remote access technologies, see Lesson 8, "Using Terminal Services," Lesson 9, "Configuring Terminal Services Clients," and Lesson 10, "Using the Terminal Services Gateway."

USING THE WEB SERVER (IIS) ROLE

Originally, Web servers were designed to respond to requests for Hypertext Markup Language (HTML) files generated by client browsers. These HTML files, when interpreted by the browser, display Web page content. Eventually, Web pages grew in complexity, incorporating images into their content, and then audio and video, and finally applications. Today, organizations use Web servers for a huge variety of applications, servicing clients on intranets, extranets, and the Internet.

While standalone applications certainly have their uses, many applications rely on the client/server model, particularly when many users have to access the same resources. For example, it would be possible to create a standalone database application that runs entirely on a single workstation and enables the user to access the company's customer list. However, to add a new customer, it would be necessary to update the database on each user's workstation, as shown in Figure 1-6, which would be highly impractical.

Figure 1-6

Running standalone applications with duplicate databases on every workstation is not a practical solution

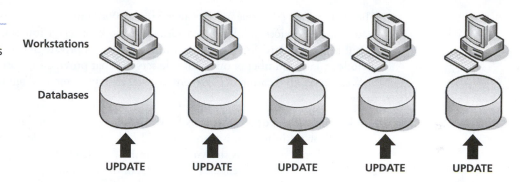

It makes far more sense to store a single copy of the customer list in a database on a central server and have each of the users run a client program that sends requests to the server, as shown in Figure 1-7. This way, administrators only have to make modifications to a single copy of the database, and all of the users can obtain the updated information immediately.

Figure 1-7

Running a single database application enables all of the workstations to retrieve updated information

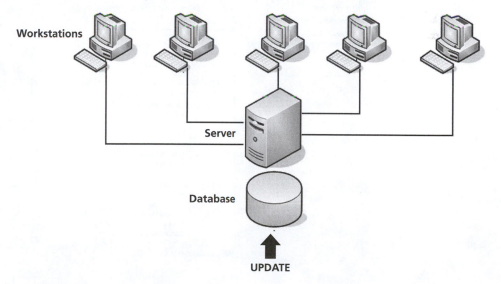

The question remains, however, of where a Web server fits into this client/server model. The simple answer is that Web servers and Web browsers eliminate the need for application developers to reinvent existing technologies. Web browsers are clients that send requests for information to Web servers, which respond by sending the requested information. To implement the client/server database application described earlier from scratch, developers would have to create a client program that generates database requests and a server program that processes those requests, accesses the desired information in the database, and generates replies.

By using the existing IIS Web server and Internet Explorer Web browser applications already incorporated in the Windows operating systems, database application developers can concentrate on the back end server application, which manages the database itself. They do not have to create a client interface or a server to receive and interpret the client requests.

The client/server model implemented by IIS and Internet Explorer can support many types of applications other than databases. Custom-designed business applications can run on the same computer as the Web server, on a different server, or on the client workstation itself.

Therefore, the client/server model in this type of arrangement consists of three elements:

- An Internet Explorer client browser running on the workstation
- An IIS server running on a Windows Server 2008 computer
- An application that makes use of the services provided by the Web server and the client browser

The Web Server (IIS) role in Windows Server 2008 implements, as its core, Internet Information Services 7.0. IIS 7 provides the basic Web server functionality that enables you to publish a standard Web site on the Internet or on a private network. However, IIS 7 also includes a large number of optional role services that provide support for virtually any type of Web-based application deployment, as well as management, diagnostic, and security functions.

Unlike some of the other Windows Server 2008 roles, installing the Web Server (IIS) role is not an all-or-nothing proposition. The Add Roles Wizard enables you to select a combination of optional role services, as shown in Figure 1-8, while enforcing any dependencies that might exist between them. This enables you to install the capabilities that your applications require, without wasting server resources running a lot of unnecessary code.

Figure 1-8

Selecting role services for the Web Server (IIS) role

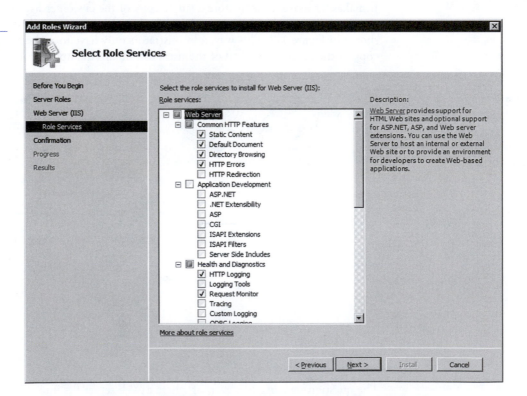

The following sections describe the various role services that you can install as part of the Web Server (IIS) role. The modules marked with an asterisk (*) are those the operating system installs with the role by default.

SELECTING IIS 7 WEB SERVER ROLE SERVICES

The Web Server role services provide basic HTTP server functionality, plus optional features that enhance the Web server's ability to support custom Web server settings, specific application environments, Web server logging functions, client access control capabilities, and Web server performance controls. The features you can select within the Web Server role service are as follows.

- Common HTTP Features — Provides support for standard Web server features, including the following:

  - Static Content (*) — Enables the Web server to publish Web sites that consist only of HTML and image files.
  - Default Document (*) — Specifies the name of the file that client browsers should load by default (such as index.html) when the Uniform Resource Locator (URL) received from a client does not include a filename.
  - Directory Browsing (*) — Enables clients to view a listing of the files in a particular directory and navigate up and down through the directory tree.
  - HTTP Errors (*) — Enables the Web server administrator to create customized messages for specific HTTP errors.
  - HTTP Redirection — Enables the Web server to forward incoming requests for a specific URL to another URL, such as when a site changes domain names.

- Application Development — Provides infrastructure support for applications developed using the following programming tools:

  - ASP.NET — Implements a server side, object-oriented programming environment based on the .NET framework.
  - .NET Extensibility — Enables developers to modify the functionality of the Web server, using the ASP.Net extensibility model and the .NET application programming interfaces (APIs).
  - ASP (Active Server Pages) — Provides a server-side scripting environment that supports both VBScript (Microsoft Visual Basic Scripting Edition) and Jscript for the development of Web sites and applications.
  - Common Gateway Interface (CGI) — Provides a scripting interface that enables a Web server to pass incoming information to another program.
  - Internet Server Application Programming Interface (ISAPI) Extensions — Enables the Web server to execute compiled ISAPI applications.
  - ISAPI Filters — Provides support for applications that use ISAPI filters to modify the functionality of the IIS Web server.
  - Server Side Includes (SSI) — Provides support for a scripting language that enables the Web server to dynamically generate HTML pages.

- Health and Diagnostics — Enables IIS to capture information that administrators can use to manage, monitor, and troubleshoot the Web server, using tools like the following:

  - Custom Logging — Enables administrators to log Web server activity using a customized format.
  - HTTP Logging (*) — Enables the Web server to maintain logs of all Web site activity.
  - Logging Tools — Provides tools for managing activity logs and automating logging tasks.
  - Open Database Connectivity (ODBC) Logging — Enables the Web server to save its logs to an ODBC-compliant database.
  - Request Monitor (*) — Captures information about HTTP requests that administrators can use to monitor the Web server's health and troubleshoot performance problems.
  - Tracing — Enables the Web server to save information about failed application requests for troubleshooting purposes.

- Security — Enables administrators to restrict access to the Web server, using tools like the following:
  - Basic Authentication — Provides support for a highly compatible and relatively unsecured form of authentication using Windows user names and passwords.
  - Client Certificate Mapping Authentication — Provides certificate-based authentication using Active Directory for one-to-one certificate mapping.
  - Digest Authentication — Authenticates users by sending a password hash to a domain controller on the network.
  - IIS Client Certificate Mapping Authentication — Provides certificate-based authentication using IIS for one-to-one or many-to-one certificate mapping.
  - IP and Domain Restrictions — Enables administrators to restrict access to the Web server by allowing only computers with certain IP addresses or domain names to connect.
  - Request Filtering (*) — Enables the Web server to block malicious traffic by filtering incoming requests based on rules the administrator creates.
  - URL Authorization — Enables administrators to restrict access to specific URLs by authorizing only specific users or groups.
  - Windows Authentication — Provides a secure NTLM- or Kerberos-based authentication method for domain users.
- Performance — Enables administrators to conserve network bandwidth by using the following data compression techniques:
  - Dynamic Content Compression — Enables the Web server to conserve network bandwidth by compressing dynamic Web site content before transmitting it to the client, at the cost of increased Web server CPU utilization.
  - Static Content Compression (*) — Enables the Web server to conserve network bandwidth by compressing static Web site content before transmitting it to the client.

SELECTING IIS 7 MANAGEMENT TOOLS

The Management Tools role service provides a variety of interfaces to the Web server administration controls, including MMC snap-ins, command-line tools, and scripting capabilities. The individual services you can select are as follows:

- IIS 6 Management Compatibility — Enables administrators to manage an IIS 7 Web server using IIS 6 tools and scripts.
  - IIS 6 Management Console — Provides the ability to manage remote IIS 6 Web servers.
  - IIS 6 Metabase Compatibility — Translates interfaces and scripts designed for the IIS 6 metabase to the new IIS 7 format.
  - IIS 6 Scripting Tools — Enables administrators to use IIS 6 scripting tools to manage IIS 7 Web servers.
  - IIS 6 WMI Compatibility — Provides support for IIS 6 Windows Management Instrumentation (WMI) scripts.
- IIS Management Console (*) — An MMC snap-in that enables administrators to manage local or remote IIS 7 Web servers.
- IIS Management Scripts and Tools — Enables administrators to automate IIS 7 management tasks using command-line tools and scripts.
- Management Service — Enables administrators to manage the Web server remotely using the IIS Management Console.

SELECTING FTP PUBLISHING SERVICES

The FTP Publishing Service included with Windows Server 2008 provides an alternative, directory-based interface that clients can use to upload and download files and perform basic file management tasks. The service, which is the same as the one included with IIS 6, consists of the following elements:

- FTP Server — Enables the Web server to host FTP sites and respond to FTP client requests.
- FTP Management Console — Enables administrators to manage local and remote IIS 7 FTP sites.

A new FTP Publishing Service for IIS7 is available as a free download from Microsoft's Web site. FTP7 is compatible with the IIS7 Management console, as well as other new IIS7 features, such as XML-based configuration files with .config extensions, shared configurations, and modular extensibility.

SELECTING ROLE SERVICES

Microsoft designed the Web server role services to support a wide variety of application development environments and administration requirements. Unless you plan to run a large number of applications that require different development environments, you will not need all of the role services that Web Server (IIS) role provides. In fact, Microsoft includes some of the role services, particularly some of those in the Application Development category, primarily to support legacy applications. If your organization is creating new applications for the server deployment, then it makes sense to select a single development environment and install only the role services needed to support those applications.

X REF

For more information on the Web Server (IIS) role, see Lesson 5, "Deploying IIS Services," Lesson 6, "Securing IIS Servers," and Lesson 7, "Deploying Web Applications."

USING THE UDDI SERVICES ROLE

Originally designed to be the basis for a worldwide directory of Internet sites and services, it is now more common for large organizations to use Universal Description, Discovery, and Integration (UDDI) as an internal catalog of their available Web services. Clients on the company intranet or a protected extranet can use a Web interface to access the catalog and search for the services the company's Web servers provide.

The UDDI Services role in Windows Server 2008 consists of the following role services:

- UDDI Services Database — Provides a central storage location for the UDDI catalog and the service's configuration settings.
- UDDI Services Web Application — Implements a Web site with which users and applications can access the UDDI catalog to search for Web services on the network.

X REF

For more information on deploying the UDDI Services role, see Lesson 7, "Deploying Web Applications."

USING THE APPLICATION SERVER ROLE

The Web Server (IIS) role provides a number of technologies that enable organizations to develop and deploy their own custom applications, using IIS to handle incoming requests from clients. The Application Server role is essentially a superset of the Web Server (IIS) role that enables IIS to host Web services developed using environments such as Windows Communication Foundation (WCF) and .NET Framework 3.0.

Installing the Application Server role automatically installs .NET Framework 3.0, and the Add Roles Wizard enables you to select from the following role services:

- Application Server Foundation — Implements the core technologies needed to support .NET 3.0 applications, including WCF, Windows Presentation Foundation (WPF), and Windows Workflow Foundation (WWF). This is the only role service installed with the role by default.

✚ **MORE INFORMATION**

Microsoft server applications, such as Exchange Server and SQL Server, do not require the Application Server role for their own functions. However, custom applications that use the services provided by Exchange and SQL Server might require the role.

- Web Server (IIS) Support — Enables the application server to host internal or external Web sites, as well as Web applications and services using technologies such as ASP.NET and WCF.
- COM+ Network Access — Enables the application server to host applications built with COM+ or Enterprise Services components.
- TCP Port Sharing — Enables multiple applications to share a single TCP port, so that they can coexist on a single computer.
- Windows Process Activation Service Support — Enables the Application Server to invoke applications remotely over the network, so that the applications can start and stop dynamically in response to incoming traffic. The individual traffic types WAS supports are as follows:
  - HTTP Activation — Enables applications to start and stop dynamically in response to incoming HTTP traffic.
  - Message Queuing Activation — Enables applications to start and stop dynamically in response to incoming Message Queuing traffic.
  - TCP Activation — Enables applications to start and stop dynamically in response to incoming TCP traffic.
  - Named Pipes Activation — Enables applications to start and stop dynamically in response to incoming named pipes traffic.
- Distributed Transactions — Implements services that help to ensure the successful completion of transactions involving multiple databases hosted by different computers. The individual services are as follows:
  - Incoming Remote Transactions — Provides support for transactions that applications on remote servers propagate.
  - Outgoing Remote Transactions — Enables the server to propagate the transactions that it generates itself to remote servers.
  - WS-Atomic Transactions — Provides support for applications that use two-phase commit transactions based on Simple Object Access Protocol (SOAP) exchanges.

For more information on using the Application Server role, see Lesson 11, "Using Network Application Services."

USING THE PRINT SERVICES ROLE

Sharing printers was one of the original applications that inspired the development of local area networks (LANs), and it is a common requirement on enterprise networks today. You can share a printer connected to a Windows Server 2008 computer without installing the Print Services role, but the role provides centralized tools that enable an administrator to monitor printer activities all over the network. The Print Services role includes the following optional role services:

- Print Server — Installs the Print Management snap-in for MMC, which provides centralized printer management for an entire enterprise network.
- LPD Service — Enables UNIX client computers running the line printer remote (LPR) application to send jobs to Windows Server 2008 printers.
- Internet Printing — Implements a Web-based printer management interface and enables remote users on the Internet to send print jobs to Windows Server 2008 printers.

USING THE FAX SERVER ROLE

For more information on using the Print Services and Fax Server roles, see Lesson 4, "Deploying Print and Fax Servers."

Sending and receiving faxes through the network can be an enormous convenience and Windows Server 2008 includes a Fax Server role that includes the Fax Service Manager application, which enables administrators to monitor fax devices, create fax rules and policies, and manage all of the faxes for the organization. The Fax Server role has no optional role services from which to choose. However, it does require the installation of the Print Services role.

USING THE STREAMING MEDIA SERVICES ROLE

The Streaming Media Services role enables an application server to provide digital audio and video content to network clients in real time, using HTTP or the Real Time Streaming Protocol (RTSP). The clients run a media player application that processes the content as they receive it from the server.

Unlike earlier versions of Windows Server, the Streaming Media Services role is not included with the operating system. You must download an update from the Microsoft Web site to add the role to the Server Manager application. When you install the role, you can choose from the following role services:

- Windows Media Server — Enables the application server to stream media to clients on the network.
- Web-based Administration — Provides a Web-based interface for managing media server functions.
- Logging Agent — Enables the media server to maintain logs of statistics received from clients.

X REF

For more information on using the Streaming Media Services role, see Lesson 11, "Using Network Application Services."

Selecting Application Server Hardware

> Choosing the correct hardware for an application server requires an understanding of the roles it will perform.

Not until you have decided how you will deploy your applications and what roles an application server will perform should you begin selecting the hardware that goes into the computer. For example, suppose your organization decides to deploy an application suite such as Microsoft Office on all of the company's workstations. If you decide to install the applications on each individual workstation, each of the computers must have sufficient memory and processor speed to run them efficiently. The application servers on the network will then only have to perform relatively simple roles, such as file and print services, which do not require enormous amounts of server resources.

By contrast, if you decide to deploy the applications using Terminal Services, you can use workstations with a minimal hardware configuration, because the terminal servers will take most of the burden. In this case, you will need an application server that is more powerful, in terms of processor and memory, or perhaps even several servers sharing the client load.

Server roles can also dictate requirements for specific subsystems within the application server computers, as in the following examples.

X REF

For more information on storage area networking, see Lesson 2, "Deploying a File Server." For more information on network load balancing and server clustering, see Lesson 12, "Using High Availability Technologies."

- Servers hosting complex applications might require more memory and faster processors.
- File servers can benefit from hard drives with higher speeds and larger caches, or even a high performance drive interface, such as SATA (Serial Advanced Technology Attachment) or SCSI (Small Computer System Interface).
- Web servers receiving large amounts of traffic might need higher-end network adapters or multiple adapters to connect to different subnets.
- Streaming media servers require sufficient hardware in all subsystems, because any performance bottleneck in the server can interrupt the client's media experience.

Finally, enterprises with extensive application server requirements might want to consider specialized server hardware, such as a storage area network, network attached storage, or server cluster.

Selecting Application Server Software

> Microsoft provides several alternative software deployments for Windows Server 2008 computers.

Microsoft provides a number of additional products and alternative installation practices that you might be able to use to minimize the cost and maximize the efficiency of your application server deployment. These alternatives are not suitable for all installations, but they can be viable solutions for some.

The following sections discuss software alternatives that require either a different Windows Server 2008 installation procedure, the installation of additional software, or the purchase of a different software product.

USING TERMINAL SERVICES

As mentioned earlier in this lesson and discussed at length later in this book, Terminal Services can provide a number of benefits in an enterprise application deployment, including substantial savings in the cost of workstation hardware and conservation of network bandwidth. Windows Server 2008 includes all of the software needed to implement a terminal server, plus new features, such as the Terminal Services Gateway.

With Windows Server 2008, Windows Vista Service Pack 1, and Windows XP Service Pack 3, Microsoft includes the Remote Desktop Connection 6.1 client application that workstations need to connect to a terminal server and utilize all of its capabilities. The license that each client needs to connect to a terminal server is the only Terminal Services component that Microsoft does not include with the operating system or make available as a free download.

Windows Server 2008 includes a two-user client license so that administrators can use Remote Desktop to configure servers from other computers, but clients using Terminal Services to run applications or desktop sessions must have additional licenses. This is an additional purchase and an additional cost that you must not forget when calculating your network deployment costs.

USING WEB EDITION

The Windows Server 2008 Standard, Enterprise, and Datacenter editions include all of the roles and features discussed in this lesson. However, another viable alternative is available for some installations: Windows Server 2008 Web Edition. Microsoft has designed the Web Edition of Windows Server 2008 for computers dedicated solely to hosting Web sites, applications, and services.

The Web Edition is essentially a subset of Windows Server 2008 Standard Edition, available at a reduced cost. When compared to the Standard edition, the Web Edition product has the following limitations:

- Windows Server 2008 Web Edition supports two-way symmetric multiprocessing (SMP), a maximum of 2 gigabytes of RAM, and 10 inbound Server Message Block (SMB) connections.
- Windows Server 2008 Web Edition can host only Web-based applications; applications that do not use IIS Web serving capabilities are prohibited.
- A Windows Server 2008 Web Edition server can be a member of an Active Directory domain, but it cannot function as a domain controller or run any of the Active Directory server roles.
- Windows Server 2008 Web Edition does not support the UDDI Services server role.
- Windows Server 2008 Web Edition cannot run Microsoft SQL Server, although it can run SQL Server 2005 Express Edition.
- Windows Server 2008 Web Edition is not available as a retail product. It is available only to Microsoft customers with an Enterprise, Select, Open, or Service Provider licensing agreement, or through Microsoft original equipment manufacturers (OEMs) and System Builder partners.

USING A SERVER CORE INSTALLATION

Computer users today have become so accustomed to graphical user interfaces (GUIs) that many are unaware that there is any other way to operate a computer. When the first version of Windows NT Server appeared, many network administrators complained about wasting the server's system resources on graphical displays and other elements that they deemed unnecessary. Until that point, server displays were usually minimal, character-based, monochrome affairs. In fact, many servers had no display hardware at all, relying instead on text-based remote administration tools, such as Telnet.

Many enterprise networks today use many servers, with each server performing one or two roles. You learned about the advantages to this arrangement earlier in this lesson. However, when a server is devoted to performing a single role, does it really make sense to have so many other processes running that contribute nothing to that role?

INTRODUCING SERVER CORE

Windows Server 2008 includes an installation option that addresses those old complaints. By using the Windows Server Core installation option of Windows Server 2008, you get a stripped-down version of the operating system. There is no Start menu, no desktop Explorer shell, no MMC console, and virtually no graphical applications. All you see when you start the computer is a single window with a command prompt.

In addition to omitting most of the graphical interface, a Server Core installation omits some of the server roles and features found in a full installation. Tables 1-2 and 1-3 list the roles and features that are available and not available in a Server Core installation.

Table 1-2

Windows Server 2008 Server Core Roles

ROLES AVAILABLE IN SERVER CORE INSTALLATION	ROLES NOT AVAILABLE IN SERVER CORE INSTALLATION
Active Directory Domain Services	Active Directory Certificate Services
Active Directory Lightweight Directory Services	Active Directory Federation Services
DHCP Server	Active Directory Rights Management Services
DNS Server	Network Policy and Access Services
File Services	Windows Deployment Services
Print Services	Application Server
Web Server (IIS)	Fax Server
	Terminal Services
	UDDI Services

Table 1-3

Windows Server 2008 Server Core Features

FEATURES AVAILABLE IN SERVER CORE INSTALLATION	FEATURES NOT AVAILABLE IN SERVER CORE INSTALLATION
BitLocker Drive Encryption	.NET Framework 3.0
Failover Clustering	BITS Server Extensions
Multipath I/O	Connection Manager Administration Kit
Network Load Balancing	Desktop Experience
QoS (Quality of Service) (qWave)	Internet Printing Client

(continued)

Table 1-3 (*continued*)

FEATURES AVAILABLE IN SERVER CORE INSTALLATION	FEATURES NOT AVAILABLE IN SERVER CORE INSTALLATION
Removable Storage Manager	Internet Storage Name Server
SNMP Services	LPR Port Monitor
Subsystem for UNIX-based Applications	Message Queuing
Telnet Client	Peer Name Resolution Protocol
Windows Server Backup	Remote Assistance
Windows Internet Name Service (WINS) Server	Remote Server Administration Tools
	RPC Over HTTP Proxy
	Simple TCP/IP Services
	SMTP Server
	Storage Manager for SANs
	Telnet Server
	Trivial File Transfer Protocol Client
	Windows Internal Database
	Windows Process Activation Service
	Windows System Resource Manager
	Wireless LAN Service

ADMINISTERING SERVER CORE

Obviously, with so much of the operating system missing, a computer running Server Core can devote more of its resources to its server functions. However, the missing elements provide most of the traditional Windows Server management and administration tools. To work with a Server Core computer, you must rely primarily on either the extensive collection of command prompt tools Microsoft includes with Windows Server 2008 or use MMC consoles on another system to connect to the server.

A few graphical applications can still run on Server Core. Notepad still works, so you can edit scripts and batch files. Task Manager runs, enabling you to load programs and monitor processes. Some elements of the Control Panel work as well, including the Date and Time application and the Regional and Language Options.

JUSTIFYING SERVER CORE

The next logical question to ask about Server Core is whether it is worth the inconvenience of learning a completely new management paradigm and giving up so much server functionality to save some memory and processor clock cycles. The answer is that there are other benefits to using Server Core besides hardware resource conservation.

As mentioned earlier, many Windows Server computers on enterprise networks are dedicated to a single role, but they still have a great many other applications, services, and processes running on them all the time. You can take it as an axiom that the more complex a system is, the more ways it can go wrong. Despite the fact that all of those extra software elements are performing no useful purpose, it is still necessary to maintain and update them, and that introduces the potential for failure. By removing many of these elements and leaving only the functions needed to perform the server's role, you diminish the failure potential, reduce the number of updates you need to apply, and increase the computer's reliability.

Another drawback to having all of those unnecessary processes running on a server is that they provide an increased attack surface for the computer. The more processes a computer is running, the more avenues there are for attacks to exploit. Removing the unneeded software elements makes the server more secure as well.

USING SERVER CORE FOR APPLICATION SERVERS

It is clear from the Tables 1-2 and 1-3, earlier in this section, that the Server Core configuration is limited when it comes to application services. The removal of the Application Server and Terminal Services roles means that you cannot use Server Core to deploy some applications or Terminal Services connections. However, the Server Core option provides a viable alternative for file and print servers, as well as streaming media servers.

USING VIRTUAL APPLICATION SERVERS

As discussed earlier in this lesson, running a large number of server roles on a single computer has distinct disadvantages, and yet distributing roles among many servers can be expensive and wasteful. However, a compromise between these two extremes is becoming an increasingly popular enterprise networking solution.

A *virtual server* is a complete installation of an operating system that runs in a software environment emulating a physical computer. Applications such as Microsoft Virtual Server 2005 and the Windows Server virtualization technology in Windows Server 2008 make it possible for a single computer to host multiple virtual machines, each of which runs in a completely independent environment.

The advantages of virtualization include the following:

For more information on Microsoft virtualization technologies and using them to deploy application servers, see Lesson 12, "Using High Availability Technologies."

- Fault tolerance — Any type of software failure on a virtual server affects only that server.
- Security — Virtual servers appear to the network as separate computers, so an attack on a virtual server has no effect on the other virtual machines or the host computer.
- Disaster recovery — Virtual servers are hardware independent, so in the event of a hardware failure, you can easily restore a backup copy of a virtual server on another computer and have it running in minutes.
- Resource allocation — As resource requirements for individual servers change, you can easily redeploy them onto other computers or adjust the physical computer resources allocated to them.
- Training and testing — Virtual servers simplify the task of creating an isolated laboratory environment in which you can test software products and train users and administrators.

Deploying Servers

THE BOTTOM LINE Windows Deployment Services enables administrators to perform attended and unattended operating system installations on remote computers.

After you have selected the application servers you need on your network and created a plan specifying the roles you will install on your servers, it is time to think about the actual server deployment process. For small networks, manual server installations, in which you run the Windows Server 2008 DVD on each computer separately, might be the most practical solution. However, if you have many servers to install, you might benefit from automating the installation process using Windows Deployment Services.

Windows Deployment Services (WDS) is a role included with Windows Server 2008, which enables you to perform unattended installations of Windows Server 2008 and other operating systems on remote computers, using network-based boot and installation media. This means that you can deploy a new computer with no operating system or local boot device on it, by installing image files stored on a server running Windows Deployment Services.

WDS is a client/server application in which the server supplies operating system image files to clients on the network. However, unlike most client/server applications, the WDS server is also responsible for providing the remote computer with the boot files it needs to run and the client side of the application.

For this to be possible, the client computer must have a network adapter that supports a ***preboot execution environment (PXE)***. In a PXE, the computer, instead of booting from a local drive, connects to a server on the network and downloads the boot files it needs to run. In the case of a WDS installation, the client downloads a boot image that loads ***Windows PE (Preinstallation Environment) 2.1***, after which it installs the operating system using another image file.

Installing Windows Deployment Services

> To use WDS, you must install the Windows Deployment Services role, configure the service, and add the images you want to deploy.

WDS is a standard role that you can install from the Initial Configuration Tasks window or the Server Manager console. The Windows Deployment Services role includes the following two role services:

- Deployment Server
- Transport Server

The Deployment Server role service provides a full WDS installation and requires the installation of the Transport Server role service as well. If you select Transport Server by itself, you install only the core networking elements of WDS, which you can use to create namespaces that enable you to transmit image files using multicast addresses. You must choose the Deployment Server role service to perform full remote operating system installations.

The Add Roles Wizard enforces no other dependencies for the Windows Deployment Services role, but the Wizard has several other requirements, as follows:

- Active Directory — The Windows Deployment Services computer must be a member of, or a domain controller for, an Active Directory domain.
- DHCP — The network must have an operational DHCP server that is accessible by the WDS clients.
- DNS — A DNS server must be on the network for the WDS server to function.
- NTFS — The WDS server must have an NTFS drive to store the image files.

The process of installing the Windows Deployment Services role does not add configuration pages to the Add Roles Wizard, but you must configure the server before clients can use it, as discussed in the following sections.

CONFIGURING THE WDS SERVER

After you install Windows Deployment Services, it remains inactive until you configure the service and add the images that the server will deploy to clients. To configure the server, use the following procedure.

 CONFIGURE A WDS SERVER

GET READY. Log on to Windows Server 2008 using an account with Administrative privileges. When the logon process is completed, close the Initial Configuration Tasks window and any other windows that appear.

1. Click **Start**, and then click **Administrative Tools** > **Windows Deployment Services**. The Windows Deployment Services console appears, as shown in Figure 1-9.

Figure 1-9

The Windows Deployment Services console

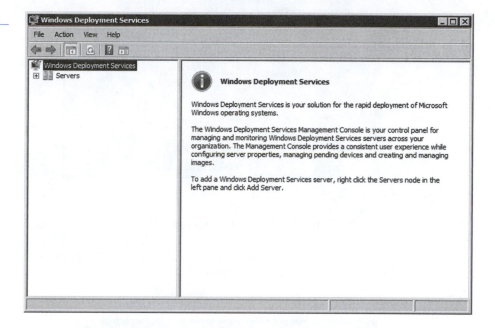

2. In the scope (left) pane, expand the **Servers** node. Right-click your server and, from the context menu, select **Configure Server**. The Windows Deployment Services Configuration Wizard appears.

3. Click **Next** to bypass the Welcome page. The Remote Installation Folder Location page appears, as shown in Figure 1-10.

Figure 1-10

The Remote Installation Folder Location page

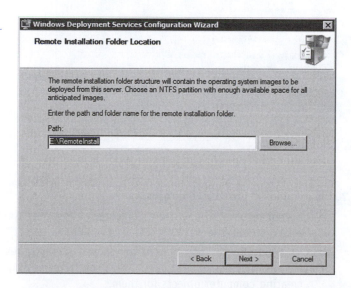

4. In the Path text box, key or browse to the folder where you want to locate the WDS image store. The folder you select must be on an NTFS drive and must have sufficient space to hold all of the images you want to deploy. Microsoft also recommends that the image store not be located on the system drive.

5. Click **Next** to continue. The DHCP Option 60 page appears, as shown in Figure 1-11.

Figure 1-11

The DHCP Option 60 page

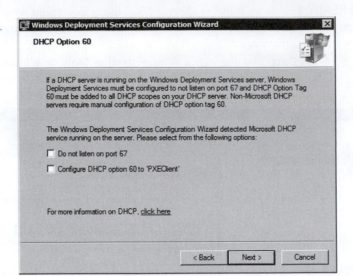

6. If the DHCP role is running on the same server as the Windows Deployment Services role, select the **Do not listen on port 67** and **Configure DHCP option 60 to 'PXEClient'** checkboxes. Then click **Next**. The PXE Server Initial Settings page appears, as shown in Figure 1-12.

Figure 1-12

The PXE Server Initial Settings page

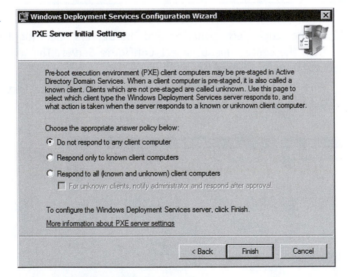

7. Select one of the following options:

a. Do not respond to any client computer — Prevents the WDS from providing boot access to any clients.

b. Respond only to known client computers — Configures the WDS server to provide boot access only to clients that you have prestaged in Active Directory by creating computer objects for them.

c. Respond to all (known and unknown) client computers — Configures the WDS server to provide access to all clients, whether you have prestaged them or not. Selecting the *For unknown clients, notify administrator and respond after approval* checkbox requires an administrator to approve each client connection attempt before the server provides it with boot access.

8. Click **Next** to complete the configuration process. The Configuration Complete page appears, as shown in Figure 1-13.

Figure 1-13

The Configuration Complete page

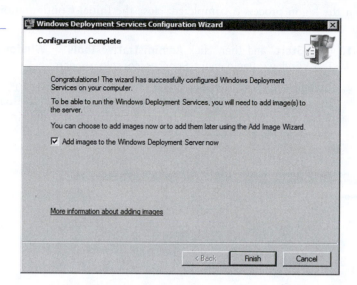

9. Select the **Add images to the Windows Deployment Server now** checkbox to launch the Add Image Wizard. Then click **Finish** to complete the Windows Deployment Services Configuration Wizard.

CLOSE the Windows Deployment Services console.

After the Windows Deployment Services Configuration Wizard has completed its tasks, the server has the proper environment to store image files and listen for incoming requests from clients. However, you still must populate the image store with image files, as described in the next section.

ADDING IMAGE FILES

Windows Deployment Services requires two types of image files to perform remote client installations: a boot image and an install image. The boot image contains the files needed to boot the computer and initiate an operating system installation. The Windows Server 2008 installation DVD includes a boot image file called boot.wim, located in the \Sources folder, which loads Windows PE 2.1 on the client computer. You can use this image file for virtually any operating system deployment without modification.

⊕ **MORE INFORMATION**

If you want to deploy an operating system to a computer that is not PXE-enabled, you can add a boot image to the store, and then convert it to a discover boot image by right-clicking the image and selecting Create a Discover Image from the context menu. A discover image is an image file that you can burn to a CD-ROM or other boot medium. When you boot the client computer using the discover image disk, the computer loads Windows PE, connects to a specified WDS server, and proceeds with the operating system installation process.

The image file contains the operating system that WDS will install on the client computer. Windows Server 2008 includes an install image in the \Sources folder on the installation DVD as well, called install.wim. This file performs a standard Windows Server 2008 setup, just as if you used the DVD to perform a manual installation.

To add the image files into the Windows Deployment Services console, use the following procedure.

⊙ ADD IMAGE FILES

GET READY. Log on to Windows Server 2008 using an account with Administrative privileges. When the logon process is completed, close the Initial Configuration Tasks window and any other windows that appear.

1. Click **Start**, and then click **Administrative Tools** > **Windows Deployment Services**. The Windows Deployment Services console appears.

2. Expand the Server node and the node for your server. Then, right-click the **Boot Images** folder and, from the context menu, select **Add Boot Image**. The Windows Deployment Services – Add Image Wizard appears, showing the Image File page, as shown in Figure 1-14.

Figure 1-14

The Image File page in the Windows Deployment Services – Add Image Wizard

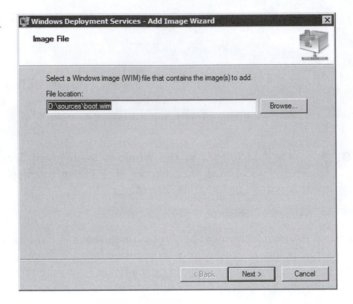

3. Key or browse to the location of the boot image you want to add to the store and then click **Next.** The Image Metadata page appears, as shown in Figure 1-15.

Figure 1-15

The Image Metadata page

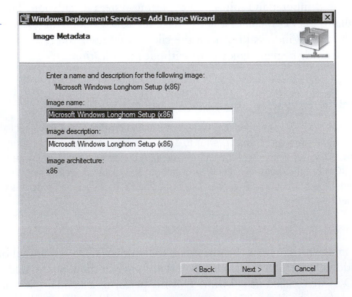

4. Specify different Image Name and Image Description values for the image file you selected, if desired. Then click **Next** to continue. The Summary page appears.

5. Click **Next** to continue. The Task Progress page appears, as the wizard adds the image to the store.

6. When the operation is complete, click **Finish**. The image appears in the detail pane of the console.

7. Right-click the **Install Images** folder and, from the context menu, select **Add Install Image**. The Windows Deployment Services – Add Image Wizard appears, showing the Image Group page, as shown in Figure 1-16.

Figure 1-16

The Image Group page in the Windows Deployment Services – Add Image Wizard

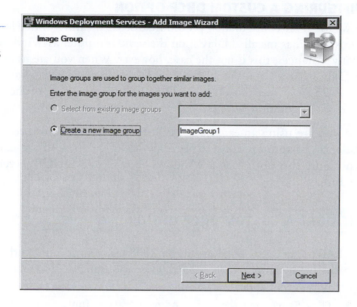

8. With the default *Create a new image group* option selected, supply a name for the group, if desired, and then click **Next**. The Image File page appears.

9. Key or browse to the location of the boot image you want to add to the store and then click **Next**. The List of Available Images page appears, as shown in Figure 1-17, containing a list of the images in the file you selected.

Figure 1-17

The List of Available Images page

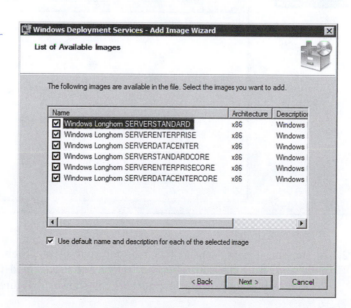

10. Select the images you want to add to the store and then click **Next**. The Summary page appears.

11. Click **Next** to continue. The Task Progress page appears, as the wizard adds the image to the store.

12. When the operation is complete, click **Finish**. The image group you created and the images you selected appear in the detail pane of the console.

CLOSE the Windows Deployment Services console.

At this point, the WDS server is ready to service clients.

CONFIGURING A CUSTOM DHCP OPTION

The WDS server configuration procedure discussed earlier in this lesson assumes that an administrator has installed DHCP on the same computer as Windows Deployment Services. In many instances, this is not the case, however. When you are using another computer as your DHCP server, you should clear the *Do not listen on port 67* and *Configure DHCP option 60 to 'PXEClient'* checkboxes on the DHCP Option 60 page of the Windows Deployment Services Configuration Wizard.

When you are using an external DHCP server, you must also configure it manually to include the custom option that provides WDS clients with the name of the WDS server. To configure this option on a Windows Server 2008 DHCP server, use the following procedure.

 CONFIGURE A CUSTOM DHCP OPTION

GET READY. Log on to Windows Server 2008 using an account with Administrative privileges. When the logon process is completed, close the Initial Configuration Tasks window and any other windows that appear.

1. Click **Start**, and then click **Administrative Tools** > **DHCP**. The DHCP console appears, as shown in Figure 1-18.

Figure 1-18

The DHCP console

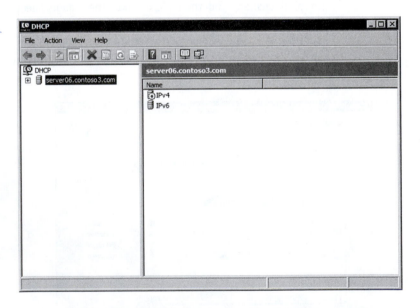

2. In the scope pane, expand the node for your server. Then, right-click the **IPv4** node and, from the context menu, select **Set Predefined Options**. The Predefined Options and Values dialog box appears, as shown in Figure 1-19.

Figure 1-19

The Predefined Options and Values dialog box

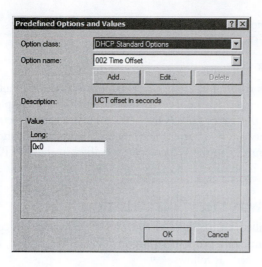

TAKE NOTE *

For a DHCP server running Windows Server 2003, you must right-click the server node (instead of the IPv4 node) and select Set Predefined Options from the context menu. You can then continue with the rest of the procedure.

3. Click **Add.** The Option Type dialog box appears, as shown in Figure 1-20.

Figure 1-20

The Option Type dialog box

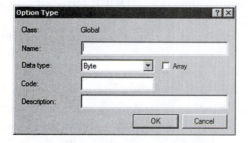

4. In the Name text box, key **PXEClient**.

5. From the Data Type drop-down list, select **String**.

6. In the Code text box, key **060**.

7. Click **OK**.

8. Click **OK** again to close the Predefined Options and Values dialog box.

9. In the scope pane, right-click the **Server Options** node and, from the context menu, select **Configure Options**. The Server Options dialog box appears.

10. In the Available Options list box, scroll down and select the **060 PXEClient** option you just created, as shown in Figure 1-21.

Figure 1-21

The Server Options dialog box

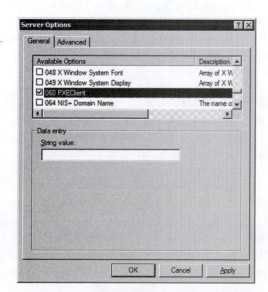

11. In the String Value text box, key the name or IP address of your WDS server. Then, click **OK**.

CLOSE the DHCP console.

This procedure adds the 060 custom option value you defined to all of the DHCPOFFER packets the DHCP server sends out to clients. When a client computer boots from a local device, such as a hard drive or CD-ROM, the 060 option has no effect. However, when a client performs a network boot, after receiving and accepting an offered IP address from the DHCP server, it connects to the WDS server specified in the 060 PXEClient option and uses it to obtain the files it needs to boot.

PERFORMING A WDS CLIENT INSTALLATION

After you have installed and configured your WDS server and added images to the store, it is ready to service clients. In a properly configured WDS installation, the client operating system deployment proceeds as follows:

1. The client computer starts and, finding no local boot device, attempts to perform a network boot.

2. The client computer connects to a DHCP server on the network, from which it obtains a DHCPOFFER message containing an IP address and other TCP/IP configuration parameters, plus the 060 PXEClient option, containing the name of a WDS server.

3. The client connects to the WDS server and is supplied with a boot image file, which it downloads using the Trivial File Transfer Protocol (TFTP).

4. The client loads Windows PE and the Windows Deployment Services client from the boot image file onto a RAM disk (a virtual disk created out of system memory) and displays a boot menu containing a list of the install images available from the WDS server.

5. The user on the client computer selects an install image from the boot menu, and the operating system installation process begins.

6. From this point, setup proceeds just like a manual installation.

Customizing WDS Client Installations

WDS enables you to deploy customized image files and use unattend scripts to perform unattended installations.

As mentioned earlier, the install.wim image file that Microsoft supplies on the Windows Server 2008 DVD performs a basic operating system installation on the client. However, the real strength of WDS in an enterprise environment is in the ability to create and deploy custom image files using unattended procedures. To do this, you must create your own image files and unattend scripts, as discussed in the following sections.

CREATING IMAGE FILES WITH WDS

An install image is basically a snapshot of a computer's hard drive taken at a particular moment in time. The image file contains all of the operating system files on the computer, plus any updates and drivers you have installed, applications you have added, and configuration changes you have made. Creating your own image files is essentially a matter of setting up a computer the way you want it and then capturing an image of the computer to a file.

You can use several tools to create image files, including the ImageX.exe command-line utility Microsoft provides in the Windows Automated Installation Kit (Windows AIK), which is available from the Microsoft Downloads Center at http://microsoft.com/downloads. To use ImageX.exe, you must boot the target computer to Windows PE and run the tool from the

command line. However, the Windows Deployment Center console provides another method for creating image files, using the same WDS infrastructure you used to install images.

WDS enables you to create your own image files by modifying an existing boot image, such as the boot.wim image Microsoft provides with Windows Server 2008, and turning it into a tool that boots the target computer and runs the Windows Deployment Service Capture Utility instead of an operating system's Setup program. The utility then creates an image file and writes it out to the computer's drive, after which you can copy it to the WDS server and deploy it to other computers in the usual manner.

MODIFYING A BOOT IMAGE

To modify a boot image to create image file captures, use the following procedure.

 MODIFY A BOOT IMAGE

GET READY. Log on to Windows Server 2008 using an account with Administrative privileges. When the logon process is completed, close the Initial Configuration Tasks window and any other windows that appear.

1. Click **Start**, and then click **Administrative Tools** > **Windows Deployment Services**. The Windows Deployment Services console appears.

2. Expand the **Server** node and the node for your server. Then, select the **Boot Images** folder.

3. If you have not done so already, add the Windows Server 2008 boot.wim image to the Boot Images store, using the procedure described earlier in this lesson.

4. In the detail pane, right-click the boot image and select **Create Capture Boot Image** from the context menu. The Windows Deployment Services – Create Capture Image Wizard appears, as shown in Figure 1-22.

Figure 1-22

The Windows Deployment Services – Create Capture Image Wizard

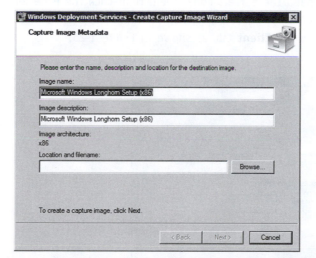

5. On the Capture Image Metadata page, specify a name and description for the new image, and a location and filename for the new image file.

6. Click **Next**. The Task Progress page appears as the wizard creates the new image file.

7. When the image is created successfully, click **Finish**.

CLOSE the Windows Deployment Services console.

You can now add the new capture image to the Boot Image store in the normal manner. To complete the imaging process, you must prepare the target computer with the Sysprep.exe utility and then reboot the system using the capture image. A wizard then appears on the computer that guides you through the process of capturing an image of the computer and uploading it to the WDS server.

DEPLOYING UNATTEND FILES

WDS by itself enables you to perform a standard operating system installation, but the setup process is still interactive, requiring someone at the workstation, like an installation from the DVD. To perform an unattended installation using WDS, you must use unattend files. An unattend file is a script containing responses to all of the prompts that appear on the client during the installation process. To create unattend files, Microsoft recommends using the Windows System Image Manager (Windows SIM) tool in the Windows AIK.

To install an operating system on a client using WDS with no interactivity, you must have two unattend files, as follows:

- WDS client unattend file — This unattend file automates the WDS client procedure that begins when the client computer loads the boot image file.

- Operating system unattend file — This is an unattend file for a standard operating system installation, containing responses to all of the prompts that appear after the client computer loads the install image file.

To use unattend files during a WDS operating system deployment, use the following procedure.

 DEPLOY AN UNATTEND FILE

GET READY. Log on to Windows Server 2008 using an account with Administrative privileges. When the logon process is completed, close the Initial Configuration Tasks window and any other windows that appear.

1. Copy your WDS client unattend file to the \RemoteInstall\WDSClientUnattend folder on the WDS server.

2. Click **Start**, and then click **Administrative Tools** > **Windows Deployment Services**. The Windows Deployment Services console appears.

3. Expand the **Servers** node. Then, right-click the node for your server and, from the context menu, select **Properties**. The server's Properties sheet appears.

4. Click the **Client** tab, as shown in Figure 1-23.

Figure 1-23

The Client tab of a WDS server's Properties sheet

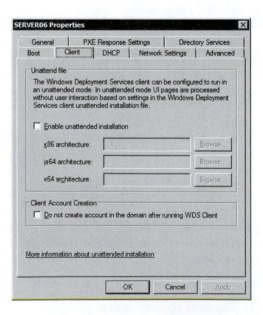

5. Select the **Enable unattended installation** checkbox.

6. Click the **Browse** button corresponding to the processor architecture of the client computer.

7. Browse to your unattend file and then click **Open**.

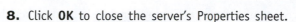

8. Click **OK** to close the server's Properties sheet.

9. Expand the node for your server and the **Install Images** node and locate the image you want to associate with an unattend file.

10. Right-click the image file and, from the context menu, select **Properties**. The Image Properties sheet appears, as shown in Figure 1-24.

Figure 1-24

The Image Properties sheet

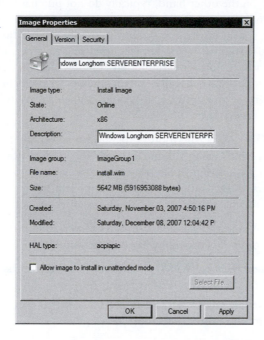

11. Select the **Allow image to install in unattended mode** checkbox.

12. Click **Select File**. The Select Unattend File dialog box appears, as shown in Figure 1-25.

Figure 1-25

The Select Unattend File dialog box

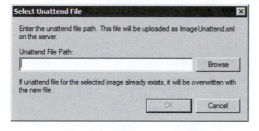

13. Key or browse to the unattend file you want to use and then click **OK**.

14. Click **OK** to close the Image Properties sheet.

CLOSE the Windows Deployment Services console.

At this point, if your unattend files are properly configured, the entire operating system installation process on the client should require no interaction, except for turning on the computer.

■ Activating Windows

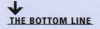

THE BOTTOM LINE

You must activate Windows Server 2008 computers within 30 days of installing them. For organizations with volume license agreements, Microsoft has designed a new program called Volume Activation 2.0, which simplifies the process of activating computers on enterprise networks.

Retail versions of Microsoft Windows include a product key that you must supply during installation. After you have installed the operating system, you must activate the product key by contacting Microsoft, either online or by telephone. Activation is the establishment of a relationship between a product key and a copy of the Windows operating system installed on a specific computer.

Enterprise networks, on the other hand, typically do not purchase retail copies of Windows. Instead, they enter into a volume licensing agreement with Microsoft that enables them to run the operating system on a specific number of computers. Until Windows Vista and Windows Server 2008, volume license keys required no activation. However, Microsoft has determined that the vast majority of counterfeit Windows installations are using volume license keys that personnel have illegally shared, whether by accident or intent. As a result, corporate customers must now activate all Windows Vista and Windows Server 2008 computers using volume license keys.

Volume Activation (VA) 2.0 is Microsoft's program for automating and managing the activation of products obtained using volume licenses. VA 2.0 does not alter the terms of your license agreement with Microsoft in any way; it is simply a tool to simplify the activation process. For end users, the activation process is completely transparent, and administrators do not have to supply individual product keys when installing Windows.

Volume licenses for Windows Vista and Windows Server 2008 now include two types of keys, which are designed to support the following two activation services:

- *Key Management Service (KMS)* — An activation service that runs on the local network, enabling clients to activate without communicating with Microsoft.
- *Multiple Activation Key (MAK)* — Enables a specified number of computers to activate using Microsoft's hosted activation services.

Using KMS

KMS enables Windows Server 2008 and Windows Vista computers to activate themselves using a KMS host on the local network.

The Key Management Service is the activation method that Microsoft recommends for medium to large networks with volume licensing agreements. To use KMS, you install the KMS key you receive with your volume license on a computer, which turns it into a KMS host. You then perform a one-time activation of the host with Microsoft, using Microsoft's online services or the telephone. The system resources consumed by the KMS host service are negligible, so you can install it on almost any Windows Vista or Windows Server 2008 computer, and a single host can support a virtually unlimited number of clients.

After you have activated a KMS host on your network, other computers running volume editions of Windows Vista and Windows Server 2008 can activate themselves by contacting the host using their built-in KMS client capabilities. These clients, therefore, do not have to communicate directly with Microsoft.

UNDERSTANDING KMS ACTIVATION

For a KMS host to activate KMS clients, it must receive a certain number of activation requests within the last 30 days. This is called the *KMS activation threshold*, and it is designed to prevent pirated KMS keys from functioning on small networks or individual computers. For a KMS host to activate a Windows Server 2008 client, it must receive at least five client activation requests within 30 days. For a host to activate a Windows Vista client, it must receive 25 activation requests within 30 days.

By default, KMS clients locate KMS hosts by an auto-discovery process that uses DNS queries. When you install a KMS host, the computer creates an SRV resource record on its local DNS server. The SRV record contains the fully-qualified domain name (FQDN) of the com-

puter functioning as a KMS host, and the port number it uses for network communications, which defaults to TCP port 1688.

> For the KMS host to successfully create or modify the SRV record, your DNS server must support dynamic updates (Dynamic DNS), like all Windows DNS servers using Windows 2000 Server or better. The host computer must also have appropriate permissions to create and modify DNS records.

When clients attempt to activate, which they do every 120 minutes until an activation is successful, they first query their local DNS server and obtain the SRV records specifying the KMS hosts on the network. The client then selects one of the hosts at random and sends an activation request to it, using the Remote Procedure Call (RPC) protocol. The KMS host counts the number of activation requests it receives within the past 30 days and sends that value back to the client. If the count is sufficient to exceed the activation threshold, the client activates itself for a period of 180 days.

If KMS clients and KMS hosts find intervening firewalls, routers, or other protective devices between them, you might have to manually configure the protective devices to allow the KMS traffic through.

While activated, the client continually attempts to renew its activation by connecting to the host every seven days. When the renewal succeeds, the client pushes its activation period forward to a full 180 days. If the client is unable to contact the host for 180 days, it begins to display recurring messages to the user, specifying the need to activate Windows, until it is able to reactivate.

On the host computer, KMS records the unique ***client machine ID (CMID)*** of each successful activation in a protected table for 30 days, after which it purges the record. When a client successfully renews its activation, the host removes the old CMID entry and creates a new one. As a safety precaution, the host caches twice the number of CMIDs it needs to meet the activation threshold, that is, ten Windows Server 2008 computers or 50 Windows Vista computers. This helps to ensure that clients on a network meeting the activation threshold are always able to activate themselves.

CONFIGURING KMS

KMS often does not require any manual configuration after you install and activate a KMS key on a computer. The host automatically creates an SRV record on the DNS server and volume editions of Windows Vista and Windows Server 2008 automatically attempt to contact the host to authenticate themselves. However, it is possible to modify the default behavior of KMS clients and hosts as needed for your environment.

KMS does not have a graphical interface; you use a script called Slmgr.vbs, which you run from the command-prompt with the Cscript.exe utility, to modify the operational parameters of clients and hosts. The Slmgr.vbs syntax is as follows:

```
Cscript C:\windows\system32\slmgr.vbs [/ipk key] [/ato] [/sprt port]

[/cdns] [/sdns] [/sai interval] [/sri interval] [/skms server{:port}]

[/ckms]
```

- /ipk *key* — Installs the specified KMS key on the computer, turning it into a KMS host.
- /ato — On a host, performs an online activation with Microsoft. On a client, triggers the local activation process.
- /sprt *port* — Configures the KMS host to use the specified TCP port, rather than the default port 1688.
- /cdns — Disables automatic DNS publishing.
- /sdns — Enables automatic DNS publishing.
- /sai *interval* — Specifies a time interval between client activation attempts other than the default 120 minutes.

- /sri *interval* — Specifies a time interval between client activation renewal attempts other than the default 7 days.
- /skms *server:port* — Disables auto-discovery on a KMS client and specifies the name or address (and, optionally, the port number) of the KMS host it will use to activate. The *server* variable can be an FQDN, a NetBIOS name, an IPv4 address, or an IPv6 address.
- /ckms — Re-enables auto-discovery on a KMS client.

Using MAK

> MAK enables individual computers to activate themselves by contacting Microsoft hosts or using a proxy.

Microsoft intends the use of Multiple Activate Keys for networks that do not have a sufficient number of computers to support KMS, or for computers that do not connect to the organization's network on a regular basis, such as laptops issued to traveling users. A MAK is a single key that enables a specified number of computers to activate, using one of the following two types of activation:

- MAK Independent Activation — Clients contact the Microsoft hosts directly, using an Internet connection or a telephone.
- MAK Proxy Activation — Multiple clients send their activation requests to a proxy called the Volume Activation Management Tool (VAMT).

MAK Independent Activation is similar to the standard retail product key activation, except that you use the same key for multiple computers. At its simplest, MAK deployment is a matter of supplying the MAK key during the operating system installation, using the standard setup interface. You can also enter a MAK key on an existing Windows installation through the Control Panel. You can install the MAK key on clients individually, or include the key as part of an image file and deploy it on multiple computers.

After you have installed a MAK on a client computer, the activation proceeds in the usual manner, with the client either contacting a Microsoft host automatically on the Internet, or activating manually, using a telephone call. After installation, the client computer stores the MAK key in encrypted form, so that it is inaccessible to the end user.

For ***MAK Proxy Activation***, you must download the Volume Activation Management Tool (VAMT) from the Microsoft Download Center (at http://microsoft.com/downloads) and install it on a computer with access to the Internet. VAMT collects the activation requests from the clients on the network, uses a single connection to the Microsoft hosts to activate them all at the same time, and then distributes the resulting activation codes to the clients using the Windows Management Instrumentation (WMI) interface. With VAMT, you can also redeploy existing activation codes to clients you have re-imaged or rebuilt.

■ Using Server Manager

THE BOTTOM LINE

> Server Manager is an MMC console that provides a selection of the most commonly used Windows Server 2008 management tools.

When you start a Windows Server 2008 computer for the first time after installing the operating system, the Initial Configuration Tasks window displays, as shown in Figure 1-26. This window presents a consolidated view of the post-installation tasks that, in previous Windows Server versions, you had to perform using various interfaces presented during and after the OS setup process.

After you complete the configuration tasks in sections 1 and 2 of the Initial Configuration Tasks window, you can use the links in the Customize This Server section to install roles

Figure 1-26

The Initial Configuration Tasks window

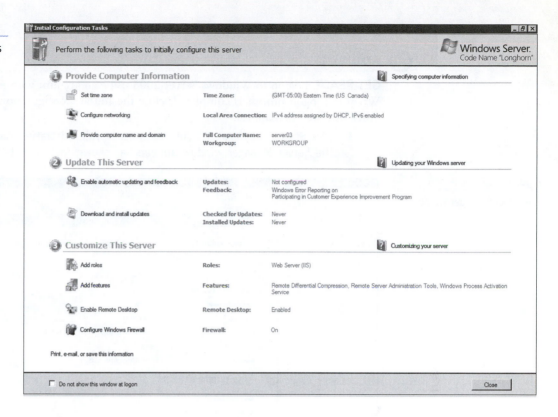

and features on the computer. The Add Roles and Add Features links launch the Add Roles Wizard and the Add Features Wizard, respectively.

You can also install and manage roles and features using the Server Manager console. Server Manager is an MMC console that contains a collection of snap-ins most commonly used by Windows Server 2008 administrators. The Server Manager console integrates the following snap-ins into a single interface:

- Component Services
- Device Manager
- Disk Management
- Event Viewer
- Local Users and Groups
- Reliability and Performance Monitor
- Routing and Remote Access
- Services
- Share and Storage Management
- Task Scheduler
- Terminal Services Configuration
- Terminal Services Manager
- Windows Firewall with Advanced Security
- Windows Server Backup
- WMI Control

Adding Roles

The Add Roles Wizard enables you to select multiple roles and role services for installation.

To add roles using Server Manager, use the following procedure.

 ADD ROLES

GET READY. Log on to Windows Server 2008 using an account with Administrative privileges. When the logon process is completed, close the Initial Configuration Tasks window and any other windows that appear.

1. Click **Start**, and then click **All Programs** > **Administrative Tools** > **Server Manager**. The Server Manager window appears, as shown in Figure 1-27.

Figure 1-27

The Server Manager window

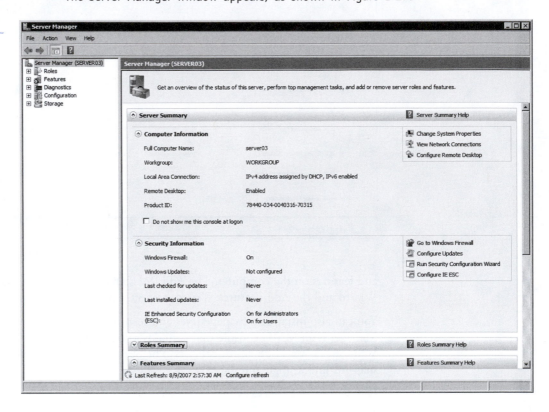

2. In the scope (left) pane, click the **Roles** node, and then click **Add Roles**. The Add Roles Wizard appears, as shown in Figure 1-28.

Figure 1-28

The Add Roles Wizard

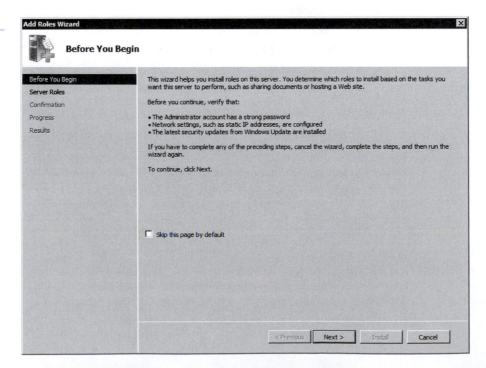

3. Click **Next** to skip the Before You Begin page. The Select Server Roles page appears, as shown in Figure 1-29.

Figure 1-29

The Select Server Roles page

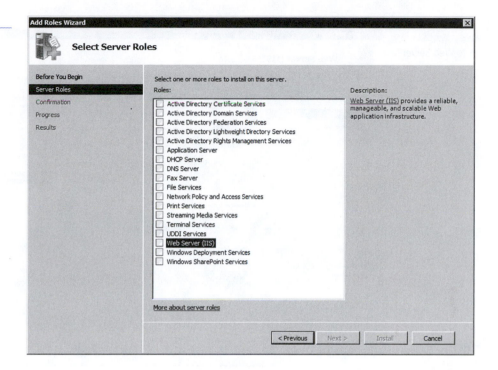

4. Select the checkbox for the role (or roles) you want to install. If the role you select is dependent on other roles or features, the Add Features Required For Web Server (IIS) dialog box appears, as shown in Figure 1-30.

Figure 1-30

The Add Features Required For Web Server (IIS) page

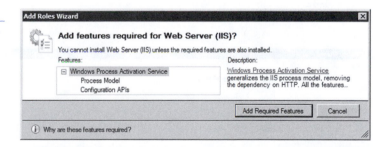

5. Click **Add Required Features**, and then click **Next**. A role-specific Introduction page appears, explaining the function of the role and providing installation notes and links, as shown in Figure 1-31.

Figure 1-31

The Introduction to Web Server (IIS) page

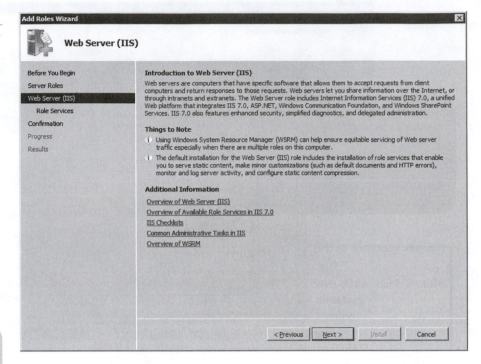

6. Click **Next**. Additional role-specific pages might appear, providing access to configuration settings or enabling you to select the role services you want to install.

7. Click **Next**. The Confirm Installation Selections page appears, as shown in Figure 1-32.

Figure 1-32

The Confirm Installation Selections page

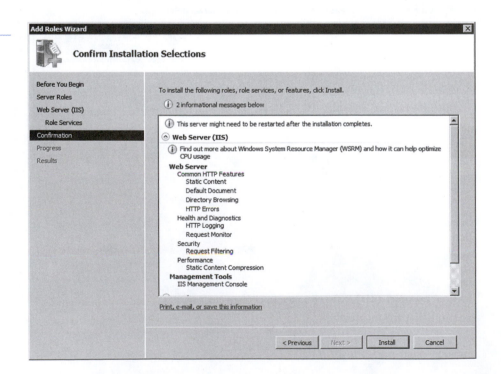

8. Click **Install**. The Installation Progress page appears as the wizard installs the selected roles, role services, and features. When the installation is completed, the Installation Results page appears, as shown in Figure 1-33.

Figure 1-33

The Installation Results page

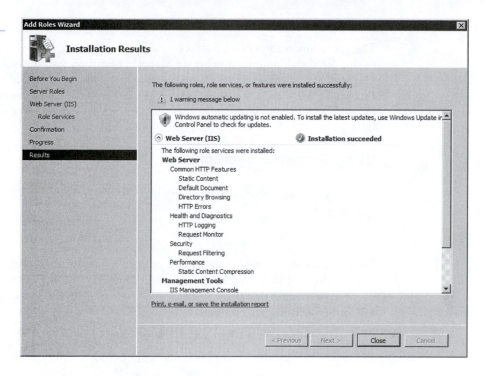

9. After you confirm that all of the installations have completed successfully, click **Close**.

CLOSE the Server Manager console.

After you have completed the Add Roles Wizard, which installed roles on the server, the Roles screen in Server Manager displays a detailed summary of the roles installed on the computer, including a list of all the role services and a status indicator, as shown in Figure 1-34.

Figure 1-34

The Roles screen in Server Manager

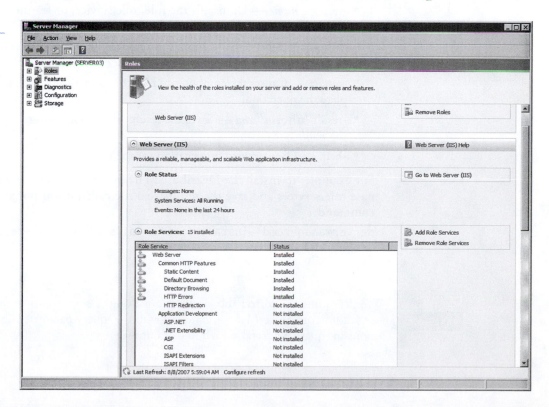

Adding Features

> The Add Features Wizard enables you to select multiple server features for installation.

The procedure for installing features on a Windows Server 2008 computer is almost identical to that for installing roles. On Server Manager's Features screen, click Add Features. The Add Features Wizard takes you through the process of selecting and configuring features. As with the Add Roles Wizard, the Add Features Wizard preserves all of the necessary dependencies by prompting you to install any other features or roles that are necessary.

Using ServerManagerCmd.exe

> The *ServerManagerCmd.exe* utility provides a command prompt alternative to Server Manager.

ServerManagerCmd.exe is a command prompt tool that can perform many of the same functions as the Add Roles Wizard and the Add Features Wizard. The benefit of the command prompt interface is that you can install roles and features from scripts or batch files. The syntax for ServerManagerCmd.exe is as follows:

```
ServerManagerCmd [-query][-install name][-remove name]
```

```
[-inputPath answer.xml][-restart][-resultPath result.xml[-help]
```

- -query — Displays a complete list of all the roles, role services, and features supported by the computer and indicates which ones are currently installed.
- -install *name* [-setting *name=value*] [-allSubFeatures] — Installs the role, role service, or feature specified by the *name* variable. Use the — setting parameter to specify values for required role settings. Use the — allSubFeatures parameter to install all of the subordinate roles, role services, or features associated with the module it is installing.
- -remove *name* — Uninstalls the role, role service, or feature specified by the *name* variable.
- -inputPath *answer.xml* — Installs or removes all of the roles, role services, or features listed in the XML file specified by the *answer.xml* variable.
- -restart — Causes the computer to restart automatically, if a restart is needed to complete the operation.
- -resultPath *result.xml* — Saves the results of the operation to an XML file specified by the *result.xml* variable.
- -help — Displays help information for the program.

For example, to install the Distributed File System role service with all of its subordinate role services and save the results to a file called dfsoutput.xml, use the following command:

```
servermanagercmd —install FS-DFS —allsubfeatures —resultpath dfsoutput
.xml
```

TAKE NOTE* To determine the correct abbreviation to use on the command line for a role, role service, or feature, run ServerManagerCmd.exe with the -query parameter. It shows the abbreviations in square brackets on each line of output.

SUMMARY SKILL MATRIX

IN THIS LESSON YOU LEARNED:

- Applications in the enterprise can take several forms, including client-run applications, client/server applications, and distributed applications.

- The Add Roles Wizard provides roles that fall into three basic categories: directory services, infrastructure services, and application services.

- Windows Server 2008 includes a collection of features, which you can select individually. You can also augment a given role by adding features that increase its capabilities.

- The number of roles a server can perform depends on the computer's hardware configuration, the hardware requirements of the role, and the size and scope of the enterprise.

- Distributing server roles among several computers has several distinct advantages, including fault tolerance, ease of resource allocation, high availability, server scalability, security configuration, dispersed network traffic, and simpler update management.

- Not until you have decided how you will deploy your applications and the roles an application server will perform should you begin selecting the hardware that goes into the computer.

- Terminal Services can provide a number of benefits in an enterprise application deployment, including substantial savings in the cost of workstation hardware and conservation of network bandwidth.

- The Windows Server Core installation option of Windows Server 2008 gives you a stripped-down version of the operating system. There is no Start menu, no desktop Explorer shell, no MMC console, and virtually no graphical applications. All you see when you start the computer is a single window with a command prompt.

- A virtual server is a complete installation of an operating system that runs in a software environment emulating a physical computer. Applications such as Microsoft Virtual Server 2005 and the Windows Server virtualization technology in Windows Server 2008 make it possible for a single computer to host multiple virtual machines, each of which runs in a completely independent environment.

- Windows Deployment Services (WDS) is a role included with Windows Server 2008, which enables you to perform unattended installations of Windows Server 2008 and other operating systems on remote computers, using network-based boot and installation media.

- Volume Activation (VA) 2.0 is Microsoft's program for automating and managing the activation of products obtained using volume licenses. VA 2.0 does not alter the terms of the license agreement with Microsoft in any way; it is simply a tool to simplify the activation process. For end users, the activation process is completely transparent, and administrators do not have to supply individual product keys when installing Windows.

- Volume licenses for Windows Vista and Windows Server 2008 now include two types of keys, which Microsoft designed to support the following two activation services: Key Management Service (KMS) and Multiple Activation Key (MAK).

■ Knowledge Assessment

Fill in the Blank

Complete the following sentences by writing the correct word or words in the blanks provided.

1. The storage area networking technology supported by Windows Server 2008 as a lower cost alternative to Fibre Channel is called _____.

2. The only server roles discussed in this lesson that are not included with the Windows Server 2008 product are _____ and _____.

3. DHCP and DNS are known as _____ services.

4. To create a searchable catalog of Web services on your network, you would install the _____ role.

5. To create Web sites that people can use to collaborate on documents and tasks, you must install the _____ role.

6. The feature that enhances fault tolerance by providing multiple data paths to a single server storage device is called _____.

7. The Windows Server 2008 file server element that conserves disk space by eliminating duplicate copies of files is called _____.

8. The Application Server role is essentially a superset of the _____ role.

9. To implement Windows Vista desktop themes on a Windows Server 2008 computer, you must install the _____ feature.

10. The type of activation recommended by Microsoft for medium to large networks with volume licensing agreements is _____.

Multiple Choice

Select the correct answer for each of the following questions. Choose all answers that are correct.

1. Which of the following *cannot* be installed from the command line by the ServerManagerCmd.exe utility?
   - **a.** Features
   - **b.** Applications
   - **c.** Roles
   - **d.** Role services

2. Which of the following provide(s) UNIX clients with Windows printing capabilities?
   - **a.** Internet Printing Client
   - **b.** Multipath I/O (MPIO)
   - **c.** LPR Port Monitor feature
   - d. LPD Service role service

3. Which of the following roles must you install with the Fax Server role on a Windows Server 2008 computer?
   - **a.** Active Directory Certificate Services
   - **b.** UDDI Services
   - **c.** Print Services
   - **d.** Web Server

4. When a client runs an application on a terminal server, which of the client computer's resources does the application utilize?
   - **a.** The client computer's memory resources
   - **b.** The client computer's processor resources
   - **c.** The client computer's hard drive resources
   - **d.** None of the above

5. Windows Server 2008 requires that you install which of the following features for the Application Server role?
   - **a.** .NET Framework 3.0 feature
   - **b.** Network Load Balancing (NLB)
   - **c.** Windows System Resource Manager (WSRM)
   - **d.** Windows Process Activation Service (WPAS)

6. Which of the following is a true statement about limitations Microsoft places on the number of roles a Windows Server 2008 computer can support?
   - **a.** There are no limitations placed on the number of roles a Windows Server 2008 computer can perform.
   - **b.** The number of roles that a Windows Server 2008 computer can run is limited only to the amount of hardware resources available to the server.
   - **c.** A Windows Server 2008 computer can perform only one role.
   - **d.** None of the above.

7. Which of the following is *not* true in reference to using the Server Manager console?
   a. The Add Roles Wizard and the Add Features Wizard are both accessible from the Server Manager.
   b. You must run a separate instance of the Add Roles Wizard for each role you want to install.
   c. Server Manager can install multiple roles at once.
   d. You must download an update from the Microsoft Downloads Web site to add the Streaming Media Services role to the Server Manager console.

8. Which feature(s) must you install when you install the Web Server (IIS) role?
   a. Windows Process Activation Service (WPAS)
   b. Telnet Client
   c. Message Queuing
   d. Peer Name Resolution Protocol (PNRP)

9. The TS Gateway role service enables clients on the Internet to access which type of server?
   a. Windows Server 2008   b. SMTP Server
   c. Telnet Server   d. Windows Server 2008 Terminal Server

10. Which of the following services does a Windows Deployment Services client computer use to locate a WDS server?
    a. DHCP   b. DNS
    c. Active Directory   d. WINS

Review Questions

1. List three reasons why it might not be a good idea to purchase the most powerful server computer you can find and install all of the roles your organization needs on that one machine. Explain your answers.

2. Explain how a distributed application works.

Case Scenarios

Scenario 1-1: Installing Roles with a Batch File

Mark Lee is an IT technician whose supervisor has assigned the task of configuring twenty new servers, which Mark is to ship to the company's branch offices around the country. He must configure each server to function as a file server with support for DFS and UNIX clients, a print server with support for Internet and UNIX printing, a fax server, and a secured, intranet Web/FTP server for domain users. Write a batch file that Mark can use to install all of the required software elements on a server.

Scenario 1-2: Hosting Applications with Terminal Services

Your company is planning to open a second office in another city, and you are part of the team that is designing the new network. The employees in the new office will be performing a wide variety of tasks, and they need a large number of applications installed on their computers. Ralph, your IT director, is having trouble meeting his budget for the new network, due to the high cost of the applications, processor, memory, and disk space resources the workstations will need to run the applications. He is also concerned about supporting and maintaining the workstations because there will be no full-time IT personnel at the new site.

You suggest using Terminal Services to host the applications. Ralph, however, knows nothing about Terminal Services. Explain how using Terminal Services can resolve all of the network design problems Ralph is experiencing.

2 LESSON

Deploying a File Server

OBJECTIVE DOMAIN MATRIX

TECHNOLOGY SKILL	OBJECTIVE DOMAIN	OBJECTIVE DOMAIN NUMBER
Adding a New Disk	Configure storage.	1.5

KEY TERMS

access control entries
  (ACEs)
access control list (ACL)
ATA (Advanced Technology
  Attachment)
authorization
basic disk
direct-attached storage
disk duplexing
disk mirroring
DiskPart.exe

dynamic disk
effective permissions
external drive array
file system
folder redirection
logical unit numbers
  (LUNs)
network attached storage
  (NAS)
Offline Files
partition style

Redundant Array of
  Independent Disks (RAID)
security identifiers (SIDs)
security principal
serial ATA (SATA)
Shadow Copies
Small Computer System
  Interface (SCSI)
special permissions
standard permissions
storage area network (SAN)

The file server, the most basic and the most universal type of application server, is found on almost every network. While Windows Server 2008 includes a role dedicated to File Services, this lesson covers the file server operations included in every server installation by default, including the following:

- Disk management
- Planning for fault tolerance
- Folder sharing
- Access control using share and NTFS permissions
- Mapping drives

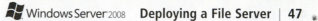

Planning a File Server Deployment

THE BOTTOM LINE

Time spent planning a file server deployment before actually configuring the computer is never wasted.

In its most basic form, configuring a Windows Server 2008 computer to function as a file server is the simplest role to implement. All you have to do is share a folder or a drive and, technically, you have a file server. However, on an enterprise network, things are almost never that simple. File sharing on a large network is subject to any or all of the following problems:

- Scalability — How much storage space do the users need now, and how much more will they need next year?
- Navigation — On a large network with many shares, how should users find the files they need?
- Protection — How do you control access to network file shares?
- Abuse — How do you prevent users from consuming too much server storage space?
- Diversity — How do you provide file-sharing support for users running operating systems other than Windows?
- Fault tolerance — How quickly can you recover from the failure of a hard drive, server, or entire facility?
- Availability — How can you ensure that users have continuous local access to critical files, even on remote networks?

The File Services role and the other storage-related features included with Windows Server 2008 provide tools that enable system administrators to address all of these problems on a scale appropriate to a large enterprise network. However, before you implement the role or use these tools, you should think about your users' needs and how they affect their file storage and sharing practices. Implementation of technologies such as Distributed File System and storage quotas requires some idea of how to use the technologies on your enterprise network. Therefore, a period of planning and design is recommended before you start the implementation.

How Many File Servers?

When is one big file server preferable to several smaller ones?

After you have a general idea of how much data you will need to store, you can begin thinking about how many file servers you will need. In Lesson 1, "Deploying an Application Server," you learned about the advantages and disadvantages of using one large server versus several smaller ones, so you should now have some idea of which arrangement would be better suited to your organization.

If you are considering one large file server, or if your organization's storage requirements are extremely large, you must also consider the inherent storage limitations of Windows Server 2008, which are listed in Table 2-1.

Table 2-1

Windows Server 2008 Storage Limitations

Storage Characteristic	Limitation
Maximum basic volume size	2 terabytes
Maximum dynamic volume size (simple and mirrored volumes)	2 terabytes
Maximum dynamic volume size (spanned and striped volumes)	64 terabytes (2 terabytes per disk, with a maximum of 32 disks)
Maximum dynamic volume size (RAID-5 volumes)	62 terabytes (2 terabytes per disk, with a maximum of 32 disks, and 2 terabytes reserved for parity information)
Maximum NTFS volume size	2^{32} clusters minus 1 cluster (Using the default 4 kilobyte cluster size, the maximum volume size is 16 terabytes minus 64 kilobytes. Using the maximum 64 kilobyte cluster size, the maximum volume size is 256 terabytes minus 64 kilobytes.)
Maximum number of clusters on an NTFS volume	2^{32} (4,294,967,296)
Maximum NTFS file size	2^{44} bytes (16 terabytes) minus 64 kilobytes
Maximum number of files on an NTFS volume	2^{32} minus 1 file (4,294,967,295)
Maximum number of volumes on a server	Approximately 2,000 (1000 dynamic volumes and the rest basic)

The number of sites your enterprise network encompasses and the technologies you use to provide network communications between those sites can also affect your plans. If, for example, your organization has branch offices scattered around the world and uses relatively expensive wide area networking (WAN) links to connect them, it would probably be more economical to install a file server at each location than to have all of your users access a single file server using the WAN links.

Within each site, the number of file servers you need can depend on how often your users work with the same files and how much fault tolerance and high availability you want to build into the system. For example, if each department in your organization typically works with its own documents and rarely needs access to other departments' files, deploying individual file servers to each department might be preferable. If everyone in your organization works with the same set of files, a single server might be a better choice.

The need for high availability and fault tolerance can also lead you to deploy additional servers, whether you initially configure them all as file servers or not. As discussed in Lesson 1, distributing roles among multiple servers enables you to redeploy roles as needed, in the event of a hardware failure or other catastrophe.

Finally, if you are upgrading file servers from an earlier version of Windows to Windows Server 2008, or replacing older servers with Windows Server 2008 servers, you can expect increased file server performance. For example, upgrading a network running Windows 2000 file servers and clients can yield a 200 to 300 percent overall improvement in performance, even without hardware or network upgrades.

Selecting File Server Hardware

In addition to estimating the amounts of processor speed, memory, and disk space you require, consider whether your needs call for specialized file server hardware.

You should select the hardware for a file server based primarily on the amount of storage your users need and their performance and availability requirements.

SELECTING PROCESSORS

Serving files in Windows Server 2008 is not a particularly processor-intensive task in itself, but additional storage-related services can add to the processor burden. For example, using a software-based *Redundant Array of Independent Disks (RAID)* implementation, such as the one included in Windows Server 2008, which enables the computer to protect its data against a disk failure, imposes an additional burden on the system processor that a hardware-based RAID implementation would not. The same holds true for encryption, compression, and other roles, features, or applications you might have installed on the computer.

The processor speed is roughly proportional to its performance level. In other words, a 3.0 gigahertz (GHz) Xeon processor will yield roughly twice the file server performance of a 1.5 GHz Xeon processor. Therefore, purchasing a file server with a faster processor is usually worth the extra expense, from a performance standpoint.

However, using multiple processors in a single server typically provides less improvement. For example, installing a second identical processor in a single-processor server will only provide 1.4 to 1.6 times the performance, and as the number of processors goes up, the improvement rate declines. Upgrading a two-processor server to four processors will only yield 1.3 to 1.4 times the performance. Therefore, two single-processor servers would increase performance more than one server with two processors.

TAKE NOTE*

To estimate the performance level increase you will achieve by a combination of operating system upgrades, processor speed increases, and adding processors, you multiply the increases provided by the individual upgrades. For example, if you replace a 1.5 GHz, single-processor server running Windows 2000 with a Windows Server 2008 dual-processor server running at 3.0 GHz, the individual performance factors would be increased by about 2.5 times for the operating system, 2 times for the processor speed, and about 1.5 times for adding the second processor. $2.5 \times 2 \times 1.5$ yields an overall increase of 7.5 times.

ESTIMATING MEMORY REQUIREMENTS

The amount of memory needed for a file server depends on the amount of storage the computer must support and the file usage habits of the server clients. Windows Server 2008 uses memory to cache frequently used files, so additional memory might improve performance. However, there are other factors to consider as well.

For example, a Windows Server 2008 file server with one gigabyte of memory can support approximately 100,000 remote file handles, meaning that all of the server's users combined can have as many as 100,000 files open simultaneously. Of that one gigabyte of memory, the server can use approximately 500 megabytes to cache files, with the rest being devoted to other operating systems tasks. Any additional memory you install in the server will be almost wholly devoted to supplementing the system's caching capability.

Whether this additional memory will actually benefit your users, however, depends on how they utilize the server's storage. If the users tend to open the same files frequently, then they are more likely to access data from the cache, and additional memory will improve the computer's file-serving performance. If, however, the users consistently open different files, then they will be accessing data directly from disk most of the time, and the server would derive greater benefit from faster disks than more memory.

ESTIMATING STORAGE REQUIREMENTS

The amount of storage space you need in a file server depends on a variety of factors, including your users' requirements. Start by allocating a specific amount of space for each user the server will support. Then, factor in the potential growth of your organization and your network, both in terms of additional users and additional space required by each user.

In addition to the space allocated to individual users, you must also consider the storage requirements for the following server elements:

- Operating system — The size of the operating system installation depends on the roles and features you choose to install. A typical Windows Server 2008 installation with the File Services role takes just over 7 GB, but the system requirements for Windows Server 2008 recommend 40 GB and state that 80 GB is optimal. For a Server Core installation, 10 GB is recommended and 40 GB is optimal.

- Paging file — By default, the paging file on a Windows Server 2008 computer is 1.5 times the amount of memory installed in the computer.

- Memory dump — When Windows Server 2008 experiences a serious malfunction, it offers to dump the contents of the system memory to a file, which technicians can use for diagnostic purposes. The maximum size for a memory dump file is the amount of memory installed in the computer plus one megabyte.

- Applications — Any additional applications you install on a file server require their own disk space, as well as space for data files, log files, and future updates.

- Log files — Be sure to consider any applications that maintain their own logs, in addition to the operating system logs. You can configure the maximum log size for the Windows event logs and for most application logs, and add those values to calculate the total log space required.

- Shadow copies — The Windows Server 2008 Shadow Copies feature can utilize up to 10 percent of a volume, by default. However, Microsoft recommends enlarging this value for volumes containing files that are frequently modified.

- Fault tolerance — Fault-tolerance technologies, such as disk mirroring and RAID, can profoundly affect disk consumption. Mirroring disks cuts the effective storage size in half, and RAID 5 reduces it by one third.

SELECTING A DISK TECHNOLOGY

As of this writing, standard hard drives up to one terabyte in size are available, and higher capacities are no doubt on the way. A basic file server uses *direct-attached storage*, that is, a computer with hard drives stored inside it. For file servers that require more storage space than a standard computer case can hold, or that have special availability requirements, a variety of storage hardware options are available.

Of the many specifications that hard disk manufacturers provide for their products, the best gauge of the drive's performance is the rotational speed of the spindle that holds the platters. Typical desktop workstation hard drives have rotational speeds of 7,200 or 10,000 revolutions per minute (rpm). For a file server, 10,000 should be considered the minimum acceptable speed; many higher-end server drives run at 15,000 rpm, which is preferable but costly.

Just as important as the speed and capacity of the hard disks you select is the interface the disks use to connect to the computer. A file server on an enterprise network often has to handle large numbers of disk I/O requests simultaneously, far more than a workstation drive with a single user ever would. For that reason, an interface that might be more than sufficient for a workstation, such as the *ATA (Advanced Technology Attachment)* interface that most workstation drives use, would perform poorly under a file server load.

TAKE NOTE*

Hard drives using the ATA interface are also commonly referred to as Integrated Drive Electronics (IDE) or Enhanced IDE (EIDE) drives.

ATA devices are limited to a maximum transmission speed of 133 megabytes/second (MB/sec), which is relatively slow by file server standards. The other big problem with ATA devices is that only a single command can be on the cable at any one time. If you have two drives connected to an ATA cable, a command sent to the first drive has to be completed before the system can send a command to the second drive. For a file server that must handle requests from many simultaneous users, this is an inherently inefficient arrangement.

The newer *serial ATA (SATA)* standard increases the maximum transmission speed to 300 MB/sec and addresses the ATA unitasking problem with a technology called Native Command

Queuing (NCQ). NCQ enables a drive to optimize the order in which it processes commands, to minimize drive seek times. However, SATA only supports a single drive per channel, and can only utilize NCQ when the computer has a motherboard and chipset that supports the Advanced Host Controller Interface (AHCI) standard. Older computers run the drives in an "IDE emulation" mode, which disables their NCQ and hot plugging capabilities. While SATA drives are more efficient than ATA, and can be a viable solution for relatively low-volume file servers, they are not suitable for large enterprise servers.

Small Computer System Interface (SCSI) is the most commonly used storage interface for enterprise servers. SCSI offers transmission rates up to 640 MB/sec, support for up to 16 devices on a single bus, and the ability to queue commands on each device. This enables multiple drives connected to one SCSI host adapter to process commands simultaneously and independently, which is an ideal environment for a high-volume file server.

SCSI standards vary, with different bus types, transmission speeds, and cable configurations. To use SCSI on file servers, all devices and host adapters must support the same standard. You connect SCSI devices to a host adapter using a daisy chain cable arrangement called a SCSI bus. Many host adapters enable you to connect both internal and external devices, so you can expand the bus as needed, even if the computer case does not have room for additional drives. Every device on a SCSI bus has an identifier called a SCSI ID, which the host adapter uses to send commands to the device. Subcomponents of a SCSI device, such as individual drives in an array, are identified using ***logical unit numbers (LUNs)***.

SCSI hard drives are usually quite a bit more expensive than those using any of the other disk interfaces, despite the fact that the disk assemblies are virtually identical; only the electronics are different. However, for most administrators of large enterprise networks, the enhanced performance of SCSI drives in a high-traffic environment is worth the added expense.

USING EXTERNAL DRIVE ARRAYS

High capacity file servers often store hard drives in a separate housing, called an ***external drive array***, which typically incorporates a disk controller, power supply, cooling fans, and cache memory into an independent unit. Drive arrays can connect to a computer using a disk interface, such as SCSI (Small Computer System Interface), IEEE 1394 (FireWire), or USB 2.0, or a network interface, such as iSCSI or Fibre Channel.

Drive arrays enable a file server to contain more hard drives than a normal computer case can hold, and often include additional fault-tolerance features, such as hot-swappable drives, redundant power supplies, and hardware-based RAID. Obviously, the more features the array has, and the more drives it can hold, the higher the cost. Large arrays intended for enterprise networks can easily run into the five figure price range.

Drive arrays typically operate in one of two configurations:

- ***Storage area network (SAN)*** — A SAN is a separate network dedicated solely to storage devices, such as drive arrays, magnetic tape autochangers, and optical jukeboxes, as shown in Figure 2-1. SANs use a high speed networking technology, such as SCSI,

TAKE NOTE *

With the introduction of the Serial ATA interface, the original ATA interface has been retroactively named Parallel ATA, in reference to the way in which these devices transmit data over 16 connections simultaneously.

Figure 2-1

A SAN is a separate network dedicated to file servers and external storage devices

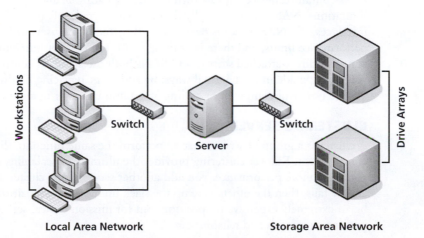

iSCSI, or Fibre Channel to enable them to transmit large amounts of file data very quickly. Therefore, a file server on a SAN will have two separate network interfaces, one to the SAN and one to the standard local area network (LAN). A SAN provides block-based storage services to the computers connected to it, just as if the storage devices were installed in the computer. The storage hardware on a SAN might provide additional capabilities, such as RAID, but the file system used to store and protect data on the SAN devices is implemented by the computer.

- *Network attached storage (NAS)* — A NAS drive array differs from a SAN array primarily in its software. NAS devices are essentially dedicated file servers that provide file-based storage services directly to clients on the network. A NAS array connects to a standard LAN, using traditional Fast Ethernet or Gigabit Ethernet hardware, as shown in Figure 2-2, and does not require a computer to implement the file system or function as a file server. In addition to the storage subsystem, the NAS device has its own processor and memory hardware, and runs its own operating system with a Web interface for administrative access. The operating system is typically a stripped-down version of UNIX designed to provide only data storage, data access, and management functions. Most NAS devices support both the Server Message Block (SMB) protocol used by Windows clients and the Network File System (NFS) protocol used by most UNIX distributions.

Figure 2-2

A NAS device connects directly to the LAN and functions as a self-contained file server

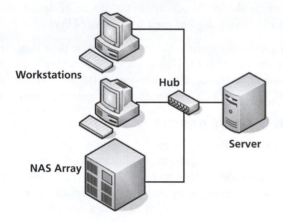

SAN and NAS are both technologies designed to provide scalability and fault tolerance to network data storage systems. Generally speaking, a SAN is more complicated and more expensive to implement, but it can provide excellent performance, due to its use of a separate network medium and virtually unlimited storage capacity. Windows Server 2008 includes several new SAN management features and tools, which are discussed later in this lesson.

Adding a NAS device to your network is a simple way to provide your users with additional storage and reduce the processing burden on your servers. Despite its almost plug-and-play convenience, however, NAS does have some significant drawbacks. Because the NAS array is a self-contained device with its own processing hardware and operating system, it has inherent limitations. NAS devices typically do not have upgradeable processors, memory, or network interfaces. If a NAS device is overburdened by too many users or I/O requests, it can reach its performance limits, and there is nothing you can do except purchase another NAS device. By contrast, direct-attached storage and SANs both use standard computers to serve files, which you can upgrade in all the usual ways: by adding or replacing hardware, moving the drives to a more powerful computer, or adding an additional server to a cluster.

CLUSTERING SERVERS

A cluster is a group of servers that all perform the same function, dividing the client load among them. Failover clustering provides the ultimate in scalability and fault tolerance. If you need more performance, you add another server to the cluster. If one of the servers in the cluster fails, then the others take up the slack until you can repair or replace it. Clustering can be an extremely expensive proposition, but for mission critical servers, it provides unmatched performance levels and reliability.

X REF

For more information on failover clustering, see Lesson 12, "Using High Availability Technologies."

Working with Disks

> When preparing a hard disk for use, Windows Server 2008 file servers often require different settings than workstations.

When you install Windows Server 2008 on a computer, the setup program automatically performs all of the preparation tasks for the hard disks in the system. However, when you install additional hard disk drives on a file server, or when you want to use settings that differ from the system defaults, you must perform the following tasks manually:

- Select a partitioning style — Windows Server 2008 supports two hard disk partition styles, on both x86- and x64-based computers: the master boot record (MBR) partition style and the GUID (globally unique identifier) partition table (GPT) partition style. You must choose one of these partition styles for a drive; you cannot use both.

- Select a disk type — Windows Server 2008 supports two disk types: basic and dynamic. You cannot use both types on the same disk drive, but you can mix disk types in the same computer.

- Divide the disk into partitions or volumes — Although many professionals use the terms partition and volume interchangeably, it is correct to refer to partitions on basic disks, and volumes on dynamic disks.

- Format the partitions or volumes with a file system — Windows Server 2008 supports the NTFS file system and the FAT file system (including the FAT16 and FAT32 variants).

The following sections examine the options for each of these tasks.

SELECTING A PARTITION STYLE

The term *partition style* refers to the method that Windows operating systems use to organize partitions on the disk. Two hard disk partition styles can be used in Windows Server 2008:

- MBR — The MBR partition style has been around as long as Windows and is still the default partition style for x86-based and x64-based computers.

- GPT — GPT has also been around for a while, but no x86 version of Windows prior to Windows Server 2008 and Windows Vista supports it. (Windows XP Professional x64 Edition does support GPT.) Now, you can use the GPT partition style on x86-, as well as x64-based, computers.

Before Windows Server 2008 and Windows Vista, all x86-based Windows computers used only the MBR partition style. Computers based on the x64 platform could use either the MBR or GPT partition style, as long as the GPT disk was not the boot disk.

MBR uses a partition table to point to the locations of the partitions on the disk. The MBR disk partitioning style supports volumes up to 2 terabytes in size, and up to either four primary partitions or three primary partitions and one extended partition on a single drive.

The following systems can use either the MBR or the GPT partition style for their disks:

- Windows Server 2003 SP1 (or later) x86-based machines
- Windows Server 2008 computers
- Windows Vista x86-based computers
- Itanium-based computers
- x64-based computers

Bear in mind, however, that unless the computer's architecture provides support for an Extensible Firmware Interface (EFI)–based boot partition, it is not possible to boot from a GPT disk. If this is the case, the system drive must be an MBR disk, and GPT must reside on a separate non-bootable disk used only for data storage.

Itanium-based computers do support EFI; in fact, developers created the EFI specification with the Itanium processor in mind. The Itanium processor's main use is driving applications that require more than 4 GB of memory, such as enterprise databases.

One of the ways that GPT differs from MBR is that partitions, rather than hidden sectors, store data critical to platform operation. In addition, GPT-partitioned disks use redundant primary and backup partition tables for improved integrity. Although GPT specifications permit an unlimited number of partitions, the Windows implementation restricts partitions to 128 per disk. The GPT disk partitioning style supports volumes up to 18 exabytes (1 exabyte = 1 billion GB, or 2^{60} bytes).

⊕ MORE INFORMATION

As far as the Windows Server 2008 disk management tools are concerned, there is no difference between creating partitions or volumes in MBR and in GPT. You create partitions and volumes for both by using the same tools to follow the same process.

Table 2-2 compares some of the characteristics of the MBR and GPT partition styles.

Table 2-2

MBR and GPT Partition Style Comparison

MASTER BOOT RECORD (MBR)	GUID PARTITION TABLE (GPT)
Supports up to four primary partitions or three primary partitions and one extended partition, with unlimited logical drives on the extended partition	Supports up to 128 primary partitions
Supports volumes up to 2 terabytes	Supports volumes up to 18 exabytes
Hidden (unpartitioned) sectors store data critical to platform operation	Partitions store data critical to platform operation
Replication and cyclical redundancy checks (CRCs) are not features of MBR's partition table	Replication and CRC protection of the partition table provide increased reliability

UNDERSTANDING DISK TYPES

Most personal computers use *basic disks* because they are the easiest to manage. A basic disk uses primary partitions, extended partitions, and logical drives to organize data. A primary partition appears to the operating system as though it is a physically separate disk and can host an operating system, in which case it is known as the *active partition*.

During the operating system installation, the setup program creates a *system partition* and a *boot partition*. The system partition contains hardware-related files that the computer uses to start. The boot partition contains the operating system files, which are stored in the Windows file folder. In most cases, these two partitions are one and the same, the active primary partition that Windows uses when starting. The active partition tells the computer which system partition and operating system it should use to start Windows.

When you work with basic disks in Windows Server 2008, you can create up to four primary partitions. For the fourth partition, you have the option of creating an extended partition instead, on which you can create as many logical drives as needed. You can format and assign driver letters to logical drives, but they cannot host an operating system. Table 2-3 compares some of the characteristics of primary and extended partitions.

Table 2-3

Primary and Extended Partition Comparison

PRIMARY PARTITIONS	EXTENDED PARTITIONS
A primary partition functions as though it is a physically separate disk and can host an operating system.	Extended partitions cannot host an operating system.
A primary partition can be marked as an active partition. You can have only one active partition per hard disk. The system BIOS looks to the active partition for the boot files it uses to start the operating system.	You cannot mark an extended partition as an active partition.
You can create up to four primary partitions or three primary partitions and one extended partition.	A basic disk can contain only one extended partition, but unlimited logical partitions.
You format each primary partition and assign a unique drive letter.	You do not format the extended partition itself, but the logical drives it contains. You assign a unique drive letter to each of the logical drives.

The alternative to using a basic disk is to convert it to a ***dynamic disk***. The process of converting a basic disk to a dynamic disk creates a single partition that occupies the entire disk. You can then create an unlimited number of volumes out of the space in that partition. Dynamic disks support several different types of volumes, as described in the next section.

UNDERSTANDING VOLUME TYPES

A dynamic disk can contain an unlimited number of volumes that function much like primary partitions on a basic disk, but you cannot mark an existing dynamic disk as active. When you create a volume on a dynamic disk in Windows Server 2008, you must choose from the following five types:

- Simple volume—Consists of space from a single disk. After you have created a simple volume, you can extend it to multiple disks to create a spanned or striped volume, as long as it is not a system volume or boot volume. You can also extend a simple volume into any adjacent unallocated space on the same disk or, with some limitations, shrink the volume by de-allocating any unused space in the volume.

- Spanned volume—Consists of space from 2 to 32 physical disks, all of which must be dynamic disks. A spanned volume is essentially a method for combining the space from multiple dynamic disks into a single large volume. Windows Server 2008 writes to the spanned volume by filling all of the space on the first disk and then fills each of the additional disks in turn. You can extend a spanned volume at any time by adding disk space. Creating a spanned volume does not increase the disk's read/write performance, nor does it provide fault tolerance. In fact, if a single physical disk in the spanned volume fails, all of the data in the entire volume is lost.

- Striped volume—Consists of space from 2 to 32 physical disks, all of which must be dynamic disks. The difference between a striped volume and a spanned volume is that in a striped volume, the system writes data one stripe at a time to each successive disk in the volume. Striping provides improved performance because each disk drive in the array has time to seek the location of its next stripe while the other drives are writing. Striped volumes do not provide fault tolerance, however, and you cannot extend them after creation. If a single physical disk in the striped volume fails, all of the data in the entire volume is lost.

- Mirrored volume—Consists of an identical amount of space on two physical disks, both of which must be dynamic disks. The system performs all read and write operations on both disks simultaneously, so they contain duplicate copies of all data stored on the volume. If one of the disks fails, the other continues to provide access to the volume until the failed disk is repaired or replaced.
- RAID-5 volume—Consists of space on three or more physical disks, all of which must be dynamic. The system stripes data and parity information across all of the disks, so that if one physical disk fails, the missing data can be recreated using the parity information on the other disks. RAID-5 volumes provide improved read performance, because of the disk striping, but write performance suffers, due to the need for parity calculations.

CHOOSING A VOLUME SIZE

Although Windows Server 2008 can support dynamic volumes as large as 64 terabytes, this does not mean that you should create volumes that big, even if you have a server with that much storage. To facilitate the maintenance and administration processes, it is usually preferable to split your file server's storage into volumes of manageable size, rather than create a single, gigantic volume.

One common practice is to choose a volume size based on the capacity of your network backup solution. For example, if you perform network backups using tape drives with an 80 GB capacity, creating volumes that can fit onto a single tape can facilitate the backup process. Creating smaller volumes will also speed up the restore process if you have to recover a volume from a tape or other backup medium.

Another factor is the amount of downtime your business can tolerate. If one of your volumes suffers a file system error, and you do not have a fault tolerance mechanism in place to take up the slack, you might have to bring it down, so that you can run Chkdsk.exe or some other disk repair utility. The larger the volume, the longer the Chkdsk process will take, and the longer your users will be without their files.

Of course, it is possible to err in the other extreme as well. Splitting a one terabyte drive into 100 volumes of 10 GB, for example, would also be an administrative nightmare, in many different ways.

UNDERSTANDING FILE SYSTEMS

To organize and store data or programs on a hard drive, you must install a *file system*. A file system is the underlying disk drive structure that enables you to store information on your computer. You install file systems by formatting a partition or volume on the hard disk.

In Windows Server 2008, three file system options are available: NTFS, FAT32, and FAT (also known as FAT16). NTFS is the preferred file system for a file server; the main benefits are improved support for larger hard drives and better security in the form of encryption and permissions that restrict access by unauthorized users.

Because the FAT file systems lack the security that NTFS provides, any user who gains access to your computer can read any file without restriction. Additionally, FAT file systems have disk size limitations: FAT32 cannot handle a partition greater than 32 GB, or a file greater than 4 GB. FAT cannot handle a hard disk greater than 4 GB, or a file greater than 2 GB. Because of these limitations, the only viable reason for using FAT16 or FAT32 is the need to dual boot the computer with a non-Windows operating system or a previous version of Windows that does not support NTFS, which is not a likely configuration for a file server.

Designing a File-Sharing Strategy

Decide where users should store their files and who should be permitted to access them.

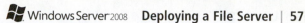

Why should the administrators of an enterprise network want users to store their files on shared server drives, rather than their local workstation drives? The answers to this question typically include the following:

- To enable users to collaborate on projects by sharing files
- To back up document files more easily
- To protect company information by controlling access to documents
- To reduce the number of shares needed on the network
- To prevent the need to share access to workstations
- To monitor users' storage habits and regulate their disk space consumption
- To insulate users from the sharing and permission assignment processes

Without these problems, file sharing would simply be a matter of creating a share on each user's workstation and granting everyone full access to it. Because of these problems, however, this practice would lead to chaos, in the form of lost files, corrupted workstations, and endless help calls from confused users.

Server-based file shares should provide users with a simplified data storage solution that they can use to store their files, share files with other users, and easily locate the files shared by their colleagues. Behind the scenes, and unbeknown to the users, administrators can use server-based storage tools to protect everyone's files, regulate access to sensitive data, and prevent users from abusing their storage privileges.

ARRANGING SHARES

The first step in designing a file-sharing strategy is to decide how many shares to create and where to create them. Simply installing a big hard drive in a server and giving everyone access to it would be as chaotic as sharing everyone's workstation drives. Depending on the size of your organization, you might have one single file server, or many servers scattered around the network.

For many large organizations, departmental or workgroup file servers are a viable solution. Each user has his or her "local" server, the directory layout of which becomes familiar. If you have separate file servers for the various departments or workgroups in your organization, it is a good idea to develop a consistent directory structure and duplicate it on all of the servers, so that if users have to access a server in another department, they can find their way around.

Generally speaking, a well-designed sharing strategy provides each user with three resources:

- A private storage space, such as a home folder, to which the user has exclusive access.
- A public storage space, where each user can store files that they want colleagues to be able to access.
- Access to a shared work space for communal and collaborative documents.

One way to implement this strategy would be to create one share called Home, with a private folder for each user on it, and a second share called Public, again with a folder for each user. Depending on your network's hardware configuration, you could create both of these shares on a separate server for each department or workgroup, split the shares and folder among multiple servers in each department, or even create one big file server for the entire company, containing all of the shares.

TAKE NOTE✱

Even if you split the Home and Public shares among multiple servers, you can still make them appear as a single unified directory tree using the Windows Server 2008 Distributed File System (DFS). See the "Using the Distributed File System" section in Lesson 3, "Using the File Services Role," for more information.

CONTROLLING ACCESS

On most enterprise networks, the principle of "least privileges" should apply. This principle states that users should have only the privileges they need to perform their required tasks, and no more.

A user's private storage space should be exactly that, private and inaccessible, if not invisible, to other users. This is a place in which each user can store his or her private files, without exposing them to other users. Each user should, therefore, have full privileges to his or her private storage, with the ability to create, delete, read, write, and modify files. Other users should have no privileges to that space at all.

TAKE NOTE*

The easiest way to create private folders with the appropriate permissions for each user is to create a home folder through each Active Directory user object.

Each user should also have full privileges to his or her public folder. This is a space where users can share files informally. For example, when Ralph asks Alice for a copy of her budget spreadsheet, Alice can simply copy the file from her private folder to her public folder. Then, Ralph can copy the file from Alice's public folder to his own private folder, and access it from there. Therefore, public and private folders differ in that other users should be able to list the contents of all public folders and read the files stored there, but not be able to modify or delete files in any folder but their own. Users should also be able to navigate throughout the Public folder tree, so that they can read any user's files and copy them to their own folders.

In the shared work space for collaborative documents, users should have privileges based on their individual needs. Some users need read access only to certain files, while others might have to modify them as well. You should limit the ability to create and delete files to managers or supervisors.

TAKE NOTE*

Although users should have full privileges to their personal folders, you should not leave their storage practices unmonitored or unregulated. Later in this lesson, you will learn how to set quotas limiting users' storage space, prohibit users from storing certain types of files on network servers, and generate reports detailing users' storage habits.

Administrators, of course, must have the privileges required to exercise full control over all users' private and public storage spaces, as well as the ability to modify permissions as needed.

NFTS permissions are most commonly used to assign these privileges on a Windows Server 2008 file server. There is no compelling reason to use the FAT (File Allocation Table) file system in Windows Server 2008. NTFS provides not only the most granular user access control but also other advanced storage features, including file encryption and compression.

To simplify the administration process, you should always assign permissions to security groups and not to individuals. Assigning permissions to groups enables you to add new users or move them to other job assignments without modifying the permissions themselves. On a large Active Directory network, you might also consider the standard practice of assigning the NTFS permissions to a domain local group, placing the user objects to receive the permissions in a global (or universal) group, and making the global group a member of a domain local group.

Except in special cases, it is usually not necessary to explicitly deny NTFS permissions to users or groups. Some administrators prefer to use this capability, however. When various administrators use different permission assignment techniques on the same network, it can become extremely difficult to track down the sources of certain effective permissions. Another way to simplify the administration process on an enterprise network is to establish specific permission assignment policies, so that everyone performs tasks the same way.

X REF

For more information on NTFS permission assignments, see "Assigning Permissions," later in this lesson.

MAPPING DRIVES

After you have created the folders for each user and assigned permissions to the folders, the next step is to make sure that users can access their folders. One way of doing this is to use the Folder Redirection settings in Group Policy to map each user's Documents folder to his

or her home folder on the network share. This process is invisible to users, enabling them to work with their files without even knowing they are stored on a network drive.

Another way to provide users with easy and consistent access to their files is to map drive letters to each user's directories with logon scripts, so they can always find their files in the same place, using Windows Explorer. For example, you might consider mapping drive F: to the user's private home folder and drive G: to the user's Public folder. A third drive letter might point to the root of the Public share, so that the user can access other people's public folders.

Many computer users do not understand the fundamental concepts of network drive sharing and file management. Often, they just know that they store their files on the F drive, and are unaware that another user's F drive might point to a different folder. However, consistent drive letter assignments on every workstation can make it easier to support users experiencing problems storing or retrieving their files.

Planning for Fault Tolerance

> How valuable is your data, and how much are you willing to spend to protect it from disaster?

Depending on the nature of your organization, fault tolerance for your file servers might be a convenience or an absolute requirement. For some businesses, a hard drive failure might mean a few hours of lost productivity. For an order entry department, it could mean lost income. For a hospital records department, it could mean lost lives. Depending on where in this range your organization falls, consider using a fault tolerance mechanism to make sure that your users' files are always available to them.

The essence of fault tolerance is immediate redundancy. If one copy of a file becomes unavailable due to a disk error or failure, another copy online can take its place almost immediately. A variety of fault tolerance mechanisms provide this redundancy in different ways. Some create redundant blocks, redundant files, redundant volumes, redundant drives, and even redundant servers.

As with many computer technologies, fault tolerance is a tradeoff between performance and expense. The mechanisms that provide the most fault tolerance are usually the most expensive. And it is up to you and your organization to decide the value of continuous access to your data.

The following sections discuss some of the most common fault tolerance mechanisms used by and for file servers.

USING DISK MIRRORING

Disk mirroring, in which the computer writes the same data to identical volumes on two different disks, is one of the simplest forms of fault tolerance to implement and manage, but it is also one of the more expensive solutions. By mirroring volumes, you are essentially paying twice as much for your storage space.

Little or no performance penalty is associated with mirroring volumes, as long as you use a hardware configuration that enables the two drives to write their data simultaneously. As discussed earlier in this lesson, SCSI and SATA drives are suitable for disk mirroring, but parallel ATA drives are not, because two ATA drives on the same interface have to write their data sequentially, and not simultaneously, slowing down the volume's performance substantially.

A variation on disk mirroring, called *disk duplexing*, uses duplicate host adapters as well as duplicate hard drives. Installing the drives on separate host adapters adds an extra measure of fault tolerance, which enables users to continue working if either a drive or a host adapter fails. Duplexing also enables the computer to mirror ATA drives effectively, because each disk is connected to a separate host adapter.

USING RAID

RAID is a group of technologies that use multiple disk drives in various configurations to store redundant data, providing increased performance or fault tolerance, or both. Table 2-4 lists some types of RAID configurations.

Table 2-4

RAID Levels

RAID Level	RAID Functionality	Number of Disks Required	Description
RAID 0	Stripe set without parity	2, minimum	Implemented in Windows Server 2008 as a striped volume, RAID 0 provides no fault tolerance, but it does enhance performance, due to the parallel read and write operations that occur on all of the drives simultaneously. RAID 0 has no error detection mechanism, so the failure of one disk causes the loss of all data on the volume.
RAID 1	Mirror set without parity	2, minimum	Implemented in Windows Server 2008 as a mirrored volume, a RAID 1 array provides increased read performance, as well as fault tolerance. The array can continue to serve files as long as one of the disks remains operational.
RAID 3	Byte-level stripe set	3, minimum	Not implemented in Windows Server with dedicated parity 2008, a RAID 3 array stripes data at the byte level across the disks, reserving one disk for parity information. A RAID 3 array can survive the loss of any one disk, but because every write to one of the data disks requires a write to the parity disk, the parity disk becomes a performance bottleneck.
RAID 4	Block-level stripe set with dedicated parity	3, minimum	Not implemented in Windows Server 2008, RAID 4 is identical in structure to RAID 3, except that a RAID 4 array uses larger, block-level stripes, which improves performance on the data disks. The parity disk can still be a performance bottleneck, however.
RAID 5	Stripe set with distributed parity	3, minimum	Implemented in Windows Server 2008 as a RAID-5 volume, RAID 5 stripes data and parity blocks across all of the disks, making sure that a block and its parity information are never stored on the same disk. Distributing the parity eliminates the performance bottleneck of the dedicated parity drive in RAID 3 and RAID 4, but the need to calculate the parity information still adds overhead to the system. A RAID 5 array can tolerate the loss of any one of its drives, and rebuild the missing data when the drive is repaired or replaced.
RAID 6	Stripe set with dual distributed parity	4, minimum	Not implemented in Windows Server 2008, RAID 6 uses the same structure as RAID 5, except that it stripes two copies of the parity information with the data. This enables the array to survive the failure of two drives. When a RAID 5 array suffers a drive failure, the array is vulnerable to data loss until the failed drive is replaced and the missing data rebuilt, which in the case of a large volume can take a long time. A RAID 6 array remains protected against data loss, even while one failed drive is rebuilding.

Parity is a mathematical algorithm that some RAID levels use to provide data redundancy in their disk write operations. To calculate the parity information for a RAID array, the system takes the values for the same data bit at a specific location on each of the drives in the array and adds them together. The resulting value becomes the parity bit for those data bits. The system then repeats the process for every bit location on the drives. If one of the drives is lost,

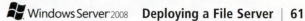

due to a hardware failure, the system can restore each lost data bit by calculating its value using the remaining data bits and the parity bit.

RAID arrays that use parity provide the same fault tolerance as mirrored disks, in that the array can survive the failure of any one drive, but they leave more storage space for data. While mirrored disks only provide half of their total storage capacity for data, the data storage capacity of a RAID array that uses parity is the size of the disks multiplied by the number of disks in the array, minus one. For example, a RAID 5 array that uses five 200 GB disks has a data storage capacity of 800 GB.

In addition to the levels listed in the table, there are also hybrid RAID solutions, such as RAID 0+1, which is an array of striped drives mirrored on a duplicate array. Windows Server 2008 only provides support for RAID levels 0, 1, and 5, although the operating system does not refer to RAID 0 and RAID 1 as such, calling them striping and mirroring, respectively. To implement these hybrid RAID solutions, or any standard RAID level other than 0, 1, or 5, you must install a third-party product.

Third-party products can implement RAID functions in software (as they are implemented in Windows Server 2008) or in hardware. Most third-party RAID implementations are hardware-based, and can range from a host adapter card that you connect to your own drives to a complete array containing drives and a host adapter. Generally speaking, hardware RAID implementations are preferable to software ones because they offload the parity calculations and disk manipulation functions from the system processor.

USING SHADOW COPIES

Shadow Copies is a Windows Server 2008 mechanism that automatically retains copies of files on a server volume in multiple versions from specific points in time. When users accidentally overwrite or delete files, they can access the shadow copies to restore earlier versions. This feature is designed to prevent administrators from having to load backup media to restore individual files for users. Shadow Copies is a file-based fault tolerance mechanism that does not provide protection against disk failures, but it does protect against the minor disasters that inconvenience users and administrators on a regular basis.

USING OFFLINE FILES

Offline Files, while technically not a form of fault tolerance, is a mechanism that individual users can employ to maintain access to their server files, even if the network service fails. Windows workstations copy server-based folders that users designate for offline use to the local drive, and the users work with the copies, which remain accessible whether the computer is connected to the network or not. If the network connection fails, or the user undocks a portable computer, access to the offline files continues uninterrupted. When the computer reconnects to the network, a synchronization procedure replicates the files between server and workstation in whichever direction is necessary. If there is a version conflict, such as when users have modified both copies of a file, the system prompts the user to specify which copy to retain.

Although an effective fault-tolerance mechanism, primary control of Offline Files rests with the user, making it a less suitable solution for an enterprise network than the other measures discussed in this section. Administrators can configure shares to prevent users from saving offline copies, but they cannot configure a file server to force a workstation to save offline copies.

BACKING UP

Server administrators should understand that none of the fault-tolerance mechanisms discussed in the previous sections substitute for a reliable backup solution. A file server can survive using mirroring or RAID, but what if the entire server is stolen or destroyed in a fire or other disaster? Or, more commonly, what if a user overwrites a critical company spreadsheet with a corrupted file? In a case like this, the mirror copy of the file or the RAID parity information is lost, so those mechanisms are no help. Regular backups to an offline, and preferably offsite, medium enable you to restore files, volumes, or entire servers when these types of disasters occur.

■ Configuring a File Server

THE BOTTOM LINE

Implementing basic file server functions requires only a default Windows Server 2008 installation.

The process of deploying and configuring a simple file server using Windows Server 2008 includes many of the most basic server administration tasks, including installing disks, creating shares, assigning permissions, and mapping drive letters. The following sections describe the procedures for these administration tasks, which form the basis of all file server implementations.

This lesson describes file server tasks that you can perform without installing the File Services role. Lesson 3, "Using the File Services Role," covers tasks that require the role. However, in a production environment, you should always install the File Services role on any Windows Server 2008 computer that you intend to use as a file server.

Using the Disk Management Snap-in

Prepare your disks by selecting a partition type, a volume type, and a file system.

Disk Management is a Microsoft Management Console (MMC) snap-in that you use to perform disk-related tasks, such as the following:

- Initializing disks
- Selecting a partition style
- Converting basic disks to dynamic disks
- Creating partitions and volumes
- Extending, shrinking, and deleting volumes
- Formatting partitions and volumes
- Assigning and changing driver letters and paths
- Examining and managing physical disk properties, such as disk quotas, folder sharing, and error checking

ANOTHER WAY

You can also use the DiskPart.exe command prompt utility to perform disk management tasks.

To access the Disk Management snap-in, use any of the following procedures:

- From the Administrative Tools program group, select Computer Management, and then click the Disk Management node.
- Click the Start button, right-click Computer, and then click Manage. When the Server Manager console appears, expand the Storage node and select Disk Management.
- Open the Run dialog box and execute the compmgmt.msc file.

In the Disk Management snap-in, the two center panes, the Top view and the Bottom view, display disk and volume information, respectively. Although Disk Management can display only two views at any one time, three views are available:

- Disk List — As shown in Figure 2-3, this view provides a summary about the physical drives in the computer. This information includes the disk number; disk type, such as Basic or DVD; disk capacity; size of unallocated space; the status of the disk device, such as online, offline, or no media; the device type, such as SCSI or IDE; and the partition style, such as MBR or GPT.

Figure 2-3

The Disk Management Disk List and Graphical views

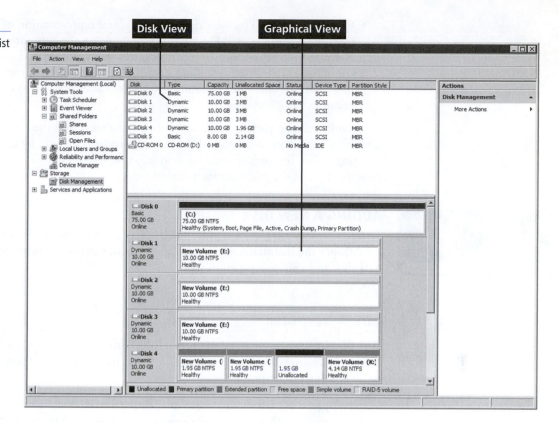

• Volume List—As shown in Figure 2-4, this view provides a more detailed summary of all the drives on the computer. This information includes the volume name; the volume layout, such as Simple, Spanned, or Striped; the disk type, such as Basic or Dynamic; the file system in use, such as NTFS or CDFS; the hard disk status, such as Healthy, Failed, or Formatting; the disk capacity; the disk available free space; the percentage of the hard disk that is free; whether the hard disk is fault tolerant; and the disk overhead percentage.

Figure 2-4

The Disk Management Volume List and Graphical views

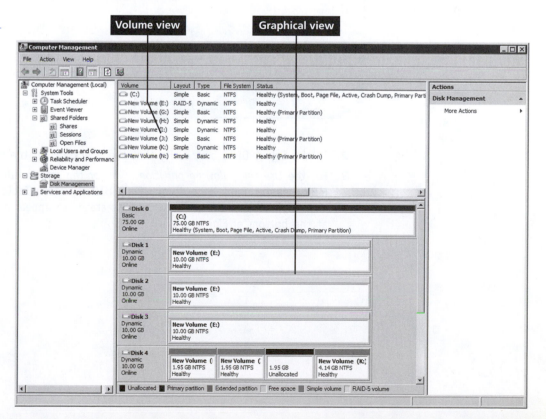

- Graphical view—This view displays a graphical representation of all the physical disks, partitions, volumes, and logical drives available on the computer. The Graphical view is divided into two columns: the disk status (left column) and the volume status (right column). The disk status column displays the number, type, capacity, and status of each disk. The volume status column displays the name, size, file system, and status of each volume.

By default, the Top pane contains the Volume List view, and the Bottom pane contains the Graphical view. You can change the views to suit your purposes by clicking the View menu, selecting either Top or Bottom, and then selecting the desired view. You can hide the Bottom view by clicking the Hidden menu option.

CERTIFICATION READY?
Configure storage
1.5

ADDING A NEW DISK

To add a new secondary disk, shut down your computer and install or attach the new physical disk per the manufacturer's instructions. Then, use the following procedure to initialize a new disk and choose a partition style.

ADD A NEW DISK

GET READY. Log on to Windows Server 2008 using an account with Administrator privileges. When the logon process is completed, close the Initial Configuration Tasks window and any other windows that appear.

1. Open the Disk Management snap-in. If the disk does not have a disk signature, the console automatically opens the Initialize Disk dialog box, as shown in Figure 2-5.

Figure 2-5

The Initialize Disk dialog box

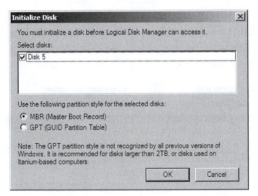

2. In the Select Disks box, verify that the checkbox for the new disk is selected.
3. For the *Use the following partition style for the selected disks* option, select either **MBR (Master Boot Record)** or **GPT (GUID Partition Table)** and click **OK.** The snap-in initializes the disk, causing its status to appear as Unallocated, as shown at the bottom of Figure 2-6.

Figure 2-6

The Disk Management snap-in, with a newly initialized disk

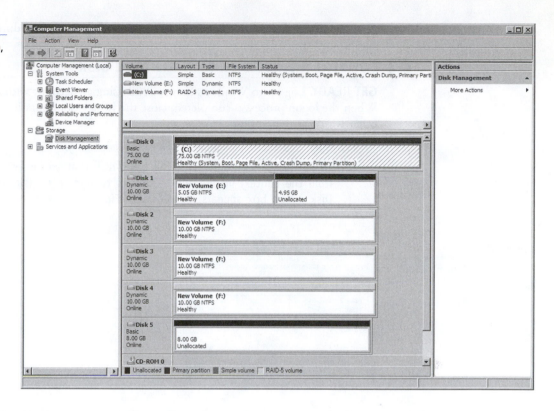

CLOSE the console containing the Disk Management snap-in.

You can convert a disk from one partition style to another at any time, by right-clicking the disk you need to convert in the Disk List view and then, from the context menu, selecting Convert to GPT Disk or Convert to MBR Disk. However, be aware that converting the disk partition style is a destructive process. You can only perform the conversion on an unallocated disk, so if the disk you want to convert contains data, you must back up the disk, and then delete all existing partitions or volumes before you begin the conversion.

CONVERTING A BASIC DISK TO A DYNAMIC DISK

Newly installed disks always appear as basic disks first. You can convert a basic disk to a dynamic disk at any time without affecting the data stored on the disk. However, before you convert a basic disk to a dynamic disk, you must be aware of the following conditions:

- Make sure that you have enough space available on the disk for the conversion. The conversion will fail if the hard drive does not have at least 1 MB of free space at the end of the disk. The Disk Management console reserves this free space when creating partitions and volumes, but you cannot presume that other disk management tools that you might use also preserve that space.

- You should not convert a basic disk to a dynamic disk if you are dual booting. If you convert to a dynamic disk, you will not be able to start an installed operating system from any volume on the disk except the current boot volume.

- You cannot convert removable media to dynamic disks. You can configure them only as basic disks with primary partitions.

- You cannot convert drives that use an allocation unit size (sector size) greater than 512 bytes unless you reformat the drive with a smaller sector size before upgrading.

- If the boot partition or system partition is part of a striped or spanned volume, you cannot convert the disk to a dynamic disk.

- Once you change a basic disk to a dynamic disk, the only way you can change it back again is to back up the entire disk and delete the dynamic disk volumes. When you delete the last volume, the dynamic disk automatically converts back to a basic disk.

To convert a basic disk to a dynamic disk, use the following procedure.

 CONVERT A BASIC DISK TO A DYNAMIC DISK

GET READY. Log on to Windows Server 2008 using an account with Administrator privileges. When the logon process is completed, close the Initial Configuration Tasks window and any other windows that appear.

1. Open the Disk Management snap-in if necessary.

2. In Disk List view, right-click the basic disk that you want to convert and then, from the context menu, select **Convert to Dynamic Disk**. The Convert to Dynamic Disk dialog box appears, as shown in Figure 2-7.

Figure 2-7

The Convert to Dynamic Disk dialog box

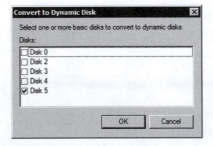

3. Select the checkbox(es) for the disk(s) you want to convert, and then click **OK**. If the disks you selected do not contain formatted partitions, clicking OK immediately converts the disks, and you do not need to follow the remaining steps. If the disks you are converting to dynamic disks have formatted partitions, clicking OK displays the Disks to Convert dialog box, as shown in Figure 2-8, which means that you need to follow the remaining steps to complete the disk conversion.

Figure 2-8

The Disks to Convert dialog box

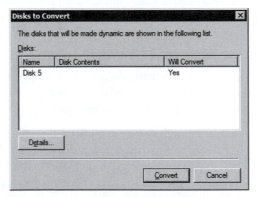

4. The Disks to Convert dialog box lists the disks you chose for conversion for your confirmation. Check the value in the Will Convert column. It should be set to Yes for each of the disks that you are converting. If any of the disks have the value No, then they may not meet Windows conversion criteria.

5. Click **Details**. The Convert Details dialog box appears, as shown in Figure 2-9. This dialog box lists the partitions on the selected drives that Disk Management will convert.

Figure 2-9

The Convert Details dialog box

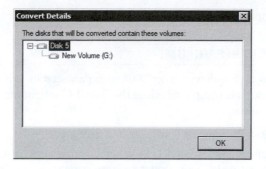

6. Click **OK** when you are ready to continue with the conversion.

7. On the Disks to Convert dialog box, click **Convert** to start the conversion. A Disk Management information box, shown in Figure 2-10, appears to warn you that after you convert the disks to dynamic disks, you will not be able to boot installed operating systems from any volume other than the current boot volume.

Figure 2-10

A Disk Management information box

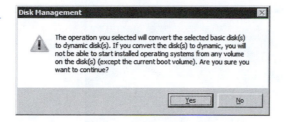

8. If a selected drive contains the boot partition, the system partition, or a partition that is in use, Disk Management prompts you to restart the computer.

CLOSE the console containing the Disk Management snap-in.

When you convert a basic disk into a dynamic disk, Disk Management performs the following tasks:

- Converts basic disk partitions to dynamic disk volumes of equal size.
- Converts basic disk primary partitions and logical drives in the extended partition to simple volumes.
- Marks any free space in a basic disk extended partition as unallocated.

CREATING A SIMPLE VOLUME

Technically speaking, you create partitions on basic disks and volumes on dynamic disks. This is not just an arbitrary change in nomenclature. Converting a basic disk to a dynamic disk actually creates one big partition, occupying all of the space on the disk. The volumes you create on the dynamic disk are logical divisions within that single partition.

Earlier versions of Windows use the correct terminology in the Disk Management snap-in. The menus enable you to create partitions on basic disks and volumes on dynamic disks. Windows Server 2008 uses the term volume for both disk types, and enables you to create any of the available volume types, whether the disk is basic or dynamic. If the volume type you select is not supported on a basic disk, the wizard converts it to a dynamic disk (with your permission) as part of the volume creation process.

Despite the menus that refer to basic partitions as volumes, the traditional rules for basic disks remain in effect. The New Simple Volume menu option on a basic disk creates up to three primary partitions. When you create a fourth volume, the wizard actually creates an extended partition and a logical drive of the size you specify. If there is any remaining space on the disk, you can create additional logical drives in the extended partition.

⚠ **WARNING** When you use **DiskPart.exe,** a command-line utility included with Windows Server 2008, to manage basic disks, you can create four primary partitions or three primary partitions and one extended partition. The DiskPart.exe utility contains a superset of the commands supported by the Disk Management snap-in. In other words, DiskPart can do everything Disk Management can do, and more. However, while the Disk Management snap-in prevents you from unintentionally performing actions that might result in data loss, DiskPart has no such safeties, and so does not prohibit you from performing such actions. For this reason, Microsoft recommends that only advanced personnel use DiskPart and that they use it infrequently and with due caution.

To create a new simple volume on a basic or dynamic disk, use the following procedure.

 CREATE A NEW SIMPLE VOLUME

GET READY. Log on to Windows Server 2008 using an account with Administrator privileges. When the logon process is completed, close the Initial Configuration Tasks window and any other windows that appear.

1. Open the Disk Management snap-in if necessary.

2. In the Graphical View, right-click an unallocated area in the volume status column for the disk on which you want to create a volume and, from the context menu, select **New Simple Volume**. The New Simple Volume Wizard appears.

3. Click **Next** to bypass the Welcome page. The Specify Volume Size page appears, as shown in Figure 2-11.

Figure 2-11

The Specify Volume Size page

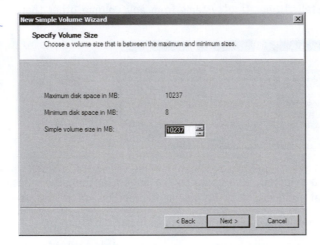

4. Select the size for the new partition or volume, within the maximum and minimum limits stated on the page, using the *Simple volume size in MB* spin box, and then click **Next**. The Assign Drive Letter or Path page appears, as shown in Figure 2-12.

Figure 2-12

The Assign Drive Letter or Path page

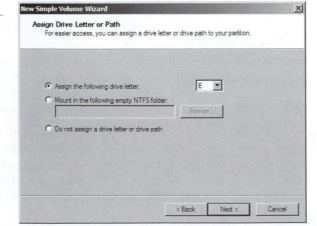

5. Configure one of the following three options, and then click **Next**. The Format Partition page appears, as shown in Figure 2-13.

• Assign the following drive letter—If you select this option, click the associated dropdown list for a list of available drive letters and select the letter you want to assign to the drive.

Figure 2-13

The Format Partition page

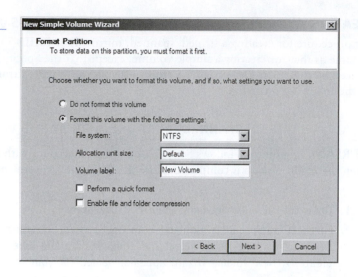

- Mount in the following empty NTFS folder—If you select this option, either key the path to an existing NTFS folder or click Browse to search for or create a new folder. The entire contents of the new drive will appear in the folder you specify.
- Do not assign a drive letter or drive path—Select this option if you want to create the partition, but are not yet ready to use it. When you do not assign a volume a drive letter or path, the drive is left unmounted and inaccessible. When you want to mount the drive for use, assign a drive letter or path to it.

6. Specify whether the wizard should format the volume, and if so, how. If you do not want to format the volume at this time, select the **Do not format this volume** option. If you do want to format the volume, select the **Format this volume with the following settings** option, and then configure the associated options, as follows. Then click **Next**. The Completing the New Simple Volume Wizard page appears.
   - File system—Select the desired file system: NTFS, FAT, or FAT32.
   - Allocation unit size—Specify the file system's cluster size. The cluster size signifies the basic unit of bytes in which the system allocates disk space. The system calculates the default allocation unit size based on the size of the volume. You can override this value by clicking the associated dropdown list and then selecting one of the values. For example, if your client uses consistently small files, you may want to set the allocation unit size to a smaller cluster size.
   - Volume label—Specify a name for the partition or volume. The default name is New Volume, but you can change the name to anything you want.
   - Perform a quick format—When selected, Windows formats the disk without checking for errors. This is a faster method with which to format the drive, but Microsoft does not recommend it. When you check for errors, the system looks for and marks bad sectors on the disk so that your clients will not use those portions of the disk.
   - Enable file and folder compression—Turns on folder compression for the disk. This option is available only for volumes being formatted with the NTFS file system.

7. Review the settings to confirm your options, and then click **Finish**. The wizard creates the volume according to your specifications.

CLOSE the console containing the Disk Management snap-in.

After you create a simple volume, you can modify its properties by extending it or shrinking it, as described later in this lesson.

CREATING A STRIPED, SPANNED, MIRRORED, OR RAID-5 VOLUME

The procedure for creating a striped, spanned, mirrored, or RAID-5 volume is almost the same as that for creating a simple volume, except that the Specify Volume Size page is replaced by the Select Disks page. To create a striped, spanned, mirrored, or RAID-5 volume, use the following procedure.

CREATE A STRIPED, SPANNED, MIRRORED, OR RAID-5 VOLUME

GET READY. Log on to Windows Server 2008 using an account with Administrator privileges. When the logon process is completed, close the Welcome Center window and any other windows that appear.

1. Open the Disk Management snap-in if necessary.

2. In the Graphical View, right-click an unallocated area on a dynamic disk and then, from the context menu, select the command for the type of volume you want to create. A New Volume Wizard appears, named for your selected volume type.

3. Click **Next** to bypass the Welcome page. The Select Disks page appears, as shown in Figure 2-14.

Figure 2-14

The Select Disks page

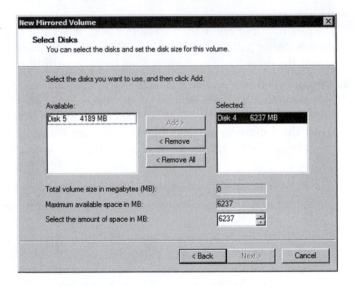

4. On the Select Disks page, select the disks you want to use for the new volume from the Available list box, and then click **Add**. The disks you chose are moved to the Selected list box, joining the original disk you selected when launching the wizard. For a striped, spanned, or mirrored volume, you must have at least two disks in the Selected list; for a RAID-5 volume, you must have at least three.

5. Specify the amount of space you want to use on each disk, using the *Select the amount of space in MB* spin box. Then click **Next**. The Assign Drive Letter or Path page appears.

   • If you are creating a spanned volume, you must click each disk in the Selected list and specify the amount of space to use on that disk. The default value for each disk is the size of the unallocated space on that disk.

   • If you are creating a striped, mirrored, or RAID-5 volume, you only specify one value, because these volumes require the same amount of space on each disk. The default value is the size of the unallocated space on the disk with the least amount of space free.

6. Specify whether you want to assign a drive letter or path, and then click **Next**. The Format Partition page appears.

X REF

See the "Create a New Simple Volume" procedure, in the preceding section, for more information about the Assign Drive Letter or Path and Format Partition pages.

TAKE NOTE *

You must be a member of the Backup Operator or the Administrators group to extend or shrink any volume.

7. Specify if or how you want to format the volume, and then click **Next**. The Completing the New Simple Volume Wizard page appears.

8. Review the settings to confirm your options, and then click **Finish**. If any of the disks you selected to create the volume are basic disks, a Disk Management message box appears, warning you that the volume creation process will convert the basic disks to dynamic disks.

9. Click **Yes**. The wizard creates the volume according to your specifications.

CLOSE the Disk Management snap-in.

The commands that appear in a disk's context menu depend on the number of disks installed in the computer and the presence of unallocated space on them. For example, at least two disks with unallocated space must be available to create a striped, spanned, or mirrored volume, and at least three disks must be available to create a RAID-5 volume.

EXTENDING AND SHRINKING VOLUMES

To extend or shrink a volume, you simply right-click a volume and select Extend Volume or Shrink Volume from the context menu or from the Action menu.

Windows Server 2008 extends existing volumes by expanding them into adjacent unallocated space on the same disk. When you extend a simple volume across multiple disks, the simple volume becomes a spanned volume. You cannot extend striped volumes.

To extend a volume on a basic disk, the system must meet the following requirements:

- A volume of a basic disk must be either unformatted or formatted with the NTFS file system.

- If you extend a volume that is actually a logical drive, the console first consumes the contiguous free space remaining in the extended partition. If you attempt to extend the logical drive beyond the confines of its extended partition, the extended partition expands to any unallocated space left on the disk.

- You can extend logical drives, boot volumes, or system volumes only into contiguous space, and only if the hard disk can be upgraded to a dynamic disk. The operating system will permit you to extend other types of basic volumes into noncontiguous space, but will prompt you to convert the basic disk to a dynamic disk.

To extend a volume on a dynamic disk, the system must meet these requirements:

- When extending a simple volume, you can use only the available space on the same disk, if the volume is to remain simple.

- You can extend a simple volume across additional disks if it is not a system volume or a boot volume. However, after you expand a simple volume to another disk, it is no longer a simple volume; it becomes a spanned volume.

- You can extend a simple or spanned volume if it does not have a file system (a raw volume) or if you formatted it using the NTFS file system. (You cannot extend volumes using the FAT or FAT32 file systems.)

- You cannot extend mirrored or RAID-5 volumes, although you can add a mirror to an existing simple volume.

When shrinking volumes, the Disk Management console frees up space at the end of the volume, relocating the existing volume's files, if necessary. The console then converts that free space to new unallocated space on the disk. To shrink basic disk volumes and simple or spanned dynamic disk volumes, the system must meet the following requirements:

- The existing volume must not be full and must contain the specified amount of available free space for shrinking.

- The volume must not be a raw partition (one without a file system). Shrinking a raw partition that contains data might destroy the data.

- You can shrink a volume only if you formatted it using the NTFS file system. (You cannot shrink volumes using the FAT or FAT32 file systems.)
- You cannot shrink striped, mirrored, or RAID-5 volumes.

CONFIGURING SHADOW COPIES

As discussed earlier in this lesson, Shadow Copies is a Windows Server 2008 feature that enables you to maintain previous versions of files on a server, so that if users accidentally delete or overwrite a file, they can access a copy. You can only implement Shadow Copies for an entire volume; you cannot select specific shares, folders, or files.

To configure a Windows Server 2008 volume to create Shadow Copies, use the following procedure.

 CONFIGURE SHADOW COPIES

GET READY. Log on to Windows Server 2008 using an account with domain administrative privileges. When the logon process is completed, close the Initial Configuration Tasks window and any other windows that appear.

1. Click **Start**, and then click **All Programs** > **Accessories** > **Windows Explorer**. The Windows Explorer window appears.

2. In the Folders list, expand the **Computer** container, right-click a volume and, from the context menu, select **Configure Shadow Copies**. The Shadow Copies dialog box appears, as shown in Figure 2-15.

Figure 2-15

The Shadow Copies dialog box

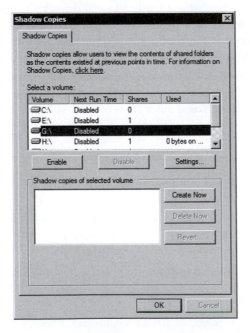

3. In the Select a Volume box, choose the volume for which you want to enable Shadow Copies. By default, when you enable Shadow Copies for a volume, the system uses the following settings:
   - The system stores the shadow copies on the selected volume.
   - The system reserves 300 megabytes of disk space for the shadow copies.
   - The system creates shadow copies at 7:00 AM and 12:00 PM every weekday.

4. To modify the default parameters, click **Settings**. The Settings dialog box appears, as shown in Figure 2-16.

Windows Server 2008 **Deploying a File Server** | 73

Figure 2-16

The Settings dialog box

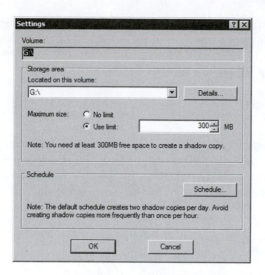

5. In the Storage Area box, specify the volume where you want to store the shadow copies. For a server operating with a high I/O load, such as a file server, Microsoft recommends that, for best performance, you create the Shadow Copies storage area on another volume, one that does not have Shadow Copies enabled.

6. Specify the Maximum Size for the storage area, or choose the **No Limit** option. If the storage area should become filled, the system begins deleting the oldest shadow copies, so if there are a lot of large files stored on the volume, increasing the size of the storage area can be beneficial. However, no matter how much space you allocate to the storage area, Windows Server 2008 supports a maximum of 64 shadow copies for each volume, after which the system begins deleting the oldest copies.

7. Click **Schedule**. The Schedule dialog box appears, as shown in Figure 2-17. Using the controls provided, you can modify the existing Shadow Copies tasks, delete them, or create new ones, based on the needs of your users. Scheduling shadow copies to occur too frequently can degrade server performance and cause copies to be aged out too quickly, while scheduling them to occur too infrequently can cause users to lose work because the most recent copy is too old.

Figure 2-17

The Schedule dialog box

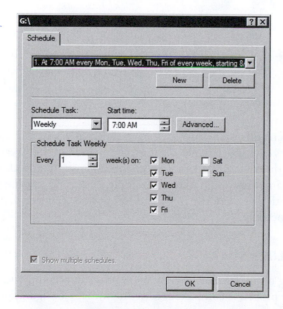

8. Click **OK** twice to close the Schedule and Settings dialog boxes.

9. Click **Enable**. The system enables the Shadow Copies feature for the selected volume and creates the first copy in the designated storage area.

CLOSE any open windows.

After you complete this procedure, users can restore previous versions of files on the selected volumes from the Shadow Copies tab of the volume's Properties sheet.

Creating Folder Shares

Sharing folders makes them accessible to network users.

After you have configured the disks on a file server, you must create shares for network users to be able to access those disks. As noted in the planning discussions earlier in this lesson, you should have a sharing strategy in place by the time you are ready to actually create your shares. This strategy should consist of the following information:

- What folders you will share
- What names you will assign to the shares
- What permissions you will grant users to the shares
- What Offline Files settings you will use for the shares

If you are the Creator Owner of a folder, you can share it on a Windows Server 2008 computer by right-clicking the folder in any Windows Explorer window, selecting Share from the context menu, and following the instructions in the File Sharing dialog box, as shown in Figure 2-18.

Figure 2-18

The File Sharing dialog box

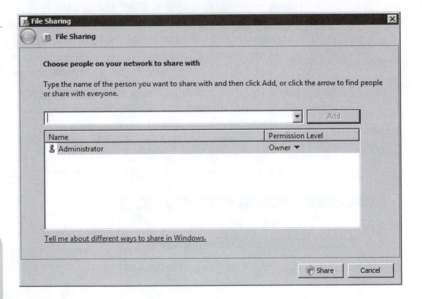

TAKE NOTE*

For the users on the network to be able to see the shares you create on the file server, you must make sure that the Network Discovery and File Sharing settings are turned on in the Network and Sharing Center control panel.

This method of creating shares provides a simplified interface that contains only limited control over elements such as share permissions. If you are not the Creator Owner of the folder, the Share tab of the folder's Properties sheet appears instead, and clicking the Share button launches the wizard. However, to create multiple shares and exercise more granular control over their properties, you can use the Share and Storage Management console, as described in the following procedure.

 CREATE A FOLDER SHARE

GET READY. Log on to Windows Server 2008 using an account with administrative privileges. When the logon process is completed, close the Initial Configuration Tasks window and any other windows that appear.

1. Click **Start** > **Administrative Tools** > **Share and Storage Management**. The Share and Storage Management console appears, as shown in Figure 2-19.

 **ANOTHER WAY**

You can also use the Shared Folders snap-in, accessible from the Computer Management console, to create and manage shares.

Figure 2-19

The Share and Storage Management console

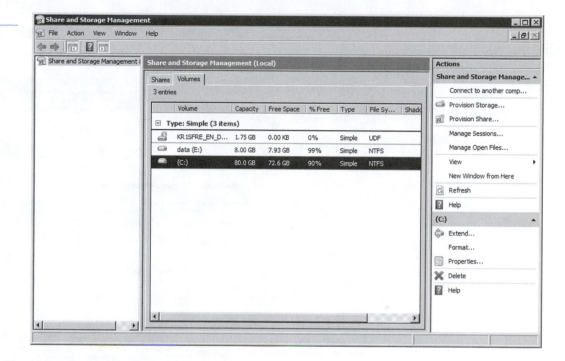

2. In the actions pane, click **Provision Share**. The Provision a Shared Folder Wizard appears, displaying the Shared Folder Location page, as shown in Figure 2-20.

Figure 2-20

The Shared Folder Location page of the Provision a Shared Folder Wizard

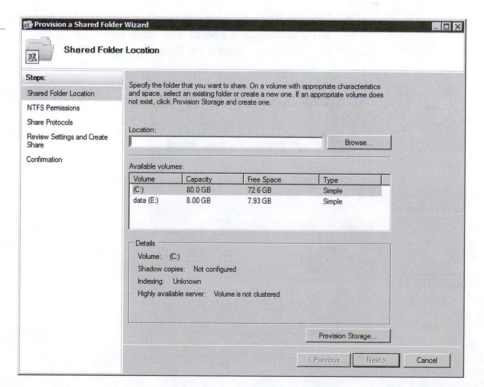

3. In the Location text box, key the name of or browse to the folder you want to share, and click **Next**. The NTFS Permissions page appears, as shown in Figure 2-21. If necessary, you can create a new volume by clicking **Provision Storage** to launch the Provision Storage Wizard.

Figure 2-21

The NTFS Permissions page of the Provision a Shared Folder Wizard

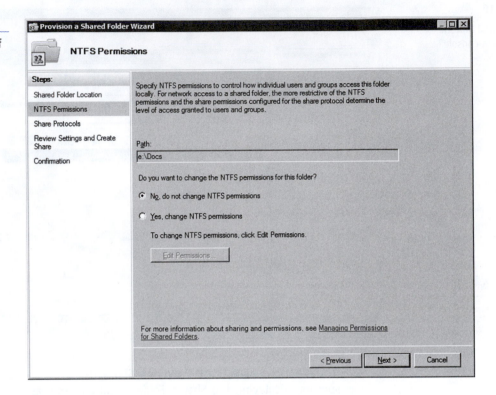

4. To modify the NTFS permissions for the specified folder, select the **Yes, change NTFS permissions option and click Edit Permissions**. A Permissions dialog box for the folder appears, as shown in Figure 2-22.

Figure 2-22

An NTFS Permissions dialog box

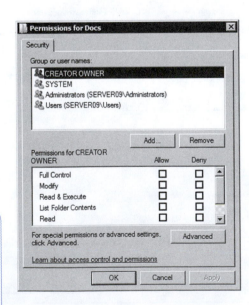

MORE INFORMATION

For more information on permissions, see "Assigning Permissions," later in this lesson. To set NTFS permissions, see "Assigning Standard NTFS Permissions" and "Assigning Special NTFS Permissions."

5. Modify the NTFS permissions for the folder as needed and click **OK** to close the Permissions dialog box and return to the NTFS Permissions page.

6. On the NTFS Permissions page, click **Next** to continue. The Share Protocols page appears, as shown in Figure 2-23.

Figure 2-23

The Share Protocols page of the Provision a Shared Folder Wizard

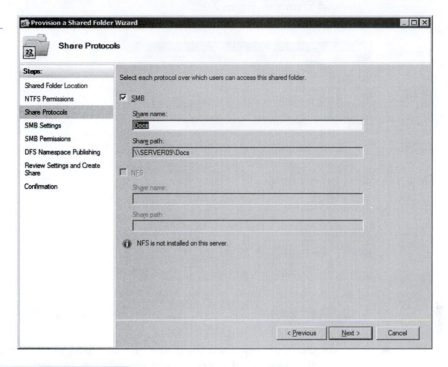

 **MORE INFORMATION**

Every disk in the computer has a root share for administrative purposes. These shares, along with the default ADMIN and IPC shares, appear with a dollar sign ("$") following the name, which hides them from users browsing the network. You can create your own hidden shares by appending a dollar sign to the end of any share name.

7. With the default SMB checkbox selected, key the name you want to assign to the share in the *Share name* text box and click **Next**. The SMB Settings page appears, as shown in Figure 2-24. If you have the File Services role installed, with the Services for Network File System role service, you can also use the Share Protocols page to create an NFS share.

Figure 2-24

The SMB Settings page of the Provision a Shared Folder Wizard

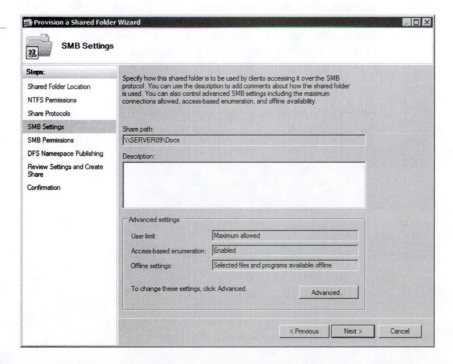

8. Key descriptive text for the share in the Description text box. To modify the default settings for the share, click **Advanced**. The Advanced dialog box appears, as shown in Figure 2-25.

Figure 2-25

The Advanced dialog box

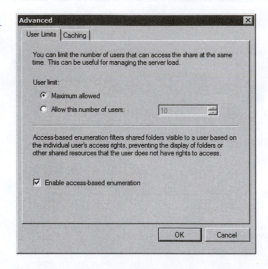

9. Modify the following settings as needed, and click **OK** to return to the SMB settings page:

- User limit—To limit the number of users that can access the share, select **Allow this number of users** and use the spin box to specify a limit.

- Access-based enumeration—To prevent users from seeing shared resources to which they have no access permissions, select the **Enable access-based enumeration** checkbox.

- Offline settings—To specify the files and programs that client workstations can save locally using Offline Files, click the **Caching** tab, as shown in Figure 2-26, and select the appropriate option.

➕ **MORE INFORMATION**

Access-based enumeration (ABE), a feature first introduced in Windows Server 2003 R2, applies filters to shared folders based on individual user's permissions to the files and subfolders in the share. Simply, users who cannot access a particular shared resource are unable to see that resource on the network. This feature prevents users from searching through files and folders they cannot access. You can enable or disable ABE for share at any time by opening the share's Properties sheet in the Sharing and Storage Management console and clicking Advanced, to display the same Advanced dialog box displayed by the Provision a Shared Folder Wizard.

Figure 2-26

The Caching tab of the Advanced dialog box

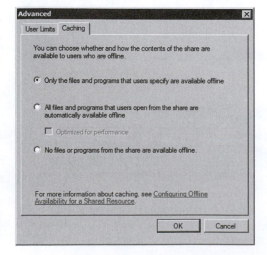

10. On the SMB Settings page, click **Next** to continue. The SMB Permissions page appears, as shown in Figure 2-27.

Figure 2-27

The SMB Permissions page of the Provision a Shared Folder Wizard

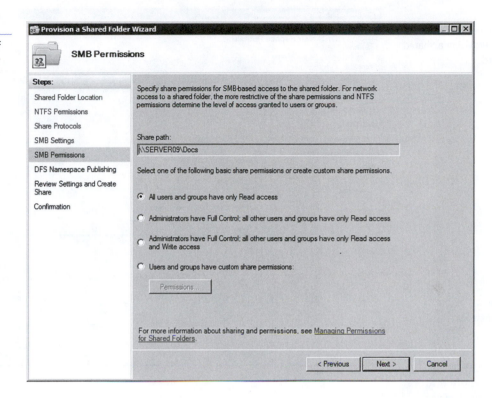

Provision a Shared Folder Wizard

SMB Permissions

Steps:

Shared Folder Location

NTFS Permissions

Share Protocols

SMB Settings

SMB Permissions

DFS Namespace Publishing

Review Settings and Create Share

Confirmation

Specify share permissions for SMB-based access to the shared folder. For network access to a shared folder, the more restrictive of the share permissions and NTFS permissions determine the level of access granted to users or groups.

Share path:

\\SERVER09\Docs

Select one of the following basic share permissions or create custom share permissions.

⦿ All users and groups have only Read access

◯ Administrators have Full Control; all other users and groups have only Read access

◯ Administrators have Full Control; all other users and groups have only Read access and Write access

◯ Users and groups have custom share permissions:

[Permissions...]

For more information about sharing and permissions, see Managing Permissions for Shared Folders.

[< Previous] [Next >] [Cancel]

11. Select one of the pre-configured share permission options, or select **Users and groups have custom share permissions** and click **Permissions**, to display the Permissions dialog box for the share, as shown in Figure 2-28.

Figure 2-28

A share Permissions dialog box

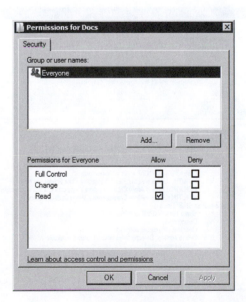

Permissions for Docs

Security

Group or user names:

Everyone

[Add...] [Remove]

Permissions for Everyone	Allow	Deny
Full Control	☐	☐
Change	☐	☐
Read	☑	☐

Learn about access control and permissions

[OK] [Cancel] [Apply]

✚ MORE INFORMATION

For more information about permissions, see "Assigning Permissions," later in this lesson. For procedures describing how to set custom share permissions, see "Setting Share Permissions."

12. Modify the share permissions as needed and click **OK** to close the Permissions dialog box and return to the SMB Permissions page.

13. On the SMB Permissions page, click **Next** to continue. The DFS Namespace Publishing page appears, as shown in Figure 2-29.

Figure 2-29

The DFS Namespace Publishing page of the Provision a Shared Folder Wizard

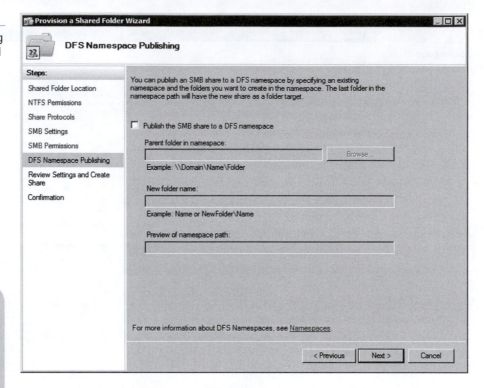

14. To add the share to a Distributed File System (DFS) namespace, select the **Publish the SMB share to a DFS namespace** checkbox and specify the parent folder and new folder names in the text boxes provided. Then click **Next**. The Review Settings and Create Share page appears, as shown in Figure 2-30.

Figure 2-30

The Review Settings and Create Share page of the Provision a Shared Folder Wizard

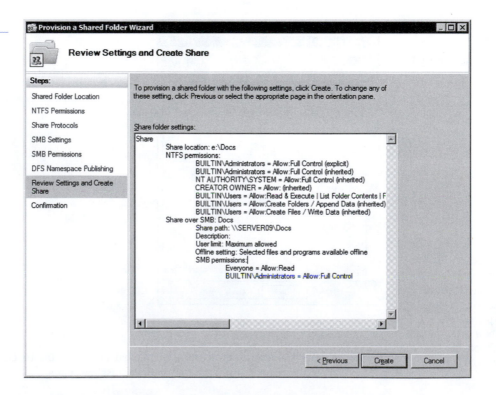

15. Click **Create**. The wizard creates the share and displays a Confirmation page.

16. Click **Close** to close the wizard.

CLOSE the Sharing and Storage Management console.

After you create a share with the wizard, the share appears on the Shares tab in the detail (middle) pane of the Share and Storage Management console. You can now use the console to manage the share by opening its Properties sheet, or stop sharing it by clicking Stop Sharing in the actions pane.

Assigning Permissions

Protect your data by controlling who can access it.

Earlier in this lesson, you learned about controlling access to a file server, to provide network users with the access they need, while protecting other files against possible intrusion and damage, whether deliberate or not. To implement this access control, Windows Server 2008 uses permissions.

Permissions are privileges granted to specific system entities, such as users, groups, or computers, enabling them to perform a task or access a resource. For example, you can grant a specific user permission to read a file, while denying that same user the permissions needed to modify or delete the file.

Windows Server 2008 has several sets of permissions, which operate independently of each other. As a server administrator, you should be familiar with the operation of the following four permission systems:

- Share permissions—Control access to folders over a network. To access a file over a network, a user must have appropriate share permissions (and appropriate NTFS permissions, if the shared folder is on an NTFS volume).

- NTFS permissions—Control access to the files and folders stored on disk volumes formatted with the NTFS file system. To access a file, whether on the local system or over a network, a user must have the appropriate NTFS permissions.

- Registry permissions—Control access to specific parts of the Windows registry. An application that modifies registry settings or a user attempting to manually modify the registry must have the appropriate registry permissions.

- Active Directory permissions—Control access to specific parts of an Active Directory hierarchy. Although file servers typically do not function as Active Directory domain controllers, server administrators might utilize these permissions when servicing computers that are members of a domain.

All of these permission systems operate independently of each other, and sometimes combine to provide increased protection to a specific resource. For example, an administrator might grant Ralph the NTFS permissions needed to access a spreadsheet stored on a file server volume. If Ralph sits down at the file server console and logs on as himself, he will be able to access that spreadsheet. However, if Ralph is working at his own computer, he will not be able to access the spreadsheet until the administrator creates a share containing the file and grants Ralph the proper share permissions as well.

TAKE NOTE *

While all of these permissions systems are operating all the time, server administrators do not necessarily have to work with them all on a regular basis. In fact, many administrators might not ever have to manually alter a Registry or Active Directory permission. However, many server administrators do have to work with NTFS and share permissions on a daily basis.

For network users to be able to access a shared folder on an NTFS drive, you must grant them both share permissions and NTFS permissions. As you saw earlier, you can grant share permissions as part of the share creation process, but you can also modify the permissions at any time afterwards.

UNDERSTANDING THE WINDOWS PERMISSION ARCHITECTURE

Files, folders, shares, registry keys, and Active Directory objects are all protected by permissions. To store the permissions, each of these elements has an *access control list (ACL)*. An ACL is a collection of individual permissions, in the form of *access control entries (ACEs)*. Each ACE consists of a *security principal* (that is, the name of the user, group, or computer granted the permissions) and the specific permissions assigned to that security principal. When you manage permissions in any of the Windows Server 2008 permission systems, you are actually creating and modifying the ACEs in an ACL.

It is important to understand that, in all of the Windows operating systems, permissions are stored as part of the protected element, not the security principal granted access. For example, when you grant a user the NTFS permissions needed to access a file, the ACE you create is stored in the file's ACL; it is not part of the user account. You can move the file to a different location, and its permissions go with it.

To manage permissions in Windows Server 2008, you use a tab in the element's Properties dialog box, like the one shown in Figure 2-31, with the security principals listed at the top and the permissions associated with them at the bottom. Share permissions are typically found on a Share Permissions tab, and NTFS permissions are located on a Security tab. All of the Windows permission systems use the same interface, although the permissions themselves differ.

Figure 2-31

The Security tab of a Properties dialog box

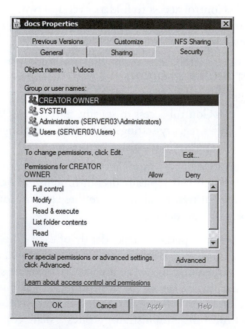

UNDERSTANDING STANDARD AND SPECIAL PERMISSIONS

The permissions protecting a particular system element are not like the keys to a lock, which provide either full access or no access at all. Permissions are designed to be granular, enabling you to grant specific degrees of access to security principals. For example, you can use NTFS permissions to control not only who has access to a spreadsheet but also the degree of access. You might grant Ralph permission to read and modify the spreadsheet, while Alice can only read it, and Ed cannot see it at all.

To provide this granularity, each of the Windows permission systems has an assortment of permissions that you can assign to a security principal in any combination. Depending on the permission system you are working with, you might have dozens of different permissions available for a single system element.

If this is all starting to sound extremely complex, don't worry. Windows provides preconfigured permission combinations suitable for most common access control chores. When you open the Properties dialog box for a system element and look at its Security tab, the NTFS permissions you see are called *standard permissions*. Standard permissions are actually combinations of *special permissions*, which provide the most granular control over the element.

For example, the NTFS permission system has 14 special permissions that you can assign to a folder or file. However, there are also six standard permissions, which are various combinations of the 14 special permissions. In most cases, administrators work only with standard permissions. Many administrators rarely, if ever, work directly with special permissions.

If you do find it necessary to work with special permissions directly, Windows makes it possible. When you click the Advanced button on the Security tab of any Properties dialog box, an Advanced Security Settings dialog box appears, as shown in Figure 2-32, which enables you to access the ACEs for the selected system element directly.

Figure 2-32

The Advanced Security Settings dialog box

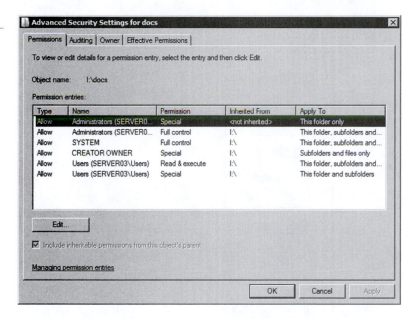

ALLOWING AND DENYING PERMISSIONS

When you assign permissions to a system element, you are, in effect, creating a new ACE in the element's ACL. There are two basic types of ACE: *Allow* and *Deny*. This makes it possible to approach permission management tasks from two directions:

- Additive—Start with no permissions and then grant Allow permissions to individual security principals to provide them with the access they need.

- Subtractive—Start by granting all possible Allow permissions to individual security principals, providing them with full control over the system element, and then grant them Deny permissions for the access you don't want them to have.

Most administrators prefer the additive approach, because Windows, by default, attempts to limit access to important system elements. In a properly designed permission hierarchy, the use of Deny permissions is often not needed at all. Many administrators frown on their use, because combining Allow and Deny permissions in the same hierarchy can often make it difficult to determine the effective permissions for a specific system element.

INHERITING PERMISSIONS

The most important principle in permission management is that permissions tend to run downwards through a hierarchy. This is called permission inheritance. Permission inheritance means that parent elements pass their permissions down to their subordinate elements. For example, when you grant Alice Allow permissions to access the root of the D: drive, all of the folders and subfolders on the D: drive inherit those permissions, and Alice can access them. The principle of inheritance simplifies the permission assignment process enormously. Without it, you would have to grant security principals individual Allow permissions for every file, folder, share, object, and key they need to access. With inheritance, you can grant access to an entire file system by creating one set of Allow permissions.

In most cases, whether consciously or not, system administrators take inheritance into account when they design their file systems and Active Directory trees. The location of a system element in a hierarchy is often based on how the administrators plan to assign permissions. For example, the section of a directory tree shown in Figure 2-33 is intended to be a place where network users can temporarily store files that they want other users to access, as discussed earlier in this lesson.

Figure 2-33

A sample xfer directory structure

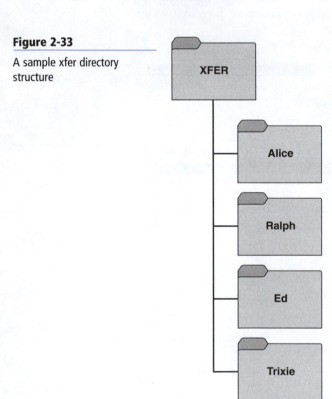

Because the administrator has assigned all users the Allow Read and Allow List Folder Contents standard permission to the xfer folder, as shown in Figure 2-34, everyone is able to read the files in the xfer directory. Because the assigned permissions run downwards, all of the subfolders beneath xfer inherit those permissions, so all of the users can read the files in all of the subfolders as well.

Figure 2-34

Granting Allow permissions to
the xfer folder

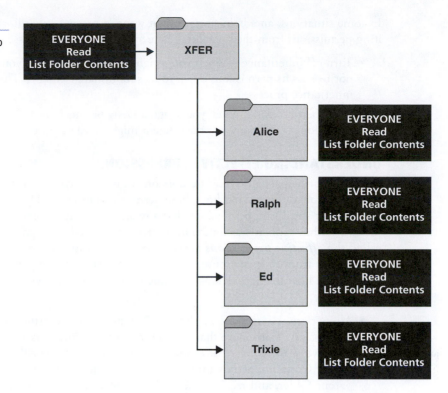

The next step for the administrator is to assign each user the Allow Full Control permission to his or her own subfolder, as shown in Figure 2-35. This enables each user to create, modify, and delete files in his or her own folder, without compromising the security of the other users' folders. Because the user folders are at the bottom of the hierarchy, there are no subfolders to inherit the Full Control permissions.

Figure 2-35

Granting Full Control to
individual user folders

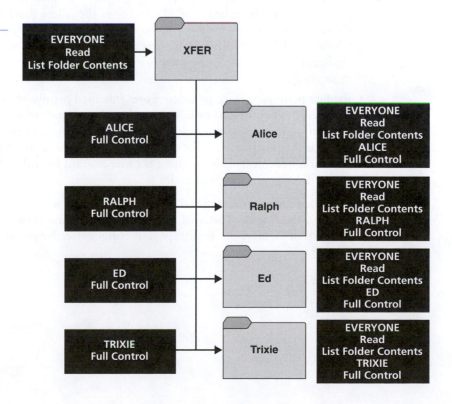

In some situations, an administrator might want to prevent subordinate elements from inheriting permissions from their parents. There are two ways to do this:

- Turn off inheritance—When you assign special permissions, you can configure an ACE not to pass its permissions down to its subordinate elements. This effectively blocks the inheritance process.

- Deny permissions—When you assign a Deny permission to a system element, it overrides any Allow permissions that the element might have inherited from its parent objects.

UNDERSTANDING EFFECTIVE PERMISSIONS

A security principal can receive permissions in many ways, and it is important for an administrator to understand how these permissions interact. The combination of Allow permissions and Deny permissions that a security principal receives for a given system element, whether explicitly assigned, inherited, or received through a group membership, is called the *effective permissions* for that element. Because a security principal can receive permissions from so many sources, it is not unusual for those permissions to conflict, so rules define how the permissions combine to form the effective permissions. These rules are as follows:

- Allow permissions are cumulative—When a security principal receives Allow permissions from more than one source, the permissions are combined to form the effective permissions. For example, if Alice receives the Allow Read and Allow List Folder Contents permissions for a particular folder by inheriting them from its parent folder, and receives the Allow Write and Allow Modify permissions to the same folder from a group membership, Alice's effective permissions for the folder are the combination of all four permissions. If you then explicitly grant Alice's user account the Allow Full Control permission, this fifth permission is combined with the other four.

- Deny permissions override Allow permissions—When a security principal receives Allow permissions, whether explicitly, by inheritance, or from a group, you can override those permissions by granting the principal Deny permissions of the same type. For example, if Alice receives the Allow Read and Allow List Folder Contents permissions for a particular folder by inheritance, and receives the Allow Write and Allow Modify permissions to the same folder from a group membership, explicitly granting the Deny permissions to that folder prevents her from accessing it in any way.

- Explicit permissions take precedence over inherited permissions—When a security principal receives permissions by inheriting them from a parent or from group memberships, you can override those permissions by explicitly assigning contradicting permissions to the security principal itself. For example, if Alice inherits the Deny Full Access permission for a folder, explicitly assigning her user account the Allow Full Access permission to that folder overrides the denial.

Of course, instead of examining and evaluating all of the possible permission sources, you can just open the Advanced Security Settings dialog box and click the Effective Permissions tab, as shown in Figure 2-36, to display your current effective permissions for the selected file or folder.

Figure 2-36

The Effective Permissions tab of the Advanced Security Settings dialog box

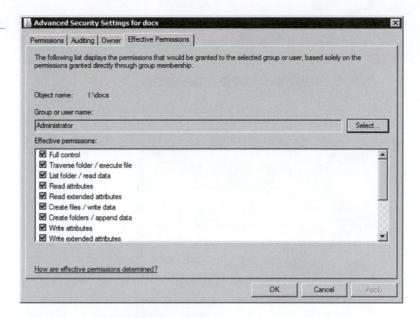

SETTING SHARE PERMISSIONS

On Windows Server 2008, shared folders have their own permission system, which is completely independent from the other Windows permission systems. For network users to access shares on a file server, you must grant them the appropriate share permissions. By default, the Everyone special identity receives the Allow Read share permission to any new volumes you create. To set additional share permissions, use the following procedure.

 SET SHARE PERMISSIONS

GET READY. Log on to Windows Server 2008 using an account with domain administrative privileges. When the logon process is completed, close the Initial Configuration Tasks window and any other windows that appear. Make sure that Network Discovery and File Sharing are turned on in the Network and Sharing Center control panel.

1. Click **Start** > **Administrative Tools** > **Share and Storage Management**. The Share and Storage Management console appears.

2. In the detail (middle) pane, click the **Shares** tab. All of the folder shares on the computer appear in the detail pane, as shown in Figure 2-37.

Figure 2-37

The Shares pane in the Share and Storage Management console

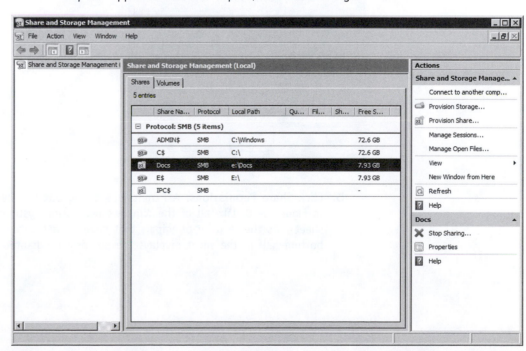

3. Select the share you want to modify and, in the actions pane, select **Properties**. The Properties sheet for the share appears, as shown in Figure 2-38.

Figure 2-38

A shared folder's Properties sheet

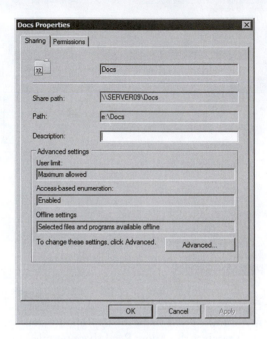

4. Click the **Permissions** tab, as shown in Figure 2-39.

Figure 2-39

The Permissions tab

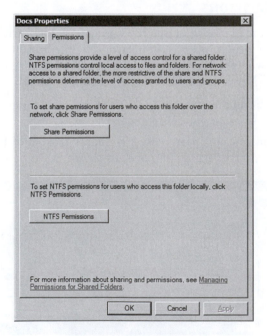

5. Click **Share Permissions**. A Permissions dialog box for the share appears, as shown in Figure 2-40. Like all of the Windows permission systems, the top half of the sheet lists the security principals that have been granted permissions, and the bottom half of the sheet displays the permissions granted to the selected principal.

Figure 2-40

A share Permissions dialog box

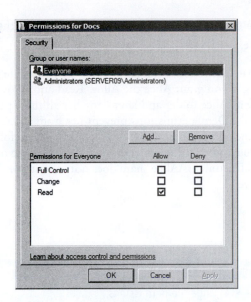

> The Permissions dialog box is also accessible from the SMB Permissions page of the console's Provision a Shared Folder Wizard, as covered in "Creating Folder Shares," earlier in this lesson.

ANOTHER WAY

6. Click **Add.** The Select Users, Computers, or Groups dialog box appears, as shown in Figure 2-41.

Figure 2-41

Select Users, Computers, or Groups dialog box

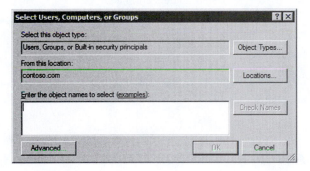

> This procedure, like all of the procedures in this book, assumes that the Windows Server 2008 computer is a member of an Active Directory domain. On a computer that is not a domain member, some of the dialog boxes are slightly different in appearance.

TAKE NOTE*

7. In the *Enter the object names to select* text box, key the name of the user or group you want to add and click **OK.** The user or group is added to the *Group or user names* list.

8. In the Permissions list for the added user or group, select or clear the checkboxes to Allow or Deny any of the permissions shown in Table 2-5 after this exercise.

TAKE NOTE*

> As discussed later in this lesson, many file server administrators simply assign the Allow Full Control share permission to the Everyone special identity, essentially bypassing the share permission system, and rely solely on NTFS permissions for granular file system protection.

9. Click **OK** twice to close the Permissions dialog box and the Properties sheet.

CLOSE the Share and Storage Management console.

When assigning the share permissions shown in Table 2-5, be aware that they do not combine like NTFS permissions. If you grant Alice the Allow Read and Allow Change permissions to the shared C:\Documents\Alice folder and later deny her all three permissions to the shared C:\Documents folder, the Deny permissions prevent her from accessing any files through the C:\Documents share, including those in the C:\Documents\Alice folder. However, she can still access her files through the C:\Documents\Alice share because of the Allow permissions. In other words, the C:\Documents\Alice share does not inherit the Deny permissions from the C:\Documents share.

Table 2-5

Share Permissions and Their Functions

SHARE PERMISSION	ALLOWS OR DENIES SECURITY PRINCIPALS THE ABILITY TO:
Full Control	• Change file permissions. • Take ownership of files. • Perform all tasks allowed by the Change permission.
Change	• Create folders. • Add files to folders. • Change data in files. • Append data to files. • Change file attributes. • Delete folders and files. • Perform all actions permitted by the Read permission.
Read	• Display folder names, filenames, file data, and attributes. • Execute program files. • Access other folders within the shared folder.

UNDERSTANDING NTFS AUTHORIZATION

The majority of Windows installations today use the NTFS file system, as opposed to FAT32. One of the main advantages of NTFS is that it supports permissions, which FAT32 does not. As described earlier in this lesson, every file and folder on an NTFS drive has an ACL that consists of ACEs, each of which contains a security principal and the permissions assigned to that principal.

In the NTFS permission system, the security principals involved are users and groups, which Windows refers to using *security identifiers (SIDs)*. When a user attempts to access an NTFS file or folder, the system reads the user's security access token, which contains the SIDs for the user's account and all of the groups to which the user belongs. The system then compares these SIDs to those stored in the file or folder's ACEs, to determine what access the user should have. This process is called *authorization*.

ASSIGNING STANDARD NTFS PERMISSIONS

Most file server administrators work with standard NTFS permissions almost exclusively because there is no need to work directly with special permissions for most common access control tasks. To assign standard NTFS permissions to a shared folder, use the following procedure.

 ASSIGN STANDARD NTFS PERMISSIONS

GET READY. Log on to Windows Server 2008 using an account with domain administrative privileges. When the logon process is completed, close the Initial Configuration Tasks window and any other windows that appear.

1. Click **Start** > **Administrative Tools** > **Share and Storage Management**. The Share and Storage Management console appears.

2. In the detail (middle) pane, click the **Shares** tab. All of the folder shares on the computer appear in the detail pane.

3. Select the share you want to modify and, in the actions pane, select **Properties**. The Properties sheet for the share appears.

4. Click the **Permissions** tab, and then click **NTFS Permissions**. An NTFS Permissions dialog box for the share appears, as shown in Figure 2-42. The top half of the display lists all of the security principals currently possessing permissions to the selected folder. The bottom half lists the permissions held by the selected security principal.

Figure 2-42

An NTFS Permissions dialog box

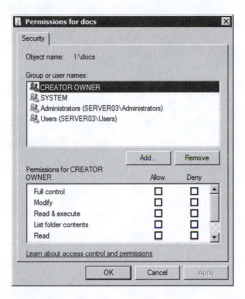

TAKE NOTE NTFS permissions are not limited to shared folders. Every file and folder on an NTFS volume has permissions. While this procedure describes the process of assigning permissions to a shared folder, you can open the Properties sheet for any folder in a Windows Explorer window, click the Security tab, and work with its NTFS permissions in the same way.

5. Click **Add**. The Select Users, Computers, or Groups dialog box appears.

6. In the *Enter the object names to select* text box, key the name of the user or group you want to add and click **OK**. The user or group appears on the Permissions dialog box in the *Group or user names* list.

7. Select the user or group you just added and, in the Permissions box, select or clear the checkboxes to Allow or Deny the user any of the standard permissions.

8. Click **OK** twice to close the Permissions dialog box and the Properties sheet.

CLOSE the Share and Storage Management console.

Table 2-6 lists the standard permissions that you can assign to NTFS files or folders, and the capabilities that they grant to their possessors.

 TAKE NOTE*

Assigning permissions to a single folder takes only a moment, but for a folder with a large number of files and subfolders subordinate to it, the process can take a long time, because the system must modify the ACL of each folder and file.

Table 2-6

NTFS Standard Permissions

STANDARD PERMISSION	WHEN APPLIED TO A FOLDER, ENABLES A SECURITY PRINCIPAL TO:	WHEN APPLIED TO A FILE, ENABLES A SECURITY PRINCIPAL TO:
Full Control	• Modify the folder permissions. • Take ownership of the folder. • Delete subfolders and files contained in the folder. • Perform all actions associated with all of the other NTFS folder permissions.	• Modify the file permissions. • Take ownership of the file. • Perform all actions associated with all of the other NTFS file permissions.
Modify	• Delete the folder. • Perform all actions associated with the Write and the Read & Execute permissions.	• Modify the file. • Delete the file. • Perform all actions associated with the Write and the Read & Execute permissions.
Read and Execute	• Navigate through restricted folders to reach other files and folders. • Perform all actions associated with the Read and List Folder Contents permissions.	• Perform all actions associated with the Read permission. • Run applications.
List Folder Contents	• View the names of the files and subfolders contained in the folder.	• Not applicable.
Read	• See the files and subfolders contained in the folder. • View the ownership, permissions, and attributes of the folder.	• Read the contents of the file. • View the ownership, permissions, and attributes of the file.
Write	• Create new files and subfolders inside the folder. • Modify the folder attributes. • View the ownership and permissions of the folder.	• Overwrite the file. • Modify the file attributes. • View the ownership and permissions of the file.

ASSIGNING SPECIAL NTFS PERMISSIONS

To view and manage the special NTFS permissions for a file, folder, or share, use the following procedure.

 ASSIGN SPECIAL NTFS PERMISSIONS

GET READY. Log on to Windows Server 2008 using an account with domain administrative privileges. When the logon process is completed, close the Initial Configuration Tasks window and any other windows that appear.

1. Open the Properties sheet for a file, folder, or share on an NTFS drive using one of the following procedures:

   • Open Windows Explorer, right-click a file or folder and, from the context menu, select **Properties**. Then, click the **Security** tab.

   • Open the Share and Storage Management console, select a share, and click **Properties**. Click the **Permissions** tab and then click the **NTFS Permissions** button.

2. Click **Advanced**. The Advanced Security Settings dialog box for the selected file or folder appears. This dialog box is as close as the Windows graphical interface can come to displaying the contents of an ACL. Each of the lines in the Permission Entries list is essentially an ACE, and includes the following information:

   • Type—Specifies if the entry allows or denies the permission.

   • Name—Specifies the name of the security principal receiving the permission.

   • Permission—Specifies the name of the standard permission assigned to the security principal. If the entry is used to assign special permissions, the word *Special* appears in this field.

   • Inherited From—Specifies if the permission is inherited and if so, where it is inherited from.

   • Apply To—Specifies if the permission is inherited by subordinate objects and if so, by which ones.

3. Click **Edit**. An editable Advanced Security Settings dialog box appears, as shown in Figure 2-43. This dialog box also contains the following two checkboxes:

   • Include inheritable permissions from this object's parent—Specifies whether the file or folder should inherit permissions from parent objects. This checkbox is selected by default. Deselecting it causes a Windows Security message box to appear, enabling you to choose whether to remove all of the inherited ACEs from the list or copy the inherited permissions from the parents to the file or folder. If you choose the latter, the effective permissions stay the same, but the file or folder is no longer dependent on the parents for permission inheritance. If you change the permissions on the parent objects, the file or folder remains unaffected.

   • Replace all existing inheritable permissions on all descendents with inheritable permissions from this object—Causes subordinate objects to inherit permissions from this file or folder, to the exclusion of all permissions explicitly assigned to the subordinate objects.

Figure 2-43

The editable Advanced Security Settings for docs Folder page

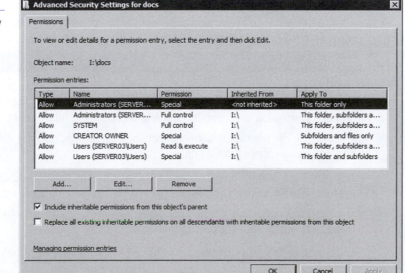

4. Click **Add**. The Select Users, Computers, or Groups dialog box appears.

5. In the *Enter the object names to select* text box, key the name of the user or group you want to add and click **OK**. The Permission Entry dialog box for the user or group appears, as shown in Figure 2-44.

Figure 2-44

The Permission Entry for docs Folder dialog box

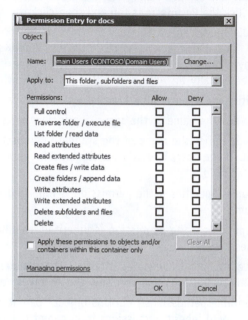

6. In the Apply To dropdown list, select which subordinate elements should receive the permissions you assign using this dialog box.

7. In the Permissions list, select or clear the checkboxes to Allow or Deny the user any of the special permissions.

8. Click **OK** four times to close all of the dialog boxes.

CLOSE Windows Explorer or the Share and Storage Management console.

Table 2-7 lists the NTFS special permissions that you can assign to files and folders, and the capabilities that they grant to their possessors.

Table 2-7

NTFS Special Permissions

SPECIAL PERMISSION	FUNCTIONS
Traverse Folder/Execute File	• The Traverse Folder permission allows or denies security principals the ability to move through folders that they do not have permission to access, so they can reach files or folders that they do have permission to access. This permission applies to folders only. • The Execute File permission allows or denies security principals the ability to run program files. This permission applies to files only.
List Folder/Read Data	• The List Folder permission allows or denies security principals the ability to view the file and subfolder names within a folder. This permission applies to folders only. • The Read Data permission allows or denies security principals the ability to view the contents of a file. This permission applies to files only.
Read Attributes	Allows or denies security principals the ability to view the NTFS attributes of a file or folder.
Read Extended Attributes	Allows or denies security principals the ability to view the extended attributes of a file or folder.

(continued)

Table 2-7 (continued)

SPECIAL PERMISSION	FUNCTIONS
Create Files/Write Data	• The Create Files permission allows or denies security principals the ability to create files within the folder. This permission applies to folders only. • The Write Data permission allows or denies security principals the ability to modify the file and overwrite existing content. This permission applies to files only.
Create Folders/Append Data	• The Create Folders permission allows or denies security principals the ability to create subfolders within a folder. This permission applies to folders only. • The Append Data permission allows or denies security principals the ability to add data to the end of the file but not to modify, delete, or overwrite existing data in the file. This permission applies to files only.
Write Attributes	Allows or denies security principals the ability to modify the NTFS attributes of a file or folder.
Write Extended Attributes	Allows or denies security principals the ability to modify the extended attributes of a file or folder.
Delete Subfolders and Files	Allows or denies security principals the ability to delete subfolders and files, even if the Delete permission has not been granted on the subfolder or file.
Delete	Allows or denies security principals the ability to delete the file or folder.
Read Permissions	Allows or denies security principals the ability to read the permissions for the file or folder.
Change Permissions	Allows or denies security principals the ability to modify the permissions for the file or folder.
Take Ownership	Allows or denies security principals the ability to take ownership of the file or folder.
Synchronize	Allows or denies different threads of multithreaded, multiprocessor programs to wait on the handle for the file or folder and synchronize with another thread that might signal it.

As mentioned earlier in this lesson, standard permissions are combinations of special permissions designed to provide frequently needed access controls. Table 2-8 lists all of the standard permissions, and the special permissions that compose them.

Table 2-8

NTFS Standard Permissions and Their Special Permission Equivalents

STANDARD PERMISSIONS	SPECIAL PERMISSIONS
Read	• List Folder/Read Data • Read Attributes • Read Extended Attributes • Read Permissions • Synchronize
Read and Execute	• List Folder/Read Data • Read Attributes • Read Extended Attributes • Read Permissions • Synchronize • Traverse Folder/Execute File
Modify	• Create Files/Write Data • Create Folders/Append Data

(continued)

Table 2-8 (*continued*)

STANDARD PERMISSIONS	SPECIAL PERMISSIONS
	• Delete • List Folder/Read Data • Read Attributes • Read Extended Attributes • Read Permissions • Synchronize • Write Attributes • Write Extended Attributes
Write	• Create Files/Write Data • Create Folders/Append Data • Read Permissions • Synchronize • Write Attributes • Write Extended Attributes
List Folder Contents	• List Folder/Read Data • Read Attributes • Read Extended Attributes • Read Permissions • Synchronize • Traverse Folder/Execute File
Full Control	• Change Permissions • Create Files/Write Data • Create Folders/Append Data • Delete • Delete Subfolders and Files • List Folder/Read Data • Read Attributes • Read Extended Attributes • Read Permissions • Synchronize • Take Ownership • Write Attributes • Write Extended Attributes

UNDERSTANDING RESOURCE OWNERSHIP

As you study the NTFS permission system, it might occur to you that it seems possible to lock out a file or folder, that is, assign a combination of permissions that permits access to no one at all, leaving the file or folder inaccessible. In fact, this is true.

A user with administrative privileges can revoke his or her own permissions, as well as everyone else's, preventing them from accessing a resource. However, the NTFS permissions system includes a "back door" that prevents these orphaned files and folders from remaining permanently inaccessible.

Every file and folder on an NTFS drive has an owner, and the owner always has the ability to modify the permissions for the file or folder, even if the owner has no permissions him- or herself. By default, the owner of a file or folder is the user account that created it. However,

any account possessing the Take Ownership special permission (or the Full Control standard permission) can take ownership of the file or folder.

The Administrator user can take ownership of any file or folder, even those from which the previous owner has revoked all of Administrator's permissions. After the Administrator user has taken ownership of a file or folder, the Administrator user cannot assign ownership back to the previous owner. This prevents the Administrator account from accessing other users' files undetected.

The other purpose for file and folder ownership is to calculate disk quotas. When you set quotas specifying the maximum amount of disk space particular users can consume, Windows calculates a user's current disk consumption by adding the sizes of all the files and folders that the user owns.

COMBINING SHARE AND NTFS PERMISSIONS

It is important for file server administrators to understand that the NTFS and share permission systems are completely separate from each other, and that for network users to access files on a shared NTFS drive, they must have both the correct NTFS and the correct share permissions. The share and NTFS permissions assigned to a file or folder can conflict. For example, if a user has the NTFS Write and Modify permissions for a folder and lacks the share Change permission, that user will not be able to modify a file in that folder.

The share permission system is the simplest of the Windows permission systems, and provides only basic protection for shared network resources. Share permissions provide only three levels of access, compared to the far more complex system of NTFS permissions. Generally speaking, network administrators prefer to use either NTFS or share permissions, but not both.

Share permissions provide limited protection, but this might be sufficient on some small networks. Share permissions might also be the only alternative on a computer with FAT32 drives, because the FAT file system does not have its own permission system.

On networks already possessing a well-planned system of NTFS permissions, share permissions are not really necessary. In this case, you can safely grant the Full Control share permission to Everyone, overriding the default Read permission, and allow the NTFS permissions to provide security. Adding share permissions to the mix would only complicate the administration process, without providing any additional security.

Mapping Drives

> Configure your users' workstation for them, because they might not know what shares and servers are.

After you have set up your disks, created your shares, and assigned permissions, the file server is ready to use. However, most network users will benefit from some simplified way of knowing that the server's resources are available to them. One of the best methods of doing this, as mentioned earlier in this lesson, is to create drive mappings on users' workstations, pointing to specific file server shares. The following sections describe several ways that administrators can deploy drive mappings on large groups of workstations.

USING FOLDER REDIRECTION

As discussed earlier in this lesson, most enterprise networks provide each user with a designated storage space on a file server for his or her exclusive use. To prevent users from searching for their storage space and from having to understand the difference between local and server storage, you can use a feature called folder redirection.

Folder redirection is a mechanism that enables administrators to store elements of user profiles on a server share instead of the local drives on individual workstations. This enables users to click what appears to be a local folder, such as Documents, and access their files, which are actually stored on a server. Because the files in the Documents folder are stored on a server, users can access them from any workstation, and administrators can back up the files easily.

To configure folder redirection, you use Group Policy settings, as described in the following procedure.

➔ REDIRECT A FOLDER

GET READY. Log on to Windows Server 2008 using an account with domain administrative privileges. When the logon process is completed, close the Initial Configuration Tasks window and any other windows that appear.

1. If you have not done so already, install the Group Policy Management feature on the computer, using the Add Features Wizard in Server Manager.

2. Click **Start**, and then click **Administrative Tools** > **Group Policy Management**. The Group Policy Management console appears.

3. In the scope (left) pane, browse to and right-click the group policy object (GPO) you want to modify and, from the context menu, select **Edit**. The Group Policy Management Editor console appears, as shown in Figure 2-45.

Figure 2-45

The Group Policy Management Editor console

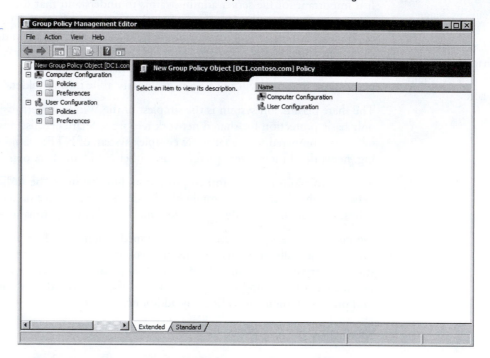

4. In the scope pane, browse to the **User Configuration** > **Policies** > **Windows Settings** > **Folder Redirection** folder, as shown in Figure 2-46.

Figure 2-46

The Folder Redirection folder in the Group Policy Management Editor console

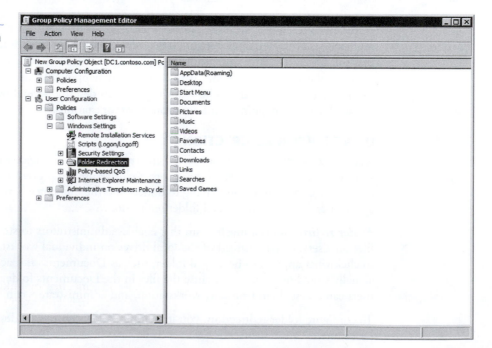

5. Right-click the folder you want to redirect and, from the context menu, select **Properties**. The Properties sheet for the folder appears, as shown in Figure 2-47.

Figure 2-47

A Folder Redirection folder's Properties sheet

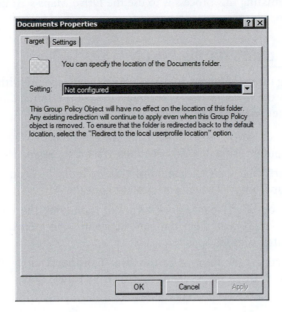

6. From the Setting dropdown list, select **Basic—Redirect everyone's folder to the same location**, as shown in Figure 2-48.

Figure 2-48

A Folder Redirection folder's Properties sheet, with the Basic option selected

7. In the Target Folder Location box, verify that the default *Create a folder for each user under the root path* option is selected and, in the Root Path text box, key or browse to the location on a server share where you want to store the redirected files.

8. Click **OK**.

CLOSE the Group Policy Management Editor console and the Group Policy Management console.

At this point, you can deploy the GPO in the normal manner, by linking it to a domain, site, or organizational unit object in your Active Directory tree. For every user to which the GPO applies, the computer will redirect the Documents folder to the server location you specified in the policy setting.

MAPPING DRIVES USING GROUP POLICY

On an enterprise network, you might want to map additional drive letters to shared folders. One way of automating this process is to use the Drive Maps settings in Group Policy, as in the following procedure.

 MAP A DRIVE USING GROUP POLICY

GET READY. Log on to Windows Server 2008 using an account with domain administrative privileges. When the logon process is completed, close the Initial Configuration Tasks window and any other windows that appear.

1. If you have not done so already, install the Group Policy Management feature on the computer, using the Add Features Wizard in Server Manager.

2. Click **Start**, and then click **Administrative Tools** > **Group Policy Management**. The Group Policy Management console appears.

3. In the scope (left) pane, browse to and right-click the group policy object you want to modify and, from the context menu, select **Edit**. The Group Policy Management Editor console appears.

4. In the scope pane, browse to the **User Configuration** > **Preferences** > **Windows Settings** > **Drive Maps** node, as shown in Figure 2-49.

Figure 2-49

The Drive Maps node in the Group Policy Management • Editor console

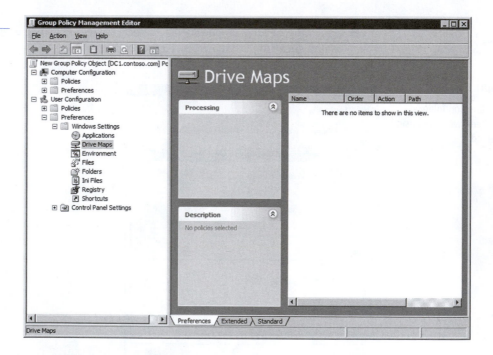

5. Right-click the **Drive Maps** node and, in the context menu, point to **New** and select **Mapped Drive.** The New Drive Properties sheet appears, as shown in Figure 2-50.

6. From the Action dropdown list, select **Create**.

7. In the Location text box, key the path to the shared server folder you want to map, using UNC notation (\\servername\sharename\foldername).

8. Select the **Reconnect** checkbox to map the drive during all subsequent user logons.

9. In the Drive Letter box, select a drive letter for the mapping, and specify if you want to use that specific drive, or the first available drive after the letter you selected.

10. Click **OK**.

Figure 2-50

The New Drive Properties sheet

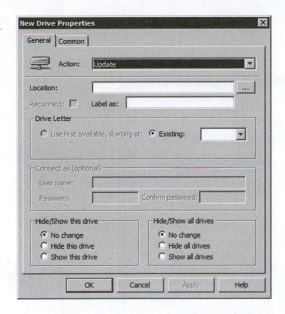

CLOSE the Group Policy Management Editor console and the Group Policy Management console.

You can now deploy the group policy object (GPO) in the normal manner, by linking it to a domain, site, or organizational unit object in your Active Directory tree. For every user to which the GPO applies, the computer will map the selected drive to the folder you specified in the policy setting.

USING LOGON SCRIPTS

Another way to automate the drive mapping process is to create batch files and use them as logon scripts for your users. You can use the Net.exe command-line utility with the Use parameter to map drive letters to folders, so your logon scripts need only contain commands like the following:

    net use *x:* *servername**sharename**foldername*

- *x:*—Specifies the drive letter you want to map to the path specified on the command line.
- *servername*—Specifies the name of the file server containing the share and the folder that you want to map to the drive letter on the command line.
- *sharename*—Specifies the name of a folder share on the specified file server containing the folder that you want to map to the drive letter on the command line.
- *foldername*—Specifies the name of a folder in the share on the file server that you want to map to the drive letter on the command line.

You can specify as many of these commands in a logon script as you have available drive letters, and employ variables such as %username% to create generic scripts suitable for multiple users.

To deploy the logon scripts, store them in a shared folder and use one of the following methods:

- To deploy a logon script to an individual user—In the Active Directory Users and Computers console, open the user object's Properties sheet, select the Profile tab, and specify the path to the logon script in the Logon Script text box, as shown in Figure 2-51.

Figure 2-51

Deploying a logon script with a user object

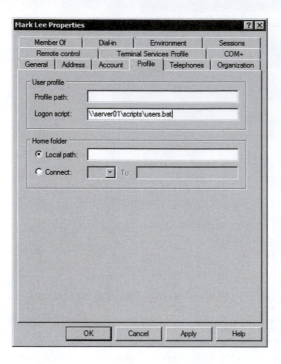

• To deploy a logon script to multiple users with Group Policy—In the Group Policy Management Editor console, create or open a GPO, browse to the User Configuration > Policies > Windows Settings > Scripts (Logon/Logoff) container, double-click the Logon policy, and add the logon script file, as shown in Figure 2-52. Then link the GPO to an appropriate domain, site, or organization unit object.

Figure 2-52

Deploying a logon script using Group Policy

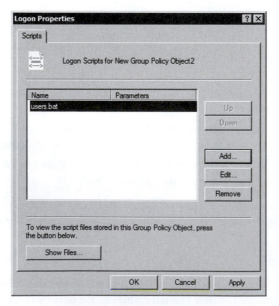

TAKE NOTE *

If the computer is a member of an Active Directory domain but is not a domain controller, you must install the Group Policy Management feature before the Group Policy Management console will appear in the Administrative Tools folder. To do this, open Server Manager, start the Add Features Wizard, and select Group Policy Management.

SUMMARY SKILL MATRIX

IN THIS LESSON YOU LEARNED:

• Planning is a critical part of a file server deployment. Your deployment plan should specify how many file servers you need, what hardware they should have, how you will configure them, how you will share the server data, and how you will protect the data.

• The Disk Management snap-in is the primary interface you use to initialize, partition, and format disks.

• Windows Server 2008 supports two hard disk partition types: MBR and GPT; two disk types: basic and dynamic; five volume types: simple, striped, spanned, mirrored, and RAID-5; and two file systems: NTFS and FAT.

• Creating folder shares makes the data stored on a file server's disks accessible to network users.

• Windows Server 2008 has several sets of permissions, which operate independently of each other, including NTFS permissions, share permissions, registry permissions, and Active Directory permissions.

• NTFS permissions enable you to control access to files and folders by specifying the tasks individual users can perform on them. Share permissions provide rudimentary access control for all of the files on a network share. Network users must have the proper share and NTFS permissions to access file server shares.

• Mapping drive letters with logon scripts makes shared folders easily available to network users.

■ Knowledge Assessment

Fill in the Blank

Complete the following sentences by writing the correct word or words in the blanks provided.

1. The feature that enables a Windows Server 2008 computer to maintain up to 64 previous versions of a file is called _____.

2. The process of granting users access to file server shares by reading their permissions is called _____.

3. In Windows, the _____ file system is limited to volumes no larger than 32 GB.

4. The drive interface that is preferred for network servers is called _____.

5. A mirrored drive installation that also uses redundant host adapters is called disk _____.

6. The combination of permissions assigned to a file, plus the permissions inherited from parent folders and group memberships, is called the file's _____ permissions.

7. The _____ utility enables you to create a fourth primary partition on a basic disk.

8. The disk interface most commonly associated with workstations is called _____.

9. _____ volumes use parity information to rebuild data in the event of a disk failure.

10. In the NTFS permission system, _____ permissions are actually combinations of _____ permissions.

Multiple Choice

Select the correct answer for each of the following questions. Choose all answers that are correct.

1. Which of the following statements are true of striped volumes?
   a. Striped volumes provide enhanced performance over simple volumes.
   b. Striped volumes provide greater fault tolerance than simple volumes.

    c. You can extend striped volumes after creation.

    d. If a single physical disk in the striped volume fails, all of the data in the entire volume is lost.

2. Which of the following statements are true of simple volumes?

    a. You create simple volumes from a single disk.

    b. You can extend a simple volume to multiple disks to create a spanned or a striped volume, even when the simple volume is a system volume or boot volume.

    c. You can shrink a simple volume by de-allocating any unused space in the volume.

    d. Once it is created, you cannot extend a simple volume into any adjacent unallocated space on the same disk.

3. Which of the following statements are *not* true in reference to converting a basic disk to a dynamic disk?

    a. You cannot convert a basic disk to a dynamic disk if you need to dual boot the computer.

    b. You cannot convert drives with volumes that use an allocation unit size greater than 512 bytes.

    c. A boot partition or system partition on a basic disk cannot be extended into a striped or spanned volume, even if you convert the disk to a dynamic disk.

    d. The conversion will fail if the hard drive does not have at least 1 MB of free space at the end of the disk.

4. Which of the following statements are *not* true about differences between network attached storage (NAS) devices and storage area network (SAN) devices?

    a. NAS devices provide a file system implementation; SAN devices do not.

    b. NAS devices must have their own processor and memory hardware; SAN devices do not require these components.

    c. NAS devices must run their own operating system and typically provide a Web interface for administrative access; SAN devices do not have to have either one.

    d. NAS devices require a specialized protocol, such as Fibre Channel or iSCSI; SAN devices use standard networking protocols.

5. A security principal is

    a. The person granting permissions to network users.

    b. The network element receiving permissions.

    c. A collection of individual special permissions.

    d. An object that assigns permissions.

6. Which of the following statements about the DiskPart command-line utility is *not* true?

    a. DiskPart contains a superset of the commands supported by the Disk Management snap-in.

    b. Using DiskPart, you can create four primary partitions or three primary partitions and one extended partition.

    c. DiskPart prohibits you from unintentionally performing actions that might result in data loss.

    d. DiskPart can manage both basic disks and dynamic disks.

7. Which of the following statements are requirements for extending a volume on a dynamic disk?

    a. If you want to extend a simple volume, you can use only the available space on the same disk if the volume is to remain simple.

    b. The volume must have a file system (a raw volume) before you can extend a simple or spanned volume.

    c. You can extend a simple or spanned volume if you formatted it using the FAT or FAT32 file systems.

    d. You can extend a simple volume across additional disks if it is not a system volume or a boot volume.

8. Which of the following statements is *not* true about effective permissions?

    a. Inherited permissions take precedence over explicit permissions.

    b. Deny permissions always override Allow permissions.

    c. When a security principal receives Allow permissions from multiple groups, the permissions are combined to form the effective permissions.

    d. Effective permissions include both permissions inherited from parents and permissions derived from group memberships.

9. Which of the following is not true in reference to resource ownership?

    a. One of the purposes for file and folder ownership is to calculate disk quotas.

    b. Every file and folder on an NTFS driver has an owner.

    c. Any user possessing the Take Ownership special permission can assume the ownership of a file or folder.

    d. You can lock out a file or folder, assigning a combination of permissions that permits access to no one at all, including the owner of the file or folder.

10. Which of the following operating systems can use either the MBR or GPT partition style?

    a. Windows Server 2003   **b.** Windows Server 2008

    c. Windows Vista   **d.** Windows XP Professional

Review Questions

1. Of the five dynamic volume types supported by Windows Server 2008, explain why each volume type either does or does not provide fault tolerance.

2. What is the main reason why many file servers uses the SCSI disk interface, rather than ATA?

■ Case Scenarios

Scenario 2-1: Assigning Permissions

While you are working the help desk for a corporate network, a user named Leo calls to request access to the files for Trinity, a new classified project. The Trinity files are stored in a shared folder on a file server, which is locked in a secured underground data storage facility in New Mexico. After verifying that he has the appropriate security clearance for the project, you create a new group on the file server called TRINITY_USERS and add Leo's user account to that group. Then, you add the TRINITY_USERS group to the access control list for the Trinity folder on the file server, and assign the group the following NTFS permissions:

- Allow Modify
- Allow Read & Execute
- Allow List Folder Contents
- Allow Read
- Allow Write

Sometime later, Leo calls you to tell you that he is able to access the Trinity folder and read the files stored there, but he has been unable to save changes back to the server. What is the most likely cause of the problem?

Scenario 2-2: Accessing Orphaned Files

Libby, a new hire in the IT department, approaches you, her supervisor, ashen-faced. A few minutes earlier, the president of the company called the help desk and asked Libby to give his new assistant the permissions needed to access his personal budget spreadsheet. As she was attempting to assign the permissions, she accidentally deleted the BUDGET_USERS group from the spreadsheet's access control list. Libby is terrified because that group was the only entry in the file's ACL. Now, no one can access the spreadsheet file, not even the president or the Administrator account. Is there any way to gain access to the file, and if so, how?

3 LESSON

Using the File Services Role

Many of the most basic capabilities of a file server, such as folder sharing, are part of a default Windows Server 2008 installation. However, the File Services role provides more advanced features, including the following:

- Distributed File System (DFS)
- DFS Replication
- File Server Resource Manager
- Network File System (NFS)

■ Installing the File Services Role

THE BOTTOM LINE

Install the File Services role on all of your file servers, to provide access to tools and services that simplify the server deployment and maintenance processes.

As discussed in Lesson 2, "Deploying a File Server," a default Windows Server 2008 installation includes all of the components needed for a basic file server deployment. You can manage the server's disk drives, share folders, map drives, and control access to those shares with no additional software installations. However, enterprise networks often have requirements that go beyond the basics and, to address those needs, Windows Server 2008 includes the File Services role, which implements the Distributed File System (DFS) and other useful tools.

Selecting Role Services

Choose the role services you need, based on the size of your network and the types of clients the server has to support.

When you install the File Services role using Server Manager, the Add Roles Wizard displays several pages specific to the File Services components. On the Select Role Services page, as shown in Figure 3-1, you choose the File Services components you want to install. Table 3-1 lists the role services for the File Services role, with the names of the pages they add to the Add Roles Wizard and the system services they install on the computer.

Figure 3-1

The Select Roles Services page in the Add Roles Wizard

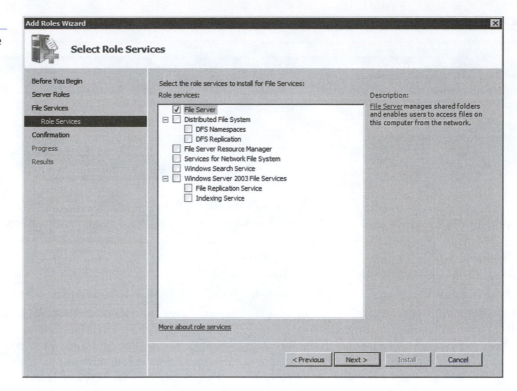

Table 3-1

Role Service Selections for the File Services Role

ROLE SERVICE	WIZARD PAGES ADDED	SYSTEM SERVICES INSTALLED	DESCRIPTION
File Server	[None]	• Server (LanmanServer)	• Installs the Share and Storage Management console for Microsoft Management Console (MMC). • The only role service required to add the File Services role.
Distributed File System: DFS Namespaces	• DFS Namespaces • Namespace Type • Credentials	• DFS Namespace (DFS)	• Enables you to create virtual namespaces that consist of actual directories located on servers all over the network. • By default, the DFS Namespace system service is in the Stopped state after installation, with the Startup Type set to Auto.
Distributed File System: DFS Replication	[None]	• DFS Replication (DFSR)	• Implements a multimaster replication engine that can keep copies of files at remote locations updated on a regular basis.
File Server Resource Manager	• Storage Monitoring	• File Server Resource Manager (SRMSVC) • File Server Storage Reports Manager (SRMReports)	• Installs an MMC console that provides centralized management of quotas, file screening policies, and storage reports. • By default, the File Server Storage Reports Manager system service is in the Stopped state after installation, with the Startup Type set to Manual.

(continued)

Table 3-1 (*continued*)

Role Service	Wizard Pages Added	System Services Installed	Description
Services for Network File System	[None]	• Server for NFS (NFSSvc)	• Enables UNIX clients to access files on the server using NFS.
Windows Search Service	• Volumes to Index	• Windows Search (wsearch)	• Creates an index of the files on selected volumes, enabling qualified clients to perform rapid file searches.
Windows Server 2003 File Services: File Replication Service	[None]	• File Replication (NTFRS)	• Provides backwards compatibility enabling Windows Server 2008 computers to synchronize folders with Windows Server 2003 computers running the File Replication Service instead of DFS Replication.
Windows Server 2003 File Services: Indexing Service	[None]	• Indexing Service (cisvc)	• Provides backwards compatibility with the Windows Server 2003 Indexing Service, which catalogs files and their properties on computers throughout the network. • You cannot install the Windows Server 2003 Indexing Service on the same computer as the Windows Search Service.

The Server service, which enables the computer to share files with network users, is installed on all Windows Server 2008 computers by default. Therefore, the wizard always selects the File Server role service by default when you install the File Services role. You can remove the File Server role service but doing so would cause all shared folders on the server to become unshared.

Configuring Role Services

Configuring your role services as you install them saves time and effort later.

In some cases, the Add Roles Wizard provides the opportunity to configure individual role services as it installs them. It does this by inserting additional pages into the wizard as you select particular role services. The additional pages appear in the left column of the wizard, which displays them in order as you page through the installation process. The following sections examine the functions of these role service-specific configuration pages.

CONFIGURING THE DFS ROLE SERVICE

Selecting the DFS Namespaces role service adds steps to the Add Roles Wizard, as follows:
  • DFS Namespaces—Enables you to create a new DFS namespace during the role installation process, as shown in Figure 3-2, or later.

Figure 3-2

The Create a DFS Namespace
page in the Add Roles Wizard

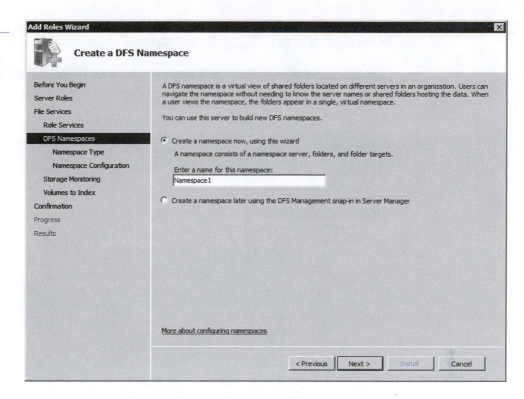

• Namespace Type—Enables you to specify whether you want to create a domain-based
namespace or a stand-alone namespace, as shown in Figure 3-3.

Figure 3-3

The Select Namespace Type
page in the Add Roles Wizard

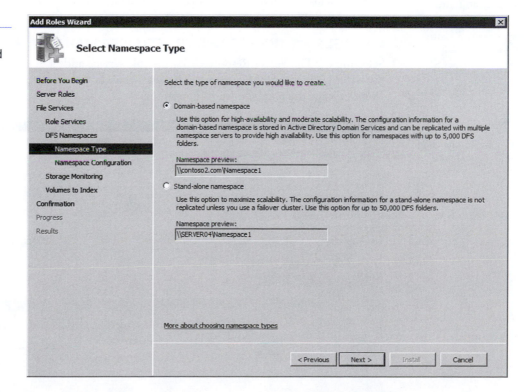

- Namespace Configuration—Enables you to build your DFS namespace, as shown in Figure 3-4, by specifying folder names and targets.

Figure 3-4

The Configure Namespace page in the Add Roles Wizard

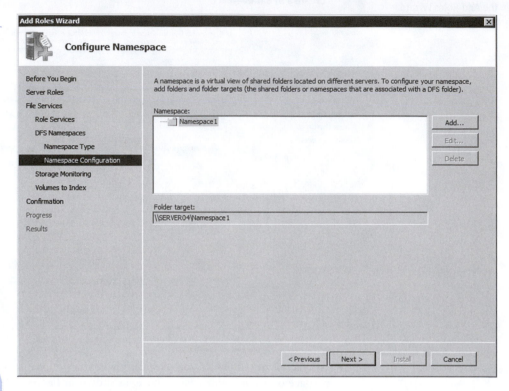

For more information on creating and configuring a DFS namespace, see "Using the Distributed File System," later in this lesson.

- Credentials—If you are not logged on using an account with the privileges needed to create the DFS namespace, the wizard prompts you to furnish a user name and password.

CONFIGURING THE FILE SERVER RESOURCE MANAGER ROLE SERVICE

Selecting the File Server Resource Manager role service adds a Storage Monitoring page to the wizard, as shown in Figure 3-5. This page enables you to select the volumes on the server whose storage capacity you want to monitor.

Figure 3-5

The Configure Storage Usage Monitoring page in the Add Roles Wizard

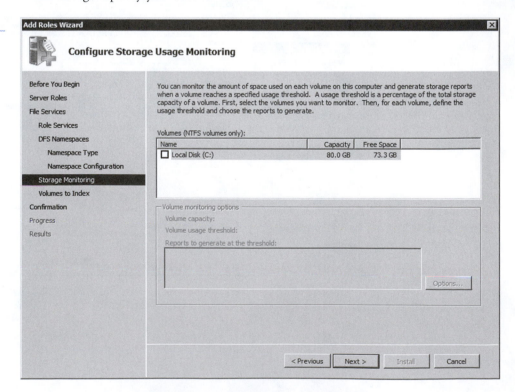

By default, the wizard configures the File Server Resource Manager service to generate a Files By Owner Report and a Files By File Group Report when the available storage space on the selected volumes drops below 85 percent of the total space.

You can modify these defaults by clicking Options to display the Volume Monitoring Options dialog box, as shown in Figure 3-6. In this dialog box, you can modify the Volume Usage Threshold value and select which reports you want the service to generate.

Figure 3-6

The Volume Monitoring Options dialog box

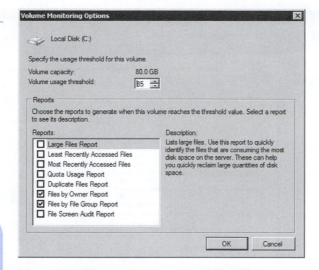

X REF

For more information on configuring File Server Resource Manager, see "Using File Server Resource Manager," later in this lesson.

CONFIGURING THE WINDOWS SEARCH SERVICE

Selecting the Windows Search Service role service adds a Select Volumes to Index for Windows Search Service page to the wizard, as shown in Figure 3-7. On this page, you can select the volumes on the computer that you want the service to keep indexed, so that clients on the network can perform faster file searches.

Figure 3-7

The Select Volumes to Index for Windows Search Service page in the Add Roles Wizard

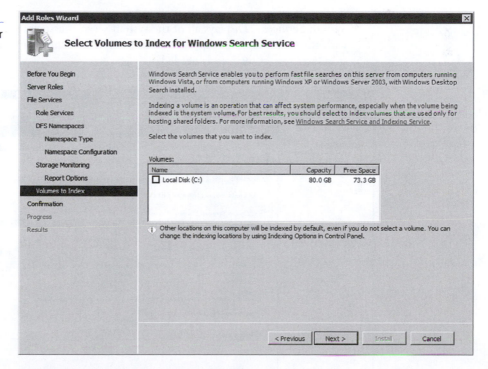

Managing the File Services Role

After the Add Roles Wizard finishes installing the File Services role, a File Services node appears under Roles in the Server Manager's scope pane.

The File Services node provides access to the following elements:

- Events—Displays a subset of the computer's System log containing all events related to the File Services role during the past 24 hours, as shown in Figure 3-8. You can configure the filter to display only events with certain levels or event IDs, or specify a different time period. You can also click the Go To Event Viewer link to display the entire Event Viewer snap-in, which is also integrated into the Server Manager console.

Figure 3-8

The Events display for the File Services role

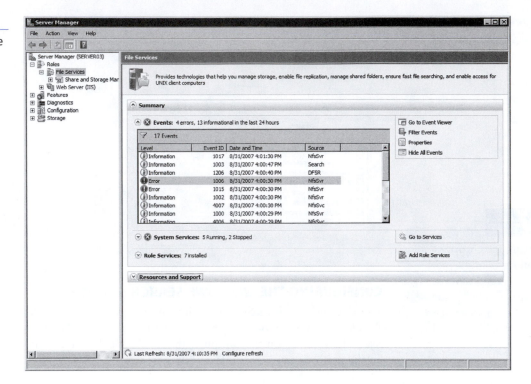

- System Services—Displays all of the system services associated with the File Services role, with the Status and Startup Type of each service, as shown in Figure 3-9. You can start, stop, and restart services as needed.

Figure 3-9

The System Services display for the File Services role

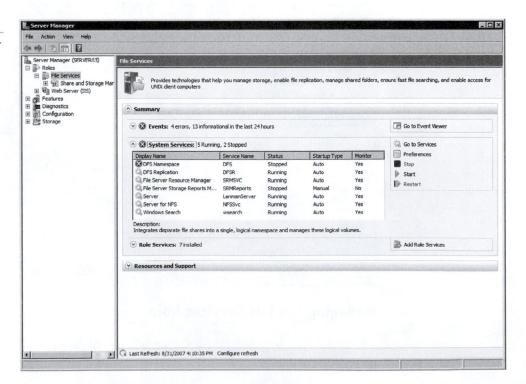

- Role Services—Displays a list of the role services for the File Services role, specifying which role services are currently installed, as shown in Figure 3-10. You can install or remove role services by clicking the provided links to launch the appropriate wizard.

Figure 3-10

The Role Services display for the File Services role

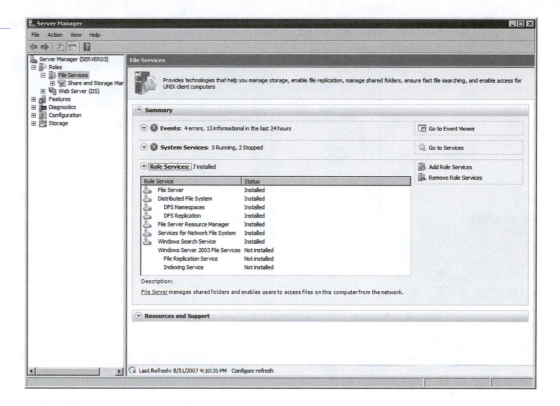

- Resources and Support—Displays a list of role-related tasks and suggestions, as shown in Figure 3-11, which are linked to help files.

Figure 3-11

The Resources and Support display for the File Services role

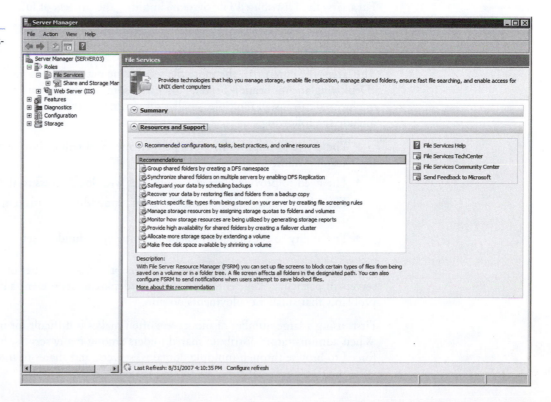

• Share and Storage Management—Provides access to the Share and Storage Management snap-in for MMC (shown in Figure 3-12) that the wizard installs with the role. Use the snap-in to manage all of the shared folders and disk volumes on the computer.

Figure 3-12

The Share and Storage Management snap-in

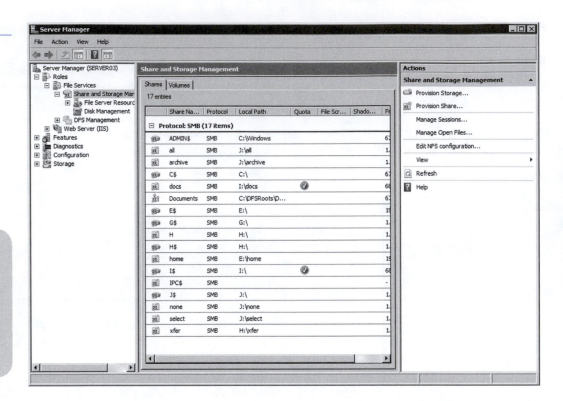

■ Using the Distributed File System

THE BOTTOM LINE

For users, the Distributed File System simplifies the process of locating files and folders on network servers. For administrators, DFS facilitates traffic control and network backups.

The larger the enterprise, the more file servers the network users are likely to need. Lesson 1, "Deploying an Application Server," discussed some of the reasons why network administrators might prefer to install multiple, smaller servers, rather than one large server. These reasons include the following:

• The desire to improve network performance and reduce internetwork bandwidth by keeping traffic local.
• The need to provide users at remote sites with local access to their files.
• The administrative convenience of giving individual departments or workgroups control over their own servers.
• The ability to provide fault tolerance by using redundant servers.

Generally speaking, deploying multiple servers provides a number of benefits, but for file servers in particular, large enterprise network deployments present administrators with several problems that smaller deployments do not.

First, using a large number of file servers often makes it difficult for users to locate their files. When administrators distribute shared folders among many servers, network users might be forced to browse through multiple domains, servers, and shares to find the files they need. For experienced users, who understand something of how a network operates, this can be an exasperating inconvenience. For inexperienced users, who are unfamiliar with basic networking principles, it can be an exercise in mystified frustration.

A second common problem for enterprise networks that have networks at multiple sites is providing users with access to their files, while minimizing the traffic passing over expensive wide area network (WAN) connections. Administrators could store files at a central location and let the remote users access them over the WAN. However, this solution allows WAN traffic levels to increase without check, and if a WAN connection fails, the remote users are cut off from their files. The other alternative is to maintain local copies of all the files needed at each location. This provides users at every site with local access to their data, minimizes WAN traffic, and enables the network to tolerate a WAN link failure with a minimal loss of productivity. However, to make this solution feasible, it is necessary to synchronize the copies of the files at the different locations, so that changes made at one site are propagated to all of the others.

Enterprise administrators also must consider how to implement a backup solution for small branch offices that do not have their own IT staffs. Even if the organization is willing to install a complete backup hardware and software solution at each site, the tasks of changing the media, running the backup jobs, monitoring their progress, and performing any restores that are needed would be left to untrained personnel. The alternative, backing up over the WAN connection to a centrally located backup server, is likely to be slow, costly, and bandwidth-intensive.

The ***Distributed File System (DFS)*** implemented in the Windows Server 2008 File Services role includes two technologies: DFS Namespaces and DFS Replication, which address these problems and enable administrators to do the following:

- Simplify the process of locating files
- Control the amount of traffic passing over WAN links
- Provide users at remote sites with local file server access
- Configure the network to survive a WAN link failure
- Facilitate consistent backups

The architecture of the DFS technologies is discussed in the following section.

Introducing DFS

Each of the two role services that make up the Distributed File System role can work with the other to provide a DFS solution scalable to almost any size network.

The DFS Namespaces role service provides basic virtual directory functionality, and the DFS Replication role service enables administrators to deploy that virtual directory on multiple servers, all over the enterprise.

UNDERSTANDING NAMESPACES

At its simplest, DFS is a virtual ***namespace*** technology that enables you to create a single directory tree that contains references to shared folders on various file servers, all over the network. This directory tree is virtual; it does not exist as a true copy of the folders on different servers. Instead, it is a collection of references to the original folders, which users can browse as though it was an actual server share. The actual shared folders are referred to as the ***targets*** of the virtual folders in the namespace.

For example, Figure 3-13 shows three file servers, each with its own shared folders. Normally, a user looking for a particular file would have to search the folders on each server individually.

Figure 3-13

File server shares integrated into a DFS namespace

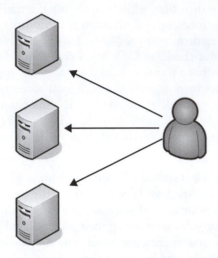

By creating a DFS namespace that contains a virtual representation of the shared folders on all three servers, as shown in Figure 3-14, the user can search through a single directory structure. When the user attempts to open a file in the DFS namespace, the namespace server forwards the access request to the file server where the file is actually stored, which then supplies it to the user.

Figure 3-14

User access requests are forwarded by the DFS server

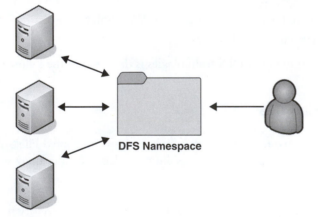

DFS Namespace

Creating a DFS namespace enables users to locate their files more easily, irrespective of where they are actually located. You can create multiple namespaces on a single server and create additional namespace servers for a single namespace.

REPLICATING SHARES

Creating a DFS namespace does not, by itself, affect the actual locations of the files and folders listed in the namespace, nor does it improve file services to remote sites. The DFS Replication role service performs these tasks. DFS Replication is a multimaster replication engine that can create and maintain copies of shared folders on different servers throughout an enterprise network.

Multimaster replication is a technique in which duplicate copies of a file are all updated on a regular basis, no matter which copy changes. For example, if a file is duplicated on four different servers, a user can access any one of the four copies and modify the file as needed. The replication engine then takes the changes made to the modified copy and uses them to update the other three copies.

➕ **MORE INFORMATION**

The alternative to multimaster replication is *single master replication,* a much simpler concept in which a user's changes to one copy of a file are propagated, in one direction only, to the other copies.

At its simplest, DFS Replication service copies files from one location to another. However, DFS Replication also works in tandem with DFS Namespaces to provide unified services, such as the following:

- Data distribution—By replicating shared folders to multiple locations, DFS enables users to access the files they need from a local server, minimizing internetwork traffic and its accompanying delays due to network latency. In addition, by integrating the replicated copies into a DFS namespace, users all over the enterprise can browse the same directory tree. When a user attempts to access a file, the namespace server directs the request to the nearest replica.

- Load balancing—A DFS namespace by itself can simplify the process by which users locate the files they need, but if people all over the network need access to the same file, the requests are still directed to the same file server, which can cause a performance bottleneck in the computer itself or on the subnet where the file server is located. By replicating shared folders to multiple servers, DFS can distribute the access requests, thus preventing any one server from shouldering the entire traffic load.

- Data collection—Instead of installing backup solutions at remote sites or performing backups over a WAN connection, DFS enables administrators to replicate data from remote file servers to a central location, where the backups can take place. Windows Server 2008 DFS uses **Remote Differential Compression (RDC)**, a protocol that conserves network bandwidth by detecting changes in files and transmitting only the modified data to the destination. This conserves bandwidth and greatly reduces the time needed for the replication process.

Configuring DFS

Implementing DFS on a Windows Server 2008 computer is more complicated than simply installing the File Services role and the Distributed File System role services.

After the role and role services are in place, you have to perform at least some of the following configuration tasks:

- Create a namespace
- Add folders to the namespace
- Configure referral order
- Create a replication group

The following sections examine these tasks in detail.

CREATING A NAMESPACE

TAKE NOTE *

All versions of the Windows Server 2008 and Windows Server 2003 operating systems can function as DFS namespace servers. However, the Standard Edition and Web Edition products can only host a single DFS namespace, while the Enterprise Edition and Datacenter Edition versions can host multiple namespaces.

To create a DFS namespace, you must have a Windows Server 2008 or Windows Server 2003 computer with the Distributed File System role and the DFS Namespace role service installed. After you have created a namespace, this computer, the *namespace server*, will maintain the list of shared folders represented in the virtual directory tree and respond to network user requests for access to those shared folders.

In essence, the namespace server functions just like a file server, except that when a user requests access to a file in the DFS directory tree, the namespace server replies, not with the file itself, but with a *referral* specifying the file's actual location. The DFS client on the user's computer then sends its access request to the file server listed in the referral, and receives the file in return.

TAKE NOTE *

To raise the domain functional level of a domain, use the Active Directory Domains and Trusts console.

Although the DFS namespace does not include the actual data files of the shared folders that populate it, it does require some storage space of its own to maintain the directory structure that forms the virtual directory tree. The namespace server must have an NTFS volume to create the shared folder that will host the namespace.

The DFS Namespaces role service supports two basic types of namespaces: stand-alone and domain-based. Domain-based namespaces come in two modes: Windows Server 2008 mode and Windows 2000 Server mode, which are based on the domain functional level of the domain hosting the namespace.

Table 3-2 summarizes the differences between these three namespace configurations.

Table 3-2

Comparison of Stand-alone and Domain-based DFS Namespaces

STAND-ALONE NAMESPACE	DOMAIN-BASED NAMESPACE (WINDOWS SERVER 2008 MODE)	DOMAIN-BASED NAMESPACE (WINDOWS 2000 SERVER MODE)
Path to namespace is \\server\root	Path to namespace is \\domain\root	Path to namespace is \\domain\root
Server name is exposed	Server name is hidden	Server name is hidden
Namespace can contain up to 50,000 folders	Namespace can contain up to 50,000 folders	Namespace can contain approximately 5,000 folders. (The Active Directory namespace object can be no larger than 5 megabytes.)
Can be a domain controller, a member server in a domain, or a stand-alone server	Must be a domain controller or member server in the domain hosting the namespace	Must be a domain controller or member server in the domain hosting the namespace
Namespace stored in system registry and memory cache	Namespace stored in Active Directory and memory cache on each namespace server	Namespace stored in Active Directory and memory cache on each namespace server
Supports the use of only one namespace server for a single namespace (except for clustered servers)	Supports the use of multiple namespace servers (in the same domain) for a single namespace	Supports the use of multiple namespace servers (in the same domain) for a single namespace
No Active Directory domain services required	Requires Active Directory using the Windows Server 2008 domain functional level	Requires Active Directory using at least the Windows 2000 Mixed domain functional level
Supports access-based enumeration	Supports access-based enumeration	Does not support access-based enumeration
Supports DFS Replication of folders when namespace server is joined to an Active Directory domain	Supports DFS Replication of folders	Supports DFS Replication of folders
Can be part of a server cluster	The namespace cannot be a clustered resource, although the namespace server can be part of a cluster	The namespace cannot be a clustered resource, although the namespace server can be part of a cluster

To select the namespace type you should use for your network, consider the following factors:

- If you are deploying DFS on an Active Directory network, you should select the domain-based namespace, unless some of the computers that will be namespace servers are running Windows Server 2003 or an earlier version, and you intend to add more than 5,000 folders to the namespace.

- If all of the computers that will be namespace servers are running Windows Server 2008, a domain-based namespace in Windows Server 2008 mode will provide the most fault tolerance and scalability.

- If you are deploying DFS on a network that does not use Active Directory, your only choice is to create a stand-alone namespace. In this case, you are limited to one namespace server and no DFS replication.

To create a new namespace, use the following procedure.

 CREATE A NAMESPACE

GET READY. Log on to Windows Server 2008 using an account with domain administrative privileges. When the logon process is completed, close the Initial Configuration Tasks window and any other windows that appear. Make sure that the File Services role, with the DFS Namespaces role service, is installed on the computer.

1. Click **Start**, and then click **Administrative Tools** > **DFS Management**. The DFS Management console appears, as shown in Figure 3-15.

Figure 3-15

The DFS Management console

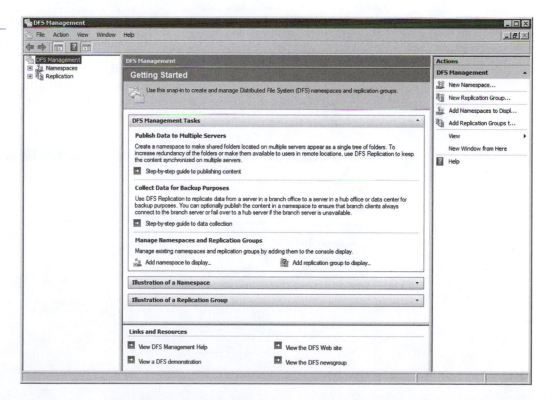

 The DFS Management snap-in can run only on Windows Server 2008, Windows Server 2003 R2, and Windows XP SP2 computers.

2. In the scope pane, right-click the **Namespaces** node and, from the context menu, select **New Namespace.** The New Namespace Wizard appears and displays the Namespace Server page, as shown in Figure 3-16.

Figure 3-16

The Namespace Server page of the New Namespace Wizard

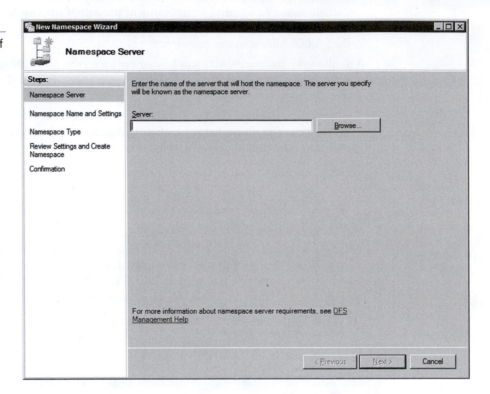

3. In the Server text box, key the name of or browse to the server that you want to host the namespace, and then click **Next.** If the DFS Namespace system service is not running on the server you specified, the wizard offers to start the service and set its Startup Type to Automatic. Click **Yes** to continue. The Namespace Name and Settings page appears, as shown in Figure 3-17.

Figure 3-17

The Namespace Name and Settings page

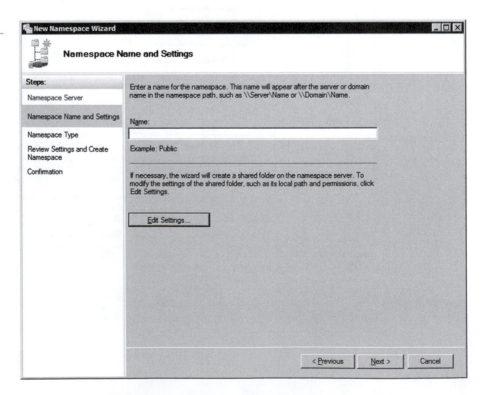

4. In the Name text box, key the name that will become the root of the namespace. Then, click **Edit Settings**. The Edit Settings dialog box appears, as shown in Figure 3-18.

Figure 3-18

The Edit Settings dialog box

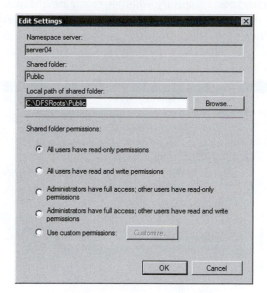

The root of the namespace is an actual share that the wizard will create on the namespace server, containing the referrals that point to the shared folders that populate the namespace. Users on the network will access the DFS namespace by browsing to this share or using its name in the form *server**root* or *domain**root*.

5. Under Shared Folder Permissions, select one of the radio buttons to configure the share permissions for the namespace root. To configure the share permissions manually, select the **Use custom permissions** option and click **Customize**. A Permissions dialog box appears, in which you can configure the share permissions in the usual manner.

6. Click **OK** to close the Permissions dialog box, and click **OK** again to close the Edit Settings dialog box. Then, click **Next.** The Namespace Type page appears, as shown in Figure 3-19.

Figure 3-19

The Namespace Type page

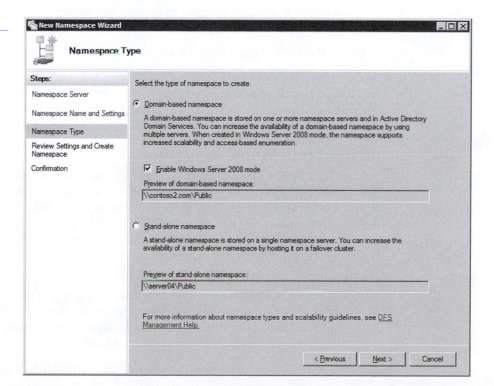

7. Select one of the option buttons to create either a Domain-based namespace or a Stand-alone namespace. If you choose the former, use the Enable Windows Server 2008 Mode checkbox to specify whether to create the namespace in Windows Server 2008 mode or Windows 2000 mode. Then, click **Next**. The Review Settings and Create Namespace page appears, as shown in Figure 3-20.

Figure 3-20

The Review Settings and Create Namespace page

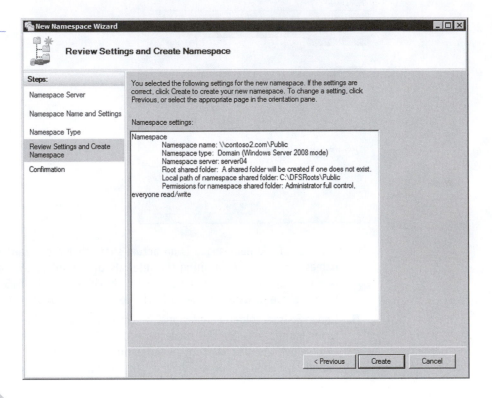

8. Review the settings you have selected and click **Create** to create and configure the namespace. After the process is completed, the Confirmation page appears, indicating that the wizard successfully created the namespace, and the namespace appears in the console's scope pane.

CLOSE the DFS Management console.

At any time after you create a domain-based namespace, you can add namespace servers, for load balancing or fault tolerance, by right-clicking the namespace and, from the context menu, selecting Add Namespace Server. Every namespace server must have the DFS Namespaces role service installed and must have an NTFS volume to store the namespace share.

TAKE NOTE *

Adding namespace servers to an existing namespace replicates only the virtual directory structure, not the target folders and files referred to by the virtual folders. To replicate the target folders, you must use DFS Replication, as discussed later in this lesson.

ADDING FOLDERS TO A NAMESPACE

After you have created a namespace, you can begin to build its virtual directory structure by adding folders. You can add two types of folders to a namespace, those with targets and those without. A folder with a target points to one or more shared folders on the same or another server. Users browsing the namespace will see the folder you add, plus all of the subfolders and files that exist in the target folder beneath it. You can also, purely for organizational purposes, create folders in the namespace that do not have targets.

You can add as many targets to a folder as you need. Typically, administrators add multiple targets to namespace folders to balance the server load and give users at different locations local access to the folders. Adding multiple targets means that you will have identical copies of the target on different servers. These duplicate targets must remain identical, so you will later configure DFS Replication to keep them updated.

To add folders to a DFS namespace, use the following procedure.

 ADD FOLDERS TO A NAMESPACE

GET READY. Log on to Windows Server 2008 using an account with domain administrative privileges. When the logon process is completed, close the Initial Configuration Tasks window and any other windows that appear.

1. Click **Start**, and then click **Administrative Tools** > **DFS Management**. The DFS Management console appears.

2. Right-click a namespace in the scope pane and, from the context menu, select **New Folder**. The New Folder dialog box appears, as shown in Figure 3-21.

Figure 3-21

The New Folder dialog box

3. In the Name text box, key the name of the folder as you want it to appear in the DFS virtual directory tree. Then, click **OK**. The new folder appears beneath the namespace.

   Because this folder has no target, it exists in the namespace only to build up the virtual directory structure and cannot contain any files.

4. Right-click the folder you just created and, from the context menu, select **New Folder**. The New Folder dialog box appears again.

5. In the Name text box, key the name of the folder you want to appear beneath the first folder you created.

6. Click **Add**. The Add Folder Target dialog box appears, as shown in Figure 3-22.

Figure 3-22

The Add Folder Target dialog box

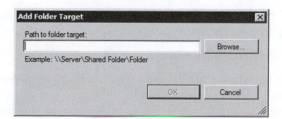

7. Click **Browse**. The Browse for Shared Folders dialog box appears, as shown in Figure 3-23.

Figure 3-23

The Browse for Shared Folders dialog box

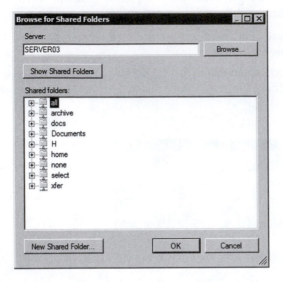

TAKE NOTE* When referring to folder targets, the term "server" refers to any Windows computer with one or more shared folders on it. Targets for a DFS namespace do not have to be running a Server version of Windows.

8. Perform one of the following procedures to specify the shared folder that you want to be the target. Then, click **OK** to close the Browse For Shared Folders dialog box.

   • Select one of the existing shares in the Shared Folders list on the current server shown in the Server text box. Then click **OK.**

   • Click **Browse** to select a different server on the network and select one of its shares. Then click **OK.**

   • Select a server and click **New Shared Folder** to display the Create Share dialog box, which you can use to create a new shared folder and set its share permissions. Then, click **OK** to close the Create Share dialog box.

9. Click **OK** to close the Add Folder Target dialog box.

10. Repeat steps 6–9 to add additional targets to the folder. When you add multiple targets to a folder, the console prompts you to create a replication group to keep the targets synchronized. Click **No,** because the process of configuring replication is covered later in this lesson.

11. Click **OK** to close the New Folder dialog box. The folder is added to the virtual directory tree in the scope pane.

   CLOSE the DFS Management console.

You can continue to populate the namespace by adding more folders to the virtual directory structure or by adding more targets to existing folders. When you select an untargeted folder in the scope pane, you can select New Folder from the context menu to create another subordinate folder (targeted or untargeted). However, to add a subfolder to a targeted folder, you must create the subfolder in the target share, and it will appear in the namespace.

CONTROLLING REFERRAL ORDER

When you add more than one target to a folder in a DFS namespace, the namespace server sends referrals containing all of the targets to clients attempting to access that folder. The

client tries to connect to the first target in any referral it receives and, if the first target is unavailable, tries to access the second, and then the third, and so forth. As a result, the order of the targets in the referrals is critical if the DFS implementation is to successfully provide users with local file access and control WAN traffic levels.

By default, when a DFS client attempts to access a folder with targets, the namespace server notes the site where the client is located and, in its referral, lists the targets at the same site first, in random order, followed by the targets at other sites, from the lowest to the highest cost. You can modify this default behavior by manipulating the referral controls found in the Properties sheet for every namespace, targeted folder, and target.

CONFIGURING NAMESPACE REFERRALS

In a namespace's Properties sheet, on the Referral tab, as shown in Figure 3-24, you can change the Ordering Method value, which alters the way in which the server specifies the targets at different sites from the client, using the following values:

- Lowest cost
- Random order
- Exclude targets outside of the client's site

Figure 3-24

The Referrals tab of a namespace's Properties sheet

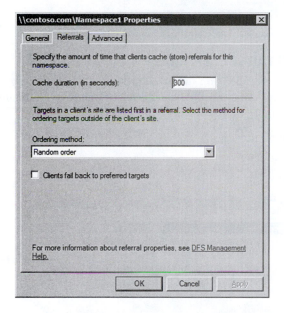

The fact that the targets in the same site as the client are supplied in random order by default effectively balances the client load among the servers at that site. Selecting the Random Order option for the Ordering Method value does the same load balancing for the targets at other sites. Selecting the *Exclude targets outside of the client's site* option prevents the clients from accessing targets at other sites, thus conserving WAN bandwidth. Note, however, that the Ordering Method value does not affect the order of the targets at the same site as the client, which always appear first in the referrals, and in random order.

CONFIGURING FOLDER REFERRALS

In a targeted folder's Properties sheet, on the Referral tab, as shown in Figure 3-25, you can configure the nameserver to restrict its referrals for that folder only to servers at the same site as the client.

Figure 3-25

The Referrals tab of a targeted folder's Properties sheet

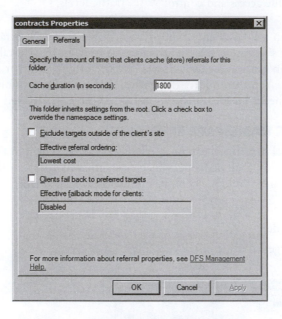

CONFIGURING TARGET REFERRALS

In a target's Properties sheet, on the Advanced tab, as shown in Figure 3-26, you can override the referral ordering values for the namespace and the folder containing the target by selecting one of the following options:

- First among all targets
- Last among all targets
- First among targets of equal cost
- Last among targets of equal cost

Figure 3-26

The Advanced tab of a target's Properties sheet

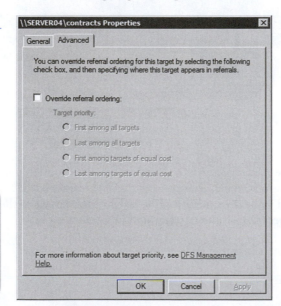

TAKE NOTE *

You can also disable referrals for the selected target entirely by clearing the checkbox on the General tab of this Properties sheet.

These individual target settings are most useful when you have copies of a target folder that you want clients to access only as a last resort. For example, you might have a hot standby file server on the network, in case another file server fails. To streamline the failover process, you add the shares on the standby server as targets to the appropriate DFS namespace folders, so that you don't have to take the time to do this if a server fails. Because you don't want users to

access the standby server unless there is a failure, you configure all of the targets with the *Last among all targets* option, so that no matter what site clients are in, they will never access the standby shares unless all of the other copies of the shares are offline.

ENABLING CLIENT FAILBACK

Client failback is the ability of DFS clients to revert to targets that were previously unavailable, when they become available again and are of lower cost than the target the client is using. For example, if a client cannot access the target at its same site, because the server is offline, it will access the lowest cost target at another site. When Client Failback is enabled, the client will revert to the target at its same site, when it becomes available.

You can enable Client Failback for an entire namespace by selecting the *Clients fail back to preferred targets* checkbox on the Referrals tab of the namespace's Properties sheet. You can also enable Client Failback for an individual folder by selecting the checkbox of the same name on the Referrals tab of its Properties sheet.

CONFIGURING DFS REPLICATION

When a folder in a DFS namespace has multiple targets, the targets should be identical, so that users can access the files from any of the targets invisibly. However, users usually modify the files in a folder as they work with them, causing the targets to differ. To resynchronize the target folders, DFS includes a replication engine that automatically propagates changes from one target to all of the others.

To enable replication for a DFS folder with multiple targets, you must create a **replication group**, which is a collection of servers, known as *members*, each of which contains a target for a particular DFS folder. In its simplest form, a folder with two targets requires a replication group with two members: the servers hosting the targets. At regular intervals, the DFS Replication engine on the namespace server triggers replication events between the two members, using the RDC protocol, so that their target folders remain synchronized.

TAKE NOTE*

Although terms such as "group" and "member" are typically associated with Active Directory, DFS Replication does not use them to refer to Active Directory objects. In fact, unlike the File Replication Service (FRS) in Windows Server 2003, DFS Replication does not require Active Directory, and can function on stand-alone, as well as domain-based, namespace servers.

DFS Replication need not be so simple, however, because it is also highly scalable and configurable. A replication group can have up to 256 members, with 256 replicated folders, and each server can be a member of up to 256 replication groups, with as many as 256 connections (128 incoming and 128 outgoing). A member server can support up to one terabyte of replicated files, with up to eight million replicated files per volume.

In addition to scaling the replication process, you can also configure it to occur at specific times and limit the amount of bandwidth it can utilize. This enables you to exercise complete control over the WAN bandwidth utilized by the replication process.

➕ MORE INFORMATION

For each member server, the number of replication groups multiplied by the number of replicated folders multiplied by the number of simultaneous replication connections should not exceed 1,024. If you are having trouble keeping below this limit, the best solution is to schedule replication to occur at different times for different folders, thus limiting the number of simultaneous connections.

The larger the DFS deployment, the more complicated the replication process becomes. By default, replication groups use a *full mesh topology*, which means that every member in a group replicates with every other member. For relatively small DFS deployments, this is a satisfactory solution, but on larger installations, the full mesh topology can generate a huge amount of network traffic. In such cases, you might want to opt for a *hub/spoke topology*, which enables you to limit the replication traffic to specific pairs of members, as shown in Figure 3-27.

Figure 3-27

The full mesh and hub/spoke replication topologies

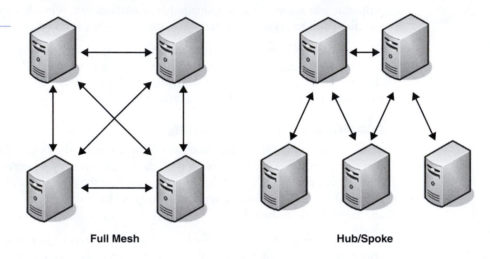

Full Mesh   Hub/Spoke

TAKE NOTE*
No matter which topology you use, DFS replication between two members is always bidirectional by default. This means that the Replicate Folder Wizard always establishes two connections, one in each direction, between every pair of computers involved in a replication relationship. This is true in a hub/spoke as well as a full mesh topology. To create unidirectional replication relationships, you can either disable selected connections between the members of a replication group in the DFS Management console or use share permissions to prevent the replication process from updating files on certain member servers.

To create a replication group and initiate the replication process, use the following procedure.

TAKE NOTE*
In addition to manually creating replication groups, the system prompts you automatically to create a group when you create a second target for a previously targeted folder.

 CREATE A REPLICATION GROUP

GET READY. Log on to Windows Server 2008 using an account with domain administrative privileges. When the logon process is completed, close the Initial Configuration Tasks window and any other windows that appear.

1. Click **Start**, and then click **Administrative Tools** > **DFS Management**. The DFS Management console appears.

2. Right-click a folder with multiple targets in the scope pane and, from the context menu, select **Replicate Folder**. The Replicate Folder wizard appears, displaying the Replication Group and Replicated Folder Name page, as shown in Figure 3-28.

Figure 3-28

The Replication Group and
Replicated Folder Name page
of the Replicate Folder wizard

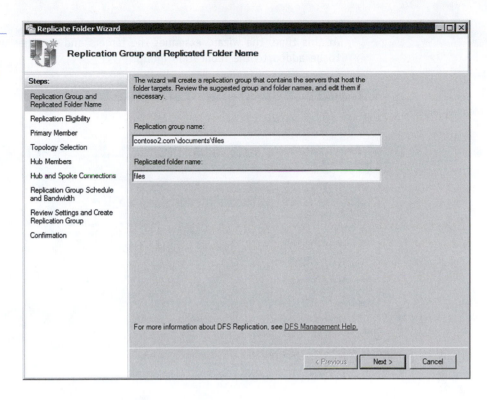

3. Click **Next** to accept the default values for the Replication Group Name and Replicated Folder Name fields. The Replication Eligibility page appears, as shown in Figure 3-29.

Figure 3-29

The Replication Eligibility page

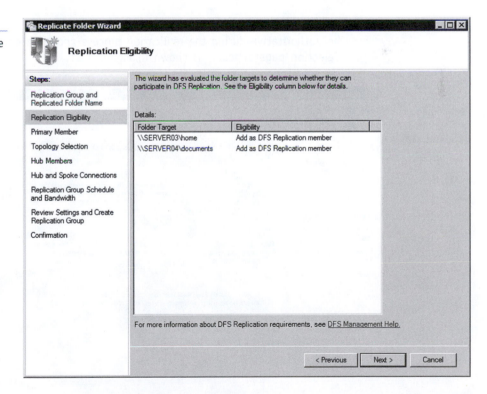

In the Replication Group Name text box, the name that the wizard suggests for the replication group consists of the full path from the domain or server to the selected folder. The suggested name for the Replicated Folder Name field is the name of the selected folder. Although it is possible to modify these values, there is usually no compelling reason to do so.

4. Click **Next** to continue. The Primary Member page appears, as shown in Figure 3-30. At this time, the wizard examines the targets and specifies whether they are eligible to be added to the replication group.

Figure 3-30

The Primary Member page

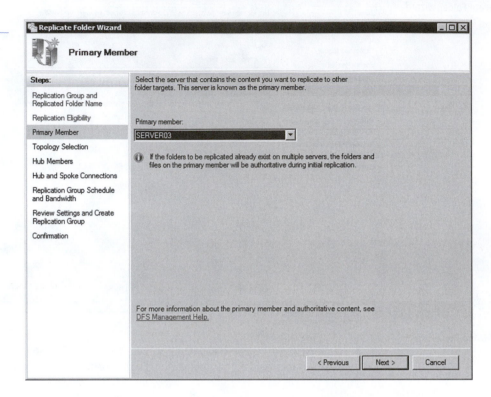

5. In the Primary Member dropdown list, select the target server that you want to be authoritative during the replication process and then click **Next**. The Topology Selection page appears, as shown in Figure 3-31.

Figure 3-31

The Topology Selection page

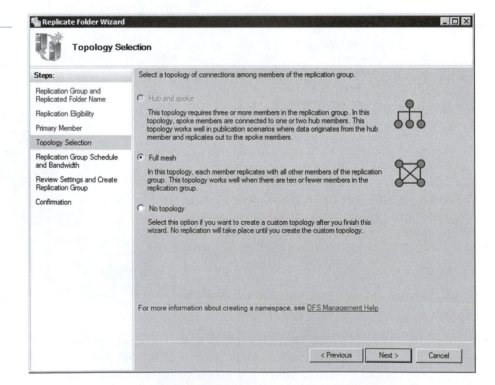

During the replication process, the files from the server that you designate as the primary member will be copied to the other targets in the replication group. If any of the files in one target folder differ from their counterparts in the others, DFS Replication will use the primary member version to overwrite all other versions.

6. Select a replication topology from one of the following options and click **Next**. The Replication Group Schedule and Bandwidth page appears, as shown in Figure 3-32.

   • Hub and Spoke—Each member is designated as a hub or a spoke. Hubs replicate with each other and with spokes, but spokes only replicate with hubs, not with each other. This topology requires the folder to have at least three member servers.

   • Full Mesh—Every member replicates with every other member. This is the default setting.

   • No topology—Indicates that you intend to create a customized topology after the wizard is completed. Replication will not occur until you create a topology.

Figure 3-32

The Replication Group Schedule and Bandwidth page

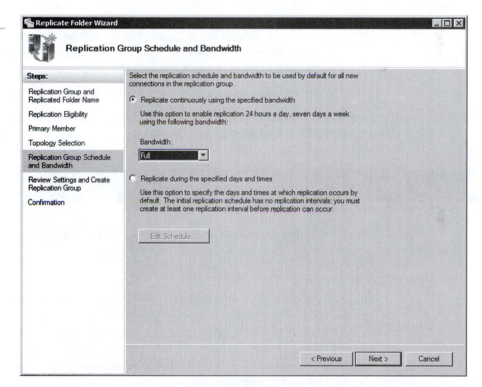

7. Configure one of the following replication scheduling/bandwidth options and then click **Next**. The Review Settings and Create Replication Group page appears.

   • Replicate continuously using the specified bandwidth—Select this option and use the Bandwidth dropdown list to specify how much network bandwidth the replication process should be permitted to use.

- Replicate during the specified days and times—Select this option and click **Edit Schedule** to display the Edit Schedule dialog box shown in Figure 3-33, in which you can specify the days of the week and the hours of the day that replication is permitted to occur.

Figure 3-33

The Edit Schedule dialog box

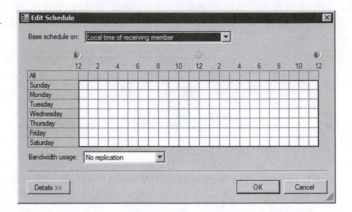

8. Review the settings you selected and click **Create**. When the wizard completes the configuration process, click **Close**. The replication group appears under the Replication node in the scope pain, and the replication process begins as soon as the configuration parameters propagate throughout the domain.

CLOSE the DFS Management console.

After you have created a replication group, it appears under the replication node in the scope pane of the DFS Management console.

Using File Server Resource Manager

THE BOTTOM LINE

File Server Resource Manager enables administrators to monitor and regulate the storage consumed by network users.

Although the price of hard disk storage continues to plummet, users still often have a habit of consuming all of the storage space that administrators give them. This is especially true when you consider the large sizes of the audio and video media files that many users store on their drives. In an enterprise environment, it is important to monitor and regulate the amount of storage space consumed by users, so that each user receives a fair share and server resources are not overwhelmed by irresponsible user storage practices.

When you install the File Server Resource Manager role service, Windows Server 2008 installs the File Server Resource Manager (FSRM) console, first introduced in Windows Server 2003 R2, which provides tools that enable file server administrators to monitor and regulate their server storage, by performing the following tasks:

- Establish quotas that limit the amount of storage space allotted to each user.
- Create screens that prevent users from storing specific types of files on server drives.
- Create templates that simplify the process of applying quotas and screens.
- Automatically send email messages to users and/or administrators when quotas are exceeded or nearly exceeded.
- Generate reports providing details of users' storage activities.

These tasks are discussed in the following sections.

Working with Quotas

> Quotas can warn administrators of excessive storage utilization trends or apply hard restrictions to user accounts.

In Windows Server 2008, a quota is simply a limit on the disk space a user is permitted to consume in a particular volume or folder. Quotas are based on file ownership. Windows automatically makes a user the owner of all files that he or she creates on a server volume. The quota system tracks all of the files owned by each user and adds their sizes. When the total size of a given user's files reaches the quota specified by the server administrator, the system takes action, also specified by the administrator.

The actions the system takes when a user approaches or reaches a quota are highly configurable. For example, administrators can configure quotas to be hard or soft. A hard quota prohibits users from consuming any disk space beyond the allotted amount, while a soft quota allows the user storage space beyond the allotted amount and just sends an email notification to the user and/or administrator. Administrators can also specify the thresholds at which the system should send notifications and configure the quota server to generate event log entries and reports in response to quota thresholds.

CREATING A QUOTA TEMPLATE

For enterprise networks, you should create quota templates to manage quota assignments on a large scale. A quota template is a collection of settings that define the following:

- Whether a quota should be hard or soft
- What thresholds FSRM should apply to the quota
- What actions FSRM should take when a user reaches a threshold

The File Server Resource Manager console includes several predefined templates, which you can use to create your own template. To create a quota template, use the following procedure.

 CREATE A QUOTA TEMPLATE

GET READY. Log on to Windows Server 2008 using an account with domain administrative privileges. When the logon process is completed, close the Initial Configuration Tasks window and any other windows that appear.

1. Click **Start**, and then click **Administrative Tools** > **File Server Resource Manager**. The File Server Resource Manager console appears, as shown in Figure 3-34.

Figure 3-34

The File Server Resource Manager console

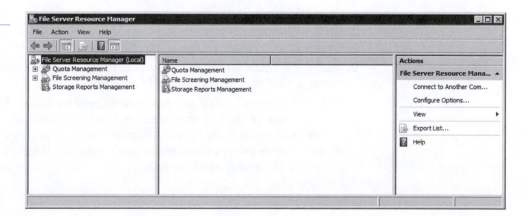

2. Expand the **Quota Management** node, right-click the **Quota Templates** node and, from the context menu, select **Create Quota Template**. The Create Quota Template dialog box appears, as shown in Figure 3-35.

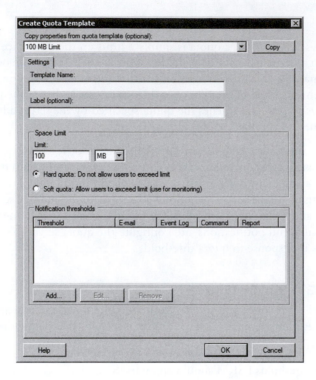

3. If you want to create a new quota template based on the settings in one of the existing templates, click the **Copy properties from quota template** dropdown list to select a template and click **Copy**. The settings from the template appear in the dialog box, so that you can modify them as needed.

4. In the Template Name text box, key the name you will use to identify the template.

5. Optionally, in the Label text box, you can key a term that will be associated with all of the quotas you create using the template.

6. In the Space Limit box, specify the amount of storage space you want to allot to each individual user and specify whether you want to create a hard quota or a soft quota.

7. In the Notification Thresholds box, click **Add**. The Add Threshold dialog box appears.

8. In the *Generate notifications when usage reaches (%)* text box, specify a threshold in the form of a percentage of the storage quota.

9. Use the controls on the following tabs to specify the actions you want taken when a user reaches the specified threshold:

   • E-mail Message—Select the appropriate checkbox to specify whether you want the system to send an email message to an administrator, to the user, or both, as shown in Figure 3-36. For administrators, you can specify the email addresses of one or more persons separated by semicolons. For the user, you can modify the text of the default email message.

Figure 3-36

The E-mail Message tab on the
Add Threshold dialog box

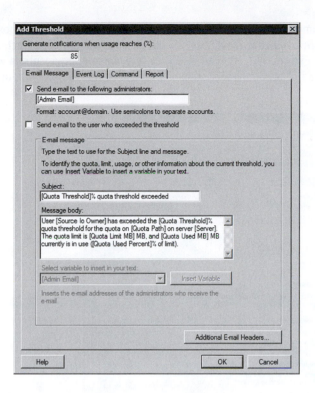

The Windows Server 2008 computer must be running the Simple Mail Transfer Protocol (SMTP) service to be able to send email messages. To install SMTP, you must use Server Manager to add the SMTP Server feature.

• Event Log—Select the **Send warning to event log** checkbox to create a log entry when a user reaches the threshold, as shown in Figure 3-37. You can modify the wording of the log entry in the text box provided.

Figure 3-37

The Event Log tab on the Add
Threshold dialog box

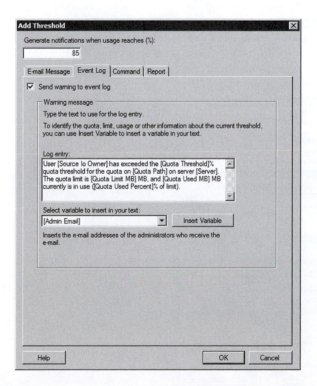

• Command—Select the **Run this command or script** checkbox to specify a program or script file that the system should execute when a user reaches the threshold, as shown in Figure 3-38. You can also specify command arguments, a working directory, and the type of account the system should use to run the program or script.

Figure 3-38

The Command tab on the Add Threshold dialog box

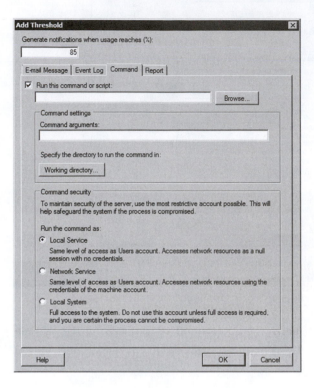

• Report—Select the **Generate reports** checkbox, and then select the checkboxes for the reports you want the system to generate, as shown in Figure 3-39. You can also specify that the system email the selected reports to an administrator or to the user who exceeded the threshold.

Figure 3-39

The Report tab on the Add Threshold dialog box

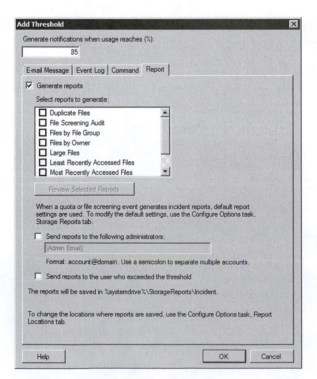

10. Click **OK** to close the dialog box and add the new threshold to the Notification Thresholds list on the Create Quota Template dialog box.

11. Repeat steps 7–10 to create additional thresholds, if desired. When you have created all of the thresholds you need, click **OK** to create the quota template.

CLOSE the File Server Resource Manager console.

Using quota templates simplifies the quota management process, in much the same way as assigning permissions to groups, rather than users. If you use a template to create quotas, and you want to change the properties of all of your quotas at once, you can simply modify the template, and the system applies the changes to all of the associated quotas automatically.

CREATING A QUOTA

After you have created your quota templates, you can create the quotas themselves. To create a quota, use the following procedure.

 CREATE A QUOTA

GET READY. Log on to Windows Server 2008 using an account with domain administrative privileges. When the logon process is completed, close the Initial Configuration Tasks window and any other windows that appear.

1. Click **Start**, and then click **Administrative Tools** > **File Server Resource Manager**. The File Server Resource Manager console appears.

2. Expand the **Quota Management** node, right-click the **Quotas** folder and, from the context menu, select **Create Quota**. The Create Quota dialog box appears, as shown in Figure 3-40.

Figure 3-40

The Create Quota dialog box

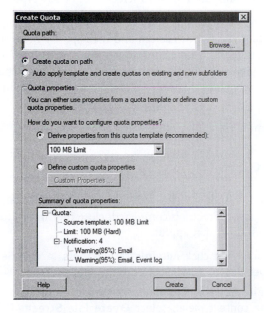

3. In the Quota Path text box, key or browse to the name of the volume or folder for which you want to create a quota.

4. Select one of the following application options:
   • Create quota on path—Creates a single quota for the specified volume or folder.
   • Auto apply template and create quotas on existing and new subfolders—Causes FSRM to automatically create a quota, based on a template, for each subfolder in the designated path, and for every new subfolder created in that path.

5. Select one of the following properties options:
   - Derive properties from this quota template—Configures the quota using the settings of the template you select from the dropdown list.
   - Define custom quota properties—Enables you to specify custom settings for the quota. Clicking the Custom Properties button opens a Quota Properties dialog box for the selected volume or folder, which contains the same controls as the Create Quota Template dialog box discussed in the previous section.
6. Click **Create**. The new quota appears in the console's details pane.

CLOSE the File Server Resource Manager console.

Even if you do not install the File Server Resource Manager role service, quotas are available on NTFS volumes, but these so-called NTFS quotas are limited to controlling storage on entire volumes on a per-user basis. When you create FSRM quotas for volumes or folders, however, they apply to all users. NTFS quotas are also limited to creating event log entries only, while FSRM quotas can also send email notifications, execute commands, and generate reports, as well as log events.

Creating a File Screen

FSRM, in addition to creating storage quotas, enables administrators to create file screens, which prevent users from storing specific types of files on a server drive.

Administrators typically use file screening to keep large audio and video files off of server drives because they consume a lot of space and users frequently obtain them illegally. Obviously, in an organization that utilizes these types of files, screening them would be inappropriate, but you can configure FSRM to screen files of any type.

The process of creating file screens is quite similar to that of creating storage quotas. You choose the types of files you want to screen and then specify the actions you want the server to take when a user attempts to store a forbidden file type. As with quotas, the server can send emails, create log entries, execute commands, and generate reports. Administrators can also create file screen templates that simplify the process of deploying file screens throughout the enterprise.

To create a file screen, use the following procedure.

 CREATE A FILE SCREEN

GET READY. Log on to Windows Server 2008 using an account with domain administrative privileges. When the logon process is completed, close the Initial Configuration Tasks window and any other windows that appear.

1. Click **Start**, and then click **Administrative Tools** > **File Server Resource Manager**. The File Server Resource Manager console appears.
2. Expand the **File Screening Management** node, right-click the **File Screens** folder and, from the context menu, select **Create File Screen**. The Create File Screen dialog box appears, as shown in Figure 3-41.

Figure 3-41

The Create File Screen dialog box

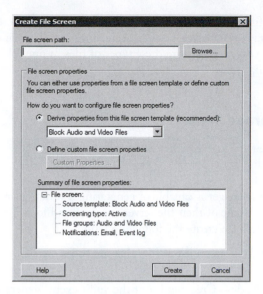

3. In the File Screen Path text box, key or browse to the name of the volume or folder that you want to screen.

4. Select one of the following properties options:

  • Derive properties from this file screen template—Configures the file screen using the settings of the template you select from the dropdown list.

  • Define custom file screen properties—Enables you to specify custom settings for the file screen. Clicking the Custom Properties button opens a File Screen Properties dialog box for the selected volume or folder, which contains the Settings tab shown in Figure 3-42, plus the same E-mail Message, Event Log, Command, and Report tabs as the Quota Properties dialog box.

Figure 3-42

The Settings tab of a File Screen Properties dialog box

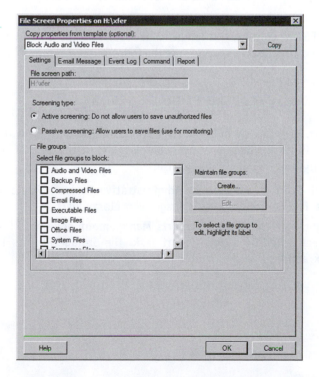

5. Click **Create**. The new file screen appears in the console's details pane.

CLOSE the File Server Resource Manager console.

You can also create file screen exceptions, which override the file screening rules inherited from a parent folder. For example, if you are screening out audio and video files from a particular volume, and you need to store these types of files in one folder, you can create an exception only for that folder.

Generating Storage Reports

Reporting is one of the keys to efficient storage management.

File Server Resource Manager is capable of generating a variety of reports that enable administrators to examine the state of their file server volumes and identify transgressors or company storage policies. FSRM can create the following reports:

- Duplicate Files—Creates a list of files that are the same size and have the same last modified date.
- File Screening Audit—Creates a list of the audit events generated by file screening violations for specific users during a specific time period.
- Files By File Group—Creates a list of files sorted by selected file groups in the File Server Resource Manager console.
- Files By Owner—Creates a list of files sorted by selected users that own them.
- Large Files—Creates a list of files conforming to a specified file spec that are a specified size or larger.
- Least Recently Accessed Files—Creates a list of files conforming to a specified file spec that have not been accessed for a specified number of days.
- Most Recently Accessed Files—Creates a list of files conforming to a specified file spec that have been accessed within a specified number of days.
- Quota Usage—Creates a list of quotas that exceed a specified percentage of the storage limit.

Using the FSRM console, you can generate reports on the fly or schedule their creation on a regular basis. To schedule a report, use the following procedure.

 GENERATE A SCHEDULED STORAGE REPORT

GET READY. Log on to Windows Server 2008 using an account with domain administrative privileges. When the logon process is completed, close the Initial Configuration Tasks window and any other windows that appear.

1. Click **Start**, and then click **Administrative Tools** > **File Server Resource Manager**. The File Server Resource Manager console appears.
2. Right-click the **Storage Reports Management** node and, from the context menu, select **Schedule a New Report Task**. The Storage Reports Task Properties dialog box appears, as shown in Figure 3-43.

Figure 3-43

The Storage Reports Task
Properties dialog box

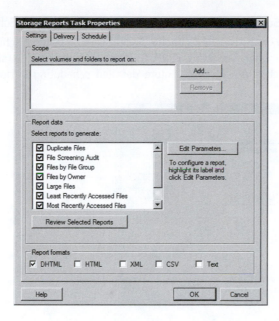

3. On the Settings tab, click **Add** and, in the Browse For Folder dialog box that
   appears, select the volume or folder on which you want a report. Repeat this step
   to select multiple volumes or folders, if desired.

4. In the Report Data box, select the reports that you want to generate. When you
   select a report and click **Edit Parameters**, a Report Parameters dialog box appears,
   in which you can configure the parameters for that specific report.

5. In the Report Formats box, select the checkboxes for the formats you want FSRM
   to use when creating the reports.

6. If you want FSRM to send the reports to administrators via email, click the **Delivery** tab, as shown in Figure 3-44, select the **Send reports to the following
   administrators** checkbox, and key one or more email addresses (separated by semicolons) in the text box.

Figure 3-44

The Delivery tab of the Storage
Reports Task Properties dialog
box

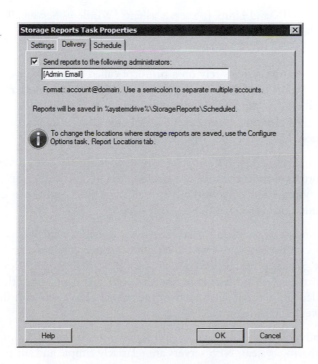

7. Click the **Schedule** tab and then click **Create Schedule**. A Schedule dialog box appears.

8. Click **New**, and use the Schedule Task, Start Time, and Schedule Task Daily controls to specify when you want FSRM to create the reports, as shown in Figure 3-45. You can also click **Advanced** for more detailed scheduling options.

Figure 3-45

The Schedule dialog box

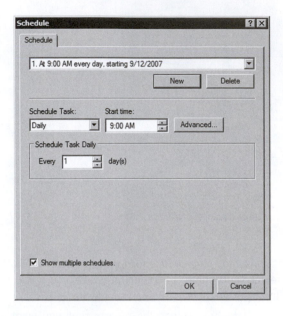

9. Click **OK** to close the Schedule dialog box and click **OK** again to close the Storage Reports Task Properties dialog box.

CLOSE the File Server Resource Manager console.

The report is now added to the schedule. The system will generate it at the specified time.

Using Services for NFS

 THE BOTTOM LINE
To support UNIX and Linux file server clients, Windows Server 2008 supports the Network File System (NFS).

Windows operating systems rely on a protocol called *Server Message Blocks (SMB)* for their file sharing, but in the UNIX world, the standard is the *Network File System (NFS)*. NFS was originally developed by Sun Microsystems in the 1980s, but they released it to the public domain, and the Internet Engineering Task Force (IETF) standardized NFS as RFC 1813, "NFS Version 3 Protocol Specification" in 1995.

As defined in RFC 1813, NFS is a "machine, operating system, network architecture, and transport protocol independent" service designed to "[provide] transparent remote access to shared file systems across networks." Virtually all UNIX and Linux distributions available today include both NFS client and server support.

To accommodate organizations that have heterogeneous networks containing both Windows and UNIX computers, Windows Server 2008 includes the Services for Network File System role service, which provides NFS Server and NFS Client capabilities. Simply stated, an NFS server exports part of its file system and the NFS client integrates the exported information, a process called "mounting," into its own file system. The client can then access the server's files as if they were a local resource.

In NFS, the bulk of the file-sharing process rests on the client. Compared to the Windows SMB file-sharing system, NFS servers are relatively simple and, in technical terms, dumb. NFS servers simply respond to file access requests from clients; they do not maintain any

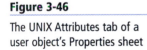

The Services for NFS implementation in Windows Server 2008 is substantially simpler than its predecessor in Windows Server 2003. The Gateway for NFS and Server for PCNFS modules, as well as the PCNFS elements of Client for NFS and the server functionality from User Name Mapping, have been removed. However, the Windows Server 2008 implementation does include some new features, including Active Directory lookup and support for 64-bit computers.

information about the client connections or the files that individual clients have open. For this reason, NFS servers are said to be *stateless*. If a server crash or a network service interruption should occur, the client just continues to resend its requests until it receives a response from the server. If the client computer fails, there is no harmful effect on the server and no need for a complex reconnection sequence.

NFS clients, on the other hand, are said to be smart, because they are responsible for integrating the files they receive from the server into their local file systems.

Obtaining User and Group Information

UNIX operating systems have their own user accounts, separate from those in Windows and Active Directory. To prevent NFS clients running on UNIX systems from having to perform a separate logon when accessing NFS shares, the Windows Server 2008 NFS Server implementation can look up the user information sent by the client and associate the UNIX account with a particular Windows account.

In UNIX, when a user successfully authenticates with an account name and password, the operating system assigns a user identifier (UID) value and a group identifier (GID) value to the user. The NFS client includes the UID and GID in the file access request messages it sends to the NFS server. For the Windows Server 2008 NFS server to grant the UNIX user access to the requested file, it must associate the UID and GID with a Windows or Active Directory account and use that account to authenticate the client.

NFS Server supports two mechanisms for obtaining user and group information, as follows:

- Active Directory lookup—NFS Server searches the Active Directory database for the UID and GID values in an NFS file access request and uses the accounts associated with those values to authenticate the client. To use this mechanism, you must install the Identity Management for UNIX and Server for Network Information Services role services in the Active Directory Domain Services role on your domain controllers. This role service extends the Active Directory schema by adding a UNIX Attributes tab containing UID and GID fields to the Properties sheet for every user and group object, as shown in Figure 3-46. You must populate these fields with the appropriate values for the UNIX clients that need access to Windows NFS shares.

Figure 3-46

The UNIX Attributes tab of a user object's Properties sheet

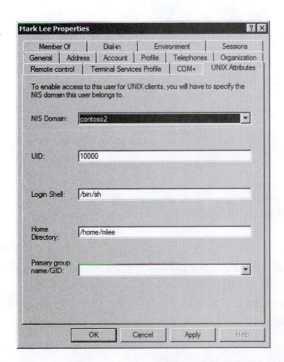

• User Name Mapping—The User Name Mapping service was the primary authentication mechanism in previous versions of Windows Services for NFS. It is essentially a lookup service that maintains a list of UNIX accounts, using their UID and GID values, and their equivalent Windows or Active Directory accounts. The server component of User Name Mapping is not included in Windows Server 2008, but NFS Server still retains the client component, which enables it to access an existing User Name Mapping server and perform account lookups.

To configure Services for NFS to use one of these lookup mechanisms, use the following procedure.

 CONFIGURE ACCOUNT LOOKUPS

GET READY. Log on to Windows Server 2008 using an account with domain administrative privileges. When the logon process is completed, close the Initial Configuration Tasks window and any other windows that appear.

1. Click **Start**, and then click **Administrative Tools** > **Services for Network File System (NFS)**. The Services for Network File System console appears, as shown in Figure 3-47.

Figure 3-47

The Services for Network File System console

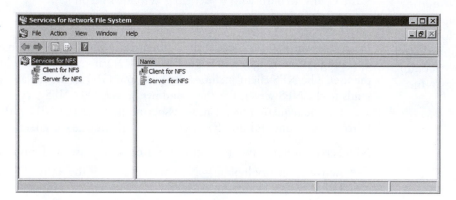

2. Right-click the **Services for NFS** node and, from the context menu, select **Properties**. The Services for NFS Properties sheet appears, as shown in Figure 3-48.

Figure 3-48

The Services for NFS Properties sheet

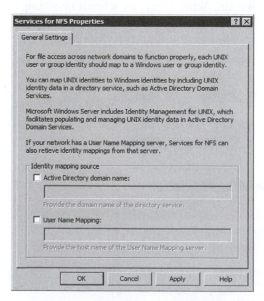

3. Select one of the following checkboxes to choose an identity mapping source:
   • Active Directory domain name—Specify the name of the domain that Services for NFS should use to look up user UIDs and GIDs.
   • User Name Mapping—Specify the name or IP address of the User Name Mapping server that Services for NFS should use to look up user UIDs and GIDs.

4. Click **OK**.

CLOSE the Services for Network File System console.

The system can now look up UIDs and GIDs with the service you specified.

Creating an NFS Share

> When you install the Services for NFS role service, the system adds an NFS Sharing tab to every volume and folder on the computer's drives.

To make a volume or folder accessible to NFS clients, you must explicitly share it, just as you would for Windows network users. To create an NFS share, use the following procedure.

CREATE AN NFS SHARE

GET READY. Log on to Windows Server 2008 using an account with domain administrative privileges. When the logon process is completed, close the Initial Configuration Tasks window and any other windows that appear.

1. Click **Start**, and then click **All Programs** > **Accessories** > **Windows Explorer**. The Windows Explorer window appears.

2. Browse to a volume or folder on a local NTFS drive, right-click it and, from the context menu, select **Properties**. The Properties sheet for the volume or folder appears.

3. Click the **NFS Sharing** tab, as shown in Figure 3-49.

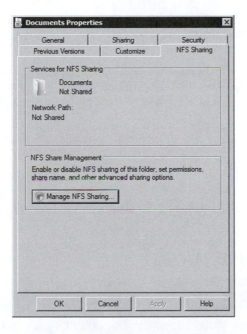

4. Click **Manage NFS Sharing**. The NFS Advanced Sharing dialog box appears, as shown in Figure 3-50.

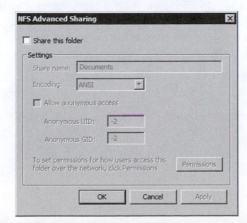

5. Select the **Share this folder** checkbox.

6. In the Share Name text box, key the name that you want NFS clients to use when accessing the folder and select one of the encoding schemes from the Encoding dropdown list.

7. If you want NFS clients to be able to access the share without authenticating, select the **Allow anonymous access** checkbox, and modify the Anonymous UID and Anonymous GID values, if necessary.

8. Click **Permissions**. The NFS Share Permissions dialog box appears, as shown in Figure 3-51.

Figure 3-51

The NFS Share Permissions dialog box

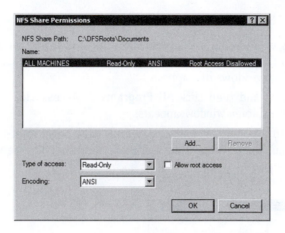

9. By default, all NFS clients have read-only access to the share. You can modify this permission by selecting different values in the *Type of access* and Encoding dropdown lists, or you can click **Add** to select users or groups and create new permission assignments.

10. Click **OK** to close the NFS Share Permissions and NFS Advanced Sharing dialog boxes.

11. Click **Close** to close the Properties sheet.

CLOSE all windows.

At this point, the share is available to NFS clients on the network.

SUMMARY SKILL MATRIX

IN THIS LESSON YOU LEARNED:

- The File Services role includes several role services that you can choose to install, including Distributed File System and Services for Network File System. Selecting individual role services can add extra configuration pages to the Add Roles Wizard.

- The Distributed File System (DFS) includes two technologies: DFS Namespaces and DFS Replication, which can simplify the process of locating files, control the amount of traffic passing over WAN links, provide users at remote sites with local file server access, configure the network to survive a WAN link failure, and facilitate consistent backups.

- DFS is a virtual namespace technology that enables you to create a single directory tree that contains references to shared folders located on various file servers, all over the network.

- A namespace server functions just like a file server, except that when a user requests access to a file in the DFS directory tree, the namespace server replies, not with the file itself, but with a referral specifying the file's actual location.

- DFS Replication works in tandem with DFS Namespaces to provide unified services, such as data distribution, load balancing, and data collection.

- To enable replication for a DFS folder with multiple targets, you must create a replication group, which is a collection of servers, known as members, each of which contains a target for a particular DFS folder.

- The File Server Resource Manager console provides tools that enable file server administrators to monitor and regulate their server storage, by establishing quotas that limit the amount of storage space allotted to each user, creating screens that prevent users from storing specific types of files on server drives, and generating reports providing details of users' storage activities.

- A quota is a limit on the disk space a user is permitted to consume in a particular volume or folder. Quotas are based on file ownership. The quota system tracks all of the files owned by each user and adds their sizes. When the total size of a given user's files reaches the quota specified by the server administrator, the system takes action.

- FSRM enables administrators to create file screens, which prevent users from storing specific types of files on a server drive. Administrators typically use file screening to keep undesirable files off of server drives.

- FSRM is capable of generating a variety of reports that enable administrators to examine the state of their file server volumes and identify transgressors or company storage policies. These reports include Duplicate Files, File Screening Audit, Files By File Group, Files By Owner, Large Files, Least Recently Accessed Files, Most Recently Accessed Files, and Quota Usage.

- NFS is a "machine, operating system, network architecture, and transport protocol independent" service designed to "[provide] transparent remote access to shared file systems across networks." Virtually all UNIX and Linux distributions available today include both NFS client and server support.

- To accommodate organizations that have heterogeneous networks containing both Windows and UNIX computers, Windows Server 2008 includes the Services for Network File System role service, which provides NFS Server and NFS Client capabilities.

- An NFS server exports part of its file system and the NFS client integrates the exported information, a process called "mounting," into its own file system. The client can then access the server's files as if they were a local resource.

■ Knowledge Assessment

Fill in the Blank

Complete the following sentences by writing the correct word or words in the blanks provided.

1. The DFS Replication engine uses a form of replication called _____.

2. In the Distributed File System, the actual shared folders referred to by the virtual folders in the namespace are known as _____.

3. Windows networks rely on a protocol called _____ for their file sharing.

4. The Distributed File System creates virtual directories in a construction known as a(n) _____.

5. Because NFS servers do not maintain any information about the client connections or the files that individual clients have open, they are said to be _____.

6. A DFS replication topology in which every server replicates with every other server is called a(n) _____.

7. The protocol that the distributed file system uses to conserve network bandwidth by detecting changes in files and transmitting only the modified data to the destination is called _____.

8. To keep a DFS folder's multiple targets synchronized, you must create a(n) _____.

9. The DFS replication topology intended for large enterprise networks is called the _____.

10. The folder-sharing mechanism most commonly used by UNIX computers is called _____.

Multiple Choice

Select the correct answer for each of the following questions. Choose all answers that are correct.

1. Which of the following statements about the Distributed File System are true?
   a. DFS is a virtual namespace technology that includes two components: DFS Namespaces and DFS Replication.
   b. DFS exists as a directory tree that contains true copies of the shared folders on different servers.
   c. DFS cannot control the amount of traffic passing over WAN links.
   d. DFS does not enable a network to tolerate a WAN link failure with minimal loss of productivity.

2. The Distributed File System enables administrators to
   a. facilitate consistent backups.
   b. simplify the process of locating files.
   c. provide users at remote sites with local file server access.
   d. do all of the above.

3. To which of the following elements does the File Services node in the Server Manager scope pane provide access?
   a. Share and Storage Management
   b. Role Services
   c. Reliability and Performance
   d. WMI Control

4. Which of the following tasks cannot be performed by file server administrators using the File Server Resource Manager (FSRM) console?
   a. Monitor file systems for access by intruders.
   b. Generate reports providing details about users' storage activities.
   c. Create quota templates and file screens.
   d. Establish quotas that limit the amount of storage space allotted to each user.

5. After installing the role and role services for DFS, which of the following configuration tasks should you perform?
   a. task scheduling
   b. adding folders to the namespace
   c. creating a replication group
   d. configuring referral order

6. Which statement about quota templates is not accurate?
   a. Quota templates limit the disk space an administrator permits a user to consume on a specified volume or folder.
   b. Quota templates specify the actions Windows Server 2008 should take when a user reaches a specified storage threshold.
   c. You can use quota templates to configure a soft quota, which prohibits users from consuming disk space beyond the allotted amount.
   d. In enterprise networks, administrators use quota templates to manage quota assignments on a large scale.

7. Which of the following statements about the Network File System is not true?
   a. NFS is used primarily by UNIX and Linux computers.
   b. To create NFS shares, use the Services for Network File System console.

    c. In NFS, the client component is primarily responsible for integrating the network files into the local file system.

    d. NFS shares must have the same names as their corresponding Windows shares.

8. Which of the following role services conflicts with the Windows Search Service role service, so that you cannot install both role services on the same computer?

    a. Distributed File System: DFS Replication

    b. Windows Server 2003 File Services: File Replication Service

    c. Windows Server 2003 File Services: Indexing Service

    d. File Server Resource Manager

9. The most common use for file screens is to

    a. prevent users from storing audio and video files on network server drives.

    b. protect database files from unauthorized access.

    c. prevent users from consuming too much storage space on network server drives.

    d. generate reports about users' storage habits.

Review Questions

1. Describe how the Distributed File System is able to conserve WAN bandwidth by replicating shared folders to file servers at remote locations.

2. Describe two ways in which NFS is able to authenticate UNIX clients with Windows user accounts to provide user access to folders on Windows file servers.

■ Case Scenarios

Scenario 3-1: Installing NFS Server Support

Several Linux workstations have been added to the company network and Randall must provide the workstations with access to the Windows file servers. After installing the Services for NFS role service on the file servers and configuring them to use Active Directory lookup, Randall creates NFS shares corresponding to each of the Windows shares. However, the Linux users report that they cannot access the NFS shares using their Active Directory user accounts. What must Randall do to provide the Linux users with Windows file server access?

Scenario 3-2: Creating FSRM Quotas

Kathleen has installed the File Server Resource Manager role service on her Windows Server 2008 file servers and created a number of quotas to limit the server disk space each user can consume. In each quota, she has configured FSRM to send email messages to the user and to the administrator if any user exceeds a quota. She has also configured FSRM to create a Quota Usage report each Friday. The next week, on examining the report, she discovers that several users have exceeded their quotas, but she has received no emails to that effect. What is the most likely reason that Kathleen did not receive the FSRM emails and what can she do about it?

4 LESSON

Deploying Print and Fax Servers

Printing and faxing are relatively simple functions that can become complicated when deployed on an enterprise scale. This lesson covers some of the printer and fax deployment and management capabilities provided with Windows Server 2008, including the following:

- Printer sharing
- Print Management console
- Printer scheduling, pooling, and security
- Fax server deployment
- Fax routing policies

■ Deploying a Print Server

THE BOTTOM LINE   Like the file-sharing functions discussed in the previous lessons, print device sharing is one of the most basic applications for which local area networks were designed.

Installing, sharing, monitoring, and managing a single network print device is relatively simple, but when you are responsible for dozens or even hundreds of print devices on a large enterprise network, these tasks can be overwhelming.

Understanding the Windows Print Architecture

It is important to understand the terms that Microsoft uses when referring to the various components of the network printing architecture.

Printing in Microsoft Windows typically involves the following four components:

- Print device—A **print device** is the actual hardware that produces hard-copy documents on paper or other print media. Windows Server 2008 supports both *local print devices*, which are directly attached to computer ports, and *network interface print devices*, which are connected to the network, either directly or through another computer.
- Printer—In Windows, a **printer** is the software interface through which a computer communicates with a print device. Windows Server 2008 supports numerous physical interfaces, including Universal Serial bus (USB), IEEE 1394 (FireWire), parallel (LPT),

serial (COM), Infrared Data Access (IrDA), Bluetooth ports, and network printing services such as lpr, Internet Printing Protocol (IPP), and standard TCP/IP ports.

- Print server—A ***print server*** is a computer (or stand-alone device) that receives print jobs from clients and sends them to print devices that are either locally attached or connected to the network.

- Printer driver—A ***printer driver*** is a device driver that converts the print jobs generated by applications into an appropriate string of commands for a specific print device. Printer drivers are designed for a specific print device and provide applications with access to all of the print device's features.

> **TAKE NOTE** * "Printer" and "print device" are the most commonly misused terms of the Windows printing vocabulary. Obviously, many sources use "printer" to refer to the printing hardware. However, in Windows, printer and print device are not equivalents. For example, you can add a printer to a Windows Server 2008 computer without a physical print device being present. The computer can then host the printer, print server, and printer driver. These three components enable the computer to process the print jobs and store them in a print queue until the print device is available.

UNDERSTANDING WINDOWS PRINTING

These four components work together to process the print jobs produced by Windows applications and turn them into hard-copy documents, as shown in Figure 4-1.

Figure 4-1

The Windows print architecture

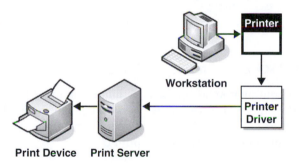

Before you can print documents in Windows, you must install at least one printer. To install a printer in Windows, you must do the following:

- Select the print device's specific manufacturer and model.
- Specify the port (or other interface) the computer will use to access the print device.
- Supply a printer driver specifically created for that print device.

When you print a document in an application, you select the printer that will be the destination for the print job.

The printer is associated with a printer driver that takes the commands generated by the application and converts them into a ***printer control language (PCL)***, a language understood by the printer. PCLs can be standardized, like the PostScript language, or they can be proprietary languages developed by the print device manufacturer.

The printer driver enables you to configure the print job to use the various capabilities of the print device. These capabilities are typically incorporated into the printer's Properties sheet. For example, your word-processing application does not know if your print device is color, monochrome, or supports duplex printing. It is the printer driver that provides support for print device features such as these.

After the printer processes a print job, it stores the job in a print queue, known as a ***spooler***. Depending on the arrangement of the printing components, the spooled jobs might be in

PCL format, ready to go to the print device, or in an interim format, in which case the printer driver must process the spooled jobs into the PCL format before sending them to the device. If other jobs are waiting to be printed, a new job might wait in the spooler for some time. When the server finally sends the job to the print device, the device reads the PCL commands and produces the hard-copy document.

WINDOWS PRINTING FLEXIBILITY

The flexibility of the Windows print architecture is manifested in the different ways that you can deploy the four printing components. A single computer can perform all of the roles (except for the print device, of course), or you can distribute them across the network. The following sections describe four fundamental configurations that are the basis of most Windows printer deployments. You can scale these configurations up to accommodate a network of virtually any size.

DIRECT PRINTING

The simplest print architecture consists of one print device connected to one computer, also *known as a locally-attached print device*, as shown in Figure 4-2. When you connect a print device directly a Windows Server 2008 computer and print from an application running on that system, the computer supplies the printer, printer driver, and print server functions.

Figure 4-2

A locally-attached print device

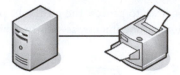

LOCALLY-ATTACHED PRINTER SHARING

In addition to printing from an application running on that computer, you can also share the printer (and the print device) with other users on the same network. In this arrangement, the computer with the locally-attached print device functions as a print server. Figure 4-3 shows the other computers on the network, the print clients.

Figure 4-3

Sharing a locally-attached printer

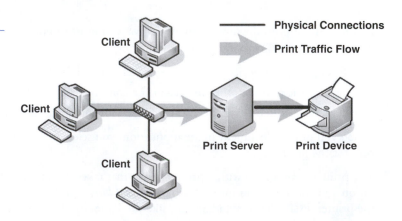

In the default Windows Server 2008 printer-sharing configuration, each client uses its own printer and printer driver. As before, the application running on the client computer sends the print job to the printer and the printer driver renders the job, based on the capabilities of the print device. In this arrangement, the printer driver creates a job file using one of two interim formats, as follows:

- ***Enhanced Metafile (EMF)***—A standardized, highly portable print job format that is the default format used by the Windows 2000, Windows XP, and Windows Server 2003 print subsystems. The printer driver converts the application data into an EMF file, and the printer sends it to the print server, which stores it in the spooler. The spooler then uses the printer driver on the print server to render the job into the final PCL format understood by the print device.

- ***XML Paper Specification (XPS)*** — A new platform-independent document format included with Windows Server 2008 and Windows Vista, in which print job files use a single XPS format for their entire journey to the print device, rather than being converted first to EMS and then to PCL.

The main advantage of this printing arrangement is that multiple users, located anywhere on the network, can send jobs to a single print device, connected to a computer functioning as a print server. The downside is that processing the print jobs for many users can impose a significant burden on the print server. Although any Windows computer can function as a print server, you should use a workstation for this purpose only when you have no more than a handful of print clients to support or a very light printing volume.

When you use a server computer as a print server, you must be aware of the system resources that the print server role will require. Dedicating a computer solely to print server duties is only necessary when you have a lot of print clients or a high volume of printing to support. In most cases, Windows servers that run the Print Services role perform other functions as well. However, you must be judicious in your role assignments.

For example, it is common practice for a single server to run both the Print Services and File Services roles. The usage patterns for these two roles complement each other, in that they both tend to handle relatively brief transactions from clients. Running the Print Services role on a domain controller is seldom a good idea, however, because network clients are constantly accessing the domain controller; their usage patterns are more conflicting than complementary.

NETWORK-ATTACHED PRINTING

The printing solutions discussed thus far involve print devices connected directly to a computer, using a USB or other port. Print devices do not necessarily have to be attached to computers, however. You can connect a print device directly to the network, instead. Many print device models are equipped with network interface adapters, enabling you to attach a standard network cable. Some print devices have expansion slots into which you can install a network printing adapter purchased separately. Finally, for print devices with no networking capabilities, stand-alone network print servers are available, which enable you to attach one or more print devices and connect to the network. Print devices so equipped have their own IP addresses and typically an embedded Web-based configuration interface.

With *network-attached print devices*, the primary deployment decision that the administrator must make is to decide which computer will function as the print server. One simple, but often less than practical, option is to let each print client function as its own print server, as shown in Figure 4-4. Each client processes and spools its own print jobs, connects to the print device using a TCP (Transmission Control Protocol) port, and sends the jobs directly to the device for printing.

Figure 4-4

A network-attached print device with multiple print servers

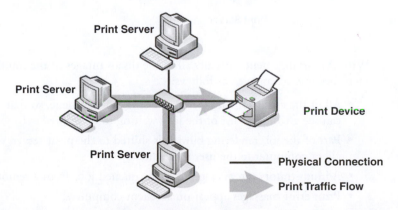

———	Physical Connection
⇒	Print Traffic Flow

Even individual end users with no administrative assistance will find this arrangement simple to set up. However, the disadvantages are many, including the following:

- Users examining the print queue see only their own jobs.
- Users are oblivious of the other users accessing the print device. They have no way of knowing what other jobs have been sent to the print device, or how long it will be until the print device completes their jobs.
- Administrators have no way of centrally managing the print queue, because each client has its own print queue.
- Administrators cannot implement advanced printing features, such as printer pools or remote administration.
- Error messages appear only on the computer that originated the job the print device is currently processing.
- All print job processing is performed by the client computer, rather than being partially offloaded to an external print server.

For these reasons, this arrangement is only suitable for small workgroup networks that do not have dedicated administrators supporting them.

NETWORK-ATTACHED PRINTER SHARING

The other, far more popular, option for network-attached printing is to designate one computer as a print server and use it to service all of the print clients on the network. To do this, you install a printer on one computer, the print server, and configure it to access the print device directly through a TCP port. Then, you share the printer, just as you would a locally-attached print device, and configure the clients to access the print share.

As you can see in Figure 4-5, the physical configuration is exactly the same as in the previous arrangement, but the logical path the print jobs take on the way to the print device is different. Instead of going straight to the print device, the jobs go to the print server, which spools them and sends them to the print device in order.

Figure 4-5

A network-attached print device with a single, shared print server

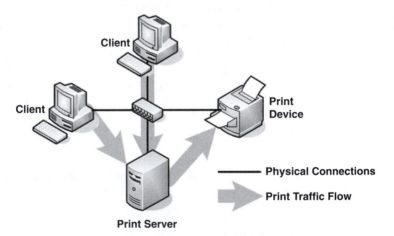

With this arrangement, virtually all of the disadvantages of the multiple print server arrangement become advantages, as follows:

- All of the client jobs are stored in a single print queue, so that users and administrators can see a complete list of the jobs waiting to be printed.
- Part of the job rendering burden is shifted to the print server, returning control of the client computer to the user more quickly.
- Administrators can manage all of the queued jobs from a remote location.
- Print error messages appear on all client computers.

- Administrators can implement printer pools and other advanced printing features.
- Administrators can manage security, auditing, monitoring, and logging functions from a central location.

ADVANCED PRINTING CONFIGURATIONS

Administrators can use the four configurations described in the previous sections as building blocks to create printing solutions for their networks. Many possible variations can be used to create a network printing architecture that supports your organization's needs. Some of the more advanced possibilities are as follows:

- You can connect a single printer to multiple print devices, creating what is called a **_printer pool_**. On a busy network with many print clients, the print server can distribute large numbers of incoming jobs among several identical print devices to provide more timely service and fault tolerance.
- You can connect multiple print devices that support different forms and paper sizes to a single print server, which will distribute jobs with different requirements to the appropriate print devices.
- You can connect multiple print servers to a single print device. By creating multiple print servers, you can configure different priorities, security settings, auditing, and monitoring parameters for different users. For example, you can create a high-priority print server for company executives, while junior users send their jobs to a lower priority server. This ensures that the executives' jobs get printed first, even if the servers are both connected to the same print device.

Sharing a Printer

> Using Windows Server 2008 as a print server can be simple or complex, depending on how many clients the server has to support and how much printing they do.

For a home or small business network, in which a handful of users need occasional access to the printer, no special preparation is necessary. However, if the computer must support heavy printer use, the following hardware upgrades might be needed:

- Additional system memory—Processing print jobs requires system memory, just like any other application. If you plan to run heavy print traffic through a Windows Server 2008 server, in addition to other roles or applications, make sure that the computer has sufficient memory to support all of its functions.
- Additional disk space—When a print device is busy, the print server spools additional incoming print jobs temporarily on a hard drive until the print device is free to receive them. Depending on the amount of print traffic and the types of print jobs, the print server might require a substantial amount of temporary storage for this purpose. In addition, be sure to plan for the extra storage space needed to support temporary print device outages. When a printer runs out of paper, ink, or toner, it remains idle until replenished, and the server must retain all incoming print jobs in the queue. This can cause the server to require even more storage space than normal.
- Make the computer a dedicated print server—In addition to memory and disk space, using Windows Server 2008 as a print server requires processor clock cycles, just like any other application. On a server handling heavy print traffic, other roles and applications are likely to experience substantial performance degradation. If you need a print server to handle heavy traffic, consider dedicating the computer to print server tasks only and deploying other roles and applications elsewhere.

Before you can share a printer on a Windows Server 2008 computer, you must enable the Printer Sharing setting in the Network and Sharing Center, just as you have to enable File

Sharing to share files and folders. Typically, you can share a printer as you are installing it, or at any time afterwards. On older printers, initiate the installation process by launching the Add Printer Wizard from the Printers control panel. However, most of the print devices on the market today use either a USB connection to a computer or an Ethernet connection to a network.

In the case of a USB-connected printer, you plug the print device into a USB port on the computer and turn on the device to initiate the installation process. Manual intervention is only required when Windows Server 2008 does not have a driver for the print device.

For network-attached print devices, an installation program supplied with the product locates the print device on the network, installs the correct drivers, creates a printer on the computer, and configures the printer with the proper IP address and other settings.

After the printer is installed on the Windows Server 2008 computer that will function as your print server, you can share it with your network clients, using the following procedure.

→ SHARE A PRINTER

GET READY. Log on to Windows Server 2008 using a domain account with Administrator privileges. When the logon process is completed, close the Initial Configuration Tasks window and any other windows that appear.

1. Click **Start**, and then click **Control Panel** > **Printers**. The Printers window appears.
2. Right-click the icon for the printer you want to share and, from the context menu, select **Sharing**. The printer's Properties sheet appears, with the Sharing tab selected, as shown in Figure 4-6.

Figure 4-6

The Sharing tab of a printer's Properties sheet

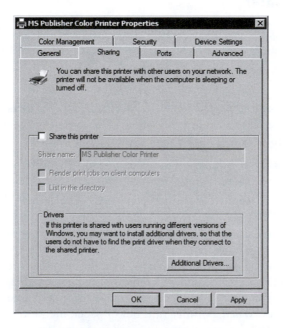

3. Select the **Share this printer** checkbox. The printer name appears in the Share Name text box. You can accept the default name or supply one of your own.
4. Select one or both of the following optional checkboxes:

   • Render print jobs on client computers—Minimizes the resource utilization on the print server by forcing the print clients to perform the bulk of the print processing.

   • List in the directory—Creates a new printer object in the Active Directory database, enabling domain users to locate the printer by searching the directory. This option only appears when the computer is a member of an Active Directory domain.

5. Click **Additional Drivers**. The Additional Drivers dialog box appears, as shown in Figure 4-7. This dialog box enables you to load printer drivers for other versions of the operating system, such as Itanium and x64. When you install the alternate drivers, the print server automatically supplies them to clients running those operating system versions.

Figure 4-7

The Additional Drivers dialog box

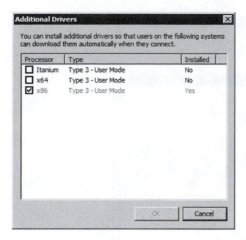

6. Select any combination of the available checkboxes and click **OK**. For each checkbox you selected, Windows Server 2008 displays a Printer Drivers dialog box.

7. In each Printer Drivers dialog box, key or browse to the location of the printer drivers for the selected operating system, and then click **OK**.

8. Click **OK** to close the Additional Drivers dialog box.

9. Click **OK** to close the Properties sheet for the printer. The printer icon in the Printers control panel now includes a symbol indicating that it has been shared.

CLOSE the control panel.

At this point, the printer is available to clients on the network.

Configuring Printer Security

Like folder shares, clients must have the proper permissions to access a shared printer.

Printer permissions are much simpler than NTFS permissions; they basically dictate whether users are allowed to merely use the printer, manage documents submitted to the printer, or manage the properties of the printer itself. To assign permissions for a printer, use the following procedure.

 ASSIGN PRINTER PERMISSIONS

GET READY. Log on to Windows Server 2008 using a domain account with Administrator privileges. When the logon process is completed, close the Initial Configuration Tasks window and any other windows that appear.

1. Click **Start**, and then click **Control Panel** > **Printers**. The Printers window appears.

2. Right-click one of the printer icons in the window and, from the context menu, select **Properties**. When the printer's Properties sheet appears, click the **Security** tab, as shown in Figure 4-8. The top half of the display lists all of the security principals currently possessing permissions to the selected printer. The bottom half lists the permissions held by the selected security principal.

Figure 4-8

The Security tab of a printer's Properties sheet

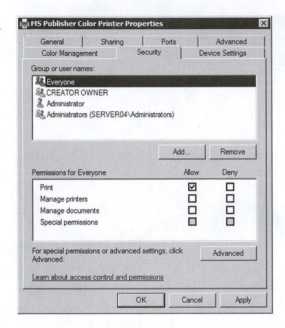

3. Click **Add.** The Select Users, Computers, or Groups dialog box appears, as shown in Figure 4-9.

Figure 4-9

The Select Users, Computers, or Groups dialog box

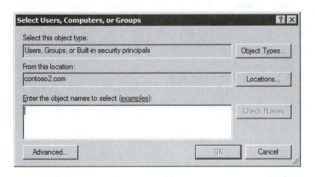

TAKE NOTE*   This procedure assumes that the Windows Server 2008 computer is a member of an Active Directory domain. When you assign printer permissions on a stand-alone server, you select local user and group accounts to be the security principals that receive the permissions.

4. In the *Enter the object names to select* text box, key a user or group name, and then click **OK.** The user or group appears in the *Group or user names* list.

5. Select the user or group you added, and select or clear the checkboxes in the bottom half of the display to Allow or Deny the user any of the standard permissions.

6. Click **OK** to close the Properties sheet.

CLOSE the control panel.

Like NTFS permissions, there are two types of printer permissions: standard and special. Each of the three standard permissions consists of a combination of special permissions, as listed in Table 4-1.

Table 4-1

Standard Printer Permissions

PERMISSION	CAPABILITIES	SPECIAL PERMISSIONS	DEFAULT ASSIGNMENTS
Print	• Connect to a printer • Print documents • Pause, resume, restart, and cancel the user's own documents	• Print • Read Permissions	Assigned to the Everyone special identity
Manage Printers	• Cancel all documents • Share a printer • Change printer properties • Delete a printer • Change printer permissions	• Print • Manage Printers • Read Permissions • Change Permissions • Take Ownership	Assigned to the Administrators group
Manage Documents	• Pause, resume, restart, and cancel all users' documents • Control job settings for all documents	• Manage Documents • Read Permissions • Change Permissions • Take Ownership	Assigned to the Creator Owner special identity

Managing Documents

By default, all printers assign the Allow Print permission to the Everyone special identity, which enables all users to access the printer and manage their own documents. Users who possess the Allow Manage Documents permission can manage any users' documents.

Managing documents refers to pausing, resuming, restarting, and cancelling documents that are currently waiting in a print queue. Windows Server 2008 provides a print queue window for every printer, which enables you to view the jobs that are currently waiting to be printed. To manage documents, use the following procedure.

 MANAGE DOCUMENTS

GET READY. Log on to Windows Server 2008 using any user account. When the logon process is completed, close the Initial Configuration Tasks window and any other windows that appear.

1. Click **Start**, and then click **Control Panel** > **Printers**. The Printers window appears.
2. Double-click one of the printer icons. A print queue window named for the printer appears, as shown in Figure 4-10.

Figure 4-10

A Windows Server 2008 print queue window

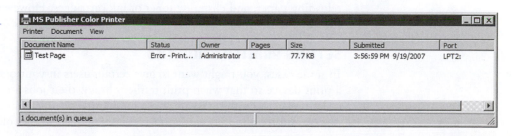

3. Select one of the menu items to perform the associated function.

4. Close the print queue window.

CLOSE the control panel.

Table 4-2 lists the document management options available in the print queue window.

Table 4-2

Document Management Menu
Commands

Menu Item	Function
Printer > Pause Printing	Causes the print server to stop sending jobs to the print device until you restart it by selecting the same menu item again. All pending jobs remain in the queue.
Printer > Cancel All Documents	Removes all pending jobs from the queue. Jobs that are in progress complete normally.
Printer > Use Printer Offline	Enables users to send jobs to the printer, where they remain unprocessed in the queue, until you select the same menu item again.
Printer > Properties	Opens the Properties sheet for the printer.
Document > Pause	Pauses the selected document, preventing the print server from sending the job to the print device.
Document > Resume	Causes the print server to resume processing a selected document that has previously been paused.
Document > Restart	Causes the print server to discard the current job and restart printing the selected document from the beginning.
Document > Cancel	Causes the print server to remove the selected document from the queue.
Document > Properties	Opens the Properties sheet for the selected job.

TAKE NOTE*

When managing documents, keep in mind that the commands accessible from the print queue window affect only the jobs waiting in the queue, not those currently being processed by the print device. For example, a job that is partially transmitted to the print device cannot be completely cancelled. The data already in the print device's memory will be printed, even though the remainder of the job was removed from the queue. To stop a job that is currently printing, you must clear the print device's memory (by resetting or power cycling the unit), as well as clear the job from the queue.

Managing Printers

Users with the Allow Manage Printers permission can go beyond manipulating queued documents; they can reconfigure the printer itself. Managing a printer refers to altering the operational parameters that affect all users and controlling access to the printer.

Generally, most of the software-based tasks that fall under the category of managing a printer are those you perform once, while setting up the printer for the first time. Day-to-day printer management is more likely to involve physical maintenance, such as clearing print jams, reloading paper, and changing toner or ink cartridges. However, the following sections examine some of the printer manager's typical configuration tasks.

SETTING PRINTER PRIORITIES

In some cases, you might want to give certain users in your organization priority access to a print device so that when print traffic is heavy, their jobs are processed before those of other users. To do this, you must create multiple printers, associate them with the same print device, and then modify their priorities, as described in the following procedure.

 SET A PRINTER'S PRIORITY

GET READY. Log on to Windows Server 2008 using an account with the Manage Printer permission. When the logon process is completed, close the Initial Configuration Tasks window and any other windows that appear.

1. Click **Start**, and then click **Control Panel** > **Printers**. The Printers window appears.
2. Right-click one of the printer icons and then, from the context menu, select **Properties**. The Properties sheet for the printer appears.
3. Click the **Advanced** tab, as shown in Figure 4-11.

Figure 4-11

The Advanced tab of a printer's Properties sheet

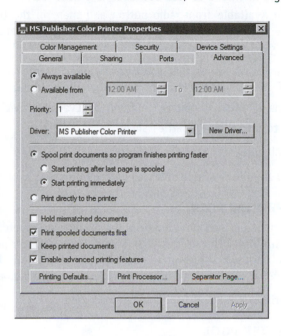

TAKE NOTE*

The values of the Priority spin box do not have any absolute significance; they are pertinent only in relation to each other. As long as one printer has a higher priority value than another, the server will process its print jobs first. In other words, it doesn't matter if the higher priority value is 9 or 99, as long as the lower priority value is less.

4. Set the Priority spin box to a number representing the highest priority you want to set for the printer. Higher numbers represent higher priorities. The highest possible priority is 99.
5. Click the **Security** tab.
6. Add the users or groups that you want to provide with high-priority access to the printer and assign the Allow Print permission to them.
7. Revoke the Allow Print permission from the Everyone special identity.
8. Click **OK** to close the Properties sheet.
9. Create an identical printer using the same printer driver and pointing to the same print device. Leave the Priority setting to its default value of 1 and leave the default permissions in place.
10. Rename the printers, specifying the priority assigned to each one.

CLOSE the control panel.

Inform the privileged users that they should send their jobs to the high-priority printer. All jobs sent to that printer will be processed before those sent to the other, low-priority printer.

SCHEDULING PRINTER ACCESS

Sometimes, you might want to limit certain users' access to a printer to specific times of the day or night. For example, your organization might have a color laser printer that the company's graphic designers use during business hours, but which you permit other employees to use after 5:00 PM. To do this, you associate multiple printers with a single print device, much as you did to set different printer priorities.

After creating two printers, both pointing to the same print device, you configure their scheduling using the following procedure.

SCHEDULE PRINTER ACCESS

GET READY. Log on to Windows Server 2008 using an account with the Manage Printer permission. When the logon process is completed, close the Initial Configuration Tasks window and any other windows that appear.

1. Click **Start**, and then click **Control Panel** > **Printers**. The Printers window appears.

2. Right-click one of the printer icons and then, from the context menu, select **Properties**. The Properties sheet for the printer appears.

3. Click the **Advanced** tab.

4. Select the **Available from** radio button and then, in the two spin boxes provided, select the range of hours you want the printer to be available.

5. Click the **Security** tab.

6. Add the users or groups that you want to provide with access to the printer during the hours you selected and grant them the Allow Print permission.

7. Revoke the Allow Print permission from the Everyone special identity.

8. Click **OK** to close the Properties sheet.

CLOSE the control panel.

The two printers are now available only during the hours you have specified.

CREATING A PRINTER POOL

As mentioned earlier, a printer pool increases the production capability of a single printer by connecting it to multiple print devices. When you create a printer pool, the print server sends each incoming job to the first print device it finds that is not busy. This effectively distributes the jobs among the available print devices, providing users with more rapid service.

To configure a printer pool, use the following procedure.

 CREATE A PRINTER POOL

GET READY. Log on to Windows Server 2008 using an account with the Manage Printer permission. When the logon process is completed, close the Initial Configuration Tasks window and any other windows that appear.

1. Click **Start**, and then click **Control Panel** > **Printers**. The Printers window appears.

2. Right-click one of the printer icons and then, from the context menu, select **Properties**. The Properties sheet for the printer appears.

3. Click the **Ports** tab, and then select all of the ports to which the print devices are connected.

4. Select the **Enable printer pooling** checkbox, and then click **OK**.

CLOSE the control panel.

To create a printer pool, you must have at least two identical print devices, or at least print devices that use the same printer driver. The print devices must be in the same location, because there is no way to tell which print device will process a given document. You must also connect all of the print devices in the pool to the same print server. If the print server is a Windows Server 2008 computer, you can connect the print devices to any viable ports.

■ Using the Print Services Role

THE BOTTOM LINE

All of the printer sharing and management capabilities discussed in the previous sections are available on any Windows Server 2008 computer in its default installation configuration. However, installing the Print Services role on the computer provides additional tools that are particularly useful to administrators involved with network printing on an enterprise scale.

When you install the Print Services role using Server Manager's Add Roles Wizard, a Role Services page appears, as shown in Figure 4-12, enabling you to select from the options listed in Table 4-3.

Figure 4-12

The Select Role Services page for the Print Services role

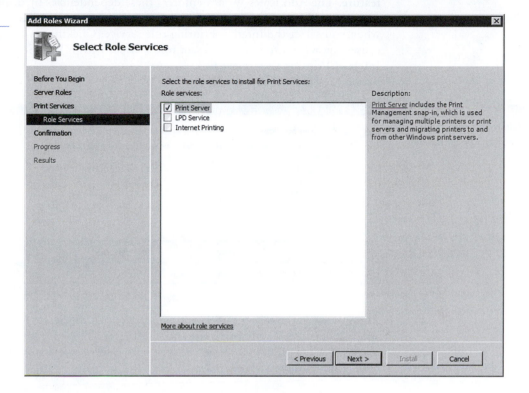

Table 4-3

Role Service Selections for the Print Services Role

ROLE SERVICE	WIZARD PAGES ADDED	SYSTEM SERVICES INSTALLED	DESCRIPTION
Print Server	[None]	Print Spooler (Spooler)	■ Installs the Print Management console for Microsoft Management Console (MMC), which enables administrators to deploy, monitor, and manage printers throughout the enterprise. ■ This is the only role service that is required when you add the Print Services role.
LPD Service	[None]	TCP/IP Print Server (LPDSVC)	■ Enables UNIX clients running the LPR (line printer remote) program to send their print jobs to Windows printers.
Internet Printing	[None]	■ World Wide Web Publishing Service (w3svc) ■ IIS Admin Service (iisadmin)	■ Creates a Web site that enables users on the Internet to send print jobs to shared Windows printers.

To install the Internet Printing role service, you must also install the Web Server (IIS) role, with certain specific role services, as well as the Windows Process Activation Service feature. The Add Roles Wizard enforces these dependencies by displaying an *Add role services and features required for Internet Printing* message box, as shown in Figure 4-13, when you select the Internet Printing role service. Clicking *Add Required Role Services* causes the wizard to select the exact role services within Web Server (IIS) role that the Internet Printing service needs.

Figure 4-13

The Add role services and features required for Internet Printing message box

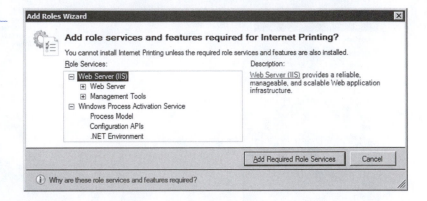

As always, Windows Server 2008 adds a new node to the Server Manager console when you install a role. The Print Services node contains a filtered view of print-related event log entries, a status display for the role-related system services and role services, and recommended configuration tasks and best practices, as shown in Figure 4-14.

Figure 4-14

The Print Services node in Server Manager

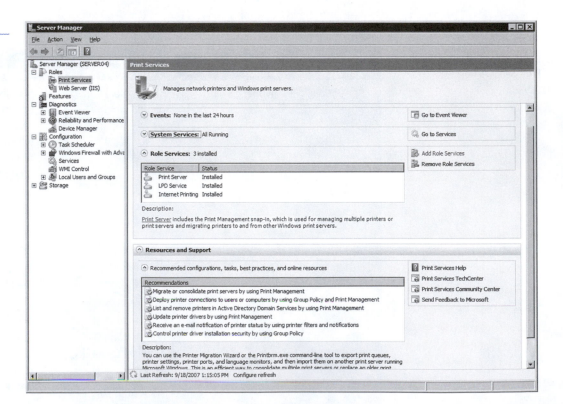

Using the Print Management Console

The Print Management snap-in for MMC, an administrative tool, consolidates the controls for the printing components throughout the enterprise into a single console. With this tool, you can access the print queues and Properties sheets for all of the network printers in the enterprise, deploy printers to client computers using Group Policy, and create custom views that simplify the process of detecting print devices that need attention due to errors or depleted consumables.

Windows Server 2008 installs the Print Management console when you add the Print Services role to the computer. You can also install the console without the role by adding the Print Services Tools feature, found under Remote Server Administration Tools > Role Administration Tools in Server Manager.

When you launch the Print Management console, the default display, shown in Figure 4-15, includes the following three nodes in the scope (left) pane:

- Custom Filters—Contains composite views of all the printers hosted by the print servers listed in the console, regulated by customizable filters.
- Print Servers—Lists all of the print servers you have added to the console, and all of the drivers, forms, ports, and printers for each print server.
- Deployed Printers—Lists all of the printers you have deployed with Group Policy using the console.

Figure 4-15

The Print Management console

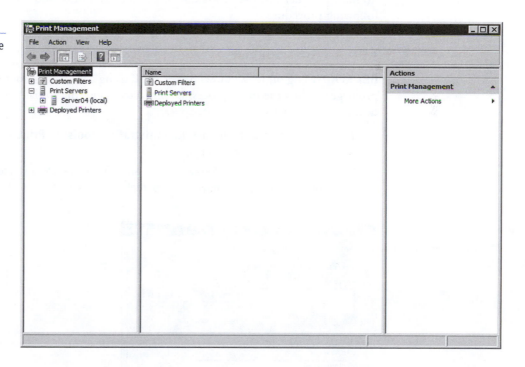

The following sections demonstrate some of the administration tasks you can perform with the Print Management console.

ADDING PRINT SERVERS

By default, the Print Management console displays only the local machine in its list of print servers. Each print server has four nodes beneath it, as shown in Figure 4-16, listing the drivers, forms, ports, and printers associated with that server.

Figure 4-16

A print server displayed in the Print Management console

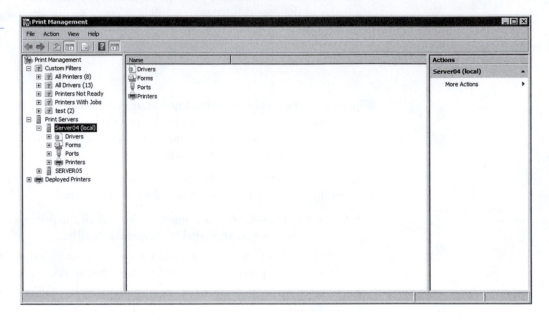

To manage other print servers and their printers, you must add them to the console, using the following procedure.

 ADD A PRINT SERVER

GET READY. Log on to Windows Server 2008 using a domain account with Administrator privileges. When the logon process is completed, close the Initial Configuration Tasks window and any other windows that appear.

1. Click **Start**, and then click **Administrative Tools** > **Print Management**. The Print Management console appears.

2. Right-click the **Print Servers** node and, from the context menu, click **Add/Remove Servers**. The Add/Remove Servers dialog box appears, as shown in Figure 4-17.

Figure 4-17

The Add/Remove Servers dialog box

3. In the Specify Print Server box, click **Browse**. The Select Print Server dialog box appears, as shown in Figure 4-18.

Figure 4-18

The Select Print Server dialog box

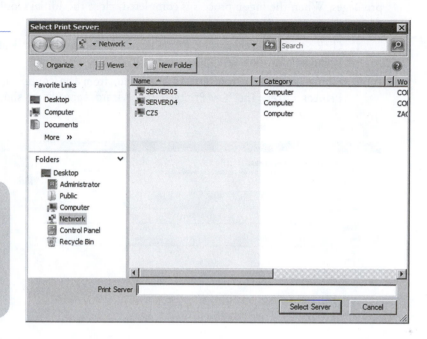

To browse for print servers on the network, you must activate the Network Discovery setting in the Network and Sharing Center control panel.

4. Select the print server you want to add to the console and click **Select Server**. The server you selected appears in the Add Servers text box on the Add/Remove servers dialog box.

5. Click **Add to List**. The server you selected appears in the Print Servers list.

6. Click **OK**. The Server appears under the Print Servers node.

CLOSE the control panel.

You can now manage the printers associated with the server you added to the console.

VIEWING PRINTERS

One of the major problems for printing administrators on large enterprise networks is keeping track of dozens or hundreds of print devices, all in frequent use, and all needing attention on a regular basis. Whether the maintenance required is a major repair, replenishing ink or toner, or just filling the paper trays, print devices will not get the attention they need until an administrator is aware of the problem.

The Print Management console provides a multitude of ways to view the printing components associated with the print servers on the network. To create views, the console takes the complete list of printers and applies various filters to it, selecting which printers to display. Under the Custom Filters node, there are four default filters, as follows:

- All Printers—Contains a list of all the printers hosted by all of the print servers added to the console.

- All Drivers—Contains a list of all the printer drivers installed on all of the print servers added to the console.

- Printers Not Ready—Contains a list of all printers that are not reporting a Ready status.

- Printers With Jobs—Contains a list of all the printers that currently have jobs waiting in the print queue.

Views such as Printer Not Ready are a useful way for administrators to identify printers that need attention, without having to browse individual print servers or search through a long list of every printer on the network. In addition to these defaults, you can create your own custom filters with the following procedure.

CREATE A CUSTOM FILTER

GET READY. Log on to Windows Server 2008 using a domain account with Administrator privileges. When the logon process is completed, close the Initial Configuration Tasks window and any other windows that appear.

1. Click **Start**, and then click **Administrative Tools** > **Print Management**. The Print Management console appears.

2. Right-click the **Custom Filters** node and, from the context menu, select **Add New Printer Filter**. The New Printer Filter Wizard appears, as shown in Figure 4-19.

Figure 4-19

The New Printer Filter Wizard

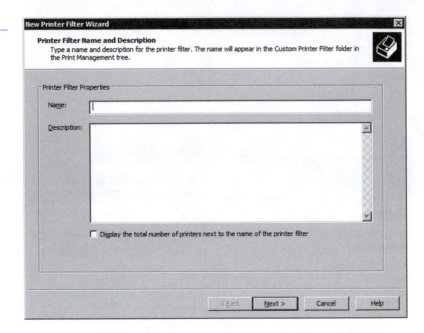

3. In the Name text box, key a name for the filter, and optionally, key a description for the filter in the Description text box. If you want the number of printers in the filtered list to appear next to the filter name, select the **Display the total number of printers next to the name of the printer filter** checkbox. Then click **Next**. The *Define a printer filter* page appears, as shown in Figure 4-20.

Figure 4-20

The Define a printer filter page

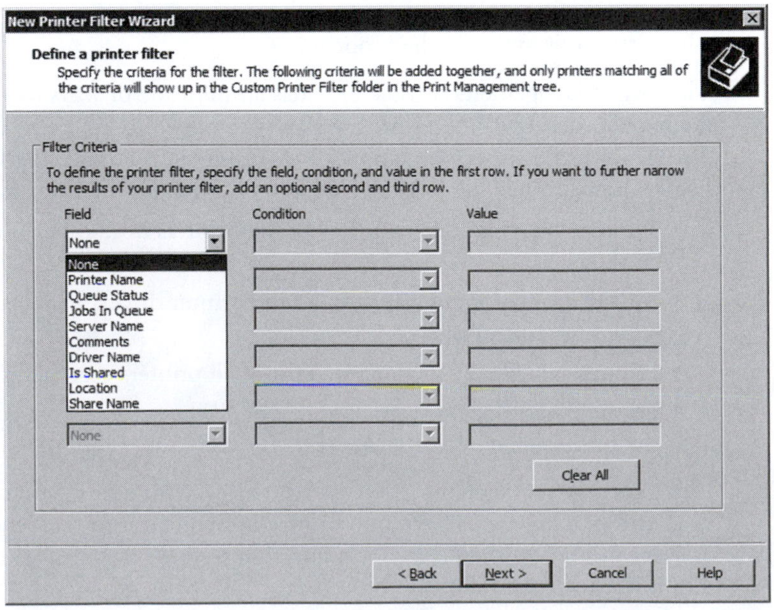

4. In the top row of boxes, select values for the Field, Condition, and Value fields. Select values for additional rows of boxes, if desired. Then, click **Next**. The Set Notifications page appears, as shown in Figure 4-21.

Figure 4-21

The Set Notifications page

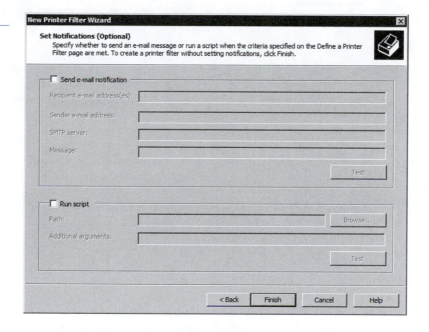

5. Select the **Send e-mail notification** checkbox to send a message to a specific person when printers meeting the criteria you specified are displayed on the *Define a printer filter* page. Use the text boxes provided to specify the sender's and recipient's email addresses, the Simple Mail Transfer Protocol (SMTP) server that will send the message, and the text of the message itself.

6. Select the **Run script** checkbox to execute a particular script file when printers meeting the criteria you specified are displayed on the *Define a printer filter* page. Use the text boxes provided to specify the path to the script and any additional arguments you want the system to pass to the script when running it.

7. Click **Finish**. The new filter appears under the Custom Filters node.

CLOSE the control panel.

When creating filters, each entry in the Field dropdown list has its own collection of possible entries for the Condition dropdown list, and each Condition entry has its own possible entries for the Value setting. This creates many thousands of possible filter combinations.

For example, when you select Queue Status in the Field list, the Condition dropdown list presents two options, *is exactly* and *is not exactly*. After you select one of these Condition settings, you choose from the Value list, which displays all of the possible queue status messages that the print server can report, as shown in Figure 4-22.

Figure 4-22

Filter status values

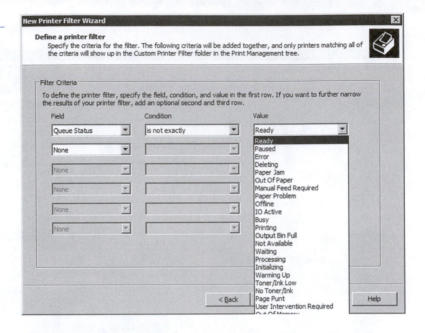

If you create a filter with the settings *Queue Status, is exactly,* and *Error,* the filter will display all of the printers that are currently reporting an error condition. A filter like this can be useful for detecting printers reporting one specific condition, but many different status messages can indicate a print device stoppage. For the busy printer administrator, a better combination might be a filter with the settings Queue Status, is not exactly, and Ready. This way, the filter will display all of the printers with abnormal conditions. These printers need administrative attention.

MANAGING PRINTERS AND PRINT SERVERS

After you have used filtered views to isolate the printers you want to examine, selecting a printer displays its status, the number of jobs currently in its print queue, and the name of the print server hosting it. If you right-click the filter in the scope pane and, from the context menu, select Show Extended View, an additional pane appears containing the contents of the selected printer's queue, as shown in Figure 4-23. You can manipulate the queued jobs just as you would from the print queue window on the print server console.

Figure 4-23

The Print Management console's extended view

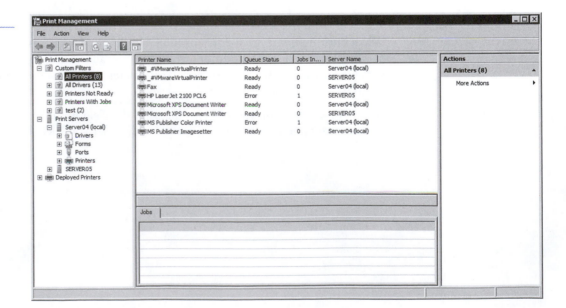

The Print Management console also enables administrators to access the configuration interface for any printer or print server appearing in any of its displays. Right-clicking a printer or print server anywhere in the console interface, and selecting Properties from the context menu, displays the same Properties sheet you would see on the print server computer itself. Administrators can then configure printers and print servers without having to travel to the site of the print server or establish a Remote Desktop connection to the print server.

DEPLOYING PRINTERS WITH GROUP POLICY

Configuring a print client to access a shared printer is a simple matter of browsing the network or the Active Directory tree and selecting the printer. However, when you have to configure hundreds or thousands of print clients, the task becomes more complicated. Active Directory helps simplify the process of deploying printers to large numbers of clients.

Publishing printers in the Active Directory database enables users and administrators to search for printers by name, location, or model (if you populate the Location and Model fields in the printer object). To create a printer object in the Active Directory database, you can either select the *List in the directory* checkbox while sharing the printer or right-click a printer in the Print Management console and, from the context menu, select List in Directory.

To use Active Directory to deploy printers to clients, you must configure the appropriate policies in a Group Policy Object (GPO). You can link a GPO to any domain, site, or organizational unit (OU) in the Active Directory tree. When you configure a GPO to deploy a printer, all of the users or computers in that domain, site, or OU will receive the printer connection when they log on, by default.

To deploy printers with Group Policy, use the following procedure.

 DEPLOY PRINTERS WITH GROUP POLICY

GET READY. Log on to Windows Server 2008 using a domain account with Administrator privileges. When the logon process is completed, close the Initial Configuration Tasks window and any other windows that appear.

1. Click **Start**, and then click **Administrative Tools** > **Print Management**. The Print Management console appears.

2. Right-click a printer in the console's scope pane and, from the context menu, select **Deploy with Group Policy**. The Deploy with Group Policy dialog box appears, as shown in Figure 4-24.

Figure 4-24

The Deploy with Group Policy dialog box

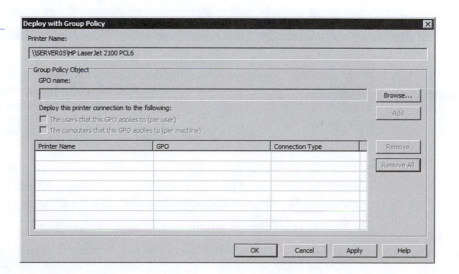

3. Click **Browse**. The Browse for a Group Policy Object dialog box appears, as shown in Figure 4-25.

Figure 4-25

The Browse for a Group Policy Object dialog box

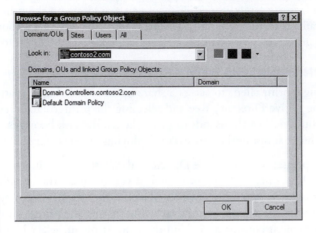

4. Select the GPO you want to use to deploy the printer and click **OK**. The GPO you selected appears in the GPO Name field.

5. Select the appropriate checkbox to select whether to deploy the printer to the users associated with the GPO, the computers, or both. Then click **Add**. The new printer/GPO associations appear in the table.

Deploying the printer to the users means that all of the users associated with the GPO will receive the printer connection, no matter what computer they use to log on. Deploying the printer to the computers means that all of the computers associated with the GPO will receive the printer connection, no matter who logs on to them.

6. Click **OK**. A Print Management message box appears, informing you that the operation has succeeded.

7. Click **OK**, then click **OK** again to close the Deploy with Group Policy dialog box.

CLOSE the control panel.

The next time the Windows Server 2008 users, Windows Vista users, and computers associated with the GPO refresh their policies or restart, they will receive the new settings and the printer will appear in the Printers control panel.

■ Deploying a Fax Server

THE BOTTOM LINE

Sending faxes, receiving faxes, waiting for faxes, and even walking back and forth to the fax machine can be an enormous drain on productivity in many organizations. Windows Server 2008 includes a Fax Server role that enables users to send faxes from and receive them to their desktops.

By installing the Fax Server role, you enable a Windows Server 2008 computer to send and receive faxes for clients. The clients send their faxes using a standard printer interface, which connects to a fax server on the network as easily as connecting to a local fax modem.

The basic steps involved in setting up a fax server are as follows:

- Add the Fax Server role—Creates the Fax printer and installs the Fax service and the Fax Service Manager console.

- Add the Desktop Experience feature—Installs the Windows Fax and Scan application.

- Share the fax printer—Makes the printer available to network users.

- Configure the fax device—Configures the fax modem or other device that will physically send and receive the fax transmissions.
- Configure incoming fax routing—Specifies the actions the server should take when incoming faxes arrive.
- Designate fax users—Specifies which users are permitted to send and receive faxes using the server.

The following sections examine each of these steps.

Using the Fax Services Role

To use a Windows Server 2008 computer as a fax server, you must add the Fax Server role, using Server Manager console.

The Fax Server role consists of only a single role service, the details of which are listed in Table 4-4. The Fax Server role is dependent on the Print Services role. You must install the Print Services role before, or with, the Fax Server role.

Table 4-4

Role Service for the Fax Server Role

ROLE SERVICE	WIZARD PAGES ADDED	SYSTEM SERVICES INSTALLED	DESCRIPTION
Fax Server	▪ Fax Users ▪ Fax Server Inbox ▪ Routing Assistants	▪ Fax (Fax)	▪ Creates a Fax printer, and installs the Fax Service Manager console.

After you install the Fax Server role, the Server Manager displays the usual events and System Services summaries, as shown in Figure 4-26, as well as a list of recommended configuration tasks. The Fax Server role also installs the Fax Service Manager console, which you can access by expanding the Roles and Fax Server nodes and clicking Fax.

Figure 4-26

The Fax Server role

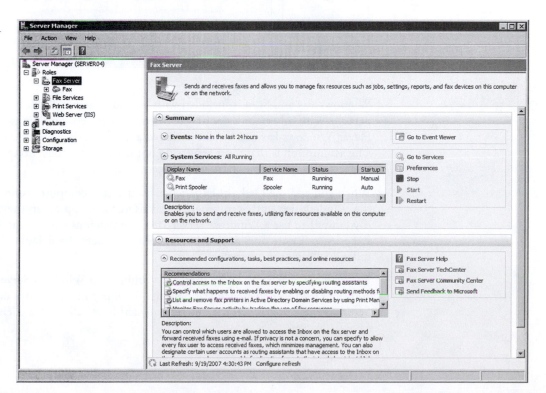

The Fax Service Manager enables administrators to perform the following tasks:

- View and configure fax devices, such as modems.
- Specify routing policies for inbound faxes.
- Specify rules for outbound faxes.
- Manage fax users.
- Configure fax logging and archiving.

Adding the Desktop Experience Feature

> The Fax Service Manager can configure various fax server functions, but it cannot actually send outgoing faxes or view incoming ones.

To send and view faxes, you must use the Windows Fax and Scan program, shown in Figure 4-27.

Figure 4-27

The Windows Fax and Scan program

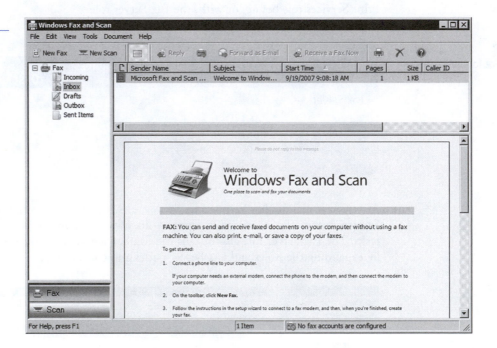

Windows Fax and Scan is included with Windows Server 2008, but it is not installed by default. With other non-essential elements, such as desktop themes and Windows Media Player, Windows Fax and Scan is packaged as part of a single feature called Desktop Experience. The assumption is that most servers do not need these applications, and administrators would prefer not to have them installed unnecessarily.

When you add the Desktop Experience feature on a computer running the Fax Server role, the Windows Fax and Scan program is activated and appears in the Start menu. However, if you want to use a Windows Server 2008 computer as a fax client, installing the Desktop Experience feature does not enable any of the elements by default. You must enable them individually as you use them.

For example, when you add a shared fax printer to a Windows Server 2008 computer and add the Desktop Experience feature, the first time you try to fax a document, a Fax Client Setup message box appears, asking if you want to install the fax client software.

Sharing the Fax Printer

Adding the Fax Server role installs a Fax printer, which is what clients use to send outgoing faxes.

When a client selects the Fax printer instead of a standard printer, the print job goes to the fax server instead of to a print server or print device. However, while adding the role creates the Fax printer, it does not share it. You must share the fax printer manually, using the same procedure described earlier in this lesson, in "Sharing a Printer."

Configuring a Fax Device

For a Windows Server 2008 computer to function as a fax server, it must have a hardware device capable of sending and receiving faxes over a telephone line, such as a modem. Depending on the fax volume it must support, a fax server's hardware can range from a standard, single fax modem to a rack-mounted device containing many modems.

The Fax printer created by the Fax Server role represents all of the fax devices installed on the computer. If there are multiple devices, the server can distribute outgoing faxes among a group of devices, but there is only a single fax job queue on the system.

When you run the Fax Service Manager console, the fax devices appear in the Devices folder automatically. By default, the server configures all devices to send faxes only. To receive faxes, you must configure the device, using the following procedure.

 CONFIGURE A FAX DEVICE

GET READY. Log on to Windows Server 2008 using a domain account with Administrator privileges. When the logon process is completed, close the Initial Configuration Tasks window and any other windows that appear.

1. Click **Start**, and then click **Administrative Tools** > **Fax Service Manager**. The Fax Service Manager console appears, as shown in Figure 4-28.

Figure 4-28

The Microsoft Fax Service Manager console

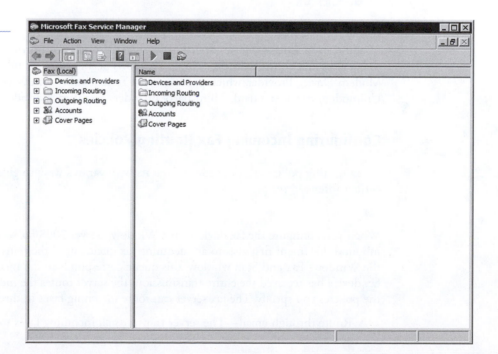

2. In the console's scope pane, expand the **Devices and Providers** folder, and then the **Devices** folder.

3. Right-click one of the devices in the details pane and, from the context menu, select **Properties**. The device's Properties sheet appears, as shown in Figure 4-29.

Figure 4-29

A fax modem's Properties sheet

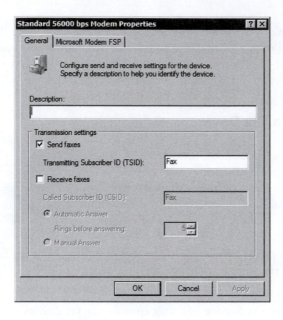

4. Select the **Receive faxes** checkbox.

5. Specify Transmitting Subscriber ID (TSID) and Called Subscriber ID (CSID) values for routing purposes, if desired.

6. Select the **Automatic Answer** or **Manual Answer** option. If you select **Automatic Answer**, specify the number of times you want the telephone to ring before the modem answers it.

7. If your modem uses adaptive answering to distinguish between incoming fax and data calls, click the **Microsoft Modem FSP** tab and select the **Enable adaptive answering if supported by the modem** checkbox.

8. Click **OK**.

CLOSE the control panel.

In addition to at least one fax device, a fax server also needs a provider, which manages the devices and controls fax processing. Windows Server 2008 includes the Microsoft Modem Device Provider, which provides basic functionality for devices that conform to the Unimodem driver standard. Third-party providers might include additional features.

Configuring Incoming Fax Routing Policies

Fax routing policies provide administrators with various ways to give incoming faxes to their intended recipients.

When you configure the fax devices on a Windows Server 2008 fax server to receive faxes, an inbound document first goes to an incoming fax queue, until the transmission is completed. In the Windows Fax and Scan window, this queue corresponds to the Incoming folder. After the fax device has received the entire transmission, the server routes the incoming fax according to the policies you specify. The fax server can route incoming faxes in three ways, as follows:

- Route through email—The server transmits all incoming faxes to a specified email address.

- Store in a folder—The server copies all incoming faxes to a specified hard disk folder.
- Print—The server sends all incoming faxes to a specified printer.

To configure incoming routing policies, use the following procedure.

 CONFIGURE INCOMING FAX ROUTING POLICY

GET READY. Log on to Windows Server 2008 using a domain account with Administrator privileges. When the logon process is completed, close the Initial Configuration Tasks window and any other windows that appear.

1. Click **Start**, and then click **Administrative Tools** > **Fax Service Manager**. The Fax Service Manager console appears.
2. Expand the **Devices and Providers** node, the **Devices** node, and the node for the device whose routing you want to configure.
3. Select the **Incoming Methods** node. The three routing methods appear in the details pane, as shown in Figure 4-30.

Figure 4-30

The Incoming Methods for a fax device

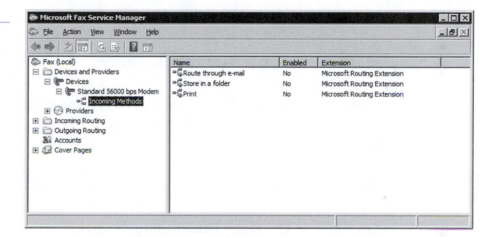

4. Right-click one of the three methods and, from the context menu, select **Properties**. The Properties sheet for the method appears.
5. Click the **E-mail**, **Store in Folder**, or **Print** tab, depending on which method you selected, as shown in Figure 4-31.

Figure 4-31

The E-mail tab of an incoming method's Properties sheet

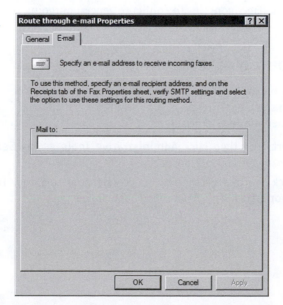

6. Specify an email address, path to a folder, or printer name in the text box provided, and then click **OK**.

7. Right-click each of the methods that you want to use and, from the context menu, select **Enable**.

8. To modify the priorities of the incoming methods, expand the **Incoming Routing** node and select **Global Methods**, as shown in Figure 4-32.

Figure 4-32

The global Incoming Routing methods

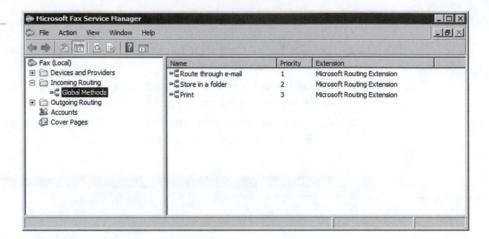

9. Right-click one of the methods and, from the context menu, select **Move Up** or **Move Down** to change its priority.

CLOSE the control panel.

You configure the incoming routing policies for each fax device individually. You can enable multiple routing methods for each device, and set their respective priorities.

Configuring Outgoing Fax Routing Policies

Outgoing fax routing policies enable you to specify the sending parameters for fax transmissions, including cover pages and dialing rules.

You can configure the properties the server should apply to outgoing faxes in two places in the Fax Service Manager console. To configure general outgoing policies, use the following procedure.

 CONFIGURE OUTGOING FAX ROUTING POLICY

GET READY. Log on to Windows Server 2008 using a domain account with Administrator privileges. When the logon process is completed, close the Initial Configuration Tasks window and any other windows that appear.

1. Click **Start**, and then click **Administrative Tools** > **Fax Service Manager**. The Fax Service Manager console appears.

2. Right-click the root of the Fax Service Manager tree and, from the context menu, select **Properties**. The Properties sheet appears.

3. Click the **Outbox** tab, as shown in Figure 4-33.

Figure 4-33

The Outbox tab of the fax
server Properties sheet

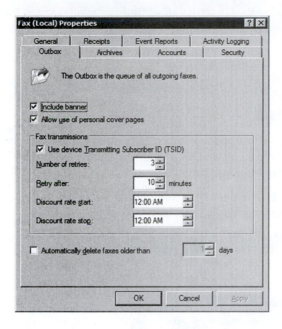

4. Configure any of the following settings:

* Include banner—Specifies whether each page of a fax should contain banner information, including the transmission date and time, the sender's TSID, the recipient's phone number, the page number, and the total number of pages.

* Allow use of personal cover pages—Specifies whether fax clients can supply their own cover pages. When cleared, clients can only use the cover pages supplied by the server.

* Use device Transmitting Subscriber ID (TSID)—Specifies whether the outgoing faxes should include the TSID for the device. When cleared, the server uses the sender's fax number, as configured in the Windows Fax and Scan program.

* Number of retries—Specifies the number of times the server should try to send a fax.

* Retry after—Specifies the number of minutes the server should wait before it retries sending a fax.

* Discount rate start—Specifies the time of day at which long distance telephone rates begin to be discounted.

* Discount rate stop—Specifies the time of day at which long distance telephone rates stop being discounted.

* Automatically delete faxes older than—Specifies the number of days that failed faxes should remain in the outgoing queue.

5. Click **OK**.

CLOSE the control panel.

The other outgoing fax policies enable you to specify which fax devices the server should use when dialing specific locations. To do this, you must create one or more routing groups and one or more rules, as in the following procedure. The routing group contains one or more of the server's fax devices, and the rule consists of a country code and/or area code, with the group that the server should use when dialing those codes.

Selecting Fax Users

For users to access the fax server, an administrator must create an account for them in the Fax Service Manager console.

To authorize user accounts, use the following procedure.

 SELECT FAX USERS

GET READY. Log on to Windows Server 2008 using a domain account with Administrator privileges. When the logon process is completed, close the Initial Configuration Tasks window and any other windows that appear.

1. Click **Start**, and then click **Administrative Tools** > **Fax Service Manager**. The Fax Service Manager console appears.

2. Right-click the **Accounts** node and, on the context menu, point to **New** and click **Account**. The Create New Account dialog box appears, as shown in Figure 4-34.

Figure 4-34

The Create New Account dialog box

3. Click **Browse**. The Select User dialog box appears, as shown in Figure 4-35.

Figure 4-35

The Select User dialog box

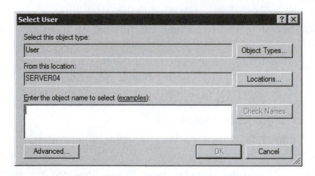

4. Key the user name in the *Enter the object name to select* text box and click **OK**.

5. Click **Create** to add the account to the fax server.

CLOSE the control panel.

The user you selected is now able to use the fax server.

SUMMARY SKILL MATRIX

IN THIS LESSON YOU LEARNED:

- Printing in Microsoft Windows typically involves the following four components: print device, printer, print server, and print driver.

- The printer driver enables you to configure the print job to use the various capabilities of the print device.

- The simplest form of print architecture consists of one print device connected to one computer, known as a locally-attached print device. You can share this printer (and the print device) with other users on the same network.

- XML Paper Specification (XPS) is a new, platform-independent document format included with Windows Server 2008 and Windows Vista, in which print job files use a single XPS format for their entire journey to the print device, rather than being converted first to EMS and then to PCL.

- With *network-attached* print devices, the administrator's primary deployment decision is which computer will function as the print server.

- Printer permissions are much simpler than NTFS permissions; they basically dictate whether users are allowed to merely use the printer, manage documents submitted to the printer, or manage the properties of the printer itself.

- The Print Management snap-in for MMC is an administrative tool that consolidates the controls for the printing components throughout the enterprise into a single console.

- To use Active Directory to deploy printers to clients, you must configure the appropriate policies in a Group Policy Object (GPO).

- Windows Server 2008 includes a Fax Server role that enables users to send faxes from and receive them to their desktops.

- You must install the Print Services role before or with the Fax Server role.

- The fax server can route incoming faxes in three ways: route through email, store in a folder, or print.

Knowledge Assessment

Fill in the Blank

Complete the following sentences by writing the correct word or words in the blanks provided.

1. Before you can share a printer on a Windows Server 2008 computer, you must enable the _____ setting in the Network and Sharing Center.

2. A(n) _____ is the software interface through which a computer communicates with a print device.

3. When you connect a single printer to multiple print devices, you create what is called a(n) _____.

4. Listing printers in the _____ enables users and administrators to search for printers by name, location, or model.

5. The _____ console enables administrators to access the configuration interface for any printer or print server.

6. When you install the Print Services role on a Windows Server 2008 computer, the two optional role services you can select are _____ and _____.

7. By default, all printers assign the _____ permission to the _____ special identity, which enables all users to access the printer and manage their own documents.

8. The _____ program enables Windows Server 2008 and Windows Vista users to send outgoing faxes or view incoming ones.

9. The three components installed when you add the Fax Server role are the _____, the _____, and the _____.

10. Users with the _____ permission can go beyond just manipulating queued documents; they can reconfigure the printer itself.

Multiple Choice

Select the correct answer for each of the following questions. Choose all answers that are correct.

1. Which of the following tasks can you perform using the printer scheduling capabilities in Windows Server 2008?
   a. Limit access to your company's color laser printer to specific hours and employees in the Graphic Designers department.
   b. Schedule the use of all company printers during specific business hours only.
   c. Associate multiple printers with a single print device to control access based on the user's department.
   d. All of the above.

2. Which of the following statements is true about deploying printer connections using Group Policy?
   a. The GPO automatically configures all users or computers in the enterprise to receive the printer connection.
   b. Only the users or computers in the domain, site, or OU linked to the GPO receive the printer connection.
   c. Printer connection deployments are limited to domains or sites.
   d. By default, neither all users nor all computers receive a printer connection when they log on.

3. Which of the following statements are true about printer control languages (PCLs)?
   a. PCLs are controlled by industry-wide standards developed by the Institute of Electrical and Electronics engineers (IEEE).
   b. PCLs ensure that spooled jobs are in PCL format, ready to go directly to the print device.
   c. PCLs can be based on industry standards.
   d. PCLs can be proprietary languages developed by print device manufacturers.

4. Which of the following statements are true about printer pools?
   a. The print server sends each incoming job to the first print device it finds that is not busy.
   b. The print server sends each incoming job to the nearest print device it finds.
   c. Printer pools must consist of multiple identical print devices.
   d. You must configure each client computer to send its print jobs to a specific print device in the pool.

5. Which of the following group(s) have the Manage Printers standard permission assigned to them by default?
   a. Power Users
   b. Domain Users
   c. Administrators
   d. Backup Operators

6. Managing a printer consists of which of the following tasks?
   a. Manipulating queued documents only.
   b. Altering the operational parameters that affect all users.

    c. Controlling access to the printer.

    d. Physical maintenance only, such as clearing paper jams and changing toner or ink cartridges.

7. Which of the following is *not* true about a fax server?

    a. You must install the Print Services role before or with the Fax Server role.

    b. Clients send faxes via the standard fax interface.

    c. If a fax server has multiple fax devices, the system can distribute outgoing faxes among a group of devices, but the entire system has only one fax job queue.

    d. The Fax Server role installs the Fax Service Manager console.

8. Which of the following steps involved in setting up a fax server should come first?

    a. Share the fax printer.   **b.** Add the Fax Server role.

    c. Configure the fax device.   **d.** Configure incoming fax routing.

9. Which of the following methods *cannot* be used by the fax server to route incoming faxes?

    a. The server sends instant messages for all incoming faxes through Windows Live Messenger.

    b. The server copies all incoming faxes to a specified hard disk folder.

    c. The server transmits all incoming faxes to a specified e-mail address.

    d. The server sends all incoming faxes to a specified printer.

10. Which of the following statements is true about a server handling heavy print traffic?

    a. Other roles and applications running on the server are likely to experience some performance degradation, but not enough for end users to notice.

    b. Other roles and applications do not experience performance degradation because the operating system provides the same priority to all of the tasks running on the server.

    c. Other roles and applications are likely to experience substantial performance degradation.

    d. Other roles and applications are likely to come to a complete standstill, causing loss of data to end users.

Review Questions

1. Explain why it is preferable to use an XPS printer driver over an EMF driver.

2. Give three reasons why it is preferable to designate a single computer as the print server for a network-attached printer as opposed to allowing each client to function as its own print server.

■ Case Scenarios

Scenario 4-1: Enhancing Print Performance

You are a desktop support technician for a law firm with a group of ten legal secretaries who provide administrative support to the attorneys. The secretaries use a single, shared, high-speed laser printer connected to a dedicated Windows Server 2008 print server. They regularly print multiple copies of large documents, and although the laser printer is fast, it runs constantly. Sometimes, the secretaries have to wait 20 minutes or more after submitting a print job for their documents to reach the top of the queue. The office manager has offered to purchase additional printers for the department. However, the secretaries are accustomed to simply clicking the Print button, and don't like the idea of having to examine multiple print queues to determine which one has the fewest jobs before submitting a document. What can you do to provide the department with a printing solution that will enable the secretaries to utilize additional printers most efficiently?

Scenario 4-2: Troubleshooting Printer Delays

One of your small business clients has a print device connected to a server running Windows Server 2008. He has shared the printer so that the other network users can access it. Often, the other users print large documents that take a long time to print, but sometimes your client and other users have important documents that need to be printed before any long documents that are waiting in the printer queue. What would you suggest to this user?

5 LESSON

Deploying IIS Services

OBJECTIVE DOMAIN MATRIX

TECHNOLOGY SKILL	OBJECTIVE DOMAIN	OBJECTIVE DOMAIN NUMBER
Creating a Web site	Manage Web sites.	3.2
Configuring Site Properties	Manage Internet Information Services (IIS).	3.5
Creating an FTP Site	Configure a File Transfer Protocol (FTP) server.	3.3

KEY TERMS

binding
File Transfer Protocol (FTP)
FTP over Secure Sockets Layer
  (SSL)
host header

Hypertext Markup Language
  (HTML)
Hypertext Transfer Protocol
  (HTTP)
protocol listener

virtual directory
virtual hosting
Windows Process Activation
  Service (WPAS)

Internet Information Services (IIS), a major component of Windows Server 2008, includes many modules and functions. This is the first of three lessons devoted to IIS, and includes the following topics:

- Installing IIS
- Creating a Web site
- Creating a virtual directory
- Configuring IIS settings
- Deploying and configuring an FTP7 server

■ Using the Web Server (IIS) Role

THE BOTTOM LINE

From its origins as a simple Web server application, Internet Information Services (IIS) has grown to be an important part of many enterprise network deployments.

In addition to hosting Web sites based on HTML (Hypertext Markup Language) pages and image files, IIS can host applications using a variety of development environments.

What's New in IIS7?

Microsoft has extensively renovated the new version of Internet Information Services included in Windows Server 2008.

Internet Information Services (IIS), now in version 7.0, has undergone major revisions for the Windows Vista and Windows Server 2008 releases. Some of the new developments are as follows:

- **Modular installation**—Compared to earlier IIS versions, which split the installation into a handful of optional components, IIS7 has more than forty individual modules for installation. For example, instead of installing all of the supported authentication methods by default, you can now select only the ones that you intend to use. This reduces the application's attack surface, minimizes the amount of memory and other system resources it needs to run, and simplifies the configuration and maintenance processes.

- **New** management interface—The IIS Manager application now uses an icon-based interface, as shown in Figure 5-1, that displays only the controls associated with the modules you have installed. The application also uses the Actions pane introduced in Microsoft Management Console 3.0 to great effect, providing context-sensitive commands for the module you have selected.

Figure 5-1

The IIS Manager interface

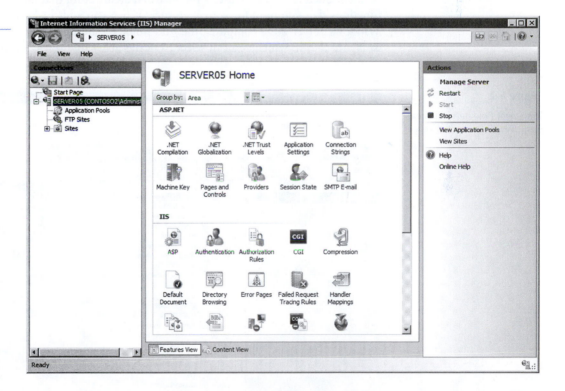

- **Command line interface**—The Virtual Basic administration scripts that IIS6 used for command line management have been replaced by a comprehensive application called AppCmd.exe, which can perform virtually any IIS configuration task from the command line.

- **Security** enhancements—As mentioned earlier, the IIS7 modular architecture enables you to install only the modules you need. By omitting the unnecessary code, you install fewer patches and attackers have fewer weaknesses to exploit. In addition, request filtering is now built into IIS7, instead of being implemented as a separate add-on product.

- **Configuration files**—IIS6 stored all of its configuration settings in the metabase, a central XML repository. IIS7 eliminates the metabase, in favor of a series of ASP.NET configuration files with .config extensions. However, IIS7 does include an IIS6 Metabase

Compatibility role service, which enables administrators to continue using any management scripts they created for the IIS6 metabase. IIS7 also provides a variety of configuration options that can help to replicate servers in a Web farm.

- Error handling—IIS7 is able to capture more information about failed requests than previous versions. The IIS log file format includes new error subcodes that provide more detailed reasons for a failure, and Failed Request Tracing capabilities, which enable IIS7 to log additional diagnostic information when an application meets specified status code, time elapsed, or error type conditions.

- Extensibility—In addition to providing control over the IIS7 modules you install, the Web server's modular architecture enables developers to create modules that plug into the same pipeline as the IIS7 components.

Selecting IIS Role Services

Internet Information Service includes a large collection of role services that you can use to customize the server installation.

As mentioned earlier, IIS7 uses a modularized architecture that enables you to install only the functions that you need for your Web sites. When you add the Web Server (IIS) role on a Windows Server 2008 computer, the Add Roles Wizard displays the Role Services page shown in Figure 5-2, in which you can select from the many role services provided with IIS.

Figure 5-2

The Select Role Services page for the Web Server (IIS) role

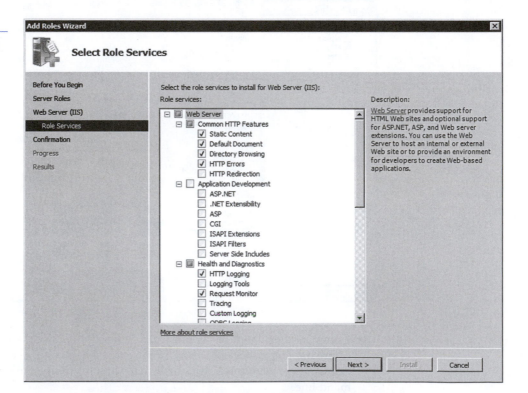

When you select the Web Server (IIS) role for installation, the wizard displays the message box shown in Figure 5-3, asking if you want to install the Windows Process Activation Service (WPAS) feature that the role requires. The default Web server (IIS) role installation requires WPAS with its Process Model and Configuration APIs components. If you select the ASP.NET or .NET Extensibility role services, the WPAS.NET Environment component is required as well.

Figure 5-3

Web Server (IIS) role dependencies

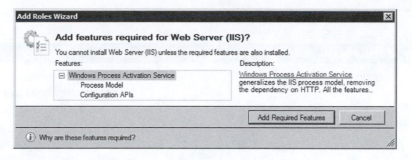

X REF

For more information about WPAS, see "Introducing the Windows Process Activation Service," later in this lesson.

The list of role services for the Web Server (IIS) role is extensive, and the default selections are minimal, consisting only of the following modules:

- Static Content
- Default Document
- Directory Browsing
- HTTP Errors
- HTTP Logging
- Request Monitor
- Request Filtering
- Static Content Compression
- IIS Management Console

These components are sufficient to create a basic, anonymous HTTP Web site. Notice that, by default, IIS has no authentication protocols, no application development environments, and only the most basic management and logging capabilities installed. To host anything beyond a simple Web site, you must install additional role services, either when you install the role or afterwards.

Fortunately, when you select additional role services, the Add Roles Wizard does not include configuration pages for each of the role services you select. The nature of the IIS architecture and the large number of role services involved precludes the possibility of using the configure-as-you-go method found in some of the other role installations. Table 5-1 lists the role services, the modules associated with them, and their functions.

Table 5-1

Web Server (IIS) Role Services and Their Functions

ROLE SERVICE	MODULE NAME	CATEGORY	FUNCTION
Static Content (*)	StaticFileModule	HTTP (Hypertext Transfer Protocol)	• Enables the Web server to publish traditional Web sites that consist only of HTML and image files. • You can omit this module if you will use only IIS to host non-HTTP sites, such as applications developed using Windows Communication Foundation (WCF).
Default Document (*)	DefaultDocumentModule	HTTP	• Specifies the name of the file that client browsers should load by default (such as index.html) when the Uniform Resource Locator (URL) received from a client does not include a filename. • Without this module, all client URLs must include filenames. • If this module is omitted and Directory Browsing is disabled or omitted, client URLs lacking a filename will result in an error.

(continued)

Table 5-1 (*continued*)

ROLE SERVICE	MODULE NAME	CATEGORY	FUNCTION
Directory Browsing (*)	DirectoryListingModule	HTTP	• Enables clients to view a listing of the files in a particular directory and navigate up and down through the directory tree. • Select this module if you want to provide Web site users with directory-based access to the files on your Web sites. • After installation, you can enable or disable this module for individual sites, as needed.
HTTP Errors (*)	CustomErrorModule	HTTP	• Enables the Web server administrator to create customized messages for specific HTTP errors. • Install this module if you want to provide specific information to clients when they experience an error, such as the email address or telephone number of the company help desk.
HTTP Redirection	HttpRedirect	HTTP	• Enables the Web server to forward incoming requests for a specific URL to another URL, such as when a site changes domain names. • This module is useful when you move a Web site to a new domain due to a product name change, company merger, or sale of a product line, and you want the Web server to automatically forward user traffic to the new URL.
ASP.NET	ASP.NET	Application Development	• Implements a server side, object-oriented programming environment, based on the .NET framework.
.NET Extensibility	NetFxExtensibility	Application Development	• Enables developers to modify the functionality of the Web server, using the ASP.Net extensibility model and the .NET application programming interfaces (APIs).
Active Server Pages (ASP)	ASP	Application Development	• Provides a server side scripting environment for the development of Web sites and applications that supports VBScript and JScript.
Common Gateway Interface (CGI)	CGIModule	Application Development	• Provides a scripting interface that enables a Web server to pass incoming information to another program.
Internet Server Application Programming Interface (ISAPI) Extensions	ISAPIModule	Application Development	• Enables the Web server to execute compiled ISAPI applications.
ISAPI Filters	ISAPIFilterModule	Application Development	• Provides support for applications that use ISAPI filters to modify the functionality of the IIS Web server.
Server Side Includes (SSI)	ServerSideIncludeModule	Application Development	• Provides support for a scripting language that enables the Web server to dynamically generate HTML pages.

(continued)

Table 5-1 (continued)

ROLE SERVICE	MODULE NAME	CATEGORY	FUNCTION
HTTP Logging (*)	HttpLoggingModule	Health and Diagnostics	• Enables the Web server to maintain logs of all Web site activity. • Virtually all Web sites can benefit from detailed examination of activity logs for troubleshooting, traffic analysis, market research, and other statistical purposes.
Logging Tools	LoggingLibraries	Health and Diagnostics	• Provides tools for managing activity logs and automating logging tasks.
Request Monitor (*)	RequestMonitorModule	Health and Diagnostics	• Captures information about HTTP requests that administrators can use to monitor the Web server's health and troubleshoot performance problems.
Tracing	HTTPTracingModule	Health and Diagnostics	• Enables the Web server to save information about failed application requests for troubleshooting purposes.
Custom Logging	CustomLoggingModule	Health and Diagnostics	• Enables administrators to log Web server activity using a customized format. • Many tools are available to analyze and interpret Web server logs in their standard format, but if you plan to use tools that require a different format, this module enables you to alter the default logs.
Open Database Connectivity (ODBC) Logging	ODBCLogging	Health and Diagnostics	• Enables the Web server to save its logs to an ODBC-compliant database. • Web server logs are typically saved as text files, but database logging can provide more advanced and automated statistical capabilities.
Basic Authentication	BasicAuthModule	Security	• Provides support for a highly compatible and relatively unsecured form of authentication, using Windows user names and passwords. • Suitable for relatively small intranet Web sites, but not for Internet sites, because it is easy to capture and decrypt the user passwords. • Use with Secure Sockets Layer (SSL).
Windows Authentication	WindowsAuthModule	Security	• Provides a secure NTLM- or Kerberos-based authentication method for domain users. • Not suitable for Web sites with clients that are not members of the domain, or who must access the site through a firewall or proxy server.
Digest Authentication	DigestAuthModule	Security	• Authenticates users by sending a password hash to a domain controller on the network. • Provides better security than Basic Authentication. • Suitable for Web sites with clients who must access the site through a firewall or proxy server.
Client Certificate Mapping Authentication	CertificateMapping-AuthenticationModule	Security	• Provides certificate-based authentication using Active Directory for one-to-one certificate mapping.

(continued)

Table 5-1 (*continued*)

ROLE SERVICE	MODULE NAME	CATEGORY	FUNCTION
IIS Client Certificate Mapping Authentication	IISCertificateMapping-AuthenticationModule	Security	• Provides certificate-based authentication using IIS for one-to-one or many-to-one certificate mapping.
URL Authorization	UrlAuthorizationModule	Security	• Enables administrators to restrict access to specific URLs by authorizing only specific users, groups, or HTTP verbs (such as GET or POST). • Suitable only for protecting intranet sites because the authorized users and groups must have a domain account or a local account on the Web server.
Request Filtering (*)	RequestFilteringModule	Security	• Enables the Web server to block malicious traffic by filtering incoming requests based on rules created by the administrator. • Replaces the URLScan utility from earlier IIS versions.
IP and Domain Restrictions	IPSecurityModule	Security	• Enables administrators to restrict access to the Web server by allowing only computers with certain IP addresses or domain names to connect.
Static Content Compression (*)	HTTPStaticCompression	Performance	• Enables the Web server to conserve network bandwidth by compressing static Web site content before transmitting it to the client.
Dynamic Content Compression	HTTPDynamic Compression	Performance	• Enables the Web server to conserve network bandwidth by compressing dynamic Web site content before transmitting it to the client, at the cost of increased Web server CPU utilization.
IIS Management Console (*)	ManagementConsole	Management Tools	• Enables administrators to manage local or remote IIS7 Web servers.
IIS Management Scripts and Tools	ManagementScripting	Management Tools	• Enables administrators to automate IIS7 management tasks using command-line tools and scripts.
Management Service	ManagementService	Management Tools	• Enables the Web server to be managed remotely using the IIS Management Console.
IIS 6 Metabase Compatibility	Metabase	Management Tools	• Translates interfaces and scripts designed for the IIS 6 metabase to the new IIS7 format.
IIS 6 WMI Compatibility	WMICompatibility	Management Tools	• Provides support for IIS 6 Windows Management Instrumentation (WMI) scripts.
IIS 6 Scripting Tools	LegacyScripts	Management Tools	• Enables administrators to use IIS 6 scripting tools to manage IIS7 Web servers.
IIS 6 Management Console	LegacySnap-in	Management Tools	• Provides the ability to manage remote IIS 6 Web servers.
FTP Server	FTPServer	FTP Publishing	• Enables the Web server to host FTP sites and respond to FTP client requests.
FTP Management Console	FTPManagement	FTP Publishing	• Enables administrators to manage local and remote IIS7 FTP sites.

Introducing the Windows Process Activation Service

WPAS enables IIS to respond to a variety of incoming message types, not just HTTP.

A Web server is essentially a program that listens for incoming requests from clients and responds to those requests by supplying data or executing an instruction. Originally, Web servers listened only for messages sent using the *Hypertext Transfer Protocol (HTTP)*, the standard application layer protocol for Web communications, which client browsers generated when a user keyed or clicked a link for a Uniform Resource Locator (URL). On receiving such a request, the server responded by transmitting a file back to the client, coded using *Hypertext Markup Language (HTML)*, a simple coding language that provides the client browser with instructions on displaying the text in the file and embedding the accompanying image files.

Today, however, Web servers can also listen for types of requests other than HTTP and respond by executing programs and sending the resulting data back to the client in any number of different forms. This means that several modules other than the HTTP listener are listening for client requests. In previous versions of IIS, the World Wide Web Publishing Service (W3SVC) managed all requests; the process was essentially HTTP-centric.

In IIS7, the modular architecture extends into the request handling process as well. Instead of a monolithic, HTTP-based request pipeline with support for additional request types tacked on to it, IIS7 uses a generic request pipeline that is modular in nature. When you select the role services that provide support for various types of applications, IIS7 plugs those modules into the pipeline.

The component that manages the request pipeline, the server's application pools, and the worker processes running in them is called the *Windows Process Activation Service (WPAS)*. As mentioned earlier in this lesson, you must install the WPAS feature, with its subfeatures, to run the Web Server (IIS) role. Because WPAS now handles incoming requests instead of the W3SVC service, those requests do not have to be based on HTTP. Therefore, you can use IIS7 to implement applications through HTTP or non-HTTP Web sites.

■ Publishing IIS Web Sites

↓
THE BOTTOM LINE
IIS creates a default Web site when you install it, but you can create as many additional sites as you wish.

After you have installed the Web Server (IIS) role, you can use the Internet Information Services (IIS) Manager application to create, configure, and secure sites, and deploy applications, if desired. These procedures are covered in the following sections, as well as in Lesson 6, "Securing IIS Services," and Lesson 7, "Deploying Web Applications."

Creating a Web Site

Any additional Web sites you create on an IIS7 server inherit the default server settings unless you modify them manually.

When you install the Web Server (IIS) role on a Windows Server 2008 system, IIS7 automatically creates a default Web site, using the modules you selected for installation with the role. You can use that default site to publish your content, reconfiguring it as needed, or you can create additional sites on the server.

To create a new IIS7 Web site, use the following procedure.

CERTIFICATION READY?
Manage Web sites

3.2

→ **CREATE A WEB SITE**

GET READY. Log on to Windows Server 2008 using a domain account with Administrator privileges. When the logon process is completed, close the Initial Configuration Tasks window and any other windows that appear.

1. Click **Start**, and then click **Administrative Tools** > **Internet Information Services (IIS) Manager**. The Internet Information Services (IIS) Manager console appears, as shown in Figure 5-4.

Figure 5-4

The Internet Information Services (IIS) Manager console

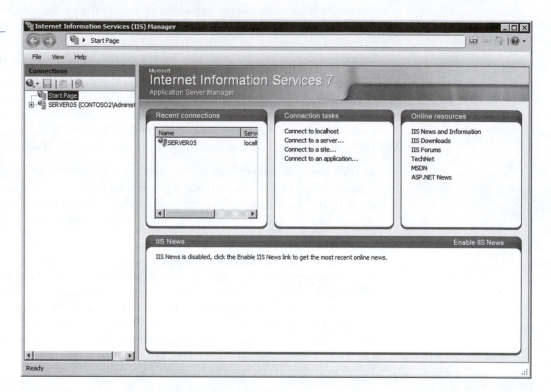

2. In the scope pane, expand the local server. Then, right-click the **Sites** node and, from the context menu, select **Add Web Site**. The Add Web Site dialog box appears, as shown in Figure 5-5.

Figure 5-5

The Add Web Site dialog box

3. In the Web Site Name text box, key the name you want to use for the site.

4. In the Physical Path text box, key or browse to the folder containing the content files for the Web site.

   If the content files are located in a folder that requires authentication for access, click **Connect as** and supply the credentials needed. Remember that IIS requires access to the content files, whether you are logged on to the computer or not.

5. In the Binding box, specify the IP Address, Port, and/or Host Header settings that IIS will use to uniquely identify this Web site.

6. To make the site active as soon as it is created, leave the *Start Web site immediately* checkbox selected.

7. Click **OK** to create the site. The name you selected appears under the Sites node.

CLOSE the Internet Information Services (IIS) Manager console.

If you have selected the *Start Web site immediately* checkbox during the Web site creation process, the site is immediately available to clients supplying the correct URL. If you have not, you must start the site by selecting Start from the actions pane.

Creating a Virtual Directory

> Virtual directories enable you to use a Web site to publish files located anywhere on the network.

When you create a Web site in IIS7, all of the files and folders in the home folder you specify in the Physical Path text box become available on the new site. However, IIS7 also enables you to create virtual directories on your sites. A ***virtual directory*** is an alias that points to a folder in another physical location, essentially a shortcut that enables you to publish content found on different drives or different computers, without copying or moving it.

For example, your company might want to host some of the same documents on several different Web sites. Rather than copy the documents to each content folder, you can create a virtual directory on each site, pointing to a central location where you stored the documents. This way, you can conserve disk space by maintaining a single copy of each document file, and you don't have to replicate the documents to each site when anyone modifies them.

In addition to providing access to content located anywhere on your network, virtual directories also hide the actual locations of your files from the Web clients, which helps to secure your server. To create a virtual directory on one of your sites, use the following procedure.

 CREATE A VIRTUAL DIRECTORY

GET READY. Log on to Windows Server 2008 using a domain account with Administrator privileges. When the logon process is completed, close the Initial Configuration Tasks window and any other windows that appear.

1. Click **Start**, and then click **Administrative Tools** > **Internet Information Services (IIS) Manager**. The Internet Information Services (IIS) Manager console appears.

2. In the scope pane, expand the local server. Then, expand the **Sites** node, right-click a site and, from the context menu, select **Add Virtual Directory**. The Add Virtual Directory dialog box appears, as shown in Figure 5-6.

Figure 5-6

The Add Virtual Directory dialog box

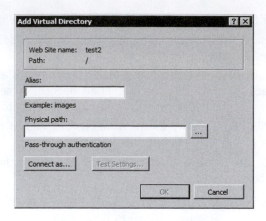

3. In the Alias text box, key the name for the virtual directory on your Web site.

4. In the Physical Path text box, key or browse to the physical location of the folder you want to add to the site as a virtual directory.

5. If the Web server needs credentials to access the folder you specified, click **Connect as**, supply a user name and password, and then click **OK**.

6. Click **OK** to close the Add Virtual Directory dialog box. The new virtual directory appears beneath the site you selected.

CLOSE the Internet Information Services (IIS) Manager console.

After you have created a virtual directory, you can configure it with its own settings for many IIS7 modules, including Default Document, Directory Browsing, and Error Pages. These settings override those the virtual directory inherits from its parent site or server.

Configuring Site Properties

> The modular architecture of IIS7 provides an icon-based interface that you can use to configure a Web site's many properties.

CERTIFICATION READY?
Manage Internet Information Services (IIS)
3.5

Assuming that you leave the *Start Web site immediately* checkbox selected, each new Web site that you create in IIS7 should be immediately accessible from a Web browser. However, you might want to configure a number of other site properties before you consider it ready for your users.

TAKE NOTE*

> The following sections discuss some of the most basic Web site configuration tasks you are likely to perform in IIS7. Remember, however, that many of these tasks are dependent on selecting the appropriate role services when you install the Web Server (IIS) role. If the controls for a particular feature do not appear in your IIS Manager console, it is probably because the dependent role service is not installed.

X REF

For information on configuring Web site permissions and other security issues, see Lesson 6, "Securing IIS Services." For information on configuring Web sites to host applications, see Lesson 7, "Deploying Web Applications."

CONFIGURING SITE BINDINGS

IIS7 is capable of hosting many separate Web sites simultaneously. However, for the Web sites to be accessible to clients, the HTTP *protocol listener*, Http.sys, must have some way of associating each incoming request with one particular Web site. The *binding* for each site determines how the listener will identify its requests.

IIS7 supports three HTTP binding options, as described in the following sections:

- IP address—You can assign multiple IP addresses to a single network connection on the Web server and use a different address for each site hosted by IIS7. For this method to function practically, you must register each IP address in a DNS domain with a different host name.

• Port number—HTTP Web sites use the well-known port number 80, but you can differentiate sites by assigning different port numbers to them. However, client browsers use the port number 80 by default, so to access the sites with alternative ports, users must specify the port number in the URL, following the server name and a colon, as in the example http://www.contoso.com:1024.

• Host header—HTTP request messages contain a Host: field containing a server name, which IIS7 uses to associate the request with one of the sites it is hosting. For this method to function, you must register each of the host header names you specify in your Web site bindings in a DNS domain, using the IP address of the server. Sometimes known as *virtual hosting*, this method enables the Web server to host multiple Web sites using a single IP address and port number, without requiring any special information from clients.

CONFIGURING IP ADDRESS HOSTING

You can assign multiple IP addresses to a single network connection on the Web server, and use a different address for each site hosted by IIS7. To set this up, use the following procedure.

 CONFIGURE IP ADDRESS HOSTING

GET READY. Log on to Windows Server 2008 using a domain account with Administrator privileges. When the logon process is completed, close the Initial Configuration Tasks window and any other windows that appear.

1. Click **Start**, and then **Control Panel**. Open the **Network and Sharing Center** and click **Manage Network Connections**. The Network Connections window appears.

2. Right-click the connection you want to modify and, from the context menu, select **Properties**. The connection's Properties sheet appears.

3. Select **Internet Protocol Version 4 (TCP/IPv4)** and click **Properties**. The Internet Protocol Version 4 (TCP/IPv4) Properties sheet appears.

4. Click **Advanced**. The Advanced TCP/IP Settings dialog box appears, as shown in Figure 5-7.

Figure 5-7

The Advanced TCP/IP Settings sheet

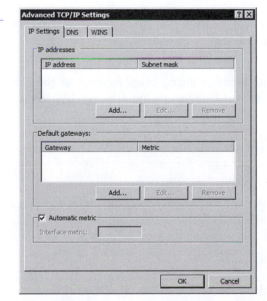

5. Click **Add**. The TCP/IP Address dialog box appears.

6. Key an IP address and subnet mask in the text boxes provided and click **OK**. The address appears in the IP Addresses box on the Advanced TCP/IP Settings sheet.

7. Create additional IP address entries as needed.

8. Click **OK** three times to close the dialog boxes. At this point, all of the IP addresses appearing in the Advanced TCP/IP Properties sheet are equally valid addresses for the computer.

9. Click **Administrative Tools** > **Internet Information Services (IIS) Manager**. The Internet Information Services (IIS) Manager console appears.

10. In the scope pane, right-click one of the Web sites on the server and, from the context menu, select **Edit Bindings**. The Site Bindings dialog box appears, like the one shown in Figure 5-8.

Figure 5-8

The Site Bindings dialog box

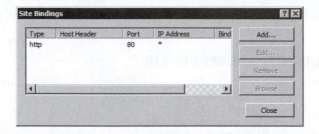

11. Select the existing binding and click **Edit**. An Edit Site Binding dialog box appears, as shown in Figure 5-9.

Figure 5-9

The Edit Site Binding dialog box

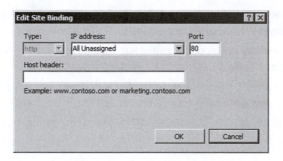

12. Using the IP Address dropdown list, select one of the IP addresses you assigned to the network connection. Click **OK**.

13. Click **Close**.

14. Open the Site Bindings dialog boxes for each of the other sites hosted by IIS7 and configure their bindings to use different IP addresses.

CLOSE the Network Connections window.

IIS7 configures the Default Web Site to use the All Unassigned setting for the IP Address binding. When you create a new Web site using IP address hosting, you must configure it with its own unique IP address binding.

After you have changed the bindings for your sites, users can access each of the Web sites on the IIS7 by keying a URL containing the appropriate IP address in a Web browser, as in http://192.168.4.58. For clients to be able to use server names in their URLs, you must create a Host (A) record in your DNS domain for each IP address, associating it with a different server name.

For example, if you have created three Web sites on an IIS7 Web server, and bound each one to a different IP address, you must create three Host records in your DNS domain, using information such as the following:

```
www          192.168.4.58
sales        192.168.4.59
support      192.168.4.60
```

After you have created the DNS records, your clients can access the Web servers using the names you specified. If your domain is called contoso.com, requests containing the three URLs http://www.contoso.com, http://sales.contoso.com, and http://support.contoso.com will all arrive at the IIS7 Web server, because each one is associated with one of the server's IP addresses. However, based on the different IP address in each request, IIS7 will send the www request to the Web site bound to 192.168.4.58, the sales request to 192.168.4.59, and the support request to 192.168.4.60.

The disadvantage of IP address hosting is that, for Internet Web servers, each site must have its own registered IP address, which can be inconvenient to manage and expensive to maintain.

CONFIGURING PORT NUMBER HOSTING

HTTP Web sites use the well-known TCP (Transmission Control Protocol) port number 80, but you can differentiate sites by assigning different port numbers to them. To do this, use the following procedure.

 CONFIGURE PORT NUMBER HOSTING

GET READY. Log on to Windows Server 2008 using a domain account with Administrator privileges. When the logon process is completed, close the Initial Configuration Tasks window and any other windows that appear.

1. Click **Start**, and then click **Administrative Tools** > **Internet Information Services (IIS) Manager**. The Internet Information Services (IIS) Manager console appears.
2. In the scope pane, right-click one of your Web sites and, from the context menu, select **Edit Bindings**. The Site Bindings dialog box appears.
3. Select the existing binding and click **Edit**. An Edit Site Binding dialog box appears.
4. In the Port text box, key the port number you want to associate with the site. Then click **OK**.
5. Click **Close**.
6. Open the Site Bindings dialog box for the other sites on the server and configure each of them to use a different port number.

CLOSE the Internet Information Services (IIS) Manager console.

The problem with port number hosting, and the reason why few Web servers use it, is that it requires clients to change their habits. All browser applications assume the port number 80 by default. When you key the URL http://www.contoso.com, the browser sends an HTTP request to port 80 on the specified Web server. To access a site using a different port, users must specify the port number in the URL, following the server name and a colon, as in http://www.contoso.com:1024. Not only are most Web users unaware of what a TCP port is and what it does, they also have no way of knowing what port number to use, unless you somehow inform them.

> **+ MORE INFORMATION**
>
> Some Web servers and administrators use alternative port number assignments to keep certain Web sites hidden from general users. These sites use a randomly chosen port number, and unless users know or guess the number, or use a port scanner to discover it, they cannot access the site. This is obviously not a secure arrangement; much more effective means of controlling access to a Web site are discussed in Lesson 6, "Securing IIS Services."

CONFIGURING HOST HEADER HOSTING

TCP/IP networks communicate using IP addresses, not computer names. When a client keys a URL into a browser, the program first sends the name of the server in the URL to a DNS server, which resolves it into an IP address. Then, the browser generates an HTTP request message and transmits it to the Web server's IP address, which it received from the DNS server.

However, the HTTP request message also contains a ***Host header*** field, which contains the name of the Web server to which the client is sending the request. IIS7 can use this Host field to associate the request with one of the Web sites it is hosting. For example, IIS7 might be hosting three Web sites, each with a different server name, as follows:

```
www.contoso.com
sales.contoso.com
support.contoso.com
```

All three names resolve to the same IP address in the DNS database, so no matter which name clients use in their URLs, the HTTP request messages all go to the same Web server. When IIS7 receives the messages, it checks the contents of the Host field, and sends the request message to the Web site associated with the server name it finds there. This is the most commonly used method for creating multiple virtual Web servers on a single computer.

To configure IIS7 sites to use host header hosting, use the following procedure.

 CONFIGURE HOST HEADER HOSTING

GET READY. Log on to Windows Server 2008 using a domain account with Administrator privileges. When the logon process is completed, close the Initial Configuration Tasks window and any other windows that appear.

1. Click **Start**, and then click **Administrative Tools** > **Internet Information Services (IIS) Manager**. The Internet Information Services (IIS) Manager console appears.
2. In the scope pane, right-click one of your Web sites and, from the context menu, select **Edit Bindings**. The Site Bindings dialog box appears.
3. Select the existing binding and click **Edit**. An Edit Site Binding dialog box appears.
4. In the *Host header* text box, key the server name that you want IIS7 to associate with that site. Then click **OK**.
5. Click **Close**.
6. Open the Site Bindings dialog boxes for the other sites on the server and configure each of them to use a different *Host header* value.

CLOSE the Internet Information Services (IIS) Manager console.

For this hosting method to function, you must register each of the host header names you specify in the Web site bindings in your DNS domain, using the IP address of the server. Sometimes known as virtual hosting, this method enables a Web server to host multiple Web sites using a single IP address and port number, without the clients requiring any special knowledge.

CONFIGURING THE DEFAULT DOCUMENT FILENAMES

The URLs that clients key into their browsers usually do not include a filename; they contain only server and directory names. When a Web server receives an HTTP request, it parses the URL and locates the directory it specifies. When the URL does not specify a filename, the Web server replies to the request with the default file specified for the Web site. When you install the Default Document role service in IIS7, you can specify default filenames for the entire Web server, and for each of the server's Web sites, individually.

The original default filename for the Web was index.html, but Web servers running on Windows computers were then constrained to the 8.3 file naming format, and frequently used index.htm instead. IIS has traditionally used the filename default.htm. The Default Document module in IIS7 includes all of the filenames, plus others supporting Active Server Pages (ASP). When the server processes a request, it checks the directory specified in the URL for each filename in the list sequentially and replies to the client with the first named file that it finds.

In IIS7, you can configure default document filenames for the entire Web server or for individual Web sites. Each Web site inherits the Default Document settings from the server, until you modify them.

To configure default document filenames, use the following procedure.

→ CONFIGURE DEFAULT DOCUMENT FILENAMES

GET READY. Log on to Windows Server 2008 using a domain account with Administrator privileges. When the logon process is completed, close the Initial Configuration Tasks window and any other windows that appear.

TAKE NOTE * Before you can configure Default Document filenames, you must install the Default Document role service in the Web Server (IIS) role.

1. Click **Start**, and then click **Administrative Tools** > **Internet Information Services (IIS) Manager**. The Internet Information Services (IIS) Manager console appears.
2. In the scope pane, select the node named for your server. The server home page appears in the details pane.
3. Double-click the **Default Document** icon in the IIS area. The Default Document pane appears, as shown in Figure 5-10, displaying the current default filenames for the server.

Figure 5-10

The Default Document pane

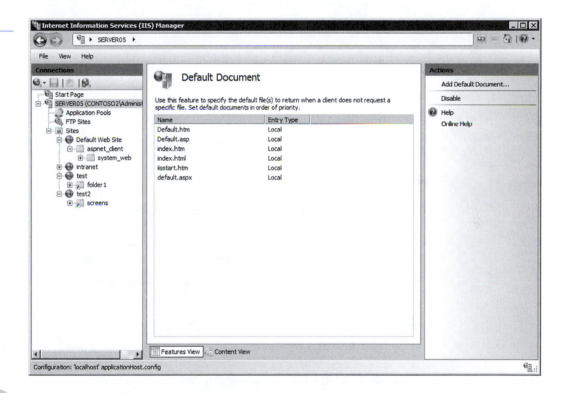

TAKE NOTE *

Like many other IIS7 parameters, you can configure Default Document settings at the site or virtual directory level, in addition to the server level. This enables you to specify different default document names for individual Web sites and virtual directories, which override the server settings.

4. Use one of the following procedures to manage the Default Document entries:
   - To delete one of the existing entries, select it and click **Remove** in the Actions pane.
   - To create a new entry, click **Add** in the Actions pane. In the Add Default Document dialog box that appears, key a filename in the Name text box and click **OK**.
   - To change the order of the files in the list, select an entry and, in the Actions pane, click **Move Up** or **Move Down**.
5. Click the **Back** arrow to return to the server home page.

CLOSE the Internet Information Services (IIS) Manager console.

To configure the default document filenames for an individual site, you simply select the site and perform the same procedure. You will notice that the Default Documents page for a site indicates that the default filename entries are inherited, not local. Any new entries you create will be local to the site.

CONFIGURING DIRECTORY BROWSING

When IIS7 receives an HTTP request containing a URL with no filename, and none of the default document filenames exist in the specified folder, the Web server has two choices: it can generate an error message, or it can display a directory listing, as shown in Figure 5-11. The directory listing enables the user to browse the site's directory structure and select files to display in the browser.

Figure 5-11

An IIS Web site directory display

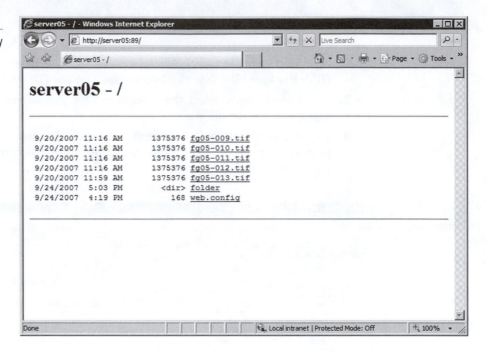

For an IIS7 Web site to provide clients with directory browsing capability, you must install the Directory Browsing role service and enable it. Like the Default Directory settings, you can configure Directory Browsing at the server level, and each of the sites on the server will inherit the setting you select, unless you explicitly change it for a particular site. You can also select different directory browsing settings for a site's virtual directories.

To configure directory browsing, use the following procedure.

 CONFIGURE DIRECTORY BROWSING

GET READY. Log on to Windows Server 2008 using a domain account with Administrator privileges. When the logon process is completed, close the Initial Configuration Tasks window and any other windows that appear.

> **TAKE NOTE★**
>
> Before you can configure Directory Browsing, you must install the Directory Browsing role service in the Web Server (IIS) role.

1. Click **Start**, and then click **Administrative Tools** > **Internet Information Services (IIS) Manager**. The Internet Information Services (IIS) Manager console appears.

2. In the scope pane, select a server, site, or virtual directory node. The home page for the element you selected appears in the details pane.

3. Double-click the **Directory Browsing** icon in the IIS area. The Directory Browsing pane appears, as shown in Figure 5-12, displaying the current Directory Browsing settings.

Figure 5-12

The Directory Browsing pane

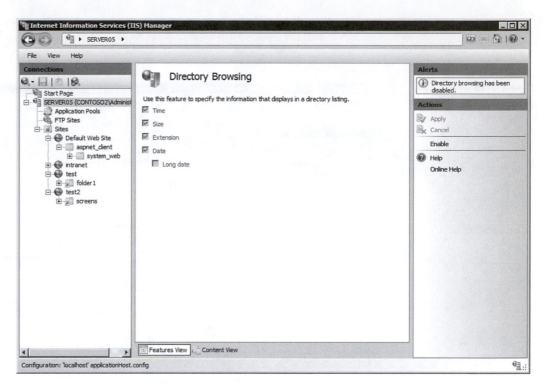

4. Use one of the following procedures to manage the Default Document entries:
- To enable or disable directory browsing, click **Enable** or **Disable** in the Actions pane.
- To specify the information the clients should see in the directory listing, select or clear the checkboxes in the Directory Browsing pane.

5. Click the **Back** arrow to return to the server home page.

CLOSE the Internet Information Services (IIS) Manager console.

For Internet Web sites, enabling directory browsing is usually considered a security breach, albeit a minor one, because it provides users with direct access to the site's files. However, for certain types of files, such as large collections of images, it can be easier to enable directory browsing than to create a page containing links to all of the images.

CONFIGURING WEB SITE LOGGING

HTTP Logging is one of the role services that Windows Server 2008 installs by default with the Web Server (IIS) role. You can configure the log format and other parameters, using the following procedure.

CONFIGURE WEB SITE LOGGING

GET READY. Log on to Windows Server 2008 using a domain account with Administrator privileges. When the logon process is completed, close the Initial Configuration Tasks window and any other windows that appear.

 TAKE NOTE*

Before you can configure Web Site Logging, you must install the HTTP Logging role service in the Web Server (IIS) role.

1. Click **Start**, and then click **Administrative Tools** > **Internet Information Services (IIS) Manager**. The Internet Information Services (IIS) Manager console appears.

2. In the scope pane, select a server, site, or virtual directory node. The home page for the server you selected appears in the details pane.

3. Double-click the **Logging** icon in the IIS area. The Logging pane appears, as shown in Figure 5-13, displaying the current Logging settings.

Figure 5-13

The Logging pane

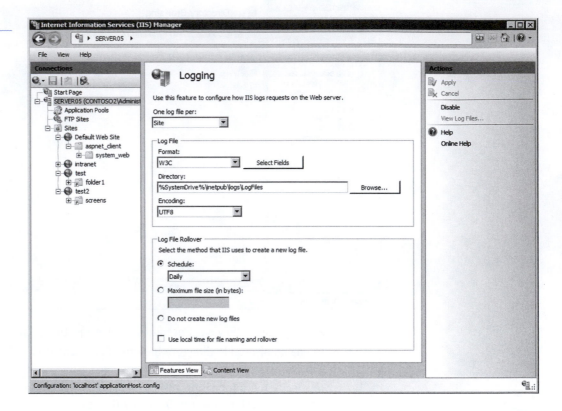

4. Using the *One log file per* dropdown list, specify whether you want IIS to create a single log for the entire server or separate logs for each site.

Selecting the Site option propagates the server's logging settings to all of the individual sites as defaults. You can then configure the logging settings for individual sites, to override the defaults.

5. Using the Format dropdown list, select the format you want IIS to use for the log files from the following options:

- Binary—Creates a single binary log file for all of the sites on the server. This option is not available for individual sites. If you select this option for the server and configure a site to use a different format, you must specify a different log filename for the site. To access binary logs, you must use a product such as Microsoft Log Parser.

- W3C—Configures the server or site to use the World Wide Web Consortium's log file format, which is space-delimited and records time stamps in Coordinated Universal Time (UTC). You can specify the information IIS saves to the log by clicking **Select Fields**, to open the W3C Logging Fields dialog box, as shown in Figure 5-14.

Figure 5-14

The W3C Logging Fields dialog box

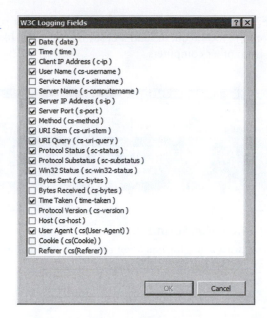

- IIS—Configures the site to use the native IIS log file format, which is comma-delimited, uses local time for time stamps, and is not customizable.

- NCSA—Configures the site to use the National Center for Supercomputing Applications log file format, which is space-delimited, uses UTC time for time stamps, and is not customizable.

- Custom—Disables the IIS logging capability, so that you can use a custom logging module.

6. In the Directory text box, key or browse to the folder where you want IIS7 to create the log files.

7. In the Encoding dropdown list, select the encoding scheme you want to use for the log files, from the following options:

- UTF-8—Supports single-byte and multibyte characters, providing support for non-English language logging.

- ANSI—Supports only single-byte characters.

8. In the Log File Rollover box, specify how and when you want IIS7 to create new log files by selecting from the following options:

- Schedule—Configures IIS to create a new log file at the interval you specify: hourly, daily, weekly, or monthly.

- Maximum file size—Configures IIS7 to create a new log file when the old file reaches a specified size, in bytes.

- Do not create new log files—Configures IIS7 to use a single log file.

9. In the actions pane, click **Apply** to save your changes.

CLOSE the Internet Information Services (IIS) Manager console.

Web server logs are text files containing raw information about the activities of the server or a particular site. With this raw data, you can use third-party products to display detailed information about your site or server traffic, often in graphical form.

CONFIGURING ERROR PAGES

When a Web server cannot process a client request, it generates an error code, which specifies the reason for the problem. For example, if a client sends a request for a filename that does not exist, the server generates an HTTP 404.0 — Not Found. The code numbers for the errors are standardized in the HTTP specifications, but how the error messages are presented is left up to the Web server implementation.

By default, when IIS7 generates a 404 error, it sends a detailed error page, like the one shown in Figure 5-15, in response to local requests, and a custom error page, like the one in Figure 5-16, for requests coming from other computers.

Figure 5-15

An IIS7 detailed error page

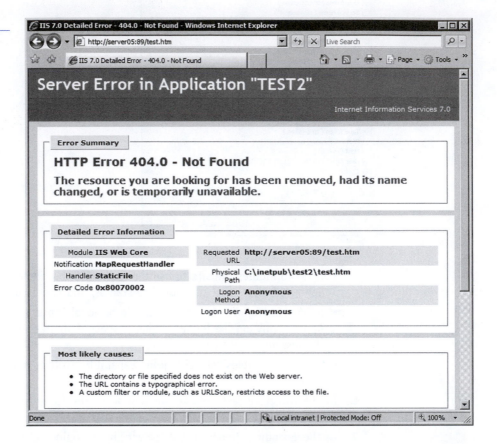

Figure 5-16

An IIS7 custom error page

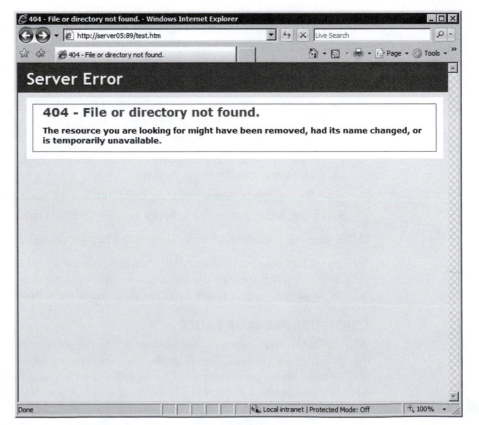

The detailed error page is designed to provide debugging information for administrators and Web site developers. For remote clients, the server uses a simpler error page that does not disclose any potentially sensitive information to outside users.

The HTTP Errors role service enables administrators to control which type of error page the server should use and specify alternatives to IIS7's preconfigured custom error pages. Like most of the other modules, the settings you configure for the server are inherited by the individual sites on that server, unless you override them by configuring the sites separately.

To configure the error pages for a server or site, use the following procedure.

CONFIGURE ERROR PAGES SETTINGS

Before you can configure error pages, you must install the HTTP Errors role service in the Web Server (IIS) role.

GET READY. Log on to Windows Server 2008 using a domain account with Administrator privileges. When the logon process is completed, close the Initial Configuration Tasks window and any other windows that appear.

1. Click **Start**, and then click **Administrative Tools** > **Internet Information Services (IIS) Manager**. The Internet Information Services (IIS) Manager console appears.

2. In the scope pane, select a server, site, or virtual directory node. The home page for the server you selected appears in the details pane.

3. Double-click the **Error Pages** icon in the IIS area. The Error Pages pane appears, as shown in Figure 5-17, displaying the current page entries.

Figure 5-17

The Error Pages pane

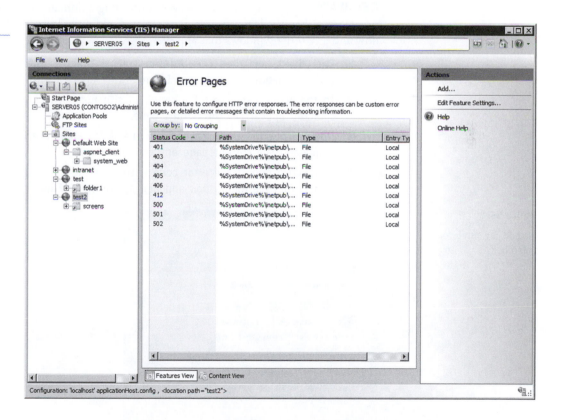

4. In the Actions pane, click **Edit Feature Settings**. The Edit Error Pages Settings dialog box appears.

5. In the Error Responses box, select one of the following options:
   • Custom error pages—Displays custom error pages for all types of requests, disabling detailed errors.

- Detailed errors—Displays detailed errors for all types of requests, disabling custom error pages.
- Detailed errors for local requests and custom error pages for remote requests—Displays detailed errors for requests generated by the local computer and custom error pages for all requests from other computers. This is the default setting.

6. In the Path text box, specify a path or URL for the custom error page you want the server to display.

7. In the Path Type dropdown list, select the type of path you specified in the Path text box, choosing from the following options:

- File—Specifies a full path to a static page, such as an HTML file.
- Execute URL—Specifies a URL to a file providing dynamic content, such as an ASP file.
- Redirect—Species the full URL of a Web page containing a custom error page.

8. Click **OK**.

CLOSE the Internet Information Services (IIS) Manager console.

Completing this procedure configures the basic settings for all of the error pages generated by a server, site, or virtual directory. To configure the custom page for a specific error code, use the following procedure.

 CONFIGURE INDIVIDUAL ERROR PAGES

GET READY. Log on to Windows Server 2008 using a domain account with Administrator privileges. When the logon process is completed, close the Initial Configuration Tasks window and any other windows that appear.

1. Click **Start**, and then click **Administrative Tools** > **Internet Information Services (IIS) Manager**. The Internet Information Services (IIS) Manager console appears.

2. In the scope pane, select a server or site node. The home page for the server you selected appears in the details pane.

3. Double-click the **Error Pages** icon in the IIS area. The Error Pages pane appears, displaying the current page entries.

4. Right-click one of the error code entries in the list and click **Edit**. The Edit Custom Error Page dialog box appears, as shown in Figure 5-18.

Figure 5-18

The Edit Custom Error Page dialog box

5. In the Response Action box, select and configure one of the following options:

- Insert content from a static file into the error response—Specifies a path to an HTML file containing content that you want to appear on the custom error page

for the selected code. To support multiple languages, create a separate content folder for each language and select the *Try to return the error file in the client language* checkbox.

- Execute a URL on this site—Specifies a relative path to another page on the same site containing content that you want to appear on the custom error page for the selected code.

- Respond with a 302 redirect—Specifies a full URL to a page on another site containing content that you want to appear on the custom error page for the selected code.

6. Click **OK** to save your changes.

CLOSE the Internet Information Services (IIS) Manager console.

By creating custom error pages, you can provide users with information about the problem they are experiencing or specify how they can contact the technical support staff.

Deploying an FTP Server

 THE BOTTOM LINE FTP7 does not ship with Windows Server 2008, but it is available as a free download.

Windows Server 2008 ships with an FTP Publishing Service role service, but if you install it, you will find that it is virtually identical to the one included in Windows Server 2003. It even requires you to use the old IIS6 Management console to create and configure FTP sites; it is not compatible with the IIS7 Management console. However, an FTP Publishing Service for IIS7 is available as a free download from Microsoft's Web site. FTP7 is compatible with the IIS7 Management console, as well as other new IIS7 features, such as XML-based configuration files with .config extensions, shared configurations, and modular extensibility.

> ⊕ **MORE INFORMATION**
> FTP7 is being released at the same time as Windows Server 2008, but development schedules made it impossible to include it on the Windows Server 2008 installation DVD.

What's New in FTP7?

> FTP7 is fully integrated with IIS7.

File Transfer Protocol (FTP) is an application layer protocol that enables a client to connect to a remote server, perform rudimentary file management tasks, and copy files in either direction between the two computers. FTP is defined by the RFC 114 document, which the Internet Engineering Task Force (IETF) published in 1971, making it one of the oldest TCP/IP protocols still in use. Originally implemented as command-line applications, FTP clients now most often use a graphical interface and are integrated into most browser applications, including Internet Explorer.

Some of the new features in FTP7 are as follows:

- IIS7 integration—FTP7 eliminates the need for the old IIS6 FTP Management console and metabase, as it is fully integrated with the modular IIS7 Manager console and its new configuration architecture.

- *FTP over Secure Sockets Layer (SSL)*—The original FTP standard has no provision for password protection or data encryption; the client transmits user names and passwords to the server in clear text, which in today's environment is highly insecure. FTP7 can use SSL to encrypt its authentication traffic before transmission, providing protection for sensitive passwords, as well as the file data itself.

- Combined FTP and Web hosting—Because FTP is now integrated into IIS7, you can allow Web and FTP access to the same site, simply by adding an FTP binding to an existing Web site.

- Virtual host naming—FTP7 supports host name hosting, just like IIS7 Web sites, enabling you to publish multiple FTP sites on a single computer, using one IP address and port number.

- Improved logging and error handling—FTP7 can now provide detailed error messages for local clients, and its logs include additional fields, session tracking, and sub-status codes.

Installing FTP7

To use FTP7, you must install it in a Windows Server 2008 computer that is already running the Web Server (IIS) role.

Before you install FTP7, make sure that IIS7 is not running the FTP Publishing Service role services that ship with Windows Server 2008. If these role services are installed, be sure to uninstall them before you install FTP7.

To install FTP7, use the following procedure.

 INSTALL FTP7

GET READY. Log on to Windows Server 2008 using a domain account with Administrator privileges. When the logon process is completed, close the Initial Configuration Tasks window and any other windows that appear.

1. Download Microsoft FTP Publishing Service for IIS 7.0 from the IIS Web site at www.iis.net/downloads.

2. Run the Windows Installer package you downloaded by double-clicking it in any Windows Explorer window. The Welcome to the Microsoft FTP Publishing Service for IIS 7.0 Setup Wizard page appears.

3. Click **Next**. The End User License Agreement page appears.

4. Select the **I accept the terms in the license agreement** checkbox and click **Next**. The Custom Setup page appears, as shown in Figure 5-19.

Figure 5-19

The Custom Setup page in the Microsoft FTP Publishing Service for IIS 7.0 RCO Setup Wizard

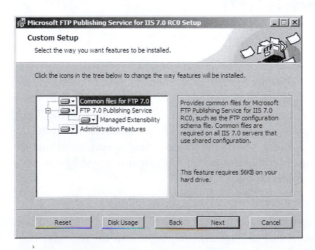

5. Modify the default setup settings to omit features, if desired, and click **Next**. The Ready to install Microsoft FTP Publishing Service for IIS 7.0 page appears.

6. Click **Install**. The Completed the Microsoft FTP Publishing Service for IIS 7.0 Setup Wizard page appears.

7. Click **Finish**.

After you have installed FTP7, the Internet Information Services (IIS) Manager console receives an FTP section, as shown in Figure 5-20, which contains the icons you use to configure the individual FTP parameters.

Figure 5-20

FTP7 icons in the Internet Information Services (IIS) Manager console

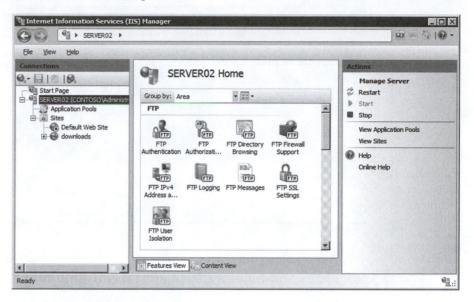

Creating an FTP Site

You can use FTP capabilities on existing Web sites or create new, independent FTP sites.

CERTIFICATION READY?
Configure a File Transfer Protocol (FTP) server
3.3

After you have installed FTP7, you can create an FTP site on your server in one of two basic ways: you can create an entirely new site, devoted to FTP, or you can add FTP capabilities to an existing Web site.

To create a new, dedicated FTP site, use the following procedure.

 CREATE AN FTP SITE

GET READY. Log on to Windows Server 2008 using a domain account with Administrator privileges. When the logon process is completed, close the Initial Configuration Tasks window and any other windows that appear.

1. Click **Start**, and then click **Administrative Tools** > **Internet Information Services (IIS) Manager**. The Internet Information Services (IIS) Manager console appears.

2. In the scope pane, expand the server node. Then, right-click the **Sites** node and, from the context menu, select **Add FTP Site**. The Add FTP Site wizard appears, displaying the Site Information page, as shown in Figure 5-21.

Figure 5-21

The Site Information page of
the Add FTP Site wizard

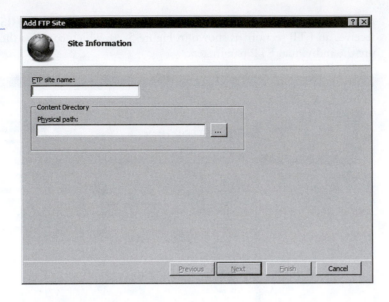

3. In the *FTP site name* text box, key the name you want to use to identify the site.

4. In the *Physical path* text box, key or browse to the folder that will be the root directory for the FTP site. Then click **Next**. The Binding and SSL Settings page appears, as shown in Figure 5-22.

Figure 5-22

The Binding and SSL Settings
page of the Add FTP Site
wizard

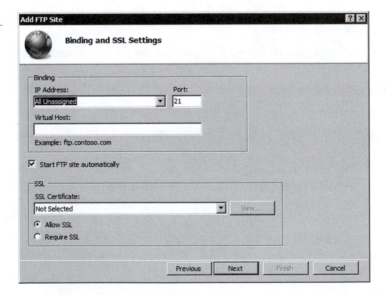

5. If you plan to host other FTP sites on the same server, use the IP Address, Port, and Host Name fields to create a unique binding for the site, just as you did in the "Configuring Site Bindings" procedures, earlier in this lesson.

6. If you want to use SSL to secure the FTP site, select the SSL Certificate you want the server to use for this site and specify whether you want to allow clients to use SSL or require them to do so. If you do not want to use SSL, leave the default values in place.

7. Click **Next**. The Authentication and Authorization Information page appears, as shown in Figure 5-23.

Figure 5-23

The Authentication and Authorization Information page of the Add FTP Site wizard

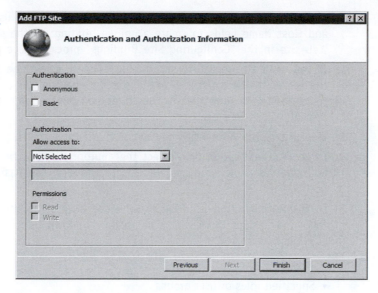

8. In the Authentication box, select the appropriate checkboxes to specify whether you want to allow anonymous access to the site, use Basic Authentication, or both.

 REF For more information on FTP security issues, including authentication, authorization, and using SSL to secure FTP sites, see Lesson 6, "Securing IIS Services."

9. In the Authorization box, specify who can access the site by selecting one of the following options in the *Allow access to* dropdown list:
- All users
- Anonymous users
- Specified roles or user groups
- Specified users

If you select one of the last two options, use the text box provided to specify the name(s) of one or more users, roles, or groups.
10. Specify whether users should have Read or Write access to the site, or both.
11. Click **Finish**. The new site appears in the scope pane.

CLOSE the Internet Information Services (IIS) Manager console.

The Add FTP Site wizard enables you to create only one binding and one authorization rule. However, you can create additional bindings and rules as needed, using the Internet Information Services (IIS) Manager console.

To add FTP access to an existing Web site, use the following procedure.

 ADD FTP TO A WEB SITE

GET READY. Log on to Windows Server 2008 using a domain account with Administrator privileges. When the logon process is completed, close the Initial Configuration Tasks window and any other windows that appear.

1. Click **Start**, and then click **Administrative Tools** > **Internet Information Services (IIS) Manager.** The Internet Information Services (IIS) Manager console appears.
2. In the scope pane, right-click a site node and, from the context menu, select **Add FTP Publishing.** The Add FTP Site Publishing wizard appears, displaying the Binding and SSL Settings page.

3. If you plan to host other FTP sites on the same server, use the IP Address, Port, and Host Name fields to create a unique binding for the site, just as you did for a Web site in the "Configuring Site Bindings" procedures, earlier in this lesson.

4. If you want to use SSL to secure the FTP site, select the SSL Certificate you want the server to use for this site and specify whether you want to allow clients to use SSL or require them to do so. If you do not want to use SSL, leave the default values in place.

5. Click **Next**. The Authentication and Authorization Information page appears.

6. In the Authentication box, select the appropriate checkboxes to specify whether you want to allow anonymous access to the site, use Basic Authentication, or both.

7. In the Authorization box, specify who can access the site by selecting one of the following options in the *Allow access to* dropdown list:
   - All users
   - Anonymous users
   - Specified roles or user groups
   - Specified users

   If you select one of the last two options, use the text box provided to specify the name(s) of one or more users, roles, or groups.

8. Specify whether users should have Read or Write access to the site, or both.

9. Click **Finish**. A message box appears, stating that FTP publishing was successfully added to the site.

10. Click **OK**.

CLOSE the Internet Information Services (IIS) Manager console.

Like Web sites, you can create virtual directories on FTP sites, which are aliases pointing to folders in other locations, by right-clicking a site and selecting Add Virtual Directory from the context menu.

Configuring FTP Properties

After you have created an FTP site or added FTP publishing to an existing Web site, you can configure a number of properties.

Many of the properties of an FTP7 site are security related, and are discussed in Lesson 6, "Securing IIS Servers." Some of the non-security properties you can configure are covered in the following sections.

CONFIGURING FTP DIRECTORY BROWSING

The FTP Directory Browsing feature in FTP7 controls the format that the server uses when sending directory listing information to a client. The original format for FTP directory listings was based on the format used by the UNIX operating systems of the time, as follows:

```
-rwxrwxrwx 1 owner group  577189 Sep 29 23:36 fg05-0000.tif
-rwxrwxrwx 1 owner group  577189 Sep 29 23:36 fg05-0001.tif
-rwxrwxrwx 1 owner group  577189 Sep 29 23:36 fg05-0002.tif
-rwxrwxrwx 1 owner group  577189 Sep 29 23:37 fg05-0003.tif
-rwxrwxrwx 1 owner group  577189 Sep 29 23:37 fg05-0004.tif
-rwxrwxrwx 1 owner group  577189 Sep 29 23:38 fg05-0005.tif
drwxrwxrwx 1 owner group       0 Oct 1 14:54 files
226-Directory has 33,985,671,168 bytes of disk space available.
226 Transfer complete.
```

You can specify whether to use that format, or one corresponding to MS-DOS directory listings, as follows.

```
09-29-07  11:36PM     577189  fg05-0000.tif
09-29-07  11:36PM     577189  fg05-0001.tif
09-29-07  11:36PM     577189  fg05-0002.tif
09-29-07  11:37PM     577189  fg05-0003.tif
09-29-07  11:37PM     577189  fg05-0004.tif
09-29-07  11:38PM     577189  fg05-0005.tif
10-01-07  02:54PM     <DIR>   files
226-Directory has 33,985,708,032 bytes of disk space available.
226 Transfer complete.
```

The primary difference between the two formats is the inclusion of UNIX-style permissions and ownership information in the former. To configure FTP Directory Browsing, use the following procedure.

 CONFIGURE FTP DIRECTORY BROWSING

GET READY. Log on to Windows Server 2008 using a domain account with Administrator privileges. When the logon process is completed, close the Initial Configuration Tasks window and any other windows that appear.

1. Click **Start**, and then click **Administrative Tools** > **Internet Information Services (IIS) Manager**. The Internet Information Services (IIS) Manager console appears.

2. In the scope pane, expand the server node and the Sites node. Then, select an FTP site node and double-click the **FTP Directory Browsing** icon. The FTP Directory Browsing pane appears, as shown in Figure 5-24.

Figure 5-24

The FTP Directory Browsing pane

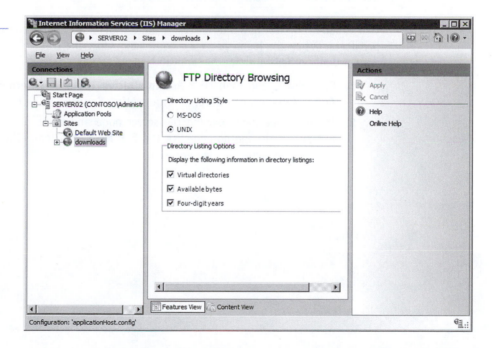

3. In the Directory Listing Style box, select either the **MS-DOS** or **UNIX** option.

4. Select any combination of the following checkboxes.

   • Virtual directories—When selected, IIS7 includes the site's virtual directories in all directory listings. When cleared, virtual directories do not appear in the listings, but are accessible to users that know of them.

   • Available bytes—Causes IIS7 to include the amount of usable storage space left on the site in all directory listings. The usable storage space can be the amount of physical space left on the hard disk or the amount of space remaining before reaching a storage quota.

- Four digit years—Causes IIS7 to display the last modified date of all files and folders using four-digit year designations. When cleared, IIS7 uses two-digit year designations.

5. In the Actions pane, click **Apply.**

CLOSE the Internet Information Services (IIS) Manager console.

Please note that the FTP Directory Browsing settings only control the format that the server uses when transmitting directory listings. If you access an IIS7 FTP site using Internet Explorer, you will not see any changes as a result of altering these settings. This is because the browser is responsible for interpreting and displaying the directory listings it receives from FTP servers. The same is true for most graphical FTP clients. To see the changes that result from alterations of the settings, you must use a command-line client, such as Ftp.exe, which displays the server output without modification.

CONFIGURING CUSTOM SITE MESSAGES

When a client first connects to an FTP server, the server transmits a banner message announcing itself before it authenticates the user, a welcome message after a successful authentication, and an exit message when the client disconnects. The server also displays a message when a client attempting to connect to the server exceeds the maximum number of allowed connections.

You can configure FTP7 to display custom messages in place of (or in addition to) the default ones, using the following procedure.

 CONFIGURE CUSTOM SITE MESSAGES

GET READY. Log on to Windows Server 2008 using a domain account with Administrator privileges. When the logon process is completed, close the Initial Configuration Tasks window and any other windows that appear.

1. Click **Start**, and then click **Administrative Tools** > **Internet Information Services (IIS) Manager.** The Internet Information Services (IIS) Manager console appears.

2. In the scope pane, expand the server node and the Sites node. Then, select an FTP site node and double-click the **FTP Messages** icon. The FTP Messages pane appears, as shown in Figure 5-25.

Figure 5-25

The FTP Messages pane

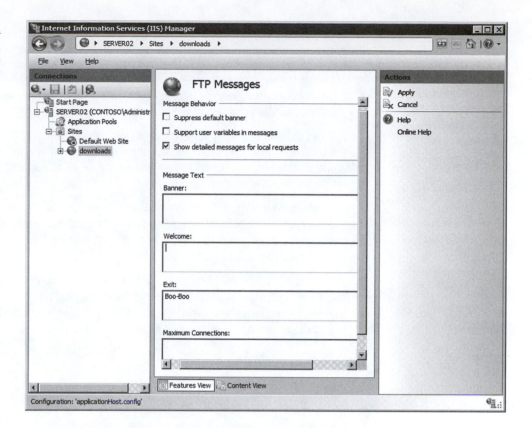

3. Select the **Suppress default banner** checkbox to prevent IIS7 from displaying its default FTP messages.

4. Select the **Support user variables in messages** checkbox to enable the use of the following variables in your custom messages:
   - %BytesReceived%
   - %BytesSent%
   - %SessionID%
   - %SiteName%
   - %UserName%

5. Select the **Show detailed messages for local requests** checkbox to configure FTP7 to display additional error information when connecting from a client on the local host.

6. In the Message Text box, key the messages you want FTP7 to display in the Banner, Welcome, Exit, and Maximum Connections text boxes.

7. In the Actions pane, click **Apply**.

CLOSE the Internet Information Services (IIS) Manager console.

When you complete the procedure, the customized messages you specified take effect in all subsequent client sessions, but not in sessions that are already running.

CONFIGURING FTP LOGGING

FTP7 sites have the same logging configuration capabilities as IIS7 Web sites. To configure FTP7 logging in the Internet Information Services (IIS) Manager console, select a site and double-click the FTP Logging icon. In the FTP Logging pane, you can configure the controls using the same procedures described in "Configuring Web site Logging," earlier in this lesson.

SUMMARY SKILL MATRIX

IN THIS LESSON YOU LEARNED:

- Internet Information Services (IIS), now in version 7.0, has undergone major revisions for the Windows Vista and Windows Server 2008 releases.

- IIS7 has over forty individual modules that you can select for installation. Selecting only the modules you intend to use reduces the application's attack surface, minimizes the amount of memory and other system resources it needs to run, and simplifies the configuration and maintenance processes.

- The default Web server (IIS) role installation requires you to also install the Windows Process Activation Server (WPAS) feature, with its Process Model and Configuration APIs components. If you select the ASP.NET or .NET Extensibility role services, the WPAS .NET Environment component is required as well.

- When you install the Web Server (IIS) role on a Windows Server 2008 system, IIS7 automatically creates a default Web site, using the modules you selected for installation with the role. You can use that default site to publish your content, reconfiguring it as needed, or you can create any number of additional sites on the server.

- A virtual directory is an alias that points to a folder in another physical location, enabling you to publish content found on different drives or different computers, without copying or moving it.

- IIS7 is capable of hosting many separate Web sites simultaneously. It is the binding for each site that determines how the protocol listener will identify incoming requests and send them to the correct site. IIS7 supports three hosting methods: IP addresses, port numbers, or host headers.

- The Internet Information Services (IIS) Manager in Windows Server 2008 uses icons to configure individual modules, rather than tabbed dialog boxes.

Knowledge Assessment

Fill in the Blank

Complete the following sentences by writing the correct word or words in the blanks provided.

1. The component that manages the IIS7 request pipeline, the server's application pools, and the worker processes running in them is called the _____.

2. The IIS component that enables the computer to recognize and react to incoming HTTP messages is called a(n) _____.

3. Web browsers typically connect to Web servers using a protocol called _____.

4. The techniques that enable multiple Web sites to run on a single computer are called _____.

5. A(n) _____ is an alias that points to a folder in another physical location.

6. The only virtual hosting method you can use for multiple sites using the same IP address and port number is called _____ hosting.

7. For clients to perform file management tasks on an IIS server, they must connect to a(n) _____ server.

8. The original coding language used for the files transmitted to client browsers by Web servers is called _____.

9. FTP7 can secure its communications by using _____.

10. To add FTP capabilities to a Web site requires that you create an additional _____.

Multiple Choice

Select the correct answer for each of the following questions. Choose all answers that are correct.

1. Which of the following statements about IIS7 hosting is/are true?
   a. IIS7 is not capable of hosting many separate Web sites simultaneously.
   b. IIS7 is limited to hosting ten Web sites simultaneously.
   c. IIS7 is not capable of hosting more than one Web site at a time.
   d. IIS7 is capable of hosting many separate Web sites simultaneously.

2. Which of the following statements is/are true about IIS7 and virtual directories?
   a. Virtual directories cannot help share information across several Web sites.
   b. Virtual directories can help share information across several Web sites, thus conserving disk space.
   c. Virtual directories replicate shared information to each Web site.
   d. Virtual directories are not capable of hiding the actual locations of shared files and folders from Web clients.

3. IIS7 stores all of its configuration settings in
   a. files with a .config extension.
   b. a central location called a metabase.
   c. a central location file you name for security purposes.
   d. files with an .iis7 extension.

4. Which of the following statements is/are true about the default IIS7 error pages?
   a. By default, IIS7 displays custom error pages for local requests.
   b. By default, IIS7 displays detailed error pages for local requests.
   c. By default, IIS7 displays custom error pages for remote requests.
   d. By default, IIS7 displays detailed error pages for remote requests.

5. Client browsers attempting to access a Web site receive an error message when the following conditions are in place:
   a. When Directory Browsing is enabled and a Web site does not have any of the default filenames in its root directory.
   b. When Directory Browsing is enabled and a Web site has a default filename in its root directory.
   c. When Directory Browsing is disabled and a Web site does not have any of the default filenames in its root directory.
   d. When Directory Browsing is disabled and a Web site has a default filename in its root directory.

6. Which of the following IIS7-supported formats can you configure by selecting fields?
   a. FTP Directory Browsing log formatting
   b. Binary log formatting
   c. HTTP log format
   d. W3C log format

7. Which of the following statements is/are true about HTTP Logging?
   a. HTTP Logging is one of the role services that Windows Server 2008 installs by default with the Web Server (IIS) role.
   b. HTTP Logging is not one of the role services that Windows Server 2008 installs by default with the Web Server (IIS) role.
   c. You must configure IIS7 to install HTTP Logging.
   d. HTTP Logging is not included with Windows Server 2008. You must download it from the Microsoft Web site.

8. Which of the following statements about File Transfer Protocol 7 (FTP7) is/are true?
   a. FTP7 enables a client to connect to a remote server.
   b. FTP7 is a transport layer protocol.
   c. FTP7 eliminates the need for the old IIS6 FTP Management console and metabase.
   d. FTP7 has no provision for password protection or data encryption.

9. IIS7 does not support which of the following hosting methods?
   a. IP addresses
   b. Proxy server filtering
   c. Port numbers
   d. Host headers

10. Which of the following IIS role services is/are not included in the HTTP category?
    a. Default Document
    b. Static Content
    c. Directory Browsing
    d. HTTP Logging

Review Questions

1. IIS7 supports three site binding solutions, which enable a single server to host multiple Web sites simultaneously. Of the three, host header hosting is the most popular. Explain why this is so, giving a specific reason why each of the other two solutions is less desirable.

2. Explain the role of the Windows Process Application Service (WPAS) with regard to how IIS7 processes incoming requests from clients.

■ Case Scenarios

Scenario 5-1: Host Header Hosting

Ralph has just installed the Web Server (IIS) role on a Windows Server 2008 computer, and has created five intranet Web sites for various departments in his company. To differentiate the sites, he has configured the bindings with five different host header values, as follows:

- sales.contoso.com
- marketing.contoso.com
- legal.contoso.com
- it.contoso.com
- hr.contoso.com

After starting up all five sites, Ralph emails the various departments to inform them that their intranet Web servers are up and running. Within minutes, emails and phone calls start coming in from users complaining that they cannot access the new Web sites. What is most likely the cause of the problem?

Scenario 5-2: Web Server Publishing

The content files for your company Web server are currently stored on the D drive of a Windows Server 2008 computer with IIS7 installed on it. The server is named Web1, and its URL is *http://intranet.contoso.com.* You have been instructed to create an IIS solution that will enable the Human Resources department to publish documents containing company benefit and policy information on the Web site, using the URL *http://intranet.contoso.com/hr.* These documents are stored on the HR department's own server and change frequently. What would be the most efficient way to make this possible?

Securing IIS Services

OBJECTIVE DOMAIN MATRIX

Technology Skill	Objective Domain	Objective Domain Number
Enabling and Configuring Authentication Methods	Configure Web site authentication and permissions.	3.7
Assigning Standard and Special NTFS Permissions	Configure Web site authentication and permissions.	3.7
Configuring Certificates	Configure SSL Security.	3.6

KEY TERMS

Anonymous Authentication
authentication
Basic Authentication
certification authority (CA)

Digest Authentication
digital certificate
Kerberos
NTLMv2

public key infrastructure
Windows Authentication

A Web server is, by definition, a doorway into your network, but this does not mean that the doorway has to be unprotected. This lesson examines some of the many security mechanisms included in IIS7, including:

- IP address and domain name restrictions
- Authentication methods
- Authorization rules
- Handler mappings
- NTFS permissions
- Secure Sockets Layer (SSL)

Understanding IIS Security

 THE BOTTOM LINE   Configuring the various security mechanisms provided by IIS7 and Windows Server 2008 is an essential element of Web server administration.

Internet Information Services (IIS) has become a key component of the Windows Server products over the years, due to the ever increasing importance of the Internet in the business world, and the increasing use of Web server technologies to deploy applications internally and externally. The primary role of an IIS server is to listen for incoming requests from clients of various types and then respond by performing some action or supplying some piece of information.

Because IIS functions, metaphorically, as an open door to a private network, it is also a potential avenue for attack. As a result, the server administrator must secure IIS against such attacks.

Attacks against an IIS server can come in many different forms and for many different reasons. Some attackers might try to use the services provided by IIS to gain access to files or data for which they are not authorized, while others might try to use the server to access the organization's internal network. Still others might only be intent on inhibiting IIS' functionality to prevent other users from accessing its services.

Because of these varied threats, IIS7 has many built-in security mechanisms and makes use of Windows Server 2008's own security features. This lesson discusses how to use these features to protect your IIS7 server against attack.

Configuring Web Site Security

THE BOTTOM LINE

IIS7 has many security mechanisms you can use to protect your Web servers individually or in combinations. Each of these mechanisms has its own configuration interface.

As mentioned earlier, IIS7 Web sites are designed to listen for incoming requests from clients and respond to those requests. However, before IIS7 processes a request and issues a response, it must determine whether the client issuing the request has the privileges needed to use the Web site. In essence, IIS7 evaluates each incoming request by asking the following questions:

- Are the client's IP address and domain name allowed access to the site?
- Who is the client sending the request?
- Is the client authorized to access the requested resource?
- Does the client have the permissions needed to access the resource?

These questions all correspond to IIS7 or Windows Server 2008 security mechanisms that administrators can use to protect their Web sites and server resources from unauthorized access.

TAKE NOTE*

While the FTP6 role services included with Windows Server 2008 are relatively limited in their security capabilities, the FTP7 module is fully integrated with IIS7 and supports most of the same security mechanisms, including IP address and domain name restrictions, Anonymous and Basic Authentication, and Secure Sockets Layer (SSL) encryption.

Configuring IP Address and Domain Name Restrictions

To restrict Web site or FTP site access to specific computers or companies, you can create a list of IP addresses and domain names to which the server will grant or deny access.

IIS7 retains a security feature from earlier IIS versions enabling you to specify IP addresses or domain names that the server should allow or deny access to a server, Web or FTP7 site, virtual directory, folder, or file. To configure IP address restrictions, use the following procedure.

TAKE NOTE*

Before you can configure IP address and domain name restrictions, you must install the IP and Domain Restrictions role service in the Web Server (IIS) role.

 CONFIGURE IP ADDRESS RESTRICTIONS

GET READY. Log on to Windows Server 2008 using a domain account with Administrator privileges. When the logon process is completed, close the Initial Configuration Tasks window and any other windows that appear.

1. Click **Start**, and then click **Administrative Tools** > **Internet Information Services (IIS) Manager**. The Internet Information Services (IIS) Manager console appears, as shown in Figure 6-1.

Figure 6-1

The Internet Information Services (IIS) Manager console

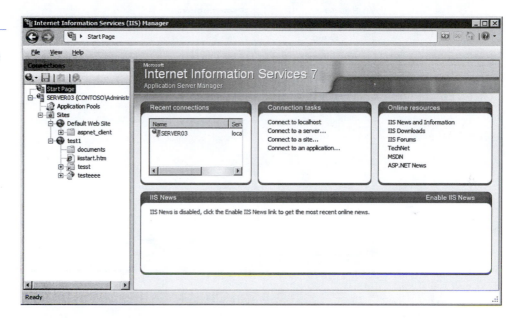

2. In the scope pane, select a server, site, folder, or virtual directory. The Home pane for the selected element appears, like the one shown in Figure 6-2.

Figure 6-2

The Home pane for an IIS7 server

3. Double-click the **IPv4 Address and Domain Restrictions** icon. The IPv4 Address and Domain Restrictions pane appears, as shown in Figure 6-3.

Figure 6-3

The IPv4 Address and Domain Restrictions pane

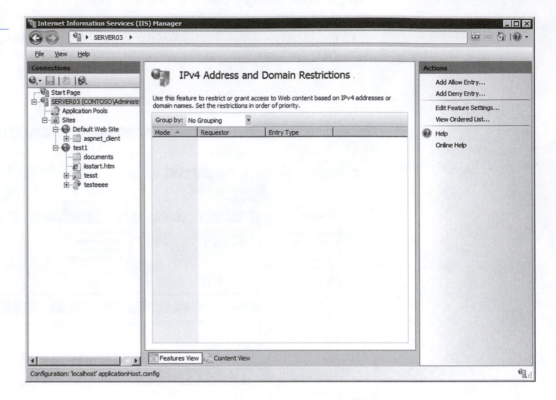

TAKE NOTE*

To configure a folder that is not a virtual directory or an individual file, select a Web site and click Content View. Then, double-click the desired folder or file, return to Features View, and double-click the IPv4 Address and Domain Restrictions icon.

4. In the actions pane, click **Edit Feature Settings**. The Edit IP and Domain Restrictions Settings dialog box appears, as shown in Figure 6-4.

Figure 6-4

The Edit IP and Domain Restrictions Settings dialog box

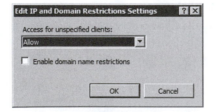

5. Select one of the following options in the *Access for unspecified clients* dropdown list:
- Allow—Permits access to all IP addresses and domain names except for those you explicitly identify in deny entries. This is the default value.
- Deny—Blocks access to all IP addresses and domain names except for those you explicitly identify in allow entries.

By default, the IPv4 Address and Domain Restrictions role service enables you to create rules specifying address restrictions only. To enable domain name restriction rules, select the **Enable domain name restrictions** checkbox. Then, confirm your action by clicking **Yes** in the **Edit** IP and Domain Restrictions Settings message box that appears.

6. Click **OK** to close the Edit IP and Domain Restrictions Settings dialog box.

7. In the actions pane, click **Add Allow Entry**. The Add Allow Restriction Rule dialog box appears, as shown in Figure 6-5.

Figure 6-5

The Add Allow Restriction Rule dialog box

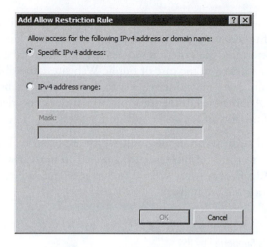

8. Select one of the following options and key an appropriate entry in the accompanying text box:

- Specific IPv4 address—Enables you to specify one IP address that will be allowed or denied access to the selected element.
- IPv4 Address Range—Enables you to specify a range of IP addresses and a subnet mask, identifying a group of systems that you will be allowed or denied access to the selected element.
- Domain name—Enables you to specify a domain name that will be allowed or denied access to the selected element.

9. Click **OK**. The new entry appears in the IPv4 Address and Domain Restrictions pane.

CLOSE the Internet Information Services (IIS) Manager console.

Although they are easy to understand and use, IP address and domain name restrictions are not particularly useful security tools. For example, if you have an intranet Web site that you want to restrict to a certain group of users, you can configure the site to deny access to all IP addresses except those of specified users. However, it is not difficult to spoof IP addresses, so this practice is not particularly secure. You can also use this feature to deny access to specific Internet addresses or domains that are the sources of attacks, but most installations have a firewall that is better at this sort of thing.

You should also consider carefully the consequences of creating domain name restrictions. As IIS7 mentions in its warning when you enable domain restrictions, this practice can slow the Web server down significantly. HTTP communications are based on IP addresses, not domain names. When you create domain name restrictions, IIS7 must perform a reverse name lookup of the IP address where each incoming request originated to determine its domain name. This adds a substantial additional burden on the server, which can negatively affect its performance.

 **MORE INFORMATION**

DNS servers typically perform name resolutions, in which they take a fully qualified domain name and resolve it into an IP address. A reverse name lookup occurs when a DNS server receives a request containing an IP address and must determine its domain name. You must configure a DNS server to perform reverse name resolutions, by creating a reverse lookup zone and creating Pointer (PTR) records for the addresses you want the server to resolve.

Enabling and Configuring Authentication Methods

The authentication methods you use for your Web sites depend on the types of clients you must support and the sensitivity of your site content.

Authentication is the process of confirming a user's identity, usually by requiring the user to supply some sort of token, such as a password or certificate. By identifying the user sending a request, IIS7 can determine the system resources the user should be permitted to access. Even though it might not seem so in the case of public Web sites accessible through the Internet, IIS7 does authenticate every incoming request to determine the sender. In the case of a public site, the server uses Anonymous Authentication, which does not identify users by name, but still completes the formality of the authentication process.

IIS7 supports several authentication methods, which are listed in Table 6-1, with the role services they require to run, and their intended uses. You must install the appropriate role services using the Add Role Services Wizard in Server Manager before you can enable or configure these authentication methods.

CERTIFICATION READY?
Configure Web site authentication and permissions
3.7

Table 6-1

Authentication Methods Supported by IIS7

AUTHENTICATION METHOD	ADDITIONAL ROLE SERVICES REQUIRED	BEST USED FOR:
Active Directory Client Certificate Authentication	Client Certificate Mapping Authentication	Intranet Web sites on networks already using Active Directory and with a server functioning as a certification authority (CA)
Anonymous Authentication	None	Internet Web or FTP sites that are open to the public with no access restrictions
ASP.NET Impersonation	ASP.NET .NETExtensibility ISAPI Extensions ISAPI Filters	Web sites with ASP.NET applications that require a non-default security context
Basic Authentication	Basic Authentication	Private Web or FTP sites with clients on the other side of firewalls or proxy servers, or that do not support any other type of non-anonymous authentication
Digest Authentication	Digest Authentication	Intranet Web servers with clients that are members of the same Active Directory domain and separated by a firewall or proxy server
Forms Authentication	ASP.NET .NET Extensibility ISAPI Extensions ISAPI Filters	High-traffic Web sites with ASP.NET applications that include application-based authentication capabilities
IIS Client Certificate Authentication	IIS Client Certificate Mapping Authentication	One-to-one and one-to-many certificate mapping on intranet Web sites not using Active Directory certificate mapping and with a server functioning as a certification authority (CA)
Windows Authentication	Windows Authentication	Intranet Web servers with clients that are members of the same Active Directory domain or who have user accounts on the IIS7 server, and are not separated by a firewall or proxy server.

Of the methods listed in the table, only Anonymous Authentication is integrated into an IIS7 installation by default. All of the other authentication methods require the selection of additional role services during the installation of the Web Server (IIS) role.

Even when you install the role services required for additional authentication methods, IIS7 leaves those methods disabled by default until you explicitly enable them. You can enable and disable authentication methods for any IIS7 server, application, site, folder, virtual directory, or individual file. For example, if you want the root folder of a site to be available to anyone, and a virtual directory beneath the root to be available only to specific users, you can enable anonymous access at the site level, and then disable it for the virtual directory. Of course, you must also enable some other form of authentication for the virtual directory, if you want anyone to be able to access it.

As is usual in IIS7, the authentication settings you configure at a particular level are inherited by all subordinate levels. IIS7 enables Anonymous Authentication at the server level by default when you install it, so all of the sites you create on the server also have Anonymous Authentication enabled. If you modify the authentication settings at the server level, you must explicitly configure each site that you want to use different settings.

To enable and disable authentication methods that you have already installed in IIS7, use the following procedure.

 ENABLE AUTHENTICATION METHODS

GET READY. Log on to Windows Server 2008 using a domain account with Administrator privileges. When the logon process is completed, close the Initial Configuration Tasks window and any other windows that appear.

1. Click **Start**, and then click **Administrative Tools** > **Internet Information Services (IIS) Manager**. The Internet Information Services (IIS) Manager console appears.

2. In the scope pane, select a server, site, or virtual directory. The Home pane for the selected element appears.

3. Double-click the **Authentication** icon. The Authentication pane appears, as shown in Figure 6-6.

Figure 6-6

The Authentication pane in the Internet Information Services (IIS) Manager console

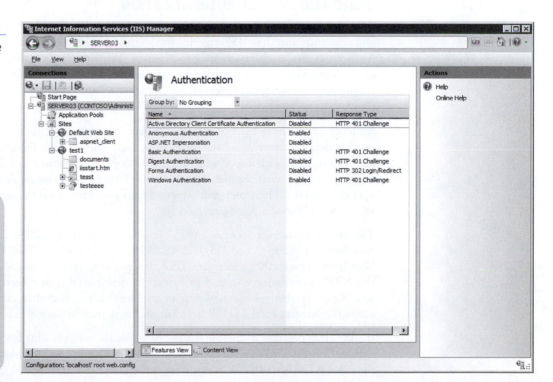

TAKE NOTE *

Before you can enable an authentication method, you must install the appropriate role service in the Web Server (IIS) role.

4. Select the authentication method you want to modify and, in the actions pane, click **Enable** or **Disable**. The Status indicator for the authentication method changes.

CLOSE the Internet Information Services (IIS) Manager console.

You can enable as many authentication methods for an IIS7 element as you need to support your clients. When a client connects to a site configured to use multiple authentication methods, it always attempts to establish an anonymous connection first. If either the client or the server does not allow Anonymous Authentication, the systems attempt to authenticate again, using the other methods from most to least secure. Therefore, IIS7 uses its various methods to authenticate clients in the following order:

1. Anonymous Authentication
2. Windows Authentication
3. Digest Authentication
4. Basic Authentication

Active Directory Client Certificate Authentication, ASP.NET Impersonation, and Forms Authentication do not fall within this authentication order. These authentication methods have special requirements that cause IIS7 to handle them differently. For more information, see the individual sections for these methods, later in this lesson.

TAKE NOTE

FTP7 supports only Anonymous Authentication and Basic Authentication. For greater security, however, you can use SSL with FTP7 to encrypt the authentication traffic as it passes over the network.

If all of the authentication methods fail, as in an improperly configured site with no methods enabled, the client receives the following error message:

```
HTTP Error 401.2 - Unauthorized: Access is denied due to server
configuration
```

The following sections examine the various authentication methods supported by IIS7, including when (or if) you should use them, and how to configure their properties.

USING ANONYMOUS AUTHENTICATION

Anonymous Authentication is the only authentication method integrated into IIS7, and the only one that IIS7 enables by default. As the name implies, Anonymous Authentication enables any user to access a Web site that employs it, without supplying an account name or password. This method of authentication is designed primarily for public Web sites on the Internet, or any internal site that you want to be available to all users.

Although anonymous users do not have to supply credentials, enabling Anonymous Authentication does not leave your Web server completely unprotected. By default, IIS7 authenticates anonymous users with a specifically created account. This account has the permissions necessary to access the Web site files, but it does not have access to other files or sensitive areas of the operating system. Therefore, your server remains protected, even though you are allowing users to access the Web site files anonymously.

The anonymous user account in IIS7 is a built-in account called IUSR, which is a member of a group called IIS_IUSRS. When you install the Web Server (IIS) role on a Windows Server 2008 computer, IIS7 creates the user and the group and assigns the group the NTFS permissions needed to access the designated root directory of the Default Web Site (C:\inetpub\wwwroot). When an anonymous client connects to the Web site, IIS7 maps the request to the IUSR account and uses that to access the necessary files.

In IIS7, it is possible to disable the use of a specific user account for Anonymous Authentication, and use the application pool identity instead. Application pools run under the NETWORKSERVICE account by default.

CHANGING THE ANONYMOUS AUTHENTICATION USER

Although IIS7 uses the IUSR account for anonymous access by default, you can change it. For example, if your Web site uses content files located elsewhere on the network, you might want to use a different account with network privileges for anonymous access. The IUSR account is local, and does not have such privileges. To change the account that IIS7 uses for Anonymous Authentication, use the following procedure.

➔ CHANGE THE ANONYMOUS AUTHENTICATION USER

> **TAKE NOTE** *
>
> To configure a folder that is not a virtual directory or an individual file, select a Web site and click Content View. Then double-click the desired folder or file, return to Features View, and double-click the Authentication icon.

GET READY. Log on to Windows Server 2008 using a domain account with Administrator privileges. When the logon process is completed, close the Initial Configuration Tasks window and any other windows that appear.

1. Click **Start**, and then click **Administrative Tools** > **Internet Information Services (IIS) Manager**. The Internet Information Services (IIS) Manager console appears.
2. In the scope pane, select a server, site, application, or virtual directory. The Home pane for the selected element appears.
3. Double-click the **Authentication** icon. The Authentication pane appears.

> **TAKE NOTE** *
>
> Before you can configure Anonymous Authentication, you must install the Anonymous Authentication role service in the Web Server (IIS) role.

4. Select **Anonymous Authentication** and, in the actions pane, click **Edit**. The Edit Anonymous Authentication Credentials dialog box appears, as shown in Figure 6-7.

Figure 6-7

The Edit Anonymous Authentication Credentials dialog box

5. Click **Set**. The Set Credentials dialog box appears, as shown in Figure 6-8. You can also select the *Application pool identity* option to override the anonymous user account.

Figure 6-8

The Set Credentials dialog box

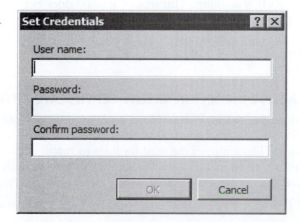

6. In the User Name text box, key the name of the account you want IIS7 to use for anonymous access to the element you selected.
7. In the Password and Confirm Password text boxes, key the password associated with the account you specified.

8. Click **OK** to close the Set Credentials dialog box.

9. Click **OK** to close the Edit Anonymous Authentication Credentials dialog box.

10. Restart the Web site.

CLOSE the Internet Information Services (IIS) Manager console.

After the Web site restarts, the server authenticates all anonymous users connecting to the site using the account you specified.

UNDERSTANDING IIS7 ANONYMOUS AUTHENTICATION

The IIS7 anonymous access user and group accounts differ from those of IIS6 and earlier versions. IIS6 uses a standard local user account called IUSR_*computername* and a built-in group called IIS_WPG. The IIS6 elements function in much the same way as IIS7's as far as anonymous request handling is concerned. However, they have caused some administrative problems, particularly in the area of scalability.

Many organizations run multiple, redundant IIS servers to support heavy traffic or provide fault tolerance. To create a duplicate Web site on another IIS server, administrators typically copy the configuration files and content files from one computer to the other, using a utility that retains the access control list (ACL) information for each file and folder, such as the Xcopy.exe program with the /O parameter. The ACL information contains the NTFS permissions that provide the anonymous user account with access to the content files.

The problem with IIS6 arises when the destination computer attempts to parse configuration metabase file and the ACL information on the copied content files. Because anonymous user accounts on the two computers have different names (due to the inclusion of the computer name), the metabase cannot function on the new server without modification.

The problem with the ACL information in the content files results from the fact that each local user and group in Windows Server has a unique security identifier (SID) that the system assigns when creating the account. ACLs use only the SIDs to reference security principals, not the user and group names. The anonymous user and group accounts on the destination computer have different SIDs than the source computer, so the ACLs are useless on the destination computer. Therefore administrators must modify the metabase for each new IIS6 Web server and recreate the NTFS permissions for the content files.

IIS7 addresses these problems in two ways. First, the anonymous user account name (IUSR) no longer includes the computer name, so it is now identical on each IIS7 computer. This makes the configuration files completely compatible, without modifications. Second, the IUSR account is now a built-in account, just like the LOCALSERVICE and NETWORKSERVICE accounts. This type of account does not need a password, which eliminates potential password expiration problems, and is not subject to the SID conflict problems that affect the IIS6 accounts. As a result, administrators can copy IIS7 configuration and content files to multiple servers and use them as is.

ENABLING ACTIVE DIRECTORY CLIENT CERTIFICATE AUTHENTICATION

If you are running an intranet Web server on an Active Directory network with its own certification authority, you can configure IIS7 to automatically authenticate domain users that have client certificates. This eliminates the need for users to supply account names and passwords, while providing a high level of security. Obviously, this form of authentication is not suitable for Internet Web sites because the clients are not members of the Active Directory domain.

To use Active Directory Client Certificate Authentication, your network must meet the following prerequisites:

• Active Directory—The network must have an Active Directory domain controller installed. All of the clients who will access the Web sites using Active Directory Client Certificate Authentication must have Active Directory user accounts.

X REF

For more information on configuring IIS7 sites to use SSL, see "Using Secure Sockets Layer," later in this lesson.

- Certification Authority—The network must have a server functioning as a certification authority (CA), as implemented in the Active Directory Certificate Services role. Certificates issued by a third-party, commercial CA can be used for this purpose, but because all of the systems involved are internal to the organization, this would be an unnecessary expense.
- Secure Sockets Layer (SSL)—To protect the certificates, you must configure all of the Web sites on the IIS7 server to require SSL communications. To do this, you must create an HTTPS binding and enable SSL in the SSL Settings pane.
- Domain server certificate—The server must have a domain server certificate, obtained from a CA.
- Map client certificates—You must map certificates to the domain user objects for the clients that will be accessing the Web sites. To map client certificates, you must obtain certificates from a CA, and then use Active Directory Users and Computers, with Advanced Features enabled, to map the certificates to specific users.

To configure IIS7 to use Active Directory Client Certificate Authentication, use the following procedure.

⊘ ENABLE ACTIVE DIRECTORY CLIENT CERTIFICATE AUTHENTICATION

GET READY. Log on to Windows Server 2008 using a domain account with Administrator privileges. When the logon process is completed, close the Initial Configuration Tasks window and any other windows that appear.

1. Click **Start**, and then click **Administrative Tools** > **Internet Information Services (IIS) Manager**. The Internet Information Services (IIS) Manager console appears.
2. In the scope pane, select a server. The Home pane for the selected element appears.
3. Double-click the **Authentication** icon. The Authentication pane appears.

TAKE NOTE* Active Directory Client Certificate Authentication only appears in the Authentication pane at the server level. You cannot configure individual sites or other IIS7 elements to use this authentication method.

TAKE NOTE*

Before you can configure Active Directory Client Certificate Authentication, you must install the Client Certificate Mapping Authentication role service in the Web Server (IIS) role.

4. Select **Active Directory Client Certificate Authentication** and, in the actions pane, click **Enable**.
5. Disable any other authentication methods that show a status of Enabled.
6. Restart the IIS7 service.

CLOSE the Internet Information Services (IIS) Manager console.

Because Active Directory Client Certificate Authentication requires the use of SSL with client certificates, it is not compatible with any of the other authentication methods IIS7 supports and, therefore, does not fall into any of the authentication methods listed earlier in this lesson. If, for any reason, the IIS7 server cannot authenticate a client, it generates an error message such as the following:

```
HTTP Error 403.7 - Forbidden: The page you are attempting to access
requires your browser to have a Secure Sockets Layer (SSL) client
certificate that the Web server recognizes.
```

IIS7 also supports its own form of client certificate authentication that does not use Active Directory. The IIS Client Certificate Mapping Authentication role service enables you to create two types of mappings, as follows:

- One-to-one mappings—Each client must have a copy of its own certificate stored on the IIS7 server.

- Many-to-one mappings—Uses wildcard matching rules to ensure that certificates submitted by clients contain specific information.

However, you cannot configure this authentication method using the Internet Information Services (IIS) Manager console. You can only configure IIS client certificate mapping by editing the IIS7 configuration files directly or by using Windows Management Instrumentation (WMI).

USING WINDOWS AUTHENTICATION

Of the three traditional, challenge/response authentication methods supported by IIS7, **Windows Authentication** is the most secure. Known by several other names in previous versions of IIS, the technology that Windows Authentication uses stretches all the way back to the NTLM authentication method in the original Microsoft LAN Manager product of the late 1980s.

IIS7's Windows Authentication module supports two authentication protocols:

- *NTLMv2*—A challenge/response authentication protocol used by Windows computers that are not members of an Active Directory domain. The client initiates the authentication process by sending a message to the server specifying its encryption capabilities and containing the user's account name. The server replies with a message containing information about its own capabilities, plus a random challenge string. The client then uses the challenge string and its password to calculate a response, which it transmits to the server. The server performs the same calculations and, if its results match the client's, the authentication is successful.

- *Kerberos*—A ticket-based authentication protocol used by Windows computers that are members of an Active Directory domain. Unlike NTLM, which involves only the IIS7 server and the client, Kerberos authentication involves an Active Directory domain controller as well. The client begins the authentication process by sending an Authentication Service Request message to the Kerberos Key Distribution Center (KDC) running on the domain controller. This message contains pre-authentication data, which the client encrypts with its user key. The KDC decrypts the data with its own copy of the user key, created when the client specified a password for the user account. If the decryption is successful, then the identity of the client is confirmed, and the KDC responds by sending a ticket granting ticket (TGT) and an encrypted session key that the client will use for all subsequent communications with the ticket granting service (TGS) on the domain controller. After authentication, the client can initiate additional exchanges with the TGS to obtain service tickets that provide access to network services, such as an IIS7 Web site.

Notice that both of these protocols are capable of authenticating clients without transmitting passwords over the network in any form. This is an extremely secure form of authentication, because even if someone with a protocol analyzer is capturing the packets transmitted over the network, no data that would be useful to them is in the packets, even if they could decrypt it.

Windows Authentication is designed for use with intranet Web sites only, because it would not be practical for Internet clients to be members of the Active Directory domain or have accounts on the Web server. In addition, the use of Windows Authentication is also subject to the following restrictions.

- Clients must be running Internet Explorer version 3.01 or later.
- The clients and Web server must be members of the same domain.
- To use Kerberos, the clients and Web server should not be separated by a firewall.
- To use Kerberos, both clients and Web server must have continuous access to an Active Directory domain controller.

- To use NTLMv2, the clients must have user accounts on the Web server.
- To use NTLMv2, the clients should not require the use of a proxy server to access the Web server.

When clients that are not members of an Active Directory domain attempt to access an IIS7 Web site using Windows Authentication, a Connect To dialog box appears, in which the user must specify an account name and password. The IIS7 server then authenticates the client using NTLMv2.

If the client and the IIS7 server are both members of a domain, the client authentication that occurs when the user logs on to the domain is usually sufficient to provide access to the Web sites on the server that is using Windows Authentication. If the client uses the server's computer name in the browser URL, such as http://*servername*, Windows recognizes the server as an internal resource and performs a Kerberos message exchange with the TGS to obtain a service ticket for IIS7. This process is invisible to the user working on the client computer, who receives access to the Web site with no further interaction.

If the client uses the server's IP address or DNS name in its URL, such as http://192.168.3.76 or http://*servername*.contoso.com, Windows might interpret the connection attempt as coming from an outside system and generate a Connect To dialog box for another authentication.

> ⊕ **MORE INFORMATION**
>
> On an IIS7 server using Windows Authentication with Active Directory, Kerberos usually makes it possible for clients to access Web site content stored on servers other than the Web server, no matter how you integrate the content into the site. However, in the absence of Active Directory and Kerberos, you must consider how you integrate the remote content, if you want to avoid forcing users to perform an additional authentication. For example, if you map a drive to a share on another server, and publish the mapped drive on a Web site, Kerberos will provide clients with access to the remote content invisibly by obtaining an extra service ticket from the TGS in the background. NTLMv2, however, will not forward the user's credentials to the remote server, so the user will have to log on again to re-authenticate. To avoid this, use virtual directories instead of mapped drives and click the Connect As button in the Add Virtual Directory dialog box to supply alternative credentials that IIS7 should always use when accessing the remote content.

ENABLING DIGEST AUTHENTICATION

Digest Authentication is also designed for use with intranet Web servers in an Active Directory environment. Unlike Windows Authentication, Digest Authentication works through firewalls and proxy servers because it actually transmits passwords over the network. However, the protocol protects the passwords using a strong MD5 encryption scheme.

> **TAKE NOTE** *
>
> The Digest Authentication method in IIS7 is comparable to the Advanced Digest Authentication method from IIS6.

The use of Digest Authentication is subject to the following restrictions:

- Clients must be running Internet Explorer version 5 or later.
- The clients and Web server must be members of the same Active Directory domain.
- All clients must have user accounts in the Active Directory domain.
- If Anonymous Authentication is installed in IIS7, it must be disabled for Digest Authentication to work.

To configure and enable Digest Authentication, use the following procedure.

 ENABLE DIGEST AUTHENTICATION

GET READY. Log on to Windows Server 2008 using a domain account with Administrator privileges. When the logon process is completed, close the Initial Configuration Tasks window and any other windows that appear.

1. Click **Start**, and then click **Administrative Tools** > **Internet Information Services (IIS) Manager**. The Internet Information Services (IIS) Manager console appears.
2. In the scope pane, select a server, site, application, or virtual directory. The Home pane for the selected element appears.

3. Double-click the **Authentication** icon. The Authentication pane appears.

To configure a folder that is not a virtual directory or an individual file, select a Web site and click Content View. Then, double-click the desired folder or file, return to Features View, and double-click the Authentication icon.

4. Select **Digest Authentication** and, in the actions pane, click **Edit.** The Edit Digest Authentication Settings dialog box appears, as shown in Figure 6-9.

Figure 6-9

The Edit Digest Authentication Settings dialog box

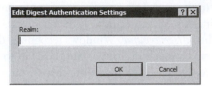

TAKE NOTE*

Before you can configure Digest Authentication, you must install the Digest Authentication role service in the Web Server (IIS) role.

5. In the Realm text box, key the name of the Active Directory domain of which the Web server is a member. Then click **OK**.

6. Select **Digest Authentication** and, in the actions pane, click **Enable**.

TAKE NOTE*

To force clients to use Digest Authentication, disable Anonymous Authentication. All clients attempt to authenticate anonymously first and, failing that, move on to alternative authentication methods.

7. Restart the IIS7 service.

CLOSE the Internet Information Services (IIS) Manager console.

Digest Authentication functions well as a backup for Windows Authentication when some clients on the network cannot use that method. Also, because it uses stronger encryption algorithms, Digest Authentication is significantly more secure than Basic Authentication.

ENABLING BASIC AUTHENTICATION

Basic Authentication is the weakest of the challenge/response authentication methods supported by IIS7. When a client authenticates to an IIS7 server using Basic Authentication, the client transmits its credentials unencrypted, using Base64 encoding, so anyone capturing the network packets can read the user's credentials. In addition, the server caches clients' user tokens for 15 minutes, so it is possible to read the credentials from the server hard disk during that time.

TAKE NOTE*

Some earlier versions of IIS required clients using Basic Authentication to have the Log On Locally user right. However, in IIS6 and IIS7, it is no longer necessary to assign this user right to clients.

To enable Basic Authentication, use the following procedure.

 ENABLE BASIC AUTHENTICATION

GET READY. Log on to Windows Server 2008 using a domain account with Administrator privileges. When the logon process is completed, close the Initial Configuration Tasks window and any other windows that appear.

1. Click **Start**, and then click **Administrative Tools** > **Internet Information Services (IIS) Manager.** The Internet Information Services (IIS) Manager console appears.

2. In the scope pane, select a server, site, application, or virtual directory. The Home pane for the selected element appears.

3. Double-click the **Authentication** icon. The Authentication pane appears.

TAKE NOTE To configure a folder that is not a virtual directory or an individual file, select a Web site and click Content View. Then, double-click the desired folder or file, return to Features View, and double-click the Authentication icon.

4. Select **Basic Authentication** and, in the actions pane, click **Edit.** The Edit Basic Authentication Settings dialog box appears, as shown in Figure 6-10.

Figure 6-10

The Edit Basic Authentication Settings dialog box

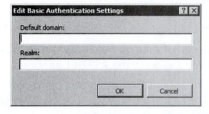

5. In the Default Domain text box, key the name of the Active Directory domain in which you want the clients to be authenticated. The default value, if you leave the field blank, is the IIS7 server's domain. Leave the Realm text box blank, or key the name value as the Default Domain text box, and click **OK.**

6. Select **Basic Authentication** and, in the actions pane, click **Enable**.

7. Restart the IIS7 service.

CLOSE the Internet Information Services (IIS) Manager console.

The advantages of Basic Authentication are that it is defined in the HTTP standard, so virtually all browsers support it, and that it works through firewalls and proxy servers. If you must use Basic Authentication, you should use it in conjunction with SSL, so that the authentication traffic is properly encrypted.

ENABLING ASP.NET IMPERSONATION

ASP.NET Impersonation is not an authentication protocol in itself, unlike most of the other options in the Authentication pane. Instead, ASP.NET is a way to configure an ASP.NET application to run in a security context different from the application's default context. To enable ASP.NET Impersonation, use the following procedure.

 ENABLE ASP.NET IMPERSONATION

GET READY. Log on to Windows Server 2008 using a domain account with Administrator privileges. When the logon process is completed, close the Initial Configuration Tasks window and any other windows that appear.

1. Click **Start**, and then click **Administrative Tools** > **Internet Information Services (IIS) Manager.** The Internet Information Services (IIS) Manager console appears.

2. In the scope pane, select a server, site, application, or virtual directory. The Home pane for the selected element appears.

3. Double-click the **Authentication** icon. The Authentication pane appears.

TAKE NOTE * To configure a folder that is not a virtual directory or an individual file, select a Web site and click Content View. Then, double-click the desired folder or file, return to Features View, and double-click the Authentication icon.

4. Select **ASP.NET Impersonation** and, in the actions pane, click **Edit.** The Edit ASP.NET Impersonation Settings dialog box appears, as shown in Figure 6-11.

Figure 6-11

The Edit ASP.NET Impersonation Settings dialog box

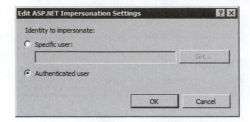

5. Select one of the following options and click **OK:**

- Specific user—Clicking **Set** opens a Set Credentials dialog box, in which you can specify the credentials you want the ASP.NET application to use.
- Authenticated user—Causes IIS7 to use the client's current security context when running the ASP.NET application. For example, if the client connects using Anonymous Authentication, the application runs using the IUSR account (unless you have changed the default Anonymous Authentication settings).

6. Select **ASP.NET Impersonation** and, in the actions pane, click **Enable.**

7. Restart the IIS7 service.

CLOSE the Internet Information Services (IIS) Manager console.

Once IIS7 restarts, users accessing the ASP.NET application connect to the server using the credentials you specified, instead of the application's default credentials.

ENABLING FORMS AUTHENTICATION

Windows Authentication, Digest Authentication, and Basic Authentication are all challenge-based authentication methods. An IIS7 server configured to use these methods transmits a challenge message to clients attempting to connect, and the client must reply with the correct response for the authentication to succeed. Forms Authentication, on the other hand, is a login/redirection-based method.

Clients attempting to connect to a site using Forms Authentication are redirected to an alternative Web page containing a logon interface. The advantage of this method is that the authentication process occurs at the application level, instead of the operating system level like challenge-based methods. If you are running a heavily trafficked intranet site or an Internet site with publicly available applications, Forms Authentication can significantly reduce the load on the operating system, diverting it to your application instead.

To configure and enable Forms Authentication, use the following procedure.

 ENABLE FORMS AUTHENTICATION

GET READY. Log on to Windows Server 2008 using a domain account with Administrator privileges. When the logon process is completed, close the Initial Configuration Tasks window and any other windows that appear.

1. Click **Start**, and then click **Administrative Tools** > **Internet Information Services (IIS) Manager.** The Internet Information Services (IIS) Manager console appears.

2. In the scope pane, select a server, site, application, or virtual directory. The Home pane for the selected element appears.

TAKE NOTE ★ To configure a folder that is not a virtual directory or an individual file, select a Web site and click Content View. Then, double-click the desired folder or file, return to Features View, and double-click the Authentication icon.

3. Double-click the **Authentication** icon. The Authentication pane appears.

4. Select **Forms Authentication** and, in the actions pane, click **Edit.** The Edit Forms Authentication Settings dialog box appears, as shown in Figure 6-12.

Figure 6-12

The Edit Forms Authentication Settings dialog box

5. Configure the following parameters and click **OK**.

- Login URL—Specify the URL of the Web page containing the authentication interface.

- Authentication cookie time-out—Specify the length of time (in minutes) that the cookie containing the Forms Authentication ticket should remain on the client computer before timing out.

- Mode—Specifies whether the client computer should use cookies to store the Forms Authentication ticket.

- Name—Specifies the name of the Forms Authentication cookie.

- Protection mode—Specifies whether the systems should protect the Forms Authentication cookie using data encryption, data validation, both, or neither.

- Requires SSL—Specifies whether the server should require an SSL connection before transmitting the Forms Authentication cookie. This option is disabled by default.

- Extend cookie expiration on every request—Enables sliding expiration, which causes the server to reset a client's Forms Authentication cookie each time the client issues a new request during an active session. This option is enabled by default.

6. Select **Forms Authentication** and, in the actions pane, click **Enable**.

7. Disable any other authentication methods that show a status of Enabled.

8. Restart the IIS7 service.

CLOSE the Internet Information Services (IIS) Manager console.

Forms Authentication is designed for use instead of challenge-based authentication methods, not in addition to them. Therefore, you must disable all of the other authentication methods when you enable Forms Authentication.

Creating URL Authorization Rules

Authorization rules specify what clients are able to do on a Web site after the server has authenticated them.

Authentication is the process of identifying users and confirming that they are who they claim to be. After the IIS7 server has authenticated a client, the next step is authorization, which determines what resources the client is allowed to access.

In previous versions of IIS, the primary authorization mechanism is NTFS permissions, which Web administrators can use to control access to site content, in the same way that file server administrators use permissions. NTFS permissions are still a viable authorization tool in IIS7, but they are complex to configure and they can complicate the process of deploying redundant IIS servers due to the unique SIDs assigned to every user and group.

IIS7 provides an alternative to NTFS permissions called URL Authorization, which enables administrators to create authorization rules for individual URLs, not for the underlying file system. IIS7 stores URL Authorization rules in the IIS configuration files, which simplifies the process of copying them to another server on the network. Therefore, URL Authorization rules can function as a replacement for NTFS permissions, providing clients with access to the resources they need and protecting everything else.

IIS7 URL Authorization uses two major guidelines to evaluate the rules that apply to a specific element:

- Deny rules supersede allow rules—If you create conflicting rules at the same level, one of which denies access and one of which allows access, the deny rule will take precedence.
- Parent rules supersede child rules—If you create a rule at one level, and a conflicting rule at a subordinate level, the high-level rule takes precedence.

To create your own URL Authorization rules, use the following procedure.

 CREATE URL AUTHORIZATION RULES

GET READY. Log on to Windows Server 2008 using a domain account with Administrator privileges. When the logon process is completed, close the Initial Configuration Tasks window and any other windows that appear.

1. Click **Start**, and then click **Administrative Tools** > **Internet Information Services (IIS) Manager**. The Internet Information Services (IIS) Manager console appears.
2. In the scope pane, select a server, site, application, or virtual directory. The Home pane for the selected element appears.
3. Double-click the **Authorization Rules** icon. The Authorization Rules pane appears, as shown in Figure 6-13.

TAKE NOTE *

To configure a folder that is not a virtual directory or an individual file, select a Web site and click Content View. Then double-click the desired folder or file, return to Features View, and double-click the Authorization Rules icon.

Figure 6-13

The Authorization Rules pane

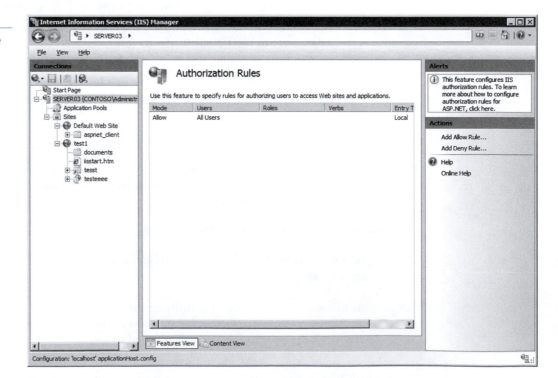

4. In the actions pane, click **Add Allow Rule** or **Add Deny Rule**. The Add Allow Authorization Rule or Add Deny Authorization Rule dialog box appears, as shown in Figure 6-14.

Figure 6-14

The Add Allow Authorization Rule dialog box

5. Specify to whom you want to apply the rule by using one of the following options:
   - All users—Allows or denies access to all clients, regardless of how they are authenticated.
   - All anonymous users—Allows or denies access only to clients using Anonymous Authentication.
   - Specified roles or user groups—Allows or denies access to the user groups or .NET roles you specify (separated by commas).
   - Specified users—Allows or denies access to the users you specify (separated by commas).

6. To limit the rule to specific types of requests, select the **Apply this rule to specific verbs** checkbox and specify the HTTP Method values to which you want the rule to apply. Common values include GET, PUT, POST, REPLY, and DELETE.

7. Click **OK**. The new rule appears in the Authorization Rules pane.

CLOSE the Internet Information Services (IIS) Manager console.

You can create URL Authorization rules for virtually every IIS7 element, including servers, sites, applications, virtual directories, folders, and individual files. By default, IIS7 creates an authorization rule at the server level, granting all users access to the Web content. All of the subordinate elements on the server inherit this rule, so you might have to delete or modify it at any subordinate element where you want to create your own, more restrictive, rules.

Configuring Handler Mappings

In previous versions of IIS, when you specified the home directory that would form the root of a Web site, you could grant clients any combination of read, write, script, and execute permissions for the site. In IIS7, this capability has been moved to a feature called Handler Mappings, which provides additional, more granular, configuration capabilities.

In addition to the general permissions, the Handler Mappings module also enables you to limit client access to specific file types in several different ways. You can limit the application of a handler mapping based on the HTTP verb specified in the request or based on whether the client request is for a file or a folder. You can also specify the permission required by the handler: read, write, script, execute, or none.

To configure handler mappings, use the following procedure.

 CONFIGURE HANDLER MAPPINGS

GET READY. Log on to Windows Server 2008 using a domain account with Administrator privileges. When the logon process is completed, close the Initial Configuration Tasks window and any other windows that appear.

1. Click **Start**, and then click **Administrative Tools** > **Internet Information Services (IIS) Manager.** The Internet Information Services (IIS) Manager console appears.
2. In the scope pane, select a server, site, application, or virtual directory. The Home pane for the selected element appears.
3. Double-click the **Handler Mappings** icon. The Handler Mappings pane appears, as shown in Figure 6-15.

 TAKE NOTE*

To configure a folder that is not a virtual directory or an individual file, select a Web site and click Content View. Then, double-click the desired folder or file, return to Features View, and double-click the Handler Mappings icon.

Figure 6-15

The Handler Mappings pane

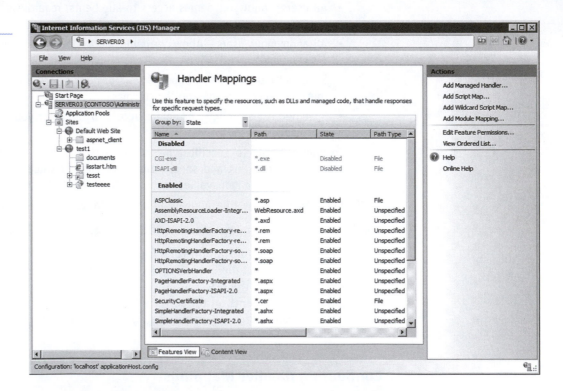

4. In the actions pane, click **Edit Feature Permissions**. The Edit Feature Permissions dialog box appears, as shown in Figure 6-16.

Figure 6-16

The Edit Feature Permissions dialog box

5. Select the checkboxes indicating the default permissions you want clients to have for the selected element. Then click **OK.**

6. Select one of the handlers listed in the pane and, in the actions pane, click **Edit.** An Edit dialog box for the selected handler appears, as shown in Figure 6-17.

Figure 6-17

The Edit dialog box for a handler

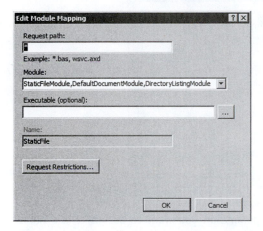

7. Click **Request Restrictions**. A Request Restrictions dialog box appears, as shown in Figure 6-18.

Figure 6-18

The Request Restrictions dialog box

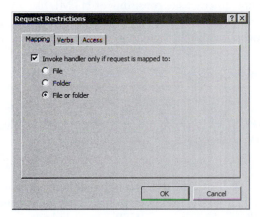

8. To limit the application of the handler, select the **Invoke handler only if request is mapped to** checkbox on the Mapping tab and specify whether you want IIS7 to invoke the handler when the request is for a file (the default), a folder, or both.

9. Click the **Verbs** tab, as shown in Figure 6-19.

Figure 6-19

The Verbs tab of the Request Restrictions dialog box

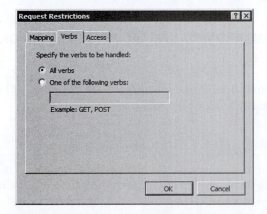

10. To limit the HTTP verbs that the handler can process, select the **One of the fol-lowing verbs** option and, in the text box, key the verbs you want to permit.

11. Click the **Access** tab, as shown in Figure 6-20.

Figure 6-20

The Access tab of the Request Restrictions dialog box

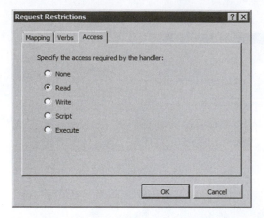

12. Select the permission you want to assign to the handler.

13. Click **OK**.

CLOSE the Internet Information Services (IIS) Manager console.

Limiting the types of client access to a Web site makes the server more secure. If, for example, you are running a simple Internet site consisting of HTML files and images, clients do not need anything other than read access. By denying the clients all access other than read, you eliminate all possibility of clients using the Web site to write to the server or execute programs and scripts.

Using NTFS Permissions

Although URL authorization rules provide an excellent alternative, NTFS permissions still factor into the IIS7 security picture, and they are still a viable means of regulating access to Web site contents.

For a client to access a Web site, the user account with which it is authenticated must have the proper NTFS permissions for the site's content files. This applies to clients that use Anonymous Authentication as well, in which case the IUSR user must have the right permissions.

Before you begin working with NTFS permissions, it is important to understand how the Windows permission system works. To review the basic principles of permission management, see "Understanding the Windows Permission Architecture" in Lesson 2, "Deploying a File Server."

ASSIGNING STANDARD AND SPECIAL NTFS PERMISSIONS

CERTIFICATION READY?
Configure Web site authentication and permissions
3.7

Most desktop technicians and Windows system administrators work with standard NTFS permissions almost exclusively because you do not need to work directly with special permissions for most common access control tasks. To assign standard NTFS permissions for a Web site element, use the following procedure.

 ASSIGN STANDARD NTFS PERMISSIONS

GET READY. Log on to Windows Server 2008 using a domain account with Administrator privileges. When the logon process is completed, close the Initial Configuration Tasks window and any other windows that appear.

TAKE NOTE

To configure a folder that is not a virtual directory or an individual file, select a Web site and click Content View. Then, double-click the desired folder or file, return to Features View, and double-click the Authentication icon.

1. Click **Start**, and then click **Administrative Tools** > **Internet Information Services (IIS) Manager**. The Internet Information Services (IIS) Manager console appears.

2. In the scope pane, select a site, application, or virtual directory. The Home pane for the selected element appears.

3. In the actions pane, click **Edit Permissions**. The Properties sheet for the file or folder corresponding to the selected element appears.

4. Click the **Security** tab. The top half of the resulting display lists all of the security principals currently possessing permissions to the file or folder. The bottom half lists the permissions held by the selected security principal.

5. Click **Edit.** A Permissions dialog box for the file or folder appears, as shown in Figure 6-21. The interface is the same as that of the previous dialog box, except that the permissions are now represented by checkboxes, indicating that you can modify their states.

Figure 6-21

A Permissions dialog box

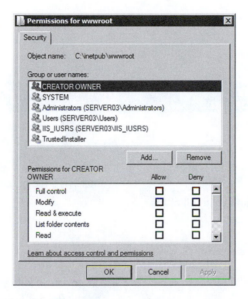

6. Click **Add.** The Select Users, Computers, or Groups dialog box appears, as shown in Figure 6-22.

Figure 6-22

The Select Users, Computers, or Groups dialog box

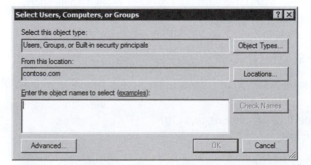

TAKE NOTE *

When you assign permissions on a stand-alone computer, you select local user and group accounts to be the security principals that receive the permissions. However, if the computer is a member of an Active Directory domain, you can also assign permissions to domain users, groups, and other objects.

7. In the *Enter the object names to select* text box, key the name of the user or group to which you want to assign permissions and then click **OK.** The user or group appears in the Permissions dialog box in the *Group or user names* list.

8. Select the user or group you just added and then, in the Permissions box, select or clear the checkboxes to Allow or Deny the user any of the standard permissions.

9. Click **OK** twice to close the Permissions dialog boxes and the Properties sheet.

CLOSE the Internet Information Services (IIS) Manager console.

The standard NTFS permissions have slightly different functions, depending on whether you apply them to a file or a folder. Table 6-2 lists all of the NTFS standard permissions and their effects on files and folders.

 TAKE NOTE* Assigning permissions to the single folder you created takes only a moment, but for a folder with a large number of files and subfolders subordinate to it, the process can take a long time because the system must modify the ACL of each folder and file.

Table 6-2

NTFS Standard Permissions

STANDARD PERMISSION	WHEN APPLIED TO A FOLDER, ENABLES A SECURITY PRINCIPAL TO:	WHEN APPLIED TO A FILE, ENABLES A SECURITY PRINCIPAL TO:
Full Control	• Modify the folder permissions. • Take ownership of the folder. • Delete subfolders and files contained in the folder. • Perform all actions associated with all of the other NTFS folder permissions.	• Modify the file permissions. • Take ownership of the file. • Perform all actions associated with all of the other NTFS file permissions.
Modify	• Delete the folder. • Perform all actions associated with the Write and the Read & Execute permissions.	• Modify the file. • Delete the file. • Perform all actions associated with the Write and the Read & Execute permissions.
Read & Execute	• Navigate through restricted folders to reach other files and folders. • Perform all actions associated with the Read and List Folder Contents permissions.	• Perform all actions associated with the Read permission. • Run applications.
List Folder Contents	• View the names of the files and subfolders contained in the folder.	• Not applicable.
Read	• See the files and subfolders contained in the folder. • View the ownership, permissions, and attributes of the folder.	• Read the contents of the file. • View the ownership, permissions, and attributes of the file.
Write	• Create new files and subfolders inside the folder. • Modify the folder attributes. • View the ownership and permissions of the folder.	• Overwrite the file. • Modify the file attributes. • View the ownership and permissions of the file.

If you ever have to work with NTFS special permissions directly, Windows Server 2008 provides the tools. To view and manage the special NTFS permissions for a file or folder, use the following procedure.

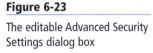 **ASSIGN SPECIAL NTFS PERMISSIONS**

GET READY. Log on to Windows Server 2008 using a domain account with Administrator privileges. When the logon process is completed, close the Initial Configuration Tasks window and any other windows that appear.

1. Click **Start**, and then click **Administrative Tools** > **Internet Information Services (IIS) Manager**. The Internet Information Services (IIS) Manager console appears.

2. In the scope pane, select a site, application, or virtual directory. The Home pane for the selected element appears.

3. In the actions pane, click **Edit Permissions**. The Properties sheet for the file or folder corresponding to the selected element appears.

4. Click the **Security** tab, and then click **Advanced**. An Advanced Security Settings page for the selected file or folder appears. This dialog box is as close as the Windows graphical interface can come to displaying the contents of an ACL. Each line in the *Permission entries* list is essentially an ACE and includes the following information:

   • Type—Specifies whether the entry allows or denies the permission.

   • Name—Specifies the name of the security principal receiving the permission.

   • Permission—Specifies the name of the standard permission being assigned to the security principal. If the entry is used to assign special permissions, the word *Special* appears in this field.

   • Inherited From—Specifies whether the permission is inherited and if so, where it is inherited from.

   • Apply To—Specifies whether the permission is inherited by subordinate objects and if so, by which ones.

5. Click **Edit**. Another Advanced Security Settings dialog box appears. This one is editable, as shown in Figure 6-23. This dialog box also contains the following two checkboxes:

Figure 6-23

The editable Advanced Security Settings dialog box

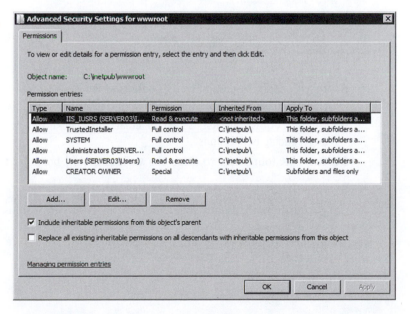

• Include inheritable permissions from this object's parent—Specifies whether the file or folder should inherit permissions from parent objects. This checkbox is selected by default. Deselecting it causes a Windows Security message box to appear, enabling you to choose whether to remove all of the inherited ACEs from the list or copy the inherited permissions from the parent to the file or folder. If you choose the latter, the effective permissions stay the same, but the file or folder no longer depends on the parent for permission inheritance. If you change the permissions on the parent objects, the file or folder remains unaffected.

- Replace all existing inheritable permissions on all descendents with inheritable permissions from this object—Causes subordinate objects to inherit permissions from this file or folder, to the exclusion of all permissions explicitly assigned to the subordinate objects.

6. Click **Add**. The Select User, Computer, or Group dialog box appears.

7. In the *Enter the object names to select* text box, key the name of the user or group to which you want to assign permissions and then click **OK**. A Permission Entry dialog box for the file or folder appears, as shown in Figure 6-24.

Figure 6-24

A Permission Entry dialog box

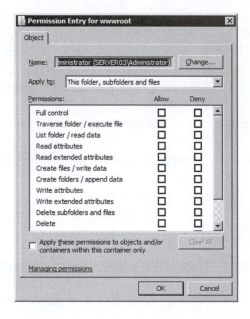

8. In the *Apply to* dropdown list, select which subordinate elements should receive the permissions you assign using this dialog box.

9. In the Permissions list, select or clear the checkboxes to Allow or Deny the user any special permissions.

10. Click **OK** four times to close the various dialog boxes and the Properties sheet.

CLOSE the Internet Information Services (IIS) Manager console.

Special permissions are slightly different from standard permissions, in that they have different names, depending on whether you apply them to a file or a folder. Table 6-3 lists all of the special permissions, along with their functions.

Table 6-3

NTFS Special Permissions

SPECIAL PERMISSION	FUNCTIONS
Traverse Folder/Execute File	• The Traverse Folder permission allows or denies security principals the ability to move through folders that they do not have permission to access to reach files or folders that they do have permission to access. This permission applies to folders only.
	• The Execute File permission allows or denies security principals the ability to run program files. This permission applies to files only.
List Folder/Read Data	• The List Folder permission allows or denies security principals the ability to view the file and subfolder names within a folder. This permission applies to folders only.
	• The Read Data permission allows or denies security principals the ability to view the contents of a file. This permission applies to files only.
Read Attributes	Allows or denies security principals the ability to view the NTFS attributes of a file or folder.
Read Extended Attributes	Allows or denies security principals the ability to view the extended attributes of a file or folder.
Create Files/Write Data	• The Create Files permission allows or denies security principals the ability to create files within the folder. This permission applies to folders only.
	• The Write Data permission allows or denies security principals the ability to modify the file and overwrite existing content. This permission applies to files only.
Create Folders/Append Data	• The Create Folders permission allows or denies security principals to create subfolders within a folder. This permission applies to folders only.
	• The Append Data permission allows or denies security principals the ability to add data to the end of the file but not to modify, delete, or overwrite existing data in the file. This permission applies to files only.
Write Attributes	Allows or denies security principals the ability to modify the NTFS attributes of a file or folder.
Write Extended Attributes	Allows or denies security principals the ability to modify the extended attributes of a file or folder.
Delete Subfolders and Files	Allows or denies security principals the ability to delete subfolders and files, even if the Delete permission has not been granted on the subfolder or file.
Delete	Allows or denies security principals the ability to delete the file or folder.
Read Permissions	Allows or denies security principals the ability to read the permissions for the file or folder.
Change Permissions	Allows or denies security principals the ability to modify the permissions for the file or folder.
Take Ownership	Allows or denies security principals the ability to take ownership of the file or folder.
Synchronize	Allows or denies different threads of multithreaded, multiprocessor programs to wait on the handle for the file or folder and synchronize with another thread that might signal it.

As mentioned earlier in this lesson, standard permissions are combinations of special permissions designed to provide frequently needed access controls. Table 2-8 in Lesson 2, "Deploying a File Server," lists all of the standard permissions, and the special permissions that compose them.

■ Using Secure Sockets Layer

THE BOTTOM LINE Secure Sockets Layer (SSL) is a security protocol that you can use to encrypt the data exchanged by clients and IIS servers.

When you click a link or key a URL containing the prefix https:// in your browser, you are establishing an SSL connection with the server. Virtually all browsers support SSL, and virtually all servers that handle sensitive data, such as e-commerce information, use it.

TAKE NOTE* When a user typing a URL omits the prefix by keying just a domain address, such as www.sitename.com, the browser automatically uses the http://prefix. To connect to the server using SSL, the URL or link must explicitly contain the https://prefix.

To use SSL on an IIS7 server, you must complete the following tasks:

- Obtain and install a server certificate.
- Create an SSL binding for your Website(s).
- Configure the Web site or FTP7 site to use SSL.

These tasks are discussed in the following sections.

Configuring Certificates

To use SSL, you must obtain a digital certificate for each of your Web servers.

CERTIFICATION READY?
Configuring SSL Security
3.6

A *digital certificate* is an electronic credential, issued by a *certification authority (CA)*, which confirms the identity of the party to which it is issued. For example, a digital certificate issued to a user contains identifying information about the individual, as well as a public key, which enables the user to participate in encrypted communications and prove his or her identity. A certificate issued to a server enables clients to verify that this really is the server it claims to be.

Participants in a *public key infrastructure* are issued two keys, one public and one private. The participant keeps the private key secret, while the public key is freely available in the digital certificate. Data encrypted with the private key can only be decrypted using the public key, and data encrypted with the public key can only be decrypted using the private key. Therefore, when a client obtains a Web server's certificate, its ability to decrypt the server's encrypted transmissions using the server's public key confirms that this is the system represented in the certificate. In addition, any data that the client encrypts using the server's public key can only be decrypted and read by the server.

A CA is simply an entity that issues certificates, which is trusted by both parties involved in the encrypted communications. If you want to use SSL on an Internet Web site, you must obtain a certificate for your Web server from a commercial CA, such as VeriSign, which is trusted both by your organization and by your clients. For intranet Web servers, you can run your own CA on a Windows Server 2008 computer and issue your own certificates. Because both the Web server and the clients are internal to the organization, both can trust an internal CA. To deploy your own CA, you must install the Active Directory Certificate Services role.

CREATING A CERTIFICATE REQUEST FILE

To obtain a server certificate for your IIS7 computer, you must either generate a request file and send it to a commercial CA or send an online request to your organization's internal CA.

To generate a request for a commercial CA, use the following procedure.

⊘ CREATE A CERTIFICATE REQUEST FILE

GET READY. Log on to Windows Server 2008 using a domain account with Administrator privileges. When the logon process is completed, close the Initial Configuration Tasks window and any other windows that appear.

1. Click **Start**, and then click **Administrative Tools** > **Internet Information Services (IIS) Manager**. The Internet Information Services (IIS) Manager console appears.

2. In the scope pane, select a server. The Home pane for the selected server appears.

3. Double-click the **Server Certificates** icon. The Server Certificates pane appears, displaying any existing certificates, as shown in Figure 6-25.

Figure 6-25

The Server Certificates pane

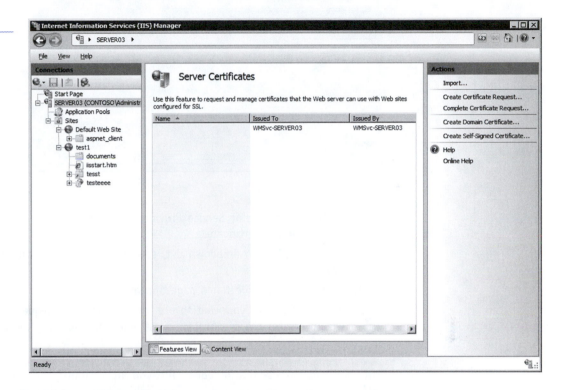

4. In the actions pane, click **Create Certificate Request**. The Request Certificate wizard appears, displaying the Distinguished Name Properties page, as shown in Figure 6-26.

Figure 6-26

The Distinguished Name Properties page of the Request Certificate wizard

5. Fill in each of the text boxes with the requested information about your organization, and then click **Next**. The Cryptographic Service Provider Properties page appears, as shown in Figure 6-27.

Figure 6-27

The Cryptographic Service Provider Properties page of the Request Certificate wizard

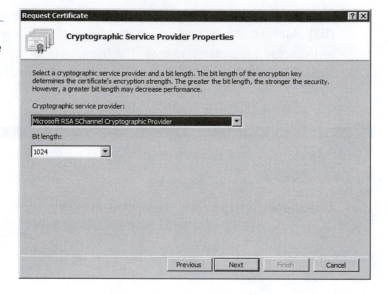

6. In the Cryptographic Service Provider dropdown list, select the provider you want to use for the certificate.

7. In the Bit Length dropdown list, specify the length for the certificate's encryption key.

8. Click **Next**. The File Name page appears.

9. Specify the name you want to use for the certificate request, and click **Finish**. The wizard creates the certificate request and stores it using the filename you specified.

CLOSE the Internet Information Services (IIS) Manager console.

After you create the certificate request file, you must submit it to your CA. The CA will send back a file containing the server certificate, which you must then install by opening the Server Certificates pane again, double-clicking Complete Certificate Request in the action pane, and specifying the name of the file the CA sent you.

If you have your own internal CA on the network, you can request a certificate from it by opening the Server Certificate pane and clicking Create Domain Certificate in the action pane. The Create Certificate wizard appears and requires you to fill out the same Distinguished Name Properties page as in the Create Certificate Request wizard. Then, you specify the name of the server hosting your CA, and the wizard submits your request and installs the certificate it receives in reply.

The computer can also create its own self-signed certificate, which you can request by selecting Create Self-Signed Certificate from the actions pane. A self-signed certificate has no real value to your clients, because it is the server itself that is verifying its own identity, but you can use this capability for testing purposes.

CREATING AN SSL BINDING

For a client to connect to an IIS7 server using SSL, the client must use the https:// prefix in its URL. For an IIS7 server to accept an SSL connection from a client, it must be able to recognize and process a URL containing the https:// prefix. To make this possible, you must create a binding for each Web site that you want to use SSL.

To create an SSL binding, use the following procedure.

 CREATE AN SSL BINDING

GET READY. Log on to Windows Server 2008 using a domain account with Administrator privileges. When the logon process is completed, close the Initial Configuration Tasks window and any other windows that appear.

1. Click **Start**, and then click **Administrative Tools** > **Internet Information Services (IIS) Manager**. The Internet Information Services (IIS) Manager console appears.
2. In the scope pane, right-click one of your Web sites and, from the context menu, select **Edit Bindings**. The Site Bindings dialog box appears.
3. Click **Add**. The Add Site Binding dialog box appears.
4. In the Type dropdown list, select **https**. The Port value changes to 443 and an SSL Certificate dropdown list appears, as shown in Figure 6-28.

Figure 6-28

The modified Add Site Binding dialog box

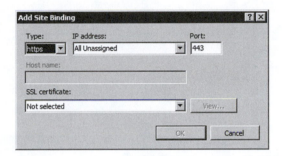

5. In the SSL certificate dropdown list, select the server certificate obtained from your CA.
6. Click **OK**. The new https binding appears in the Site Bindings list.
7. Select the existing http binding and click **Remove**. A Site Bindings message box appears, prompting you to confirm the removal.
8. Click **Yes**.
9. Click **Close**.

CLOSE the Internet Information Services (IIS) Manager console.

As you learned in Lesson 5, "Deploying IIS Services," Web servers use port number 80 by default, but you can select another port number for a site, as long as the clients include that port number in their URLs. The same is true for SSL bindings, except that the default port number for an SSL connection is 443.

ENABLING SSL

With a server certificate installed on the IIS7 server and the https binding in place, you are only required to enable SSL for your Web site, as in the following procedure.

 ENABLE SSL

GET READY. Log on to Windows Server 2008 using a domain account with Administrator privileges. When the logon process is completed, close the Initial Configuration Tasks window and any other windows that appear.

1. Click **Start**, and then click **Administrative Tools** > **Internet Information Services (IIS) Manager**. The Internet Information Services (IIS) Manager console appears.
2. In the scope pane, select a Web site. The Home pane for the selected site appears.

3. Double-click the **SSL Settings** icon. The SSL Settings pane appears, as shown in Figure 6-29.

Figure 6-29

The SSL Settings pane

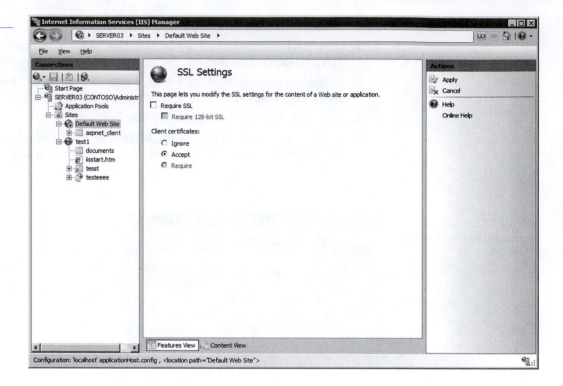

4. Select the **Require SSL** checkbox. If your clients support it, you can also select the **Require 128-bit SSL** checkbox.

5. Select one of the Client Certificates options, indicating whether you want to ignore, accept, or require client certificates.

6. In the action pane, click **Apply**.

CLOSE the Internet Information Services (IIS) Manager console.

After you have completed this procedure, clients can only connect to the Web site using the https:// URL prefix.

Enabling SSL for FTP7

The ability to encrypt FTP traffic using SSL is one of the major advantages of the FTP7 add-on module for Windows Server 2008.

SSL for FTP7 eliminates one of the major shortcomings of FTP: the transmission of passwords in clear text. To use SSL with FTP, you still need a certificate, although you can use a self-signed certificate. You do not need to create a special binding, but you do have to enable SSL for the FTP site, using the following procedure.

ENABLE SSL FOR FTP7

GET READY. Log on to Windows Server 2008 using a domain account with Administrator privileges. When the logon process is completed, close the Initial Configuration Tasks window and any other windows that appear.

1. Click **Start**, and then click **Administrative Tools** > **Internet Information Services (IIS) Manager.** The Internet Information Services (IIS) Manager console appears.

2. In the scope pane, select an FTP site. The Home pane for the selected site appears.

3. Double-click the **FTP SSL Settings** icon. The FTP SSL Settings pane appears, as shown in Figure 6-30.

Figure 6-30

The FTP SSL Settings pane

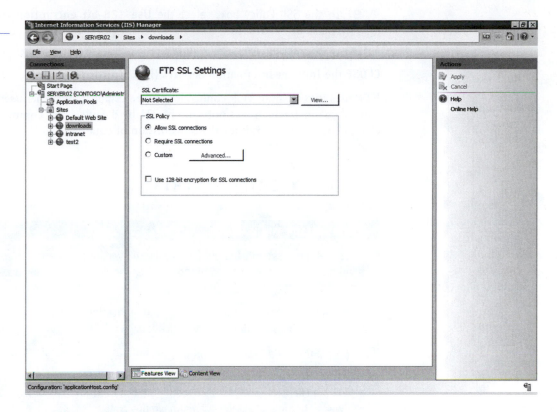

4. In the SSL Certificate dropdown list, select the certificate you want to use.

5. In the SSL Policy box, select the **Custom** option and click **Advanced**. The Advanced SSL Policy dialog box appears, as shown in Figure 6-31.

Figure 6-31

The Advanced SSL Policy dialog box

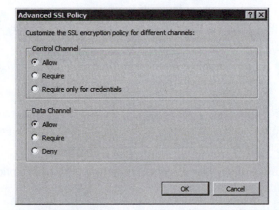

6. In the Control Channel box, select one of the following options:

- Allow—Enables FTP clients that support it to connect to the site using SSL. Clients that do not support SSL can still connect without it.

- Require—Permits only clients supporting SSL to connect to the site.

- Require only for credentials—Permits only clients supporting SSL to connect to the site, but the SSL encryption is limited to authentication traffic.

7. In the Data Channel box, select one of the following options:

- Allow—Enables FTP clients that support it to transfer data files using SSL. Clients that do not support SSL can still transfer files without it.

- Require—Permits only clients supporting SSL to transfer data files.
- Deny—Forbids clients to use SSL encryption for data transfers.

8. Click **OK**.

9. In the SSL Policy box, select the **Use 128-bit encryption for SSL connection** checkbox, if desired.

10. In the action pane, click **Apply**.

CLOSE the Internet Information Services (IIS) Manager console.

FTP uses two separate TCP connections when establishing a client/server connection. The control channel, which uses port number 21 by default, is for commands, while the data channel, using port 23, is for the transmission of data files.

SUMMARY SKILL MATRIX

IN THIS LESSON YOU LEARNED:

- IIS7 retains a security feature from earlier IIS versions that enables you to specify IP addresses or domain names that the server should allow or deny access to a server, site, virtual directory, folder, or file.

- IIS7 supports several password-based authentication methods, including anonymous, Windows, digest, and basic authentication.

- In IIS7, the authentication settings you configure at a particular level are inherited by all subordinate levels.

- When a client connects to a site configured to use multiple authentication methods, it always attempts to establish an anonymous connection first.

- The anonymous user account in IIS7 is a built-in account called IUSR, which is a member of a group called IIS_IUSRS.

- If you are running an intranet Web server on an Active Directory network with its own certification authority, you can configure IIS7 to automatically authenticate domain users that have client certificates.

- Because Active Directory Client Certificate Authentication requires the use of SSL with client certificates, it is not compatible with any of the other authentication methods IIS7 supports.

- Of the three traditional, challenge/response authentication methods supported by IIS7, Windows Authentication is the most secure.

- The Digest Authentication method in IIS7 is comparable to the Advanced Digest Authentication method from IIS6.

- Windows Authentication, Digest Authentication, and Basic Authentication are all challenge-based authentication methods.

- The NTFS permissions protecting a particular file system element are not like the keys to a lock, which provide either full access or no access at all. Permissions are designed to be granular, enabling you to grant specific degrees of access to security principals.

- NTFS permissions are realized as access control lists (ACLs), which consist of two basic types of access control entries (ACEs): Allow and Deny.

- Permissions tend to run down through a hierarchy. This is called permission inheritance.

- A digital certificate contains identifying information about the party to which it is issued, as well as a public key, which enables the issuee to participate in encrypted communications and prove its identity.

- If you want to use SSL on an Internet Web site, you must obtain a certificate for your Web server from a commercial CA, such as VeriSign, which is trusted both by your organization and by your clients. For intranet Web servers, you can use a certificate from an internal CA.

- To protect a Web site using SSL, you must have a server certificate and an https binding. Then you must enable SSL for the site.

Knowledge Assessment

Fill in the Blank

Complete the following sentences by writing the correct word or words in the blanks provided.

1. The most secure of the challenge/response authentication methods supported by IIS7 is _____ Authentication.

2. IIS7's Windows Authentication module uses the _____ authentication protocol for computers that are members of an Active Directory domain.

3. A(n) _____ is an electronic credential that confirms the identity of the party to which it is issued.

4. The process of confirming a user's identity, usually by requiring the user to supply some sort of token such as a password or certificate, is called _____.

5. The weakest of the challenge/response authentication methods supported by IIS7 is called _____.

6. When clients connect to a Web server using the _____ method, the server logs them on using the IUSR account, by default.

7. _____ Authentication is designed for use with Active Directory Web servers whose clients are on the other side of a proxy server or firewall.

8. Digital certificates are issued by internal or external resources called _____.

9. To authenticate clients that are not members of Active Directory domains, the IIS7 Windows Authentication module uses the _____ protocol.

10. Digital certificates are required for a Web server to participate in a(n) _____ infrastructure.

Multiple Choice

Select the correct answer for each of the following questions. Choose all answers that are correct.

1. Which of the following statements is/are *not* true about the IIS7 Handler Mappings module?
   a. The Handler Mappings module replaces NTFS permissions for IIS Web sites.
   b. The Handler Mappings module enables you to specify the permission required by the handler: read, write, script, execute, or none.
   c. The Handler Mappings module enables you to limit both the general permissions for a Web site and client access to specific file types.
   d. The Handler Mappings module enables you to limit the application of mappings based on the HTTP verb specified in the request.

2. The IIS7 Digest Authentication method
   a. works through firewalls and proxy servers, because it actually transmits passwords over the network.
   b. protects the passwords using a strong Kerberos encryption scheme.
   c. can be used with any version of Internet Explorer.
   d. is new to IIS7 and so is not comparable to authentication methods available in previous IIS versions.

3. Place the following methods that IIS7 uses to authenticate clients in the correct sequence.
   a. Digest Authentication
   b. Windows Authentication
   c. Basic Authentication
   d. Anonymous Authentication

4. Which of the following authentication methods is/are integrated into an IIS7 installation by default?
   a. Basic Authentication
   b. Windows Authentication
   c. Digest Authentication
   d. Anonymous Authentication

5. Anonymous users of an IIS7 Web server are authenticated using a local user account named
   a. Anonymous
   b. Authenticated User
   c. IUSR
   d. IUSR_*computername*

6. Which of the following authentication protocols can the IIS7 Windows Authentication module use?
   a. NTLMv2
   b. KDC
   c. Kerberos
   d. TGS/TGT

7. Which of the following statements about the IIS7 URL authorization rules is/are *not* true?
   a. URL Authorization rules are designed to function on concert with NTFS permissions.
   b. IIS7 stores URL Authorization rules in the IIS configuration files.
   c. Deny rules supersede allow rules.
   d. Parent rules supersede child rules.

8. Which of the following statements about the public key infrastructure is/are true?
   a. Private keys are distributed in digital certificates.
   b. A message encrypted using one user's private key can only be decrypted by another user's private key.
   c. Sending a message encrypted with a private key enables the recipient to confirm that the message actually came from the sender.
   d. Data encrypted using a public key can be decrypted by any user possessing that same public key.

9. Which of the following statements is/are prerequisites for using Active Directory Client Certificate Authentication?
   a. The network must have an Active Directory domain controller installed.
   b. The domain must use the Windows Server 2008 domain functional level.
   c. The network must have a server functioning as a certification authority (CA).
   d. All of the Web sites on the IIS7 server must require SSL communications.

Review Questions

1. List the tasks you must perform to implement SSL encryption for an IIS7 Web site.

2. What is the primary advantage of using Forms Authentication for a high-traffic Web site, rather than Windows, Digest, or Basic Authentication?

■ Case Scenarios

Scenario 6-1: Using Kerberos Authentication

Adam is deploying an intranet Web site on an IIS7 server, to provide company documents to internal users. To secure the site, Adam wants to use the Kerberos authentication capabilities provided by Active Directory, so he installs the Windows Authentication role service. After the site is live, Adam examines the log files and discovers that the clients accessing the server are using Anonymous Authentication, not Windows Authentication. What could be the problem, and what must Adam do to resolve it?

Scenario 6-2: Authorizing Web site Users

Tom is trying to secure the Web sites on his IIS7 server using URL authorization rules instead of NTFS permissions. To do this, he has modified the default rule at the server level to deny all users access. Then, he created new allow rules for each Web site on the server, granting specific users and groups the access they need. When the users attempt to access the sites, they receive error messages. What is the problem, and what changes must Tom make to the rules to correct it?

Deploying Web Applications

OBJECTIVE DOMAIN MATRIX

TECHNOLOGY SKILL	OBJECTIVE DOMAIN	OBJECTIVE DOMAIN NUMBER
Adding an Application to a Site	Configure Web applications.	3.1
Configuring SMTP Settings	Configure Simple Mail Transfer Protocol (SMTP).	3.4

KEY TERMS

Active Server Pages (ASP)
application pool
ASP.NET
Common Gateway Interface (CGI)
FastCGI

Internet Server Application Programming Interface (ISAPI)
ISAPI extensions
ISAPI filters
Server Side Includes (SSI)
Simple Mail Transfer Protocol (SMTP)

Universal Discovery, Description, and Integration (UDDI)
Web garden
worker process
worker process isolation mode

Application hosting is one of the primary areas in which Microsoft has improved Internet Information Services. This lesson examines the application-hosting capabilities built into IIS7, including the following:

- Understanding IIS7 application hosting support
- Creating and configuring application pools
- Deploying UDDI Services
- Deploying SMTP

Understanding Web Applications

THE BOTTOM LINE
Applications are now a major part of most Web server implementations. Instead of creating a completely new client, application developers can take advantage of the Web browser's capabilities and use them to access programs deployed on Web servers.

Web servers were originally designed as relatively simple applications that supplied clients with static content, in response to their requests. The static content most often took the form of Hypertext Markup Language (HTML) and image files. HTML is a simple scripting language that uses tags to specify how the client Web browser should display the text in the file and where it should insert images, which the server supplies as separate files. The HTML code is interpreted entirely by the browser application on the client computer. To the Web server, HTML files are simply text files that they supply to clients on demand.

As the Web grew in popularity, it also grew in complexity. Web site owners soon wanted to use their servers to provide more than just static content files. They wanted to perform more complicated tasks. They wanted to provide the information in their company databases to Web clients on demand. They wanted clients to be able to select products from a catalog and pay for them with a credit card. As a result, developers began to create Web servers with application capabilities.

As the years passed, developers devised various ways to implement applications in a Web environment by taking advantage of both clients' and servers' capabilities. Some types of Web-based applications execute scripts or compiled code on the server, while in others, the server supplies the script code to the client. Many Web development solutions combine the two. In any case, the primary advantage of Web applications over traditional client/server applications is that you do not need to develop, install, configure, or maintain complicated application packages on every client computer. Developers wanting to update their applications make all of their changes on the server, instead of distributing new files to hundreds or thousands of clients.

Most of the Web application environments in use today enable a server to dynamically generate Web pages and send them to clients, rather than use static, preconfigured pages. For example, when a user on a client computer keys a term into a search engine, the browser sends a request message containing the term to a Web server. The server cannot possibly hold the millions of static pages it would need to satisfy every possible search term, but it can access a database containing that information. After searching the database using the term supplied by the client, the Web server takes the resulting information, builds a new Web page containing that information, and sends it to the client.

Generally speaking, Web applications use a three-tiered architecture. The first tier is the client browser application running on the end user's computer. The second tier is a Web server with some type of dynamic content generation capability, and the third tier is a database server that stores the information the Web server uses to dynamically generate Web pages.

In addition to the information derived from a database, a dynamically generated Web page might also contain script code that runs on the client and implements dynamic elements on the user interface. Client-side scripting languages such as JavaScript, with other technologies, such as Java and Flash, enable the Web pages on client browsers to emulate virtually any function that a standalone client application can perform. Web pages can display virtually any type of content, including audio and video, and provide familiar keyboard and mouse controls, such as drag and drop.

No matter what appears in the client browser, the primary function of the Web server is still to send and receive text-based messages containing requests and replies. The added complexity lies in the technologies that the server uses to create those text messages and the browser uses to interpret them.

Understanding IIS7's Application Hosting Capabilities

IIS7 includes a wide variety of application environments that enable administrators to deploy applications created with many different development tools and languages.

With the increasing demand for Web applications came an increasing demand for Web application development solutions. Products like Microsoft Visual Studio provide simplified application development environments, but many of these products require the Web server to supply an environment in which the applications can run. As a result, Internet Information Systems version 7 (IIS7) includes role services that support a variety of development environments. Some of these role services represent cutting-edge Web development technologies, while others are relatively archaic, included with IIS7 primarily to support legacy applications.

The application role services supplied with IIS7 are discussed in the following sections.

UNDERSTANDING CGI

The *Common Gateway Interface (CGI)* is one of the earliest mechanisms designed to provide Web servers with application hosting capabilities. CGI is essentially a protocol that enables a Web server to run an application specified in a client request and pass the request to that application for processing. The Web server then receives the output from the application and packages it as a reply to the client in the form of a Web page.

The primary drawback of CGI is that the Web server, in most cases, must launch a separate process to satisfy each request. Depending on the complexity of the program, the language used to write it, and the number of concurrent incoming requests, this can place a substantial burden on the server that increases with the Web site's traffic volume. CGI can also be a security risk, especially on Internet Web servers. By allowing Web pages to call CGI programs, you are essentially permitting anyone on the Internet to run a program on your server.

Developers can create CGI programs using any language that the server is capable of executing. This includes compiled languages, such as C and C++, and scripting languages, such as Perl. Although it is possible to use CGI for major application processes, such as accessing an external database, many CGI programs still in common use on the Internet are small applications that perform relatively simple tasks, such as displaying Web page counters. For more complicated applications that have to run continuously, developers today use other technologies.

Starting with IIS version 5.1, Microsoft provided an alternative to CGI, which overcomes its most serious problem. Called *FastCGI*, this extension to the CGI engine enables the Web server to maintain a pool of processes that new clients can reuse. In standard CGI processing, each client connection causes the operating system on the server to create a new process and map the Standard Input (stdin) and Standard Output (stdout) handles to that client. When the transaction is completed, the client disconnects and the server terminates the process.

In FastCGI, the server allocates each incoming client connection to one of the existing processes in the pool and remaps the stdin and stdout handles to the new client. When the transaction is completed, the server removes the mappings and returns the process to the pool. This eliminates the need for the server to create a new process for each client connection, which boosts CGI performance considerably.

UNDERSTANDING ISAPI

Internet Server Application Programming Interface (ISAPI) was designed to be an alternative to CGI, enabling a Web server to execute applications without spawning a separate process for each incoming request. Written primarily in C++, ISAPI applications can take two forms:

- *ISAPI extensions*—Fully-realized, in-process applications that can generate dynamic HTML pages using information from a database or supplied by the client using a form.
- *ISAPI filters*—A routine that operates between the HTTP server and the HTTP listener, providing additional functionality, such as application-based authentication, encryption, and data compression services. The ISAPI implementation in IIS6 virtually eliminates the need for ISAPI filters, because it can run ISAPI extensions, more efficiently, in their place.

As originally designed, ISAPI programs run in the same address space as the Web server's HTTP engine. ISAPI applications take the form of dynamic link libraries (DLLs) instead of executables (EXEs), which load with the IIS server engine, using the same address space. All of the resources available to the IIS server are also available to the ISAPI DLLs. This eliminates the need for calls between processes, as used in CGI, which enhances performance. It also means that if an ISAPI application crashes, the entire Web server goes with it. Beginning with IIS6, however, ISAPI applications can run in a separate address space, which reduces the danger of crashing the Web server while maintaining its performance levels.

If CGI can be said to represent the first generation of Web application programming, ISAPI must be seen as the second generation. While ISAPI provides improved levels of performance, its reliance on C++ means that developing ISAPI applications requires a high-level programming effort. CGI, by comparison, was more amenable to grass roots programming using Perl and other scripting languages.

In IIS6, ISAPI extensions function as the interface between the IIS engine and other, more flexible, application technologies, such as Active Server Pages (ASP) and ASP.NET. For example, IIS and ASP.NET each maintain their own separate request pipelines, and an ISAPI extension shuttles information between the two. In this arrangement, ISAPI facilitates these other application technologies, but it also constrains them. An application running on an IIS Web site can never run faster than the ISAPI extension that enables it.

IIS7 can use ISAPI in the same way, a compatibility feature that it calls "Classic" mode, but its more efficient "Integrated" mode eliminates the need for ISAPI as the middleman. Instead, IIS, ASP.NET, and other development technologies take the form of modules that plug into a single, generic request pipeline. ISAPI is not needed to provide an interface between IIS and other application types, so the applications are not reliant on, or constrained by, it.

UNDERSTANDING SERVER SIDE INCLUDES

Server Side Includes (SSI) is another relatively old Web server technology that enables HTML pages to contain directives that the server parses and executes. In the original client/server paradigm for the Web, clients, in the form of Web browsers, send requests to a server for specific text files. The server replies to the requests by accessing the appropriate files and sending the text to the client. The server is completely oblivious of the files' contents; it simply packages the text into an HTTP reply and transmits it to the client. The browser is wholly responsible for reading and interpreting the text.

SSI changes this paradigm by forcing the Web server to read the text of the pages it is about to transmit to clients, and act upon specific commands it finds in that text.

SSI consists of two elements:

- a collection of directives that Web designers can include in their HTML pages
- a component that causes the server to scan the outgoing text for directives and take the appropriate action.

For example, to make a Web server insert the contents of a file called filename.txt into a Web page, you insert the following code into the HTML file:

```
<! -#include virtual="filename.txt"- - >
```

The bracketed enclosure is the HTML tag indicating a command, so the browser ignores the contents of the brackets while parsing the file. However, the server does just the opposite, ignoring the rest of the file and paying attention to the SSI directives and their parameters.

SSI is an easy way of updating static HTML files with frequently changing data. For example, if you want to create a Web page that contains mostly static content, but which also specifies the latest price of gold, you can use an #include directive to insert a file containing the gold price into the page. Then, you only have to modify the included file when the price of gold changes. The main Web page file remains unchanged.

SSI, though old, is a useful technology but it does increase the workload on the server. Remember, the server not only has to execute the directives, it also has to scan every outgoing HTTP reply for those directives. If you have only a few Web pages that use SSI, and a great many that do not, it might not be practical to enable SSI for the entire server.

UNDERSTANDING ACTIVE SERVER PAGES

Microsoft designed *Active Server Pages (ASP)*, a server-side script processing engine, to provide dynamic Web content with better performance than CGI and simpler development than ISAPI. ASP files have an .asp extension, and function in much the same way as Server Side Includes, with scripting commands embedded in standard HTML code. Instead of appearing within comment delimiters, however, ASP commands are enclosed within angle brackets and ampersands, such as the following example, which displays the text "Hello, World." in the client browser window:

```
<& Response.Write("Hello, World.") &>
```

Most ASP pages use Microsoft's VBScript scripting language, but it is also possible to use Jscript, Microsoft's version of JavaScript. Third-party products provide support for other active scripting engines.

+ MORE INFORMATION

Although designed and implemented by Microsoft for the Windows server operating systems, ASP has been ported to other platforms. For example, a version for Apache Web servers is called Apache::ASP, and uses Perl scripting.

UNDERSTANDING ASP.NET

Much of IIS7's application hosting capability is geared towards the ASP.NET development environment. ASP.NET is the successor to ASP and is still based on server-side scripting, but it is more than just an upgrade. Based on the .NET Framework, *ASP.NET* enables developers to create dynamic Web pages, Web applications, and XML (Extensible Markup Language) Web services, using a wide variety of programming languages and development tools.

ASP.NET files have the extension .aspx, and can contain HTML code, XML code, or scripting code for execution by the server. Now that ASP.NET applications can plug directly into the IIS7 request processing pipeline, instead of using an ISAPI extension like IIS6, the services provided by ASP.NET applications can apply to any type of content handled by the Web server.

Understanding IIS7 Application Hosting

In Windows Server 2008, application hosting has become a primary function of IIS7. As mentioned earlier, previous versions of IIS are HTTP-centric. IIS6 only provides access to application hosting environments such as ASP and ASP.NET by way of ISAPI extensions. The modular architecture of IIS7 enables applications to participate on an equal footing with traditional HTTP request processing.

The fundamental job of an IIS server, or any server, is to receive requests from clients and process them. The server therefore has to "listen" for incoming requests arriving over specific ports. IIS6 introduced a specialized HTTP protocol listener module, called HTTP.sys, which replaced the Windows Sockets API used in earlier IIS versions.

In IIS6, HTTP.sys is responsible for accepting all incoming client requests. If the request is a standard HTTP message, then HTTP.sys hands it off to the World Wide Web Publishing Service (W3SVC) for processing. If the request is directed at an application, HTTP.sys uses ISAPI extensions to pass the request to the appropriate application pipeline. In essence, IIS is enabling multiple applications to share the single TCP port (port 80) dedicated to HTTP traffic.

IIS7 still includes the HTTP.sys module, which now includes support for Secure Sockets Layer (SSL) communications, but as mentioned earlier, there is now a single, generic request pipeline into which W3SVC and the optional application support modules can connect. However, in addition to HTTP.sys, IIS7 also adds three new protocol listeners: NET.TCP, NET.PIPE, and NET.MSMQ. These listeners enable IIS7 to receive client requests using protocols other than HTTP, and ports other than port 80. In other words, it is now possible to use IIS7 to host applications without running the W3SVC service, that is, without a Web server.

UNDERSTANDING APPLICATION POOLS

One of the inherent problems with hosting Web applications on Web sites is the possibility of an unstable application affecting the entire Web server, or worse, the entire computer. This is especially true for a commercial Web hosting operation, in which customers supply their own applications. IIS7, to protect its own server functions, as well as those of other Web sites and Windows Server 2008 itself, can isolate Web applications in separate address spaces called application pools.

An *application pool* is an operational division within IIS7 that consists of a request queue and one or more worker processes. A *worker process* is a host for user-developed application code, which is responsible for processing requests it receives from the protocol listeners and returning the results to the client. Because each application pool occupies its own protected address space, a crashed application cannot affect any process running outside of that pool. This is known as *worker process isolation mode*.

The Windows Process Activation Service (WPAS) is responsible for managing application pools and worker processes. In a typical IIS7 configuration, the request handling process proceeds as follow:

1. An incoming request from a client arrives at the computer.

2. IIS7 forwards the request to the appropriate site, based on its IP address, port number, or host header.

3. If the request contains an application call, such as a URL containing a file with the .aspx extension denoting an ASP.NET application, it goes into the request queue for the application pool associated with the application.

4. WPAS examines the state of the application pool to see if a running worker process can handle the request.

5. If a worker process is available, the request goes directly to that worker process. If no worker process is available, WPAS spawns a new worker process to handle the request.

6. The worker process executes the code and generates the calls necessary to process the request.

7. The worker process packages the results of its activities into a reply message and transmits it to the client.

The configuration of the application pools, worker processes, and applications is highly flexible in IIS7. You can create as many application pools as you need, and configure them in any one of the following three ways:

- Isolated process—A single application, serviced by a single worker process
- Medium (Pooled) process—Multiple applications, serviced by a single worker process
- Web garden—Multiple applications, serviced by multiple worker processes

When you install the Web Server (IIS) role, the wizard creates two application pools in IIS7, called DefaultAppPool and Classic .NET AppPool, both of which are configured to use a single worker process. All applications that you add to the Default Web Site on the server use DefaultAppPool, resulting in a Medium (Pooled) process configuration. When you create a new Web site, IIS7 automatically creates a new application pool with the same name as the site and the same configuration settings as DefaultAppPool. You can modify these pools to use more than one worker process, or create a new pool so configured, to form what is known as a *Web garden*.

UNDERSTANDING MANAGED PIPELINE MODES

As discussed earlier in this lesson, and in more detail in Lesson 5, "Deploying IIS Services," the new modular architecture of IIS7 includes multiple protocol listener modules, all of which can plug into a single, generic request pipeline. This streamlines the application request handling process and eliminates the need for ISAPI extensions linking the HTTP request pipeline with, for example, the ASP .NET pipeline.

However, some legacy applications might not be compatible with the new architecture, and so IIS7 enables you to configure each application pool to use one of the following managed pipeline modes:

- Integrated application pool mode—IIS7 uses the new, generic request pipeline for all protocol listeners and application development environments.
- Classic application pool mode—IIS7 uses the ISAPI-based interface between the HTTP pipeline and the ASP.NET pipeline from IIS6. This mode is intended only for applications that cannot run in Integrated mode.

DefaultAppPool uses the Integrated mode, and Classic .NET AppPool uses Classic mode.

Configuring IIS7 Application Settings

Now that you have learned how IIS7 implements, supports, and processes Web applications, consider how these application development technologies affect you as an administrator of IIS7 Web servers. In many cases, the honest answer is: not very much at all. As the administrator of a Web server, it is your job to provide application developers with the environments they need to run their applications.

You must be familiar with the application hosting capabilities of IIS7 so that you can determine whether it can run a particular application. You must also be familiar with the procedures for implementing and configuring those application hosting capabilities so that you can create Web sites that are appropriately equipped to run the applications that developers supply to you.

The following sections discuss those implementation and configuration procedures.

CREATING AN APPLICATION POOL

Application pools are IIS7 components that you can create as needed, just like you create Web sites and virtual directories. To use an application pool, you then associate it with a particular Web site by adding an application to that site and selecting the appropriate pool.

To create a new application pool, use the following procedure.

 CREATE AN APPLICATION POOL

GET READY. Log on to Windows Server 2008 using a domain account with Administrator privileges. When the logon process is completed, close the Initial Configuration Tasks window and any other windows that appear.

1. Click **Start**, and then click **Administrative Tools** > **Internet Information Services (IIS) Manager**. The Internet Information Services (IIS) Manager console appears.

2. Expand the server node and select the **Application Pools** node. The Application Pools pane appears, as shown in Figure 7-1.

Figure 7-1

The Application Pools pane

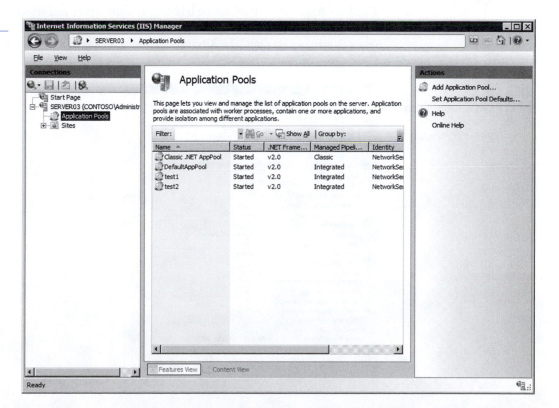

3. Right-click the **Application Pools** node and, from the context menu, select **Add Application Pool.** The Add Application Pool dialog box appears, as shown in Figure 7-2.

Figure 7-2

The Add Application Pool dialog box

4. In the Name text box, key a name for the new application pool.

5. In the *.NET Framework version* dropdown list, select the version of the .NET Framework that you want the application pool to load.

6. In the *Managed pipeline mode* dropdown list, specify whether you want to use Integrated or Classic mode.

7. If you do not want to start the application pool at this time, clear the *Start application pool immediately* checkbox.

8. Click **OK**.

CLOSE the Internet Information Services (IIS) Manager console.

After you have created an application pool, it appears in the Application Pools pane, and you can configure its settings at any time using the IIS Manager console.

CONFIGURING AN APPLICATION POOL

When you select an entry in the Applications Pool pane, you can select either Basic Settings or Advanced Settings from the actions pane.

The Edit Application Pool dialog box that appears when you select Basic Settings contains the same controls as the Add Application Pool dialog box you used to create the pool. When you select Advanced Settings, the Advanced Settings dialog box, shown in Figure 7-3, appears.

Figure 7-3

The Advanced Settings dialog box

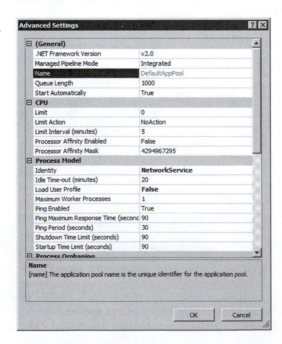

This dialog box, in addition to providing access to the basic settings, enables you to configure the resources allotted to the application pool and the actions IIS7 should take when the pool exceeds those resources. These settings are particularly useful in a commercial Web hosting environment when you want to ensure that one Web site does not monopolize the computer's resources. The parameters you can configure are listed in Table 7-1.

Table 7-1

Application Pool Advanced Settings

SETTING	DEFAULT VALUE	DESCRIPTION
(General)		
.NET Framework version	v2.0	Specifies the version of the .NET Framework that the application pool will load.
Managed Pipeline Mode	Integrated	Specifies whether IIS7 will use the new, generic request pipeline for all protocol listeners and application development environments or the IIS6 ISAPI-based interface between the HTTP pipeline and the ASP.NET pipeline.
Queue length	1000	Specifies the number of requests that HTTP.sys can hold in its queue before IIS7 begins returning error messages to clients.
Start automatically	True	Specifies whether the application pool should start when IIS7 starts.
CPU		
Limit	0	Specifies the maximum percentage of CPU time (in 1/1000s of a percent) that the worker processes in the application pool are allowed to consume.
Limit Action	NoAction	Specifies the action that IIS7 should take when the application pool exceeds its CPU time limit. The NoAction value generates an event log entry, and the KillW3wp value shuts down the application pool for a designated time interval and creates an event log entry.
Limit Interval	5	Specifies the time interval (in minutes) during which the Limit value is imposed and the application pool remains shut down in the event of a KillW3p incident.
Processor Affinity Enabled	False	Specifies whether the application pool should be forced to use specific processors on a multi-processor system.
Processor Affinity Mask	[Varies]	Specifies which processor(s) the application pool should use on a multi-processor system.
Process Model Identity	Network Service	Specifies the built-in or user account that the application pool should use to run.
Idle Time-out	20	Specifies the amount of time (in minutes) that a worker process can remain idle before IIS7 shuts it down.
Load User Profile	False	Specifies whether IIS7 should load the user profile for the account specified in the Identity value.
Maximum Worker Processes	1	Specifies the number of worker processes the application pool can use. Specifying a value greater than 1 configures the pool as a Web garden.
Ping Enabled	True	Activates health monitoring, in which IIS7 pings each worker process periodically to ensure that it is active.

(continued)

Table 7-1 (*continued*)

Setting	Default Value	Description
Ping Maximum Response Time	90	Specifies the amount of time (in seconds) that a worker process has to reply to a ping before IIS7 terminates the worker process.
Ping Period	30	Specifies the interval (in seconds) between health monitoring pings.
Shutdown Time Limit	90	Specifies the amount of time (in seconds) allotted to worker processes to finish processing all outstanding requests and shut down. If a worker process exceeds this time limit, IIS7 terminates it.
Startup Time Limit	90	Specifies the amount of time (in seconds) allotted to worker processes to start up and initialize. If a worker process exceeds this time limit, IIS7 terminates it.
Process Orphaning		
Enabled	False	Specifies whether IIS7 should abandon unresponsive worker processes instead of terminating them.
Executable	[None]	Specifies the name of a program that IIS7 should run when it abandons a worker process.
Executable Parameters	[None]	Specifies parameters that IIS7 should include when running the program specified in the Executable value.
Rapid Fail Protection		
"Service Unavailable" Response Type	HttpLevel	Specifies whether a stopped application pool should cause IIS7 to generate HTTP 503 errors or reset the TCP connection.
Enabled	True	Specifies whether IIS7 should shut down an application pool when a specified number of worker process crashes occur within a specified time interval.
Failure Interval	5	Specifies the time interval (in minutes) during which a specified number of worker process crashes must occur for IIS7 to shut down an application pool.
Maximum Failures	5	Specifies the number of worker process crashes that must occur during the time period specified by the Failure Interval value for IIS7 to shut down an application pool.
Shutdown Executable	[None]	Specifies the name of a program that IIS7 should run when it shuts down an application pool.
Shutdown Executable Parameters	[None]	Specifies parameters that IIS7 should include when running the program specified in the Shutdown Executable value.
Recycling		
Disable Overlapped Recycle	False	Specifies whether the application pool should wait for a worker process to terminate before it creates a new worker process.
Disable Recycling for Configuration Changes	False	Specifies whether the application pool should recycle worker processes when its configuration changes.
Generate Recycle Event Log Entry	[Various]	Specifies whether IIS7 should create event log entries when individual specified recycle events occur.
Private Memory Limit	0	Specifies the amount of private memory (in KB) that a worker process can consume before IIS7 recycles the application pool.

(*continued*)

Table 7-1 (*continued*)

SETTING	DEFAULT VALUE	DESCRIPTION
Regular Time Interval	1740	Specifies the time interval (in minutes) between application pool recycles.
Request Limit	0	Specifies the maximum number of requests an application pool can process before it recycles.
Specific Times	TimeSpan[] Array	Contains a list of specified times that the application pool should recycle.
Virtual Memory Limit	0	Specifies the amount of virtual memory (in KB) that a worker process can consume before IIS7 recycles the application pool.

CERTIFICATION READY?
Configure Web
applications
3.1

ADDING AN APPLICATION TO A SITE

After you create an application pool, you must associate it with the applications that will run within it. To add an application to a Web site in IIS7, use the following procedure.

 ADD AN APPLICATION TO A SITE

GET READY. Log on to Windows Server 2008 using a domain account with Administrator privileges. When the logon process is completed, close the Initial Configuration Tasks window and any other windows that appear.

1. Click **Start**, and then click **Administrative Tools** > **Internet Information Services (IIS) Manager**. The Internet Information Services (IIS) Manager console appears.

2. Expand the server node and then expand the Sites folder.

3. Right-click a Web site and, from the context menu, select **Add Application**. The Add Application dialog box appears, as shown in Figure 7-4.

Figure 7-4

The Add Application dialog box

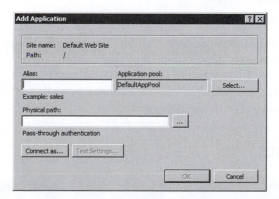

4. In the Alias text box, key the name that you want clients to use in their URLs to access the application.

5. Click **Select**. The Select Application Pool dialog box appears, as shown in Figure 7-5.

Figure 7-5

The Select Application Pool dialog box

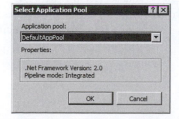

6. In the Application Pool dropdown list, select the application pool in which you want the application to run. Then click **OK**.

7. In the Add Application dialog box, in the Physical Path text box, key or browse to the folder where the application content is located. The folder can be on the local or a remote computer, and you can use drive letter notation (c:\foldername) or Universal Naming Convention (UNC) notation (\\servername\foldername).

8. By default, IIS7 uses the client user account to access application content on other systems. If the client needs alternative credentials to access the application, click **Connect As** and specify a user name and password.

9. Click **OK**.

CLOSE the Internet Information Services (IIS) Manager console.

An application node appears, subordinate to the selected Web site. When requests for the application arrive at the Web site, IIS7 passes them to the specified application pool for processing, and WPAS allocates a worker process to the task.

■ Deploying UDDI Services

THE BOTTOM LINE

Universal Discovery, Description, and Integration (UDDI) is an XML-based directory service that enables businesses to publish listings about their activities and the services they offer.

Windows Server 2008 includes a UDDI Services role that organizations can use to share information about their Web sites and services with clients on an intranet, extranet, or the Internet.

The UDDI Services role consists of the following two role services:

- UDDI Services Database
- UDDI Services Web Application

You can install both of the role services on one computer, for a stand-alone installation, the only installation type supported on Windows Server 2008 Standard. If you are running Windows Server 2008 Enterprise or Datacenter, you can choose to install the role services on two different computers, which is called a distributed installation. For performance reasons, Microsoft recommends the latter arrangement.

Installing UDDI

The UDDI Services Database is where the service stores information about Web sites, as well as its configuration settings.

The UDDI Services role supplied with Windows Server 2008 can store its database on a computer running Microsoft SQL Server, as long as you perform a distributed installation and install the UDDI Services Database role service on the SQL Server computer. Therefore, when you select only one of the two role services in the Add Roles Wizard, a SQL Server Instance page appears, as shown in Figure 7-6, on which you specify where the SQL Server is installed.

Figure 7-6

The SQL Server Instance page
in the Add Roles Wizard

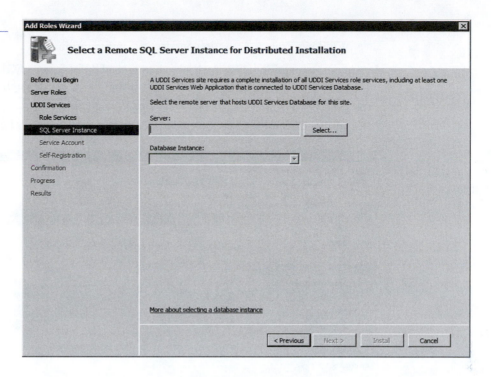

When you select both of the role services to perform a stand-alone installation, there is no
SQL Server Instance page because the UDDI Services Database role service uses the Windows
Internal Database, a version of SQL Server included with Windows Server 2008.

The UDDI Services Web Application role service uses IIS to deploy a Web site providing
access to UDDI functions. Therefore, you must have IIS installed on the same computer
where you install UDDI Services Web Application. On a computer that is not yet running
IIS when you select the UDDI Services Web Application role service, the Add Roles Wizard
prompts you to install the following required role services and features:

- Web Server (IIS) > Common HTTP Features > Static Content
- Web Server (IIS) > Common HTTP Features > Default Document
- Web Server (IIS) > Common HTTP Features > Directory Browsing
- Web Server (IIS) > Common HTTP Features > HTTP Errors
- Web Server (IIS) > Common HTTP Features > HTTP Redirection
- Web Server (IIS) > Application Development > ASP.NET
- Web Server (IIS) > Application Development > .NET Extensibility
- Web Server (IIS) > Application Development > ISAPI Extensions
- Web Server (IIS) > Application Development > ISAPI Filters
- Web Server (IIS) > Health and Diagnostics > HTTP Logging
- Web Server (IIS) > Health and Diagnostics > Logging Tools
- Web Server (IIS) > Health and Diagnostics > Request Monitor
- Web Server (IIS) > Health and Diagnostics > Tracing
- Web Server (IIS) > Security > Basic Authentication
- Web Server (IIS) > Security > Windows Authentication
- Web Server (IIS) > Security > Request Filtering
- Web Server (IIS) > Performance > Static Content Compression
- Web Server (IIS) > Management Tools > IIS Management Console
- Web Server (IIS) > Management Tools > IIS 6 Management Compatibility > IIS 6
  Metabase Compatibility
- Windows Process Activation Service > Process Model

- Windows Process Activation Service > .NET Environment
- Windows Process Activation Service > Configuration APIs

In addition to requiring these modules, selecting the UDDI Services Web Application role service adds the following pages to the wizard, which enable you to configure the basic service parameters:

- SSL Encryption Options—Specifies whether clients publishing data to the UDDI site must use Secure Sockets Layer (SSL) encryption, as shown in Figure 7-7.

Figure 7-7

The Secure Sockets Layer (SSL) Encryption Options page in the Add Roles Wizard

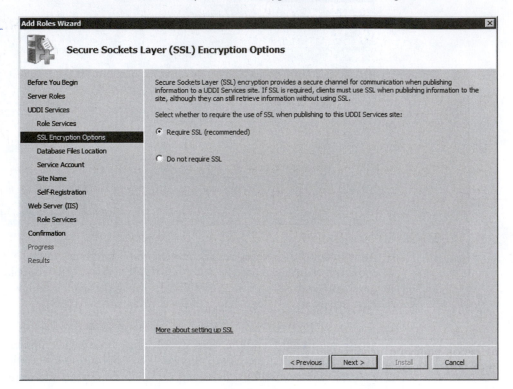

- Database Files Location—On a stand-alone installation, specifies where UDDI Services should store its database and log files, as shown in Figure 7-8.

Figure 7-8

The Specify Database and Log Files Locations page in the Add Roles Wizard

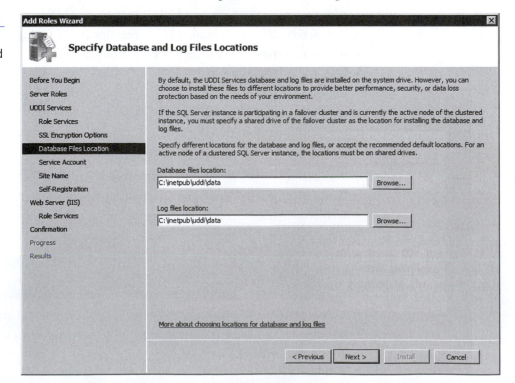

• Service Account—Specifies whether UDDI Services should communicate with other services using the Local Service account (the default) or a user account that you specify, as shown in Figure 7-9.

Figure 7-9

The Choose Service Account page in the Add Roles Wizard

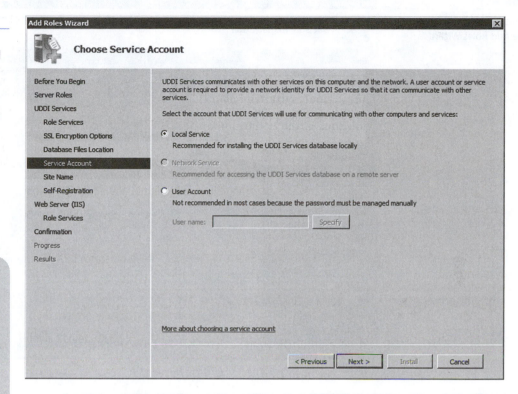

< ></>

TAKE NOTE*

The combination of the UDDI Services Database and UDDI Services Web Application role services, when the two share the same configuration, is known as a site.

• Site Name—Specifies the name that you want to assign to the UDDI site, as shown in Figure 7-10.

Figure 7-10

The Specify Site Name page in the Add Roles Wizard

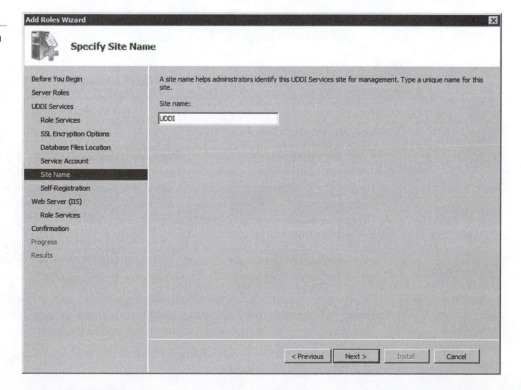

- Self-Registration—Specifies whether you want UDDI Services to enter itself into the UDDI registry, as shown in Figure 7-11.

Figure 7-11

The Set Self-Registration page in the Add Roles Wizard

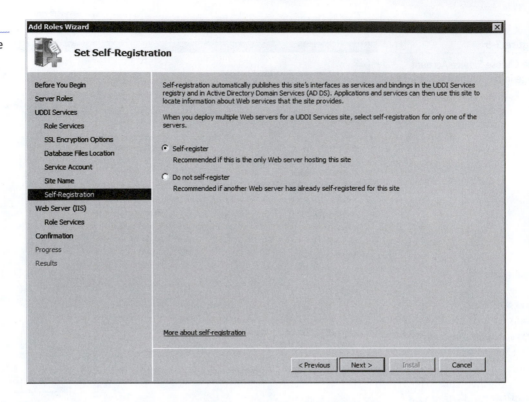

Deploying an SMTP Server

THE BOTTOM LINE

The *Simple Mail Transfer Protocol (SMTP)* is the standard email protocol for the Internet. Email clients send their outgoing messages to an SMTP server specified in their configuration settings, and the SMTP server forwards the messages to other mail servers on the way to their destinations,

Windows Server 2008 includes a feature that implements an SMTP server, which you can configure to handle all of the outgoing email messages sent by the system's various roles and features. The SMTP server is integrated into IIS because the sites you host on a Web server also can require its services.

For example, if your IIS server is hosting a Web page containing a form that clients can use to communicate with the webmaster, the application processing the form accepts the information submitted by clients, packages it as an email message, and sends it to an SMTP server to be forwarded to the webmaster's own mail server. As such, SMTP Server is essentially the Windows counterpart to the sendmail program used by most UNIX Web servers.

In addition, several of the server roles included with Windows Server 2008 have the ability to notify administrators and/or users when certain events occur by sending them automated email messages. The computer can use the SMTP Server feature to send these messages.

When you use the Add Features Wizard in Server Manager to install SMTP Server on a computer with no other roles or features installed, the message box shown in Figure 7-12 appears, informing you that the following additional modules are required:

- Web Server (IIS) > Management Tools > IIS 6 Management Compatibility > IIS 6 Metabase Compatibility

- Web Server (IIS) > Management Tools > IIS 6 Management Compatibility > IIS 6 Management Console
- Remote Server Administration Tools > Feature Administration Tools > SMTP Server Tools

Figure 7-12

The *Add role services and features required for SMTP Server?* message box in the Add Features Wizard

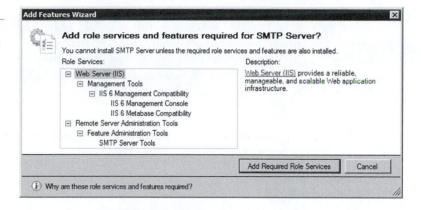

Configuring SMTP Settings

As you might surmise from the IIS6 compatibility modules required, the Windows Server 2008 SMTP Server is essentially unchanged from the Windows Server 2003 version.

CERTIFICATION READY?
Configure Simple Mail Transfer Protocol (SMTP)
3.4

To configure the SMTP Server, you use the Internet Information Services (IIS) 6.0 Manager, which employs the tabbed Properties sheet interface from IIS6, rather than IIS7's icon-based interface.

To configure the IIS7 SMTP Server module, use the following procedure.

 CONFIGURE SMTP SETTINGS

GET READY. Log on to Windows Server 2008 using a domain account with Administrator privileges. When the logon process is completed, close the Initial Configuration Tasks window and any other windows that appear.

1. Click **Start**, and then click **Administrative Tools** > **Internet Information Services (IIS) 6.0 Manager.** The Internet Information Services (IIS) 6.0 Manager console appears, as shown in Figure 7-13.

Figure 7-13

The Internet Information Services (IIS) 6.0 Manager console

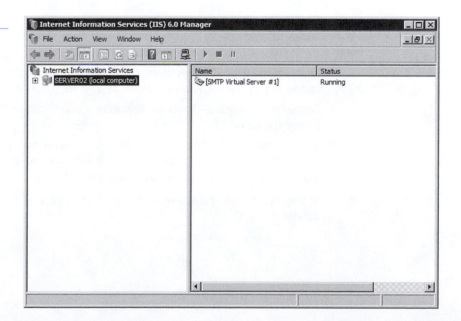

2. In the scope pane, expand the server node. Then, right-click the **SMTP Virtual Server #1** node and, from the context menu, select **Properties**. The SMTP Virtual Server #1 Properties sheet appears.

 TAKE NOTE*

When you install the SMTP Server feature, the Add Features Wizard creates one virtual server. However, you can create additional virtual servers as needed, assigning each to a different one of the computer's IP addresses. In a Web hosting situation, this enables you to create individual, dedicated SMTP server instances for each Web site hosted by IIS.

3. Click the **General** tab if necessary. On the General tab, shown in Figure 7-14, you can configure the following parameters:

Figure 7-14

The General tab of an SMTP virtual server's Properties sheet

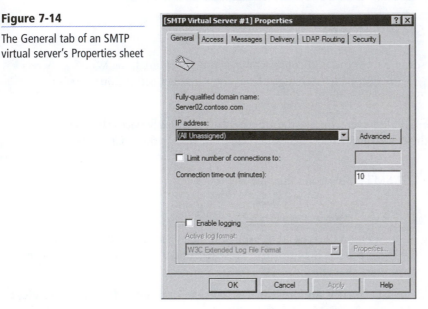

- IP address—Select the address you want clients to use to access the SMTP virtual server. If only one SMTP virtual server is running on the computer, you can leave the default All Unassigned value in place.
- Limit the number of connections to—Specifies the number of clients that can be connected to the SMTP virtual server at any one time. By default, there is no limit.
- Connection time-out—Specifies how long a client connection can remain inactive before the server disconnects it.
- Enable logging—Configures the SMTP virtual server to log its activities. You can select the log file format, and by clicking **Properties**, specify the location for the logs and when the server should create a new log file.

4. Click the **Access** tab. As shown in Figure 7-15, you can configure the following parameters:

Figure 7-15

The Access tab of an SMTP virtual server's Properties sheet

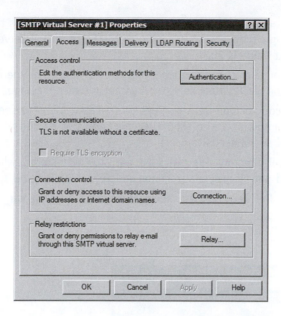

- Authentication—By default, the SMTP virtual server permits anonymous access. Click **Authentication** to enable Basic Authentication or Integrated Windows Authentication.
- Secure Communication—Configures servers with appropriate certificates to require Transport Layer Security (TLS) encryption for all client connections.
- Connection control—Enables you to control access to the SMTP virtual server by specifying IP addresses or domain names.
- Relay restrictions—Enables you to control which systems can relay mail through the SMTP virtual server by specifying IP addresses or domain names.

5. Click the **Messages** tab. As shown in Figure 7-16, you can configure the following parameters:

Figure 7-16

The Messages tab of an SMTP virtual server's Properties sheet

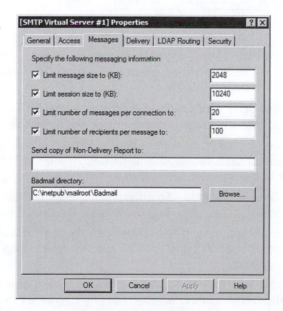

- Limit message size to—Specifies the size (in KB) of the largest message that the SMTP virtual server will accept. The default value is 2048.
- Limit session size to—Specifies the maximum amount of data (in KB) that a client can send to the SMTP virtual server in one session. The default value is 10240.

- Limit number of messages per connection to—Specifies the maximum amount of messages that a client can send to the SMTP virtual server in one connection. The default value is 20.
- Limit number of recipients per message to—Specifies the maximum number of recipients the SMTP virtual server will accept for each message. The default value is 100.
- Send copy of Non-Delivery Report to—Enables you to specify the email address of an administrator who should receive copies of all non-delivery reports the SMTP virtual server sends to users.
- Badmail directory—Specifies the path to the directory where the SMTP virtual server should put all mail that remains undeliverable after the specified number of retries.

6. Click the **Delivery** tab. As shown in Figure 7-17, you can configure the following parameters:

Figure 7-17

The Delivery tab of an SMTP virtual server's Properties sheet

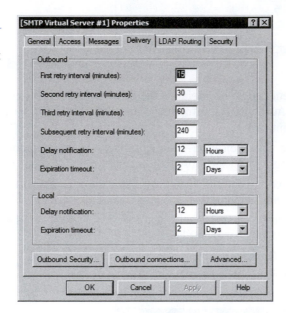

- Retry intervals—Specifies the time intervals between the first, second, third, and subsequent retries of failed message deliveries. The default values are 15, 30, 60, and 240 minutes, respectively.
- Outbound Delay notification—Specifies when the SMTP virtual server should notify the user that a message is undeliverable. The default value is 12 hours.
- Outbound Expiration timeout—Specifies when the SMTP virtual server should abandon attempts to resend an undeliverable message and transmit a non-delivery report to the user.
- Local Delay notification—Specifies when the SMTP virtual server should notify a local user that a message is undeliverable. The default value is 12 hours.
- Local Expiration timeout—Specifies when the SMTP virtual server should abandon attempts to resend an undeliverable message from a local user and transmit a non-delivery report.
- Outbound Security—Enables you to configure the authentication settings the SMTP virtual server should use when attempting to connect to another SMTP server.
- Outbound Connections—Specifies the maximum number of connections permitted and the time-out interval for the SMTP virtual server's communications with other SMTP servers.
- Advanced—Specifies the maximum number of routers for outgoing SMTP traffic, the masquerade domain name the server should insert into all outgoing messages, the

fully qualified domain name of the computer, and the name of a smart host that will provide alternate routing options.

7. Click the **LDAP Routing** tab. As shown in Figure 7-18, you can configure the following parameters:

- Enable LDAP routing—Enables the SMTP virtual server to use a Lightweight Directory Access Protocol (LDAP) server to resolve email addresses, instead of a Domain Name System (DNS) server.

Figure 7-18

The LDAP Routing tab of an SMTP virtual server's Properties sheet

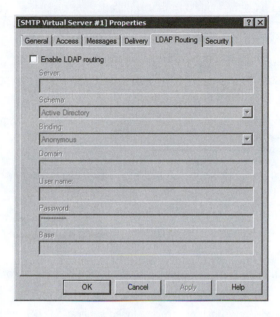

8. Click the **Security** tab. As shown in Figure 7-19, you can configure the following parameters:

- Operators—Enables you to assign operator permissions to specific Windows or domain users.

Figure 7-19

The Security tab of an SMTP virtual server's Properties sheet

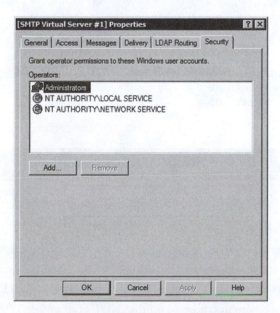

9. Click **OK** to close the Properties sheet.

CLOSE the Internet Information Services (IIS) Manager console.

At this point, the SMTP Server is ready to receive outgoing mail requests from applications running on the server, or from other Windows Server 2008 services.

SUMMARY SKILL MATRIX

IN THIS LESSON YOU LEARNED:

- Internet Information Systems version 7 (IIS7) includes role services that support a variety of development environments.

- CGI is a protocol that enables a Web server to run an application specified in a client request and pass the request to that application for processing. FastCGI is a new variant of CGI that enables IIS7 to provide clients with access to applications without creating a new process for each client.

- Internet Server Application Programming Interface (ISAPI) is designed to be an alternative to CGI, enabling a Web server to execute applications without spawning a separate process for each incoming request.

- Server Side Includes (SSI) is a relatively old Web server technology that enables HTML pages to contain directives that the server parses and executes.

- Active Server Pages (ASP) is a server-side script processing engine designed by Microsoft to provide dynamic Web content with better performance than CGI and simpler development than ISAPI.

- ASP.NET enables developers to create dynamic Web pages, Web applications, and XML (Extensible Markup Language) Web services, using a wide variety of programming languages and development tools.

- An application pool is an operational division within IIS7 that consists of a request queue and one or more worker processes.

- A worker process is a host for user-developed application code, which is responsible for processing requests it receives from the protocol listeners and returning the results to the client.

- IIS7 enables you to configure each application pool to use one of the following managed pipeline modes: Integrated or Classic.

- Universal Discovery, Description, and Integration (UDDI) is an XML-based directory service that enables businesses to publish listings about their activities and the services they offer.

- The Simple Mail Transfer Protocol (SMTP) is the standard email protocol for the Internet. Email clients send their outgoing messages to an SMTP server specified in their configuration settings, and the SMTP server forwards the messages to other mail servers on the way to their destinations.

■ Knowledge Assessment

Matching

Complete the following exercise by matching the terms with their corresponding definitions.

a. Application hosting technology that launches a separate process for each request

b. Provides the interface between IIS and ASP.NET in IIS7's Classic mode

c. The first Web technology to enable servers to process code in HTML files

d. Programming environment based on the .NET Framework 3.0

e. Sends information keyed by clients into Web forms to server administrators

f. Prevents unstable Web applications from crashing the server

g. Created and terminated as needed by Windows Process Activation Service

h. Uses commands enclosed within angle brackets and ampersands

i. An application pool with multiple worker processes

j. Allocates processes to clients from a pool rather than creating new ones

_____ **1.** Active Server Pages (ASP)

_____ **2.** application pool

_____ **3.** ASP.NET

_____ **4.** Common Gateway Interface (CGI)

_____ **5.** Internet Server Application Programming Interface (ISAPI)

_____ **6.** FastCGI

_____ **7.** Server Side Includes (SSI)

_____ **8.** Simple Mail Transfer Protocol (SMTP)

_____ **9.** Web garden

_____ **10.** worker process

Multiple Choice

Select the correct answer for each of the following questions.

1. The primary function of a Web server is to:
   a. store client information
   b. provide data storage for Web-based applications
   c. receive and send text-based messages, using the HTTP protocol syntax
   d. authenticate clients

2. When you install the Web Server (IIS) role in Windows Server 2008, the Add New Roles Wizard creates which application pools in IIS7? (Choose all answers that are correct.)
   a. DefaultNETPool
   b. Classic .NET DefaultAppPool
   c. Classic .NET AppPool
   d. DefaultAppPool

3. The Windows Process Activation Service (WPAS) is responsible for creating and terminating what IIS7 components?
   a. worker processes
   b. directory browsing
   c. request filtering
   d. application pools

4. Web applications typically use a three-tiered architecture. Which of the following is not one of those three tiers?
   a. A Web server with some type of dynamic content generation capability.
   b. A Web server that acts as a database server to store application information.
   c. A database server that stores the information the Web server uses to dynamically generate Web pages.
   d. The client browser application running on the end user's computer.

5. The UDDI Services role consists of which of the following role services? (Choose all answers that are correct.)
   a. UDDI Services Database
   b. UDDI Services Web Application
   c. UDDI Services Database Security
   d. UDDI Services Web Browser

6. The Windows Process Activation Service (WPAS) is responsible for managing application pools and worker processes. In a typical IIS7 configuration, the request handling process proceeds as follows: (Place all five answers in the correct order.)
   a. WPAS examines the state of the application pool to see if there is a worker process running that can handle the request.
   b. A worker process performs the tasks necessary to process the request.
   c. An incoming request from a client arrives at the computer.
   d. IIS7 sends the request to the application pool associated with the application.
   e. The worker process transmits a reply message to the client.

7. Which of the following provides the interface between the IIS request pipeline and the ASP.NET pipeline when an application pool is running in Classic mode?
   a. CGI
   b. .NET Framework
   c. ASP
   d. ISAPI

8. Which of the following authentication methods is not supported by the SMTP Server service in Windows Server 2008?
   a. Anonymous Authentication
   b. Basic Authentication
   c. Digest Authentication
   d. Integrated Windows Authentication

9. Which of the following application pool settings would you modify to create a Web garden?
   a. Managed Pipeline Mode
   b. .NET Framework Version
   c. Maximum Worker Processes
   d. Failure Interval

10. What term is used to describe the combination of the UDDI Services Database and UDDI Services Web Application role services when the two share the same configuration?
   a. site
   b. UDDI pool
   c. worker process
   d. XML

Review Questions

1. Explain how the development of application technologies such as Server Side Includes and Active Server Pages modified the fundamental role of the Web server.

2. List the three types of application pool configurations and describe how they differ.

■ Case Scenarios

Scenario 7-1: Configuring Application Pools

Amanda is the owner and operator of a small Web hosting company. She is using Windows Server 2008 computers as her Web servers, with IIS7 hosting multiple Web sites on each computer. One of Amanda's clients is a game manufacturer who has released a hot new product. Their Web site contains an online demo, created using ASP.NET, which is experiencing a dramatic increase in traffic. Unfortunately, this one site is starting to monopolize the server's resources, to the detriment of the other sites running on the same computer. Which of the following options can prevent the game application from affecting the other sites? Explain your answer.

A. Increase the maximum number of worker processes allowed in the game site's application pool.
B. Set a value other than zero for the application pool's Private Memory Limit setting.
C. Change the application pool's Managed Pipeline Mode setting from Integrated to Classic.
D. Set a value other than zero for the application pool's Limit setting.

Scenario 7-2: Deploying UDDI

Robert wants to deploy a UDDI site on his company network. He has two Windows Server 2008 computers running IIS7, but he is afraid that neither one has the resources to run both of the UDDI role services. Therefore, he decides to install the UDDI Services Web Application role service on one computer and the UDDI Services Database role service on the other, using the Windows Internal Database to store the UDDI site information.

What is wrong with this plan and what must Robert do to make it work?

Using Terminal Services

OBJECTIVE DOMAIN MATRIX

Technology Skill	Objective Domain	Objective Domain Number
Monitoring Terminal Server Loads	Configure and monitor Terminal Services resources.	2.4
Using Network Level Authentication	Configure Terminal Services server options.	2.7
Using RemoteApp	Configure Windows Server® 2008 Terminal Services RemoteApp™ (TS RemoteApp).	2.1

KEY TERMS

client-side caching
copy-on-write data
  sharing
Credential Security Service
  Provider (CredSSP)

Network Level Authentication
  (NLA)
Remote Desktop Connection
Remote Desktop Protocol
  (RDP)

RemoteApp
session
Session ID
thin client computing

Terminal Services is a Windows Server 2008 feature that enables administrators to deliver applications and entire desktop environments to users running a relatively simple client program. This first of three lessons about Terminal Services examines its basic functionality, including the following topics:

- Terminal Services architecture
- Deploying Terminal Services
- Selecting server hardware
- Configuring Terminal Services
- Using RemoteApp

■ Introducing Terminal Services

THE BOTTOM LINE

Terminal Services is the modern equivalent of mainframe computing, in which servers perform most of the processing and clients are relatively simple devices that provide the user interface.

In the early days of computing, applications ran on a mainframe computer and users accessed those applications from terminals. A terminal is a device with a display and a keyboard that provides the interface to the mainframe. Often called *dumb terminals* then, these devices did no computing themselves; they simply sent the user's keystrokes to the mainframe and displayed the data that they received from it. Because the applications were centralized on the mainframe, all administration took place there.

In the mid-1980s, use of personal computers (PCs) introduced the client/server computing paradigm. In client/server computing, each user has a computer, and applications are divided into separate client and server components. As a result, the computing tasks are distributed among smaller computers, instead of centralized in one big mainframe. Because each user is running a separate instance of the client application, the central server can be smaller and cheaper than a mainframe, while achieving an aggregate computing capability equal to or surpassing mainframe capacity.

Despite its advantages, however, client/server computing raises a number of serious administrative problems. For example, instead of installing and maintaining a single application on a mainframe, client/server network administrators might be responsible for hundreds or thousands of copies of the client application, which they must install and maintain on the individual client computers. As a result, deploying a simple update to the client application can be a major undertaking.

In Terminal Services, Microsoft has essentially created a throwback to the mainframe computing paradigm, albeit with features that mainframes never had, such as a graphical interface and mouse support. With Terminal Services, client computers can connect to a server and run individual applications or an entire desktop environment. In this arrangement, the server does all of the application computing; the clients function only as terminals. Because the only application running on the client computer is a small communications program, this is also known as *thin client computing*.

Understanding Terminal Services Architecture

At the highest level Terminal Services works by running applications on a Windows Server 2008 server and enabling desktop computers to operate those applications from a remote location. A client program running on the desktop computer establishes a connection to a terminal server, and the server creates a session for that client. The session can provide the client with a full-featured Windows desktop, a desktop containing one application, or (new to Windows Server 2008) a single application in its own window, appearing exactly as if the application was running on the client computer.

A single terminal server can support multiple clients. The number depends on the hardware resources in the server and the clients' application requirements. Thus, the server functions as the equivalent of a mainframe and the clients, as terminals.

To make the desktop or application appear on the client computer, the server transmits data and instructions that enable the client to render the graphical interface on its own display. In return, to manipulate the applications running on the server, the client program transmits the user's keystrokes and mouse movements. As a result, no application data passes between the client and the server; instead, only the client user's input and the application's output is transmitted in graphical form.

The preceding description of Terminal Services outlines only its most basic architectural concepts. It is relatively simple to install Terminal Services on a server and configure it to

provide clients with a simple application. However, implementing a fully functional production environment using Terminal Services can be much more complicated because it raises many additional issues, such as the following:

- Security—How secure are the individual client sessions? How secure is the server from the clients?

- Licensing—How does Terminal Services handle client licensing? Are application licenses necessary for individual sessions?

- Local resources—How can clients use locally attached printers, drives, and other devices while working in a Terminal Services session?

- Memory management—How does the terminal server keep multiple copies of the same application separated?

Configuring Terminal Services to be as secure as necessary and to provide clients with all the resources they need can require a lot of configuration and testing. The remainder of this lesson, and the next two lessons, are devoted to deploying and configuring an effective Terminal Services installation.

Examining the Terminal Services Components

All client/server applications, by definition, require three basic elements: a server program, a client program, and a protocol that enables the two programs to communicate.

Windows Server 2008 Terminal Services implements these elements in the following three components:

- Terminal Server—A service that runs on a Windows Server 2008 computer, which enables multiple clients to connect to the server and run individual desktop or application sessions.

- *Remote Desktop Connection* client—In most cases, a program running on a desktop computer that establishes a connection to a terminal server using Remote Desktop Protocol (RDP) and displays a session window containing a desktop or application. Thin clients, which are terminals designed specifically to connect to terminal servers, are also available.

- *Remote Desktop Protocol (RDP)*—A networking protocol that enables communication between the terminal server and the client.

The following sections examine these components in more detail.

INTRODUCING TERMINAL SERVER

To configure a Windows Server 2008 computer to function as a terminal server, you install the Terminal Services role using the Add Roles Wizard in Server Manager, as shown in

Figure 8-1. Like any server application, a terminal server listens for incoming client requests. In this case, client connection requests arrive over TCP port 3389, which is the well-known port number for the RDP protocol.

Figure 8-1

Installing Terminal Services

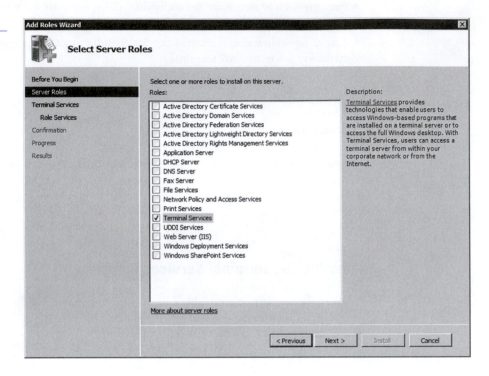

The Terminal Services role provides the computer with multi-session capability. A **session** is a collection of processes that form an individual user environment running on the server. When two or more Terminal Services clients connect to the terminal server, each client has its own session, complete with individual instances of processes like the following:

- User authentication module—Provides the WinLogon application that enables the client to supply logon credentials, which the server passes to the appropriate domain or local security subsystem for authentication.

- Win32 subsystem—Provides the Windows graphical user interface and the environment in which the client runs Win32 applications.

- Executable environment for applications—Provides a separate area of memory in which the client's applications run.

- Additional processes—A client session also includes other processes, depending on the applications it is running.

This means that every Terminal Services client has an individual desktop, with its user profile settings, which remain completely separated from those of other clients. Even when two clients are running the same application, the processes are completely separate.

USING SESSION IDS

To keep the client processes for individual sessions separate, the terminal server assigns each session a unique identifier called a **Session ID**. In Windows Server 2008, Session ID 0 is always dedicated to the system services running on the computer, which isolates them from applications for security reasons. The system then assigns Session IDs, starting with number 1, to each interactive user logging on to the computer from the local console or a remote system.

⊕ MORE INFORMATION

This dedication of Session ID 0 to the system services, called *session 0 isolation*, is a new feature in Windows Server 2008 and Windows Vista. In Windows Server 2003, the system services and the local console user share Session ID 0, which allows applications to run in the same session as the system services. This is inherently dangerous because an application could take advantage of the elevated privileges assigned to the services. By isolating the services in their own session, Windows Server 2008 and Windows Vista protect those elevated privileges from unruly or malicious applications.

When the Terminal Services service starts, it always creates two new sessions with unique IDs before any users connect. These two sessions remain dormant until Terminal Services clients connect to the server. As the clients connect, the server creates additional dormant sessions, so it is always ready to accept new clients and connect them as quickly as possible.

When a session is connected to a *terminal*, that is, a keyboard, mouse, and display, whether local or remote, the session is said to be in the active, or connected, state. The local session is always connected, but remote sessions are associated with a Terminal Services connection, which defines the protocol and other elements that the remote client uses to connect to the terminal server. When a remote client disconnects from a session, it reverts to the inactive, or disconnected, state until the user reconnects. If the user logs off, whether by choice or an administrator's intervention, the session terminates.

Despite the separate sessions and processes, the clients connected to a terminal server still share a single computer's processor(s), memory, disk space, and operating system. Obviously, the server must allocate sufficient resources to each client session to keep them running smoothly. Each session has a high-priority thread for its server-to-client display output and its client-to-server keyboard/mouse input, to which the server allocates resources on a round-robin basis.

ALLOCATING RESOURCES FOR APPLICATIONS

Allocating resources to applications, however, can be a bit trickier. While each session has individual instances of certain processes, such as those listed earlier, applications usually do not. For example, if several clients connect to a terminal server and run a word processing application, loading a complete and separate copy of the entire application for each client would consume an enormous amount of memory to no real benefit.

Most of the application files remain unchanged while users work with a word processor, so there is no reason to load multiple copies of these files into memory when the client sessions could just as easily share access to a single copy of each file. However, this is not a perfect solution either. What happens to the few files that do change? When one client modifies an application file, the modifications should logically affect all of the other clients running that application as well. They do not, though, because Windows Server 2008 uses a memory management technique called ***copy-on-write data sharing***.

As the name implies, copy-on-write means that when a client attempts to write to a shared application file, the operating system creates a copy of that file, allocates it for the exclusive use of that client, and writes the changes to the copy. This minimizes the amount of memory utilized by each client and enables the applications to run normally.

TAKE NOTE* Not all applications are suitable for use on terminal servers. Some applications might not function properly with multiple clients sharing a single set of files. Some require a full copy of the application in each client session, while others might not function at all. An extensive testing period is imperative for all Terminal Services deployments.

INTRODUCING REMOTE DESKTOP CONNECTION (RDC)

Remote Desktop Connection (also known as Terminal Services Client) is a Win32 application that enables a Windows computer to establish a connection to a terminal server, authenticate a user, and access an application or desktop session running on the server. The latest version of Remote Desktop Connection, version 6.1, as shown in Figure 8-2, is included with all versions of Windows Server 2008 and Windows Vista Service Pack 1. A release for Windows XP is also imminent.

Figure 8-2

Remote Desktop Connection

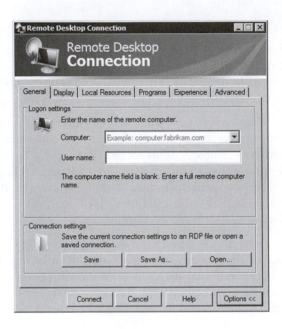

Basically, the RDC program sends the user's keystrokes and mouse movements to the terminal server, and receives information from the server to create the display. However, as noted earlier, many aspects of the Terminal Services model can complicate this relatively simple process.

One factor is the sheer amount of data required to create the display on the client. During an active Terminal Services session, the client display refreshes approximately 20 times per second. When the session is idle, the server reduces the refresh rate to 10 per second. Depending on the client's configured display resolution, transmitting an entire screen of graphic information 10 or 20 times per second can add up to a tremendous amount of data. To avoid flooding the network with display data, RDC uses a technique called client-side caching.

In *client-side caching*, RDC stores screen elements that remain unchanged from one refresh to the next in a cache on the client system. This way, the terminal server transmits only new display elements to the client during each refresh. As the cache grows in size, the client deletes the oldest elements.

In addition to the stand-alone client, Terminal Services supports a Web-based client based on an ActiveX control that is now supplied with the Remote Desktop Connection program. In previous versions of Windows, users had to download the ActiveX control from an IIS Web site on the terminal server. This caused problems because many administrators prefer to configure client computers to block ActiveX downloads for security reasons. With RDC version 6.0 and later, clients do not have to download anything; they can access Web-equipped terminal servers using Internet Explorer at any time.

TAKE NOTE*

By default, Windows Server 2008 Terminal Services includes the downloadable ActiveX control for clients that are not running Remote Desktop Connection 6.0 or later. This includes all computers running Windows operating systems prior to Windows XP SP2, and Windows XP SP2 computers that don't have RDC 6.0 installed. For more information on accessing Terminal Services Web servers, see Lesson 10, "Using the Terminal Services Gateway."

In addition to the integrated ActiveX control, RDC version 6.1 includes the following improvements over previous versions:

- Display improvements—RDC now supports display resolutions up to 4096 x 2048, custom aspect ratios for wide screen displays, 32-bit color depth, spanning of the display across multiple monitors, and font smoothing.

- Display Data Prioritization—By default, RDC 6.1 allocates 70 percent of its communication bandwidth to keyboard, mouse, and display traffic to prevent other types of Terminal Services traffic from interfering with the client's connection to the server.

- Device redirection—Applications running in Terminal Services sessions can access Plug and Play devices connected to the client computer, including media players and digital cameras.

- Easy Print—Enables applications running in Terminal Services sessions to send jobs to print devices connected to the client computer without installing printer drivers on the terminal server.

INTRODUCING REMOTE DESKTOP PROTOCOL (RDP)

After you have a server and a client, the only remaining component is the protocol that the two use to communicate. RDP, now in version 6.0, is based on the T.120 protocol standards published by the International Telecommunications Union (ITU). It provides multi-channel communication between Terminal Services clients and servers.

Multi-channel means that the protocol separates the traffic for the Terminal Services functions into logical divisions called channels, as shown in Figure 8-3. The keyboard, mouse, and display traffic occupies one channel, and the various additional features supported by Terminal Services use others. For example, a separate RDP channel carries audio output from the server to the client, enabling the client to play the audio through its local speakers. Traffic for local device mapping and features, such as 32-bit graphics color depth and clipboard mapping, also utilize separate channels. RDP can support up to 64,000 separate channels, although nowhere near that many are currently in use.

Figure 8-3

Multi-channel communications in the RDP

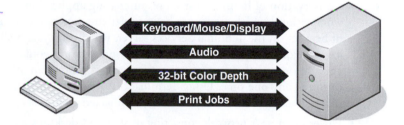

The development of new RDP versions coincides with the development of the Terminal Services client and server components. To implement a new feature, all three of the components have to support it. As a result, version control is an important part of administering a Terminal Services installation. When you install Terminal Services on a Windows Server 2008 computer, you can't take advantage of its new features unless you are running the RDC 6.0 client or later, both of which implement the RDP 6.0 protocol.

Using Terminal Services

Terminal Services represents a fundamental shift in PC networking philosophy. Some people think of it as a step backwards, while others consider it to be a return to the good old mainframe days.

You can use Terminal Services in various ways on your network. You can solve specific problems with the technology or completely change the way your network operates.

IDENTIFYING THE ADVANTAGES OF TERMINAL SERVICES

Deploying Terminal Services offers several advantages to the network administrator, including the following:

- Reduced client hardware requirements. Terminal Services client computers have to run only a single application: the RDC program. The hardware requirements for the client computer are therefore minimal. This enables administrators to purchase inexpensive computers for desktop users and avoid constant hardware upgrades to support the latest versions of desktop operating systems and applications.

- Simplified application deployment. Deploying applications on a large fleet of computers can be a long and difficult undertaking, even with distribution tools such as Group Policy and Microsoft Systems Management Services (SMS). Terminal Services enables administrators to deploy applications to as many clients as needed by installing them only on servers.

- Easy configuration and updates. Terminal Services eliminates the need to install, configure, and update applications on individual desktop computers. When an administrator configures or updates a single copy of an application on a terminal server, all of the clients reap the benefits.

- Low network bandwidth consumption. Terminal Services connections use relatively little network bandwidth because most of the data exchanged by the clients and servers consist of keystroke, mouse, and display instructions, instead of large application and data files. For remote users accessing terminal servers over the Internet, much less bandwidth is required than that required for a virtual private network (VPN) or direct dial-up connection.

- Support for thin clients. The availability of thin client devices enables administrators to install terminals in environments that are unsuitable for standard PCs. Dusty environments, such as warehouses, can clog a computer's air intakes. Public environments, such as airports and lobbies, invite computer misuse and theft. Sterile environments, such as clean rooms, can be contaminated by a computer's air circulation. Thin clients are more suitable for these, and many other, problematic locations.

- Conservation of licenses. Instead of purchasing application licenses for all individual workstations, which might not be in use at any given time, you can maintain a pool of licenses on the Terminal Services server, which the system allocates to users as they log on. For example, an office with 100 workstations would require 100 licenses for an application installed on each computer, even if more than 50 users never run the application at any one time. Using Terminal Services, 50 application licenses would be sufficient because only the users actually connected to the server need a license.

- Power savings. A network consisting of standard desktops and servers consumes substantially greater power than a typical Terminal Services installation, which can use client computers with slower processors and less memory. The use of thin clients can increase the savings even more.

- No client backups. In a typical Terminal Services installation, users access all of their applications and data files from servers. As a result, it is usually not necessary to back up the client computers, which yields savings in time and backup media.

- Remote control help and training. Terminal Services enables administrators to tap into a client session (with the client's permission) to observe the user's activity or to interact with the user in real time. Administrators can, therefore, demonstrate procedures to a user for help and training purposes without travelling to the user's location.

USING TERMINAL SERVICES IN VARIOUS SCENARIOS

Network administrators use the capabilities that Terminal Services provides in various ways. Some adopt Terminal Services wholeheartedly, as a complete client solution. Instead of installing and configuring applications on each desktop computer, they run an RDC client,

connect to a terminal server, and access a remote desktop. When you configure Terminal Services properly, many users do not know that the applications are not running on the local computer.

Whether this is a practical solution for a particular network depends largely on the hardware in the computers involved. If you spent large amounts of money purchasing high-end desktop computers for your users, then it makes little sense to use that powerful hardware just to run the RDC program. However, if you are building a new network, or if your desktops are low-powered or outdated, Terminal Services can be a viable and economical alternative to purchasing new desktops or upgrading the old ones.

TAKE NOTE *

Keep in mind that while Terminal Services might save money on desktop hardware, you might have to upgrade your servers (or purchase additional ones) to support the Terminal Services traffic, and you will certainly have to purchase client access licenses (CALs) for your users or devices.

Even if it is not practical to adopt Terminal Services for your clients' entire desktops, you might use it for individual applications. You can use Terminal Services to deploy some of your applications, automatically deploy a desktop containing only a single application, or use Terminal Services RemoteApp role service to deploy applications directly to client windows without remoting the entire desktop.

Generally, however, you should deploy desktops with individual applications only when users need just one Terminal Services application. You can, for example, have clients open individual Terminal Services sessions for each application they run. From a user perspective, this might seem like a viable solution. However, from an administrative standpoint, it is highly wasteful of server resources because each session has a separate copy of the Win32 subsystem. By comparison, a single Terminal Services session running multiple applications uses only one copy of the Win32 subsystem and therefore requires much less server memory.

RemoteApp applications handle memory differently, however. When a single user opens multiple RemoteApp applications, they all run within the same session.

In addition to using the RDC client, users can access Terminal Services sessions with a standard Web browser, such as Internet Explorer. The Terminal Services Web Access role service configures a terminal server to use Internet Information Services (IIS) to publish a Web page that provides access to remote desktop sessions or individual RemoteApp applications, as shown in Figure 8-4. When a user double-clicks an icon for a RemoteApp application on the Web page, the application launches in a separate window, just like the RDC client, not in the browser window.

Figure 8-4

A Terminal Services (TS) Web Access Web page

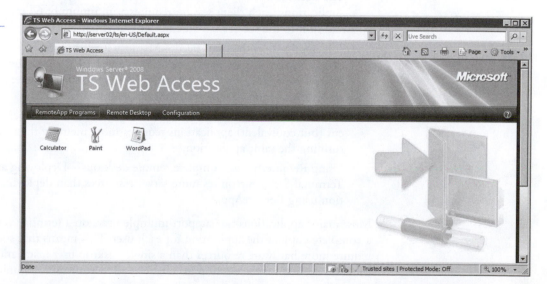

For relatively unsophisticated users, TS Web Access greatly simplifies the process of connecting to Terminal Services desktops and applications. Instead of instructing users how to connect to a particular terminal server and access applications using RDC, simply provide a URL in any of the usual ways, including shortcuts, favorites, hyperlinks, or an icon.

For administrators that don't want or need Terminal Services as an internal solution, it can also enable remote users to access applications and desktops. The new Terminal Services Gateway role service enables users on the Internet to connect to terminal servers, despite the existence of intervening firewalls and Network Address Translation (NAT) routers.

■ Deploying Terminal Services

THE BOTTOM LINE

Deploying Terminal Services can be a simple solution to a minor requirement or a fundamental shift in the way you deploy applications to your network users.

As mentioned earlier, you can deploy Terminal Services relatively simply at the high level, but configuring the details can become complicated. Many of these details are dependent on the number of clients you must support, the number and types of applications the clients will run, and the user's other needs.

Selecting Server Hardware

The basic philosophy of Terminal Services calls for client applications to run on servers instead of client desktops, which leads naturally to the need for more powerful servers and less powerful clients.

How much more powerful the servers need to be and how much less power is needed for the clients is a difficult question that is better answered through testing and experience than hard and fast rules.

The system requirements that Microsoft specifies for Windows Server 2008 are sufficient to run the Terminal Services role, but not enough to support more than one or perhaps two Terminal Services clients. When you run applications on a server instead of a client, you must shift the resources the applications require from the client to the server as well.

The selection of appropriate hardware for a terminal server should be based on the following factors:

- The number of users connected to the server at any one time—Before you consider the applications, each client session requires a minimum of 64 megabytes of memory in addition to the server's base memory requirements.
- The applications the users need—Memory loads for applications can vary greatly, depending on the size of the application and how the user runs it. Using a word processor to type a letter, for example, probably requires far less memory than spell-checking, embedding graphics, and performing a mail merge.
- The number of users who access each application—A number of clients running different (but equivalent) applications requires more memory than the same number of clients running the same application.
- Using RemoteApp vs. complete remote desktops—Deploying an entire desktop using Terminal Services requires more server resources than deploying an individual application using RemoteApp.

Most major applications can support multiple users on a terminal server without loading a complete copy of the application for each user. This means that such an application will require more hardware resources than a single desktop user installation needs, but less than the total needed for the desktop installations of all your users combined.

TAKE NOTE*

While Terminal Services usually requires servers with large amounts of hardware resources, practical limitations determine how big a terminal server can get. If you are planning to implement Terminal Services on a large scale, supporting hundreds or thousands of users, it is usually more practical to create a server farm consisting of several medium to large servers, rather than a few truly gigantic ones. For more information on using multiple terminal servers on a single network, see Lesson 12, "Using High Availability Technologies."

As for any computer, selecting hardware for a terminal server is a matter of achieving a balance of performance across all of the major components to avoid any component creating a performance bottleneck. When selecting the hardware for a terminal server, consider the following:

- **Processor.** A fast processor with a lot of cache benefits a terminal server, but the processor is the component least likely to be the performance bottleneck. Additional cache is preferable to a slight increase in speed. When considering multiple processors, be sure that your applications are capable of using them.

- **Memory.** Memory is the component that is mostly likely to be a bottleneck on a terminal server. The server requires additional memory for each client and application you plan to support. Because it is difficult to determine in advance how much memory a terminal server needs, purchase a server with plenty of room for memory upgrades.

- **Disks.** Despite the new disk technologies available, SCSI (Small Computer System Interface) drives are still the best choice for servers that must support a great deal of user traffic. SCSI host adapters can send commands to multiple drives, which queue the commands until they can execute them, unlike ATA adapters, which can only process one command at a time.

- **Network.** A Terminal Services connection in itself does not consume a large amount of network bandwidth, but if you plan to service a large number of clients with a single server, the combined bandwidth of all the connections can be significant. In addition, features like the redirection of print jobs to mapped local printers can increase the total amount of network traffic required by Terminal Services enormously. The network interface adapters in your terminal servers should use, at minimum, the PCI interface and run at 100 or 1,000 megabits per second. To provide greater throughput, consider installing multiple adapters in a terminal server, either balancing the traffic load between them or dedicating one adapter to Terminal Services traffic.

CERTIFICATION READY?
Configure and monitor Terminal Services resources
2.4

MONITORING TERMINAL SERVER LOADS

The only sure way to determine the load that your Terminal Services clients and applications will place on a computer is to deploy a test server and monitor the effect of the load. The Reliability and Performance Monitor console in Windows Server 2008 includes a wide variety of counters that you can use for this purpose, including counters that can monitor the properties of specific Terminal Services sessions. Table 8-1 lists these counters.

Table 8-1

Performance Monitor Counters for Monitoring Terminal Services

COUNTER	DESCRIPTION
PhysicalDisk:% Disk Time	The percentage of time that the selected disk drives(s) spend servicing read or write requests. This value should be as low as possible. Use this counter with the PhysicalDisk:% Idle Time counter to accurately interpret usage on a multiple-disk system.
PhysicalDisk:% Idle Time	The percentage of time that the disk was idle during the sample time interval. Use this counter with the PhysicalDisk:% Disk Time counter to interpret usage on a multiple-disk system.
PhysicalDisk:Avg. Disk Queue Length	For selected disk(s) during the sample time interval, the average number of queued read and write requests. The preferred value is less than 4. This counter identifies disk bottlenecks.
Terminal Services:Active Sessions	Reports the number of active Terminal Services sessions during the sample time interval. An Active Session indicates that a session is connected and a user is logged on to the server.
Terminal Services:Inactive Sessions	Reports the number of inactive Terminal Services sessions during the sample time interval. An Inactive Session is a session that is idle and without client activity. Even though inactive, these sessions can consume valuable system resources.

(continued)

Table 8-1 (*continued*)

COUNTER	DESCRIPTION
Terminal Services Session: % Processor Time	The percentage of elapsed processor time that all of the session threads are using to execute instructions. An instruction is the basic unit of execution. A thread is the object that executes instructions. Included in this percentage is code that the system executes to handle certain hardware interrupts and trap conditions.
Terminal Services Session: % User Time	The percentage of user mode elapsed time that processor threads are using to execute code. Applications, environment subsystems, and integral subsystems execute in user mode.
Terminal Services Session: Handle Count	A handle is a token or a pointer that identifies and accesses an object or resource for a program. This counter is the sum of the total number of handles currently opened by each thread in this process.
Terminal Services Session: Input Bytes	Number of bytes input during this sample session. This number includes all protocol overhead.
Terminal Services Session: Input Compressed Bytes	Number of bytes input after compression. Compare this number with the Total Bytes value to get the compression ratio.
Terminal Services Session: Total Bytes	Number of total bytes processed during this session, including all protocol overhead.
Terminal Services Session: Output Bytes	Number of bytes produced during this session, including all protocol overhead.
Terminal Services Session: Output Compressed Bytes	Number of bytes produced during this session after compression. Compare this number with the Total Bytes value for the compression ratio.
Terminal Services Session: Page File Bytes	The paging file, also referred to as the swap file, stores pages of memory used by a session (such as parts of programs and data files) that the system cannot place into primary memory because of space constraints. The paging file is shared by all of the sessions on the computer. The system continually moves pages from the paging file to RAM to create free space for new pages. The lack of space in paging files may prevent other processes from allocating memory.
Terminal Services Session: Private Bytes	Private bytes is the current number of bytes the swap file allocates to hold the contents of private memory (allocated bytes that cannot be shared with other processes).
Terminal Services Session: Thread Count	The number of threads currently active. A thread is the object that executes instructions. Each running process possesses at least one thread.
Terminal Services Session: Total Protocol Cache Hit Ratio	Overall hit ratio for all protocol caches. The hit ratio, in this instance, is the percentage of all accesses satisfied by the objects in the protocol cache. The protocol cache stores Windows objects (such as icons) that the operating system is most likely to reuse, thus avoiding having to resend them on the transmission line.
Terminal Services Session: Virtual Bytes	The current virtual address size, measured in bytes, that the session is using. Although virtual address space is often associated with virtual memory (disk), this counter does not imply a distinction between the use of virtual memory or physical memory (RAM) pages. Virtual memory is finite and so, if the session uses too much, it limits the ability to load its libraries.
Terminal Services Session: Working Set	Specifies the current total size, in bytes, of the memory pages accessed by the threads in the selected session.

Installing Terminal Services

> After your hardware is in place, the first step in deploying a terminal server is installing the Terminal Services role.

You must install the Terminal Services role before you install the applications that you plan to deploy on the terminal server. If you install the applications first, they might not function properly in the multi-user terminal server environment.

You install the Terminal Services role in the usual manner described in Lesson 1, "Deploying an Application Server." When you select the Terminal Services role, the Add Roles Wizard enables you to select from the following role services.

- Terminal Server—Provides the core Terminal Services functionality that enables users running the RDC client to run full desktop sessions. This role service also includes the RemoteApp feature, which enables clients to run individual applications in separate windows.

- TS Licensing—Configures the computer to function as a Terminal Services Licensing Server, which enables it to allocate client access licenses (CALs) to clients. You must have a Licensing Server on your network to use Terminal Services. You can install TS Licensing on the same computer as the other role services or another computer.

- TS Session Broker—Balances the client load among multiple terminal servers and saves session state information so that clients can reconnect to the same session from which they disconnected.

- TS Gateway—Enables RDC clients on the Internet to connect to a terminal server through a firewall or NAT router by tunneling RDP traffic within Secure Hypertext Transfer Protocol (HTTPS) packets.

- TS Web Access—Creates an IIS Web site that enables users to access Terminal Services desktops and RemoteApp applications without running the RDC client.

Selecting from the available Terminal Services role services causes the Add Roles Wizard to prompt you to install dependent roles and features, generate additional wizard pages, install system services, and add snap-ins for the Microsoft Management console. Table 8-2 lists these elements for each of the role services.

Table 8-2

Terminal Services Role Services

Role Services	Dependencies	Wizard Pages	System Services	Snap-ins
Terminal Server	[None]	• Application Compatibility • Authentication Method • Licensing Mode • User Groups	• Terminal Services (TermService)	• TS RemoteApp Manager • Terminal Services Configuration • Terminal Services Manager
TS Licensing	[None]	• TS Licensing Configuration	• Terminal Services Licensing (TermServLicensing)	• Terminal Services Configuration • Terminal Services Manager • TS Licensing Manager
TS Session Broker	[None]	[None]	• Terminal Services Session Broker (tssdis)	• Terminal Services Configuration • Terminal Services Manager

(continued)

Table 8-2 (*continued*)

ROLE SERVICES	DEPENDENCIES	WIZARD PAGES	SYSTEM SERVICES	SNAP-INS
TS Gateway	▪ Web Server (IIS) ▪ Network Policy and Access Services > Network Policy Server ▪ RPC Over HTTP Proxy ▪ Windows Process Activation Service > Process Model ▪ Windows Process Activation Service > Configuration APIs	▪ Server Authentication Certificate ▪ Authorization Policies: TS Gateway User Groups, TS CAP, TS RAP ▪ Network Policy and Access Services: Role Services ▪ Web Server (IIS): Role Services	▪ IIS Admin Service (iisadmin) ▪ Network Policy Server (IAS) ▪ RPC/HTTP Load Balancing Service (rpchttplbs) ▪ Terminal Services Gateway (TSGateway) ▪ World Wide Web Publishing Service (w3svc) ▪ Application Host Helper Service (apphostsvc) ▪ Windows Process Activation Service (WAS)	▪ Terminal Services Configuration ▪ Terminal Services Manager ▪ TS Gateway Manager
TS Web Access	▪ Web Server (IIS) ▪ Windows Process Activation Service > .NET Environment	▪ Web Server (IIS): Role Services	▪ IIS Admin Service (iisadmin) ▪ World Wide Web Publishing Service (w3svc)	▪ TS Web Access Administration ▪ Terminal Services Configuration ▪ Terminal Services Manager

Installing Applications

After you have installed the Terminal Services role, you can install the applications that the terminal server will deploy to your clients. Install the applications in the usual manner, typically by using the application's setup program.

Install applications that are designed to work together on the same terminal server. For example, install the entire Microsoft Office suite on one terminal server; do not install Microsoft Word on one server and Microsoft Excel on another.

Terminal Services has two operational modes: Execution and Install. By default, the Add Roles Wizard leaves newly installed terminal servers in Execution mode. Before you begin to install applications, you must switch the server to Install mode, using the following procedure.

 INSTALL AN APPLICATION

GET READY. Log on to Windows Server 2008 using a domain account with Administrator privileges. When the logon process is completed, close the Initial Configuration Tasks window and any other windows that appear.

1. Click **Start**, and then click **All Programs** > **Accessories** > **Command Prompt**. A command-prompt window appears.

2. In the command-prompt window, key **change user /install** and press (**Enter**). A *User session is ready to install applications* message appears.

3. Install your application using the setup program supplied by the manufacturer.

4. In the command-prompt window, key **change user /execute** and press (**Enter**). A *User session is ready to execute applications* message appears.

CLOSE the command-prompt window.

If your application is packaged as a Microsoft Installer (msi) file, you do not have to change Terminal Services to Install mode before installing it.

■ Configuring Terminal Server

 THE BOTTOM LINE
To create a minimally functional terminal server, add the Terminal Server role service and install applications.

When you select the Terminal Server role service, the Add Roles Wizard adds several new pages to configure some of the most important Terminal Services parameters, as discussed in the following sections.

Using Network Level Authentication

When a Terminal Services client connects to a terminal server, the traditional sequence of events is for the client to establish a connection to the server, and then for the server to authenticate the client by prompting for a username and password.

CERTIFICATION READY?
Configure Terminal
Services server options
2.7

As you can see when you run the RDC client, the unauthenticated client is connected to the server for a period of time. For unauthorized individuals attempting to gain access to the network or cause other kinds of trouble, this period is a window of opportunity. Attackers can use the unauthenticated connection to launch denial of service attacks that block access to the server or attempt to steal the credentials of legitimate users by setting up their own servers that masquerade as the real ones. To prevent these types of attacks, the Terminal Services components in Windows Server 2008 and Windows Vista include a new feature called Network Level Authentication.

Network Level Authentication (NLA) confirms the user's identity with the ***Credential Security Service Provider (CredSSP)*** protocol before the client and server establish the Terminal Services connection, eliminating that potentially dangerous window of opportunity. To use Network Level Authentication, the client and server must meet the following requirements:

- The terminal server must be running Windows Server 2008.
- The client computer must be running Windows Vista or another operating system that supports CredSSP.
- The client computer must be running Remote Desktop Connection version 6.0 or later.

When you install the Terminal Server role service, the Add Roles Wizard adds the Specify Authentication Method for Terminal Server page shown in Figure 8-5. On this page, you specify whether the Terminal Services clients must use NLA to connect to the server. If you have clients on the network that are running RDC versions prior to 6.0 or operating systems prior to Windows Vista, you should select the *Do not require Network Level Authentication* option.

Figure 8-5

The Specify Authentication Method for Terminal Server page of the Add Roles Wizard

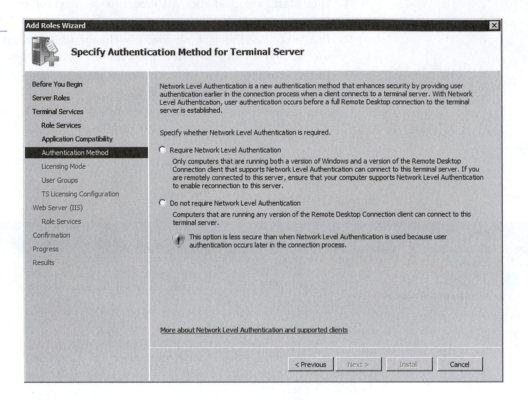

To configure NLA using the Control Panel, use the following procedure.

 CONFIGURE NLA USING CONTROL PANEL

GET READY. Log on to Windows Server 2008 using a domain account with Administrator privileges. When the logon process is completed, close the Initial Configuration Tasks window and any other windows that appear.

1. Click **Start** and then click **Control Panel**. The Control Panel window appears.
2. Double-click **System**. The System window appears.
3. In the Tasks list, click **Remote Settings**. The System Properties sheet appears with the Remote tab selected, as shown in Figure 8-6.
4. Select one of the following options:
   - Allow connections from computers running any version of Remote Desktop — Disables NLA.
   - Allow connections only from computers running Remote Desktop with Network Level Authentication—Enables NLA.
5. Click **OK**.

CLOSE the Control Panel window.

Regardless of the option you select during the Terminal Services installation, you can reconfigure NLA later using any of the following tools:

- System Control Panel
- Terminal Services Configuration
- Group Policy

Figure 8-6

The Remote tab in the System Properties sheet

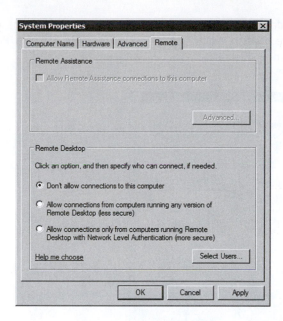

To configure NLA using the Terminal Services Configuration snap-in for MMC, use the following procedure.

 CONFIGURE NLA USING TERMINAL SERVICES CONFIGURATION

GET READY. Log on to Windows Server 2008 using a domain account with Administrator privileges. When the logon process is completed, close the Initial Configuration Tasks window and any other windows that appear.

1. Click **Start**, and then click **Administrative Tools** > **Terminal Services** > **Terminal Services Configuration.** The Terminal Services Configuration console appears, as shown in Figure 8-7.

Figure 8-7

The Terminal Services Configuration console

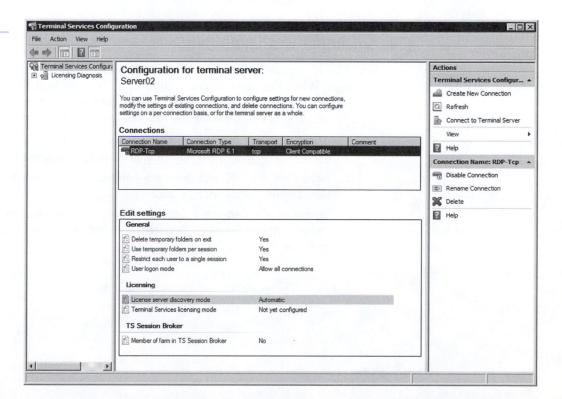

2. In the details pane, right-click the **RDP-Tcp** entry in the Connections list and, from the context menu, select **Properties**. The RDP-Tcp Properties sheet appears, as shown in Figure 8-8.

Figure 8-8

The RDP-Tcp Properties sheet

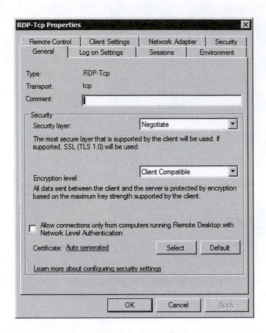

3. On the General tab, select or clear the **Allow connections only from computers running Remote Desktop with Network Level Authentication** checkbox.

4. Click **OK**.

CLOSE the Terminal Services Configuration console.

Rather than configure NLA on individual computers, you can deploy configuration settings to multiple servers simultaneously using Group Policy. To configure NLA using Group Policy, use the following procedure.

 CONFIGURE NLA USING GROUP POLICY

GET READY. Log on to Windows Server 2008 using a domain account with Administrator privileges. When the logon process is completed, close the Initial Configuration Tasks window and any other windows that appear. If you have not done so already, install the Group Policy Management console using the Add Features Wizard in Server Manager.

1. Open the Group Policy Management console, and create or locate a Group Policy Object (GPO) that will apply to your Terminal Services clients.

2. Right-click the GPO and, from the context menu, select **Edit**. The Group Policy Management Editor window appears.

3. Browse to the **Computer Configuration** > **Administrative Templates** > **Windows Components** > **Terminal Services** > **Terminal Server** > **Security** folder, as shown in Figure 8-9.

Figure 8-9

Terminal server security policies

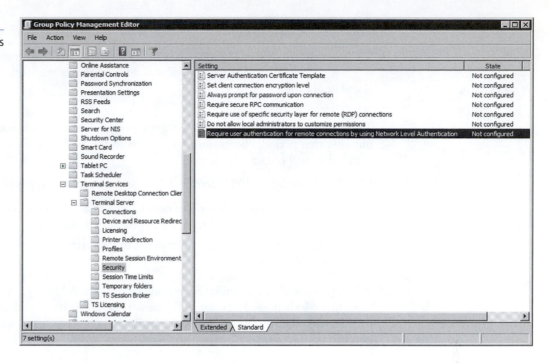

4. Double-click the **Require user authentication for remote connections by using Network Level Authentication** policy. The *Require user authentication for remote connections by using Network Level Authentication Properties* sheet appears, as shown in Figure 8-10.

Figure 8-10

The Require user authentication for remote connections by using Network Level Authentication Properties sheet

5. Select one of the following options:
   - Not Configured—The GPO applies no registry modification to the setting.
   - Enabled—The GPO modifies the registry to enable the setting.
   - Disabled—The GPO modifies the registry to disable the setting.
6. Click **OK**.

CLOSE the Group Policy Management Editor and Group Policy Management consoles.

You can configure NLA using either a local or domain GPO. Configuring NLA using Group Policy overrides the NLA settings in the System control panel and the RDP-Tcp Properties sheet.

Specifying a Licensing Mode

Clients connecting to a Windows Server 2008 terminal server must have Terminal Services client access licenses, in addition to any licenses needed for their operating system and applications.

Terminal Services provides a 120-day grace period, during which licenses are not necessary, but after that period, clients must have access to the Terminal Services License Server, from which they will obtain a license.

Like Windows Server 2008, Terminal Services supports two types of licensing:

- Per Device—Permits one client device, such as a computer, terminal, or handheld, to connect to the terminal server, no matter who is using it.
- Per User—Permits one user to connect to the terminal server, no matter what device the user is running.

When you install the Terminal Server role service, the Add Roles Wizard displays a Specify Licensing Mode page, as shown in Figure 8-11. On this page, you specify whether you want to have your clients retrieve Per Device or Per User licenses from your License Server. You can also choose to configure the licensing mode later.

Figure 8-11

The Specify Licensing Mode page in the Add Roles Wizard

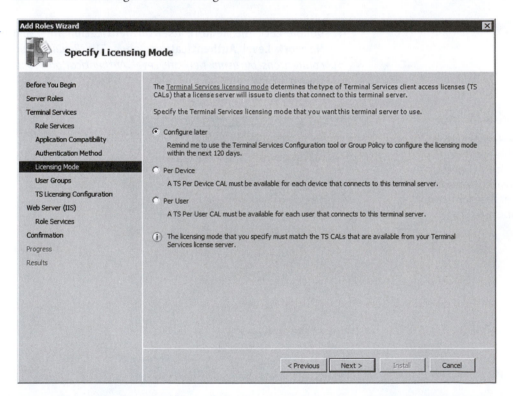

 For more information on setting up a Terminal Services License Server, see Lesson 9, "Configuring Terminal Services Clients."

No matter which option you select during the Terminal Services installation, you can reconfigure the licensing mode later using one of the following tools:

- Terminal Services Configuration
- Group Policy

To configure the licensing mode using the Terminal Services Configuration snap-in for MMC, use the following procedure.

 CONFIGURE THE LICENSING MODE USING TERMINAL SERVICES CONFIGURATION

GET READY. Log on to Windows Server 2008 using a domain account with Administrator privileges. When the logon process is completed, close the Initial Configuration Tasks window and any other windows that appear.

1. Click **Start**, and then click **Administrative Tools** > **Terminal Services** > **Terminal Services Configuration**. The Terminal Services Configuration console appears.

2. In the details pane, under Edit Settings > Licensing, double-click **Terminal Services licensing mode**. The Properties sheet for the terminal server appears, with the Licensing tab selected, as shown in Figure 8-12.

Figure 8-12

The Licensing tab of a terminal server's Properties sheet

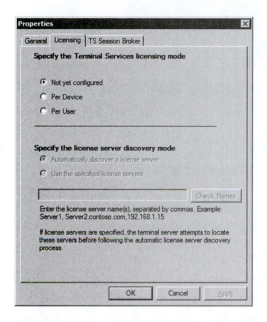

3. Select one of the following licensing mode options:
   - Not yet configured
   - Per Device
   - Per User

4. You can also specify whether the server should try to automatically detect a license server or supply the name or IP address of the license server on your network.

5. Click **OK**.

CLOSE the Terminal Services Configuration console.

 TAKE NOTE

The licensing mode you select must correspond to the type of licenses you have purchased and deployed with your license server.

Rather than configure the licensing mode on individual computers, you can deploy settings to multiple servers simultaneously using Group Policy. To configure the licensing mode using Group Policy, use the following procedure.

 CONFIGURE THE LICENSING MODE USING GROUP POLICY

GET READY. Log on to Windows Server 2008 using a domain account with Administrator privileges. When the logon process is completed, close the Initial Configuration Tasks window and any other windows that appear. If you have not done so already, install the Group Policy Management console using the Add Features Wizard in Server Manager.

1. Open the Group Policy Management console, and create or locate a GPO that will apply to your Terminal Services clients.

2. Right-click the GPO and, from the context menu, select **Edit.** The Group Policy Management Editor window appears.

3. Browse to the **Computer Configuration** > **Administrative Templates > Windows Components** > **Terminal Services** > **Terminal Server** > **Licensing** folder.

4. Double-click the **Set the terminal server licensing mode** policy. The *Set the Terminal Services licensing mode Properties* sheet appears, as shown in Figure 8-13.

Figure 8-13

The Set the Terminal Services licensing mode Properties sheet

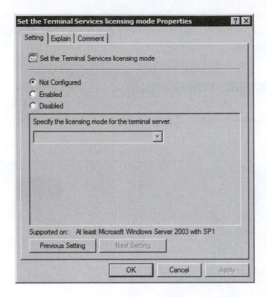

5. Select one of the following options:
   - Not Configured—The GPO applies no registry modification to the setting.
   - Enabled—The GPO modifies the registry to enable the setting.
   - Disabled—The GPO modifies the registry to disable the setting.

6. Click **OK.**

CLOSE the Group Policy Management Editor and Group Policy Management consoles.

You can configure the licensing mode using either a local or domain GPO. Configuring the licensing mode using Group Policy overrides the settings in the Terminal Services Configuration console.

Selecting User Groups

Users must have the appropriate privileges to access a terminal server, and the easiest way to provide those privileges is to add the users to the Remote Desktop Users group.

Remote Desktop Users is a local group on the computer running the Terminal Services role. When you install the Terminal Server role service, the Add Roles Wizard includes a Select User Groups Allowed Access To This Terminal Server page, as shown in Figure 8-14, on which you can select your clients' user accounts or groups.

Figure 8-14

The Select User Groups
Allowed Access To This
Terminal Server page

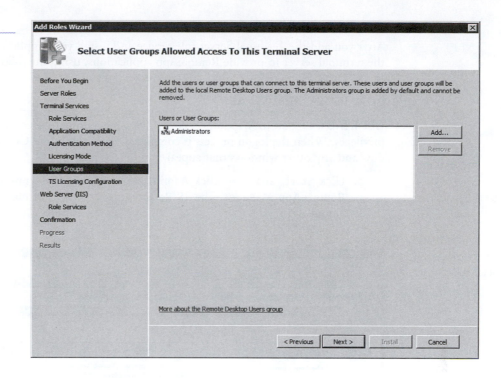

Because Remote Desktop Users is a local group, you can add domain global groups to it, as well as local or domain users. To add members to the Remote Desktop Users group after the Terminal Services installation, you can use any of the following tools:

- Local Users and Groups
- Active Directory Users and Groups
- System Control Panel

Using RemoteApp

> By eliminating the Terminal Services desktop, RemoteApp does away with much of the confusion that plagues users and support personnel. Users no longer have to switch back and forth between the local and remote desktops; they can combine local applications and RemoteApp applications in the same workspace, just as if all the applications were local.

CERTIFICATION READY?
Configure Windows
Server® 2008 Terminal
Services RemoteApp™
(TS RemoteApp)
2.1

RemoteApp is a new Terminal Services feature that enables clients to run terminal server applications within individual windows. The windows are resizable; they have standard taskbar buttons, and they are not constrained by a Terminal Services desktop. In fact, a RemoteApp window is, in most cases, indistinguishable from a window containing a local application.

RemoteApp is part of the Terminal Server role service, and includes a separate configuration tool, the TS RemoteApp Manager snap-in for MMC. To use RemoteApp, you must complete the following steps:

- Configure the terminal server by specifying the applications you want to provide to your clients.
- Package the applications by creating Remote Desktop Protocol (.rdp) files or Microsoft Installer (.msi) packages.
- Deploy the application packages using shared drives or Group Policy.

Clients can also access RemoteApp programs through a Terminal Services Web Access site.

CONFIGURING REMOTEAPP

After you add the Terminal Server role service and install your applications, you can configure the terminal server to provide RemoteApp applications, using the following procedure.

 CONFIGURE REMOTEAPP

GET READY. Log on to Windows Server 2008 using a domain account with Administrator privileges. When the logon process is completed, close the Initial Configuration Tasks window and any other windows that appear.

1. Click **Start**, and then click **Administrative Tools > Terminal Services > TS RemoteApp Manager**. The TS RemoteApp Manager console appears, as shown in Figure 8-15.

Figure 8-15

The TS RemoteApp Manager console

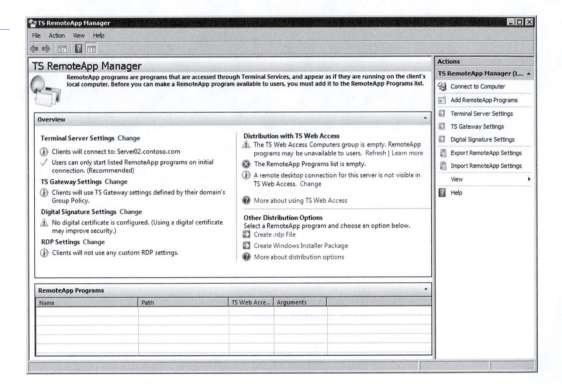

2. In the actions pane, click **Add RemoteApp Programs**. The RemoteApp Wizard appears.

3. Click **Next** to bypass the Welcome page. The *Choose programs to add to the Remote-App Programs list* page appears, as shown in Figure 8-16.

4. Select the checkbox for an application and click **Properties**. The RemoteApp Properties sheet for the application appears, as shown in Figure 8-17.

5. Modify the following settings, if desired:

   • RemoteApp program is available through TS Web Access—Specifies whether the icon for the program will appear in the default TS Web Access Web page.

   • Do not allow command-line arguments—Prevents remote users from adding command-line arguments when they launch the program.

   • Allow any command-line arguments—Enables remote users to add command-line arguments when they launch the program.

   • Always use the following command-line arguments—Specifies command-line arguments that the program will use when remote users launch it.

   • Change Icon—Enables you to select a different icon for the program.

Figure 8-16

The Choose programs to add to
the RemoteApp Programs list
page in the RemoteApp Wizard

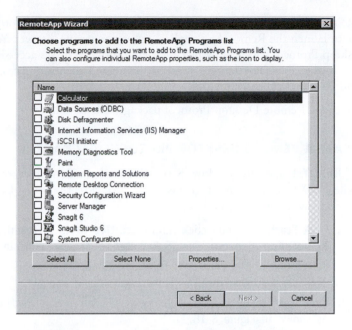

Figure 8-17

The RemoteApp Properties
sheet

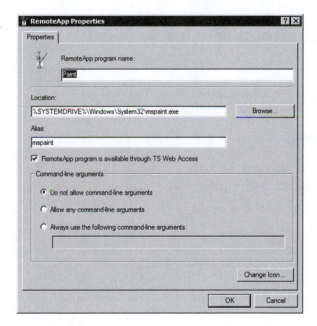

6. Click **OK** to close the RemoteApp Properties sheet.

7. Click **Next**. The Review Settings page appears.

8. Click **Finish**. The program you selected appears in the RemoteApp Programs list.

CLOSE the TS RemoteApp Manager console.

At this point, the selected applications are ready to be deployed by the terminal server. If you selected the *RemoteApp program is available through TS Web Access* checkbox, the program will appear on the default Terminal Services Web page.

PACKAGING REMOTEAPP APPLICATIONS

After you configure the terminal server to run the selected applications using RemoteApp, you must deploy them to your Terminal Services clients. The RDC client can only provide a full desktop; it cannot host RemoteApp applications. Instead, you use the TS RemoteApp Manager console to create either Remote Desktop Protocol or Microsoft Installer packages.

A Remote Desktop Protocol package is a file with an .rdp extension, which users can execute to launch the RemoteApp application on the terminal server. You can deploy Remote Desktop Protocol packages by placing them on shared drives accessible to your users, copying them to the clients' local drives, sending them as email attachments, or by using any other standard file distribution method.

To create a Remote Desktop Protocol package, use the following procedure.

 CREATE A REMOTE DESKTOP PROTOCOL PACKAGE

GET READY. Log on to Windows Server 2008 using a domain account with Administrator privileges. When the logon process is completed, close the Initial Configuration Tasks window and any other windows that appear.

1. Click **Start**, and then click **Administrative Tools** > **Terminal Services** > **TS RemoteApp Manager**. The TS RemoteApp Manager console appears.

2. Select one of the entries in the RemoteApp Programs list and, in the actions pane, click **Create .rdp File**. The RemoteApp Wizard appears.

3. Click **Next** to bypass the Welcome page. The *Specify Package Settings* page appears, as shown in Figure 8-18.

Figure 8-18

The Specify Package Settings page in the RemoteApp Wizard

4. In the *Enter the location to save the packages* text box, specify where you want to create the Remote Desktop Protocol package file.

5. Modify the Terminal Server settings, TS Gateway settings, or Certificate settings as needed. Then, click **Next**. The Review Settings page appears.

6. Click **Finish**. The wizard creates the package file in the location you specified.

CLOSE the TS RemoteApp Manager console.

Microsoft Installer packages have an msi extension and can be another means of distributing Remote Desktop Protocol packages. When a client computer executes a Microsoft Installer package, the installation program copies the rdp file contained within to the local drive and creates a shortcut for it that enables the user to launch the RemoteApp program from the Start menu. You can distribute Microsoft Installer packages to clients as files, like Remote Desktop Protocol packages, but the real advantage in this method is to use Group Policy to automatically distribute and install the packages to large groups of clients.

To create a Microsoft Installer package file, use the following procedure.

➔ CREATE A MICROSOFT INSTALLER PACKAGE

GET READY. Log on to Windows Server 2008 using a domain account with Administrator privileges. When the logon process is completed, close the Initial Configuration Tasks window and any other windows that appear.

1. Click **Start**, and then click **Administrative Tools** > **Terminal Services** > **TS RemoteApp Manager**. The TS RemoteApp Manager console appears.

2. Select one of the entries in the RemoteApp Programs list and, in the actions pane, click **Create Windows Installer Package**. The RemoteApp Wizard appears.

3. Click **Next** to bypass the Welcome page. The Specify Package Settings page appears.

4. In the *Enter the location to save the packages* text box, specify where you want to create the Remote Desktop Protocol package file.

5. Modify the Terminal Server settings, TS Gateway settings, or Certificate settings as needed. Then click **Next**. The Configure Distribution Package page appears, as shown in Figure 8-19.

Figure 8-19

The Configure Distribution Package page in the RemoteApp Wizard

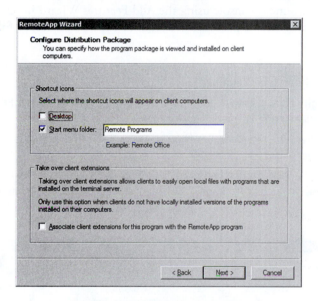

6. Configure the following settings, as needed:
   - Shortcut Icons: Desktop—Specifies whether an icon for the selected application should appear on the client's desktop.
   - Shortcut Icons: Start menu folder—Specifies whether an icon for the selected application should appear in the client's Start menu, and if so, the name of that Start menu folder.
   - Associate client extensions for this program with the RemoteApp program—Specifies whether the file types normally associated with the selected application should be associated on the client system.

7. Click **Next**. The Review Settings page appears.

8. Click **Finish**. The wizard creates the package file in the location you specified.

CLOSE the TS RemoteApp Manager console.

After you create a Microsoft Installer package, users can install it simply by executing the file, or you can deploy it using Group Policy, as discussed in the following section.

DEPLOYING REMOTEAPP APPLICATIONS

When a user executes a Remote Desktop Protocol file by double-clicking it or opening it in the Run dialog box, a RemoteApp window appears, containing the icon for the application. Depending on the circumstances, the user might have to confirm the desire to run the program and supply credentials for authentication. After the user completes these steps, the RemoteApp window disappears and the application launches on the desktop. From this point on, the application functions like it was running on the local computer.

If the user executes a Microsoft Installer package file, a brief installation procedure copies an RDP file to the local drive and creates a shortcut for the application in the client computer's Start menu. When the user clicks the shortcut, the connection procedure is the same as for any RDP file.

To deploy a Microsoft Installer package with Group Policy, use the following procedure.

 DEPLOY AN MSI FILE USING GROUP POLICY

GET READY. Log on to Windows Server 2008 using a domain account with Administrator privileges. When the logon process is completed, close the Initial Configuration Tasks window and any other windows that appear. If you have not done so already, install the Group Policy Management console using the Add Features Wizard in Server Manager and place the Microsoft Installer packages you want to deploy in a shared folder to which your clients have access.

1. Open the Group Policy Management console, and create or locate a GPO that will apply to your Terminal Services clients.
2. Right-click the GPO and, from the context menu, select **Edit**. The Group Policy Management Editor window appears.
3. Browse to the **User Configuration** > **Software Settings** > **Software Installation** folder.
4. Right-click the **Software Installation** node and, on the context menu, point to **New** and click **Package**. The Open combo box appears, as shown in Figure 8-20.

Figure 8-20

The Open combo box

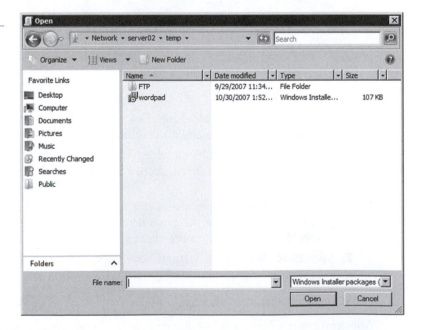

5. Open the **Network** container and browse to the folder containing the Microsoft Installer package you want to deploy. Select the package file and click **Open**. The Deploy Software dialog box appears, as shown in Figure 8-21.

Figure 8-21

The Deploy Software dialog box

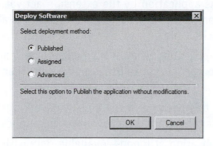

6. Select the **Advanced** option and click **OK**. The Properties sheet for the application you selected appears, as shown in Figure 8-22.

Figure 8-22

An application's Properties sheet

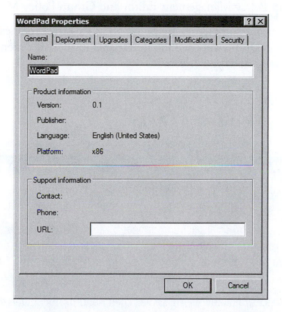

7. Click the **Deployment** tab, as shown in Figure 8-23, and select the following options, as needed:

Figure 8-23

The Deployment tab of an application's Properties sheet

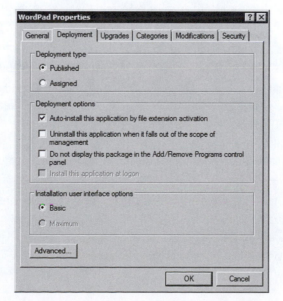

- Published—Makes the application available for installation by users, but does not require it.

- Assigned—Automatically installs the application on the user's computer.

- Auto-install this application by file extension activation—Available only with the Published option, causes the user's computer to install the application when the user double-clicks a file of a type associated with the application.

- Uninstall this application when it falls out of the scope of management—Causes the user's computer to uninstall the application when the GPO no longer applies to the user.

- Do not display this package in the Add/Remove Programs control panel—Specifies whether the user should be able to install the application from the control panel.

- Install this application at logon—Available only with the Assigned option, causes the user's computer to install the application when the user logs on.

   8. Click **OK.** The new Software Installation policy appears in the console's details pane.

CLOSE the Group Policy Management Editor and Group Policy Management consoles.

After this procedure is completed, the policy will take effect the next time the user logs on, installing the RDP file and making it available in the Start menu or the Control Panel, depending on the options you selected.

SUMMARY SKILL MATRIX

IN THIS LESSON YOU LEARNED:

- Terminal Services works by running applications on a Windows Server 2008 server and enabling desktop computers to operate those applications from a remote location.

- To make the desktop or application appear on the client computer, the server transmits data and instructions that enable the client to render the graphical interface on its display. In return, to manipulate the applications running on the server, the client program transmits the user's keystrokes and mouse movements.

- Terminal Services implements the server, client, and protocol elements with the following three components: Terminal Server, the Remote Desktop Connection client, and the Remote Desktop Protocol (RDP).

- To keep the client processes for individual sessions separate, the terminal server assigns each session a unique identifier, called a Session ID.

- Remote Desktop Connection (also known as Terminal Services Client) is a Win32 application that enables a Windows computer to establish a connection to a terminal server, authenticate a user, and access an application or desktop session running on the server.

- Remote Desktop Protocol 6.0 is based on the T.120 protocol standards published by the International Telecommunications Union (ITU), and provides multi-channel communication between Terminal Services clients and servers.

- The basic philosophy of Terminal Services calls for client applications to run on servers instead of client desktops, which leads naturally to the need for more powerful servers and less powerful clients.

- To deploy a terminal server, install the Terminal Services role before you install the applications to be deployed on the terminal server.

- Network Level Authentication (NLA) confirms the user's identity with the Credential Security Service Provider (CredSSP) protocol before the client and server establish the Terminal Services connection.

- Clients connecting to a Windows Server 2008 terminal server must have client access licenses, in addition to any licenses needed for their operating system and applications. Terminal Services provides a 120-day grace period, during which licenses are not necessary.

- RemoteApp is a new Terminal Services feature that enables clients to run terminal server applications within individual windows. The windows are resizable; they have standard taskbar buttons, and they are not constrained by a Terminal Services desktop.

■ Knowledge Assessment

Matching

Complete the following exercise by matching the terms with their corresponding definitions.

   a. Client applications running on servers
   b. Transmits keystrokes, mouse movements, and display data
   c. Enables one copy of an application to service multiple clients
   d. Reduces the network bandwidth requirements of Terminal Services
   e. Uniquely identifies a client's processes on a terminal server
   f. Carries user credentials from the client to the server
   g. Confirms the user's identity before establishing a Terminal Services connection
   h. Launches Terminal Services programs without a remote desktop
   i. Client that provides users with access to terminal servers
   j. A collection of processes that form an individual user environment running on a terminal server

_____ **1.** client-side caching
_____ **2.** copy-on-write data sharing
_____ **3.** Credential Security Service Provider (CredSSP)
_____ **4.** Network Level Authentication (NLA)
_____ **5.** RemoteApp
_____ **6.** Remote Desktop Connection
_____ **7.** Remote Desktop Protocol (RDP)
_____ **8.** session
_____ **9.** Session ID
_____ **10.** Thin client computing

Multiple Choice

Select the correct answer for each of the following questions.

1. Session 0 on a Windows Server 2008 terminal server is always devoted to which of the following?
   a. The local console user
   b. The system services running on the computer
   c. The first terminal services client to connect to the server
   d. The first user to log on locally

2. How many days can clients access a Terminal Services server before they require a client access license?
   a. 14 days
   b. 30 days
   c. 90 days
   d. 120 days

3. Which of the following Terminal Services role services enables clients of a terminal server farm to resume working with the same environment after a disconnection?
   a. TS Licensing
   b. TS Gateway
   c. TS Session Broker
   d. TS Web Access

4. Which of the following features is designed to conserve memory on a terminal server?
   a. thin client computing
   b. copy-on-write data sharing
   c. client-side caching
   d. Execution mode

5. Which of the following is generally not considered to be a component of a terminal?
   a. keyboard
   b. mouse
   c. display
   d. printer

6. Which of the following does the Remote Desktop Protocol NOT carry between a terminal server and a client?
   a. keystrokes
   b. mouse movements
   c. display information
   d. application data

7. Which of the following is not a requirement for using network level authentication?
   a. The terminal server must run Windows Server 2008.
   b. The terminal server must be a member of a domain.
   c. The client computer must run Windows Vista.
   d. The client computer must run Remote Desktop Connection version 6.0 or above.

8. A client running four RemoteApp applications on the desktop is utilizing how many sessions on the terminal server?
   a. None
   b. One
   c. Four
   d. Five

9. For users to access a Windows Server 2008 terminal server, they must be members of which of the following groups?
   a. Power Users
   b. Users
   c. Domain Users
   d. Remote Desktop Users

10. The Remote Desktop Protocol is based on which of the following?
    a. ITU T.120
    b. CredSSP
    c. Win32
    d. HTTPS

Review Questions

1. Explain the steps of the process by which you deploy RemoteApp applications to Remote Desktop Connection clients.

2. List five possible advantages to using Terminal Services to deploy applications to clients, rather than running them on individual desktops.

■ Case Scenarios

Scenario 8-1: Configuring RemoteApp Applications

Howard set up a terminal server on his network by installing Windows Server 2008, adding the Terminal Services role, and installing Microsoft Office on the server. He added the individual Office applications to the RemoteApp Programs list in the TS RemoteApp Manager console. However, when clients connect to the server using the Remote Desktop Connection client, they see an entire Terminal Services desktop instead of the individual RemoteApp applications in separate windows. What must Howard do to resolve the problem?

Scenario 8-2: Deploying Terminal Services

Several months ago, Kathleen installed the Terminal Services role on one of her Windows Server 2008 servers and has been using it to provide clients with access to a custom-designed credit reporting application. This morning, she began receiving calls from users complaining that they could no longer access their Terminal Services desktops. What is the most likely cause of the problem, and what must Kathleen do to resolve it?

9 **LESSON**

Configuring Terminal Services Clients

OBJECTIVE DOMAIN MATRIX

TECHNOLOGY SKILL	OBJECTIVE DOMAIN	OBJECTIVE DOMAIN NUMBER
Configuring RDC Options	Configure Terminal Services client connections.	2.6
Planning a TS Licensing Deployment	Configure Terminal Services licensing.	2.5

KEY TERMS

bitmap caching
Easy Print
font smoothing
Licensing server discovery
  mode

Mstsc.exe
Terminal Services client access
  license (TS CAL)
Terminal Services licensing
  mode

TS Licensing server
Windows CE
Windows XPe

Configuring a terminal server is only half of the equation. To complete a Terminal Services connection, you must configure the client as well. This lesson examines Terminal Services client-related topics, such as:

- Selecting client hardware
- Configuring the RDC client
- Deploying a TS Licensing server

Deploying Terminal Services Clients

THE BOTTOM LINE

In Lesson 8, "Using Terminal Services," you learned how to install and configure a Windows Server 2008 terminal server. After the server is ready to accept client connections, you must deploy the client computers that will initiate those connections.

When you deploy Windows Server 2008 computers to function as terminal servers, you equip them with additional hardware resources, such as faster processors, more memory, and hard disks that can support many simultaneous network users. For large Terminal Services deployments, you could build a server farm consisting of several high-powered computers, which balance the client load between them.

The tradeoff for this increased server capability is that you can use lower-powered computers for your Terminal Services clients. As mentioned in Lesson 8, if you plan to use Terminal Services to deploy all of your applications, the client computers only need sufficient hardware to run a Remote Desktop Protocol (RDP) client program. A Terminal Services client can take the form of a desktop computer or a thin client terminal.

Using Desktop Clients

To minimize the client hardware requirements, administrators should run all applications not included with the desktop operating system on terminal servers, with the sole exception of the RDC client program, which provides the desktop users with access to all of the other applications. The RDC client requires no additional hardware beyond that recommended for the operating system, enabling administrators to deploy relatively inexpensive computers on the desktop.

The primary platform for a Terminal Services client is a desktop PC running Windows Vista or Windows XP SP2 or higher, with the Remote Desktop Connection (RDC) 6.*x* client installed. Obviously, the base hardware requirements for the operating system you select still apply. Any additional requirements depend on the applications the desktop computer must run.

REDUCING HARDWARE COSTS

To be designated as Windows Vista Capable, a PC requires at least an 800 MHz processor and 512 megabytes of memory. With this hardware, the computer will run the operating system effectively. If you install a typical suite of productivity applications on the computer, including an email client, a word processor, and a spreadsheet, the official system requirements might not increase, but you will notice a distinct reduction in system performance, particularly when you run multiple applications simultaneously. However, running the RDC client instead of the productivity applications will yield virtually no performance degradation on this minimal computer.

Consider the following real-life scenario. Table 9-1 lists two typical business desktop computer configurations. The computers are virtually identical, except for the listed components. System 2 has a faster processor with more cache and twice as much memory as System 1.

Table 9-1

Two Typical Business Desktop Computer Configurations

COMPONENT	SYSTEM 1	SYSTEM 2
Operating System	Windows® XP Professional 32	Windows® XP Professional 32
Processor	Intel® Pentium® Dual-Core processor E2160 1.80 GHz 1 MB L2 cache 800 MHz front side bus	Intel® Core™2 Duo processor E4400 2.00 GHz 2 MB L2 cache 800 MHz front side bus
Memory	512 MB 667 MHz DDR2 SDRAM	1 GB 667 MHz DDR2 SDRAM
Hard Disk	80 GB 7200 rpm SATA 3.0 Gb/s	80 GB 7200 rpm SATA 3.0 Gb/s
Optical Drive	16X/48X SATA DVD	48X/32X SATA DVD/CD-RW combo
Price	$579	$789

 TAKE NOTE * Table 9-1 provides examples of common business desktop configurations. Processor speeds and other specifications change frequently and these configurations might not be available today. Also, many other computers would perform adequately in this scenario, at higher or lower prices. These examples are not recommendations of specific components or price points.

Both computers exceed the minimum requirements of the Windows XP operating system. However, if you install Microsoft Office Professional on both computers and open several of the applications at the same time, System 2 would run adequately, while System 1 would probably slow down as Windows runs out of memory and begins paging to the hard disk.

By comparison, in a Terminal Services deployment, System 1 would run the Remote Desktop Connection client adequately without needing additional hardware resources to run several memory-intensive terminal server applications. In this scenario, you could save $210 per client in hardware costs by deploying applications using Terminal Services. Of course, other economic factors are involved when calculating the total cost of ownership, such as the cost of Terminal Services client access licenses (TS CALs), but this scenario demonstrates the substantial savings for an organization with an enterprise Terminal Services deployment.

REDUCING ADMINISTRATION COSTS

The economic advantages to using Terminal Services are reduced if you do not deploy all applications using terminal servers. The desktop computers must have sufficient resources to run any local applications you install on them, regardless of how many Terminal Services applications they run as well. However, even if you cannot realize substantial savings on client hardware, you can significantly reduce the cost of installing, configuring, maintaining, and updating your applications by deploying them using Terminal Services.

Deploying applications on a large fleet of desktop computers is a complicated undertaking, no matter how you approach the task. The simplest, and perhaps the most time-consuming, method is to install each application on each desktop computer manually by travelling to each computer, inserting a disk, and running the application's installation program. The time this takes depends on the number and type of applications involved, and of course, on the number of computers you have to deploy.

You can streamline this manual installation process by installing applications from network distribution points instead of disks and by using additional staff to install the applications on multiple computers at the same time. However, when you are dealing with multiple applications and large numbers of computers, it can still be an extremely lengthy and tedious process. In addition, when you reconfigure an application or install an update, the entire manual process starts again, with another round of trips to individual computers.

For small networks, manual application installations might be a viable solution. For large networks, it is better to automate application installation. A variety of products and technologies can automate installations, ranging from Group Policy, included with the Windows Server operating systems, to third-party products, such as Microsoft Systems Management Server. Even automated deployment tools require administrators for preparation and configuration tasks, which can range from prepackaging the applications to installing a management client on each workstation. Often, additional licensing costs must be considered for desktop management products.

By contrast, deploying an application using Terminal Services requires you to install it only once on each terminal server, no matter how many clients will run the application. Configuring and updating the application likewise require only single iterations of the procedure. You do not need to travel to each client computer to install the software. Updates take minutes instead of days, and supporting the application users is simplified by the assurance that everyone is running the same version of the applications.

REDUCING NETWORK BANDWIDTH REQUIREMENTS

In addition to savings on hardware and administration costs, deploying applications using Terminal Services can drastically reduce the network bandwidth consumed by the client computers. Because the applications run on the terminal servers, you do not need to transfer large executables and other application files over the network to each client. Most of the network bandwidth that the RDC client program uses is devoted to keystrokes, mouse movements, and display information, resulting in less network traffic.

If you use an older Ethernet network running at 10 megabits per second (Mbps), deploying your applications using Terminal Services can prevent you from performing costly infrastructure upgrades. The same is true if your network must support remote users connecting with dial-up links or other low-speed connections. For users, running a major application over a dial-up virtual private network (VPN) connection can be agonizingly slow. Whether the client computer

has to use the connection to download the application files or access a database or other resource on the network, the amount of data transmitted over the connection can be enormous.

Using Terminal Services, the application loads on the server and can access network resources using high-speed internal links. The only traffic passing over the VPN connection is a small amount of terminal data.

The Terminal Services paradigm also increases the security of the client/server connection. Instead of transmitting sensitive company information over potentially vulnerable links, the RDP traffic contains only innocuous keystrokes and bitmap data that would be far more difficult to compromise.

USING OTHER PLATFORMS

The typical desktop platform for a Terminal Services client is a Windows PC, but RDP client alternatives enable computers running non-Windows operating systems to run terminal server applications. In addition to the Windows versions, Microsoft Remote Desktop Connection Client for Mac 2.0 is available as a free download, and third-party clients are available for Macintosh and UNIX/Linux computers.

Using Thin Client Terminals

> As discussed in Lesson 1, a thin client is a terminal that is more complex than the dumb terminals of old, but less so than a desktop computer.

As mentioned earlier in this lesson, deploying all of your applications using Terminal Services enables you to reduce the hardware requirements of your client computers. However, even if you buy low-end computers, some hardware is extraneous. Does a computer running all of its applications on terminal servers need an 80 gigabyte hard drive or a DVD burner? Remember, in Lesson 8, you learned how, in the early days of computing, users accessed mainframe computers with terminals that consisted of little more than a keyboard and a display screen. You can do the same thing today by using terminal devices called thin clients.

A thin client device uses a keyboard and mouse like a regular computer and supports a standard color display. Physically, thin clients are typically much smaller than the average desktop computer, with connectors for a standard keyboard, mouse, and monitor. Some are even small enough to mount on the back of a monitor.

Technically, a thin client is a computer; it has a processor and memory, and runs an operating system and a client application that enable it to connect to terminal servers. However, most thin clients are network-dependent devices; the operating system is dedicated primarily (and in some cases exclusively) to running the RDP client. As a result, the device does not typically need much memory or an extremely fast processor. They also do not have a hard drive or CD/DVD drive, so users cannot store their own data, install their own applications, or use the device for anything other than connecting to a terminal server or running specified applications, which is a huge security benefit. The lack of moving parts, such as spinning disk drives, means that the device is completely solid state and requires no cooling fans.

Thin clients require an operating system, like any other computer, but they are not designed to run a full Windows installation. The minimal hardware resources of a thin client device and its minimal application requirements call for a smaller operating system that provides only the needed terminal capabilities.

Four basic operating system options are used in the thin client market, as follows:

- **Proprietary OS.** An embedded operating system, locked down and stored in flash memory, provides access to terminal servers and limited support for local peripherals. All applications, including Web browsers, must run on a terminal server. By stripping down the operating system to its minimal components, the thin client avoids exposing a Windows-based application programming interface (API) to potential attackers,

TAKE NOTE*

Because thin clients do not require fans, they can be used in environments that would contaminate, or be contaminated by, a standard computer, such as dusty factories and clean rooms, respectively.

increasing the overall security of the system. This terminal type is ideal for use in kiosks and by workers who need access only to server-based applications, such as order entry.

- *Windows CE*. A real-time, modular operating system designed for devices with minimal amounts of memory. Windows CE is not based on the NT kernel, but it provides users with a familiar Windows graphical user interface (GUI) and has been adapted to a variety of devices, including handhelds, smart phones, and game consoles. Windows CE terminals provide local Internet Explorer browser support, which enables users to access Web sites and Web-based applications with greater efficiency than with a server-based browser. The operating system can also support a wider array of Windows drivers and peripheral devices, including smart cards for authentication, wireless networking, and USB devices. Designed to support users who need Web access in addition to terminal server applications, this is the most popular type of thin client device.

- *Windows XPe*. Windows XP Embedded is a more full-featured operating system based on the standard Windows XP kernel. Windows XPe terminals include more local computing capabilities than terminals using Windows CE or a proprietary OS, including support for local browsers and Java applications, as well as embedded Win32 applications. Windows XPe also supports the full range of Windows drivers and peripherals. The result is a more powerful and efficient workstation that can continue to function when disconnected from the network; this makes it appropriate for business critical applications and environments in which network connectivity might be intermittent. The disadvantages of Windows XPe terminals include the additional expense for the operating system and their more powerful hardware, and an increased attack surface due to the device's local processing capability and its use of the standard Win32 API.

- Linux. Linux is the wild card entry in the terminal operating system category because it can fulfill any of the roles performed by proprietary OSes, Windows CE, and Windows XPe. The open source paradigm on which the operating system is based makes it possible to modify it to support virtually any thin client capability.

Clearly, the dividing line between thin clients and desktop computers is blurring. A Windows XPe terminal with local application support is not terribly different from a Windows XP workstation with a locked-down user interface, and their respective initial hardware costs are comparable. However, designing and deploying a locked-down desktop configuration can require a great deal of effort, while thin clients are locked down by default.

Generally, thin clients are most practical when you want to restrict user access to the local computing device. For example, a thin client might be better than a standard Windows computer running Remote Desktop Connection in a kiosk in a public location, such as a hotel lobby, because it prevents potential abusers from using the client for their own purposes. You can exercise full control over what applications the system can run and eliminate virtually all possible exploits from the local hardware and software.

For situations in which client security is not as important, such as trusted office workers, thin clients can be a viable administrative solution because fewer things can go wrong. They have fewer or no operating system controls for experimentation and no way for users to install their own software, which reduces the technical support burden. However, from the standpoint of hardware economy, thin clients are not much cheaper than desktop computers, and desktops can provide greater flexibility and more application deployment options.

■ Using Remote Desktop Connection 6.1

THE BOTTOM LINE

The first version of the Remote Desktop Connection client was included with the Terminal Server Edition of Windows NT 4.0 Server released in 1998. Subsequent versions of the NT-based Windows operating systems included updated versions of the client that gradually added new features.

The development of the RDC client coincides with that of Remote Desktop Protocol, which carries traffic between the client and the terminal server. Table 9-2 lists all of the major RDP versions, the operating systems in which they were first released, and the major features added in each version.

> **TAKE NOTE*** Despite its name, Remote Desktop Connection is the client for Terminal Services, as well as for Remote Desktop.

Table 9-2

Remote Desktop Protocol Version History

VERSION NUMBER	FIRST OPERATING SYSTEM	FEATURES ADDED
4.0	Windows NT 4.0 Server, Terminal Server Edition	Initial release
5.0	Windows 2000 Server	• Local printer redirection • Improved network bandwidth consumption
5.1	Windows XP Professional	• 24-bit color • Redirection of audio, drives, ports, and network printers • Smart card authentication
5.2	Windows Server 2003	• Local resource mapping • Group Policy management • 128-bit encryption
6.0	Windows Vista	• RemoteApp • TS Gateway • Display enhancements
6.1	Windows Server 2008 Windows Vista SP1 Windows XP SP3	• Easy Print driver • TS Web Access • Network Level Authentication • Transport Layer Security

The core functionality of the RDP protocol and the RDC client have remained unchanged throughout their history, so you can establish a basic connection to a Windows Server 2008 terminal server using a 5.x version of the client. However, using an older client will limit your ability to redirect local resources and you will not be able to use new features such as RemoteApp and TS Web Access.

The Remote Desktop Connection 6.1 client included with all versions of Windows Server 2008 supports all of the new Terminal Services features in Windows Server 2008. Windows Vista includes RDC version 6.0, which supports most of the Windows Server 2008 Terminal Services features, but not all of them. Microsoft is planning to release RDC version 6.1 for Windows Vista as part of Service Pack 1.

To support RDP 6.x on the Windows Server 2003 and Windows XP platforms, Microsoft has released add-on versions of the Remote Desktop Connection client as free downloads. The downloadable version of Remote Desktop Connection 6.0 provides Windows Server 2008 Terminal Services connectivity for computers running Windows Server 2003 (with Service Pack 1 or 2 installed) and Windows XP (with Service Pack 2 installed). Microsoft will release an RDC 6.1 client as part of Windows XP Service Pack 3.

> **TAKE NOTE***
> The Remote Desktop Connection 6.0 release for Windows Server 2003 and Windows XP is available from the Microsoft Downloads Center at http://microsoft.com/downloads.

Connecting to a Terminal Server Using RDC

Establishing a connection to a terminal server is basically a matter of specifying the server name in the RDC client and supplying the appropriate logon credentials.

You can use the same credentials to open a Terminal Services session as to log on at the remote computer's keyboard. The only special requirement is that the user has either administrative privileges or membership in the Remote Desktop Users group on the terminal server.

To connect to a terminal server, use the following procedure.

CONNECT TO A TERMINAL SERVER USING RDC

GET READY. Log on to Windows Server 2008. When the logon process is completed, close the Initial Configuration Tasks window and any other windows that appear.

1. Click **Start**, and then click **All Programs** > **Accessories** > **Remote Desktop Connection**. The Remote Desktop Connection dialog box appears, as shown in Figure 9-1.

Figure 9-1

The Remote Desktop Connection dialog box

2. In the Computer text box, specify the terminal server to which you want to connect, using a fully-qualified domain name (FQDN), such as *computer01.contoso.com*; a NetBIOS name, such as *computer01*; or an IP address, such as *192.168.76.124*.

3. Click **Connect**. A Windows Security dialog box appears, as shown in Figure 9-2.

Figure 9-2

The Windows Security dialog box

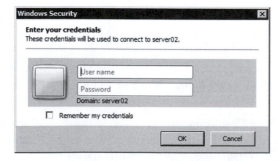

4. In the User Name text box, key the name of the account you will use to log on to the terminal server, using the format *servername\username* or *domainname\username*.

5. In the Password text box, key the password associated with the user account you specified.

6. To configure the RDC client to retain your logon credentials, click the **Remember My Credentials** checkbox.

7. Click **OK.** The terminal server desktop appears, occupying the entire display, except for a connection bar at the top, which you can use to control the terminal session.

CLOSE the Remote Desktop Connection window to disconnect from the Terminal Services session.

The RDC client displays the terminal server desktop in full screen mode by default. After the desktop appears, you can use the standard controls at the top right of the connection bar to reduce it to a window or minimize it.

Configuring RDC Options

Although the RDC client seems simple at first, clicking the Options button expands the Remote Desktop Connection dialog box into a tabbed dialog box containing a variety of configuration settings.

CERTIFICATION READY?
Configure Terminal
Services client connections
2.6

While some of the RDC options are best left to the end user, administrators can use them to improve the client's performance and optimize network bandwidth consumption. The following sections examine these options and their functions.

CONFIGURING GENERAL OPTIONS

On the General tab, shown in Figure 9-3, in addition to specifying the name or address of a terminal server, you can specify a default *User name* value that will appear in the Windows Security dialog box when the user attempts to connect. This can be useful if you intend to create RDP files or shortcuts for users confused by the domain\user name format.

Figure 9-3

The General tab on the expanded Remote Desktop Connection dialog box

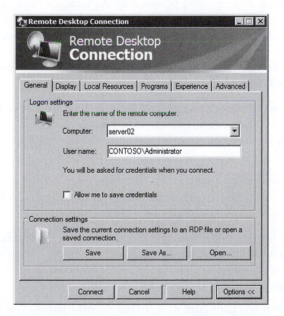

REF

For more information on using the Connection Settings controls to create RDP files, see "Creating an RDP File," later in this lesson.

CONFIGURING DISPLAY OPTIONS

On the Display tab, shown in Figure 9-4, you can specify the size of the terminal server desktop, as it appears on the client computer. By default, the *Remote Desktop size* slider is set to Full Screen, which causes the client to occupy the client computer's entire display, using the computer's configured display resolution.

Figure 9-4

The Display tab on the expanded Remote Desktop Connection dialog box

ANOTHER WAY

Another way to eliminate the dual desktop is to deploy applications using RemoteApp, which eliminates the Terminal Services desktop. For more information, see Lesson 8, "Using Terminal Services."

One of the long-term problems with Terminal Services is that some users are confused by having two separate desktops: one provided by the local operating system and one by the terminal server. If you are using Terminal Services to deploy complete desktop environments to your clients, leave the *Remote Desktop size* control set to Full Screen and clear the *Display the connection bar when in full screen mode* checkbox. This will configure the RDC client to completely overlap the local desktop with the one provided by the terminal server. Users will not be aware that two desktops are involved.

Of course, if client users require access to the local desktop, this strategy is not practical. You can either leave the checkbox selected so that the user can resize or minimize the terminal server desktop with the connection bar, or adjust the *Remote Desktop size* control to make the terminal server desktop appear in a window.

In addition to the desktop size, you can adjust the color depth of the RDC display, using the Colors dropdown list. The settings available in this dropdown list depend on the capabilities of the video display adapter installed in the client computer.

One of the new features implemented in RDP 6.*x* is support for 32-bit color, which enables clients to run graphic-intensive applications, such as image editors, with a full color palette. However, the tradeoff for this ability is the increased network bandwidth required to transmit the display information from the terminal server to the client.

For example, when you configure RDC to use 32-bit color, the client and the terminal server open a special RDP channel just for that color information. This enables the client to assign a lower priority to the extra color information, so that it does not interfere with the basic functionality of the client. However, 32-bit color increases the overall bandwidth consumed by the connection substantially. As a general rule, you should set the Colors parameter to the High Color (16-bit) setting, unless the client will be running terminal server applications that can benefit from the additional color information.

CONFIGURING LOCAL RESOURCES OPTIONS

On the Local Resources tab, shown in Figure 9-5, you configure how the RDC client should reconcile the resources on the terminal server with those on the client computer.

Figure 9-5

The Local Resources tab on the expanded Remote Desktop Connection dialog box

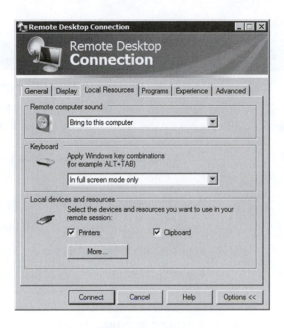

CONFIGURING AUDIO REDIRECTION

In the *Remote computer sound* box, select one of the following options to specify how the client should interact with the terminal server's audio capabilities:

- Bring to this computer. Causes all sounds generated by the applications running in the client session on the terminal server to play on the client computer and suppresses those sounds on the terminal server. This is the default setting.
- Do not play. Suppresses all sounds on the client computer and the server generated by the applications running in the client session on the terminal server.
- Leave at remote computer. Causes all sounds generated by the applications running in the client session on the terminal server to play on the terminal server only.

In most cases, the default setting for the *Remote computer sound* parameter is appropriate. For Terminal Services installations that support multiple simultaneous client sessions, you typically want to avoid playing sounds on the server because a cacophony of overlapping sounds can result.

CONFIGURING KEYBOARD REDIRECTION

Another of the long-standing problems for Terminal Services users is how the client computer should interpret system keyboard combinations during a terminal session. For example, when you press Alt+Tab to switch between the programs running on the computer, do you want to switch the terminal server programs or those on the client computer?

In the Keyboard box, you can control this behavior by selecting one of the following options:

- On the local computer. Causes the client computer to process all system keystrokes.
- On the remote computer. Causes the terminal server computer to process all system keystrokes.
- In full screen mode only. Causes the terminal server computer to process all system keystrokes, but only when the *Remote desktop size* parameter is set to Full Screen. This is the default setting.

If you select the *On the local computer* option, you can use alternative key combinations in the RDC session window, as shown in Table 9-3.

Table 9-3

Terminal Services Key Combinations

TERMINAL SERVICES KEY COMBINATION	WINDOWS KEY COMBINATION EQUIVALENT	FUNCTION
ALT+PAGE UP	ALT+TAB	Switches to the next program to the right in the task list
ALT+PAGE DOWN	ALT+SHIFT+TAB	Switches to the next program to the left in the task list
ALT+HOME	CTRL+ESC	Displays the Start menu
CTRL+ALT+BREAK	N/A	Toggles the client session between a full screen and a window
CTRL+ALT+END	CTRL+ALT+DEL	Displays the Windows Security screen
ALT+INSERT	N/A	Cycles through running programs in the order you launched them
ALT+DELETE	ALT+SPACE	Displays the system menu for the current active window
CTRL+ALT+Plus Sign	PRINT SCREEN	Copies the graphical contents of the desktop to the clipboard
CTRL+ALT+Minus Sign	ALT+PRINT SCREEN	Copies the graphical contents of the active window to the clipboard

CONFIGURING LOCAL RESOURCE REDIRECTION

Terminal Services users often have peripherals connected to their local computers, and over the years, Microsoft has gradually developed the device redirection capabilities of the RDC client. With RDC 6.*x*, you can use almost any device connected to the client computer in a terminal session.

In the Local Devices and Resources box, you can select which of the following resources on the client computer you want to use in the terminal session:

- Printers. Enables terminal server applications to send print jobs to printers on the client computer.
- Clipboard. Enables terminal server applications to copy data to, and paste data from, the clipboard on the client computer.

Click the More button to display the dialog box shown in Figure 9-6, which contains the following additional options:

Figure 9-6

The Remote Desktop Connection Local Devices and Resources dialog box

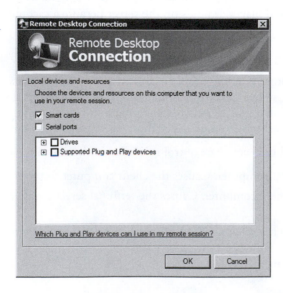

- Smart cards. Enables RDC to use a smart card reader on the client computer for authentication within a terminal session.
- Serial ports. Enables terminal server applications to access devices connected to serial ports on the client computer.
- Drives. Enables terminal server applications to access selected drives on the client computer.
- Supported Plug and Play devices. Enables terminal server applications to access selected Plug and Play devices on the client computer.

INTRODUCING EASY PRINT

In previous versions of Terminal Services, for a client to use a printer connected to the client computer in a terminal session, both the client and the terminal server must have the appropriate printer driver installed. In Windows Server 2008 Terminal Services, a new feature called *Easy Print* eliminates the need for the printer driver on the terminal server. Instead, the terminal server has a generic Easy Print driver based on the XML Paper Specification (XPS) document format introduced in Windows Vista and Windows Server 2008.

When you open a printer's Properties sheet in Windows, the printer-specific controls you see are provided by the printer driver. When a user in a terminal session tries to print a document, it is accessing a driver on the terminal server. In the past, it was necessary to install the driver on both computers, so you could access those printer-specific controls within the terminal session. With Easy Print, the driver on the terminal server redirects user interface calls back to the printer driver on the client computer, so the user sees printer-specific controls without having a printer-specific driver on the terminal server.

When you print the document, the terminal server creates a print job in the XPS format and transmits it to the client computer, which prints it using the local driver.

CONFIGURING PROGRAMS OPTIONS

On the Programs tab, shown in Figure 9-7, you can specify a program that you want to launch in the terminal session when it is established. If you are using Terminal Services to deploy a single application, you can configure the RDC client to load the application automatically, eliminating the need for users to do it themselves.

➕ **MORE INFORMATION**

Support for XPS is built in to Windows Server 2008 and Windows Vista but not Windows XP. To use Easy Print on a Windows XP computer, you must use the RDC 6.1 client and install .NET Framework 3.0, which provides the support for XPS. For more information on XPS, see Lesson 4, "Deploying Print and Fax Servers."

Figure 9-7

The Programs tab on the expanded Remote Desktop Connection dialog box

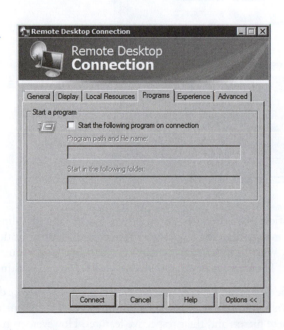

To configure a program to load automatically, select the *Start the following program on connection* checkbox and, in the *Program path and file name* text box, key the full path to the program's executable in the terminal session. In the *Start in the following folder* text box, you can specify the default folder for the documents or files the user will open in the application.

CONFIGURING EXPERIENCE OPTIONS

On the Experience tab, shown in Figure 9-8, you can specify which standard Windows desktop performance features you want the client to use within a terminal session. These features are as follows:

- Desktop background. Displays the selected desktop wallpaper in the RDC session. When deselected, the desktop appears with only a black background.
- ***Font smoothing***. Also called anti-aliasing, enables the client to display screen fonts without jagged lines.
- Desktop composition. Enables the RDC client to duplicate the graphics-rendering capabilities of Windows Vista, most notably the Aero "glass" effect.
- Show contents of window while dragging. Causes the client to move windows fluidly across the desktop when you drag them.
- Menu and window animation. Enables the client to display menu and window effects, such as fades.
- Themes. Enables the client to display the theme elements configured on the terminal server, including backgrounds and icons.
- ***Bitmap caching***. Enables the client to store display information in a cache in local memory, so that the server does not have to repeatedly transmit the same data.

Figure 9-8

The Experience tab on the expanded Remote Desktop Connection dialog box

With one exception, these features are strictly cosmetic, and enabling them can degrade the client's performance and increase its network bandwidth consumption. The only exception is bitmap caching, which improves the client's performance and reduces the amount of bandwidth it utilizes. Therefore, you should always enable bitmap caching.

The presets in the *Choose your connection speed to optimize performance* dropdown list enable you to select various combinations of features based on the speed of the client/terminal server connection. Table 9-4 lists these presets and their respective features. However, even on a fast network, you should disable some of the features to minimize the amount of bandwidth consumed by each terminal session. To configure your own combination of features, select Custom in the dropdown list.

Table 9-4

RDC Performance Presets

	MODEM (28.8 KBPS)	MODEM (56 KBPS)	BROADBAND (128 KBPS–1.5 MBPS)	LAN (10 MBPS OR HIGHER)
Desktop background				X
Font smoothing				X
Desktop composition			X	X
Show contents of window while dragging			X	X
Menu and window animation			X	X
Themes		X	X	X
Bitmap caching	X	X	X	X

 For information on configuring the settings that appear on the Advanced tab of the Remote Desktop Connection client, see Lesson 10, "Using the Terminal Services Gateway."

Creating an RDP File

RDP files store Remote Desktop Client settings in a recallable and portable form.

After you configure the settings in the RDC client, you can save them as a file with an rdp extension to avoid reconfiguring them each time you connect to that particular terminal server. To create an RDP file, use the following procedure.

 CREATE AN RDP FILE

GET READY. Log on to Windows Server 2008. When the logon process is completed, close the Initial Configuration Tasks window and any other windows that appear.

1. Click **Start**, and then click **All Programs** > **Accessories** > **Remote Desktop Connection**. The Remote Desktop Connection dialog box appears.
2. Click **Options**. The Remote Desktop Connection dialog box expands.
3. Configure the options on any or all of the tabs in the Remote Desktop Connection dialog box.
4. Click the **General** tab.
5. Click **Save As**. A Save As dialog box appears.
6. Specify a name for the RDP file and click **Save**.
7. Click **Connect** to establish a terminal server connection or **Cancel** to close the dialog box.

After you have created an RDP file, you can use it in several ways to initiate a terminal session, including the following:

- Load the RDP file into the RDC client by clicking Open on the General tab.
- Double-click the RDP file in any Windows Explorer window.
- Create a shortcut or a batch file loading the RDP file and place it in a user's Startup folder.

Using Mstsc.exe Command-Line Parameters

The executable program file for the RDC client, *Mstsc.exe*, is located in the C:\Windows\System32 folder by default.

When you run the Mstsc.exe program with no parameters, the Remote Desktop Connection window appears with its default settings intact. However, you can use parameters on the Mstsc.exe command line to control the behavior of the client. These command-line parameters are as follows:

```
Mstsc [filename] [/v:servername:portnumber] [/admin] [/f]
[/w:pixels /h:pixels] [/public] [/span] [/edit filename]
[/migrate]
```

- *filename*—Specifies the name of an RDP file that the program will use to establish a terminal server connection.
- /v:*servername:portnumber*—Specifies the name or IP address of the terminal server to which you want to connect and, optionally, the port number of a terminal server that is using a port other than 3389.
- /admin—Configures the RDC client to connect to the console session of the specified terminal server, that is, the session being used to locally administer the server.
- /f—Starts the terminal session in full screen mode.
- /w:*pixels* /h:*pixels*—Specifies the width and height of the Remote Desktop Connection session window in pixels.
- /public—Establishes a connection to the specified terminal server in a mode suitable for use on a computer in a public place that does not cache passwords or bitmaps.
- /span—Causes the RDC client to open a terminal session window that occupies the entire virtual desktop of a system with two or more monitors. The monitors must be the same size and be placed side-by-side.
- /edit *filename*—Opens a specified RDP file for editing in the Remote Desktop Connection dialog box. To save any changes you make to the settings, click Save on the General tab.
- /migrate—Converts connection files created with the Client Connection Manager utility to RDP files.

TAKE NOTE*

In previous Terminal Services implementations, you could use Mstsc.exe with the /console switch to connect the RDC client to the default session 0 on the terminal server. In Windows Server 2008, however, the /console switch has been deprecated and replaced by the /admin switch.

Configuring Client Settings on a Terminal Server

In addition to configuring the RDC client interactively, terminal server administrators can set client limitations on the server itself.

To configure RDC client settings on a terminal server, use the following procedure.

 CONFIGURE CLIENT SETTINGS ON A TERMINAL SERVER

GET READY. Log on to Windows Server 2008 using an account with administrative privileges. When the logon process is completed, close the Initial Configuration Tasks window and any other windows that appear.

1. Click **Start**, and then click **All Programs** > **Administrative Tools** > **Terminal Services** > **Terminal Services Configuration**. The Terminal Services Configuration console appears, as shown in Figure 9-9.

Figure 9-9

The Terminal Services Configuration console

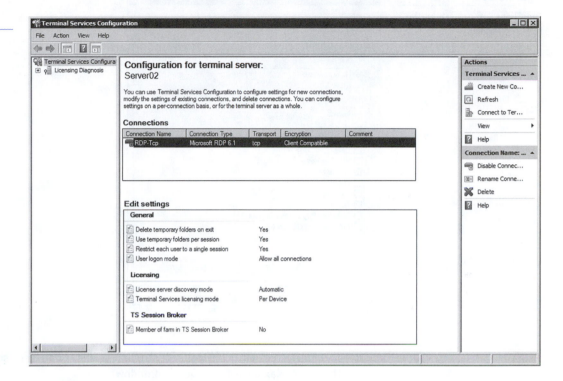

2. In the Connection list, right-click the **RDP-Tcp** connection and, from the context menu, select **Properties**. The RDP-Tcp Properties sheet appears, as shown in Figure 9-10.

Figure 9-10

The RDP-Tcp Properties sheet

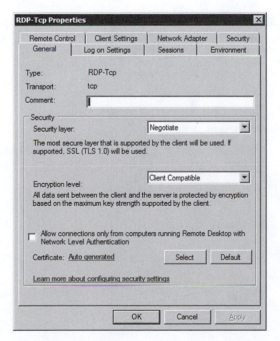

3. Click the **Client Settings** tab, as shown in Figure 9-11.

Figure 9-11

The Client Settings tab on the
RDP-Tcp Properties sheet

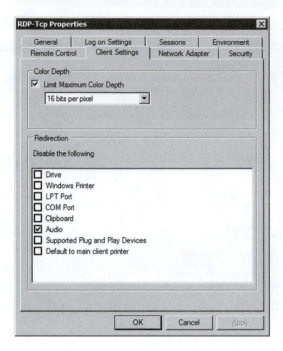

4. To modify the maximum color depth that a client can use, select a setting from the Limit Maximum Color Depth dropdown list.

5. To disable the redirection of client devices to the terminal session, select any or all of the checkboxes in the Redirection box.

6. Click the **Environment** tab, as shown in Figure 9-12.

Figure 9-12

The Environment tab on the
RDP-Tcp Properties sheet

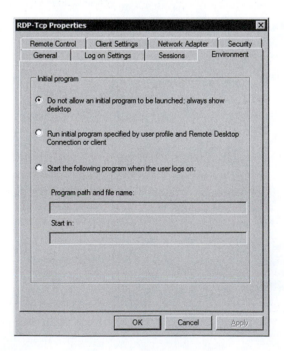

7. To configure the Programs options at the server level, select one of the following options:

- Do not allow an initial program to be launched; always show desktop—Overrides the RDC Programs settings and prevents applications from launching automatically.

- Run initial programs specified by user profile and Remote Desktop Connection or client—Enables the RDC client to use its Programs settings or the user profile settings.

- Start the following program when the user logs on—Overrides the RDC Programs settings and causes all clients to run the specified program.

8. Click **OK**.

CLOSE the Terminal Services Configuration console.

These settings enable administrators to exercise control over the client environment and the amount of bandwidth clients use without configuring each workstation individually.

Configuring RDC Options Using Group Policy

While Terminal Services administrators can control client behavior by configuring the Remote Desktop Connection program manually, this is not a practical solution for a large installation. Instead, administrators can use Group Policy to control many aspects of Terminal Services client behavior.

The Terminal Services Group Policy settings, as listed in Table 9-5, are located in the Administrative Templates/Windows Components/Terminal Services folders in both the Computer Configuration and User Configuration nodes.

Table 9-5

Terminal Services Group Policy Settings

GROUP POLICY SETTING	COMPUTER OR USER CONFIGURATION	DESCRIPTION
Remote Desktop Connection Client/Allow .rdp files from valid publishers and user's default .rdp settings	Both	By default, clients can run RDC with their default settings or with RDP files signed using a valid certificate. Disabling this setting prevents clients from doing both of these things.
Remote Desktop Connection Client/Allow .rdp files from unknown publishers	Both	By default, clients can run RDC with unsigned RDP files. Disabling this setting prevents clients from doing this.
Remote Desktop Connection Client/Do not allow passwords to be saved	Both	Controls whether RDC clients can save user passwords. For installations where users share computers, enabling this setting prevents users from using other users' passwords.
Remote Desktop Connection Client/ Specify SHA1 thumbprints of certificates representing trusted .rdp publishers	Both	Enables you to specify trusted RDP file publishers by entering their thumbprints. This setting enables you to restrict clients to specific RDP files.
Remote Desktop Connection Client/ Prompt for credentials on the client computer	Computer	Specifies which computer should prompt the user for authentication credentials, the client or the terminal server. The client can prompt for credentials only on Windows Vista and Windows Server 2008 computers.
Remote Desktop Connection Client/ Configure server authentication for client	Computer	Enables you to specify whether a client is allowed to connect to the terminal server when server authentication fails.

(continued)

Table 9-5 (*continued*)

GROUP POLICY SETTING	COMPUTER OR USER CONFIGURATION	DESCRIPTION
Terminal Server/Connections/Automatic reconnection	Computer	Specifies whether clients should attempt to automatically reconnect to a terminal server when their network connections are interrupted. This behavior is enabled in the client by default.
Terminal Server/Connections/Allow users to connect remotely using Terminal Services	Computer	Specifies whether clients can connect to the computer using Terminal Services. This setting enables you to disable Terminal Services and Remote Desktop capability on specific computers.
Terminal Server/Connections/Deny logoff to an administrator logged in to the console session	Computer	Prevents one administrator from being forcibly logged off by another administrator trying to connect to the same terminal server.
Terminal Server/Connections/Configure keep-alive connection interval	Computer	Specifies the amount of time that must elapse before an unused session reverts to a disconnected state. This prevents sessions from remaining active after the client is physically disconnected.
Terminal Server/Connections/Limit number of connections	Computer	Specifies the maximum number of clients that can connect to a terminal server. This setting enables you to limit the amount of system resources and network bandwidth devoted to Terminal Services.
Terminal Server/Connections/Set rules for remote control of Terminal Services user sessions	Both	Enables you to specify the level of remote control permitted by Terminal Services. This setting enables you to limit remote control capability to View Session only, for demonstration purposes.
Terminal Server/Connections/Allow remote start of unlisted programs	Computer	Specifies whether clients are limited to starting programs in the RemoteApp Programs list. This setting enables you to prevent clients from running other programs available from the terminal session desktop.
Terminal Server/Device and Resource Redirection/Allow audio redirection	Computer	Controls redirection of audio from the terminal server to the client.
Terminal Server/Device and Resource Redirection/Do not allow clipboard redirection	Both	Controls redirection of clipboard data between the terminal server and the client.
Terminal Server/Device and Resource Redirection/Do not allow COM port redirection	Computer	Controls redirection of the client COM ports to the terminal session.
Terminal Server/Device and Resource Redirection/Do not allow drive redirection	Computer	Controls redirection of the client drives to the terminal session.
Terminal Server/Device and Resource Redirection/Do not allow LPT port redirection	Computer	Controls redirection of the client LPT ports to the terminal session.
Terminal Server/Device and Resource Redirection/Do not allow supported Plug and Play device redirection	Computer	Controls redirection of client Plug and Play devices to the terminal session.
Terminal Server/Device and Resource Redirection/Do not allow smart card device redirection	Computer	Controls redirection of the client's smart card device to the terminal session.

(*continued*)

Table 9-5 (continued)

GROUP POLICY SETTING	COMPUTER OR USER CONFIGURATION	DESCRIPTION
Terminal Server/Device and Resource Redirection/Allow time zone redirection	Both	Controls redirection of the client time zone information to the terminal session.
Terminal Server/Licensing/Use the specified Terminal Services license servers	Computer	Enables you to specify the TS Licensing server that the client should use.
Terminal Server/Licensing/Hide notifications about TS Licensing problems that affect the terminal server	Computer	Enables you to suppress TS Licensing notifications on the terminal server.
Terminal Server/Licensing/Set the terminal services licensing mode	Computer	Specifies whether the terminal server should use Per Device or Per User licenses.
Terminal Server/Printer Redirection/Do not set default client printer to be default printer in a session	Computer	Specifies whether the terminal session should use the client computer's default printer as its default.
Terminal Server/Printer Redirection/Do not allow client printer redirection	Computer	Controls redirection of the client's printers to the terminal session.
Terminal Server/Printer Redirection/Specify terminal server fallback printer driver behavior	Computer	Specifies the behavior of the terminal server when Easy Print is disabled and the server cannot locate a printer driver to match the one on the client computer.
Terminal Server/Printer Redirection/Use Terminal Services Easy Print driver first	Both	This setting enables you to disable the Easy Print feature, causing the terminal server to try to locate a printer driver that matches the one on the client computer.
Terminal Server/Printer Redirection/ Redirect only the default client printer	Both	Limits printer redirection to the default printer only.
Terminal Server/Profiles/Set TS User Home Directory	Computer	Specifies the location of the user's home directory when connected to a terminal server.
Terminal Server/Profiles/Use mandatory profiles on the terminal server	Computer	Specifies whether clients should use a mandatory user profile, that is, one that the user cannot modify.
Terminal Server/Profiles/Set path for TS Roaming User Profile	Computer	Specifies the location on the network for users' profiles.
Terminal Server/Remote Session Environment/Limit maximum color depth	Computer	Enables you to limit the amount of network bandwidth devoted to color depth information.
Terminal Server/Remote Session Environment/Enforce Removal of Remote Desktop Wallpaper	Computer	Enables you to override the client settings and suppress the display of desktop wallpaper in terminal sessions.
Terminal Server/Remote Session Environment/Remove Remote Desktop Wallpaper	User	Enables you to override the client settings and suppress the display of desktop wallpaper in terminal sessions.
Terminal Server/Remote Session Environment/Remove "Disconnect" option from Shut Down dialog	Computer	Control whether clients can use the Shut Down Windows dialog box to disconnect from a terminal server.
Terminal Server/Remote Session Environment/Remove Windows Security item from Start menu	Computer	Removes the Windows Security item from the Start menu on client computers, preventing users from disconnecting terminal sessions accidentally.

(continued)

Table 9-5 (*continued*)

GROUP POLICY SETTING	COMPUTER OR USER CONFIGURATION	DESCRIPTION
Terminal Server/Remote Session Environment/Set compression algorithm for RDP data	Computer	Enables you to balance the trade-off between client memory and network bandwidth utilization by specifying which compression algorithm the client should use.
Terminal Server/Remote Session Environment/Start a program on connection	Both	Enables you to specify whether a client should run a program on connecting to a terminal server, overriding the Programs settings in the RDC client.
Terminal Server/Remote Session Environment/Always show desktop on connection	Computer	Specifies whether a specified program can run when a client connects to a terminal server.
Terminal Server/Security/Server Authentication Certificate Template	Computer	Requires Server Authentication to use a certificate created using the specified certificate template.
Terminal Server/Security/Set client connection encryption level	Computer	Specifies whether the client/terminal server connection should use 128-bit encryption or the highest level of encryption supported by the client.
Terminal Server/Security/Always prompt for password upon connection	Computer	Specifies whether the terminal server will prompt the user for logon credentials, even if the user already completed a client-side authentication.
Terminal Server/Security/Require secure RPC communication	Computer	Enables you to ensure the security of terminal server connections by requiring authentication and encryption.
Terminal Server/Security/Require use of specific security layer for remote (RDP) connections	Computer	Specifies the type of security that clients should use when connecting to terminal servers.
Terminal Server/Security/Do not allow local administrators to customize permissions	Computer	Specifies whether administrators can modify the Permissions settings in the Terminal Services configuration console.
Terminal Server/Security/Require user authentication for remote connections by using Network Level Authentication	Computer	Specifies whether clients should use Network Level Authentication when connecting to terminal servers.
Terminal Server/Session Time Limits/Set time limit for disconnected sessions	Both	Specifies how long a disconnected session remains active on a terminal server.
Terminal Server/Session Time Limits/Set time limit for active but idle Terminal Services sessions	User	Specifies how long a terminal session can remain idle before it is disconnected.
Terminal Server/Session Time Limits/Set time limit for active Terminal Services sessions	Both	Specifies how long a terminal session can remain active before it is disconnected.
Terminal Server/Session Time Limits/Terminate session when time limits are reached	Both	Causes terminal servers to terminate timed-out sessions rather than disconnecting them.
Terminal Server/Session Time Limits/Set time limit for logoff of RemoteApp sessions	Both	Specifies how long a RemoteApp session remains in a disconnected state before it is logged off from the terminal server.

■ Understanding Terminal Services Licensing

THE BOTTOM LINE
To facilitate the deployment of your terminal servers and clients, Windows Server 2008 provides a grace period during which clients can connect to a terminal server. It begins when the first client connects to the terminal server and lasts a maximum of 120 days. After the grace period has expired, all clients must have a license to connect to the terminal server.

Windows Server 2008 includes a limited form of Terminal Services that you can use for remote administration, whether you install the Terminal Services role or not. This feature enables up to two users to connect to the server, using the Remote Desktop Connection client, with no licenses or restrictions. To use the Terminal Services role for multiple user connections, you must purchase the appropriate number of ***Terminal Services client access licenses (TS CALs)*** and install a ***TS Licensing server*** to deploy them. A client access license (CAL) is a document that grants a single client access to a specific software program, in this case, a Terminal Services server.

When a client without a TS CAL attempts to connect, the terminal server directs it to the TS Licensing server, which issues a permanent license. If a TS Licensing server is not available or if the TS Licensing server does not have available TS CALs, the connection attempt fails.

Planning a TS Licensing Deployment

A Terminal Services deployment needs only one TS Licensing server for the entire installation regardless of the number of terminal servers on your network.

The process of installing a TS Licensing server and preparing it for use consists of the following basic steps:

1. Install the TS Licensing role service.
2. Activate the TS Licensing server.
3. Install the TS CALs on the TS Licensing server.
4. Configure the licensing settings on the terminal servers.

CERTIFICATION READY?
Configure Terminal
Services licensing
2.5

The resource requirements for the TS Licensing role service are minimal. TS Licensing does not check whether a client possesses a license; the Terminal Services service performs that task. The TS Licensing service requires only about 10 megabytes of memory and the license database requires one megabyte of storage space for every 1,200 licenses. The processor requirements are negligible because the service issues a license to each client only once.

⊕ **MORE INFORMATION**

The TS Licensing role service included with Windows Server 2008 can provide licensing services for terminal servers running on Windows Server 2003 and Windows 2000 Server computers. However, a down-level server cannot provide licensing services for Windows Server 2008 terminal servers. If you are running a Windows Server 2008 terminal server, you must install a Windows Server 2008 TS Licensing server.

When planning a TS Licensing server deployment, you must consider how your terminal servers will locate the licensing server. While it is possible to manually configure each terminal server with the name or IP address of a specific TS Licensing server, automatic licensing server detection is a more convenient alternative.

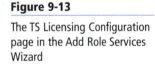

To issue licenses to clients in other domains, the computer running the license server must be a member of the Terminal Server License Servers group in each domain.

When clients trying to connect to a terminal server require licenses, the terminal server attempts to discover a TS Licensing server in the following order:

1. A licensing server specified in the terminal server configuration or a Group Policy setting.
2. A licensing server installed on the same computer as the terminal server.
3. A license server that is published in the Active Directory database.
4. A license server running on a domain controller in the terminal server's domain.

For a small Terminal Services deployment, you can run the TS Licensing role service on the same computer as the other Terminal Services role services. A terminal server can always locate a TS Licensing server running on the same computer. For larger deployments with multiple terminal servers, you can install TS Licensing on one of the terminal servers or any other server.

Another important part of the Terminal Services planning process is deciding whether you want the TS Licensing server to issue Per Device or Per User TS CALs. The license types are the same as those used for Windows Server 2008 clients. You can issue Per Device licenses that enable any user working at a licensed computer to access terminal servers, or Per User licenses that enable specific users to access terminal servers with any computer. After you decide which type of licenses to use, you must purchase the appropriate type and configure your terminal servers to accept it.

Deploying a TS Licensing Server

To deploy a TS Licensing server, you must run the Server Manager console, add the Terminal Services role, and select the TS Licensing role service.

When you add the TS Licensing role service, a TS Licensing page appears in the Add Role Services Wizard, as shown in Figure 9-13.

Figure 9-13

The TS Licensing Configuration page in the Add Role Services Wizard

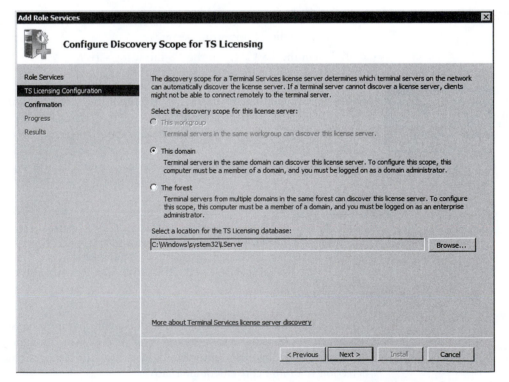

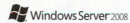

When you install the TS Licensing role service, you must specify the server's discovery scope, by selecting one of the following options.

- **Workgroup.** Enables terminal servers to discover a licensing server that is a member of the same workgroup. This is the only option for a computer that is not a member of a domain; it is not an option for domain members.
- **Domain.** Enables terminal servers that are domain members to discover a licensing server that is running on a domain controller in the same domain. To select this option, you must be logged on to the domain using an account with domain administrator privileges.
- **Forest.** Publishes license server information in the Active Directory database, enabling terminal servers to discover licensing servers running on any computer in the same forest. Microsoft recommends this scope setting for domain members.

You can also specify an alternate location for the TS Licensing database, which appears by default in the C:\Windows\System32\LServer folder.

Activating a TS Licensing Server

After you install the TS Licensing role service, you must activate the licensing server before it can be fully functional.

An unactivated licensing server can issue only temporary, 90-day Per Device TS CALs or Per User TS CALs. When you activate the server, Microsoft issues it a digital certificate that certifies the identity of the server and its owner.

To activate a TS Licensing server, use the following procedure.

 ACTIVATE A TS LICENSING SERVER

GET READY. Log on to Windows Server 2008 using an account with Administrator privileges. When the logon process is completed, close the Initial Configuration Tasks window and any other windows that appear.

1. Click **Start**, and then click **All Programs** > **Administrative Tools** > **Terminal Services** > **TS Licensing Manager.** The TS Licensing Manager console appears, as shown in Figure 9-14.

Figure 9-14

The TS Licensing Manager console

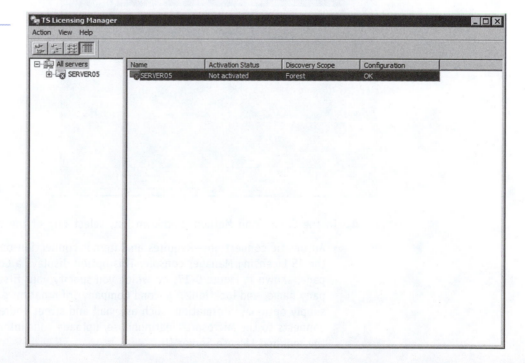

2. Right-click the server in the details pane and, from the context menu, select **Activate Server**. The Activate Server Wizard appears, as shown in Figure 9-15.

Figure 9-15

The Activate Server Wizard

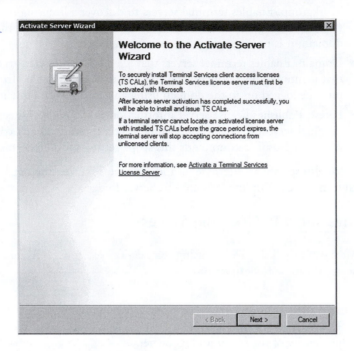

3. Click **Next** to bypass the Welcome page. The Connection Method page appears, as shown in Figure 9-16.

Figure 9-16

The Connection Method page

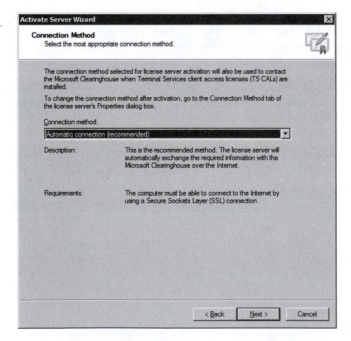

4. In the Connection Method dropdown list, select one of the following options.

- Automatic connection—Requires an Internet connection on the computer running the TS Licensing Manager console. This option displays a Company Information page, shown in Figure 9-17, on which you specify your first and last name, company name, and location. A second Company Information page enables you to supply optional information, such as email and street addresses. The console then connects to the Microsoft Clearinghouse, uploads your information, and downloads the required License Server ID.

Figure 9-17

The Company Information page

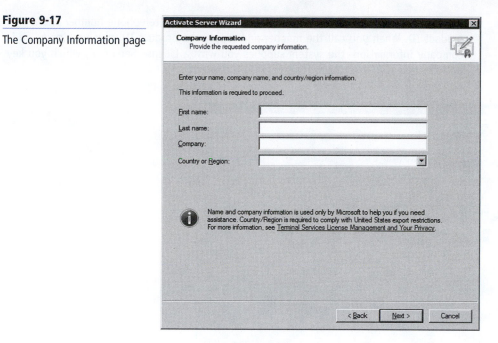

• Web browser—Requires an Internet connection on any computer. This option displays a License Server Activation page, shown in Figure 9-18, containing a hyperlink to a Microsoft activation Web site and a product ID. On any computer with an Internet connection, open the linked Web site, select **Activate a license server**, and supply the product ID and your name and company information. The Web site displays a License Server ID that you key into the License Server Activation page in the wizard.

Figure 9-18

The Web-based License Server Activation page

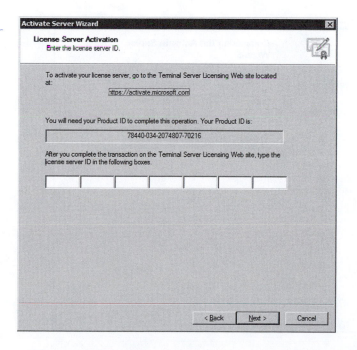

• Telephone—Requires a standard voice telephone line. This option displays a Country or Region Selection page, on which you select your location. A License Server Activation page then appears, as shown in Figure 9-19, specifying a telephone number and a product ID. When you call the number and supply the product ID, plus your name and company information, the system supplies you with a License Server ID, which you key into the License Server Activation page in the wizard.

Figure 9-19

The telephone-based License Server Activation page

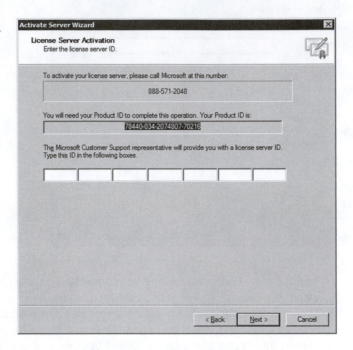

5. When the activation process is completed, click **Next**. The Completing the Activate Server Wizard page appears, as shown in Figure 9-20.

Figure 9-20

The Completing the Activate Server Wizard page

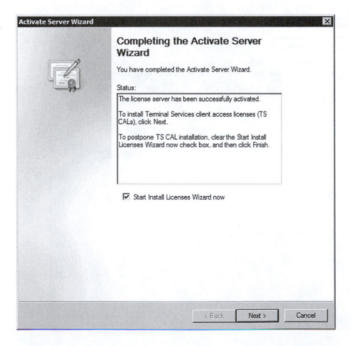

6. Clear the **Start Install Licenses Wizard now** checkbox. Then click **Finish**.

CLOSE the TS Licensing Manager console.

At this point, the TS Licensing server is activated and ready to have client access licenses installed.

Installing TS CALs

> Client access licenses are available from Microsoft through a number of channels, including retail License Packs and various volume licensing programs.

When you purchase TS CALs, you must select either Per Device or Per User licenses and configure your terminal servers accordingly. After you purchase the TS CALs, you must install them on the TS Licensing server so the server can distribute them to your clients.

To install the TS CALs you have purchased into the TS Licensing server, use the following procedure.

 **INSTALL TS CALS**

GET READY. Log on to Windows Server 2008 using an account with Administrator privileges. When the logon process is completed, close the Initial Configuration Tasks window and any other windows that appear.

1. Click **Start**, and then click **All Programs** > **Administrative Tools** > **Terminal Services** > **TS Licensing Manager.** The TS Licensing Manager console appears.
2. Right-click the server in the details pane and, from the context menu, select **Install Licenses.** The Install Licenses Wizard appears, as shown in Figure 9-21.

Figure 9-21

The Install Licenses Wizard

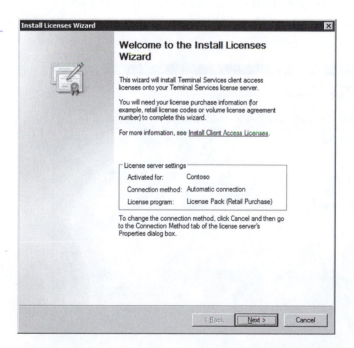

3. Click **Next** to bypass the Welcome page. The License Program page appears, as shown in Figure 9-22.

Figure 9-22

The License Program page

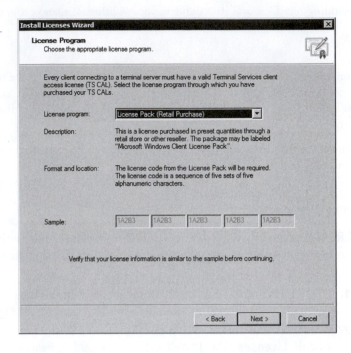

4. In the License Program dropdown list, select the method you used to purchase your TS CALs. The Sample field changes to display the format of the license number you should have received with your purchase.

5. Click **Next**. The License Code page appears, as shown in Figure 9-23.

Figure 9-23

The License Code page

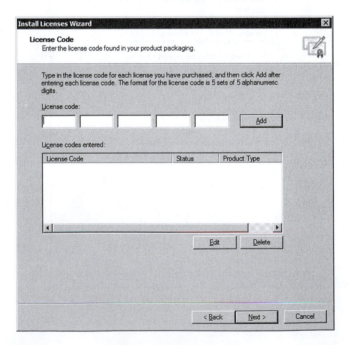

6. In the *License code* text boxes, key the license number you received with your TS CAL purchase and click **Add**. The number appears in the *License codes entered* box, as shown in Figure 9-24.

Figure 9-24

The License Code page, with license number

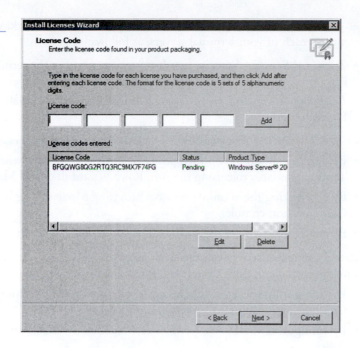

7. Click **Next**. The wizard verifies the license number you entered and the Completing the Install Licenses Wizard page appears, as shown in Figure 9-25.

Figure 9-25

The Completing the Install Licenses Wizard page

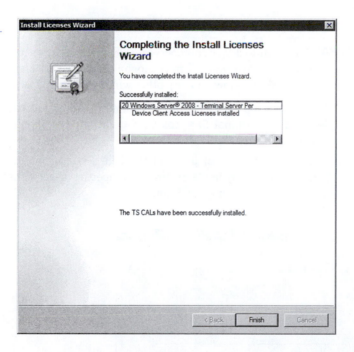

8. Click **Finish**. The licenses are now available for distribution by the TS Licensing server.

CLOSE the TS Licensing Manager console.

At this point the TS Licensing server is ready to distribute TS CALs to the Terminal Services clients that require them.

Configuring Terminal Server Licensing Settings

To utilize a TS Licensing server, terminal servers must identify the licensing server on the network.

After you have an operational TS Licensing server on your network, you must configure two elements on each of your terminal servers, as follows:

- **Terminal Services licensing mode**—Specifies whether the terminal server should issue Per Device or Per User licenses to clients attempting to connect.
- **Licensing server discovery mode**—Specifies how the terminal server will locate a TS Licensing server.

You can configure the Terminal Services licensing mode in three ways, which are as follows:

- By selecting an option on the Specify Licensing Mode page when you install the Terminal Services role using the Add Roles Wizard in Server Manager.
- By configuring the Terminal Services Licensing Mode setting in the Terminal Services Configuration console.
- By configuring the *Set the Terminal Services licensing mode* setting in Group Policy.

By default, terminal servers attempt to discover a licensing server automatically. You can use two methods to change this default behavior, which are as follows:

- By configuring the *Specify the license server discovery mode* setting in the Terminal Services Configuration console.
- By configuring the *Use the specified Terminal Services license servers* setting in Group Policy.

To configure the Terminal Services Licensing setting in the Terminal Services Configuration console, use the following procedure.

For more information on configuring the licensing mode during Terminal Services installation, see Lesson 8, "Using Terminal Services."

 CONFIGURE TERMINAL SERVER LICENSING SETTINGS

GET READY. Log on to a Windows Server 2008 terminal server using an account with Administrator privileges. When the logon process is completed, close the Initial Configuration Tasks window and any other windows that appear.

1. Click **Start**, and then click **All Programs** > **Administrative Tools** > **Terminal Services** > **Terminal Services Configuration**. The Terminal Services Configuration console appears.

2. In the details (middle) pane, in the Edit Settings box, double-click the **Terminal Services licensing mode** setting. A Properties sheet appears with the Licensing tab selected, as shown in Figure 9-26.

Figure 9-26

The Licensing tab on a terminal server's Properties sheet

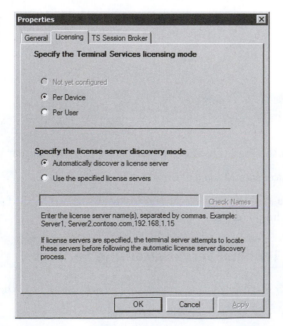

3. Under *Specify the Terminal Services licensing mode*, select **Per Device** or **Per User**. The option you select must correspond to the type of TS CALs you purchased and installed in your TS Licensing server.

   When you select a licensing mode, the *Specify the license server discovery mode* setting activates.

4. If you want to configure the terminal server to access a specific TS Licensing server, select the **Use the specified license servers** option. In the text box, key the name or address of the licensing server using an FQDN, a NetBIOS name, or an IP address.

   You can also specify multiple server names or addresses by separating them with commas.

5. Click **OK**.

CLOSE the Terminal Services Configuration console.

To test the connection between your terminal server and the TS Licensing server, select Licensing Diagnosis in the scope (left) pane of the Terminal Services Configuration console. After the terminal server detects the licensing server, the console should specify the number of TS CALs you have available, as shown in Figure 9-27.

Figure 9-27

The Licensing Diagnosis display in the Terminal Services Configuration console

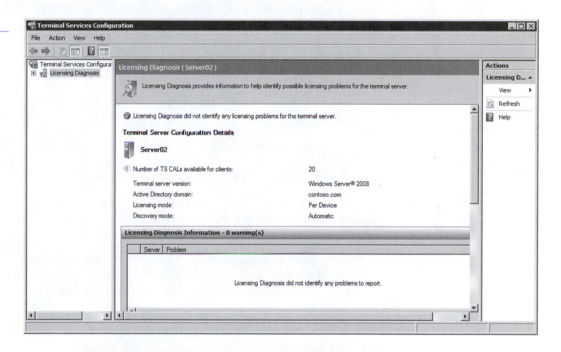

SUMMARY SKILL MATRIX

IN THIS LESSON YOU LEARNED:

- The primary platform for a Terminal Services client is a desktop PC running Windows Vista or Windows XP SP2, with the Remote Desktop Connection (RDC) 6.*x* client installed.

- To minimize the client hardware requirements, administrators should run all applications not included with the desktop operating system on terminal servers, with the sole exception of the RDC client program.

- Deploying applications on a large fleet of desktop computers is a complicated undertaking. The simplest, and perhaps the most time-consuming, method is to install each application on each desktop computer manually. For larger networks, automating the application installation process is nearly always preferable. However, deploying an application using Terminal Services requires you to install it only once on each terminal server, no matter how many clients will be running the application.

- Deploying applications using Terminal Services can drastically reduce the network bandwidth consumed by the client computers.

- Microsoft Remote Desktop Connection Client for Mac 2.0 is available as a free download, and third-party clients are available for Macintosh and UNIX/Linux computers.

- Thin clients require an operating system, just like any other computer, but they are not designed to run a full Windows installation. Operating system options include proprietary OSes, Windows CE, Window XPe, and Linux.

- The Remote Desktop Connection 6.1 client included with all versions of Windows Server 2008 supports all of the new Terminal Services features in Windows Server 2008.

- One of the long-term problems with Terminal Services is the confusion caused by having two separate desktops: one provided by the local operating system and one by the terminal server. You can configure the RDC client to completely overlap the local desktop with the one provided by the terminal server.

- Over the years, Microsoft has gradually developed the device redirection capabilities of the RDC client. With RDC 6.*x*, it is possible to use almost any device connected to the client computer in a terminal session.

- In Windows Server 2008 Terminal Services, a new feature called Easy Print eliminates the need for the printer driver on the terminal server.

- After you configure the settings in the RDC client, you can save them as a file with an rdp extension.

- In addition to configuring the RDC client interactively, terminal server administrators can set client limitations on the server. Administrators can also use Group Policy to control many aspects of Terminal Services client behavior.

- To use the Terminal Services role for multiple user connections, you must purchase the appropriate number of Terminal Services client access licenses (TS CALs) and install a TS Licensing server to deploy them.

- To facilitate the deployment of your terminal servers and clients, Windows Server 2008 provides a grace period during which clients can connect to a terminal server. This grace period begins when the first client connects to the terminal server and lasts a maximum of 120 days.

- When you install the TS Licensing role service, you must specify the server's discovery scope by selecting the workgroup, domain, or forest option.

- After you install the TS Licensing role service, you must activate the licensing server before it can be fully functional. When you activate the server, Microsoft issues it a digital certificate that certifies the identity of the server and its owner.

- When you purchase TS CALs, you must select either Per Device or Per User licenses and configure your terminal servers accordingly. After you purchase the TS CALs, you must install them on the TS Licensing server so the server can distribute them to your clients.

Knowledge Assessment

Matching

Complete the following exercise by matching the terms with their corresponding definitions.

a. Supports embedded Win32 applications

b. Not based on the NT kernel

c. Enables clients to connect to terminal servers indefinitely

d. Reduces network bandwidth consumption

e. Replaces a terminal server driver

f. Services multiple terminal servers

g. Converts Client Connection Manager files to RDP files

h. Also called anti-aliasing

i. Specifies whether to issue Per Device or Per User licenses

j. Specifies how to locate a TS Licensing server

_____ **1.** bitmap caching

_____ **2.** Terminal Services client access license (TS CAL)

_____ **3.** Easy Print

_____ **4.** font smoothing

_____ **5.** Licensing server discovery mode

_____ **6.** Mstsc.exe

_____ **7.** Terminal Services licensing mode

_____ **8.** TS Licensing server

_____ **9.** Windows CE

_____ **10.** Windows XPe

Multiple Choice

Select the correct answer for each of the following questions.

1. Which of the following thin client operating systems requires the least amount of hardware resources?
   - **a.** A proprietary OS
   - **b.** Windows CE
   - **c.** Windows XPe
   - **d.** Windows XP

2. Which of the following commands enables a Remote Desktop Connection terminal session to utilize two monitors?
   - **a.** mstsc /admin
   - **b.** mstsc /w:2048 /h:768
   - **c.** mstsc /span
   - **d.** mstsc /f

3. Which of the following TS Licensing discovery scope settings requires you to install the TS Licensing role service while logged on to a domain?
   - **a.** Workgroup only
   - **b.** Domain only
   - **c.** Forest only
   - **d.** Domain and Forest

4. Which of the following thin client operating systems cannot provide support for a local Internet browser?
   - **a.** A proprietary OS
   - **b.** Windows CE
   - **c.** Windows XPe
   - **d.** Windows XP

5. Which of the following Remote Desktop Protocol versions was the first to support Network Level Authentication?
   - **a.** 5.0
   - **b.** 5.2
   - **c.** 6.0
   - **d.** 6.1

6. What is the name of the process in which a TS Licensing server obtains a digital certificate from Microsoft?
   a. installation
   b. activation
   c. certification
   d. configuration

7. Which of the following tools can you use to configure client settings on a terminal server?
   a. TS Licensing Manager
   b. Terminal Services Manager
   c. TS RemoteApp Manager
   d. Terminal Services Configuration

8. Which of the following Remote Desktop Connection client display elements decreases network bandwidth consumption when activated?
   a. Desktop composition
   b. Bitmap caching
   c. Font smoothing
   d. Menu and window animation

9. The Easy Print feature in Remote Desktop Protocol 6.1 uses XPS as a replacement for which of the following?
   a. The printer-specific driver on the terminal server
   b. The printer-specific driver on the client computer
   c. The generic printer driver on the terminal server
   d. The generic printer driver on the client computer

10. When a Terminal Services installation does not have a TS Licensing server installed, clients can still connect to the terminal servers for _____ days.
   a. 10
   b. 30
   c. 90
   d. 120

Review Questions

1. List the four primary steps involved in deploying a TS Licensing server.

2. List three ways to configure the Terminal Services licensing mode setting.

■ Case Scenarios

Scenario 9-1: Accessing a Licensing Server

Wingtip Toys is installing three Windows Server 2008 terminal servers to provide their outside sales force with network access. The IT team also installed the TS Licensing role service on one of the three servers. Howard is responsible for the Terminal1 server, which also has TS Licensing installed. When he installed the TS Licensing server, Howard selected the Domain discovery scope option. He also configured Terminal1 to use the automatic license server discovery mode option. Richard installed Terminal2 and configured it to access a specific license server using Terminal1's IP address. Mark installed Terminal3, also using the automatic license server discovery mode option.

Which of the three servers will fail to locate the TS Licensing server and why? What must the IT team do to resolve the problem?

Scenario 9-2: Configuring the Remote Desktop Connection Client

Robert is experimenting with Windows Server 2008 Terminal Services on a lab network, attempting to gauge how much network bandwidth a terminal session utilizes. In one experiment, Robert configures the Remote Desktop Connection client to minimize its bandwidth utilization. On the Display tab, he sets the *Remote desktop size* slider to the minimum value and the color depth to 256 colors. On the Local Resources tab, he sets the *Remote computer sound* option to *Do not play*, and clears all of the *Local devices and resources* checkboxes. On the Experience tab, he clears all of the Performance checkboxes.

What can Robert do to minimize the client's bandwidth requirement even further?

10 LESSON

Using the Terminal Services Gateway

OBJECTIVE DOMAIN MATRIX

Technology Skill	Objective Domain	Objective Domain Number
Deploying a TS Gateway Server	Configure Terminal Services Gateway.	2.2

KEY TERMS

connection authorization policy (CAP)

resource authorization policy (RAP)

Terminal Services Gateway
Terminal Services (TS) Web Access

tunneling
virtual private networking (VPN)

In Lesson 9, "Configuring Terminal Services Clients," you learned how to configure client computers to access terminal servers using the Remote Desktop Connection client. You also learned in Lesson 8, "Using Terminal Services," how you can use the new RemoteApp features to deploy individual terminal server applications to client computers. However, Windows Server 2008 Terminal Services includes another new feature that enables clients to access terminal server desktops and launch RemoteApp applications directly from a Web page in Internet Explorer.

In this lesson, you learn about the following:

- Installing TS Web Access
- Publishing Terminal Services applications on Web sites
- Installing a TS Gateway server

▪ Using TS Web Access

THE BOTTOM LINE

Terminal Services (TS) Web Access is a role service that works with Internet Information Services (IIS) 7.0 to create an alternative client interface to your terminal servers.

The *Terminal Services (TS) Web Access* interface is particularly useful with RemoteApp because it enables users to launch applications by double-clicking icons on a Web page. Instead of creating RDP files and deploying them to clients using Group Policy or some other method, you can simply select a checkbox for the RemoteApp applications you want to deploy using TS Web Access, and the service adds the appropriate icons to its default Web page, as shown in Figure 10-1.

Figure 10-1

The default TS Web Access interface

TAKE NOTE *

You can also use TS Web Access with the TS Gateway role service to provide Internet users with secure access to terminal server applications behind a corporate firewall. For more information, see "Using Terminal Services Gateway," later in this lesson.

Installing TS Web Access

To install TS Web Access on a Windows Server 2008 computer, you must use Server Manager to add the Terminal Services role, and then select the TS Web Access role service.

X REF

For more information on the components of the TS Web Access role service, see Table 8-2 in Lesson 8, "Using Terminal Services."

You can install TS Web Access on the same computer as the other Terminal Services role services, or on a separate computer. When you install TS Web Access on a computer that is not a terminal server, you must configure it later to access the resources of another Windows Server 2008 computer that is a terminal server.

TS Web Access requires Internet Information Services 7.0 to run and IIS 7, in turn, requires the Windows Process Activation Service. If you have not installed these components on your computer, the Add Roles Wizard prompts you to add the Web Server (IIS) role and the Windows Process Activation Service feature, as shown in Figure 10-2.

Figure 10-2

The Add role services and features required for TS Web Access? dialog box

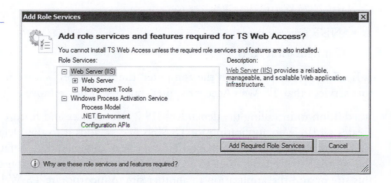

➕ MORE INFORMATION

The ability to install TS Web Access on a server other than a terminal server is particularly useful if you plan to deploy Terminal Services applications to users on the Internet. Many organizations run their Web servers on perimeter networks separated from their internal servers by a firewall. With Windows Server 2008 Terminal Services, you can install your terminal servers on an internal network and add TS Web Access to a separate Web server on a perimeter network.

The IIS 7 configuration that TS Web Access requires includes many role services and features. TS Web Access requires the following Web Server (IIS) role services:

- Common HTTP Features
  - Default Document
  - Directory Browsing
  - HTTP Errors
  - HTTP Redirection
  - Static Content
- Application Development
  - ASP .NET
  - Internet Server Application Programming Interface (ISAPI) Extensions
  - ISAPI Filters
  - .NET Extensibility
- Security
  - Request Filtering
  - Windows Authentication
- Health and Diagnostics
  - HTTP Logging
  - Logging Tools
  - Request Monitor
  - Tracing
- Performance
  - Static Content Compression
- Management Tools
  - IIS 6 Management Compatibility\IIS 6 Metabase Compatibility
  - IIS Management Console

TS Web Access requires the following Windows Process Activation Service features:

- Process Model
- .NET Environment
- Configuration APIs

If IIS 7 is already present on the computer, the Add Roles Wizard will install any additional role services that TS Web Access requires, but it will not remove existing role services.

In addition to installing the dependent IIS 7 role services and features, the Add Roles Wizard creates an IIS Web application for TS Web Access, adds it to the Default Web site, and assigns to it the URL http://*servername*/ts. This application generates a default Web page containing the controls that enable users to access terminal server features. You can, of course, modify this site or add the application to another site to incorporate TS Web Access functionality into your existing Web content.

X REF

For more information on IIS 7 role services and their functions, see Lesson 5, "Deploying IIS Services."

Configuring TS Web Access Properties

If you install the TS Web Access role service on the same computer as the Terminal Server role service, the Add Roles Wizard automatically populates the TS Web Access Web page with the RemoteApp applications and terminal services desktops hosted by the local server. To use TS Web Access with a terminal server running on another Windows Server 2008 computer, you must configure both computers to work together.

For TS Web Access to deploy terminal server sessions from another computer, it must have the appropriate permissions. Therefore, you must add the TS Web Access computer to the TS Web Access Computers local security group on the terminal server computer, using the following procedure.

 CONFIGURE A TERMINAL SERVER TO USE TS WEB ACCESS

GET READY. Log on to your Windows Server 2008 terminal server using an account with administrative privileges. When the logon process is completed, close the Initial Configuration Tasks window and any other windows that appear.

1. Click **Start**, and then click **Administrative Tools** > **Computer Management**. The Computer Management console appears, as shown in Figure 10-3.

Figure 10-3

The Computer Management console

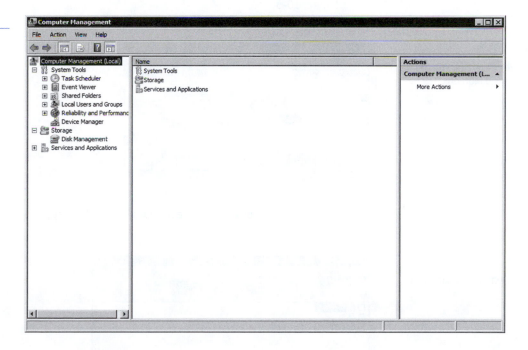

2. In the scope (left) pane, expand the **Local Users and Groups** node and select the **Groups** folder.

3. Double-click the **TS Web Access Computers** security group. The TS Web Access Computers Properties sheet appears, as shown in Figure 10-4.

Figure 10-4

The TS Web Access Computers Properties sheet

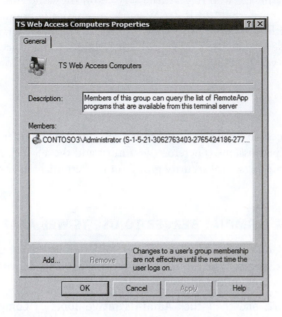

4. Click **Add**. The Select Users, Computers, or Groups dialog box appears, as shown in Figure 10-5.

Figure 10-5

The Select Users, Computers, or Groups dialog box

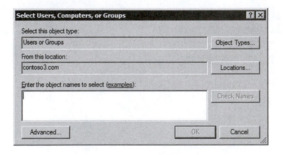

5. Click **Object Types**. The Object Types dialog box appears, as shown in Figure 10-6.

Figure 10-6

The Object Types dialog box

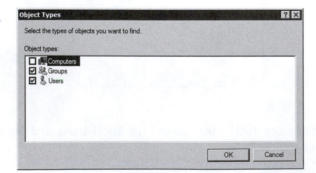

6. Select the **Computers** checkbox and click **OK**.

7. In the Select Users, Computers, or Groups dialog box, in the *Enter the object names to select* text box, key the name of the computer running the TS Web Access role service and click **OK**. The server name appears in the Members list on the TS Web Access Computers Properties sheet.

8. Click **OK**.

CLOSE the Computer Management console.

After the TS Web Access computer has the permissions needed to access the terminal server, you can configure TS Web Access to access the terminal server using the following procedure.

CONFIGURE TS WEB ACCESS TO USE AN EXTERNAL TERMINAL SERVER

GET READY. Log on to your Windows Server 2008 TS Web Access server using an account with administrative privileges. When the logon process is completed, close the Initial Configuration Tasks window and any other windows that appear.

1. Click **Start**, and then click **Administrative Tools** > **Terminal Services** > **TS Web Access Administration**. An Internet Explorer window appears, showing the TS Web Access Configuration Web page, as shown in Figure 10-7.

Figure 10-7

The Configuration interface on the TS Web Access home page

2. In the Terminal Server Name text box, key the name of the Windows Server 2008 terminal server to use with TS Web Access.

3. Click **Apply**.

CLOSE the Internet Explorer window.

At this point, the TS Web Access server can publish the terminal server's applications on the default Web page.

Publishing Terminal Server Resources on the Web

TS Web Access enables you to publish terminal server desktops and RemoteApp programs on Web pages. The following sections discuss the procedures for configuring terminal servers to supply their resources to TS Web Access.

PUBLISHING REMOTEAPP APPLICATIONS

TS Web Access can simplify the process of deploying RemoteApp applications to your clients by publishing them on your Web site. When you add applications to the RemoteApp Programs list in the TS RemoteApp Manager console, you must select the *RemoteApp program is available through TS Web Access* checkbox (shown in Figure 10-8) on the Properties sheet for each application that you want to appear on the TS Web Access Web page.

Figure 10-8

A RemoteApp Program's Properties sheet

After you install and configure the TS Web Access role service, all of the selected applications in the RemoteApp Programs list on the terminal server appear on the TS Web Access home page.

PUBLISHING A TERMINAL SERVER DESKTOP

In addition to RemoteApp programs, TS Web Access can provide clients with access to standard terminal server desktops. To configure a terminal server to display a remote access icon on the TS Web Access Web page, use the following procedure.

 PUBLISH A TERMINAL SERVER DESKTOP

GET READY. Log on to your Windows Server 2008 terminal server using an account with administrative privileges. When the logon process is completed, close the Initial Configuration Tasks window and any other windows that appear.

1. Click **Start**, and then click **Administrative Tools** > **Terminal Services** > **TS RemoteApp Manager**. The TS RemoteApp Manager console appears, as shown in Figure 10-9.
2. In the actions pane, click **Terminal Server Settings**. The RemoteApp Deployment Settings dialog box appears, as shown in Figure 10-10.
3. In the Remote Desktop Access box, select the **Show a remote desktop connection to this terminal server in TS Web Access** checkbox.
4. Click **OK**.

CLOSE the TS RemoteApp Manager console.

At this point, a Remote Desktop icon appears on the RemoteApp Programs page of the TS Web Access Web site.

TAKE NOTE*

Although it uses a different client interface, TS Web Access uses the same connection technology as the Remote Desktop Connection client, and the user requirements are identical. For a client to open a terminal session using TS Web Access, the user must be a member of the Remote Desktop Users group on the terminal server computer.

Figure 10-9

The TS RemoteApp Manager console

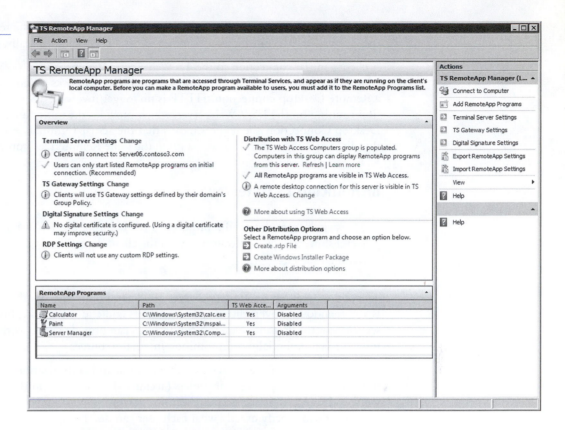

Figure 10-10

The RemoteApp Deployment Settings dialog box

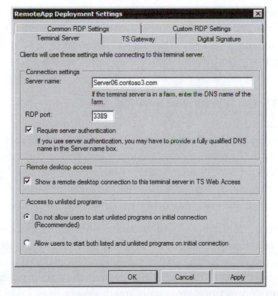

■ Using Terminal Services Gateway

THE BOTTOM LINE

Terminal Services Gateway is a new Windows Server 2008 Terminal Services role service that enables Internet users to access terminal servers on private networks, despite intervening firewalls and network access translation (NAT) servers. This section explains how TS Gateway works and how to configure terminal servers and clients to use it.

TS Web Access enables clients to connect to Windows Server 2008 terminal services using a Web browser. It might appear as though the computer is using a standard Hypertext Transfer Protocol (HTTP) connection to run RemoteApp programs and remote desktops. This would mean that TS Web Access could enable any client to connect to the terminal server, whether the client is located on the same intranet or on the Internet. Actually, this is not the case.

A client's initial connection to the TS Web Access Web page involves a standard HTTP connection using port TCP 80. However, after the user clicks a RemoteApp icon or establishes a Remote Desktop connection, HTTP is no longer involved. TS Web Access is an application running on the IIS 7 Web server, which provides the same functionality as the Remote Desktop Connection client. This means that the actual Terminal Services connection between the client and the terminal server is using the same Remote Desktop Protocol traffic as an RDC/terminal server connection.

Introducing TS Gateway

The switch from the HTTP protocol to RDP during the TS Web Access connection establishment process is transparent to the client, but it is critical to the security of the terminal server.

The ability to access a Windows Server 2008 computer from another location on the network is a tremendous convenience to administrators and end users alike, but it can be an alarming security hazard. Remote Desktop connections can provide clients with full control over a terminal server, potentially compromising internal resources.

Controlling the Terminal Services authentication and authorization processes protects terminal servers from potential intruders (accidental or not) within the organization. In other words, administrators use account security to control who can access a terminal server and permissions to specify exactly what each user can do.

Fortunately, protecting terminal servers from Internet intrusion is not a special consideration because the port number that the RDP protocol uses (TCP port 3389) is blocked by default on most firewalls. This means that Internet users might be able to connect to the TS Web Access Web page using port 80 (assuming the Web server is accessible from the Internet), but they are not able to connect to port 3389 to launch a terminal server application.

COMPARING TS GATEWAY WITH VPNs

But what about administrators who want to provide Internet users with access to terminal servers? As mentioned in Lesson 8, this could be an extremely useful capability. Generally, the technology of choice for remote network access has, in recent years, been *virtual private networking (VPN)*. In a VPN connection, computers use a technique called *tunneling*, which encapsulates an entire client/server session within another protocol. Because another protocol carries the internal, or payload, protocol, it is protected from most standard forms of attack.

One of the inherent problems with VPN connections is the amount of bandwidth they require. A VPN connection between an Internet user and a host network requires slightly more bandwidth than a standard LAN connection. Typically, the client and server must exchange application and/or document files, which in some cases can be extremely large. However, Internet connections are usually much slower than LAN connections. A broadband Internet connection typically provides satisfactory performance for most network applications, but VPN over a dial-up connection can be an extremely slow and frustrating experience.

Because Terminal Services clients and servers exchange a minimal amount of data, however, a terminal server connection can function well over a low-bandwidth connection such as a dial-up. This makes Terminal Services a good solution for Internet client connections. The biggest problem, of course, is security. Opening port 3389 in your Internet firewall enables remote clients to access your terminal servers but invites abuse.

The TS Gateway role service enables Terminal Services to support Internet clients securely using the same tunneling concept as a VPN connection; except in this case, the computers encapsulate RDP traffic within Secure Sockets Layer (SSL) packets. SSL uses TCP port number 443, which most organizations with an Internet presence leave open in their firewalls so Internet clients can establish secure connections to their Web servers.

Deploying a TS Gateway Server

The TS Gateway role service is essentially a tunnel through your network's defenses, which enables specific users on the Internet to pass through your firewalls, proxy servers, NAT routers, and other protective devices to reach the terminal servers on your private, internal network.

TS Gateway must run on a computer that is accessible to the Internet and your internal network. This area of dual accessibility is called a perimeter network, as shown in Figure 10-11.

Figure 10-11

A TS Gateway server on a perimeter network

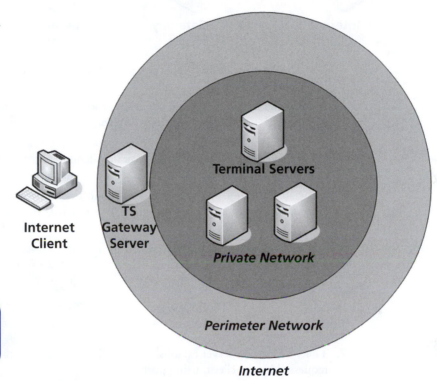

CERTIFICATION READY?
Configure Terminal
Services Gateway
2.2

A typical TS Gateway deployment consists of three basic elements: Internet clients, a TS Gateway server, and terminal servers, the latter of which can use the Terminal Services role or Remote Desktop. Table 10-1 lists these three elements and their characteristics.

Table 10-1

Components of a TS Gateway Deployment

	CLIENTS	TS GATEWAY SERVER	TERMINAL SERVERS
Supported Operating Systems	• Windows Vista • Windows XP SP2 • Windows Server 2008	• Windows Server 2008	• Windows Server 2008 • Windows Vista (Remote desktop only) • Windows XP SP2 (Remote desktop only)
Terminal Services Software	• Remote Desktop Connection 6.x client • TS Web Access home page	• TS Gateway role service	• Terminal Server role service • Remote Desktop
Location	Internet	Perimeter network	Private network

The Internet client uses the TS Gateway server to access a terminal server on a private network to establish a connection as follows:

1. The Internet client initiates the Terminal Services connection process by executing an RDP file, clicking a RemoteApp icon, or accessing a TS Web Access Web site.

2. The client initiates an SSL connection to the TS Gateway server using port 443, as shown in Figure 10-12.

Figure 10-12

A client connects to the TS Gateway server using SSL on port 443

3. The TS Gateway authenticates and authorizes the client using connection authorization policies (CAPs).

4. If the authentication and authorization processes succeed, the client requests a connection from the TS Gateway server to a terminal server on the private network.

5. The TS Gateway server authorizes the request using resource authorization policies (RAPs) to confirm the terminal server's availability and the client's permission to access that terminal server.

6. If the authorization succeeds, the SSL connection between the client and the TS Gateway server is established, forming the tunnel, as shown in Figure 10-13.

Figure 10-13

An authenticated and authorized client, connected to the TS Gateway server

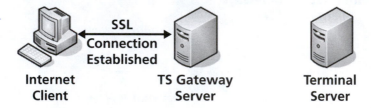

7. The TS Gateway server establishes an RDP connection with the terminal server requested by the client, using port 3389.

8. The client initiates a session with the terminal server by encapsulating its RDP traffic within SSL packets and sending them to port 443 on the TS Gateway server.

9. The TS Gateway server strips off the SSL header and relays the client's RDP traffic to the terminal server using port 3389, as shown in Figure 10-14.

Figure 10-14

The TS Gateway server establishes an RDP connection to the terminal server, using port 3389

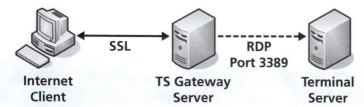

10. At this point, the client and the terminal server exchange standard RDP messages as if both were located on the same local network. The TS Gateway server continues to function as an intermediary during the terminal session, communicating with the client using SSL and the terminal server using RDP, as shown in Figure 10-15.

Figure 10-15

The TS Gateway server connects to clients using SSL and terminal servers using RDP

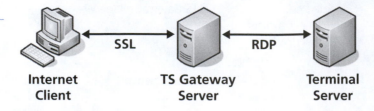

To deploy a TS Gateway server, you must perform the following tasks:
- Install the TS Gateway role service.
- Obtain and install a certificate for the TS Gateway server.
- Create connection authorization policies.
- Create resource authorization policies.
- Configure the client to use the TS Gateway.

The following sections examine the procedures for performing these tasks.

INSTALLING THE TS GATEWAY ROLE SERVICE

As you can see in Table 8-2 of Lesson 8, "Using Terminal Services," the TS Gateway role service is the most complex in the Terminal Services role. It requires many dependent roles and features, as shown in Figure 10-16, installs eight system services, and adds four pages to the Add Roles Wizard. Like TS Web Access, the TS Gateway role service requires the Web Server (IIS) role, but with a slightly different selection of role services, which are as follows:

Figure 10-16

TS Gateway role service dependencies

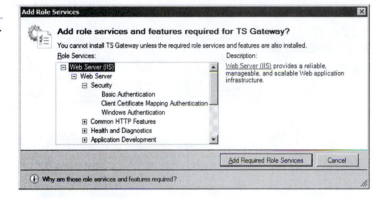

- Security
  - Basic Authentication
  - Client Certificate Mapping Authentication
  - Windows Authentication
- Common HTTP Features
  - Default Document
  - Directory Browsing
  - HTTP Errors
  - HTTP Redirection
  - Static Content
- Health and Diagnostics
  - HTTP Logging
  - Logging Tools
  - Request Monitor
  - Tracing
- Application Development
  - Internet Server Application Programming Interface (ISAPI) Extensions
- Performance
  - Static Content Compression
- Management Tools
  - IIS 6 Management Compatibility\IIS 6 Metabase Compatibility
  - IIS Management Console

In addition, TS Gateway requires the following roles and features:
- Network Policy and Access Service
  - Network Policy Server
- RPC Over HTTP Proxy
- Windows Process Activation Service
  - Process Model
  - Configuration APIs

Selecting the TS Gateway role service adds the following pages to the Add Roles Wizard. All of these pages contain controls for TS Gateway settings that you can configure later, using the TS Gateway Manager console.

- Server Authentication Certificate—Enables you to select, import, or create a digital certificate for the SSL encryption that the TS Gateway server uses when communicating with clients, as shown in Figure 10-17.

Figure 10-17

The TS Gateway Server Authentication Certificate page in the Add Role Services Wizard

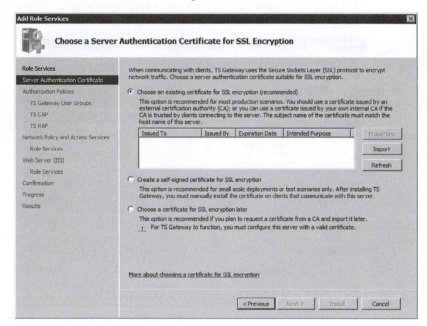

- Authorization Policies—Enables you to specify whether you want to create TS Gateway authorization policies now or later, as shown in Figure 10-18. Selecting Later disables the following three pages.

Figure 10-18

The TS Gateway Authorization Policies page in the Add Role Services Wizard

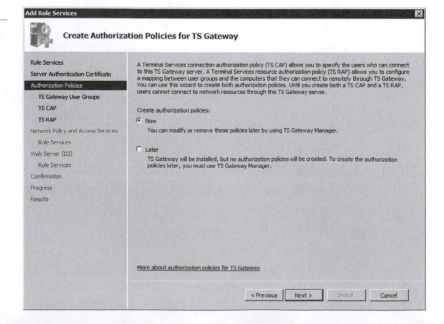

• TS Gateway User Groups—Enables you to specify the user groups allowed to connect to network resources through the TS Gateway server, as shown in Figure 10-19.

Figure 10-19

The TS Gateway User Groups page in the Add Role Services Wizard

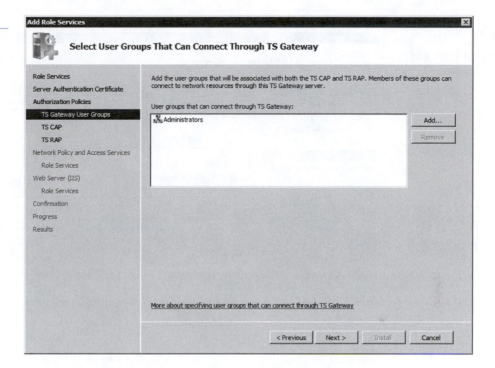

• TS CAP—Enables you to create a CAP, as shown in Figure 10-20, by specifying a policy name and whether the users in your selected groups can authenticate using passwords, smart cards, or either one.

Figure 10-20

The TS CAP page in the Add Role Services Wizard

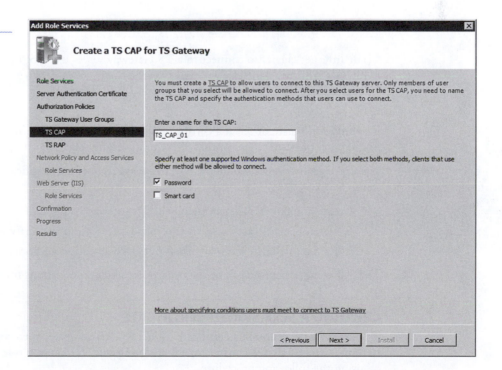

• TS RAP—Enables you to create a RAP, as shown in Figure 10-21, by specifying a policy name and whether clients can connect to any computer on the network or to the computers in a specified group only.

Figure 10-21

The TS RAP page in the Add Role Services Wizard

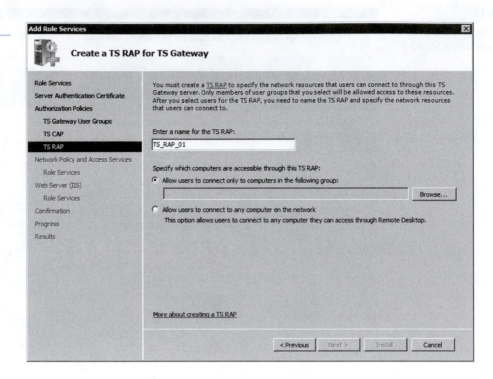

When the wizard finishes installing the TS Gateway, it adds the Terminal Services Configuration, Terminal Services Manager, and TS Gateway Manager consoles to the computer.

Obtaining and Installing a Certificate

For Internet clients to connect to a TS Gateway server using SSL, the server must have a digital certificate issued by a source that the client computers trust.

For more information about certificates and SSL, see "Configuring Certificates" in Lesson 6, "Securing IIS Services."

If you do not create or select a certificate during the TS Gateway installation process, you will find critical event messages to that effect in the computer's event logs.

You can use any one of the following three ways to obtain a certificate for a TS Gateway server.

• Create a self-signed certificate on the TS gateway computer.
• Generate a certificate using an enterprise certification authority (CA) on your network.
• Obtain a certificate from a trusted public certification authority.

The following sections describe the procedures and complications for each of these options.

CREATING A SELF-SIGNED CERTIFICATE

The easiest way to obtain a certificate for a TS Gateway server is to configure the computer to issue its own self-signed certificate, either during the TS Gateway role service installation or by using the following procedure.

 CREATE A SELF-SIGNED CERTIFICATE

GET READY. Log on to your Windows Server 2008 TS Gateway server using an account with administrative privileges. When the logon process is completed, close the Initial Configuration Tasks window and any other windows that appear.

1. Click **Start**, and then click **Administrative Tools** > **Terminal Services** > **TS Gateway Manager**. The TS Gateway Manager console appears, as shown in Figure 10-22.

Figure 10-22

The TS Gateway Manager console

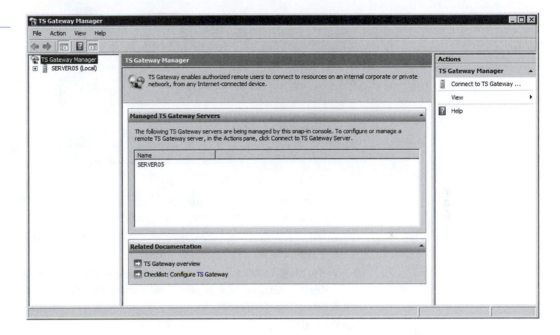

2. In the scope (left) pane, right-click your server and, from the context menu, select **Properties**. The server's Properties sheet appears.
3. Click the **SSL Certificate** tab, as shown in Figure 10-23.

Figure 10-23

The SSL Certificate tab of a TS Gateway server's Properties sheet

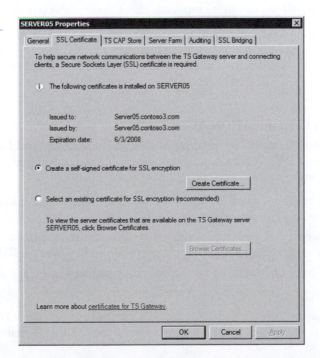

4. Select the **Create a self-signed certificate for SSL encryption** option, and then click **Create Certificate**. The Create Self-Signed Certificate dialog box appears, as shown in Figure 10-24.

Figure 10-24

The Create Self-Signed Certificate dialog box

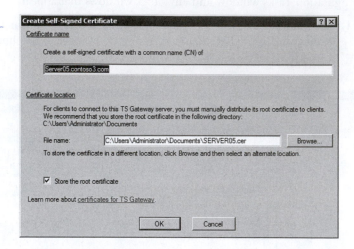

5. In the Certificate Name text box, you must specify the DNS name that your clients will use to connect to the TS Gateway server.

6. In the File Name text box, key or browse to the folder where you want to store the new certificate.

7. Verify that the **Store the root certificate** checkbox is selected and click **OK**. A TS Gateway message box appears, informing you that the server has successfully created the certificate.

8. Click **OK**.

9. Click **OK** again to close the server's Properties sheet.

CLOSE the TS Gateway Manager console.

When you create a self-signed certificate, the console installs and maps it for you, eliminating two of the manual steps you must perform when you obtain a certificate from an external CA. However, because Internet clients do not trust the TS Gateway that issued the certificate, you must install the certificate into each client computer's certificate store.

While creating a self-signed certificate simplifies the process of configuring the TS Gateway server, the need to install the certificate on every client computer usually makes it an impractical solution. In most cases, administrators limit the use of self-signed certificates to test deployments and lab servers.

X REF

For more information about installing certificates on terminal server clients, see "Configuring a TS Gateway Client" later in this lesson.

USING A CERTIFICATION AUTHORITY

TS Gateway servers can use certificates obtained from an external CA; either a commercial, public CA or a CA deployed on your network. To use a certificate on a TS Gateway server, you must make sure it meets the following requirements.

- The certificate name must be the same as the DNS name that clients will use to connect to the TS Gateway server.
- The certificate must be a computer certificate with an Extended Key Usage (EKU) OID value of 1.3.6.1.5.5.7.3.1, indicating that it will be used for SSL server authentication.
- The certificate must have a corresponding private key.
- All of your clients must trust the certificate.

For a client to trust a TS Gateway server's certificate, the client's Trusted Root Certification Authorities store must contain a certificate for the CA that issued the TS Gateway server's certificate. If you obtain your certificate from one of the trusted public CAs in the list of Microsoft root certificate program members, your Windows clients already have the required CA certificate, which enables them to trust your TS Gateway server without additional configuration.

> ➕ **MORE INFORMATION**
>
> A list of public CAs that are Microsoft root certificate program members is available in Microsoft's KnowledgeBase, at http://support.microsoft.com.

TAKE NOTE *

You cannot use the Certificate Request Wizard to obtain a TS Gateway certificate from a Windows enterprise CA. You must use the Certreq.exe command-line utility instead.

If you generate a certificate for your TS Gateway server using an enterprise CA on your own network, Internet clients that are not members of the same domain will not trust that certificate. To avoid installing the certificate on each client, you must configure your enterprise CA to issue certificates that are co-signed by a CA that your clients trust.

When you obtain a certificate from an external CA, either public or local, you must complete the following tasks:

- Install the certificate on the TS Gateway server.
- Map the certificate to the TS Gateway server.

The following sections discuss the procedures for these tasks.

INSTALLING A TS GATEWAY CERTIFICATE

After you obtain a certificate from your certification authority, copy it to a folder accessible from the TS Gateway server and use the following procedure to install the certificate.

➡️ **INSTALL A TS GATEWAY CERTIFICATE**

GET READY. Log on to your Windows Server 2008 TS Gateway server using an account with administrative privileges. When the logon process is completed, close the Initial Configuration Tasks window and any other windows that appear.

1. Click **Start**, and then click **Run**. The Run dialog box appears.
2. In the Open text box, key **mmc** and click **OK**. An empty Microsoft Management Console window appears.
3. From the File menu, select **Add/Remove Snap-in**. The Add or Remove Snap-ins dialog box appears, as shown in Figure 10-25.

Figure 10-25

The Add or Remove Snap-ins dialog box

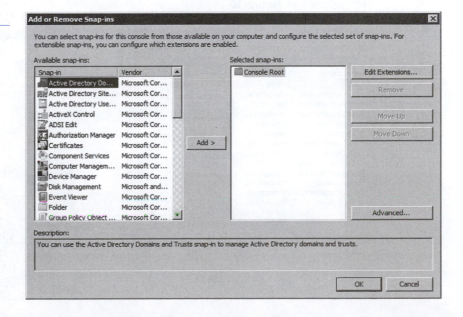

4. In the Available Snap-ins list, select **Certificates** and click **Add**. The Certificates snap-in page appears, as shown in Figure 10-26.

Figure 10-26

The Certificates snap-in page

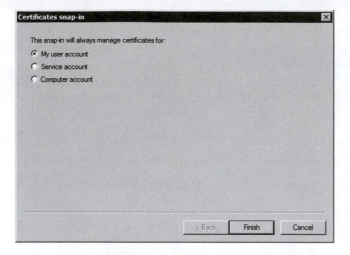

5. Select **Computer account** and click **Finish**. The Select Computer page appears, as shown in Figure 10-27.

Figure 10-27

The Select Computer page

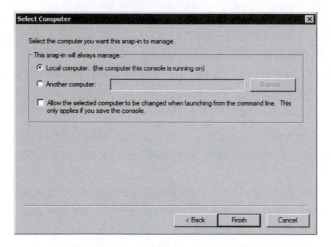

6. Verify that the default Local computer option is selected and click **Finish**. The Certificates (Local Computer) snap-in appears in the Selected snap-ins list, as shown in Figure 10-28.

Figure 10-28

The Add or Remove Snap-ins dialog box with the Certificates snap-in selected

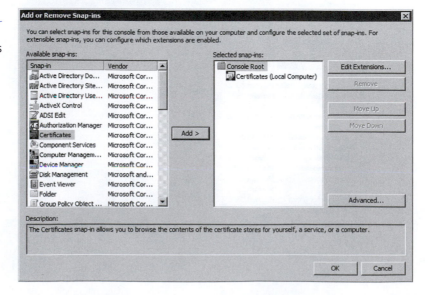

7. Click **OK**. The Certificates (Local Computer) snap-in appears in the console.

8. In the console's scope pane, expand the **Certificates (Local Computer)** node, as shown in Figure 10-29.

Figure 10-29

The Certificates snap-in's subfolders

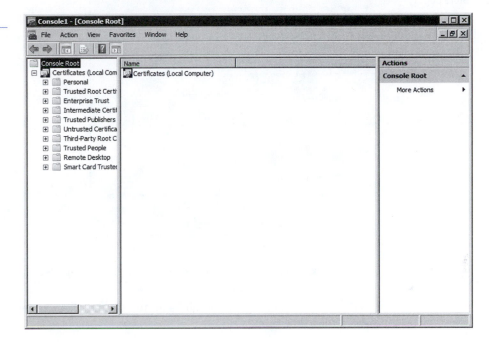

9. Right-click the **Personal** folder and, in the context menu, point to **All Tasks** and select **Import**. The Certificate Import Wizard appears.

10. Click **Next** to bypass the Welcome page. The File to Import page appears, as shown in Figure 10-30.

Figure 10-30

The File to Import page

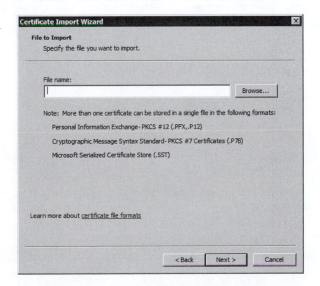

11. Key the name of or browse to the certificate file you want to import, and then click **Next**. The Certificate Store page appears, as shown in Figure 10-31.

Figure 10-31

The Certificate Store page

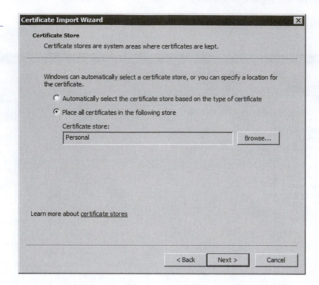

12. Click **Next** to accept the default option. The Completing the Certificate Import Wizard page appears.

13. Click **Finish**. A message box appears, stating that the wizard successfully imported the certificate.

CLOSE the MMC console.

The certificate you imported appears in the Personal\Certificates folder in the console, as shown in Figure 10-32.

Figure 10-32

The Certificates snap-in with an imported certificate

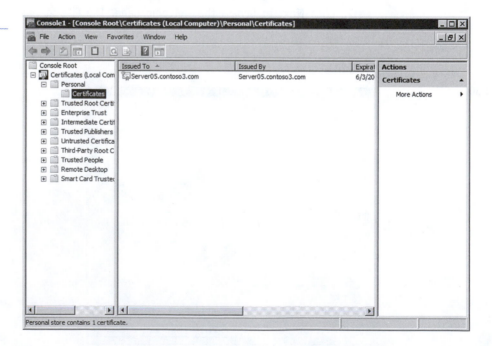

MAPPING A TS GATEWAY CERTIFICATE

After you import your certificate into the TS Gateway computer's Certificates store, you must map the certificate to the TS Gateway server so the gateway can use it. To map the certificate, use the following procedure.

 MAP A TS GATEWAY CERTIFICATE

GET READY. Log on to your Windows Server 2008 TS Gateway server using an account with administrative privileges. When the logon process is completed, close the Initial Configuration Tasks window and any other windows that appear.

1. Click **Start**, and then click **Administrative Tools** > **Terminal Services** > **TS Gateway Manager**. The TS Gateway Manager console appears.

2. In the scope page, select your TS Gateway server. Notice that a warning appears in the TS Gateway Server Status box, shown in Figure 10-33. The warning indicates that a certificate for the server has not been installed or selected.

Figure 10-33

The TS Gateway Manager console, displaying the TS Gateway Server Status box

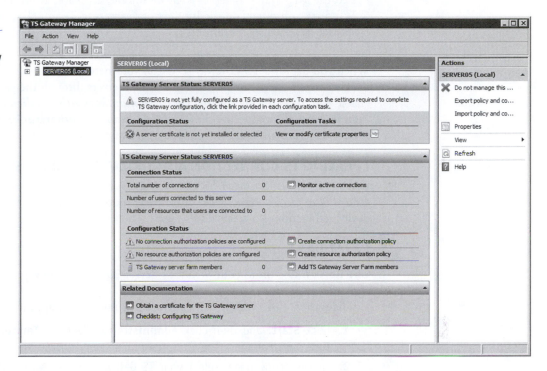

3. Right-click the server and, from the context menu, select **Properties**. The server's Properties sheet appears.

4. Click the **SSL Certificate** tab.

5. Select the **Select an existing certificate for SSL encryption** option, and then click **Browse Certificates**. The Install Certificate dialog box appears, as shown in Figure 10-34.

Figure 10-34

The Install Certificate dialog box

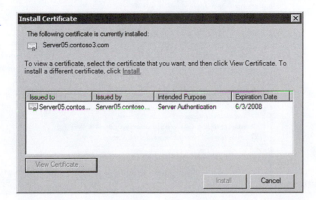

6. Select the certificate for the TS Gateway server and click **Install**.

7. Click **OK** to map the certificate and close the Properties sheet. Notice that the warning that appeared earlier in the TS Gateway Server Status box is no longer displayed.

CLOSE the TS Gateway Manager console.

You have configured the TS Gateway server to use the selected certificate. To complete the server configuration process, you must create connection authorization policies and resource authorization policies.

Creating TS Gateway Authorization Policies

> Because a TS Gateway server is, by definition, accessible from the Internet, and all Windows computers on the Internet have access to Terminal Services client software, security is a critical concern.

When you deploy a TS Gateway server on your network, you want to make sure that only the clients you select can access your terminal servers through the gateway. TS Gateway servers enable you to do this by creating *connection authorization policies (CAPs),* which specify the Internet users allowed to use the server, and *resource authorization policies (RAPs),* which specify the terminal servers on the private network that the users are permitted to access.

CREATING TS CONNECTION AUTHORIZATION POLICIES (CAPs)

CAPs enable you to restrict TS Gateway access to members of specific local or domain user groups. You can also specify the authentication method that clients must use and limit client device redirection. To create a CAP, use the following procedure.

 CREATE A TS CAP

GET READY. Log on to your Windows Server 2008 TS Gateway server using an account with administrative privileges. When the logon process is completed, close the Initial Configuration Tasks window and any other windows that appear.

1. Click **Start**, and then click **Administrative Tools** > **Terminal Services** > **TS Gateway Manager**. The TS Gateway Manager console appears.

2. In the scope page, select your TS Gateway server. Notice that a warning appears in the TS Gateway Server Status box, shown in Figure 10-35. The warning indicates that no connection authorization policies are configured.

Figure 10-35

The TS Gateway Manager console, displaying the TS Gateway Server Status box

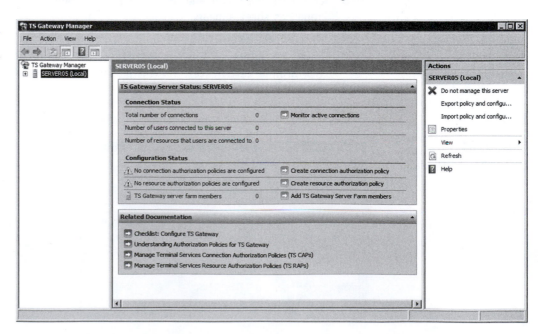

3. Expand the server node and the **Policies** node, and then select the **Connection Authorization Policies** node. The Connection Authorization Policies pane appears, as shown in Figure 10-36.

Figure 10-36

The TS Gateway Manager console, displaying the Connection Authorization Policies pane

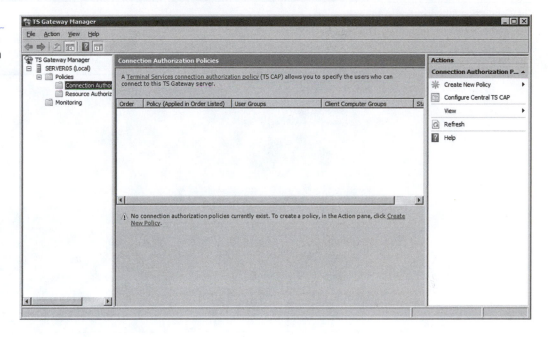

4. In the actions pane, click **Create New Policy** and, from the context menu, select **Wizard.** The Authorization Policies wizard appears, with the Create Authorization Policies for TS Gateway page displayed, as shown in Figure 10-37.

Figure 10-37

The Create Authorization Policies for TS Gateway page

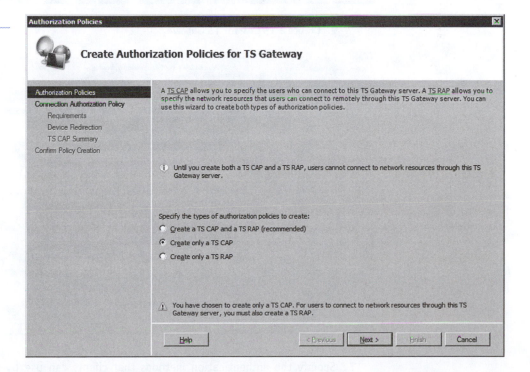

5. Leave the default *Create only a TS CAP* option selected and click **Next**. The Connection Authorization Policy page appears, as shown in Figure 10-38.

Figure 10-38

The Connection Authorization Policy page

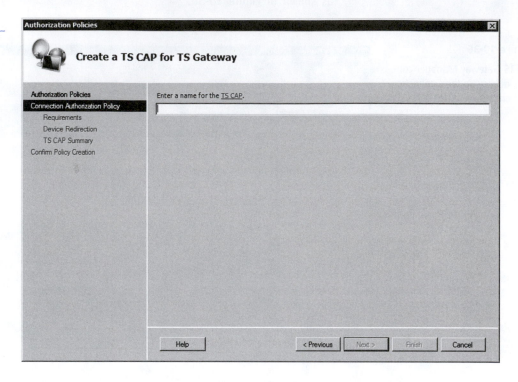

6. In the *Enter a name for the TS CAP* text box, specify the name you want to assign to the policy and click **Next**. The Requirements page appears, as shown in Figure 10-39.

Figure 10-39

The Requirements page

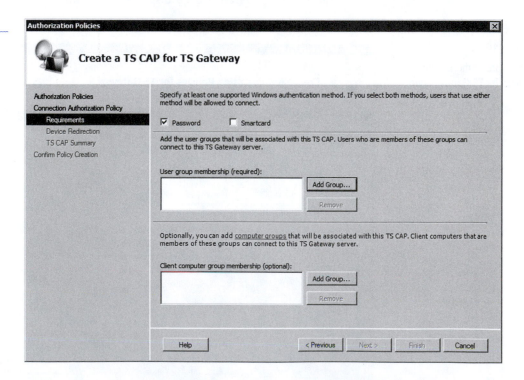

7. Specify the authentication methods that clients can use by selecting the **Password** checkbox, the **Smartcard** checkbox, or both.

8. In the User group membership box, click **Add Group**. The Select Groups dialog box appears, as shown in Figure 10-40.

Figure 10-40

The Select Groups dialog box

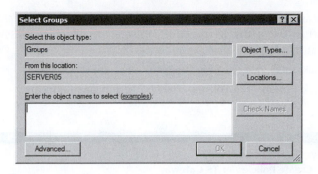

TAKE NOTE*

You can add domain or local groups to a CAP. To add a local group, you must first click Locations in the Select Groups dialog box and select the computer name in the Locations dialog box.

9. In the *Enter the object names to select* text box, specify the name of a group containing the users you want to grant access to the TS Gateway server and click **OK**. The group appears in the *User group membership* box.

10. Optionally, in the Client computer group membership box, you can click **Add Group** and select a group containing the computers that you want to grant access to the TS Gateway server.

11. Click **Next**. The Device Redirection page appears, as shown in Figure 10-41.

Figure 10-41

The Device Redirection page

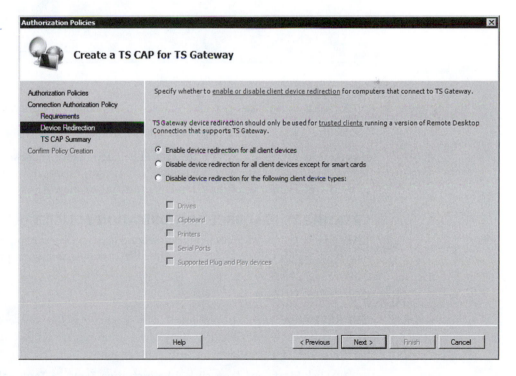

WARNING Limiting client access to redirected devices at the TS Gateway does not guarantee a specific level of security. It is the Terminal Services client that is responsible for enforcing the local device redirection settings supplied by the server. A potential attacker could, therefore, modify the client to override the settings supplied by the TS Gateway server.

12. Select one of the following options:
   - Enable device redirection for all client devices—Enables clients to use all supported local devices in a terminal session. Use this option only with trusted clients.
   - Disable device redirection for all client devices except for smartcards—Prevents clients from using local devices, except for smartcards, in a terminal session. Use for clients you do not trust that must authenticate with a smartcard.

- Disable device redirection for the following client device types—Prevents clients from using the selected local devices in a terminal session. Use for clients that authenticate with passwords.

13. Click **Next**. The TS CAP Summary page appears.

14. Click **Finish**. The Confirm Policy Creation page appears, as shown in Figure 10-42.

Figure 10-42

The Confirm Policy Creation page

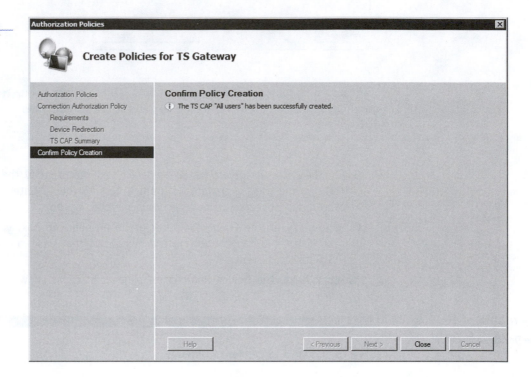

15. Click **Close**. The new CAP appears in the Connect Authorization Policies pane.

CLOSE the TS Gateway Manager console.

If you create multiple CAPs on the same TS Gateway server, the server processes each user attempting to access the gateway using the CAPs in numerical order. The server denies access to users who do not meet the requirements of any of the CAPs.

CREATING TS RESOURCE AUTHORIZATION POLICIES (RAPs)

RAPs enable you to restrict clients connecting to a TS Gateway server to specific terminal servers on the private network. To create a RAP, use the following procedure.

 CREATE A TS RAP

GET READY. Log on to your Windows Server 2008 TS Gateway server using an account with administrative privileges. When the logon process is completed, close the Initial Configuration Tasks window and any other windows that appear.

1. Click **Start**, and then click **Administrative Tools** > **Terminal Services** > **TS Gateway Manager**. The TS Gateway Manager console appears.

2. In the scope page, select your TS Gateway server. A warning appears in the TS Gateway Server Status box, shown in Figure 10-43. The warning indicates that no resource authorization policies are configured.

Figure 10-43

The TS Gateway Manager console, displaying the TS Gateway Server Status box

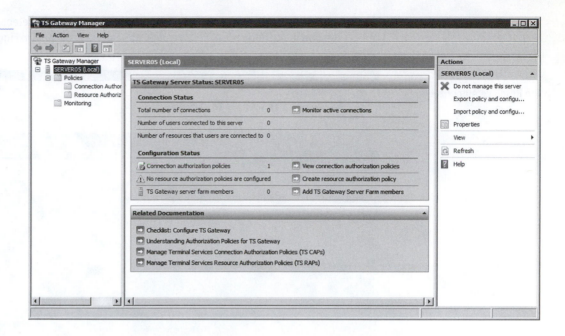

3. Expand the server node and the Policies node, and then select the **Resource Authorization Policies** node. The Resource Authorization Policies pane appears, as shown in Figure 10-44.

Figure 10-44

The TS Gateway Manager console, displaying the Resource Authorization Policies pane

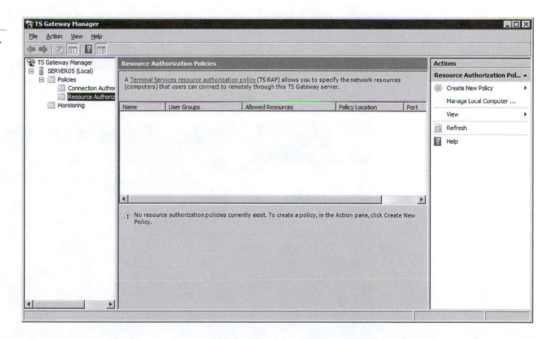

4. In the actions pane, click **Create New Policy** and, from the context menu, select **Wizard**. The Authorization Policies wizard appears with the Create Authorization Policies for TS Gateway page displayed.

5. Verify that the default Create only a TS RAP option is selected and click **Next**. The Resource Authorization Policy page appears, as shown in Figure 10-45.

Figure 10-45

The Resource Authorization Policy page

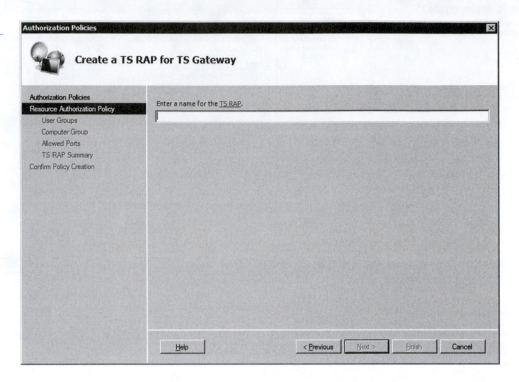

6. In the *Enter a name for the TS RAP* text box, specify the name you want to assign to the policy and click **Next**. The User Groups page appears, as shown in Figure 10-46.

Figure 10-46

The User Groups page

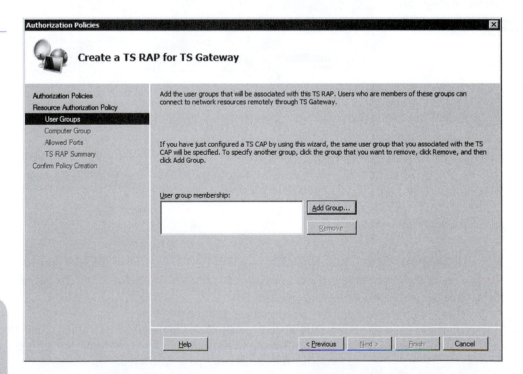

7. In the *User group membership* box, click **Add Group**. The Select Groups dialog box appears.

8. In the *Enter the object names to select* text box, specify the name of a group containing the users you want to access network resources through the TS Gateway server and click **OK**. The group appears in the *User group membership* box.

9. Click **Next**. The Computer Group page appears, as shown in Figure 10-47.

Figure 10-47

The Computer Group page

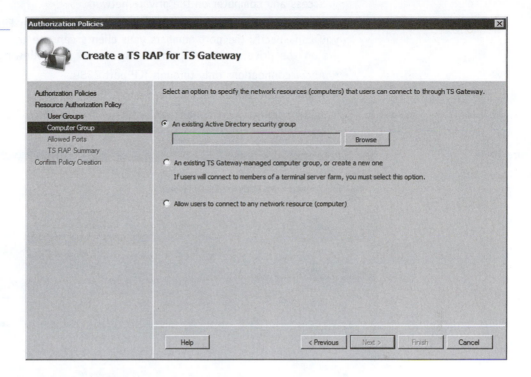

10. To specify a computer group, select one of the following options:

- An existing Active Directory security group—Enables you to select an existing Active Directory group containing the computers that your TS Gateway clients should access.
- An existing TS Gateway-managed computer group, or create a new one—Enables you to create or select a proprietary TS Gateway group containing the computers that your TS Gateway clients should be able to access. Selecting this option adds a TS Gateway-Managed Group page to the wizard, as shown in Figure 10-48, in which you can name and populate a new group or select an existing one.

Figure 10-48

The TS Gateway-Managed Group page

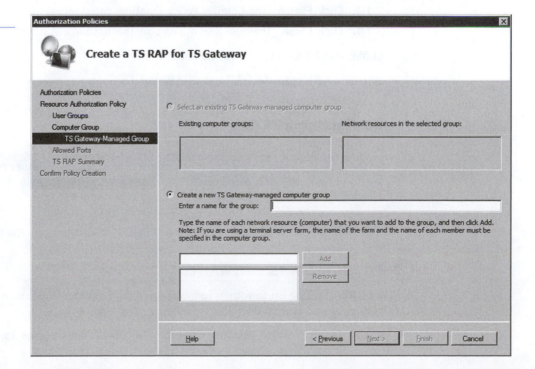

- Allow users to connect to any network resource—Allows TS Gateway clients to access any computer on the private network.

11. Click **Next**. The Allowed Ports page appears, as shown in Figure 10-49, on which you can specify the port numbers your clients can use to access the terminal servers on the private network by selecting one of the following options:

- Allow connections only through TCP port 3389.
- Allow connections through these ports.
- Allow connections through any port.

Figure 10-49

The Allowed Ports page

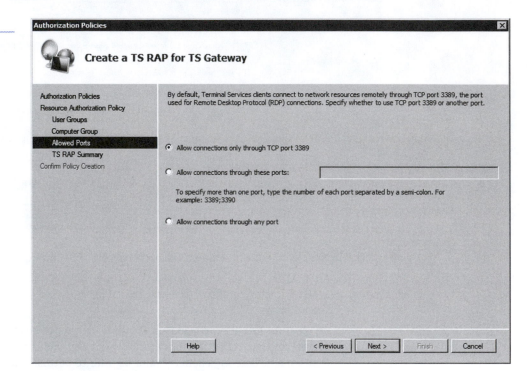

12. Click **Next**. The TS RAP Summary page appears.
13. Click **Finish**. The Confirm Policy Creation page appears.
14. Click **Close**. The new RAP appears in the Resource Authorization Policies pane.

CLOSE the TS Gateway Manager console.

After you have created a CAP and a RAP, your TS Gateway server is configured and ready to use.

Configuring a TS Gateway Client

To access a terminal server on a private network from the Internet using a TS Gateway server, first you must configure Remote Desktop Connection on the client computer.

To configure the TS Gateway settings on the RDC 6.x client, use the following procedure.

 CONFIGURE A TS GATEWAY CLIENT

GET READY. Log on to your Windows Server 2008, Windows Vista, or Windows XP SP2 computer and launch the RDC 6.x client.

1. In the Remote Desktop Connection window, click **Options** to display the tabbed interface, as shown in Figure 10-50.

Figure 10-50

The Remote Desktop Connection window

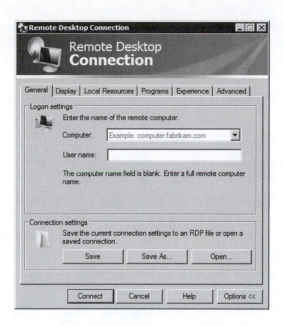

2. Click the **Advanced** tab and then click **Settings**. The TS Gateway Server Settings dialog box appears, as shown in Figure 10-51.

Figure 10-51

The TS Gateway Server Settings dialog box

3. In the Connection Settings box, select **Use these TS Gateway server settings**.

4. In the Server Name text box, key the DNS name of the TS Gateway server you will use to connect to your terminal server.

5. In the Logon Method dropdown list, specify whether you will authenticate using a password or a smartcard.

6. Verify that the **Bypass TS Gateway server for local addresses** checkbox is selected if you will also be connecting to terminal servers on your local network.

7. Verify that the **Use my TS Gateway credentials for the remote computer** checkbox is selected if you will be using the same account to log on to the TS Gateway server and the terminal server.

8. Click **OK**.

CLOSE the Remote Desktop Connection window.

If the certificate you are using for your TS Gateway server is not trusted by your clients, such as when you create a self-signed certificate, you must install it into the client computer's certificate store using the following procedure.

INSTALL A CERTIFICATE

GET READY. Log on to your Windows Server 2008, Windows Vista, or Windows XP SP2 computer, using an account with administrative privileges.

1. Open an empty Microsoft Management Console window and add the Certificates snap-in pointed to the local computer account.
2. In the console's scope pane, expand the **Certificates (Local Computer)** node.
3. Right-click the **Trusted Root Certification Authorities** folder and, in the context menu, point to **All Tasks** and select **Import**. The Certificate Import Wizard appears.
4. Click **Next** to bypass the Welcome page. The File to Import page appears.
5. Key the name of or browse to the certificate file you want to import, and then click **Next**. The Certificate Store page appears.
6. Click **Next** to accept the default option. The Completing the Certificate Import Wizard page appears.
7. Click **Finish**. A message box appears, stating that the wizard successfully imported the certificate.

CLOSE the MMC console.

At this point, the RDC client is ready to connect to the terminal server in the usual manner. The client will connect to the TS Gateway server first, and the gateway will connect to the terminal server, producing an interface that includes an icon you can use to display the Terminal Services gateway settings, as shown in Figure 10-52.

Figure 10-52

A Terminal Services session, using a TS Gateway server

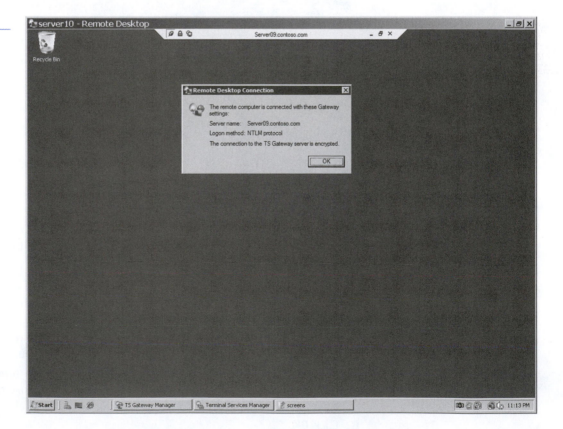

SUMMARY SKILL MATRIX

IN THIS LESSON YOU LEARNED:

- Terminal Services (TS) Web Access is a role service that, with IIS 7, creates an alternative client interface to your terminal servers.

- TS Web Access enables users to launch RemoteApp programs simply by double-clicking icons on a Web page.

- If you install the TS Web Access role service on the same computer as the Terminal Server role service, the Add Roles Wizard automatically populates the TS Web Access Web page. If you want to use TS Web Access with a terminal server running on another Windows Server 2008 computer, you must configure both computers to work together.

- Terminal Services Gateway is a new Windows Server 2008 Terminal Services role service that enables Internet users to access terminal servers on private networks despite intervening firewalls and network access translation (NAT) servers.

- The TS Gateway role service enables Terminal Services to support Internet clients securely using the same tunneling concept as a VPN connection, except that the computers encapsulate RDP traffic within Secure Sockets Layer (SSL) packets.

- To deploy a TS Gateway server, you must perform the following tasks: install the TS Gateway role service, obtain and install a certificate for the TS Gateway server, create connection authorization policies, create resource authorization policies, and configure the client to use the TS Gateway.

- TS Gateway uses connection authorization policies (CAPs), which specify the Internet users that are allowed to use the server, and resource authorization policies (RAPs), which specify the terminal servers on the private network that the users are permitted to access.

■ Knowledge Assessment

Matching

Complete the following exercise by matching the terms with their corresponding definitions.

a. Specifies who can use a TS Gateway server

b. Middleman between TS clients and servers

c. Must be installed on every Internet client when used on a TS Gateway server

d. Used for communications between Internet clients and TS Gateway servers

e. Specifies which terminal servers a TS Gateway can access

f. Issues certificates

g. Launches RemoteApp programs from Web pages

h. Uses tunneling without SSL

i. Used by VPNs and TS Gateway servers

j. Used for communications between TS Gateway servers and terminal servers

_____ **1.** Terminal Services (TS) Web Access

_____ **2.** Secure Sockets Layer (SSL)

_____ **3.** tunneling

_____ **4.** certification authority

_____ **5.** Remote Desktop Protocol (RDP)

_____ **6.** Terminal Services Gateway

_____ **7.** connection authorization policy (CAP)

_____ **8.** virtual private networking (VPN)

_____ **9.** resource authorization policy (RAP)

_____ **10.** self-signed certificate

Multiple Choice

Select the correct answer for each of the following questions. Choose all answers that are correct.

1. TS Gateway servers can use certificates obtained from which of the following external certification authorities (CAs)?
   a. An enterprise CA on a remote client's network
   b. An enterprise CA on your network
   c. A public CA
   d. A commercial CA

2. Which of the following is not a page that the TS Gateway role service adds to the Add Roles Wizard?
   a. TS Gateway User Groups
   b. Server Authentication Certificate
   c. TS MAP
   d. Authorization Policies

3. Which of the following is not one of the basic elements of a typical TS Gateway deployment?
   a. Terminal servers
   b. Internet clients
   c. a TS Gateway server
   d. a TS Web Access server

4. Which of the following is not one of the requirements for a certificate used on a TS Gateway server?
   a. The certificate must be a computer certificate.
   b. The certificate name must match the NetBIOS name of the TS Gateway server.
   c. The certificate must have a corresponding private key.
   d. All of your clients must trust the certificate.

5. Which of the following is not a Windows Process Activation Service feature that TS Web Access requires?
   a. Request Filtering
   b. Process Model
   c. .NET Environment
   d. Configuration APIs

6. Which of the following is the port number that the RDP protocol uses for terminal server applications?
   a. 3378
   b. 80
   c. 3389
   d. 3334

7. What is the area of dual accessibility on an enterprise network that provides access both to the Internet and your internal network called?
   a. a VPN
   b. a firewall
   c. a certification authority
   d. a perimeter network

8. Which of the following enable you to select the clients that can access your terminal servers through your TS Gateway?
   a. connection authorization policies
   b. network authorization policies
   c. Internet authorization policies
   d. resource authorization policies

9. Which of the following operating systems are not supported as Internet clients in a TS Gateway deployment?
   a. Windows Vista
   b. Windows XP
   c. Windows 2000 Workstation
   d. Windows 98

10. Which of the following is not one of the tasks you must perform when deploying a TS Gateway server?
    a. Install the TS Gateway role service
    b. Obtain a certificate for the TS Gateway server
    c. Add the certificate to the TS Gateway computer's Trusted Root Certification Authorities store
    d. Create connection authorization and resource authorization policies

Review Questions

1. Place the following steps of the TS Gateway connection establishment process in the correct sequence.
   a. A tunnel is established between the client and the TS Gateway server.
   b. The TS Gateway authenticates and authorizes the client.
   c. The TS Gateway server establishes an RDP connection with the terminal server.
   d. The client initiates a session with the terminal server.
   e. The client initiates an SSL connection to the TS Gateway server.
   f. The client requests a connection to a terminal server on the private network.
   g. The TS Gateway server strips off the SSL header and relays the client's RDP traffic to the terminal server.
   h. The TS Gateway server authorizes the client's request.
   i. The Internet client clicks a RemoteApp icon.

2. List the three types of groups that you can use in an RAP to specify the terminal servers that are accessible through a TS Gateway server.

■ Case Scenario

Scenario 10-1: Deploying a TS Gateway Server

Harold is installing a TS Gateway server to enable his company's outside sales staff to access the corporation's terminal servers from the Internet while traveling. Harold installed the TS Gateway role service, created a self-signed certificate, and created a CAP and a RAP specifying the Outside Sales user group and the Terminal Servers computer group, respectively. He also sent an email to the outside sales staff containing instructions on how to configure the TS Gateway settings in the Remote Desktop Connection client. The next day, Harold begins receiving emails from the salespeople complaining that they cannot access the terminal servers. Specify the most likely cause of the problem and give two possible resolutions.

Using Network Application Services

OBJECTIVE DOMAIN MATRIX

TECHNOLOGY SKILL	OBJECTIVE DOMAIN	OBJECTIVE DOMAIN NUMBER
Installing the Streaming Media Services Role	Configure Windows Media® server.	4.1
Installing Windows SharePoint Services	Configure Microsoft Windows SharePoint® Services server options.	4.3
Configuring Email Integration	Configure Windows SharePoint Services email integration.	4.4
Using Digital Rights Management	Configure Digital Rights Management (DRM).	4.2

KEY TERMS

broadcast streams
differential backup
Digital Rights Management (DRM)
Fast Streaming
multicast

on-demand streams
protocol rollover
publishing points
Real Time Streaming Protocol (RTSP)
unicast

Windows Media Encoder
Windows Media Player
Windows Media Services
Windows SharePoint Services 3.0

Windows Server 2008 supports add-on modules that implement network applications you can use to provide multimedia content and workspace collaboration capabilities for users. In this lesson, you learn about the following:

- Deploying multimedia content using Windows Media Services
- Installing and configuring Windows SharePoint Services
- Protecting information resources with Digital Rights Management

■ Using Windows Media Services

THE BOTTOM LINE

Windows Media Services enables a Windows Server 2008 server to stream multimedia content in real time, using either live or pre-recorded content.

In most cases, the role of an application server is to provide data to clients on the network. File servers and Web servers, for example, provide clients with data in the form of files. The server stores the files on its drives, transmits them to the client, and then the client either displays them or stores them on its own drive. In these cases, the client cannot make use of the data until the entire file containing it arrives at the client computer.

Windows Media Services is a Windows Server 2008 role that provides a twist to this formula. With Windows Media Services, a server can stream audio and video content to network clients in real time. A player on the client computer establishes a direct connection with the server and plays the audio or video content as it arrives.

Audio and video content is particularly well-suited to real-time streaming over a network. Unlike application or document files, audio and video data does not have to arrive at the client in bit-perfect condition to be usable. If, for example, a client runs an application from a file server drive, just one lost bit means that the application will not run. On the other hand, a few bits lost from a video data stream will result only in a few bad pixels, or at most a dropped frame or two, not enough to ruin the user experience.

A computer running Windows Media Services is responsible for publishing audio/video content to network users, but it is only one part of the equation. The front end of a Windows Media installation is the Windows Media Player client running on a user's computer, as shown in Figure 11-1. The Media Player client and the Media Services server establish a connection that enables the server to transmit content data to the client and the client to play the content as the data arrives.

Figure 11-1

A Windows Media Services server and a Windows Media Player client

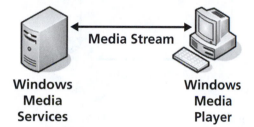

This arrangement seems simple; the server sends the content and the client receives it. However, the process involves other elements as well. The other component visible to the end user is the means by which the systems initiate the client/server connection. In most cases, this is a Web server publishing a home page that contains a link to the audio/video content on the server, as shown in Figure 11-2. In Windows Media Services, the Web server is a completely separate entity and need not be running on the same computer as Windows Media Services. The only role of the Web server is to provide a hyperlink to the streaming content. When a user clicks the link, ***Windows Media Player*** launches on the client and establishes a direct connection to the Windows Media Services server. The Web server is, from this point, out of the picture.

Figure 11-2

A Web server provides users with a link to content published by a Windows Media Services server

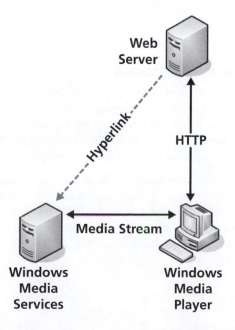

At the back end of the installation, invisible to the end user, there can be a variety of mechanisms that generate the streaming content published by Windows Media Services. The content might be pre-recorded and stored on the Windows Media Services server or located on another server. The content can also be a live event, captured using a digital video camera and sent to a server running **Windows Media Encoder**, which converts it into the Windows Media format and sends it to the Windows Media Services server for real-time distribution, as shown in Figure 11-3.

Figure 11-3

A Windows Media Encoder server, processing live video data and sending it to Windows Media Services for streaming to clients

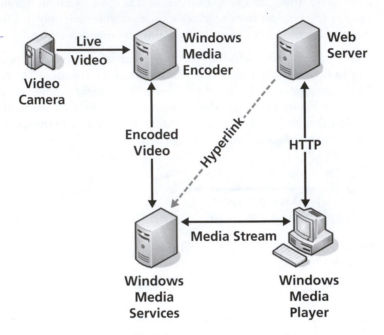

Planning a Windows Media Services Deployment

Deploying Windows Media Services largely consists of managing and regulating the large amounts of bandwidth that multimedia streams can consume.

Setting up a Windows Media Services deployment is not difficult. It can be more difficult, however, to design an effective Media Services deployment for your network. Audio and video streams often consist of large amounts of data; video files can be hundreds or even thousands of megabytes, and they can overwhelm even the fastest networks.

UNDERSTANDING MEDIA STREAMING

Media streaming is always a tradeoff between bandwidth and signal quality. As you increase the quality and/or resolution of the video image, you also increase the amount of bandwidth the stream consumes. A low-bit-rate video that appears in a postage stamp-sized window on the client's monitor might require 100 kilobytes per minute of content, whereas a high-definition, full-screen video might require ten megabytes per minute or more.

As mentioned earlier, network users access applications and documents by downloading them to their computers and then launching them. For audio/video content, network administrators can choose between publishing the files in the usual manner or streaming them. As a general rule, however, you should not use the download method for this type of content. Table 11-1 lists the reasons for this recommendation.

Table 11-1

Differences Between Downloading and Streaming Multimedia Content

DOWNLOADING	STREAMING
Multimedia content cannot begin playing until the file download is complete.	Multimedia content can begin playing soon after the file begins streaming.
The server transmits the file to the clients as quickly as possible, utilizing all of the available network bandwidth and possibly degrading the performance of other network functions.	The server streams the multimedia content to the clients, using only the speed needed to render the content properly, thus conserving network bandwidth.
Cannot be used to publish live multimedia content because the entire file must download before the client can play it.	Can transmit live multimedia content in real time as the event occurs.
Multimedia content always plays at full quality because the client does not begin rendering until it completely downloads the file.	If the bandwidth required to render the content adequately is more than the amount available on the network, the server can drop frames or otherwise thin the stream to keep the content playing on the client computer.

To provide the end user with a smooth, uninterrupted multimedia experience, a media player must receive a continuous stream of data. Because network performance can fluctuate, player applications maintain a data buffer, which is a staging area for the multimedia rendering process. The player stores arriving data in the buffer and feeds it to the rendering engine at a steady rate. In its basic configuration, the player cannot start displaying the content until the buffer is full, but Windows Media Player has a feature called *Fast Streaming*, which includes several techniques that enable the player to begin displaying content more quickly, improving the user experience. These techniques include the following:

- Fast Start—Causes the player to begin streaming data at full network speed until the buffer is filled, at which point the rendering process can begin. Then, the stream slows down to the player's normal rendering speed.

- Advanced Fast Start—The player begins streaming at an accelerated rate and starts rendering as soon as possible, before the buffer is filled. After the buffer is full, the player reverts to its normal rendering speed.

- Fast Cache—The player streams all data at the highest possible speed, filling the buffer first and then storing the rest of the data in a temporary cache on the computer's local drive.

- Fast Recovery—Enables Forward Error Correction (FEC) on the Windows Media Services server, which enables the Windows Media Player client to recover from lost or damaged packets without requesting a resend.

- Fast Reconnect—Enables a client to reconnect to a Windows Media Services server and resume an interrupted stream after a temporary network outage.

CREATING A DEPLOYMENT PLAN

When you plan a Windows Media Services deployment, you must decide how much signal quality you can afford with the bandwidth you have to expend. To do this, consider the following three elements:

- Client bandwidth—How much network bandwidth does each of your clients have available? A client that accesses a Windows Media Services server using a dial-up connection cannot possibly receive the same high-quality media stream as a LAN (local area network) client.

- Number of clients—Multiply the bandwidth required for each of your media streams by the number of concurrent clients you want to serve simultaneously. If the resulting product is near to or greater than your total network bandwidth, then you must reduce the signal quality of your data streams to lower their bandwidth requirements.

• **Content requirements**—How much signal quality do your media streams require to effectively service your clients? To reduce the bandwidth required for each stream, you can lower the signal resolution or use a different format, such as variable-bit-rate encoding (VBR). How you package your media content directly affects the user experience and the bandwidth the service consumes.

SELECTING A STREAM TYPE

Another important element of a deployment plan should be the type of streams you intend to publish. To publish content on a Windows Media Services server, you create *publishing points*, the components through which clients access specific content streams. Windows Media Services supports two types of publishing points: *on-demand streams* and *broadcast streams*. Table 11-2 summarizes the differences between on-demand and broadcast streams.

Table 11-2

Differences Between On-demand Streams and Broadcast Streams

ON-DEMAND STREAMS	BROADCAST STREAMS
Streaming begins when the user requests it	Streaming begins at a pre-arranged time
Typically used for pre-recorded content	Typically used for live content
Supports unicast transmissions only	Supports unicast or multicast transmissions
End user can employ playback controls to pause, resume, rewind, and fast forward	End user can start and stop the stream playback, but cannot control the transmission, which proceeds uninterrupted from beginning to end
The server establishes a separate connection with each client	The server can use a single transmission to service multiple clients

SELECTING A TRANSMISSION TYPE

The type of transmissions you configure Windows Media Services to use when streaming multimedia content can impact the bandwidth the service consumes. Windows Media Services uses *unicast* transmissions by default. In a unicast transmission, each client establishes its own connection to the Windows Media Services server and has its own data stream, as shown in Figure 11-4.

Figure 11-4

Unicast data streams between Windows Media Services servers and clients

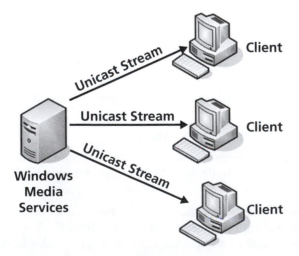

The use of unicast transmissions enables end users to control the playback of the multimedia content. When the user pauses, rewinds, or fast-forwards the playback, the server actually alters the stream by changing its speed or its content. This is possible because these changes in the stream affect only that one user.

The biggest drawback of unicast streaming is the bandwidth it can consume. Because each unicast client has its own separate stream, the Windows Media Services server can use five times the bandwidth for five clients that are playing the same video. Even when multiple clients are playing the same content, the server must transmit a separate stream for each one, with each stream containing the same data.

Multicast transmissions prevent this wastage. Multicasting is a TCP/IP (Transmission Control Protocol/Internet Protocol) feature that provides one-to-many transmission capabilities. In TCP/IP communications, IP addresses typically represent individual systems called unicast addresses. However, a special class of multicast IP addresses is called Class D addresses, each of which represents a group of computers on a network.

When you configure Windows Media Services to use multicast transmissions, the server creates a single stream directed to a single multicast address. Multiple clients can then subscribe to that address and receive the stream, as shown in Figure 11-5. No matter how many clients access the content, only a single stream is provided, which can save a vast amount of bandwidth.

Figure 11-5

Multicast data streams between Windows Media Services servers and clients

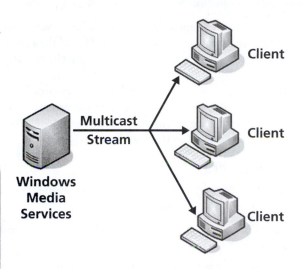

TAKE NOTE*

Windows Media Services only supports multicast streaming when it is running on Windows Server 2008 Enterprise or Windows Server 2008 Datacenter. Multicasting is not supported on Windows Server 2008 Standard or Windows Web Server 2008.

Because many clients rely on a single stream when you use multicast transmissions, individual users cannot manipulate the playback as they can with unicasts. A user can stop the playback by disconnecting from the stream, but the stream continues transmitting to the other clients. When the user restarts the playback, it reconnects to the stream at its current point, skipping any data the server transmitted in the interim.

Because multicast transmissions are designed to service multiple clients simultaneously, you can use them only for broadcast streams, not on-demand streams.

SELECTING A DATA TRANSFER PROTOCOL

Windows Media Services can stream multimedia content, using a variety of protocol combinations, to support different Windows Media Player versions. When you add the Windows Media Services role on a Windows Server 2008 computer, the Select Data Transfer Protocols page enables you to select ***Real Time Streaming Protocol (RTSP)***, Hypertext Transfer Protocol (HTTP), or both.

The Windows Server 2008 version of Windows Media Services uses the RTSP protocol by default. Any client computer running Windows Media Player 9 or later can use RTSP to stream multimedia content, with either TCP or UDP (User Datagram Protocol) at the transport layer. RTSP is actually a control protocol, which carries commands between the client and server using the connection-oriented TCP protocol and port number 554. For the actual data streaming, Windows Media Services uses the Real Time Protocol (RTP).

HTTP is the same protocol that Web servers use to send HTML (Hypertext Markup Language) and image files to client browsers. Windows Media Services includes HTTP primarily to support Windows Media Players prior to version 9, which cannot use RTSP, or clients that must stream content through a firewall. Windows Media Services uses TCP port 80 to stream multimedia content with HTTP, the same port that Web servers use, which is why most firewalls allow traffic using port 80 to pass through them.

USING PROTOCOL ROLLOVER

When you enable both the RTSP and the HTTP protocols on a Windows Media Services server, the clients and the server use a process called ***protocol rollover*** to negotiate the most efficient protocol they have in common. A client establishing a connection to a Windows Media Services server sends information about the protocols it can use, and the server selects the best protocol it is capable of using. If, for any reason, the client cannot use the selected protocol, the server reverts to the next best protocol in its list.

To use protocol rollover, administrators should publish their multimedia content using URLs with a Microsoft Media Server (MMS) URL moniker (mms:// prefix), as in *mms://servername/video*. If you use announcements to publish content instead, the player uses the mms:// prefix automatically.

When the client computer is running Windows Media Player version 9 or later, a Windows Media Services server attempts to connect using RTSP. If the server is configured to use Fast Cache (which it is by default), it tries to connect to the client using RTSP with the TCP transport layer protocol. If this connection attempt does not succeed, the server then tries RTSP with UDP. If Fast Cache is not enabled, the server tries RTSP with UDP first, and then RTSP with TCP. If both of the RTSP connection attempts fail, the server reverts to HTTP. When a client is running a version of Windows Media Player older than version 9, the server uses HTTP to connect to the player.

SPECIFYING A PROTOCOL

Administrators can specify the protocol they want a multimedia stream to use by employing protocol-specific URL prefixes, as follows:

- rtsp://—Causes the server to initiate an RTSP connection, and then negotiate whether to use UDP or TCP.
- rtspt://—Causes the server to initiate an RTSP connection using TCP.
- rtspu://—Causes the server to initiate an RTSP connection using UDP.
- http://—Causes the server to initiate an HTTP connection.

Installing the Streaming Media Services Role

Originally, the Streaming Media Services role was included with the Windows Server 2008 product. At some point during the development process, however, Microsoft decided to remove the role from the operating system and supply it as a free download instead.

CERTIFICATION READY?
Configure Windows
Media® Server
4.1

When you find Windows Media Services 2008 at the Microsoft Downloads Center (http://microsoft.com/downloads), you see three Microsoft Standalone Update (MSU) files for each of the x86 and x64 platforms. The contents of the files are as follows:

- Admin—Contains only the Windows Media Services console, enabling you to administer a server running the Streaming Media Services role from another computer.
- Core—Contains the Windows Media Services console and the Streaming Media Services role for the Windows Server Core installation option of Windows Server 2008 Standard or Enterprise Edition.
- Server—Contains the Windows Media Services console and the Streaming Media Services role for a full installation of Windows Server 2008 Standard or Enterprise Edition.

To perform a full Windows Media Services installation on a Windows Server 2008 computer, first you must run the Server or Core MSU file. Executing the file does not activate the

Streaming Media Services role, however; it merely installs it on the computer. You must add the role in the usual manner using the Server Manager console.

Use the following complete procedure for installing Windows Media Services on a full installation of Windows Server 2008.

 INSTALL WINDOWS MEDIA SERVICES

GET READY. Log on to Windows Server 2008 using an account with administrative privileges. When the logon process is completed, close the Initial Configuration Tasks window and any other windows that appear.

1. Open Internet Explorer and download the appropriate Windows Media Services 2008 file for your server's architecture (x86 or x64) from http://microsoft.com/downloads.

2. Click **Start**, and then click **Run**. The Run dialog box appears.

3. Browse to the Windows Media Services Server MSU file on your local drive and click **OK**. A Windows Update Standalone Installer message box appears, confirming that you want to install the update.

4. Click **OK**. A Read These License Terms window appears.

5. Click **I Accept** to agree to the terms. A progress indicator page appears.

6. When the Installation Complete page appears, click **Close**.

7. Click **Start**, and then click **Administrative Tools** > **Server Manager**. The Server Manager console appears.

8. Start the Add Roles Wizard. The Streaming Media Services role should now appear on the Select Server Roles page.

9. Select the **Streaming Media Services** role, as shown in Figure 11-6.

Figure 11-6

The Select Server Roles page of the Add Roles Wizard

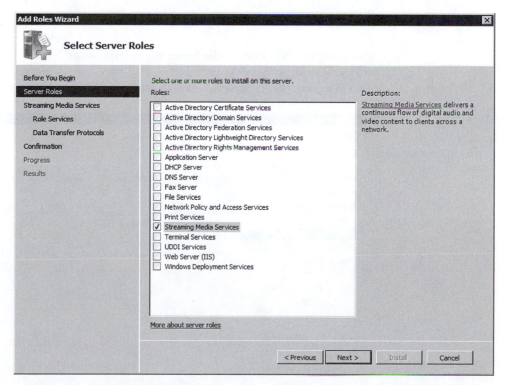

10. Complete the installation, using the procedure documented in Lesson 1, "Deploying an Application Server."

The Streaming Media Services role includes three role services. Table 11-3 lists the dependencies for each role service, the wizard pages each role service adds to the Add Roles Wizard, and the system services and Microsoft Management Console (MMC) snap-ins each role service installs.

Table 11-3

Windows Media Services Role Services

ROLE SERVICES	DEPENDENCIES	WIZARD PAGES	SYSTEM SERVICES	SNAP-INS
Windows Media Server	[None]	• Streaming Media Services > Data Transfer Protocols	• Windows Media Services (WMServer)	• Windows Media Services
Web-Based Administration	• Web Server (IIS) • Windows Process Activation Service > Process Model	• Web Server (IIS) > Role Services	• Application Host Helper Service (apphostsvc) • IIS Admin Service (iisadmin) • Windows Process Activation Service (WAS) • World Wide Web Publishing Service (w3svc)	[None]
Logging Agent	• Web Server (IIS) > ISAPI Extensions • Web Server (IIS) > ISAPI Filters • Windows Process Activation Service > Process Model	• Web Server (IIS) > Role Services	• Application Host Helper Service (apphostsvc) • Windows Process Activation Service (WAS) • World Wide Web Publishing Service (w3svc)	[None]

Selecting the Windows Media Server role service adds the Select Data Transfer Protocols page to the wizard, as shown in Figure 11-7. This page enables you to specify whether you want the Windows Media Services server to support Real Time Streaming Protocol (the default),

Figure 11-7

The Select Data Transfer Protocols page of the Add Roles Wizard

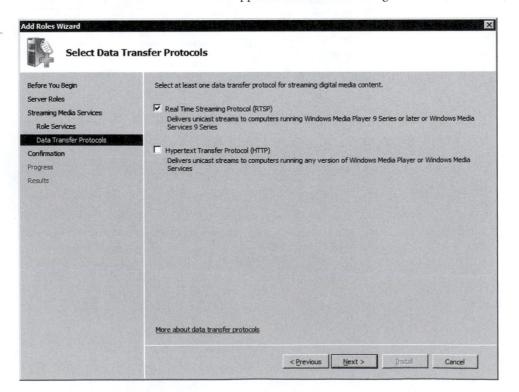

Hypertext Transfer Protocol, or both, for streaming multimedia content. If you are certain that all of your clients are computers on the local network running Windows Media Player version 9 or higher, you can safely select RTSP only. However, if any of your clients are running older versions of Windows Media Player or connecting to the server through a firewall, you should enable HTTP streaming as well.

Creating a Publishing Point

> Installing the Streaming Media Services role creates two default publishing points, but you can add as many additional publishing points as you need.

After you install the Streaming Media Services role, you can begin deploying multimedia content by creating new publishing points that specify the stream and transmission types you want the server to use.

To create a publishing point, use the following procedure.

 CREATE A PUBLISHING POINT

GET READY. Log on to Windows Server 2008 using an account with administrative privileges. When the logon process is completed, close the Initial Configuration Tasks window and any other windows that appear.

1. Click **Start**, and then click **Administrative Tools** > **Windows Media Services**. The Windows Media Services console appears, as shown in Figure 11-8.

Figure 11-8

The Windows Media Services console

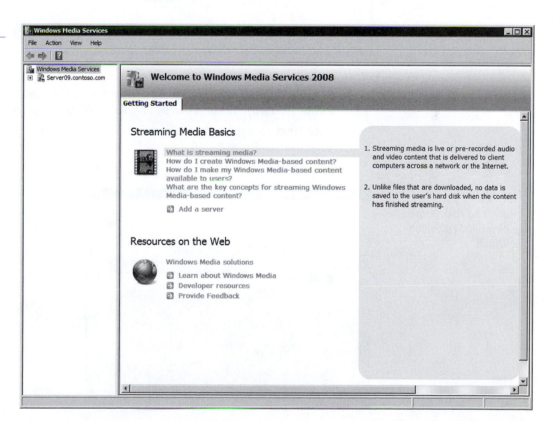

2. In the scope pane, expand the server node and select the **Publishing Points** node. The default on-demand and broadcast publishing points appear in the detail pane, as shown in Figure 11-9.

Figure 11-9

The default publishing points in the Windows Media Services console

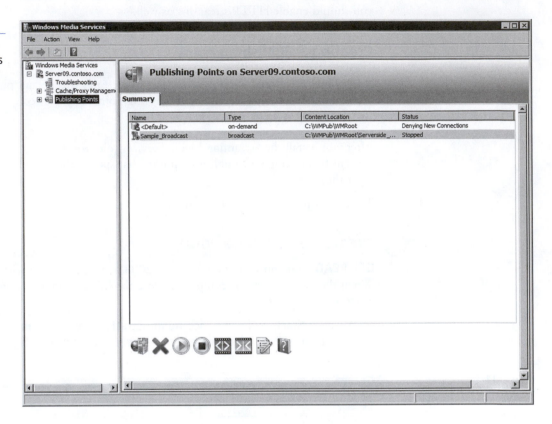

3. Right-click **Publishing Points** and, from the context menu, select **Add Publishing Point (Wizard)**. The Add Publishing Point Wizard appears.

4. Click **Next** to bypass the Welcome page. The Publishing Point Name page appears, as shown in Figure 11-10.

Figure 11-10

The Publishing Point Name page of the Add Publishing Point Wizard

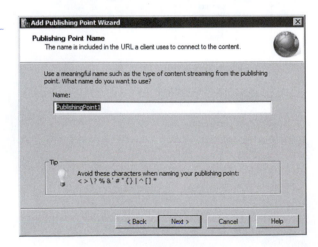

5. Key a name for the publishing point in the Name text box and click **Next**. The Content Type page appears, as shown in Figure 11-11.

Figure 11-11

The Content Type page of the
Add Publishing Point Wizard

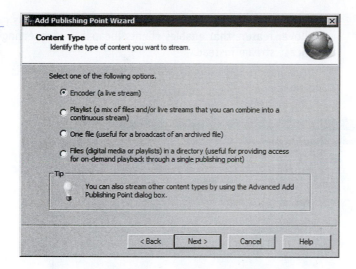

6. Select one of the following options:

- Encoder—Indicates that the content is a live stream, encoded in real time.
- Playlist—Indicates that the content is a playlist file containing a collection of files and/or live streams that will play consecutively.
- One file—Indicates that the content is a single, prerecorded file.
- Files (digital media or playlists) in a directory—Specifies the name of a single folder containing all of the content files.

7. Click **Next**. The Publishing Point Type page appears, as shown in Figure 11-12.

Figure 11-12

The Publishing Point Type page
of the Add Publishing Point
Wizard

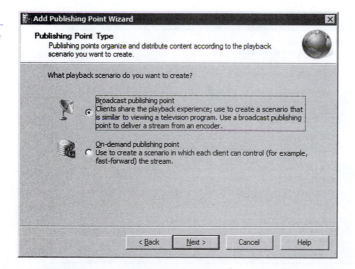

8. Select one of the following options:

- Broadcast publishing point—Creates a single, scheduled stream that multiple clients can view simultaneously. If you select this option, an additional Delivery Options for Broadcast Publishing Points page appears in the wizard, enabling you to specify whether the publishing point should use unicast or multicast transmissions, as shown in Figure 11-13. Multicast transmissions can also include a unicast rollover feature that enables clients incapable of receiving multicasts to receive a unicast stream instead.

- On-demand publishing point—Creates individual streams for individual users, as needed.

Figure 11-13

The Delivery Options for Broadcast Publishing Points page of the Add Publishing Point Wizard

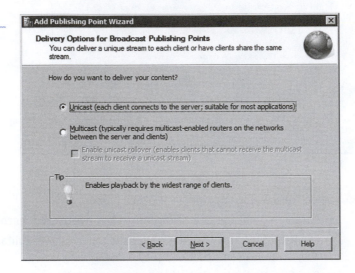

9. Click **Next**. A page appears, prompting you for the location of the content you want to publish. The exact appearance of this and the following pages depends on the Content Type and Publishing Point Type values you selected. For example, if you select Files for the content type, the Directory Location page appears, as shown in Figure 11-14.

Figure 11-14

The Directory Location page of the Add Publishing Point Wizard

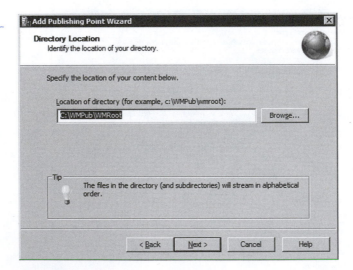

10. Specify the location of the file or folder containing the content and click **Next**. If you selected the *Files in a directory* Content Type option, the Content Playback page appears, as shown in Figure 11-15.

11. Select one of the following options, if desired:

- Loop—Causes the server to replay the content continuously.
- Shuffle—Causes the server to play the various files and/or live streams in the content in random order.

12. Click **Next**. If you are creating a unicast stream, the Unicast Logging page appears, as shown in Figure 11-16.

Figure 11-15

The Content Playback page of the Add Publishing Point Wizard

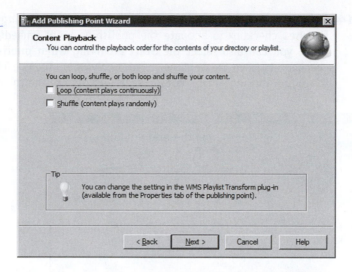

Figure 11-16

The Unicast Logging page of the Add Publishing Point Wizard

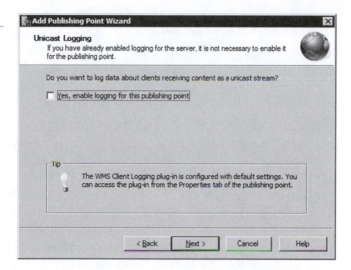

13. Select the **Yes, enable logging for the publishing point** checkbox if you want the server to log unicast client connections. Then, click **Next**. The Publishing Point Summary page appears, as shown in Figure 11-17.

Figure 11-17

The Publishing Point Summary page of the Add Publishing Point Wizard

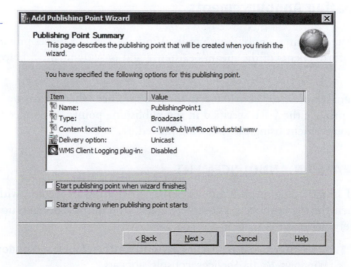

14. For broadcast publishing points, select the **Start publishing point when wizard finishes** checkbox to activate the publishing point immediately; for unicast broadcasts, you can also select the **Start archiving when publishing point starts** checkbox to save the content to an archive file. Then, click **Next**. The Completing the Add Publishing Point Wizard page appears, as shown in Figure 11-18.

Figure 11-18

The Completing the Add Publishing Point Wizard page of the Add Publishing Point Wizard

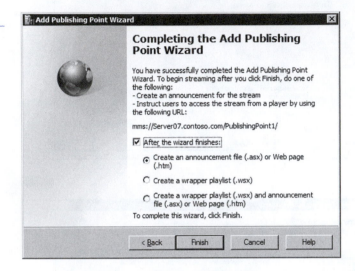

15. To perform additional tasks, select the **After the wizard finishes** checkbox and choose one of the following options:

   • Create an announcement file (.asx) or Web page (.htm)—Launches the appropriate announcement wizard for the transmission type, which enables you to create a file that users can click to load the multimedia stream.

   • Create a wrapper playlist (.wsx)—Launches the Create Wrapper Wizard, which enables you to create a playlist that includes additional content (such as announcements or advertisements) before and/or after your main content.

   • Create a wrapper playlist (.wsx) and announcement file (.asx) or Web page (.htm) —Launches both the announcement wizard and the Create Wrapper Wizard.

16. Click **Finish**. The new publishing point appears in the console's detail pane.

CLOSE the Windows Media Services console.

At this point, the content you specified while creating the publishing point is available for streaming.

Creating Announcements

> After creating a publishing point, Windows Media Services provides several ways to inform clients of the stream's existence and provide them with access to it.

To enable users to access the content you specified when creating a publishing point, you can provide the URL specified in the publishing point's Announce tab or you can create an announcement using the following procedure.

 CREATE AN ANNOUNCEMENT

GET READY. Log on to Windows Server 2008 using an account with administrative privileges. When the logon process is completed, close the Initial Configuration Tasks window and any other windows that appear.

1. Click **Start**, and then click **Administrative Tools** > **Windows Media Services**. The Windows Media Services console appears.

2. Add your server to the console, if needed. In the scope pane, expand the server node and the Publishing Points node, and select the publishing point you want to announce.

3. In the detail pane, click the **Announce** tab, as shown in Figure 11-19.

Figure 11-19

A publishing point's Announce tab

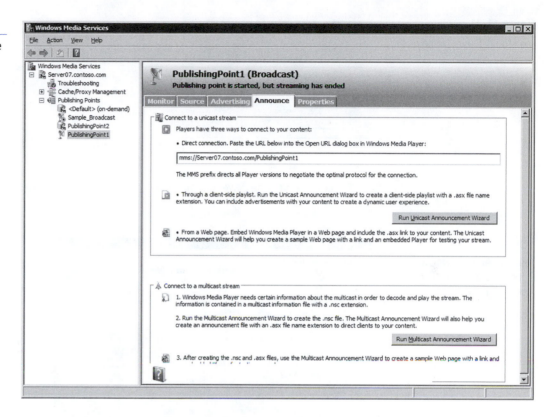

4. Click the **Run Unicast Announcement Wizard** button. The Unicast Announcement Wizard appears.

TAKE NOTE * This procedure creates an announcement for a unicast stream. To create an announcement for a multicast stream, click the Run Multicast Announcement Wizard button instead.

5. Click **Next** to bypass the Welcome page. The Access the Content page appears, as shown in Figure 11-20.

Figure 11-20

The Access the Content page of the Unicast Announcement Wizard

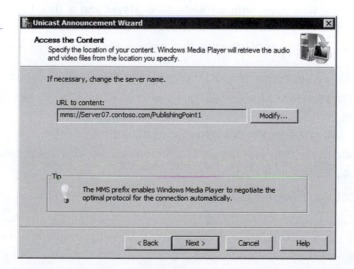

6. If you want the announcement to use a different name for the server or an IP address instead of a name, click **Modify** and, in the Modify Server Name dialog box shown in Figure 11-21, key the name or address. Then, click **OK.**

Figure 11-21

The Modify Server Name dialog box

7. Click **Next.** The Save Announcement Options page appears, as shown in Figure 11-22.

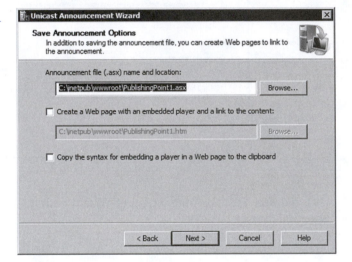

8. In the *Announcement file (.asx) name and location* text box, specify the name you want to assign to the announcement file and the folder where you want to create it.

9. To create an HTML file containing code that embeds the media player interface and a link to the content you specified into the Web page, select the **Create a Web page with an embedded player and a link to the content** checkbox. Specify the name and location for the .htm file.

10. To copy the HTML code that embeds the media player interface into the clipboard so you can paste it into an existing Web page file, select the **Copy the syntax for embedding a player in a Web page to the clipboard** checkbox.

11. Click **Next.** The Edit Announcement Metadata page appears, as shown in Figure 11-23.

12. Specify title, author, copyright, banner, and/or log URL information about the content in the publishing point as desired.

13. Click **Next.** The Completing the Unicast Announcement Wizard page appears.

14. Click **Finish.**

CLOSE the Windows Media Services console.

If you select the *Test files when the wizard finishes* checkbox, the Test Unicast Announcement dialog box appears, as shown in Figure 11-24, with which you can execute both the announcement file and the Web page created by the wizard.

Figure 11-23

The Edit Announcement
Metadata page of the Unicast
Announcement Wizard

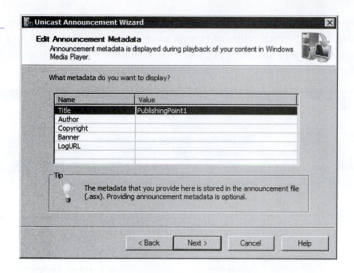

Figure 11-24

The Test Unicast Announcement
dialog box

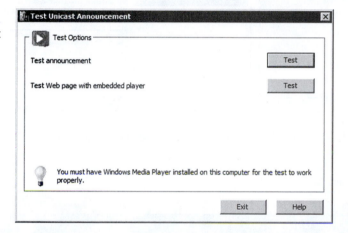

TAKE NOTE ✱ To perform the announcement tests, the computer must have Windows Media Player installed. On a Windows Server 2008 computer, you must add the Desktop Experience feature using Server Manager to install Windows Media Player.

Controlling Bandwidth Utilization

Heavily used multimedia streams can easily consume all of a network's bandwidth. Administrators should understand the impact that streaming media can have on network performance, and be familiar with the controls they can use to regulate the bandwidth that the streams utilize.

Earlier in this lesson, you learned about several factors that can affect the amount of network bandwidth consumed by Windows Media Services. In addition to these design factors, you can specify values for configuration parameters that control bandwidth utilization.

Every component on a Windows Media Services server has a Properties tab, as shown in Figure 11-25, which contains several categories, with properties in each one. The Limits category contains the properties that control bandwidth utilization, which you can configure at the server level or the publishing point level.

Figure 11-25

The Limits parameters for a Windows Media Services server

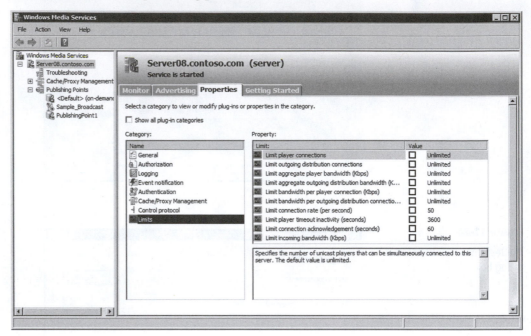

Table 11-4 lists the Limits parameters and their functions.

Table 11-4

Windows Media Services Limits Parameters

Properties	Applies to	Unit of Measurement	Default Value	Description
Limit player connections	Server and publishing points	Connections	Unlimited	Specifies the maximum number of clients that can establish unicast connections to the server or publishing point at any one time.
Limit outgoing distribution connections	Server and publishing points	Connections	Unlimited	Specifies the maximum number of connections to other servers that the server or publishing point can establish at any one time.
Limit aggregate player bandwidth	Server and publishing points	Kbps	Unlimited	Specifies the total amount of bandwidth that clients connected to the server or publishing point can use at any one time.
Limit aggregate outgoing distribution bandwidth	Server and publishing points	Kbps	Unlimited	Specifies the total amount of bandwidth that the server or publishing point can use for connections to cache/proxy servers at any one time.
Limit bandwidth per player connection	Server and publishing points	Kbps	Unlimited	Specifies the maximum amount of bandwidth that each client connected to the server or publishing point can use when receiving a stream.
Limit bandwidth per outgoing distribution connection	Server and publishing points	Kbps	Unlimited	Specifies the maximum amount of bandwidth that the server or publishing point can use for each connection to another server.

(continued)

Table 11-4 (*continued*)

Properties	Applies to	Unit of Measurement	Default Value	Description
Limit connection rate	Server only	Per second	50	Specifies the maximum number of connections the server can resolve each second.
Limit player timeout activity	Server only	Seconds	3600	Specifies how long a client can remain connected to the server without activity. After the specified time period expires, the server disconnects the inactive client.
Limit connection acknowledgment	Server only	Seconds	60	Specifies how long the server will wait for an acknowledgment from a client before disconnecting it.
Limit incoming bandwidth	Server only	Kbps	Unlimited	Specifies the maximum amount of bandwidth each incoming connection to the server can use.
Limit Fast Cache content delivery rate	On-demand publishing points only	Multiple of encoded bit rate	5	Specifies the maximum accelerated delivery factor for connections to players. The value (1 to 5) designates a multiple of the encoded bit rate of the content.
Limit Fast Start bandwidth per player connection	Publishing points only	Kbps	3500	Specifies the maximum amount of bandwidth a client supporting Fast Start can use during the initial accelerated buffering phase of a connection.

Using Windows SharePoint Services

THE BOTTOM LINE

Windows SharePoint Services 3.0 is, essentially, a database-enabled Web application that runs on an Internet Information Services server.

By accessing the ***Windows SharePoint Services 3.0*** site, users can employ browser-based workspaces to share information in a variety of ways, such as storing documents, creating calendar appointments and task lists, and contributing to newsgroup-style discussions. You can create individual Web sites for specific projects, departments, or workgroups that contain some or all of these features.

Windows SharePoint Services relies on Microsoft SQL Server 2005 technology to manage the database that stores user documents and information. For small deployments, you can use a single Windows Server 2008 computer to host the IIS Web server and the SQL database, in addition to the Windows SharePoint Services application. Windows Server 2008 includes Windows Internal Database, which is an SQL-based data store for Windows roles and features.

For large organizations, you can scale up the Windows SharePoint Services deployment by creating a server farm that distributes the functions among several computers and replicates the servers using failover clustering. For example, you can run Microsoft SQL Server 2005 on a computer separate from the Web server or even separate the Web server from the SharePoint search service and other application server features.

Installing Windows SharePoint Services

Windows SharePoint Services was included as part of Windows Server 2003, but for Windows Server 2008, Microsoft has released it as a separate product, available as a free download.

Unlike Windows Media Services, Windows SharePoint Services is not a role; it has its own installation program and requires you to install its dependent features manually.

To install a stand-alone Windows SharePoint Services 3.0 server, use the following procedure.

INSTALL WINDOWS SHAREPOINT SERVICES

GET READY. Log on to Windows Server 2008 using an account with administrative privileges. When the logon process is completed, close the Initial Configuration Tasks window and any other windows that appear.

1. Click **Start**, and then click **Administrative Tools** > **Server Manager**. The Server Manager console appears.

2. In the scope pane, right-click the **Features** node and, from the context menu, select **Add Features**. The Add Features Wizard appears, as shown in Figure 11-26.

Figure 11-26

The Add Features Wizard

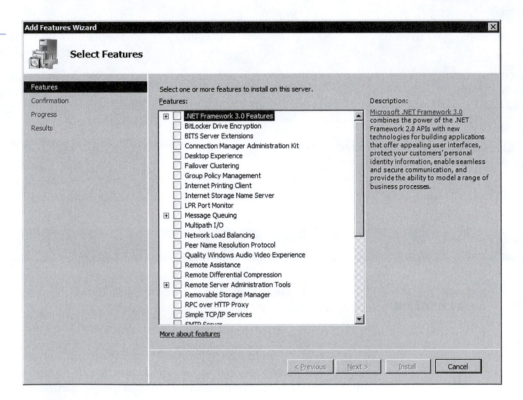

3. On the Select Features page, select the **.NET Framework 3.0 Features** checkbox. The *Add role services and features required for .NET Framework 3.0 Features?* dialog box appears, as shown in Figure 11-27.

Figure 11-27

The *Add role services and features required for .NET Framework 3.0 Features?* dialog box

4. Click **Add Required Role Services**.

5. Click **Next**.

6. Click **Next** again to bypass the Web Server (IIS) page. The Select Role Services page appears.

7. Click **Next** to accept the selected Web Server (IIS) role services. The Confirm Installation Selection page appears.

8. Click **Install**.

9. When the installation procedure finishes, click **Close**.

10. Download Windows SharePoint Services 3.0 with Service Pack 1 from the Microsoft Download Center.

 TAKE NOTE* To install Windows SharePoint Services 3.0 on Windows Server 2008, you must download the product with Service Pack 1 integrated into it. Although Windows SharePoint Services 3.0 and Service Pack 1 are available as separate downloads, you cannot install the two separately on Windows Server 2008.

11. Run the SharePoint.exe file you downloaded. An Open File—Security Warning dialog box appears, prompting you to confirm that you want to run the file.

12. Click **Run**. The Microsoft Windows SharePoint Services 3.0 wizard appears, displaying the Read the Microsoft Software License Terms page, as shown in Figure 11-28.

Figure 11-28

The Read the Microsoft Software License Terms page

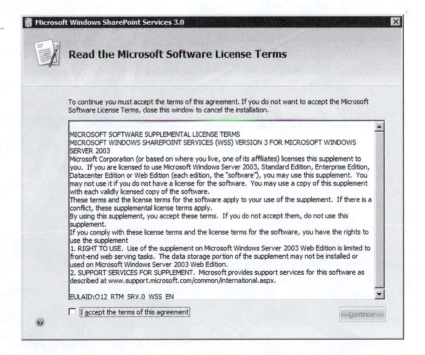

13. Select the **I accept the terms of this agreement** checkbox and click **Continue**. The *Choose the installation you want* page appears, as shown in Figure 11-29.

Figure 11-29

The *Choose the installation you want* page

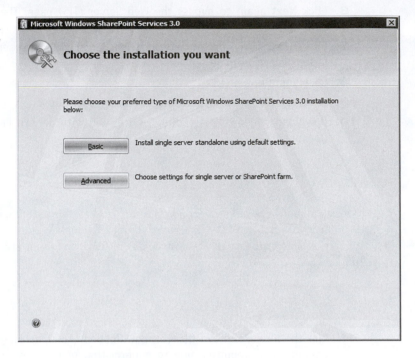

14. Click **Basic**. The Installation Progress page appears.

 TAKE NOTE＊ Click Advanced to specify an alternate location for the Windows SharePoint Services files or to install a server farm.

15. When the installation is complete, verify that the **Run the SharePoint Products and Technologies Configuration Wizard** checkbox is selected and click **Close**. The SharePoint Products and Technologies Configuration Wizard appears, as shown in Figure 11-30.

Figure 11-30

The SharePoint Products and Technologies Configuration Wizard

16. Click **Next** to bypass the Welcome page. A SharePoint Products and Technologies Configuration Wizard message box appears, as shown in Figure 11-31, warning you of the services that have to be started or reset during the configuration process.

Figure 11-31

The SharePoint Products and Technologies Configuration Wizard message box

17. Click **Yes**. The configuration process begins. When the process is complete, the Configuration Successful page appears.

18. Click **Finish**.

CLOSE the Server Manager console.

When the configuration process is completed, an Internet Explorer window appears and, after prompting you to log on, displays the server's default Web page, as shown in Figure 11-32. Windows SharePoint Services calls this default Web page the Team Site page. You can, of course, customize this page any way you wish, using standard HTML coding and Web development tools.

Figure 11-32

The Team Site Web page

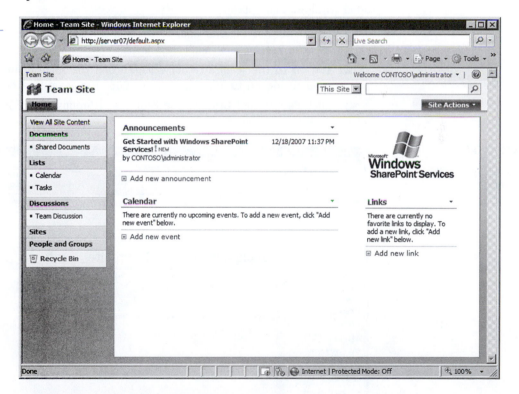

Configuring SharePoint Server Options

After you install and configure Windows SharePoint Services, you can access the administration interface by selecting SharePoint 3.0 Central Administration from the Administrative Tools program group in the Start menu.

Using the Windows SharePoint Services administration interface and the main home page, you can configure a wide array of server settings, as discussed in the following sections.

MORE INFORMATION

SharePoint 3.0 Central Administration is a separate Web site running on the same IIS server as the Team Site. During the installation, the Windows SharePoint Services setup program assigns a random port number over 1024 to the administration site to keep it separated from the user site, which uses the standard HTTP port number 80. The SharePoint 3.0 Central Administration shortcut in the Administration Tools program group simply loads Internet Explorer with a URL containing the server name and the assigned port number. While the use of the alternate port number effectively keeps the administrative site hidden from most users, you should not consider it an adequate security measure. Control access to the administrative site using accounts with secure passwords, just as you would any other administrative feature on the server.

ADDING USERS

As you saw when the SharePoint Products and Technologies Configuration Wizard finished running and launched Internet Explorer, you must log on to access the Team Site home page. For other users to access the site, you must add the users to the SharePoint server and assign appropriate permissions. The accounts you add to a SharePoint server can be local users, local groups, domain users, or domain groups, using the form *server\user*, *domain\user*, or *user@domain.com*.

To add users to the default SharePoint Team Site and assign permissions to them, use the following procedure.

➔ ADD USERS

GET READY. Log on to Windows Server 2008 using an account with administrative privileges. When the logon process is completed, close the Initial Configuration Tasks window and any other windows that appear.

1. Open Internet Explorer and, in the address box, key the URL for your server, such as *http://servername*, and press (**Enter**).
2. Log on to the Team Site home page using the same administrative account you used to log on to Windows Server 2008. The Team Site home page appears.
3. Click **People and Groups**. The People and Groups: Team Site Members page appears, as shown in Figure 11-33.

Figure 11-33

The People and Groups: Team Site Members page

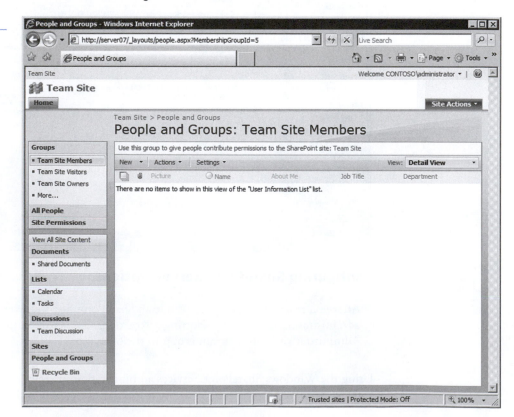

4. Click **New** and, from the context menu, select **Add Users**. The Add Users: Team Site page appears, as shown in Figure 11-34.

Figure 11-34

The Add Users: Team Site page

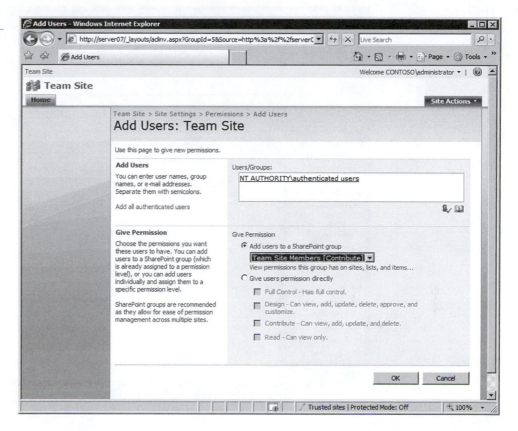

5. In the Users/Groups text box, key the names of the users and/or groups you want to add, separated by semicolons.

6. To add the users/groups you specified to an existing SharePoint group, select the **Add users to a SharePoint group** option and select one of the following groups from the dropdown list:

- Team Site Owners [Full Control]—Provides complete administrative and operational control over the site
- Team Site Visitors [Read]—Provides the user only with view capabilities for the site
- Team Site Members [Contribute]—Provides the user with view, add, update, and delete capabilities for the site

7. To assign permissions to the users/groups you specified, select the **Give users permission directly** option and choose from the following permissions:

- Full Control—Provides complete administrative and operational control over the site
- Design—Provides the user with view, add, update, delete, approve, and customize capabilities for the site
- Contribute—Provides the user with view, add, update, and delete capabilities for the site
- Read—Provides the user only with view capabilities for the site

8. Click **OK**. The People and Groups: Team Site Members page appears, as shown in Figure 11-35.

Figure 11-35

The People and Groups: Team Site Members page

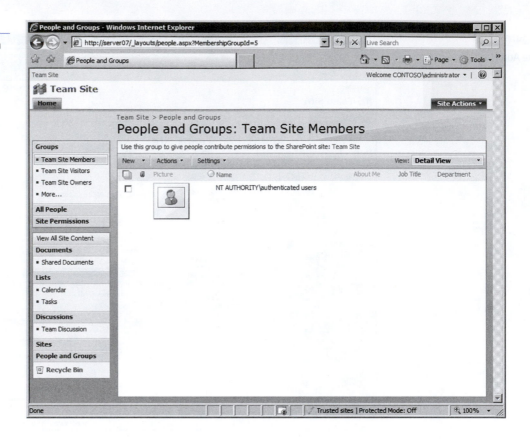

CLOSE the Internet Explorer window.

You can also click the *Add all authenticated users* link to assign permissions to the Authenticated Users special identity, which enables all users who successfully log on to access the Windows SharePoint Services site.

CONFIGURING ANTIVIRUS SETTINGS

Because Windows SharePoint Services is, by nature, a collaboration tool that enables users to share documents, you should consider using an antivirus product to protect against the spread of infections via those documents. When you install an antivirus software product compatible with Windows SharePoint Services, you can use SharePoint 3.0 Central Administration to configure its activity, using the following procedure.

 CONFIGURE ANTIVIRUS SETTINGS

GET READY. Log on to Windows Server 2008 using an account with administrative privileges. When the logon process is completed, close the Initial Configuration Tasks window and any other windows that appear.

1. Click **Start**, and then click **Administrative Tools** > **SharePoint 3.0 Central Administration**. A Connect To dialog box appears, prompting you for administrative credentials.

2. Key an appropriate user name and password in the text boxes provided and click **OK**. An Internet Explorer window appears, displaying the Central Administration home page, as shown in Figure 11-36.

Figure 11-36

The Central Administration
home page

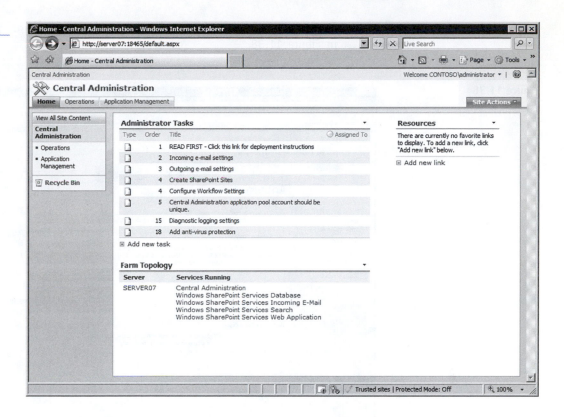

3. Click the **Operations** tab. The Operations page appears, as shown in Figure 11-37.

Figure 11-37

The Operations page

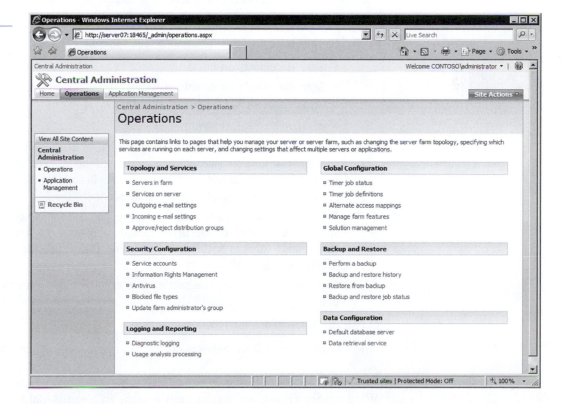

4. Under Security Configuration, click **Antivirus**. The Antivirus page appears, as shown in Figure 11-38.

Figure 11-38

The Antivirus page

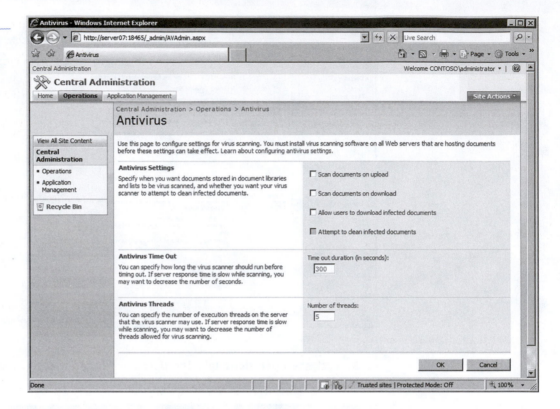

5. In the Antivirus Settings area, select some or all of the following options:

- Scan documents on upload
- Scan documents on download
- Allow users to download infected documents
- Attempt to clean infected documents

6. In the Antivirus Time Out area, key a number in the *Time out duration* box to specify how long (in seconds) the virus scanner should attempt to run before timing out. The default value is 300 seconds. Decreasing the value reduces the processor resources utilized by the antivirus scanner.

7. In the Antivirus Threads area, key a number in the *Number of threads* box to specify the number of execution threads you want the antivirus scanner to use. The default value is 5 threads. Decreasing the value reduces the processor resources utilized by the antivirus scanner.

8. Click **OK**. After saving the settings, Internet Explorer returns to the Operations page.

CLOSE the Internet Explorer window.

Now, Windows SharePoint Services can use your antivirus software to scan user documents.

BACKING UP WINDOWS SHAREPOINT SERVICES

Windows SharePoint Services can easily become an essential tool for your end users, one in which they store large amounts of important data. Like any application of this type, one of the most important administrative tasks is protecting that data by performing regular database backups. Because standard backup programs cannot back up an SQL database while it is running, Windows SharePoint Services includes its own backup function, which copies all or

part of the database to an alternate location. Then, you can back up the copy to an alternate medium using your regular network backup utility.

To back up Windows SharePoint Services, use the following procedure.

 BACK UP WINDOWS SHAREPOINT SERVICES

GET READY. Log on to Windows Server 2008 using an account with administrative privileges. When the logon process is completed, close the Initial Configuration Tasks window and any other windows that appear.

1. Click **Start**, and then click **Administrative Tools** > **SharePoint 3.0 Central Administration**. A Connect To dialog box appears, prompting you for administrative credentials.

2. Key an appropriate user name and password in the text boxes provided and click **OK**. An Internet Explorer window appears, displaying the Central Administration home page.

3. Click the **Operations** tab. The Operations page appears.

4. Under Backup and Restore, click **Perform a backup**. The Perform a Backup—Step 1 of 2: Select Component to Backup page appears, as shown in Figure 11-39.

Figure 11-39

The Perform a Backup—Step 1 of 2: Select Component to Backup page

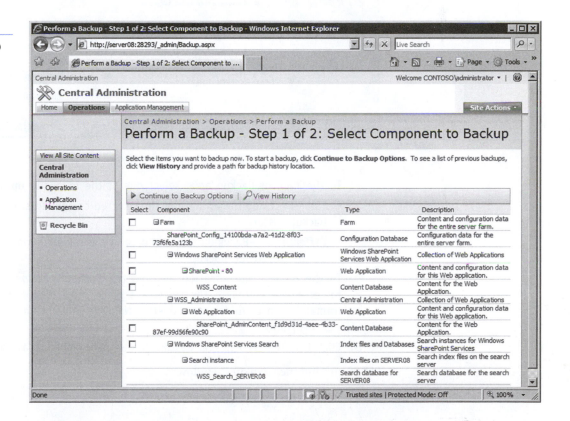

5. Select the component(s) that you want to back up. Selecting the Farm option backs up the entire Windows SharePoint Services installation, including the content database, configuration settings, and search indices. The other options let you select various combinations of individual SharePoint components.

6. Click **Continue to Backup Options**. The Start Backup—Step 2 of 2: Select Backup Options page appears, as shown in Figure 11-40.

Figure 11-40

The Start Backup—Step 2 of 2: Select Backup Options page

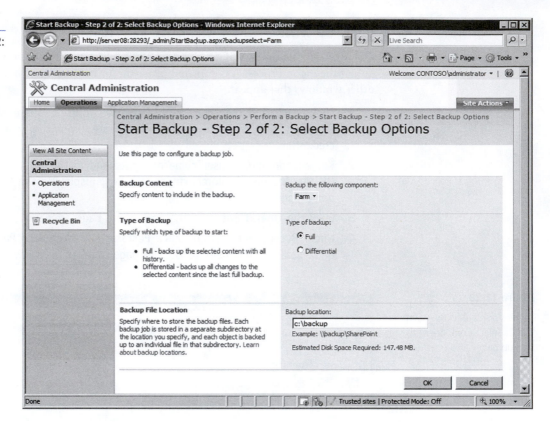

7. In the Type of Backup area, select one of the following options:
- Full—Backs up the entirety of the selected components, regardless of the previous backup history.
- *Differential*—Backs up only the data in the selected components that has changed since the last full backup.

8. In the Backup File Location area, in the *Backup location* box, specify the folder where you want the system to place the backups. Use drive letter format, as in *c:\folder*, or Universal Naming Convention (UNC) format, as in *\\server\share*.

9. Click **OK**. The Backup and Restore Status page appears, as shown in Figure 11-41.

CLOSE the Internet Explorer window.

Figure 11-41

The Backup and Restore Status page

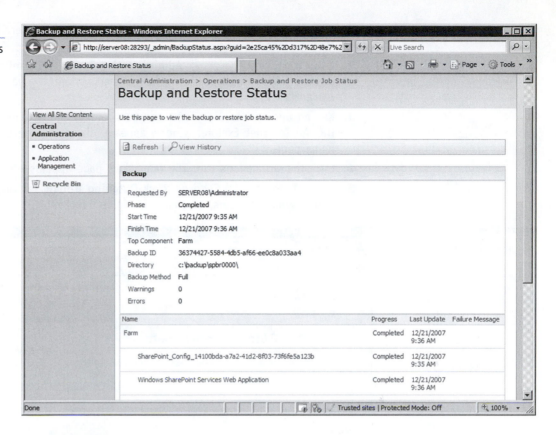

When Windows SharePoint Services performs a backup, it creates a new subdirectory beneath the folder you specified in the Backup File Location box and begins copying the application data to that subdirectory. After the backup is complete, you can back up the subdirectory to magnetic tape or any other storage medium for addition protection.

CONFIGURING EMAIL INTEGRATION

Windows SharePoint Services can integrate with email in a variety of ways, enabling users to set up calendar appointments, post announcements, add documents, and contribute to blogs and discussion forums. To provide users with these email capabilities, you must install a Simple Mail Transfer Protocol (SMTP) server and configure the incoming and outgoing email settings in Windows SharePoint Services.

Windows SharePoint Services uses incoming email to enable users to contribute content to the site. To do this, you must install an SMTP server on the SharePoint computer. Outgoing email enables SharePoint to send email-based alerts, invitations, and notifications to users and administrators. Outgoing email requires an SMTP server as well, but it does not have to be running on the SharePoint computer.

CERTIFICATION READY?
Configure Windows SharePoint Services email integration
4.4

 REF

SMTP Server is a feature included with Windows Server 2008 that you can install using the Add Features Wizard in Server Manager. See "Deploying an SMTP Server" in Lesson 7, "Deploying Web Applications," for more information.

To configure the Windows SharePoint Services incoming and outgoing email settings, use the following procedure.

 CONFIGURE EMAIL INTEGRATION

GET READY. Log on to Windows Server 2008 using an account with administrative privileges. When the logon process is completed, close the Initial Configuration Tasks window and any other windows that appear.

1. If you have not done so already, add the SMTP Server service using the Server Manager console.

2. Click **Start**, and then click **Administrative Tools** > **SharePoint 3.0 Central Administration**. A Connect To dialog box appears, prompting you for administrative credentials.

3. Key an appropriate user name and password in the text boxes provided and click **OK**. An Internet Explorer window appears, displaying the Central Administration home page.

4. Click the **Operations** tab. The Operations page appears.

5. Under Topology and Services, click **Outgoing e-mail settings**. The Outgoing E-Mail Settings page appears, as shown in Figure 11-42.

Figure 11-42

The Outgoing E-Mail Settings page

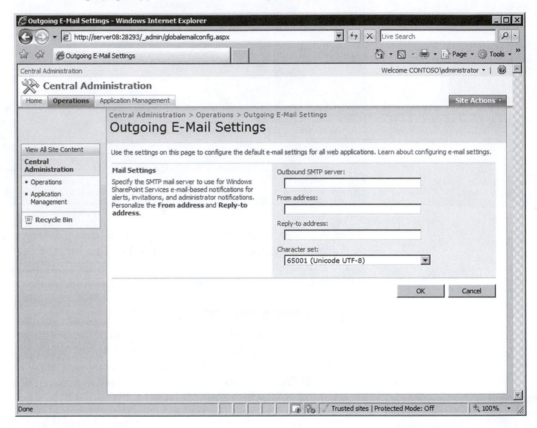

6. In the *Outbound SMTP server* text box, key the name or IP address of a Windows Server 2008 computer running the SMTP Server feature.

TAKE NOTE* For outgoing SMTP traffic, you can use any mail server that conforms to the SMTP standard, whether it runs on Windows or not.

7. In the *From address* text box, key the address that you want email recipients to see as the sender of the message.

8. In the *Reply-to address* text box, key the address that you want email recipients to use when replying to a message.

9. In the *Character set* dropdown list, select the appropriate character set for the language your server is using.

10. Click **OK**. The Operations page reappears.

11. Click **Incoming e-mail settings**. The Configure Incoming E-Mail Settings page appears, as shown in Figure 11-43.

12. In the Enable Incoming E-Mail box, click **Yes** in response to the *Enable sites on this server to receive e-mail?* prompt.

Figure 11-43

The Configure Incoming E-Mail Settings page

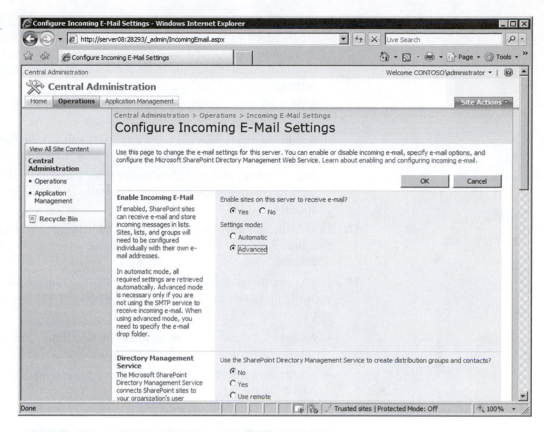

13. For *Settings mode,* select one of the following options:

- Automatic—Select this option if the SMTP Server feature included with Windows Server 2008 is installed on the computer.

- Advanced—Select this option if the computer is running an SMTP server other than the one included with Windows Server 2008.

14. In the Directory Management Service box, shown in Figure 11-44, select **Yes** to enable Windows SharePoint Services to interact with Active Directory. Then, configure the following settings:

Figure 11-44

The Directory Management Service box on the Configure Incoming E-Mail Settings page

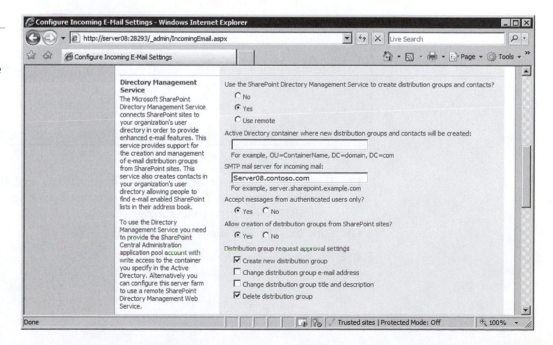

- Active Directory container where new distribution groups and contacts will be created—Specifies the location in the Active Directory hierarchy where SharePoint will create new objects. You must grant the SharePoint Central Administration application pool account with the Write permission for the container you specify in this setting.
- SMTP mail server for incoming mail—Specifies the FQDN of the SMTP server that SharePoint should use for incoming mail.
- Accept messages from authenticated users only—Specifies whether users must log on successfully to send email messages to a SharePoint site.
- Allow creation of distribution groups from SharePoint sites—Enables SharePoint sites to create distribution group objects in the Active Directory container you specified earlier.

15. In the Incoming E-Mail Server Display Address box, specify the email address the SharePoint should display in Web pages when users create incoming mail addresses.

16. If you selected the Automatic Settings mode option, a Safe E-Mail Servers box appears, as shown in Figure 11-45, in which you can select one of the following options:

- Accept mail from all e-mail servers—Enables SharePoint to receive mail from any server
- Accept mail from these safe e-mail servers—Enables SharePoint to receive mail only from the servers you specify

Figure 11-45

The Safe E-Mail Servers box on the Configure Incoming E-Mail Settings page

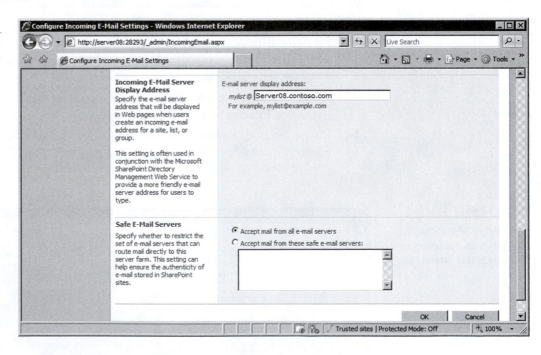

17. If you selected the Advanced Settings mode option, an E-Mail Drop Folder box appears, as shown in Figure 11-46, in which you must specify the location where your SMTP server stores incoming email.

18. Click **OK**. The Operations page reappears.

CLOSE the Internet Explorer window.

Figure 11-46

The E-Mail Drop Folder box on the Configure Incoming E-Mail Settings page

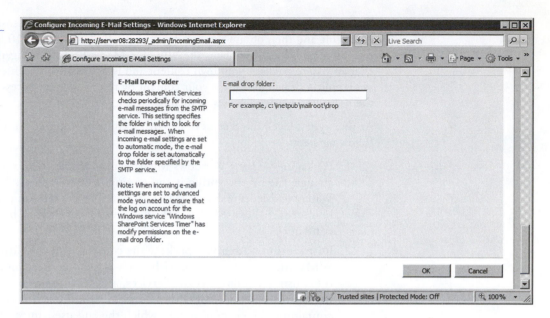

Users can now interact with Windows SharePoint Services by using their email clients to send messages to the server.

■ Using Digital Rights Management

THE BOTTOM LINE

Digital rights management (DRM) enables administrators to protect specific types of information from unauthorized consumption and distribution, even by users who have the appropriate credentials and permissions to access the information.

Throughout this book, you have learned how to protect applications and data by authenticating users to confirm their identities and authorizing users to allow them access to specific resources. However, security doesn't stop there. How do you protect information after a user has been granted access to it? An administrator might grant a specific user access to a confidential document, but what prevents the user from giving the document to others or printing and distributing copies? Digital rights management is one possible solution to this problem.

CERTIFICATION READY?
Configure Digital Rights Management (DRM)
4.2

Windows Server 2008 includes several technologies that enable you to restrict access to specific documents by specifying what users can do with them. These components include Windows Media Rights Manager, which you can use to protect multimedia files from unauthorized copying and distribution, and Active Directory Rights Management Services (AD RMS), which is a client/server application that can apply persistent protection to individual documents. The following sections examine these two technologies.

Using Windows Media Rights Manager

In some cases, multimedia content publishers might want to control access to their content by imposing limitations on it, such as who can play it, what devices they can use, how often they can play it, and so forth. To do this, you can use Windows Media Rights Manager (WMRM). WMRM is a Microsoft technology that enables you to package your content in a secure form and issue licenses that provide authorized users with limited access to the content.

To protect your content using WMRM, you must enter into a license agreement with Microsoft and then obtain the Windows Media Rights Manager 10 Software Development Kit (SDK). This SDK contains the Windows Media Rights Manager application, which enables you to package your own content and issue your own licenses. WMRM also functions as an online clearinghouse for your content by receiving users' access requests, authenticating the users, and issuing licenses to them.

At the highest level, the process of deploying content protected with WMRM consists of the following steps:

1. Packaging—Using Windows Media Rights Manager, you package your content into a single file by encrypting it and storing it in a Windows Media Audio (WMA) or Windows Media Video (WMV) format. The encryption process uses a key, stored in a separate license file, which the end users must have before they can play the content.

2. Distribution—After you package the content, you can distribute the WMA or WMV files in any way you wish, such as posting them on a Web site, streaming them using Windows Media Services, attaching them to email messages, or burning them to CD or DVD disks. These distributions do not include the license file containing the encryption key, which the end users must obtain separately. The separate distribution of the content and the license is the basis for the entire DRM security paradigm.

3. Licensing—The user requests a license for the content by establishing contact with your server running Windows Media Rights Manager. The license acquisition process can begin either when users attempt to obtain the content or after they obtain it, when they attempt to open the content file in Windows Media Player. Depending on how you configure Windows Media Rights Manager, the end user might be able to obtain a license invisibly or might be referred to a Web site requiring registration and/or payment of a fee.

4. Playback—After a user has obtained both the content file and the appropriate license file, Windows Media Player can play back the content, limited only by the rights the license terms grant.

Using the licensing capabilities of WMRM, you can restrict access to your content files in many different ways, using a variety of business rules, such as the following:

- Time limits—You can restrict the content to play back only between specific start and end times or specify a license duration limit, which begins when the user obtains the license.

- Count limits—You can limit users to a specified number of content playbacks, after which they must obtain an additional license.

- Transfer limits—You can specify whether users are able to copy the content file to a portable playback device and limit the transfer to a single device by binding the license to a device identifier.

- Copy limits—Users can freely copy the content files to other computers, but each computer requires its own license. You can limit the number of licenses you issue for a particular content file.

- Burn limits—You can specify whether users are able to burn the content to a CD or DVD. Disk-burning software products that support Windows Media content files are required to adhere to the terms of the licenses issued with the content. After the user burns the content to a disk, it is no longer protected by WMRM.

- Multiple licenses—You can create licenses with different rights for a single content file, enabling users to choose between single-playback and unlimited-playback licenses, for example.

Using Active Directory Rights Management Services

Active Directory Rights Management Services (AD RMS) is a Windows Server 2008 role that enables you to create usage policies for specific types of information that specify what authorized users can do with that information.

With Active Directory Rights Management Services, you can, for example, enable users to read a document, but prevent them from modifying or printing it. The protection provided by AD RMS is persistent, meaning that it remains a part of the document no matter where anyone moves it.

UNDERSTANDING THE AD RMS ARCHITECTURE

AD RMS consists of three components, as follows:

- AD RMS server—A Windows Server 2008 computer responsible for issuing certificates that enable users and services to assign AD RMS protection to documents by creating publishing licenses. The server also functions as a clearinghouse for client access requests.
- AD RMS client—A Windows Vista or Windows Server 2008 computer running an AD RMS-enabled application, such as Internet Explorer 7.0 or 2007 Microsoft Office system applications. When the client attempts to open a protected document, the application sends an access request to the AD RMS server, which issues a user license specifying the limitations of the user's access.
- Database server—A computer running a database manager, such as Microsoft SQL Server 2005, which stores configuration, logging, and directory services information for the AD RMS cluster.

INSTALLING THE ACTIVE DIRECTORY RIGHTS MANAGEMENT SERVICES ROLE

AD RMS is a Windows Server 2008 role that you can install like any other role using the Server Manager console. However, you must consider several prerequisites. Before you begin the installation, you must do the following:

- Add the server to the Active Directory domain that will be hosting the users of the protected content.
- Create a domain user for AD RMS to use as a service account.
- Create an IIS Web site that AD RMS will use for its virtual directory.
- Log on to Windows Server 2008 using an account that is a member of the Enterprise Admins group and that has the permissions needed to create a new database on the database server.

The AD RMS role installation process is one of the most complex in Windows Server 2008. Selecting the role adds many pages to the Add Roles Wizard, which you use to configure the server's database access and security settings. The pages that the AD RMS role adds to the wizard and the options each page provides are as follows:

- Select Role Services—Enables you to select which of the AD RMS role services you want to install, as shown in Figure 11-47, by selecting from the following options:
  - Active Directory Rights Management Server—A required role service that enables the server to identify authorized users and issue the licenses they need to access protected information.
  - Identity Federation Support—Enables AD RMS protection to cross organizational boundaries using trust relationships created with Active Directory Federation Services (AD FS). To install this role service, you must also install the AD FS role. Selecting this role service also adds a Configure Identity Federation Support page to the end of the wizard, on which you specify the name of your federation server.

Figure 11-47

The Select Role Services page
of the Add Roles Wizard

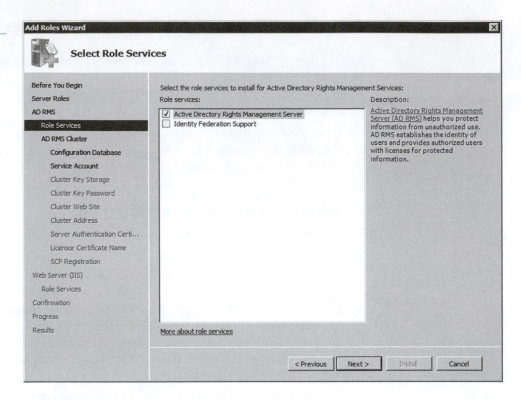

- Create or Join an AD RMS Cluster—Enables you to specify whether you want to create a new AD RMS root cluster or join the server to an existing AD RMS cluster, as shown in Figure 11-48, by selecting one of the following options:
  - Create a New AD RMS Cluster—Configures the computer to be the first server in a new AD RMS cluster. The first AD RMS server in an Active Directory forest is called the root cluster. To scale the AD RMS service, you can add more servers to the root cluster. For larger installations, you can create additional, licensing-only clusters.
  - Join an Existing AD RMS Cluster—Configures the server to be a part of a previously created AD RMS cluster.

Figure 11-48

The Create or Join an AD RMS
Cluster page of the Add Roles
Wizard

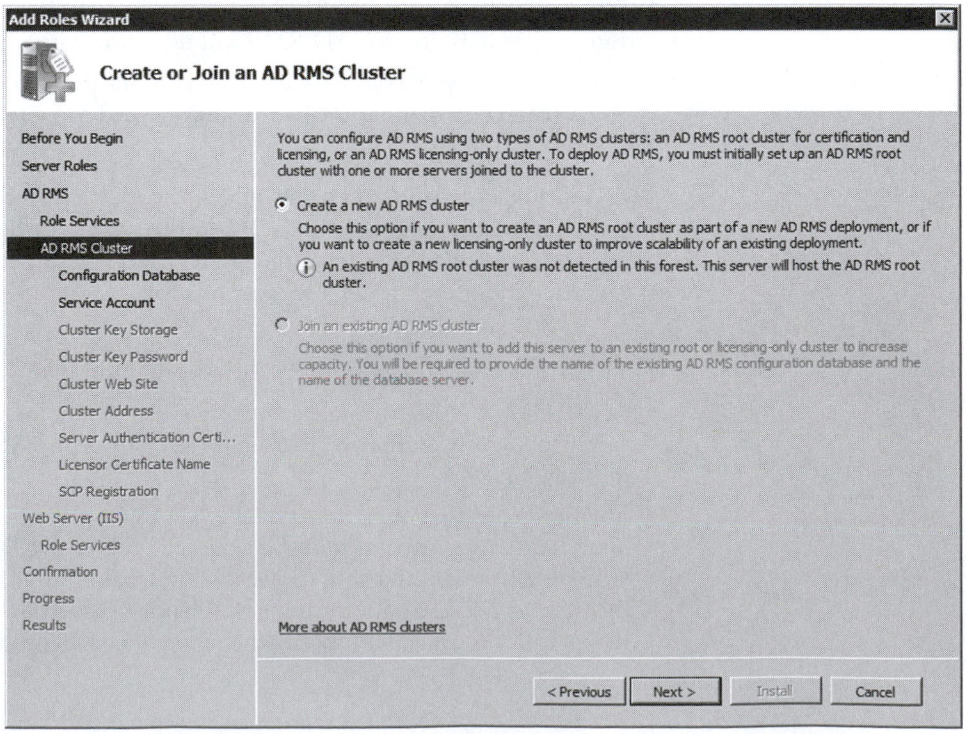

- Select Configuration Database—Enables you to specify the type and location of the database manager that AD RMS will use, as shown in Figure 11-49, by selecting from the following options:

  - Use Windows Internal Database on this server—Installs and enables AD RMS to use Windows Internal Database, a reduced version of SQL Server included with Windows Server 2008. Selecting this option limits AD RMS to a single-server cluster. Microsoft recommends using this option for testing purposes only; production AD RMS deployments should use an external database server.

  - Use a different database server—Enables AD RMS to use an external database server to store AD RMS data. Selecting this option activates the text boxes in which you must specify the name (or IP address) of the database Server and the Database Instance on that server. You must be logged on using an account that has the permissions needed to create a new database.

Figure 11-49

The Select Configuration Database page of the Add Roles Wizard

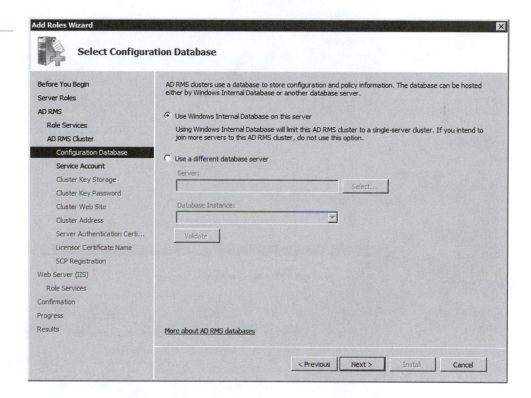

- Specify Service Account—Enables you to specify the domain user account you want AD RMS to use when communicating with other services, as shown in Figure 11-50. You should create a domain user account for this purpose. The account does not require any additional permissions.

Figure 11-50

The Specify Service Account page of the Add Roles Wizard

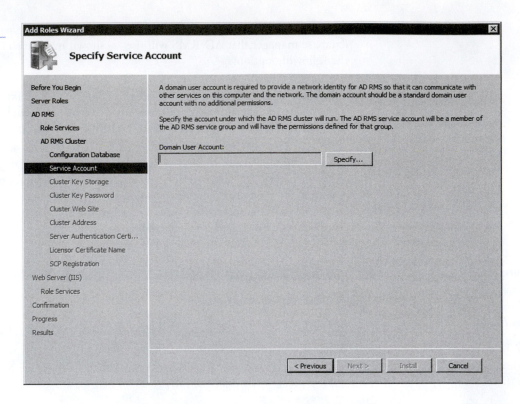

• Configure AD RMS Cluster Key Storage—Enables you to specify what method AD RMS should use to create the cluster key with which it will digitally sign the certificates and licenses it issues, as shown in Figure 11-51, by selecting one of the following options:

Figure 11-51

The Configure AD RMS Cluster Key Storage page of the Add Roles Wizard

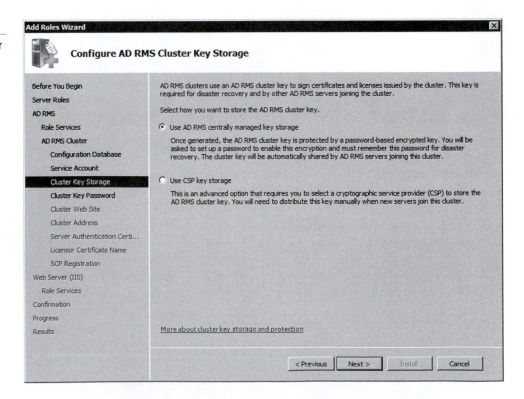

• Use AD RMS centrally managed key storage—Causes AD RMS to create a cluster key using password-based encryption. When you select this option, a Specify AD RMS Cluster Key Password page appears in the wizard, on which you must specify the password you want the server to use when creating the key.

- Use CSP key storage—Causes AD RMS to store the cluster key using a cryptographic service provider (CSP). When you select this option, a Specify AD RMS Cluster Key page appears in the wizard, on which you must select a CSP and specify whether you want to create a new key or use an existing one, as shown in Figure 11-52.

Figure 11-52

The Specify AD RMS Cluster Key Password page of the Add Roles Wizard

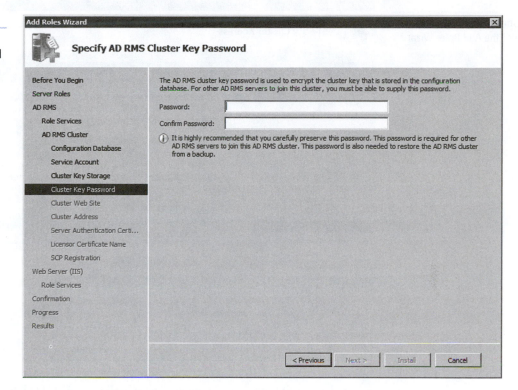

- Select AD RMS Cluster Web Site—Enables you to select the Internet Information Services (IIS) Web site that AD RMS will use to host its virtual directory, as shown in Figure 11-53. The page contains a list of all of the sites currently hosted by IIS, from which you can choose.

Figure 11-53

The Select AD RMS Cluster Web Site page of the Add Roles Wizard

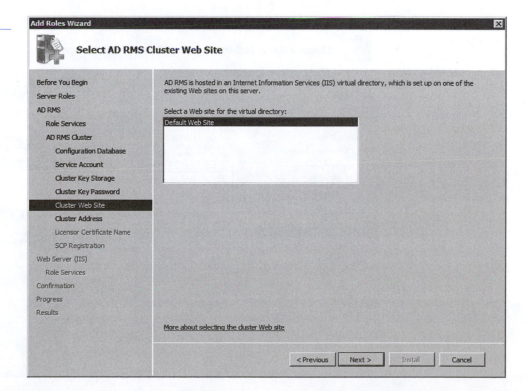

- Specify Cluster Address—Enables you to specify the fully-qualified domain name (FQDN) that clients will use to communicate with the AD RMS cluster, as shown in Figure 11-54. The settings on this page are as follows:

Figure 11-54

Figure 11-54

The Specify Cluster Address page of the Add Roles Wizard

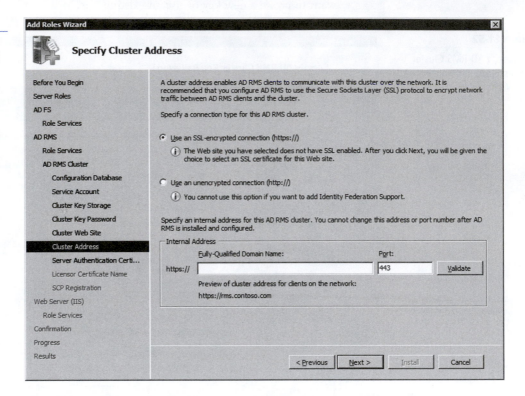

- Use an SSL-encrypted connection—Configures AD RMS to require client connections that are encrypted using Secure Sockets Layer (SSL). If you select this option, a Choose a Server Authentication Certificate for SSL Encryption page appears in the wizard, as shown in Figure 11-55, on which you can select an existing server certificate for SSL encryption or create a new one.

Figure 11-55

The Choose a Server Authentication Certificate for SSL Encryption page of the Add Roles Wizard

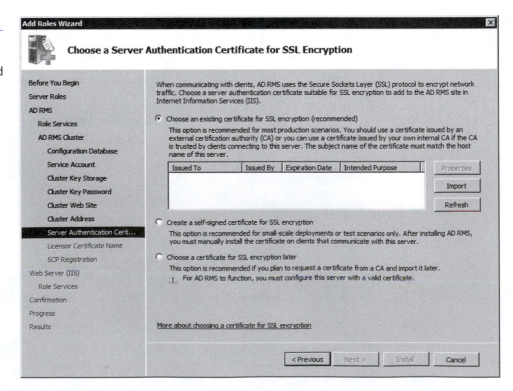

- Use an unencrypted connection—Configures AD RMS to use unencrypted client connections. You cannot select this option if you are installing the Identity Federation Support role service.
- Specify an internal address for this AD RMS cluster—Enables you to specify the FQDN and port number for the AD RMS cluster.
- Name the Server Licensor Certificate—Enables you to specify a name for the certificate that the AD RMS cluster will use to identify itself to clients, as shown in Figure 11-56.

Figure 11-56

The Name the Server Licensor Certificate page of the Add Roles Wizard

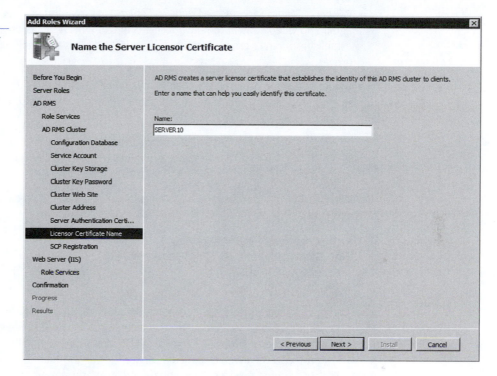

- Register AD RMS Service Connection Point—Enables you to create a service connection point for the AD RMS cluster in the Active Directory domain, either now or later, as shown in Figure 11-57. To create the connection point, you must be logged on using an account that is a member of the Enterprise Admins group.

Figure 11-57

The Register AD RMS Service Connection Point page of the Add Roles Wizard

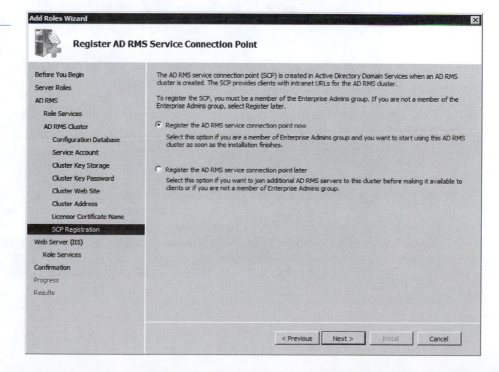

After you complete the installation of the AD RMS role, the server is ready to process AD RMS client requests.

SUMMARY SKILL MATRIX

IN THIS LESSON YOU LEARNED:

- Windows Media Services is a Windows Server 2008 role that enables a server to stream audio and video content to network clients in real time. A player on the client computer establishes a direct connection with the server and plays the audio or video content as it arrives.

- Media streaming is always a tradeoff between bandwidth and signal quality. As you increase the quality and/or resolution of the video image, you also increase the amount of bandwidth the stream consumes.

- Windows Media Player has a feature called Fast Streaming, which includes several techniques that enable the player to begin displaying content more quickly, improving the user experience.

- Windows Media Services supports two types of publishing points: on-demand streams and broadcast streams.

- Windows Media Services uses unicast transmissions by default. In a unicast transmission, each client establishes its own connection to the Windows Media Services server. To conserve bandwidth, use multicast transmissions. Multicasting is a TCP/IP feature that provides one-to-many transmission capabilities.

- Windows Media Services can stream multimedia content using different protocols to support different Windows Media Player versions, including Real Time Streaming Protocol (RTSP) and Hypertext Transfer Protocol (HTTP). When you enable both the RTSP and the HTTP protocols on a Windows Media Services server, the clients and the server use a process called protocol rollover to negotiate the most efficient protocol they have in common.

- To control access to your multimedia content, you can use Windows Media Rights Manager. WMRM is a Microsoft technology that enables you to package your content in a secure form and issue licenses that provide authorized users with limited access to the content.

- Active Directory Rights Management Services (AD RMS) is a Windows Server 2008 role that enables you to create usage policies for specific types of information that specify what authorized users can do with that information.

- Windows SharePoint Services 3.0 is a database-enabled Web application that runs on an Internet Information Services server. By accessing the site, users can employ browser-based workspaces to share information in a variety of ways, such as storing documents, creating calendar appointments and task lists, and contributing to newsgroup-style discussions.

- After you install and configure Windows SharePoint Services, you can access the administration interface by selecting SharePoint 3.0 Central Administration from the Administrative Tools program group.

- Windows SharePoint Services can integrate with email in a variety of ways, enabling users to set up calendar appointments, post announcements, add documents, and contribute to blogs and discussion forums. To provide users with these email capabilities, you must install a Simple Mail Transfer Protocol (SMTP) server and configure the incoming and outgoing email settings in Windows SharePoint Services.

■ Knowledge Assessment

Matching

Complete the following exercise by matching the terms with their corresponding definitions.

    a. Converts live multimedia content for real-time streaming.

    b. Enables media players to start displaying content sooner.

    c. Can only use unicast transmissions.

    d. Can use unicast or multicast transmissions.

    e. Enables users to rewind and fast forward streamed content.

    f. Uses Class D IP addresses.

    g. Requires Windows Media Player version 9 or higher.

    h. Enables any version of Windows Media Player to connect to a Windows Media Services server.

    i. Controls access to Windows Media content.

    j. Uses an SQL server database to store content.

    _____ **1.** unicast

    _____ **2.** Digital Rights Management (DRM)

    _____ **3.** broadcast streams

    _____ **4.** protocol rollover

    _____ **5.** Fast Streaming

    _____ **6.** on-demand streams

    _____ **7.** Windows SharePoint Services 3.0

    _____ **8.** Real Time Streaming Protocol (RTSP)

    _____ **9.** Windows Media Encoder

    _____ **10.** multicast

Multiple Choice

Select the correct answer for each of the following questions.

1. Before you install Windows SharePoint Services 3.0, you must install which of the following Windows Server 2008 elements?
   a. The .NET Framework 3.0 feature
   b. The Web Server (IIS) role
   c. Microsoft SQL Server 2005
   d. SharePoint 3.0 Central Administration

2. Which of the following is not a benefit of streaming multimedia content rather than downloading it?
   a. Playback begins sooner with streaming than with downloading.
   b. Streaming uses lower transmission rates than downloading.
   c. Streaming provides better playback quality than downloading.
   d. Streaming supports live content, while downloading does not.

3. Which of the following Fast Streaming technologies does not enable the client playback to begin sooner?
   a. Fast Reconnect
   b. Fast Start
   c. Advanced Fast Start
   d. Fast Cache

4. Which of the following is not true about broadcast streaming?
  a. Broadcast streams can use unicast or multicast transmissions.
  b. Users cannot rewind or fast forward a broadcast stream.
  c. Multiple clients can receive a single broadcast stream.
  d. Streaming can only be used for live content.

5. Which of the following URL prefixes enables a Windows Media Player client and a Windows Media Services server to use protocol rollover to negotiate the most efficient streaming protocol?
  a. rtsp://
  b. mms://
  c. http://
  d. rtspt://

6. To configure a Windows SharePoint Services 3.0 server to receive user content via incoming email, you must do which of the following?
  a. Install the Microsoft SMTP Server feature on the computer running Windows SharePoint Services.
  b. Install the Microsoft SMTP Server feature on any computer on the network.
  c. Install any SMTP server on the computer running Windows SharePoint Services.
  d. Install any SMTP server on any computer on the network.

7. Which of the following is a Windows Media Services parameter that you can adjust to limit the bandwidth utilized by client/server connections?
  a. Limit connection rate
  b. Limit player connections
  c. Limit outgoing distribution connections
  d. Limit connection acknowledgment

8. Which of the following is not true about Windows Media Services and multicast transmissions?
  a. Media streams that use multicast transmissions conserve bandwidth.
  b. Multicast transmissions send streams to multiple IP addresses simultaneously.
  c. Multicast transmissions use Class D IP addresses.
  d. Windows Media Services can only use multicast transmissions for broadcast streams.

9. Which of the following tools do you use to configure Windows SharePoint Services 3.0 settings?
  a. A SharePoint 3.0 Central Administration Web page that uses a different IP address than the Team Site page.
  b. A SharePoint 3.0 Central Administration snap-in for Microsoft Management Console.
  c. A password-protected link on the Team Site home page.
  d. A SharePoint 3.0 Central Administration Web page using a randomly selected port number.

10. During the planning phase of Windows Media Services deployment, which of the following is not one of the elements you should consider when deciding how much signal quality you can afford with the bandwidth you have to expend?
  a. How much network bandwidth your clients have available.
  b. How many clients you must service simultaneously.
  c. How much signal quality your media streams require to effectively service your clients.
  d. How many publishing points you need to create.

Review Questions

1. List the four steps involved in deploying DRM-protected content in the correct order.

2. List and explain five limitations that you can apply to a DRM license to control client access to a protected content file.

■ Case Scenario

Scenario 11-1: Installing Windows Media Services

Ralph just installed Windows Server 2008 on a new computer that he wants to use to stream training videos to clients on the local network. When he opens Server Manager for the first time, Ralph is surprised to discover that Streaming Media Services is not listed in the Add Roles Wizard. After checking on the Internet, Ralph learns that Windows Media Services no longer ships with Windows Server 2008. Ralph downloads the Windows Media Services files from the Microsoft Download Center and executes the Server file on the computer. After the installation process is completed, however, Ralph can find no indication that Windows Media Services has been installed. There is no console in the Administrative tools group and no new system services running. What must Ralph do to install Windows Media Services on the computer?

12 LESSON

Using High Availability Technologies

OBJECTIVE DOMAIN MATRIX

TECHNOLOGY SKILL	OBJECTIVE DOMAIN	OBJECTIVE DOMAIN NUMBER
What is High Availability?	Configure high availability.	1.4
Creating a Terminal Server Farm	Configure Terminal Services load balancing.	2.3
Using Virtualization	Configure Windows Server Hyper-V and virtual machines.	1.3

KEY TERMS

Arbitrated loop (FC-AL)
block I/O access
DNS round robin
failover cluster
Fibre Channel
Fibre Channel Protocol (FCP)
file-based I/O
hybrid virtualization

Hyper-V
hypervisor
Internet Storage Name Service (iSNS)
iSCSI initiator
iSCSI target
JBOD (Just a Bunch of Disks)
network load balancing (NLB)

server farm
Switched fabric (FC-SW)
VDS hardware provider
virtual instance
virtual machines (VMs)
virtualization
witness disk

In this lesson, you learn about the various technologies that Windows Server 2008 networks can use to provide high availability for their resources, including the following:

- Deploying a storage area network
- Using Windows Server 2008 SAN tools
- Using failover clustering
- Using Network Load Balancing with Terminal Services
- Understanding virtualization
- Introducing Hyper-V

■ What Is High Availability?

THE BOTTOM LINE

Application servers often provide network users with tools they need to perform their jobs. If a vital server fails, productivity suffers. For that reason, many organizations implement high availability technologies that ensure the continued performance of their server applications. High availability typically takes the form of redundant hardware, software, or data components, which enable an application to continue running despite disasters such as a drive failure, a power outage, or data loss. In many cases, high availability is the main characteristic that distinguishes a server from a computer with a faster processor and a lot of memory.

RAID (Redundant Array of Independent Disks) is one of the most basic and commonly used high availability technologies. As discussed in Lesson 2, "Deploying a File Server," a RAID array consists of multiple hard disks, with a controller that enables the array to automatically store redundant copies of data on different drives. RAID implementations come in many forms, ranging from workstation solutions, to server controllers, to stand-alone disk arrays that can connect directly to a computer or a storage area network.

Other high availability components often found in servers include redundant power supplies, active cooling systems, simultaneous connections to multiple networks, and hot-swappable components that you can replace without shutting down the computer. These are all relatively low-cost solutions that can enable a server to continue running despite a component failure or a service outage. The remainder of this lesson discusses some of the more elaborate high availability technologies that you can use to provide even greater amounts of fault tolerance.

■ Deploying a Storage Area Network

↓ **THE BOTTOM LINE**   Storage area networks are typically high-end solutions, which enterprise networks use to deploy large amounts of storage and make this storage available to other connected devices.

RAID is a proven high availability technology that was first defined in 1988, but server-attached RAID arrays are subject to scalability problems. You can only install so many drives into a single computer. Also, the terminated SCSI (Small Computer System Interface) bus that was originally used for connections to external drive arrays is limited to 16 devices and a maximum length of 25 yards.

At the highest level, a storage area network (SAN) is simply a network dedicated solely to high-speed connections between servers and storage devices. Instead of installing disk drives into servers or connecting them using a SCSI bus, a SAN consists of one or more drive arrays equipped with network interface adapters, which you connect to your servers using standard twisted pair or fiber optic network cables. A SAN-connected server, therefore, has a minimum of two network adapters, one for the standard LAN connection, and one for the SAN, as shown in Figure 12-1.

Figure 12-1

A server connected to a storage area network

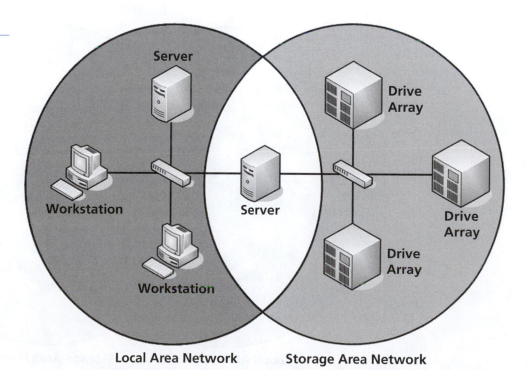

The storage devices on a SAN are nearly always drive arrays, not individual drives, and can include hard disks, optical jukeboxes, tape libraries, or any other type of storage. In most cases, SANs use **block I/O access**, which means that a server accesses the storage media on the SAN a block at a time, just as if the storage media were installed in the server computer. This is in contrast to the **file-based I/O**, which means that a server accesses the storage media on the SAN a file at a time, typically used by network attached storage.

> ✚ **MORE INFORMATION**
>
> Block I/O access is preferable for applications that use large data files, such as databases and email stores. With file-based I/O, a database manager application has to retrieve some or all of the database file from the storage device before it can access the information requested by a client. With block I/O access, the database manager can retrieve only the parts of the database file containing the requested information, enhancing the speed at which data is retrieved.

SANs have many advantages. By connecting the storage devices to a network instead of to the servers themselves, you avoid the limitations imposed by the maximum number of devices you can connect directly to a computer. SANs also provide added flexibility in their communication capabilities. Because any device on a SAN can communicate with any other device on the same SAN, high-speed data transfers can occur in any of the following ways:

- Server to storage—Servers can access storage devices over the SAN as if they are connected directly to the computer.
- Server to server—Servers can use the SAN to communicate directly with each other at high speeds to avoid flooding the LAN with traffic.
- Storage to storage—Storage devices can communicate amongst themselves without server intervention, such as to perform backups from one medium to another or to mirror drives on different arrays.

Although a SAN is not in itself a high availability technology, you can make it into one by connecting redundant servers to the same network, as shown in Figure 12-2, enabling them to access the same data storage devices. If one server should fail, another can assume its roles by accessing the same data.

Figure 12-2

Multiple servers connected to a SAN

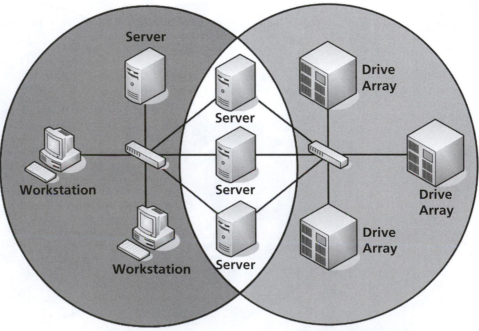

Understanding SAN Technologies

> Because they use standard networking technologies, SANs can also greatly extend the distances between servers and storage devices. You can design a SAN that spans different rooms, different floors, or even different buildings, just as you would with a standard computer network.

External hard drives are now common on servers and workstations alike. The simplest devices consist of a single Parallel or Serial ATA (Advanced Technology Attachment) drive in a housing that includes a power supply and a Universal Serial Bus (USB) interface. These are suitable for local computer use, but not for the storage of shared data, as on a server.

Hard drive arrays that connect directly to a server are more complex, usually consisting of multiple drives and a SCSI interface. Some arrays include a RAID controller, while others use a simpler arrangement amusingly called ***JBOD (Just a Bunch of Disks)***. This type of array connects to the server using an external SCSI cable, which, when compared to a standard network cable, is thick, heavy, inflexible, and limited in length. Also, the server must have a SCSI host adapter that provides the other connection for the array.

SCSI is still the interface of choice for internal server drives because it enables each drive connected to the SCSI bus to maintain its own command queue, independent of the other drives. The ATA interfaces, by comparison, can handle only one command at a time, which makes them unsuitable for use in servers that might receive dozens or hundreds of I/O requests each minute. However, many of the external hard drive arrays on the market now combine the two interface technologies to form hybrid units. The hard drives might use the high-speed Serial ATA (SATA) interface, but the array communicates with servers and other storage devices using SCSI commands.

The drive arrays designed for SANs are more complex than those connecting directly to servers, because in addition to the RAID and SCSI functionality, they include support for networking protocols and intelligent agents that provide advanced functions, such as serverless backups. In a serverless backup, a server is responsible for initiating the backup job, but after the backup begins, the data travels directly from one storage medium on the SAN to another, such as from a hard disk array to a tape library. This type of backup not only eliminates the potential LAN bottleneck by using the SAN for the data transfer, it eliminates the backup server itself as a possible bottleneck.

Servers and storage devices cannot exchange SCSI commands over a SAN connection the way they do when the devices are directly connected using a SCSI cable. The lower level SCSI protocols use parallel signaling and call for a bus topology and relatively short cables with 50 or 68 conductors. To communicate over a SAN, servers and storage devices map their SCSI communications onto another protocol, in most cases either Fibre Channel or iSCSI.

USING FIBRE CHANNEL

Fibre Channel is a high-speed serial networking technology, originally designed for use with supercomputers but now associated primarily with storage area networking. Fibre Channel is a versatile technology, supporting various network media, transmission speeds, topologies, and upper level protocols. Its primary disadvantage is that it requires specialized hardware that can be extremely expensive.

Installing a Fibre Channel SAN means building an entirely new network with its own special medium, switches, and network interface adapters. In addition to the hardware costs, which can easily be ten times that of a traditional Ethernet network, you must consider installation and maintenance expenses. Fibre Channel is a specialized technology, with few experts in the field. To install and maintain a Fibre Channel SAN, an organization must hire experienced staff or train existing personnel on the new technology.

> **+ MORE INFORMATION**
>
> The British spelling of the word "fibre" in Fibre Channel is deliberate, to distinguish the term from "fiber optic." Fibre Channel can run on twisted pair copper or optical cables. The spelling "fiber" always refers to an optical medium.

FIBRE CHANNEL MEDIA

A Fibre Channel network can use a variety of network media. Copper alternatives include video or miniature coaxial cable and, more commonly, shielded twisted pair (STP) with DB-9 or HSSDC (High Speed Serial Data Connection) cable connectors. These are distinctly different from the standard unshielded twisted pair (UTP) cables and RJ-45 connectors used for an Ethernet network and require a specialized installation. Fiber optic alternatives include 62.5- or 50-ohm multimode and 7- or 9-ohm singlemode, all using LC or SC connectors. They are standard fiber optic media options, familiar to any qualified fiber optic contractor. Because Fibre Channel uses serial instead of parallel signaling, it can span much longer distances than a pure SCSI connection, up to 50 kilometers or more in some cases.

FIBRE CHANNEL SPEEDS

Transmission speeds for Fibre Channel networks range from 133 Mbps (megabits per second) to 1 Gbps (gigabit per second) for copper cables, and up to 10 Gbps for fiber optic. Maximum speeds depend on the type of cable the network uses, the lengths of the cable segments, and, in the case of fiber optic, the type of laser used to transmit the signals.

FIBRE CHANNEL TOPOLOGIES

Fibre Channel networks can use any one of the following three topologies:

- Point-to-point (FC-P2P)—Consists of two devices only, directly connected with a single cable.
- *Arbitrated loop (FC-AL)*—Consists of up to 127 devices, connected in a loop topology, similar to that of a token ring network. The loop can be physical, with each device connected to the next device, or virtual, with each device connected to a hub that implements the loop.
- *Switched fabric (FC-SW)*—Consists of up to 16,777,216 (2^{24}) devices, each of which is connected to a Fibre Channel switch. Unlike Ethernet switches, Fibre Channel switches provide redundant paths between the connected devices, forming a topology called a *mesh* or *fabric*. If a switch or a connection between switches fails, data can find an alternate path through the fabric to its destination.

Until recently, FC-AL was the most popular of the three topologies, because few SANs require more than 127 connections, and the arbitrated loop eliminates the need for expensive switches. However, as of 2007, the prices of Fibre Channel switches have dropped considerably (perhaps due to competition from low-cost iSCSI components) and FC-SW has become the more popular Fibre Channel solution.

FIBRE CHANNEL PROTOCOLS

The Fibre channel standards define five protocol layers, as follows:

- FC0—Defines the physical elements of a Fibre Channel network, including cables, connectors, pinouts, and optical and electrical specifications.
- FC1—Defines the data-link layer transmission protocol, including the 8b/10b encoding method used to generate Fibre Channel network signals.
- FC2—Defines the basic transport mechanism of a Fibre Channel network, including the frame format and three service classes: a connection-oriented class, a connectionless class with acknowledgments, and a connectionless class without acknowledgments.
- FC3—Defines a collection of common services often required by applications using Fibre Channel networks, including data striping, multicasting, and multiport hunt groups.
- FC4—Defines the upper layer protocol mapping rules, which enable Fibre Channel networks to carry SCSI and other types of application layer traffic.

The most critical layer in the operation of a SAN is FC4, which enables the network to carry the SCSI traffic generated by the server and storage devices, replacing the lower layers native to the SCSI protocol. SANs typically use the *Fibre Channel Protocol (FCP)* to transmit SCSI traffic over the network. However, Fibre Channel networks can use a number of other protocols at the FC4 layer for storage area networking, as well as other applications.

USING ISCSI

Fibre Channel networks provide excellent SAN performance, but the expense and special skills required to install and maintain them have made them a rarity in all but the largest enterprise installations. iSCSI is an alternative storage area networking technology that enables servers and storage devices to exchange SCSI traffic using a standard IP network instead of a dedicated Fibre Channel network. This makes iSCSI a far more economical and practical solution, placing SAN technology within reach of small and medium installations.

Because iSCSI uses a standard IP network for its lower layer functionality, you can use the same cables, network adapters, switches, and routers for a SAN as you would for a LAN or wide area network (WAN), without any modifications. You simply connect your servers and storage devices to an existing Ethernet network or build a new one using low-cost, widely available components.

Because of its relatively low cost and its simplicity, iSCSI has come to dominate the SAN industry. The addition of widespread support for iSCSI in the Windows Server and other operating systems has led to the introduction of many iSCSI storage device products in a wide range of price points. Whereas a SAN at one time required a huge investment in money and time, the technology is now available to modest organizations.

INITIATORS AND TARGETS

iSCSI communication is based on two elements: initiators and targets. An *iSCSI initiator*, so-called because it initiates the SCSI communication process, is a hardware or software device running on a computer that accesses the storage devices on the SAN. On an iSCSI network, the initiator takes the place of the host adapter that traditional SCSI implementations use to connect storage devices to a computer. The initiator receives I/O requests from the operating system and sends them, in the form of SCSI commands, to specific storage devices on the SAN. The only difference between an iSCSI initiator and a SCSI host adapter is that the initiator packages the SCSI traffic in TCP/IP packets, instead of using the native SCSI protocols.

Hardware-based initiators typically take the form of a host bus adapter (HBA), an expansion card that includes the functionality of a SCSI host adapter and a Gigabit Ethernet network adapter in one device. Hardware-based initiators offload some of the SCSI processing from the computer's main processor.

Initiators can also be software-based, such as the iSCSI Initiator module included in Windows Server 2008. When using a software initiator, you connect the computer to the SAN using a standard Ethernet network adapter.

The other half of the iSCSI equation is the *iSCSI target*, which is integrated into a drive array or computer. The target receives SCSI commands from the initiator and passes them to a storage device, which is represented by a logical unit number (LUN). A LUN is essentially an address that SCSI devices use to identify a specific storage resource. A single LUN can represent an entire hard disk, part of a disk, or a slice of a RAID array. Therefore, a single computer or drive array can have many LUNs, represented by multiple targets.

Drive arrays supporting iSCSI have targets implemented in their firmware, automatically making the various volumes in the array available to iSCSI initiators on the SAN. It is also possible for iSCSI targets to be implemented in software, in the form of a service or daemon that makes all or part of a hard disk in a computer available to initiators. You can use various third-party products, both commercial and public domain, to deploy the drives in a computer as iSCSI targets, making them available to initiators on the SAN using block I/O access.

TAKE NOTE*

Windows Server 2008 includes the iSCSI Initiator by default, but for a Windows Server 2003 R2 computer, you must download iSCSI Software Initiator 2.0 from the Microsoft Download Center at www.microsoft.com.

USING ISNS

After the initiators and targets are in place, the only problem remaining in iSCSI communications is how the two locate each other. The ***Internet Storage Name Service (iSNS)*** makes this possible by registering the presence of initiators and targets on a SAN and responding to queries from iSNS clients. Windows Server 2008 includes an iSNS implementation as a feature, which can provide the identification service for an entire SAN.

iSNS consists of four components, as follows:

- iSNS server—Receives and processes registration requests and queries from clients on the SAN, using the iSNS database as an information store.
- iSNS database—Information store on an iSNS server that contains data supplied by client registrations. The server retrieves the data to respond to client queries.
- iSNS clients—Component in iSCSI initiators and targets that registers information about itself with an iSNS server and sends queries to the server for information about other clients.
- iSNS Protocol (iSNSP)—Protocol used for all registration and query traffic between iSNS servers and clients.

Using Windows Server 2008 with SANs

Windows Server 2008 provides support for both iSCSI and Fibre Channel SANs and includes the tools and services you need to manage them.

Windows Server 2008 includes several components that enable the computer to interact with devices on a SAN, as follows:

- iSCSI Initiator—Establishes connections with iSCSI targets on the SAN.
- Internet Storage Name Server—Registers and locates iSCSI initiators and targets.
- Storage Manager for SANs—Enables administrators to manage storage devices on Fibre Channel or iSCSI SANs that are compatible with the Virtual Disk Service (VDS) using a standardized interface.
- Storage Explorer—Enables administrators to view and manage the devices on Fibre Channel or iSCSI SANs.

These components are discussed in greater detail in the following sections.

INSTALLING ISNS SERVER

iSCSI Initiator is part of the default Windows Server 2008 installation; you don't have to add any roles or features to use it. However, if many devices are on your SAN, you should use an iSNS server to register your targets and initiators. If you do not have an iSNS server on your SAN already, you can deploy one on your Windows Server 2008 computer by using the following procedure.

 INSTALL ISNS SERVER

GET READY. Log on to Windows Server 2008 using an account with administrative privileges. When the logon process is completed, close the Initial Configuration Tasks window and any other windows that appear.

1. Click **Start**, and then click **Administrative Tools** > **Server Manager**. The Server Manager console appears.
2. Right-click the **Features** node and, from the context menu, select **Add Features**. The Add Features Wizard appears, displaying the Select Features page.

3. Select the **Internet Storage Name Server** feature, as shown in Figure 12-3, and click **Next**. The Confirm Installation Selections page appears.

Figure 12-3

The Add Features Wizard

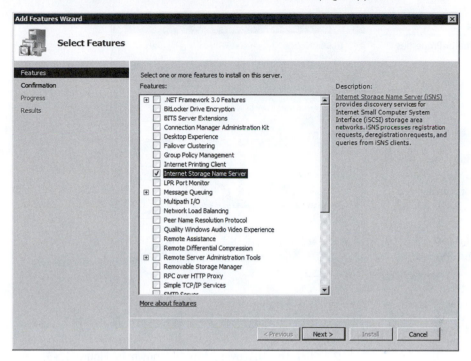

4. Click **Install**. When the installation process is completed, the Installation Results page appears.

5. Click **Close**.

CLOSE the Server Manager console.

When the installation process is complete, the iSNS server is ready to accept registrations from iSCSI targets and initiators. After the targets are registered, initiators can send queries to the iSNS server to discover them.

USING ISCSI INITIATOR

Whether or not you plan to use an iSNS server on your SAN, you have to create and/or configure iSCSI targets before your initiators can access the storage devices on the SAN. How you do this depends on the types of storage devices you are using and their iSCSI target capabilities. Drive arrays that support iSCSI have built-in targets and can use a variety of administrative interfaces to configure their functions and register them with the iSNS server. Software-based iSCSI targets that run on Windows and UNIX/Linux computers are also available from third-party vendors.

⊕ **MORE INFORMATION**

Windows Server 2008 does not include iSCSI target capabilities, but an embedded version of Windows Storage Server, called Microsoft Windows Unified Data Storage Server, does include iSCSI target capabilities. Windows Unified Data Storage Server is based on Windows Server 2003 and is only available as a part of turnkey storage server solutions from original equipment manufacturers (OEMs). As of this writing, Microsoft has not announced plans for a Windows Server 2008 version.

When your targets are configured and registered, you can access them with Windows Server 2008 by configuring iSCSI Initiator, as detailed in the following procedure.

 USE ISCSI INITIATOR

GET READY. Log on to Windows Server 2008 using an account with administrative privileges. When the logon process is completed, close the Initial Configuration Tasks window and any other windows that appear.

1. Click **Start**, and then click **Administrative Tools** > **iSCSI Initiator**. The iSCSI Initiator Properties sheet appears, as shown in Figure 12-4.

Figure 12-4

The iSCSI Initiator Properties sheet

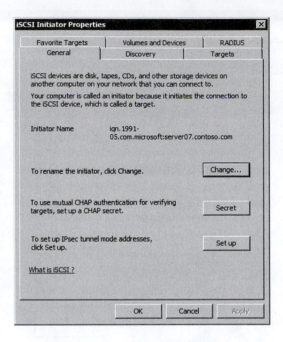

TAKE NOTE *

The first time you launch iSCSI Initiator, the system prompts you to start the iSCSI service automatically each time you start the computer and configure Windows Firewall to unblock the port used by the Internet Storage Name Service (iSNS).

2. Click the **Discovery** tab, as shown in Figure 12-5.

Figure 12-5

The Discovery tab of the iSCSI Initiator Properties sheet

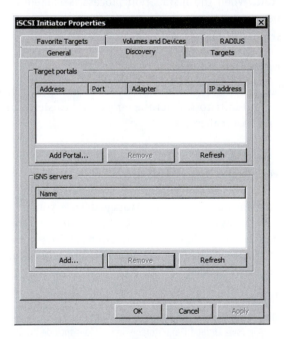

3. To use an iSNS server to discover the targets on the network, click **Add**. The Add iSNS Server dialog box appears, as shown in Figure 12-6.

Figure 12-6

The Add iSNS Server dialog box

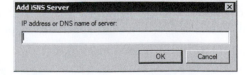

4. In the *IP address or DNS name of server* text box, key the name or address of the iSNS server on your SAN. Then, click **OK**. The server appears in the *iSNS servers* box.

5. To connect to a specific target using a target portal, click **Add Portal**. The Add Target Portal dialog box appears, as shown in Figure 12-7.

Figure 12-7

The Add Target Portal dialog box

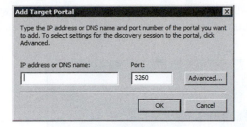

6. In the *IP address or DNS name* text box, key the name or address of the storage device containing the target to which you want to connect. Leave the Port value set to the default of 3260, unless you changed the port number on your target device. Click **OK**. The new entry appears in the *Target portals* box.

7. Click the **Targets** tab, as shown in Figure 12-8. All of the targets accessible through the iSNS servers and/or target portals you added appear in the Targets box.

Figure 12-8

The Targets tab of the iSCSI Initiator Properties sheet

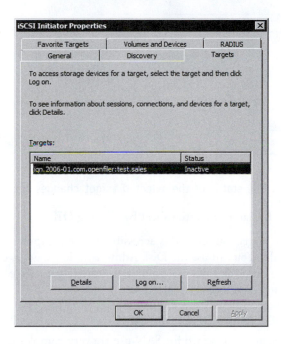

8. Select one of the available targets and click **Log on**. The Log On to Target dialog box appears, as shown in Figure 12-9.

Figure 12-9

The Log On to Target dialog box

9. Configure the following options, if desired:

- **Automatically restore this connection when the computer starts**—Creates a persistent connection that enables the computer to access the SCSI target immediately upon starting.

- Enable multi-path—Enables the iSCSI initiator to access the target using redundant paths through the SAN so that, if a cable breaks or a component fails, the computer can still access the data stored on the target device.
- Advanced—Displays an Advanced Settings dialog box, as shown in Figure 12-10, in which you can configure connection, authentication, and encryption settings.

Figure 12-10

The Advanced Settings dialog box

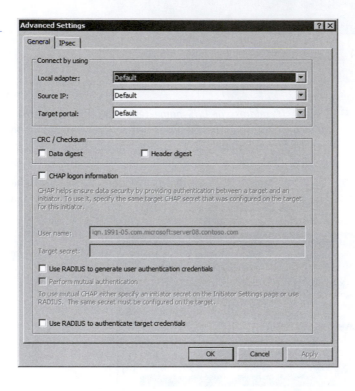

10. Click **OK**. The status of the selected target changes from Inactive to Connected.

CLOSE the iSCSI Initiator Properties sheet by clicking **OK**.

At this point, the target you selected is accessible to the computer, just as if the storage device was installed locally. You can use the Disk Administration snap-in or the Diskpart.exe command-line tool to create and manage volumes on the target device, and then access the volumes using any standard tool or application.

USING STORAGE MANAGER FOR SANS

Many of the drive arrays designed for SAN use are very complex devices, not just a bunch of drives in a case. However, they are not full-fledged computers either. SCSI LUNs, RAID, and other features require configuration, but drive arrays do not have their own monitors and keyboards, so they must use other means to provide an administrative interface.

Some drive arrays have RS-232 ports, to which you can connect a terminal, whereas others provide Web-based interfaces that you can access from a browser on any computer connected to the same network. Others use proprietary software interfaces. Windows Server 2008 provides another alternative, however, in the form of Storage Manager for SANs, a Microsoft Management Console (MMC) snap-in that enables you to manage the LUNs and iSCSI targets on a network-attached storage device.

Storage Manager for SANs is limited, however, because it can only manage storage devices that include support for the Microsoft Virtual Disk Service. To be accessible to Storage Manager for SANs, the storage device manufacturer must supply a software component called a *VDS hardware provider*, which you install on the computer you want to use to manage the device. Storage Manager for SANs is therefore not a required tool; it is just one option you can use to manage your storage devices.

TAKE NOTE *

Depending on the configuration parameters you set on the iSCSI target, you might have to supply credentials to complete the logon process or configure matching parameters on the iSCSI initiator.

⊕ MORE INFORMATION

In addition to Storage Manager for SANs, VDS enables you to use the Disk Management snap-in, as well as the Diskpart.exe and Diskraid.exe command-line utilities to manage SAN storage devices.

Storage Manager for SANs is supplied with Windows Server 2008 as a feature. To manage a storage device, you must install the VDS hardware provider supplied by the device's manufacturer and add the Storage Manager for SANs feature using the Add Features Wizard in Server Manager. Then, when you select Storage Manager for SANs from the Administrative Tools program group, the console loads the Virtual Disk Service and the VDS hardware provider, and displays the interface shown in Figure 12-11.

Figure 12-11

The Storage Manager for SANs console

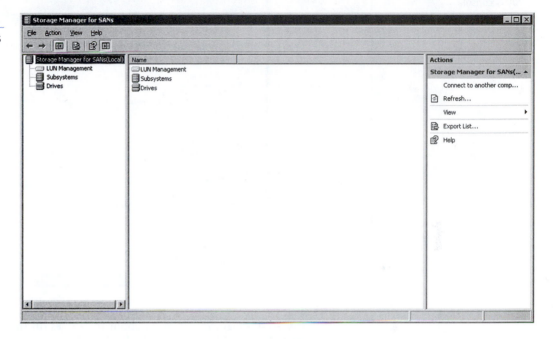

The Storage Manager for SANs console has three nodes, as follows:

- LUN Management—Enables you to manage your iSCSI targets and create LUNs on those targets, as shown in Figure 12-12.

Figure 12-12

Creating LUNs in the Storage Manager for SANs console

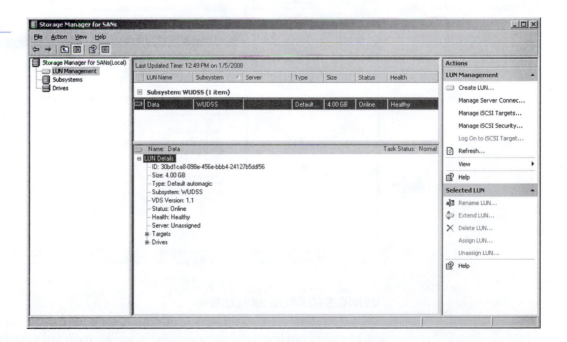

• Subsystems—Displays information about the storage devices on the SAN, including their drives, targets, and portals, as shown in Figure 12-13.

Figure 12-13

Displaying subsystem information in the Storage Manager for SANs console

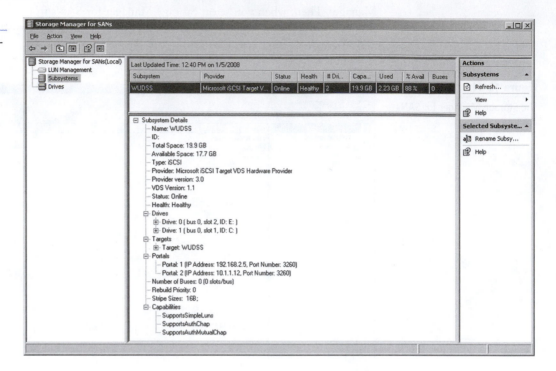

• Drives—Displays information about the drives on the SAN, as shown in Figure 12-14. This option can make the drive light blink, so you can associate the drive listings with the correct physical devices.

Figure 12-14

Displaying drive information in the Storage Manager for SANs console

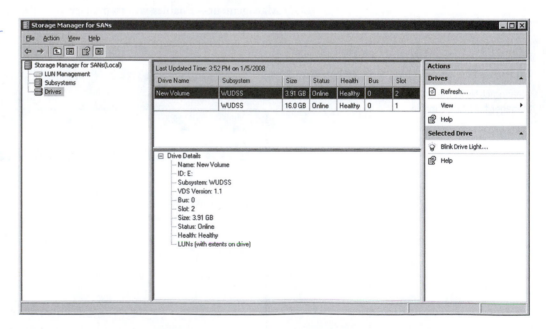

USING STORAGE EXPLORER

Storage Explorer is an MMC console that provides information about SAN resources and enables administrators to perform a variety of management tasks. The console is included in the default Windows Server 2008 installation; it is not part of a role or feature. When you launch Storage Explorer, it crawls the SAN and enumerates the devices it finds there, including servers, storage devices, and such infrastructure components as switches and iSNS servers, as shown in Figure 12-15.

Figure 12-15

The Storage Explorer console

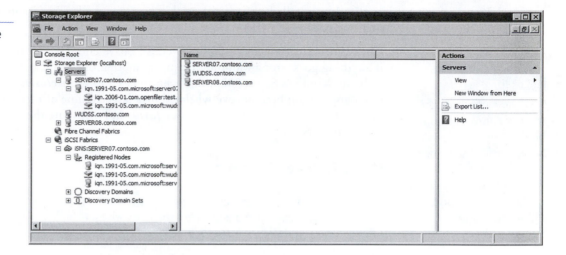

By selecting certain SAN components in the scope (left) pane, you can manipulate their properties by performing such tasks as configuring initiators, as shown in Figure 12-16, and managing iSNS records.

Figure 12-16

Configuring an iSCSI initiator in Storage Explorer

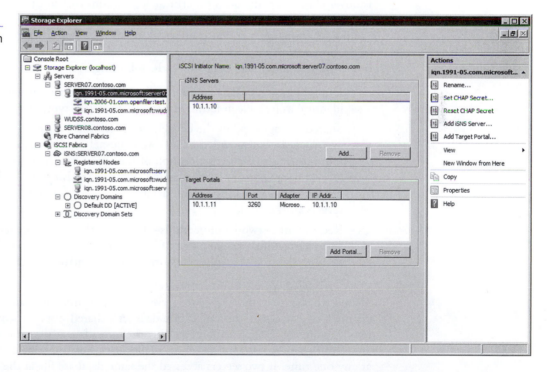

■ Clustering Servers

THE BOTTOM LINE

Server clustering can perform two services on an enterprise network. In addition to providing fault tolerance in the event of a server failure, it can provide network load balancing for busy applications.

As mentioned earlier in this lesson, high availability is typically a matter of using redundant components to ensure the continued functionality of a particular network resource. A server with redundant power supplies can continue running if one malfunctions. A database stored on a RAID array remains available to users, even if one of the hard drives fails. An application installed on a virtual machine is easily deployable on another computer if the first one crashes.

The ultimate in fault tolerance, however, is to have entire servers that are redundant, so that if anything goes wrong with one computer, another one can take its place almost immediately. In Windows Server 2008, this is known as a *failover cluster*. When a Web server or other application becomes overwhelmed by a large volume of users, you can deploy multiple identical servers, also known as a *server farm*, and distribute the user traffic evenly among the computers.

Using Failover Clustering

> A failover cluster is a collection of two or more servers that perform the same role or run the same application and appear on the network as a single entity.

Windows Server 2008 includes a Failover Cluster Management console that enables you to create and configure failover clusters after you have set up an appropriate environment. Before you can create a failover cluster in Windows Server 2008, you must install the Failover Clustering feature using the Add Features Wizard in Server Manager.

UNDERSTANDING FAILOVER CLUSTER REQUIREMENTS

Failover clusters are intended for critical applications that must keep running. If an organization is prepared to incur the time and expense required to deploy a failover cluster, Microsoft assumes that the organization is prepared to take every possible step to ensure the availability of the application. As a result, the recommended hardware environment for a failover cluster calls for an elaborate setup, including the following:

- Duplicate servers—The computers that will function as cluster nodes should be as identical as possible in terms of memory, processor type, and other hardware components.
- Shared storage—All of the cluster servers should have exclusive access to shared storage, such as that provided by a Fibre Channel or iSCSI storage area network. This shared storage will be the location of the application data, so that all of the cluster servers have access to it. The shared storage can also contain the *witness disk*, which holds the cluster configuration database. This too should be available to all of the servers in the cluster.
- Redundant network connections—Connect the cluster servers to the network in a way that avoids a single point of failure. You can connect each server to two separate networks or build a single network using redundant switches, routers, and network adapters.

Shared storage is a critical aspect of server clustering. In a pure failover cluster, all of the servers must have access to the application data on a shared storage medium, but you cannot have two instances of the application accessing the same data at the same time. For example, if you are running a database application on a failover cluster, only one of the cluster servers is active at any one time. If two servers accessed the same database file at the same time, they could modify the same record simultaneously, causing data corruption.

In addition to the hardware recommendations, the cluster servers should use the same software environment, which consists of the following elements:

- Operating system—All of the servers in a cluster must be running the same edition of the same operating system.
- Application—All of the cluster servers must run the same version of the redundant application.

- Updates—All of the cluster servers must have the same operating system and application updates installed.
- Active Directory—All of the cluster servers must be in the same Active Directory domain, and they must be either member servers or domain controllers. Microsoft recommends that all cluster servers be member servers, not domain controllers. Do not mix member servers and domain controllers in the same failover cluster.

Before you create a failover cluster using the Failover Cluster Management console, you should connect all of the hardware to the networks involved and test the connectivity of each device. Make sure that every cluster server can communicate with the other servers and the shared storage device.

VALIDATING A FAILOVER CLUSTER CONFIGURATION

The Failover Cluster Management console is included with Windows Server 2008 as a feature. You must install it using the Add Features Wizard in Server Manager. Afterward, you can start to create a cluster by validating your hardware configuration. The Validate a Configuration Wizard performs an extensive battery of tests on the computers you select, enumerating their hardware and software resources and checking their configuration settings. If any elements required for a cluster are incorrect or missing, the wizard lists them in a report.

To validate a cluster configuration, use the following procedure.

 VALIDATE A FAILOVER CLUSTER CONFIGURATION

GET READY. Log on to Windows Server 2008 using an account with administrative privileges. When the logon process is completed, close the Initial Configuration Tasks window and any other windows that appear.

1. Click **Start**, and then click **Administrative Tools** > **Failover Cluster Management**. The Failover Cluster Management console appears, as shown in Figure 12-17.

Figure 12-17

The Failover Cluster Management console

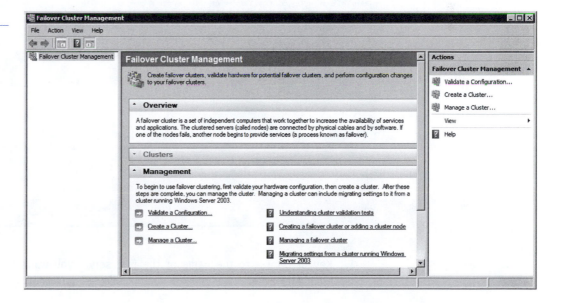

2. In the detail (middle) pane, in the Management box, click **Validate a Configuration.** The Validate a Configuration Wizard appears, as shown in Figure 12-18.

Figure 12-18

The Validate a Configuration Wizard

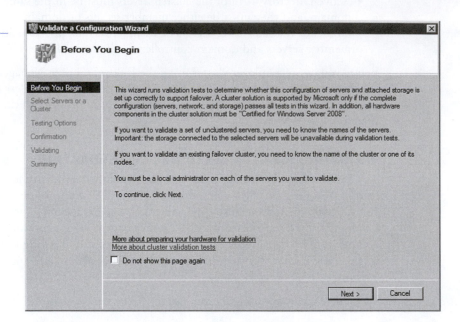

3. Click **Next** to bypass the Before You Begin page. The Select Servers or a Cluster page appears, as shown in Figure 12-19.

Figure 12-19

The Select Servers or a Cluster page of the Validate a Configuration Wizard

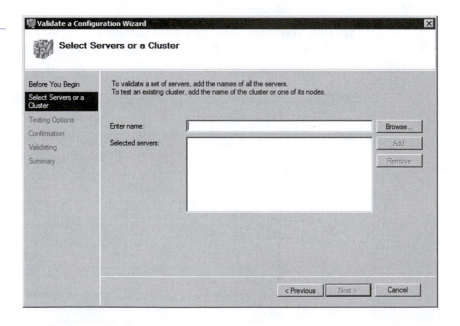

4. Key or browse to the name of the first server you want to add to the cluster and click **Add.** The server appears in the *Selected servers* list.

5. Repeat the process to add the rest of the cluster servers to the *Selected servers* list. Then, click **Next**. The Testing Options page appears, as shown in Figure 12-20.

Figure 12-20

The Testing Options page of the Validate a Configuration Wizard

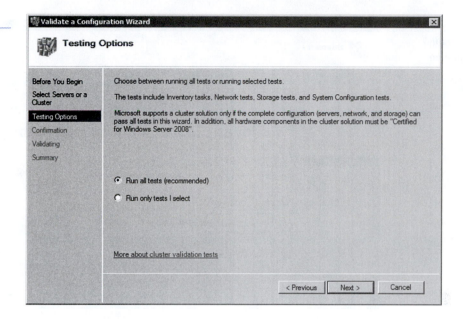

6. Leave the *Run all tests* option selected and click **Next**. The Confirmation page appears, as shown in Figure 12-21.

Figure 12-21

The Confirmation page of the Validate a Configuration Wizard

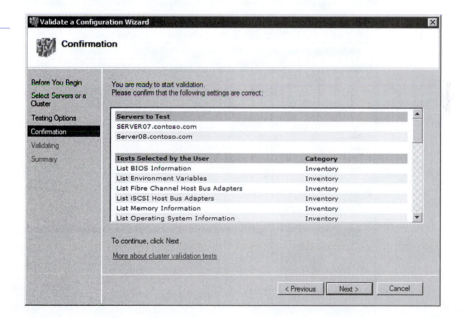

7. Click **Next**. The Validating page appears as the wizard performs the testing process. When the testing process is completed, the Summary page appears, as shown in Figure 12-22.

Figure 12-22

The Summary page of the Validate a Configuration Wizard

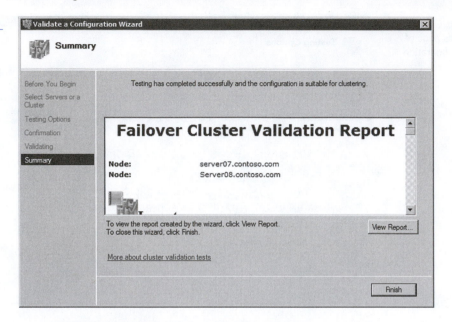

8. Click **View Report**. An Internet Explorer window appears, as shown in Figure 12-23, containing a detailed report of the validation tests.

Figure 12-23

A Failover Cluster Validation Report

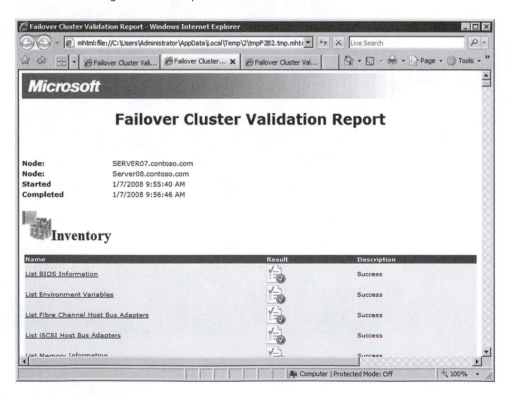

9. Click **Finish**.

CLOSE the Failover Cluster Management console.

Examine the validation report carefully, especially any listed warnings or test failures, and take appropriate actions to correct them before you create the cluster. You can repeat the entire validation process as needed or perform specific tests by selecting *Run only tests I select* on the Testing Options page.

TAKE NOTE*

You can use the Validate a Configuration Wizard to check a cluster that already exists to ensure that all of the requisite components are still operational.

CREATING A FAILOVER CLUSTER

After you validate your cluster configuration and correct any problems, you can create the cluster. A failover cluster is a logical entity that exists on the network, with a name and an IP address, just like a physical computer.

To create a failover cluster, use the following procedure.

 CREATE A FAILOVER CLUSTER

GET READY. Log on to Windows Server 2008 using an account with administrative privileges. When the logon process is completed, close the Initial Configuration Tasks window and any other windows that appear.

1. Click **Start**, and then click **Administrative Tools** > **Failover Cluster Management**. The Failover Cluster Management console appears.

2. In the detail (middle) pane, in the Management box, click **Create a Cluster**. The Create Cluster Wizard page appears, as shown in Figure 12-24.

Figure 12-24

The Create Cluster Wizard

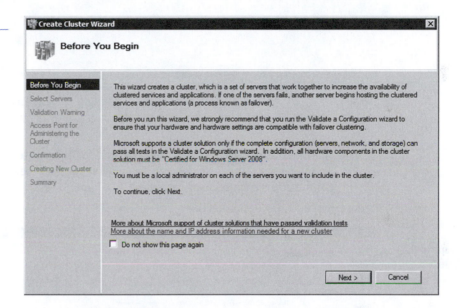

3. Click **Next** to bypass the Before You Begin page. The Select Servers page appears, as shown in Figure 12-25.

Figure 12-25

The Select Servers page of the Create Cluster Wizard

4. Key or browse to the name of the first server you want to add to the cluster and click **Add**. The server appears in the *Selected servers* list.

5. Repeat the process to add the rest of the cluster servers to the *Selected servers* list. Then, click **Next**. The Access Point for Administering the Cluster page appears, as shown in Figure 12-26.

Figure 12-26

The Access Point for Administering the Cluster page of the Create Cluster Wizard

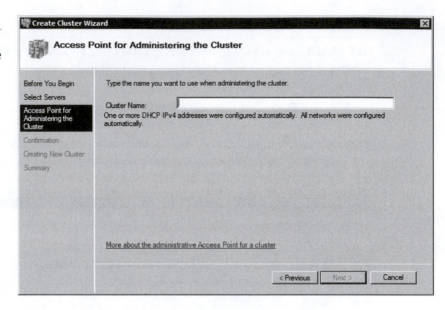

6. In the Cluster Name text box, key a name for the cluster and click **Next**. The Wizard obtains an IP address for the cluster on each network using DHCP and the Confirmation page appears, as shown in Figure 12-27.

Figure 12-27

The Confirmation page of the Create Cluster Wizard

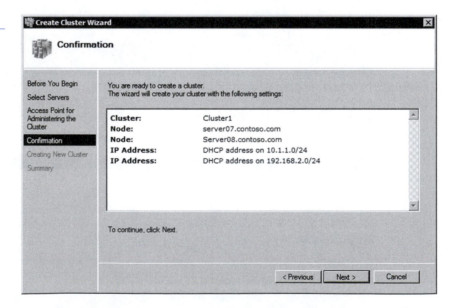

7. Click **Next**. The Creating New Cluster page appears.

8. When the cluster creation process is completed, the Summary page appears. Click **Finish**. The cluster appears in the console's scope (left) pane, as shown in Figure 12-28.

Figure 12-28

A newly created cluster in the Failover Cluster Management console

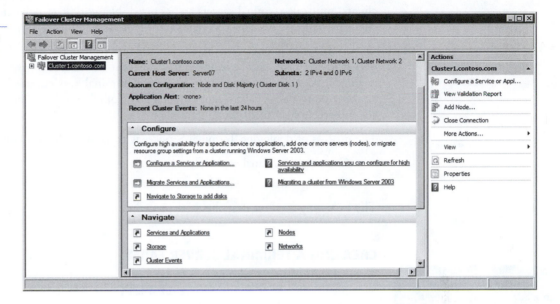

CLOSE the Failover Cluster Management console.

After you create the cluster, you can use the Failover Cluster Management console to specify the applications the cluster will manage. If a server fails, the applications you select are immediately executed on another server to keep them available to clients at all times.

Using Network Load Balancing

> Network load balancing (NLB) differs from failover clustering because its primary function is not fault tolerance, but rather more efficient support of heavy user traffic.

If, for example, you have an Internet Web site that experiences a sudden increase in traffic, the Web server could be overwhelmed, causing performance to degrade. To address the problem, you can add another Web server that hosts the same site, but how do you ensure that the incoming traffic is split equally between the two servers? *Network load balancing (NLB)* is one possible answer.

In a failover cluster, only one of the servers is running the protected application at any given time. In network load balancing, all of the servers in the cluster are operational and service clients. The NLB cluster itself, like a failover cluster, is a logical entity with its own name and IP address. Clients connect to the cluster, rather than the individual servers; the cluster distributes the incoming requests evenly among its component servers.

Because all of the servers in an NLB cluster can actively service clients at the same time, this type of cluster is not appropriate for database and email applications, which require exclusive access to a data store. NLB is more appropriate for applications such as Web servers. You can easily replicate a Web site to multiple servers on a regular basis, enabling each computer to maintain a separate copy of the data it provides to clients.

LOAD BALANCING TERMINAL SERVERS

Windows Server 2008 also supports the use of network load balancing for terminal servers. In Lesson 8, "Using Terminal Services," you learned how to deploy Windows desktops to clients using Terminal Services. For any organization with more than a few Terminal Services clients, multiple terminal servers are required. Network load balancing can ensure that the client sessions are distributed evenly among the servers.

One problem inherent in the load balancing of terminal servers is that a client can disconnect from a session and be assigned to a different terminal server when he or she attempts to reconnect later. To address this problem, the Terminal Services role includes the TS Session Broker role service, which maintains a database of client sessions and enables a disconnected client to reconnect to the same terminal server.

The process of deploying Terminal Services with network load balancing consists of two parts:

- Creating a terminal server farm
- Creating a network load balancing cluster

The following sections describe these procedures.

CREATING A TERMINAL SERVER FARM

CERTIFICATION READY?
Configure Terminal
Services load balancing
2.3

To create a load balanced terminal server farm, you must install the Terminal Services role with the Terminal Server role service on at least two Windows Server 2008 computers. You must also install the TS Session Broker role service on one computer. The computer running TS Session Broker can be, but does not have to be, one of the terminal servers. The Terminal Services computers are subject to the following requirements:

- The Terminal Services computers must be running Windows Server 2008.
- The terminal servers and the computer running TS Session Broker must be members of the same Active Directory domain.
- The terminal servers must be configured identically, with the same installed applications.
- Clients connecting to the terminal server farm must run Remote Desktop Connection (RDC) version 5.2 or later.

When you install the TS Session Broker role service, the Add Roles Wizard installs the Terminal Services Session Broker system service and creates a local group called Session Directory Computers. For a computer to participate in a terminal server farm, you must add it to the Session Directory Computers group and then complete the following procedure on each of your terminal servers.

→ CREATE A TERMINAL SERVER FARM

GET READY. Log on to Windows Server 2008 using an account with administrative privileges. When the logon process is completed, close the Initial Configuration Tasks window and any other windows that appear.

1. Click **Start**, and then click **Administrative Tools** > **Terminal Services** > **Terminal Services Configuration**. The Terminal Services Configuration console appears, as shown in Figure 12-29.

Figure 12-29

The Terminal Services Configuration console

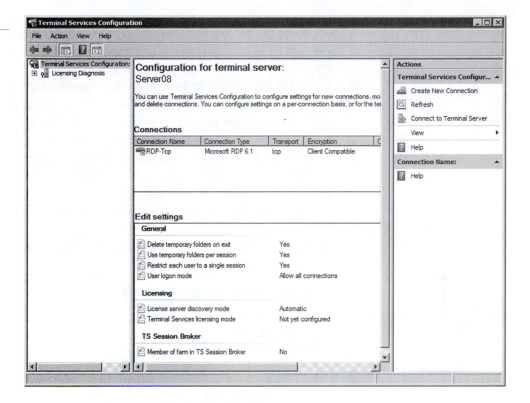

2. In the detail (middle) pane, under TS Session Broker, double-click **Member of farm in TS Session Broker**. The Properties sheet appears, displaying the TS Session Broker tab, as shown in Figure 12-30.

Figure 12-30

The TS Session Broker tab in the Properties sheet

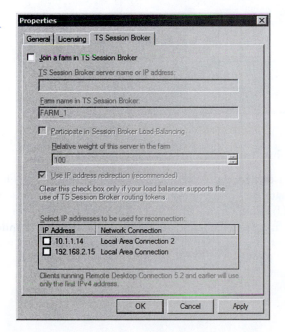

3. Select the **Join a farm in TS Session Broker** checkbox.

4. In the *TS Session Broker server name or IP address* text box, specify the name or address of the computer on which you installed the TS Session Broker role service.

5. In the *Farm name in TS Session Broker* text box, key the name of the server farm you want to use. If a farm by the name you specify does not exist on the TS Session Broker server, the console creates it. If the farm does exist, the console adds the terminal server to it.

6. Select the **Participate in Session Broker Load-Balancing** checkbox.

7. In the *Relative weight of this server in the farm* spin box, specify the priority of this terminal server in relation to the others in the farm.

8. If you use DNS round robin or Network Load Balancing redirection, leave the default *Use IP address redirection* checkbox selected. Clear this checkbox if you use a network load balancing solution that supports routing token redirection.

9. If the terminal server is connected to more than one network, select the checkbox for the IP address you want TS Session Broker to use when redirecting sessions to the server.

10. When the configuration is complete, as shown in Figure 12-31, click **OK**.

Figure 12-31

A completed TS Session Broker tab in the Properties sheet

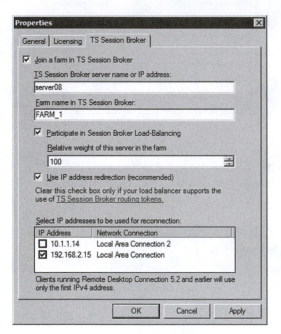

CLOSE the Terminal Services Configuration console.

You must repeat this procedure on each of your terminal servers to join them to the server farm. To automate the configuration process, you can apply these settings to an organization unit (OU) using Group Policy. The TS Session Broker settings are located in the Computer Configuration/Policies/Administrative Templates/Windows Components/Terminal Services/Terminal Server/TS Broker Session node of a group policy object, as shown in Figure 12-32.

Figure 12-32

Group Policy settings for TS
Session Broker

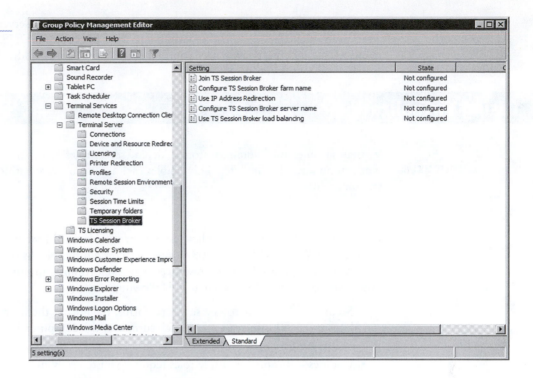

BALANCING THE TRAFFIC LOAD

When you configure your terminal servers to use the load balancing capability built in to TS Session Broker, the client connection process proceeds as follows:

1. A client attempts to connect to one of the terminal servers in the server farm.
2. The terminal server sends a query to the TS Session Broker server, identifying the client attempting to connect.
3. The TS Session Broker searches its database to see if the specified client is already in an existing session.
4. The TS Session Broker server sends a reply to the terminal server, instructing it to redirect the connection to one of the servers in the farm. If a session already exists for the client, the TS Session Broker server redirects it to the terminal server running that session. If a session does not exist for the client, the TS Session Broker server redirects it to the terminal server with the fewest sessions.
5. The terminal server forwards the client connection to the computer specified by the TS Session Broker server.

While this procedure is effective in keeping the sessions balanced among the terminal servers, it does nothing to control which terminal server receives the initial connection requests from clients on the network. When a client connects to a terminal server, the user typically specifies the server by name. The client's computer then uses the Domain Name System (DNS) to resolve the name into an IP address, which it uses to establish a terminal server connection.

Under normal circumstances, the DNS server always resolves a given name into the same IP address, thereby causing all terminal services clients to connect initially to the same terminal server. If there are enough clients, this traffic can negatively affect the performance of that one server. To prevent this from happening, Microsoft recommends the use of a secondary load balancing mechanism to distribute the initial connection attempts among the various terminal servers.

The most common way to do this is to use the *DNS round robin* technique, in which you create an individual resource record for each terminal server in the server farm using the server's own IP address and the name of the farm (instead of the server name). When clients attempt to establish a Terminal Services connection to the farm, DNS is responsible for distributing the incoming name resolution requests among the IP addresses.

■ Using Virtualization

 THE BOTTOM LINE   Virtualization enables administrators to deploy server roles on separate virtual machines that run on a single computer. This enables each role to operate within its own protected environment.

In Lesson 1, "Deploying an Application Server," you learned how you can distribute roles among your Windows Server 2008 computers, combining roles as needed to take full advantage of the computers' hardware resources. However, running multiple roles on a single computer can lead to problems, such as the following:

- Security—The more roles a server performs, the greater the number of ports you have to leave open. This increases the attack surface of the computer, making it more vulnerable to unauthorized intrusion.
- Updates—Running multiple roles requires you to apply more updates, resulting in a greater potential for software conflicts that can affect the system's performance.
- Peak usage—Different roles have different usage cycles, and the more roles a computer performs, the more complex the convergence of those cycles becomes. A system might have sufficient resources to support multiple roles when they are at rest or one role is running at its peak, but can the system support several roles operating at their peaks simultaneously?

Virtualization is a potential solution to these problems that is becoming increasingly popular in an enterprise. Available for some time in the form of separate applications such as Microsoft Virtual Server and Virtual PC, Windows Server 2008 is the first Windows version to include support for virtualization at the operating system level, using a new feature called Hyper-V.

Virtualization is the process of deploying and maintaining multiple instances of an operating system, called *virtual machines (VMs)*, on a single computer. Each virtual machine contains a completely separate copy of the operating system with its own virtual hardware resources, device drivers, and applications. To the network, each virtual machine looks like a separate computer with its own name and IP address. As a result, you are not combining the security risks of multiple roles in a single operating system instance. You update each instance of the operating system separately.

Using virtual machines also makes it easier to manage the distribution of your roles among your physical servers. On a virtualized computer, the hardware resources allocated to each virtual machine are abstracted from the actual physical resources in the computer. This means that you can copy a virtual machine from one computer to another, and it will run without modification, even if the two computers have different physical hardware. Therefore, if you have three roles installed on a single computer in three separate virtual machines, you can simply move one virtual machine to another computer if their combined usage levels begin to overwhelm the hardware.

Virtualization provides other advantages as well, including the following:

- Backups—Backing up individual virtual machines is no more difficult than backing up multiple roles on a single computer. However, virtual machines can greatly simplify the process of restoring a server in the event of a disaster. If a Hyper-V server goes down, you can restore the virtual machines to other Hyper-V servers immediately, as a temporary measure or a permanent solution. You can also maintain dormant copies of your virtual machines on other servers, which you can activate any time they're needed.

- Testing and education—Virtual machines enable you to test software products on a clean operating system installation without contaminating or being contaminated by other software components. Instead of using multiple computers to test networking functions, you can create many virtual machines on a single computer and build a virtual network in one box.
- Compatibility—A single host computer can run virtual machines with different operating systems. Therefore, if you want to upgrade your servers to the latest operating system version, you can still maintain downlevel virtual machines to support applications that require a previous version.

Understanding Virtualization Architectures

Virtualization products can use several different architectures that enable them to share a computer's hardware resources among several virtual machines.

Virtualization products, including Microsoft Virtual PC and Virtual Server, have been available for several years. With these products, you first install a standard operating system on a computer. This becomes the "host" operating system. Then, you install the virtualization product, which adds a component called a virtual machine manager (VMM). The VMM essentially runs alongside the host OS, as shown in Figure 12-33, and enables you to create as many virtual machines as you have hardware to support.

Figure 12-33

A hybrid VMM sharing hardware access with a host OS

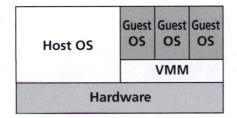

With the VMM, you create a virtual hardware environment for each virtual machine. You can specify how much memory to allocate to each VM, create virtual disk drives using space on the computer's physical drives, and provide access to peripheral devices. You then install a "guest" OS on each virtual machine, just as if you were deploying a new computer.

This type of arrangement is called *hybrid virtualization*. The host OS essentially shares access to the computer's processor with the VMM, with each taking the clock cycles it needs and passing control of the processor back to the other. Hybrid virtualization is an improvement over an earlier technology called *Type 2 virtualization*, which virtualized individual guest applications, not entire operating system installations.

While hybrid virtualization provides adequate virtual machine performance, particularly in educational and testing environments, it does not provide the same performance as separate physical computers. Therefore, it is not generally recommended for high-traffic servers in production environments.

The virtualization capability built into Windows Server 2008, called *Hyper-V*, uses a different type of architecture. Hyper-V uses *Type 1 virtualization*, in which the VMM is called a *hypervisor*, an abstraction layer that interacts directly with the computer's physical hardware. The hypervisor creates individual environments called *partitions*, each of which has its own operating system installed, and accesses the computer's hardware via the hypervisor. Unlike hybrid virtualization, no host OS shares processor time with the VMM. Instead, the hypervisor designates the first partition it creates as the parent partition, and all subsequent partitions as child partitions, as shown in Figure 12-34.

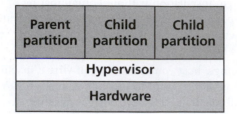

The parent partition accesses the system hardware through the hypervisor, just like the child partitions do. The only difference is that the parent runs the virtualization stack, which creates and manages the child partitions. The parent partition is also responsible for the subsystems that directly affect the performance of the computer's physical hardware, such as Plug and Play, power management, and error handling. These subsystems run in the operating systems on the child partitions as well, but they address only virtual hardware, while the parent, or root, partition handles the real thing.

There are two different forms of Type 1, or hypervisor, virtualization. One form uses a *monolithic hypervisor*, which has the device drivers for the physical hardware installed in the hypervisor layer. The primary disadvantage of this model is that any driver problems affect all of the partitions on the computer. The other form of Type 1 virtualization uses a *microkernelized hypervisor*, in which each individual partition has its own device drivers. This way, a problem driver affects only the partition in which it is running.

Introducing Hyper-V

While Microsoft has designed Hyper-V to be a role included with the Windows Server 2008 operating system, Hyper-V is not included in the initial Windows Server 2008 release. Instead, Microsoft provides it as a separate download that adds the Hyper-V role to the operating system.

Hyper-V is a Windows Server 2008 role like any other, which you can install using the Server Manager console. However, Hyper-V has hardware and licensing requirements that go beyond those for the Windows Server 2008 operating system. In practice, the technology will largely be limited to enterprise deployments that are willing to make a substantial hardware investment in virtualization technology.

Hyper-V is included in the Windows Server 2008 Standard, Enterprise, and Datacenter products, but only in the 64-bit versions, for computers with x64 processors. There will be no Hyper-V support for computers with 32-bit x86 processors. In addition, the hypervisor requires a processor with hardware support for virtualization, which limits the use of Hyper-V to computers with processors that have a virtualization extension, as well as chipset and BIOS support for virtualization. Intel has named their virtualization extension VT, while AMD calls theirs AMD-V.

In addition to the specialized hardware requirements for Hyper-V, Microsoft has added a licensing requirement. For licensing purposes, Microsoft refers to each virtual machine that you create on a Hyper-V server as a **virtual instance**. Each Windows Server 2008 version includes a set number of virtual instances; you must purchase licenses to create additional ones. Table 12-1 lists the Windows Server 2008 versions, the number of virtual instances included with each, and its manufacturer's suggested retail price (MSRP), which of course is subject to change.

Table 12-1

Windows Server 2008 Versions and Their Hyper-V Support

OPERATING SYSTEM VERSION	NUMBER OF VIRTUAL INSTANCES INCLUDED	MSRP (IN U.S. DOLLARS) WITH HYPER-V
Windows Server 2008 Standard	1	$999
Windows Server 2008 Enterprise	4	$3,999
Windows Server 2008 Datacenter	Unlimited	$2,999 per processor

After you have the appropriate hardware and the required licenses, you can add the Hyper-V role using Server Manager. Microsoft recommends that you do not install other roles with Hyper-V. Adding the role installs the hypervisor software, as well as the management interface, which takes the form of a Microsoft Management Console (MMC) snap-in called Hyper-V Manager, as shown in Figure 12-35. The Hyper-V Manager MMC snap-in provides administrators with a list of all the virtual machines registered on a Windows Server 2008 system and enables administrators to perform actions on both the Hyper-V server and the virtual machines.

Figure 12-35

The Hyper-V Manager console

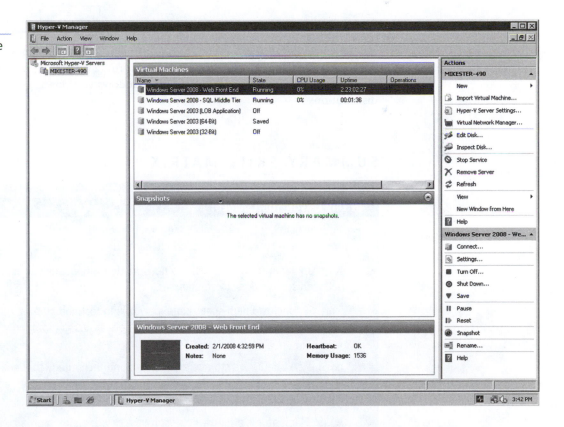

Using Hyper-V Manager, you can create new virtual machines and define the hardware resources that the system should allocate to them, as shown in Figure 12-36. In the settings for a particular virtual machine, depending on the physical hardware available in the computer and the limitations of the guest operating system, administrators can specify the number of processors and the amount of memory a virtual machine should use, install virtual network adapters, and create virtual disks using a variety of technologies, including SANs.

CERTIFICATION READY?
Configure Windows Server Hyper-V and virtual machines
1.3

Figure 12-36

The Settings configuration interface for a Hyper-V virtual machine

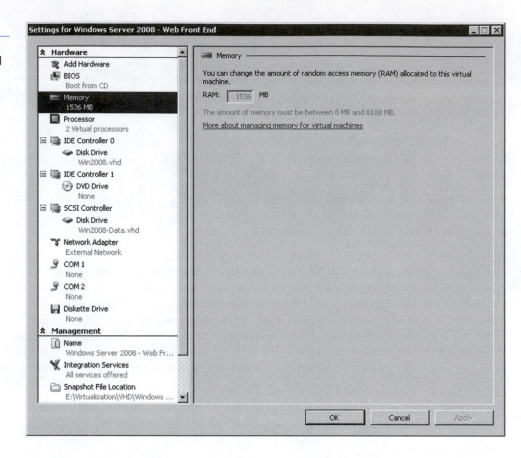

Each virtual machine on a Hyper-V server can run a different operating system, if necessary. Hyper-V supports both 32-bit and 64-bit Windows versions as guest OSes, as well as Linux distributions.

SUMMARY SKILL MATRIX

IN THIS LESSON YOU LEARNED:

- High availability typically takes the form of redundant hardware, software, or data components, which enable an application to continue running even if a disaster occurs.

- A storage area network (SAN) is a network dedicated solely to high-speed connections between servers and storage devices.

- Fibre Channel is a high-speed serial networking technology that was originally designed for use with supercomputers but which is now associated primarily with storage area networking.

- iSCSI is an alternative storage area networking technology that enables servers and storage devices to exchange SCSI traffic using a standard IP network instead of a dedicated Fibre Channel network.

- An iSCSI initiator is a hardware or software device running on a computer that accesses the storage devices on the SAN. The other half of the iSCSI equation is the iSCSI target, which receives SCSI commands from the initiator and passes them to a storage device, represented by a logical unit number (LUN).

- The Internet Storage Name Service (iSNS) registers the presence of initiators and targets on a SAN and responds to queries from iSNS clients.

- Storage Manager for SANs can manage only storage devices that include support for the Microsoft Virtual Disk Service. The storage device manufacturer must supply a software component called a VDS hardware provider, which you install on the computer that will manage the device.

- Storage Explorer is an MMC console that provides information about SAN resources and enables administrators to perform a variety of management tasks.

- The ultimate in fault tolerance is to have entire servers that are redundant, so that if anything goes wrong with one computer, another one can take its place almost immediately. In Windows Server 2008, this is known as a failover cluster.

- Network load balancing (NLB) differs from failover clustering because its primary function is not fault tolerance, but rather more efficient support of heavy user traffic.

- In a failover cluster, only one server is running the protected application at any given time. In network load balancing, all of the servers in the cluster are operational and service clients.

- The Terminal Services role includes the TS Session Broker role service, which maintains a database of client sessions and enables a disconnected client to reconnect to the same terminal server.

- Hyper-V is a new server role that provides hypervisor-based virtualization on 64-bit Windows Server 2008 computers. This enables the administrator to create multiple virtual machines on a single physical computer, each of which runs a separate operating system.

Knowledge Assessment

Matching

Complete the following exercise by matching the terms with their corresponding definitions.

a. Enables a database application to access specific records in a database file stored on a SAN drive array.

b. Supports copper and fiber optic media.

c. A Fibre Channel topology.

d. Installed by default in Windows Server 2008.

e. Provided with some SAN drive arrays.

f. Maintains a database of targets and initiators.

g. Uses redundant servers to ensure application availability.

h. A load balancing technique that assigns multiple IP addresses to a single DNS name.

i. Contains the configuration settings for a failover cluster.

j. Distributes traffic among identical servers.

_____ 1. Switched fabric

_____ 2. VDS hardware provider

_____ 3. failover cluster

_____ 4. witness disk

_____ 5. network load balancing (NLB)

_____ 6. block I/O access

_____ **7.** Internet Storage Name Service (iSNS)

_____ **8.** Fibre Channel

_____ **9.** iSCSI initiator

_____ **10.** DNS round robin

Multiple Choice

Select the correct answer for each of the following questions. Choose all answers that are correct.

1. Which of the following is not a viable medium for a Fibre Channel network?
   a. singlemode fiber optic
   b. multimode fiber optic
   c. shielded twisted pair
   d. unshielded twisted pair

2. Which of the following is the application layer protocol used for all communications between Internet Storage Name Service clients and servers?
   a. iSCSI
   b. iSNSP
   c. IP
   d. FCP

3. To manage a storage device using Storage Manager for SANs, you must have which of the following?
   a. A Fibre Channel switch
   b. An iSCSI target
   c. A VDS hardware provider
   d. An iSNS server

4. Which of the following Fibre Channel layers contains the SCSI commands destined for storage devices on the SAN?
   a. FC1
   b. FC2
   c. FC3
   d. FC4

5. In addition to the application data, which of the following is stored on a failover cluster's shared storage?
   a. The iSNS database
   b. The witness disk
   c. The TS Session Broker database
   d. The iSCSI initiator

6. Which of the following Fibre Channel topologies supports the largest number of devices?
   a. Switched fabric
   b. Token ring
   c. Arbitrated loop
   d. Point-to-point

7. Which of the following components is not included in the Windows Server 2008 product?
   a. iSCSI initiator
   b. iSCSI target
   c. iSNS Server
   d. Storage Manager for SANs

8. A JBOD drive array is an alternative to which of the following?
   a. SAN
   b. SCSI
   c. RAID
   d. iSCSI

9. Which of the following Windows Server 2008 components are intended for use with iSCSI and Fibre Channel SANs?
   a. Internet Storage Name Server
   b. Storage Manager for SANs
   c. Storage Explorer
   d. iSCSI initiator

10. An iSCSI target receives commands from an initiator and passes them to a storage device, which is represented by a(n) _____.
   a. logical unit number
   b. iSNS database entry
   c. VDS hardware provider
   d. RS-232 port

Review Questions

1. Explain the primary difference between a failover cluster and a network load balancing cluster.
2. Explain why the block I/O access provided by a storage area network is preferable to the file-based I/O provided by network-attached storage when you are running a database or email application.

■ Case Scenarios

Scenario 12-1: Deploying a Terminal Services Server Farm

Wingtip Toys has recently decided to deploy all office productivity applications to its internal users with terminal servers. Robert, a member of the IT staff, has been given the responsibility for installing and configuring a server farm on the company network that consists of 12 new terminal servers running Windows Server 2008. Robert installs the Terminal Services role, with the Terminal Server role service, on all 12 computers. He also installs the TS Session Broker role service on one of the computers. After adding each of the 12 terminal servers to a TS Session Broker farm and installing the office applications on the server, Robert begins a test deployment, adding groups of users to gradually increase the terminal server traffic load. Later, when examining the traffic statistics, Robert notices that one of the servers is experiencing much higher traffic levels than the others and it is not the server running TS Session Broker. What could be the problem and how should Robert resolve it?

Scenario 12-2: Deploying a Test Storage Area Network

Mackenzie is responsible for deploying a test storage area network, using a Windows Server 2008 computer and an iSCSI drive array with a standard Ethernet networking infrastructure. After connecting the server and the drive array to the SAN and configuring an iSCSI target using the Web-based interface provided by the array, Mackenzie uses iSCSI initiator on the server to establish a connection to a target. Mackenzie can now use the Disk Administration snap-in to partition and format the volume on the drive array. Next, Mackenzie attempts to use the Storage Manager for SANs console to create additional LUNs on the drive array, but the console fails to load the Virtual Disk Service. What must Mackenzie do to use Storage Manager for SANs to manage the LUNs on the drive array?

Windows Server 2008 Applications Infrastructure Configuration (Exam 70-643)

Matrix Skill	Skill Number	Lesson Number
Deploying Servers		
Deploy images by using Windows Deployment Services.	1.1	1
Configure Microsoft Windows activation.	1.2	1
Configure Windows Server Hyper-V and virtual machines.	1.3	12
Configure high availability.	1.4	12
Configure storage.	1.5	2
Configuring Terminal Services		
Configure Windows Server 2008 Terminal Services RemoteApp (TS RemoteApp).	2.1	8
Configure Terminal Services Gateway.	2.2	10
Configure Terminal Services load balancing.	2.3	12
Configure and monitor Terminal Services resources.	2.4	8
Configure Terminal Services licensing.	2.5	9
Configure Terminal Services client connections.	2.6	9
Configure Terminal Services server options.	2.7	8
Configuring a Web Services Infrastructure		
Configure Web applications.	3.1	7
Manage Web sites.	3.2	5
Configure a File Transfer Protocol (FTP) server.	3.3	5
Configure Simple Mail Transfer Protocol (SMTP).	3.4	7
Manage Internet Information Services (IIS).	3.5	5
Configure SSL security.	3.6	6
Configure Web site authentication and permissions.	3.7	6
Configuring Network Application Services		
Configure Windows Media server.	4.1	11
Configure Digital Rights Management (DRM).	4.2	11
Configure Microsoft Windows SharePoint Services server options.	4.3	11
Configure Windows SharePoint Services email integration.	4.4	11

The *Windows Server 2008 Applications Infrastructure Configuration* title of the Microsoft Official Academic Course (MOAC) series includes two books: a textbook and a lab manual. The exercises in the lab manual are designed for classroom use under the supervision of an instructor or a lab aide.

■ Classroom Setup

This course should be taught in a classroom containing networked computers where students can develop their skills through hands-on experience with Microsoft Windows Server 2008. The exercises in the lab manual require the computers to be installed and configured in a specific manner. Failure to adhere to the setup instructions in this document can produce unanticipated results when the students perform the exercises.

Classroom Configuration

The following configurations and naming conventions are used throughout the course and are required for completing the labs as outlined in the lab manual.

The classroom network consists entirely of computers running Windows Server 2008, including a single classroom server and a number of student servers. The classroom server performs several roles for the student servers, including the following:

- Active Directory Domain Services domain controller
- Domain Name System (DNS) server
- Dynamic host Configuration Protocol (DHCP) server

Use the following information when setting up the classroom server:

- Active Directory domain name: contoso.com
- Computer name: ServerDC
- Fully qualified domain name (FQDN): ServerDC.contoso.com
- Administrator password: P@ssw0rd

The student computers are also servers running Windows Server 2008, which the students will join to the contoso.com domain. Each student computer in the domain is to be named Server##, where ## is a unique number assigned to each computer by the instructor. Each student server will also have a corresponding domain user account called Student##, where ## is the same number assigned to the computer.

As they work through the lab manual, the students will install and remove several different roles and features. In some of the exercises, students will initiate communication with another server on the network. To make this possible, the lab manual is designed to support the following three classroom configurations.

- Dedicated computers—Each student computer has a single instance of Windows Server 2008 installed. To complete the lab exercises that require interaction between two servers, you can provide each student with two computers or assign a lab partner to each student. In the latter case, each student will complete the exercise and provide the services required by his or her partner.

- Local virtual machines—Each student computer has a virtualization product, such as Microsoft Virtual PC, installed, enabling you to create two virtual machines, each running an instance of Windows Server 2008. With this configuration, each student can perform all of the exercises on one computer, using the two virtual machines to perform the required roles.

- Web-hosted virtual machines—Each student computer uses a Web browser to access two Windows Server 2008 virtual machines hosted by a commercial service on the Internet. With this configuration, each student can perform all of the exercises on one computer, using the two virtual machines to perform the required roles.

To support these classroom configurations, students must begin each lab in the manual with the same baseline operating system configuration on the student computers. Therefore, each lab begins with an exercise that sets up the server for that lab and concludes with an exercise that returns the server to the baseline configuration. Depending on your classroom configuration, the students might be able to skip the first and last exercises in each lab.

Classroom Server Requirements

The computer running Windows Server 2008 in the classroom requires the following hardware and software:

Hardware Requirements

- Processor: 1 GHz (minimum); 2 GHz or faster (recommended)
- RAM: 512 MB (minimum); 2 GB or more (recommended)
- Disk space requirements: 10 GB (minimum); 40 GB or more (recommended)
- DVD-ROM drive
- Super VGA (800 × 600) or higher-resolution monitor
- Keyboard and mouse (or other pointing device)
- One network interface adapter

Software Requirements

- Microsoft Windows Server 2008, Standard or Enterprise

Student Computer Requirements

Each student computer requires the following hardware and software:

Hardware Requirements

- Processor: 1 GHz (minimum); 2 GHz or faster (recommended)
- RAM: 512 MB (minimum); 2 GB or more (recommended)
- First hard drive: 50+ GB, sufficient disk space for one 40 GB system partition and at least 10 GB of unpartitioned space
- Second hard drive: 10+ GB with no partitions
- DVD-ROM drive
- Super VGA (800 × 600) or higher-resolution monitor
- Keyboard and mouse (or other pointing device)
- One network interface adapter

TAKE NOTE*

If you are using Web-hosted virtual machines in your classroom, you might not have to perform any of the setup procedures described in this document because the students will be able to access preconfigured virtual machines over the Web.

TAKE NOTE*

If you plan to create virtual machines on your student computers, each virtual machine must meet these hardware requirements.

SOFTWARE REQUIREMENTS

- Windows Server 2008, Standard or Enterprise

■ Classroom Server Setup Instructions

Before you begin, do the following:

- Read this entire document.
- Verify that you have the Instructor CD provided with the course materials and the installation disk for Microsoft Windows Server 2008.

 WARNING By performing the following setup instructions, your computer's hard disks will be repartitioned and reformatted. You will lose all existing data on the system.

Installing Windows Server 2008

Using the following setup procedure, install Windows Server 2008 on ServerDC.

 INSTALL WINDOWS SERVER 2008

1. Boot the computer from the Windows Server 2008 Installation disk. When you boot from the disk, the Windows Server 2008 Setup program starts automatically and the Install Windows page appears.
2. Modify the *Language to install, Time and currency format*, and *Keyboard or input method* settings, if necessary. Click **Next**.
3. Click **Install now**. The *Type your product key for activation* page appears.
4. Enter your product key in the *Product key* text box and click **Next**. The *Please read the license terms* page appears.

TAKE NOTE*

If you plan to use evaluation versions of Windows Server 2008 in the classroom, you can leave the Product key field blank and, in the *Select the edition of Windows that you purchased* window that subsequently appears, select Windows Server 2008 Enterprise (Full Installation) for the version you want to install.

5. Select the **I accept the license terms** checkbox and click **Next**. The *Which type of installation do you want?* page appears.
6. Click **Custom**. The *Where do you want to install Windows?* page appears.
7. Select the disk where you want to install Windows Server 2008 and click **Next**. The *Installing Windows* page appears.
8. When the installation process is complete, the computer restarts and prompts you to change the Administrator password. Click **OK**.
9. Key **P@ssw0rd** in the New Password and Confirm Password text boxes and click the right arrow button. Then click **OK**. Windows Server 2008 starts and the Initial Configuration Tasks window appears.
10. Install any updates needed to keep the operating system current.

TAKE NOTE*

If your computer supports booting from CD/DVD, the computer might try to boot from the Windows Server 2008 disk after Windows Server 2008 Setup restarts. If this happens, you should be prompted to press a key to boot from the disk. However, if Setup restarts automatically, simply remove the disk and restart the computer.

PROCEED to the following section to continue the server configuration process.

Before you proceed with the server configuration, install any required updates to keep the operating system current. Use Automatic Updates, the Windows Update Web site, or any other mechanism to locate, download, and install the updates.

Completing Post-Installation Tasks on ServerDC

After the installation is complete and the Initial Configuration Tasks window has appeared, complete the following procedures to prepare the computer to function as the classroom server.

PERFORMING INITIAL CONFIGURATION TASKS

Use the following procedure to prepare the server for the course.

PERFORM INITIAL CONFIGURATION TASKS

1. In the Initial Configuration Tasks window, click **Set time zone**. The Date and Time dialog box appears.

2. Verify that the date, time, and time zone shown in the dialog box are correct. If they are not, click **Change date and time** or **Change time zone** and correct them. Then click **OK**.

3. Click **Configure Networking**. The Network Connections window appears.

4. Right-click the **Local Area Connection** icon and, from the context menu, select **Properties**. The Local Area Connection Properties sheet appears.

5. Clear the Internet Protocol Version 6 (TCP/IPv6) checkbox.

6. Select **Internet Protocol Version 4 (TCP/IPv4)** and click **Properties**. The Internet Protocol Version 4 (TCP/IPv4) Properties sheet appears.

7. Configure the TCP/IP parameters using the following values:

    - IP Address: 10.1.1.100
    - Subnet Mask: 255.255.255.0
    - Preferred DNS Server: 127.0.0.1

TAKE NOTE *

The IP addresses supplied in this setup document and in the lab manual are suggestions. You can use any IP addresses for the computers in your classroom, as long as all of the systems are located on the same subnet. If the classroom network is connected to a school network or the Internet, you can specify the address of the router providing the network connection in the Default Gateway field. Otherwise, leave it blank.

8. Click **OK** twice to close the two Properties sheets. Close the Network Connections window.

9. In the Initial Configuration Tasks window, click **Provide computer name and domain**. The System Properties dialog box appears with the Computer Name tab selected.

10. Click **Change**. The Computer Name/Domain Changes dialog box appears.

11. In the Computer name text box, key **ServerDC** and click **OK**. A message box appears, prompting you to restart your computer.

12. Click **OK**, then click **Close** to close the System Properties dialog box. Another message box appears, informing you again that you must restart the computer.

13. Click **Restart Now**. The computer restarts.

The ServerDC computer must be an Active Directory domain controller. After the computer restarts, you can install the Active Directory Domain Services role and the Active Directory Domain Services Installation Wizard.

INSTALL ACTIVE DIRECTORY

To install Active Directory on ServerDC, use the following procedure.

INSTALL ACTIVE DIRECTORY

1. Log on with the local Administrator account, using the password **P@ssw0rd**.

2. When the Initial Configuration Tasks window appears, click **Add Roles**. The Add Roles Wizard appears.

3. Using the Add Roles Wizard, install the Active Directory Domain Services role.

4. When the role installation is complete, click the **Close this wizard and launch the Active Directory Domain Services Installation Wizard (dcpromo.exe)** link. The *Welcome to the Active Directory Installation Wizard* page appears.

5. Click **Next** to proceed with the Active Directory installation.

6. On the *Operating System Compatibility* page, click **Next**.

7. On the *Choose a Deployment Configuration* page, select **Create a new domain in a new forest** and click **Next**.

8. On the *Name the Forest Root Domain* page, key **contoso.com** and click **Next**.

9. On the *Set the Forest Functional Level* page, click **Next** to accept the default setting.

10. On the *Set Domain Functional Level* page, click **Next** to accept the default setting.

11. On the *Additional Domain Controller Options* page, verify that the **DNS server** checkbox is selected and click **Next**. A Static IP Assignment message box appears, warning you that the computer has a dynamically assigned IP address.

12. For the purposes of this manual, you can ignore the warning. Click **Yes, the computer will use a dynamically assigned IP address** to continue. A message box appears, warning you that the system cannot locate an existing DNS infrastructure.

13. Because you will be creating a new DNS infrastructure, you can ignore this warning and click **Yes**.

14. On the *Location for Database, Log Files, and SYSVOL* page, click **Next** to accept the default settings.

15. On the *Directory Services Restore Mode Administrator Password* page, key **P@ssw0rd** in the Password and Confirm Password text boxes and click **Next**.

16. On the *Summary* page, click **Next**.

17. When the installation process is complete, restart the server.

After the server restarts, it functions as the domain controller for the contoso.com domain. Students must log on to the domain in all of the lab exercises.

INSTALLING THE DHCP SERVER ROLE

To install the DHCP server on ServerDC, use the following procedure.

 INSTALL THE DHCP SERVER ROLE

1. Log on with the domain Administrator account using the password **P@ssw0rd**.

2. When the Initial Configuration Tasks window appears, click **Add Roles**. The Add Roles Wizard appears.

3. Using the Add Roles Wizard, install the DHCP Server role.

4. On the *Select Network Connection Bindings* page, click **Next** to accept the default settings.

5. On the *Specify IPv4 DNS Server Settings* page, click **Next** to accept the default settings.

6. On the *Specify IPv4 WINS Server Settings* page, click **Next** to accept the default settings.

7. On the *Add or Edit DHCP Scopes* page, click **Add**.

8. In the Add Scope dialog box, create a scope using the following values:
   - Scope Name: Classroom
   - Starting IP Address: 10.1.1.101
   - Ending IP Address: 10.1.1.199
   - Subnet Mask: 255.255.255.0
   - Subnet Type: Wired

TAKE NOTE

If the classroom network is connected to a school network or the Internet, you can specify the address of the router providing the network connection in the Default Gateway field. Otherwise, leave it blank.

9. Select the **Activate this scope** checkbox and click **OK**. Then click **Next**.

10. On the Configure DHCPv6 Stateless Mode pane, click **Next** to accept the default settings.

11. On the *Authorize DHCP Server* page, click **Next** to accept the default settings.

12. On the *Confirm Installation Selections* page, click **Install**.

CLOSE the Initial Configuration Tasks window when the installation is complete.

After the DHCP role is installed, all student servers will obtain their IP addresses and other TCP/IP configuration settings via DHCP.

Creating User Accounts

Each student must have a domain user account called Student##, where ## is the same number as the computer the student is using. To create the student accounts, use the following procedure.

 CREATE USER ACCOUNTS

1. Click **Start**, and then select **Administrative Tools** > **Active Directory Users and Computers**. The Active Directory Users and Computers console appears.

2. Expand the contoso.com domain.

3. Right-click the **Users** container and select **New** > **User**. The New Object-User wizard appears.

4. Key **Student##** in the First Name and User Logon Name text boxes, where ## is the number assigned to the first student computer in the classroom. Then click **Next**.

5. In the Password and Confirm Password text boxes, key **P@ssw0rd**.

6. Clear the **User Must Change Password At Next Logon** checkbox and select the **Password Never Expires** checkbox. Then click **Next**.

7. Click **Finish** to create the user account.

8. Repeat Steps 3–7 to create a Student## user account for each computer in the classroom.

9. Right-click the **Users** container and select **New** > **Group**. The New Object-Group wizard appears.

10. In the Group Name text box, key **Students**. Then click **Next**.

11. Click **Finish** to create the group.

12. In the Users container, double-click the Students group you just created. The Students Properties sheet appears.

13. Click the **Members** tab.

14. Click **Add**, key the name of the first Student## user you created, and click **OK**.

15. Repeat Step 14 to add all the Student## accounts you created to the Students group.

16. Click **OK** to close the Students Properties sheet.

17. Using the same procedure, open the Properties sheet for the Domain Admins group and add each of the Student## user accounts you created as members of that group.

CLOSE the Active Directory Users and Computers console.

The students will use these Student## accounts to log on to the domain as they complete the exercises in the lab manual. Their membership in the Students group provides domain administrator privileges, as well as local Administrator privileges on their individual servers.

PREPARING THE FILE SYSTEM

From the Microsoft Web site, download the following add-on modules for Windows Server 2008:

- Windows Media Services 2008 for Windows Server 2008 – Server MSU file
- Windows SharePoint Services 3.0 with Service Pack 1
- Microsoft FTP Publishing Service for IIS 7.0

Windows Media Services 2008 and Windows SharePoint Services 3.0 with Service Pack 1 are available from the Microsoft Download Center at http://microsoft.com/downloads. Microsoft FTP Publishing Service for IIS 7.0 is available from Microsoft's Internet Information Services site at http://iis.net/downloads.

Complete the following procedure to make these modules available to the students and provide the students with storage on the classroom server.

 PREPARE THE FILE SYSTEM

1. On the server's C drive, create a new folder called *\Install* and three subfolders called *\Install\MediaSvcs*, *\Install\FTP7*, and *Install\SharePoint*.
2. Copy the add-on modules you downloaded to the appropriate folders.
3. Share the C:\Install folder using the share name *Install*, and then grant only the Allow Read share permission to the Everyone special identity.
4. Using Windows Explorer, grant the Students group the Allow Read, Allow Read & Execute, and Allow List Folder Contents NTFS permissions for the C:\Install folder.
5. Also on the server's C drive, create a new folder called *\Students* and copy the \Worksheets folder from your instructor disk to the C:\Students folder.
6. Grant the Students group the Allow Full Control NTFS permission for the C:\Students folder.
7. Share the C:\Students folder using the share name Students, and then grant the Everyone special identity the Allow Full Control share permission.

CLOSE the Windows Explorer window.

These folders provide students with the additional software they need to complete the lab exercises and storage space to keep their lab worksheet files.

CONFIGURING FILE REDIRECTION

To complete the lab exercises, each student must be able to store files on the classroom server. Use Group Policy to redirect each user's Documents folder to the classroom server drive, using the following procedure.

 CONFIGURE FILE REDIRECTION

1. Click **Start**, and then select **Administrative Tools** > **Group Policy Management**. The Group Policy Management console appears.
2. In the scope (left) pane, expand the console tree to display and select the **Group Policy Objects** node under the contoso.com domain.
3. In the detail (right) pane, right-click the **Default Domain Policy GPO** and, from the context menu, select **Edit**. The Group Policy Management Editor window appears.
4. Navigate to the **User Configuration** > **Policies** > **Windows Settings** > **Folder Redirection** folder. Then, right-click the **Documents** subfolder and, from the context menu, select **Properties**. The Documents Properties sheet appears.
5. From the Setting dropdown list, select **Basic – Redirect Everyone's folder to the same location**.

6. In the Target Folder Location box, verify that the default **Create a folder for each user under the root path option** is selected.

7. In the Root Path text box, key **\\ServerDC\Students**.

8. Click the **Settings** tab and clear the **Grant the user exclusive rights to Documents** checkbox.

9. Click **OK** to close the Documents Properties sheet.

CLOSE the Group Policy Management Editor and Group Policy Management consoles.

The computer is ready to function as the classroom server. You can install the student servers.

Student Server Setup

The setup for the student computers depends on your classroom configuration. The result is a bare Windows Server 2008 installation, which students can configure. However, the tasks you must complete before the students arrive vary, as follows:

- Dedicated computers—If each student computer in your classroom will have a single copy of Windows Server 2008 installed on it, proceed directly to the following Install Windows Server 2008 procedure.

- Local virtual machines—If you plan to use a virtualization product on the student computers to enable each system to run multiple copies of Windows Server 2008, first you must install the virtualization software on each computer according the manufacturer's instructions and create a virtual machine for each copy of Windows Server 2008 you plan to install. Then, install the operating system on each virtual machine, using the following Install Windows Server 2008 procedure.

- Web-hosted virtual machines—If your students will access virtual machines provided by a commercial service over the Web, then your classroom computers can run any operating system that provides the appropriate Web browser application. All of the operating systems are preinstalled, so you can skip the following procedure.

INSTALLING WINDOWS SERVER 2008 ON A STUDENT COMPUTER

Using the following setup procedure, install Windows Server 2008 on the student computers.

 INSTALL WINDOWS SERVER 2008

1. Boot the computer from the Windows Server 2008 Installation disk. When you boot from the disk, the Windows Server 2008 Setup program starts automatically, and the *Install Windows* page appears.

2. Modify the *Language to install*, *Time and currency format*, and *Keyboard or input method* settings, if necessary, and click **Next**.

3. Click **Install now**. The *Type your product key for activation* page appears.

4. Enter your product key in the *Product key* text box and click **Next**. The *Please read the license terms* page appears.

> **TAKE NOTE** *
> If you plan to use unregistered evaluation versions of Windows Server 2008 in the classroom, you can leave the Product key field blank and, in the *Select the edition of Windows that you purchased* window that subsequently appears, select Windows Server 2008 Enterprise (Full Installation) for the version you want to install.

5. Select the **I accept the license terms** checkbox and click **Next**. The *Which type of installation do you want?* page appears.

6. Click **Custom**. The *Where do you want to install Windows?* page appears.

> **TAKE NOTE** *
> Depending on the capabilities of your virtualization software and the type of licensing your school provides, you can perform a Windows Server 2008 installation on a single virtual machine and then clone multiple instances of that virtual machine, rather than perform each OS installation individually.

> **⚠ WARNING** By performing the following setup instructions, your computer's hard disks will be repartitioned and reformatted. You will lose all existing data on the system.

7. Select the disk where you want to install Windows Server 2008 and click **Drive Options**.

8. Click **New**. In the Size text box, key **40000**. Click **Apply**.

9. Select the partition you just created and click **Next**. The *Installing Windows* page appears.

10. When the installation process is complete, the computer restarts and prompts you to change the Administrator password. Click **OK**.

> **TAKE NOTE** *
>
> If your computer supports booting from CD/DVD, the computer might try to boot from the Windows Server 2008 disk after Windows Server 2008 Setup restarts. If this happens, you should be prompted to press a key to boot from the disk. However, if Setup restarts automatically, simply remove the disk and restart the computer.

11. Key **P@ssw0rd** in the New Password and Confirm Password text boxes and click the right arrow button. Then click **OK**. Windows Server 2008 starts and the Initial Configuration Tasks window appears.

12. Install any updates needed to keep the operating system current.

CLOSE the Initial Configuration Tasks window.

The computer is ready for a student to begin working through the lab manual. The student will perform all of the initial configuration tasks that the computer requires.

Glossary

A

access control entry (ACE) An entry in an object's access control list (ACL) that grants permissions to a user or group. Each ACE consists of a security principal (the name of the user, group, or computer being granted the permissions) and the specific permissions assigned to that security principal. When you manage permissions in any of the Windows Server 2008 permission systems, you are creating and modifying the ACEs in an ACL.

access control list (ACL) A collection of access control entries that defines the access that all users and groups have to an object.

Active Directory Microsoft's directory service that automates network management, such as user data, resources, and security.

Active Server Pages (ASP) A server-side script processing engine designed by Microsoft to provide dynamic Web content with better performance than the Common Gateway Interface (CGI) and simpler development than Internet Server Application Programming Interface (ISAPI). ASP files have an .asp extension and function like Server Side Includes, with scripting commands embedded in standard HTML code.

Anonymous Authentication In Internet Information Services, an authentication mechanism that enables any user to access a Web site that employs it, without supplying an account name or password. This authentication method is designed primarily for public Web sites on the Internet or any internal site available to all users.

application Computer program designed to aid users in the performance of specific tasks.

application pool In Internet Information Services, an operational division that consists of a request queue and one or more worker processes.

application services Software components that provide communications services, operating environments, or programming interfaces for specific applications.

Arbitrated loop (FC-AL) A Fibre Channel topology that consists of up to 127 devices, connected in a loop, similar to that of a token ring network. The loop can be physical, with each device connected to the next device, or virtual, with each device connected to a hub that implements the loop.

ASP.NET The successor to Active Server Pages (ASP), ASP.NET is based on server-side scripting and enables developers to create dynamic Web pages, Web applications, and XML (Extensible Markup Language) Web services using a wide variety of programming languages and development tools. ASP.NET files have the extension .aspx, and can contain HTML code, XML code, or scripting code for execution by the server.

ATA (Advanced Technology Attachment) A disk interface that uses parallel communications to connect multiple hard disk drives and other devices to a computer.

authentication The process by which Windows Server 2008 verifies that the user matches the user account employed to gain access.

authorization The process of determining whether an identified user or process is permitted access to a resource and the user's appropriate level of access.

B

Basic Authentication The weakest of the challenge/response authentication methods supported by Internet Information Services. Clients transmit unencrypted credentials using Base64 encoding, so anyone capturing the network packets can read the user's password.

basic disk The default disk type in Windows Server 2008. A basic disk supports up to four partitions, typically three primary and one extended, with logical drives to organize data.

binding In Internet Information Services, the mechanism by which the protocol listener associates each incoming request with one particular Web site hosted by the server.

bitmap caching In Terminal Services, a Windows desktop performance feature that enables a client to store display information in a cache in local memory, so that the server does not have to repeatedly transmit the same data.

block I/O access In storage area networking, a type of storage in which a computer accesses the stored data one block at a time.

broadcast stream In Windows Media Services, a multimedia stream that typically consists of live content delivered according to a prearranged schedule.

C

certification authority (CA) A software component or a commercial service that issues digital certificates. Windows Server 2008 includes a CA as part of the Active Directory Certificate Services role.

client access license (CAL) A document that grants a single client access to a specific software program, such as a Terminal Services server.

client machine ID (CMID) A unique identifier assigned to each computer that the Key Management Service host records when it successfully activates the computer.

client-side caching A Remote Desktop Connection feature that enables a client to store screen elements that remain unchanged from one refresh to the next in a cache on the computer.

Common Gateway Interface (CGI) A protocol that enables a Web server to run an application specified in a client request and pass the request to that application for processing. The Web server then receives the output from the application and packages it as a reply to the client in the form of a Web page.

connection authorization policy (CAP) A Terminal Services Gateway component that specifies the Internet users allowed to use the TS Gateway server.

copy-on-write data sharing A Windows Server 2008 Terminal Services memory management technique used by the operating system that, when a client attempts to write to a shared application file, creates a copy of that file, allocates it for the exclusive use of that client, and writes the changes to the copy.

Credential Security Service Provider (CredSSP) In Terminal Services, the protocol that Network Level Authentication (NLA) uses to confirm clients' identities.

D

differential backup A type of backup that saves only the data in the selected components that has changed since the last full backup.

Digest Authentication In Internet Authentication Services, an authentication protocol designed for use with intranet Web servers in an Active Directory environment. Unlike Windows Authentication, Digest Authentication works through firewalls and proxy servers because it transmits passwords over the network. However, the protocol protects the passwords using a strong MD5 encryption scheme.

digital certificate An electronic credential, issued by a certification authority (CA), which confirms the identity of the party to which it is issued.

Digital Rights Management (DRM) A collection of Windows technologies that enable administrators to protect specific types of information from unauthorized consumption and distribution by all users, including users with the appropriate credentials and permissions to access the information.

direct-attached storage Hard disk drives and other storage media connected to a computer using one of the standard disk interfaces, as opposed to network-connected storage.

directory services Software components that store, organize, and supply information about a network and its resources.

disk duplexing A fault tolerance mechanism in which the computer stores duplicate data on two separate disks, each on a separate host adapter, so the data remains available if one disk fails.

disk mirroring A fault tolerance mechanism in which the computer stores duplicate data on two separate disks so the data remains available if a disk fails.

DiskPart.exe A Windows Server 2008 command-line program that you can use to perform disk management tasks.

Distributed File System (DFS) A Windows Server 2008 File Services role service that includes two technologies: DFS Namespaces and DFS Replication. These technologies enable administrators to create virtual directories for shared network files and automatically copy files and folders between duplicate virtual directories.

DNS round robin A load-balancing technique in which you create an individual resource record for each terminal server in the server farm using the server's IP address and the name of the farm (instead of the server name). When clients attempt to establish a Terminal Services connection to the farm, DNS distributes the incoming name resolution requests among the IP addresses.

domain A set of network resources available for a group of users who can authenticate to the network to gain access to those resources.

domain controller A Windows server with Active Directory directory service installed. Each workstation computer joins the domain and is represented by a computer object. Administrators create user objects that represent human users. A domain differs from a workgroup because users log on to the domain once, rather than to each individual computer.

dynamic disk The alternative to the basic disk type in Windows Server 2008. Dynamic disks can have an unlimited number of volumes using various configurations. The process of converting a basic disk to a dynamic disk creates a single partition that occupies the entire disk. You can create an unlimited number of volumes out of the space in that partition.

E

Easy Print A Windows Server 2008 Terminal Services feature that eliminates the need for the printer driver on the terminal server. Instead, the terminal server has a generic Easy Print driver based on the XML Paper Specification (XPS) document format introduced in Windows Vista and Windows Server 2008.

effective permissions A combination of allowed, denied, inherited, and explicitly assigned permissions that provides a composite view of a security principal's functional access to a resource.

Enhanced Metafile (EMF) A standardized, highly portable print job format that is the default format used by the Windows 2000, Windows XP, and Windows Server 2003 print subsystems.

Execution mode One of two operational modes in Terminal Services; used when running applications.

external drive array Hard disk drives and other storage media connected to a computer using a network medium, such as Ethernet or Fibre Channel.

F

failover cluster A collection of redundant servers configured to perform the same tasks, so that if one server fails, another server can take its place almost immediately.

FastCGI An extension to the Common Gateway Interface (CGI) that enables a Web server to maintain a pool of processes that new clients can reuse.

Fast Streaming A collection of techniques that enables Windows Media Player to begin displaying streamed multimedia content more quickly.

feature An individual Windows Server 2008 component designed to perform a specific administrative function.

Fibre Channel A high-speed serial networking technology that was originally designed for use with supercomputers, but is now associated primarily with storage area networking.

Fibre Channel Protocol (FCP) The protocol that Fibre Channel storage area networks use to transmit SCSI traffic between devices.

file system An operating system component that provides a means for storing and organizing files so that users can easily locate them.

File Transfer Protocol (FTP) An application layer protocol that enables a client to connect to a remote server, perform rudimentary file management tasks, and copy files in either direction between the two computers.

file-based I/O In storage area networking, a type of storage in which a computer accesses the stored data one file at a time.

firewall A software routine that acts as a virtual barrier between a computer and the attached network. A firewall is essentially a filter that enables certain types of incoming and outgoing traffic to pass through the barrier, while blocking other types.

folder redirection A Windows service that enables workstations to store user profile data on a shared network drive instead of a local drive.

font smoothing In Terminal Services, a Windows desktop performance feature that enables the client to display screen fonts without jagged lines. Also called anti-aliasing.

FTP over Secure Sockets Layer (SSL) A method by which computers use the SSL protocol to encrypt FTP communications.

full mesh topology In the Distributed File System, a replication scheme in which every member in a group replicates with every other member.

G

globally unique identifier (GUID) partition table (GPT) You can use GPT as a boot disk if the computer's architecture provides support for an Extensible Firmware Interface (EFI)-based boot partition. Otherwise, you can use it as a non-bootable disk for data storage only. When used as a boot disk, it differs from the master boot record because platform operation critical data is located in partitions rather than unpartitioned or hidden sectors.

H

host header In Internet Information Services, a Web site property that specifies the name of the Web server to which clients send requests. IIS uses this Host field to associate incoming requests with one of the Web sites hosted by the server. See also virtual hosting.

hub/spoke topology In the Distributed File System, a replication scheme in which replication traffic is limited to specific pairs of members.

hybrid virtualization A type of virtualization in which a host OS shares access to the computer's processor with the virtual machine manager, with each taking the clock cycles it needs and passing control of the processor back to the other.

Hypertext Markup Language (HTML) A simple tagged coding language that provides a client Web browser with instructions on how to display the text in the file and embed the accompanying media files into the display.

Hypertext Transfer Protocol (HTTP) The standard application layer protocol for Web communications.

Hyper-V A Windows Server 2008 role that implements hypervisor virtualization on the computer.

hypervisor In virtualization, an abstraction layer that interacts directly with the computer's physical hardware.

I

infrastructure services Software components that provide support functions for network clients.

Install mode One of two operational modes in Terminal Services; used when installing applications.

Internet Server Application Programming Interface (ISAPI) An application processing alternative to the Common Gateway Interface (CGI), which enables a Web server to execute applications without spawning a separate process for each incoming request. ISAPI applications take the form of dynamic link libraries (DLLs) instead of executables (EXEs), which load with the IIS server engine using the same address space.

Internet Storage Name Service (iSNS) In storage area networking, a software component that registers the presence of iSCSI initiators and targets on a SAN and responds to queries from iSNS clients.

IP (Internet Protocol) address A unique 32-bit numeric address used as an identifier for a device, such as a computer, on a TCP/IP network.

ISAPI extension A fully realized, in-process application that can generate dynamic HTML pages using information from a database or a form supplied by the client.

ISAPI filter A routine that operates between the HTTP server and the HTTP listener, providing additional functionality, such as application-based authentication, encryption, and data compression services.

iSCSI initiator In storage area networking, a hardware or software device running on a computer that accesses the storage devices on the SAN.

iSCSI target In storage area networking, a component integrated into a drive array or computer that receives SCSI commands from the initiator and passes them to a storage device.

J

JBOD (Just a Bunch of Disks) A colloquial term for a drive array that is not configured to use RAID or any other type of special fault tolerance mechanism.

K

Kerberos A ticket-based authentication protocol used by Windows computers that are members of an Active Directory domain. Unlike NTLM, which involves only the IIS7 server and the client, Kerberos authentication involves an Active Directory domain controller as well.

Key Management Service (KMS) An activation service that runs on the local network, enabling clients to activate without communicating with Microsoft.

KMS activation threshold The number of activation requests that a Key Management Service host must receive within the last 30 days to activate KMS clients.

L

Licensing server discovery mode A Terminal Services configuration setting that specifies how the terminal server will locate a TS Licensing server.

logical unit number (LUN) An identifier assigned to a specific component within a SCSI device, such as an individual disk drive in an array, which enables the SCSI host adapter to send commands to that component.

M

MAK Independent Activation Clients contact Microsoft hosts directly, using an Internet connection or a telephone, to activate a product. It is similar to the standard retail product key activation, except that a single key activates multiple computers.

MAK Proxy Activation Multiple clients send activation requests to a proxy, the Volume Activation Management Tool (VAMT).

master boot record (MBR) The default partition style used since Windows was released. Supports up to four primary partitions or three primary partitions and one extended partition, with unlimited logical drives on the extended partition.

Mstsc.exe A Windows program that provides command-line access to the Remote Desktop Connection client.

multicast In Windows Media Services, a type of transmission in which a single stream is delivered to multiple clients at the same time.

multimaster replication A technique in which duplicate copies of a file are updated on a regular basis, no matter which copy changes. For example, if a file is duplicated on four different servers, a user can access any of the four copies and modify the file as needed. The replication engine uses the changes made to the modified copy to update the other three copies. Compare to single master replication.

Multiple Activation Key (MAK) A product key that enables a specified number of computers to activate using Microsoft's hosted activation services.

N

namespace In the Distributed File System, a virtual directory tree that contains references to shared folders located on network file servers. This directory tree does not exist as a true copy of the folders on different servers. Instead, it is a collection of references to the original folders, which users can browse like an actual server share.

network attached storage (NAS) A dedicated file server device, containing disk drives, which connects to a network and provides clients with direct, file-based access to storage resources. Unlike a storage area network, NAS devices include a rudimentary operating system and a file system implementation.

Network File System (NFS) An open standard, application layer, file sharing protocol, commonly used by UNIX and Linux operating systems. Windows Server 2008 includes an NFS server implementation, in the form of the Services for Network File System role service, part of the File Services role.

Network Level Authentication (NLA) A Terminal Services feature that confirms the user's identity with the Credential Security Service Provider (CredSSP) protocol before the client and server establish the Terminal Services connection.

network load balancing (NLB) A clustering technology in which a collection of identical servers run simultaneously, sharing incoming traffic equally among them.

NTFS permissions Controls access to the files and folders stored on disk volumes formatted with the NTFS file system. To access a file on the local system or over a network, a user must have the appropriate NTFS permissions.

NTLMv2 A challenge/response authentication protocol used by Windows computers that are not members of an Active Directory domain.

O

Offline Files A Windows feature that enables client computers to maintain copies of server files on their local drives. If the computer's connection to the network is severed or interrupted, the client can continue to work with the local copies until network service is restored, at which time the client synchronizes its data with the data on the server.

on-demand stream In Windows Media Services, a multimedia stream of pre-recorded content delivered at the user's request.

P

partition style The method that Windows operating systems use to organize partitions on a disk. Two hard disk partition styles can be used in Windows Server 2008: master boot record (MBR) and GUID partition table (GPT).

preboot execution environment (PXE) A network adapter feature that enables a computer to connect to a server on the network and download the boot files it needs to run, rather than booting from a local drive.

print device The hardware that produces hard copy documents on paper or other print media. Windows Vista supports *local print devices*, which are directly attached to the computer's parallel, serial, Universal Serial Bus (USB), or IEEE 1394 (FireWire) ports; and *network interface print devices*, which are connected to the network directly or through another computer.

print server A computer or stand-alone device that receives print jobs from clients and sends them to print devices that are attached locally or connected to the network.

printer The software interface through which a computer communicates with a print device. Windows Vista supports numerous interfaces, including parallel (LPT), serial (COM), USB, IEEE 1394, Infrared Data Access (IrDA), and Bluetooth ports; and network printing services such as lpr, Internet Printing Protocol (IPP), and standard TCP/IP ports.

printer control language (PCL) A language understood by the printer. Each printer is associated with a printer driver that converts the commands generated by an application into the printer's PCL.

printer driver A device driver that converts the print jobs generated by applications into an appropriate string of commands for a specific print device. Printer drivers are designed for specific print devices and provide applications that access all of the print device's features.

printer pool A single print server connected to multiple print devices. The print server can distribute large numbers of incoming jobs among several identical print devices to provide timely service. Alternatively, you can connect print devices that support different forms and paper sizes to a single print server, which distributes jobs with different requirements to the appropriate print devices.

private key In public key infrastructure (PKI), the secret key in a pair of keys, which is known only to the message or file recipient and used to decrypt the item. When a message is encrypted using the private key, only the public key can decrypt it. The ability to decrypt the message using the public key proves that the message originated from the holder of the private key.

protocol listener In Internet Information Services, the component that awaits incoming requests from clients and forwards them to the appropriate server applications.

protocol rollover In Windows Media Services, the technique by which clients and servers negotiate the most efficient streaming protocol they have in common. A client establishing a connection to a Windows Media Services server sends information about the protocols it can use and the server selects the best protocol it is capable of using. If, for any reason, the client cannot use the selected protocol, the server reverts to the next best protocol in its list.

public key infrastructure (PKI) A security relationship in which participants are issued two keys: public and private. The participant keeps the private key secret, while the public key is freely available in the digital certificate. Data encrypted with the private key can only be decrypted using the public key and data encrypted with the public key can only be decrypted using the private key.

publishing points In Windows Media Services, the components on a server through which clients access specific content streams.

R

Real Time Streaming Protocol (RTSP)
A control protocol, used by default in Windows Media Services running on Windows Server 2008, which carries commands between a client and server using the connection-oriented TCP protocol and port number 554. For the actual data streaming, Windows Media Services uses the Real Time Protocol (RTP).

Redundant Array of Independent Disks (RAID) A series of data storage technologies that use multiple disks to provide computers with increased storage, I/O performance, and/or fault tolerance.

Remote Desktop Connection A program running on a desktop computer that establishes a connection to a terminal server using Remote Desktop Protocol (RDP) and displays a session window containing a desktop or application.

Remote Desktop Protocol (RDP) The protocol used to transmit screen information, keystrokes, and mouse movements between the Remote Desktop Connection client and a Remote Desktop or Terminal Services server.

Remote Differential Compression (RDC) In the Distributed File System, a protocol that conserves network bandwidth by detecting changes in files and transmitting only the modified data to the destination. This conserves bandwidth and greatly reduces the time needed for the replication process.

RemoteApp A Terminal Services feature that enables clients to run terminal server applications within individual, resizable windows.

replication group In the Distributed File System, a collection of servers, known as members, each of which contains a target for a particular DFS folder.

resource authorization policy (RAP) A Terminal Services Gateway component that specifies the terminal servers users are permitted to access on the private network.

role A collection of Windows Server 2008 modules and tools designed to perform specific tasks for network clients.

S

security identifier (SID) A unique value assigned to every Active Directory object when it is created.

security principal The user, group, or computer to which an administrator assigns permissions.

serial ATA (SATA) A newer version of the ATA disk interface that uses serial instead of parallel communications, improves transmission speeds, and provides the ability to queue commands at the drive.

server farm A collection of identical servers used to balance a large incoming traffic load.

ServerManagerCmd.exe A Windows Server 2008 command-line tool used to install roles and features.

Server Message Blocks (SMB) The default application layer, file sharing protocol used by the Windows operating systems.

Server Side Includes (SSI) A relatively old Web server technology that enables HTML pages to contain directives that the server parses and executes.

session In Terminal Services, a collection of client processes that form an individual user environment running on the server.

Session ID In Terminal Services, a unique identifier that a terminal server assigns to each client session to keep the processes for individual clients separate.

Shadow Copies A Windows Server 2008 feature that maintains a library containing multiple versions of selected files. Users can select a version of a file to restore as needed.

Simple Mail Transfer Protocol (SMTP) The standard Transmission Control Protocol/Internet Protocol (TCP/IP) email protocol for the Internet. Email clients send outgoing messages to an SMTP server specified in their configuration settings and the SMTP server forwards the messages to other mail servers on the way to their destinations.

simple volume Consists of space from a single disk. After you create a simple volume, you can extend it to multiple disks to create a spanned or striped volume if it is not a system volume or boot volume.

single master replication. A technique in which duplicate copies of a file are updated on a regular basis from one master copy. For example, if a file is duplicated on four different servers, users can modify one copy and the replication engine propagates the changes to the other three copies. Compare with multimaster replication.

Small Computer System Interface (SCSI) A storage interface that enables computers

to transfer data to multiple storage devices connected to a bus.

spanned volume A method for combining the space from multiple (2 to 32) dynamic disks into a single large volume. If a single physical disk in the spanned volume fails, all the data in the volume is lost.

special permissions An element providing a security principal with a specific degree of access to a resource.

spooler A service running on a print server that temporarily stores print jobs until the print device can process them.

standard permissions A common combination of special permissions used to provide a security principal with a level of access to a resource.

stateless Descriptive term for a server that does not maintain information about the client connections or the files opened by individual clients. NFS servers are stateless.

storage area network (SAN) A dedicated, high-speed network that connects block-based storage devices to servers. Unlike NAS devices, SANs do not provide a file system implementation. SANs require a server to provide clients with access to the storage resources.

striped volume A method for combining the space from multiple (2 to 32) dynamic disks into a single large volume. If a single physical disk in the striped volume fails, all the data in the volume is lost. A striped volume differs from a spanned volume in that the system writes data one stripe at a time to each successive disk in the volume.

subnet mask In TCP/IP networking, a 32-bit value that specifies which bits of an IP address form the network identifier and which bits form the host identifier.

Switched fabric (FC-SW) A Fibre Channel topology that consists of up to 16,777,216 (2^{24}) devices, each of which is connected to a Fibre Channel switch.

T

target In the Distributed File System, a physical folder on a shared server drive that is represented by a virtual directory in a DFS namespace.

Terminal Services client access license (TS CAL) A document that grants a single client access to a specific software program, in this case, a Terminal Services server.

Terminal Services Gateway A Terminal Services role service that enables Internet users to access terminal servers on private networks, despite the presence of intervening firewalls and network access translation (NAT) servers.

Terminal Services licensing mode A Terminal Services configuration parameter that specifies whether the terminal server should issue Per Device or Per User licenses to clients.

Terminal Services (TS) Web Access A Terminal Services role service that enables users to launch an application by double-clicking an icon on a Web page.

thin client A software program or hardware device that connects to a terminal server and accesses applications running on the server.

thin client computing A variation on the mainframe computing paradigm, in which clients function only as terminals and servers do all of the application computing.

TS Licensing server A Terminal Services software component that issues client access licenses to Terminal Services clients on a network.

tunneling A networking technique in which one protocol is encapsulated within another protocol. In virtual private networking (VPN), an entire client/server session is tunneled within another protocol. Because the internal, or payload, protocol is carried by another protocol, it is protected from most standard forms of attack.

U

unicast In Windows Media Services, a type of transmission in which each client establishes its own connection to the Windows Media Services server and has its own data stream.

Universal Discovery, Description, and Integration (UDDI) An XML-based directory service that enables businesses to publish listings about their activities and the services they offer.

V

VDS hardware provider In storage area networking, a software component that enables you to use the Storage Manager for SANs snap-in to manage LUNs on an external storage device.

virtual directory In Internet Information Services, an alias that points to a folder in another physical location. This shortcut enables you to publish

content found on different drives or different computers without copying or moving it.

virtual hosting In Internet Information Services, a binding method in which each Web site hosted by a server is assigned a unique name, called a host header value, which differentiates it from the server's other sites. This binding method enables the Web server to host multiple Web sites using a single IP address and port number without requiring any special information from clients.

virtual instance A guest OS installed on a virtual machine in a Windows Server 2008 computer using Hyper-V.

virtual machine (VM) In virtualization, one of multiple separate operating environments on a single computer, in which you can install a separate copy of an operating system.

virtual private networking (VPN) A technique for connecting to a network at a remote location using the Internet as a network medium.

virtual server A complete installation of an operating system that runs in a software environment emulating a physical computer.

virtualization The process of deploying and maintaining multiple instances of an operating system on a single computer.

Volume Activation (VA) 2.0 Microsoft's program for automating and managing the activation of products obtained using volume licenses.

Volume Activation Management Tool (VAMT) A Microsoft program that collects activation requests from clients on the network. It uses a single connection to the Microsoft hosts to activate all of the clients at the same time, and then distributes the resulting activation codes to the clients using the Windows Management Instrumentation (WMI) interface.

W

Web garden A Web site with an application pool that uses more than one worker process.

Windows Authentication The most secure of the challenge/response authentication methods supported by Internet Information Services 7. Supports two authentication protocols: NTLMv2 and Kerberos.

Windows CE A real-time, modular operating system designed for devices with minimal amounts of memory. Windows CE is not based on the NT

kernel, but it does provide users with a familiar Windows graphical user interface (GUI), and has been adapted to a variety of devices, including handhelds, smart phones, and game consoles.

Windows Deployment Services (WDS) A role included with Windows Server 2008, which enables you to perform unattended installations of Windows Server 2008 and other operating systems on remote computers, using network-based boot and installation media.

Windows Media Encoder A Windows application that converts captured digital content into the Windows Media format and sends it to a Windows Media Services server for real time distribution.

Windows Media Player A client application supplied with the Windows operating system that enables the computer to request, receive, and display multimedia streams.

Windows Media Services A Windows Server 2008 role that can stream audio and video content to network clients in real time. A player on the client computer establishes a direct connection with the server and plays the audio or video content as it arrives.

Windows PE (Preinstallation Environment) 2.1 A subset of Windows Server 2008 that provides basic access to the computer's network and disk drives, making it possible to perform an in-place or a network installation. This eliminates DOS from the installation process by supplying its own preinstallation environment.

Windows Process Activation Service (WAS) Windows Server 2008 feature that manages the Internet Information Services 7 request pipeline, the server's application pools, and the worker processes running in them.

Windows SharePoint Services 3.0 A Microsoft service that enables users to employ browser-based workspaces to share information in a variety of ways, such as storing documents, creating calendar appointments and task lists, and contributing to newsgroup-style discussions.

Windows XPe A full-featured operating system based on the standard Windows XP kernel. Windows XPe terminals include more local computing capabilities than terminals using Windows CE or a proprietary OS, including support for local browsers and Java applications, as well as embedded

Win32 applications. Windows XPe also supports the full range of Windows drivers and peripherals. The result is a powerful and efficient workstation that can continue to function when disconnected from the network.

witness disk In failover clustering, a shared storage medium that holds the cluster configuration database.

worker process In Internet Information Services, a host for user-developed application code, which is responsible for processing requests from the protocol listeners and returning the results to the client.

worker process isolation mode In Internet Information Services, an arrangement in which each application pool occupies its own protected address space. As a result, a crashed application cannot affect any process running outside of that pool.

X

XML Paper Specification (XPS) A new, platform-independent document format included with Windows Server 2008 and Windows Vista, in which print job files use a single XPS format for their entire journey to the print device, rather than being converted first to EMS and then to PCL.

Index